Parallel Processing
and
Parallel Algorithms

Springer

New York
Berlin
Heidelberg
Barcelona
Hong Kong
London
Milan
Paris
Singapore
Tokyo

Seyed H. Roosta

Parallel Processing
and
Parallel Algorithms

Theory and Computation

With 194 Illustrations

Springer

Seyed H. Roosta
Department of Computer Science
State University of New York
Oswego, NY 13126
USA

Library of Congress Cataloging-in-Publication Data
Roosta, Seyed H.
    Parallel processing and parallel algorithms: theory and computation / Seyed H. Roosta
      p.   cm.
    Includes bibliographical references.
    ISBN 0-387-98716-9 (hardcover : alk. paper)
    1. Parallel processing (Electronic computers)   2. Parallel programming (Computer science)
    3. Computer algorithms.   I. Title.
    QA76.58R66   1999
    004′.35—dc21   99-13243

Printed on acid-free paper.

Production managed by Jenny Wolkowicki; manufacturing supervised by Jeffrey Taub.
Photocomposed copy prepared from the author's Microsoft Word files.
Printed and bound by Hamilton Printing Co., Rensselaer, NY.
Printed in the United States of America.

9 8 7 6 5 4 3 2 1

ISBN 0-387-98716-9 Springer-Verlag New York Berlin Heidelberg   SPIN 10708016

This book is dedicated with affection and respect to the memory of my father, Seyed Abolghasem Roosta. To my mother, Mahjabin, for her generosity and to my wife, Sima, for her affectionate support and encouragement. She endured the long hours I spent on this book. Without her understanding and support, this book would not be a reality.

Preface

Motivation

It is now possible to build powerful single-processor and multiprocessor systems and use them efficiently for data processing, which has seen an explosive expansion in many areas of computer science and engineering. One approach to meeting the performance requirements of the applications has been to utilize the most powerful single-processor system that is available. When such a system does not provide the performance requirements, pipelined and parallel processing structures can be employed. The concept of parallel processing is a departure from sequential processing. In sequential computation one processor is involved and performs one operation at a time. On the other hand, in parallel computation several processors cooperate to solve a problem, which reduces computing time because several operations can be carried out simultaneously. Using several processors that work together on a given computation illustrates a new paradigm in computer problem solving which is completely different from sequential processing. From the practical point of view, this provides sufficient justification to investigate the concept of parallel processing and related issues, such as parallel algorithms. Parallel processing involves utilizing several factors, such as parallel architectures, parallel algorithms, parallel programming languages and performance analysis, which are strongly interrelated.

In general, four steps are involved in performing a computational problem in parallel. The first step is to understand the nature of computations in the specific application domain. The second step involves designing a parallel algorithm or parallelizing the existing sequential algorithm. The third step is to map the parallel algorithm into a suitable parallel computer architecture, and the last step involves writing the parallel program utilizing an applicable parallel programming approach.

Parallel Processing

Parallel processing is making a tremendous impact in many areas of computer applications. A growing number of applications in science, engineering, business and medicine are requiring computing speeds that hardly can be achieved by the current conventional computers. These applications involve processing huge amount of data or performing a large number of iterations. Parallel processing is one of the approaches known today which would help to make these computations feasible. It includes the study of parallel architectures and algorithms.

Another reason to utilize parallel processing whose importance has been recognized can be illustrated by the real-time applications. In a real-time application a computer needs certain data from the other resources in order to solve a computational problem. The system receives data from several resources at the same time and it is not feasible to store data arriving from the resources for later processing, because the data become meaningless if not used immediately. The foregoing applications are representative of a host of situations in which the probability of success in performing a computational task is increased through the use of a parallel computer utilizing parallel processing. Many factors contribute to the performance of parallel systems, such as interaction among processors, hardware architecture and parallel programming approach.

Parallel Algorithms

The most important ingredient for parallel processing is parallel algorithms or parallel solution methods, and there has been considerable interest in the development of parallel algorithms. Given a problem to be solved in parallel, a parallel algorithm describes how the problem can be solved on a given parallel architecture by dividing the problem into subproblems, by communicating among processors, and by joining the partial solutions to produce the final result.

Several rough taxonomies of parallel architectures and parallel languages are beginning to emerge, but there remains a lack of understanding of how to classify parallel algorithms and applications and how a class of parallel algorithms relates to a given architecture or programming language, or even to another class of parallel algorithms.

A good parallel algorithm results from looking for parallelism that might be inherent in a sequential algorithm for a given problem. For example, algorithms based on divide-and-conquer strategy usually have an inherent parallel nature.

There are two approaches in designing parallel algorithms with respect to the number of processors available. The first is to design an algorithm in which the number of processors utilized by the algorithm is an input parameter, which means that the number of processors does not depend on the input size of the problem. The second approach is to allow the number of processors used by the parallel algorithm to grow with the size of the input, which means that the number of processors is not an input parameter but is a function of the input size. By using a division-of-labor scheme, an algorithm designed utilizing the second approach can always be converted into an algorithm suitable for the first approach.

A number of constraints arise in the design of parallel algorithms which are not present in the design of sequential algorithms. These constraints have to be highlighted together with the development of various performance measures for parallel algorithms.

Parallel Programming Languages

It has become clear in recent years that parallel programming is a subject of study in its own right, primarily because it is now recognized that the use of parallelism can be beneficial as much to the applications programmer as to the systems programmer.

The parallel programming languages are based on two categories, parallel programming abstractions that are based on mutual exclusion of access to an individual memory location and those that raise the level of abstraction to processes which communicate by sending messages to each other. Sending a message is a higher level action that can be implemented on physically distributed processors.

Each parallel programming approach suggests a particular hardware configuration which best matches its language primitives. In designing primitives for programming, a wide variety of issues must be considered, Asynchronous programming can be used for programming multiprocessors or distributed systems whereas synchronous parallel solutions are suitable for use on array and vector processors.

Book Organization

This book advocates the concept of parallel processing and parallel algorithms. It aims to cover well one aspect of the analysis of parallel computers, which is the essence of the architectures. It attempts to cover the relationship between parallel programming approaches and machines, or algorithms and architectures.

Chapter 1 (Computer Architecture) establishes a hardware theme that runs through the book. Since a knowledge of architecture features helps in the explanation of some of the programming concepts, a broad hardware overview is given in this chapter which covers the basic parallel computer architectures.

Chapter 2 (Components of Parallel Computers) introduces primitives of parallel computers, including memory, interconnection networks, compilers, operating systems and input/output constraints.

Chapter 3 (Principles of Parallel Programming) examines the principles of parallel programming with regard to issues that are involved, such as message passing compared with shared-address-space parallelism, mapping the algorithms into specific architectures, level of parallelism and granularity problems.

Chapter 4 (Parallel Programming Approaches) covers different parallel programming languages for transforming sequential programs into parallel forms. The parallel programming approaches are used in different parallel systems.

Chapter 5 (Principles of Parallel Algorithm Design) focuses on the structure of the parallel algorithms with regard to design, performance measures and complexities. The theory of parallel algorithms is becoming very important in the area of parallel processing. So, from the theory's point of view, this issue provides a challenging range of problems with new rules for the design and analysis of algorithms.

The next three chapters are dedicated to a variety of parallel algorithms. We have selected the important area of interest in the field of parallel processing which concentrates on determining and taking advantage of the inherently parallel nature of the problems. In this regard we essentially concentrate on problems which are known to have efficient parallel solutions.

Chapter 6 (Parallel Graph Algorithms) treats a variety of parallel graph algorithms. The chapter is devoted to a discussion of a number of basic graph problems and presents the design and analysis of efficient parallel algorithms for them.

Chapter 7 (Parallel Search Algorithms) focuses on the most prominent search methods. In this chapter, we deal with two basic problems concerned with finite lists of elements in the context of parallel processing. These are the problems of selection and searching.

Chapter 8 (Parallel Computational Algorithms) deals with computational algorithms that are of fundamental importance in scientific computations. We informally classify parallelism in computational algorithms demonstrating various types of parallelism such as matrix multiplication and systems of linear equations.

Chapter 9 (Data flow and Functional Programming) describes data flow computing, which is a fundamentally different issue in parallel processing and can be achieved by data flow languages. The purpose of this contribution is to deal with the architecture of data flow computers. SISAL is a functional language with no explicit parallel control constructs, but its data types and its constructs for expressing parallelism and operations are specifically chosen to produce efficient code for large-scale scientific computations.

Chapters 10 (Asynchronous Parallel Programming) focuses on asynchronous computations when all program fragments are initially regarded as parallel, independent and unordered. Any constraint on their interactions is formulated as explicit or implicit individual conditions associated with fragments. The chapter introduces three different languages, of which Modula-2 is used in hybrid systems of SIMD-MIMD computers.

Chapter 11 (Data Parallel Programming) introduces a high-level notation that simplifies parallel programming and enhances portability. This provides compilers with enough information to allow them to generate efficient parallel code for both shared-memory multiprocessors and distributed-memory multicomputers. The languages presented are Dataparallel C, a variant of the original

C* language developed by Thinking Machines Corporation and Fortran 90, which has vector and array operations.

Chapter 12 (Artificial Intelligence and Parallel Processing) discusses knowledge processing, which is a fast-growing area of computer science and engineering and how the processing speed of rule-based expert systems may be increased by utilizing parallel processing. We discuss Concurrent Prolog as a parallel logic language and Multilisp, which is a modification of an existing language (Lisp). The basic idea behind Multilisp is parallel expression evaluation.

Audience

The intended audience includes advanced undergraduate and beginning graduate students as well as anyone interested in the wonder of parallel processing. Some knowledge of design and analysis of algorithms is helpful but is not necessary. The book provides many references from which such background can be obtained.

Features

Some of the book's most distinctive features are:

- It covers the majority of the important approaches in parallel processing and algorithms.
- The book raises a number of research issues. This indicates that the book may serve as a source of inspiration for students and researchers who want to.be engaged in the area of parallel processing.
- One of the most important features provided is to enhance the reader's ability to create new algorithms or to modify existing algorithms in order to make them suitable for parallel processing.
- Since parallel algorithms and parallel processing are treated in separate sections, one is able to study as much of the parallel material as desired and use the book in the design and analysis of algorithms or principles of parallel processing.
- A comparison of the different parallel programming languages and architectures is presented to address the efficiency and applicability of the languages with regard to the processing environment.

Acknowledgments

I want to express my gratitude to the staff of Springer-Verlag Publishing Company for an excellent job with editing and production of this book. On the production side, I have benefitted by the diligence and help of Jenny Wolkowicki and Hal Henglein. I am grateful for their valuable assistance and professional editing support. A special thanks is reserved for Dr. Bill Sanders and Mr. John Kimmel, my editors, for encouragement and support of this project.

I would like to send personal thanks to my family members, my wife Sima, my children Nasim, Maryam, and Mahsa, my mother, my brother, my sisters, my father- and mother-in-law, and my brothers-in-law, for their reliable and unconditional love and understanding. The State University of New York at Oswego and the Department of Computer Science provided an active and nurturing environment to conduct this project.

State University of New York   Seyed H. Roosta
Oswego, NY
September 1999

Contents

CHAPTER 1
Computer Architecture

Computer architecture is the study of the organization and interconnection of components of computer systems. The computer can be constructed from the basic building blocks such as memories, arithmetic units, processing elements and buses. From these building blocks any one of a number of different types of computers, ranging from the smallest to the largest supercomputers, can be constructed. The functional behavior of the components of different computers are similar to each other. For instance, the memory system performs the storage functions, the central processing unit performs operations, and the input and output interfaces transfer data from a processor to appropriate devices.

The major differences among computers are in the way the modules are connected together, the performance characteristics of the modules and the method by which the computer system is controlled by operations. The two key elements of a conventional computer system are the processor and the memory. A processor manipulates data stored in the memory as dictated by the instructions. Instructions are stored in the memory modules and always flow from memory to processor. Data movement in a system is bidirectional, which means that data may be read from or written to the memory modules. Figure 1.1 represents the memory-processor interconnection known as the Von Neumann model of computation. Another natural extension of the Von Neumann model is a network of computers. In this scheme, each node in the network is a self-contained computer, which can be considerably complex and operates completely autonomously from the other nodes. A computer network may be geographically distributed.

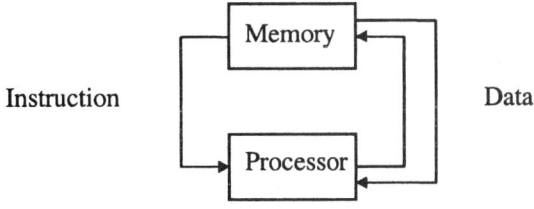

Figure 1.1. Memory-processor interconnection.

In addition to this natural extension of the Von Neumann model, it is possible to take a more fundamental approach and to design new computation models exclusively for parallel processing. These models include systolic processors, data flow models, logic-inference models, reduction models and neural networks. The number of instructions read and data items manipulated simultaneously by the processor form the basis for architecture classifications, which is the topic of the following sections in this chapter.

1.1   Classification of Computer Architectures

Michael Flynn [Flynn 66] classified computer architectures by a variety of characteristics, including number of processors, number of programs they can execute, and memory structure. In addition to Flynn's classification, which has been proved to be a good method for the taxonomy of computer architectures, several taxonomies have been proposed [Dasgupta 90, Hockney 87, Skillicorn 88, Bell 92].

Treleaven, Brownbridge and Hopking [Treleaven 82] have suggested that conventional computers can be examined from two points of view:

- Control mechanism, which defines the order of execution.
- Data mechanism, which defines the way operands are used.

Flynn's classification included the following categories:

1. Single Instruction Stream, Single Data Stream (SISD). SISD computers have one CPU that executes one instruction at a time (single instruction stream) and fetches or stores one item of data at a time (single data stream). Figure 1.2 shows a general structure of the SISD architecture. All SISD computers utilize a single register, called the program counter, which enforces serial execution of instructions. As each instruction is fetched from the memory, this register is updated to the address of the next instruction to be fetched and executed, resulting in a serial order of execution.

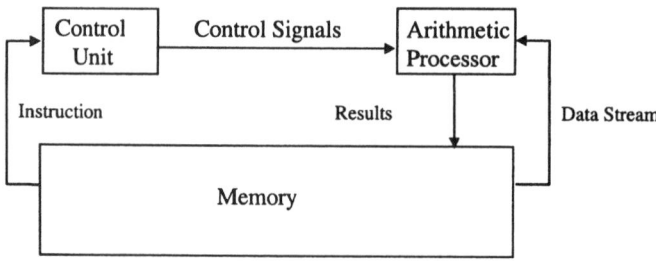

Figure 1.2. Model of an SISD architecture.

2. Single Instruction Stream, Multiple Data Stream (SIMD). SIMD machines have one Control Unit that executes a single instruction stream, but they have more than one Processing Element. The control unit generates the control signals for all of the processing elements, which execute the same operation on different data items (thus multiple data stream), meaning that they execute programs in a lock-step mode, in which each processing element has its own data stream. In other words, many separate processing elements are invoked by a single control unit. These computers are used mostly for problems having high degrees of small-grain parallelism. Some popular commercial SIMD computers are ILLIAC IV, DAP and Connection Machine CM-2. SIMD computers can also support vector processing, which can be accomplished by assigning vector elements to individual processing elements for concurrent computation. Figure 1.3 presents a general view of an SIMD architecture, which, when only one processing element is active, can be a Von Neumann machine.

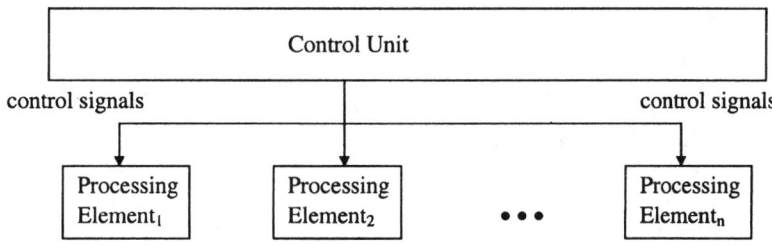

Figure 1.3. Model of an SIMD architecture.

3. Multiple Instruction Stream, Single Data Stream (MISD). Machines in this category may execute several different programs on the same data item. This implies that several instructions are operating on a single piece of data. This architecture can be illustrated two different categories:

1. A class of machines that would require distinct processing units that would receive distinct instructions to be performed on the same data. This was a big challenge for many designers and there are currently no machines of this type in the world.
2. A class of machines such that data flows through a series of processing elements. Pipelined architectures such as systolic arrays fall into this group of machines. Pipeline architectures perform vector processing through a series of stages, each of which performs a particular function and produces an intermediate result. The reason that such architectures are grouped as MISD machines is that elements of a vector may be considered to belong to the same piece of data, and all pipeline stages represent multiple instructions that are being applied to that vector. Figure 1.4 represents the general structure of an MISD architecture.

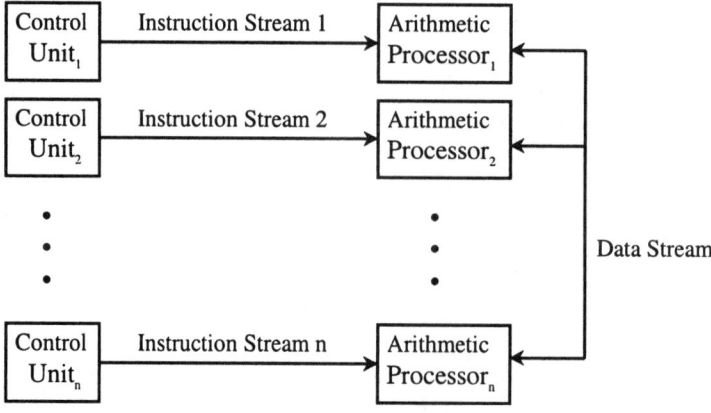

Figure 1.4. Model of an MISD architecture.

4. Multiple Instruction Stream, Multiple Data Stream (MIMD). MIMD machines are also called multiprocessors. They have more than one processor and each one can execute a different program (multiple instruction stream), on its own data item (multiple data stream). In most MIMD systems, each processor has access to a global memory, which may reduce processor communication delay. In addition, each processor possesses a private memory, which assists in avoiding memory contention. Most of the MIMD architectures take advantage of medium- and large-grain parallelism. In current MIMD parallel architectures, the number of processors is smaller than in SIMD systems. MIMD computers are the most complex, but they hold great promise for efficiency accomplished via concurrent processing. It is very likely that in the future, small MIMD systems with a limited number of processors will be built with complete connectivity, meaning that each processor will be connected to every other one. Some popular commercial MIMD computers are the BBN Butterfly, the Alliant FX series, Intel Corporation's iPSC series, and New York University's Ultracomputer. Figure 1.5 represents the general structure of an MIMD architecture.

1.2   Parallel Architectures

In the previous section, Flynn's classification addressed two important families of parallel architectures, SIMD and MIMD computers. Most of the other proposed taxonomies preserve the SIMD and MIMD features to represent a complete characterization of parallel architectures. Figure 1.6 shows a taxonomy that represents some of the features of the parallel architectures. This section concentrates on SIMD and MIMD parallel architectures.

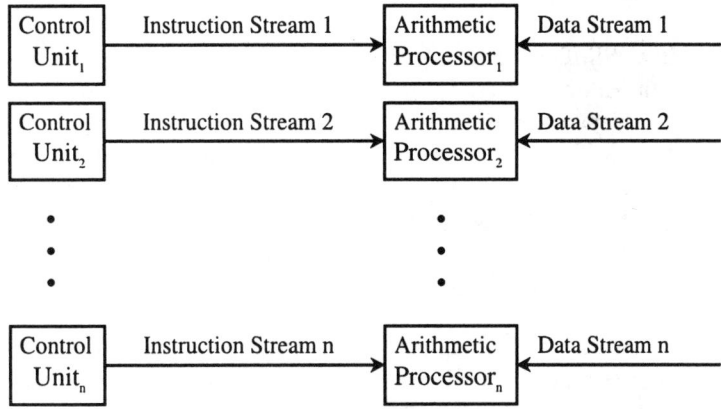

Figure 1.5. Model of an MIMD architecture.

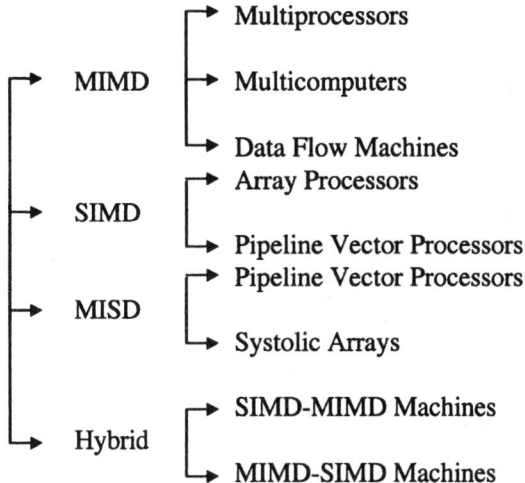

Figure 1.6. Taxonomy of parallel processing architectures.

Note that in pipelined processors, multiple instruction streams exist. If the definition of the single data stream is stretched to include the conglomeration of all data elements in a pipeline stage, then pipelined processors fit in MISD. This indicates that pipelined vector processors belong in MISD rather than SIMD as we have classified them.

1.2.1   SIMD Architectures

In an SIMD machine, several processing elements are supervised by one control unit. All the processing units receive the same instruction from the control unit but operate on different data sets, which come from different data flows. A general SIMD machine is shown in Figure 1.7 with the following characteristics:

- It distributes processing over a large amount of hardware.
- It operates concurrently on many different data elements.
- It performs the same computation on all data elements.

As each processing unit executes the same instruction at the same time, the processors are operating synchronously. The potential speedup of SIMD machines is proportional to the amount of available hardware. The resulting parallelism enables SIMD machines to achieve tremendous speeds.

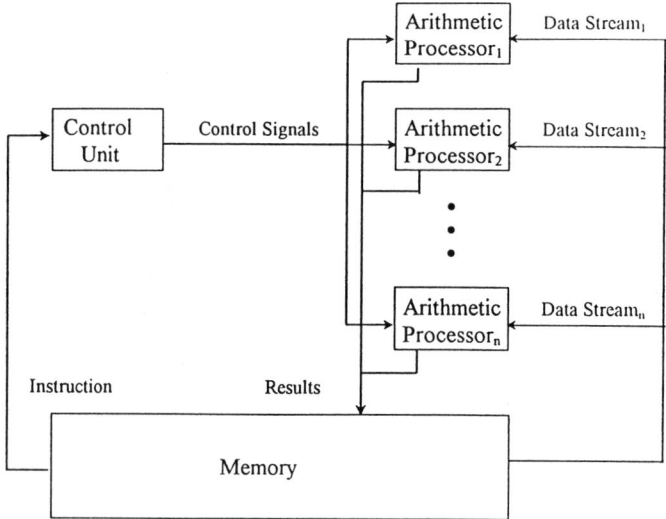

Figure 1.7. Model of an SIMD architecture.

Consider a program segment presented by the flowchart in Figure 1.8(a). Here, X_1, X_2, X_3, and X_4 represent blocks of instructions. In SISD system, after executing X_1, depending upon the value of X, X_2 or X_3 is executed and then the system executes X_4. In an SIMD system, some data streams satisfy X=???, and the others satisfy X≠???. This indicates that some processing elements execute X_3 and others execute X_2 and all processing elements eventually execute X_4. To identify the computation on SIMD systems, the branch operation is converted into a sequential operation as shown in Figure 1.8(b). Note that all the processing elements are not active during the execution of blocks X_2 and X_3. The potential speedup of SIMD machines is proportional to the amount of available hardware. The resulting parallelism enables SIMD machines to achieve tremendous speeds.

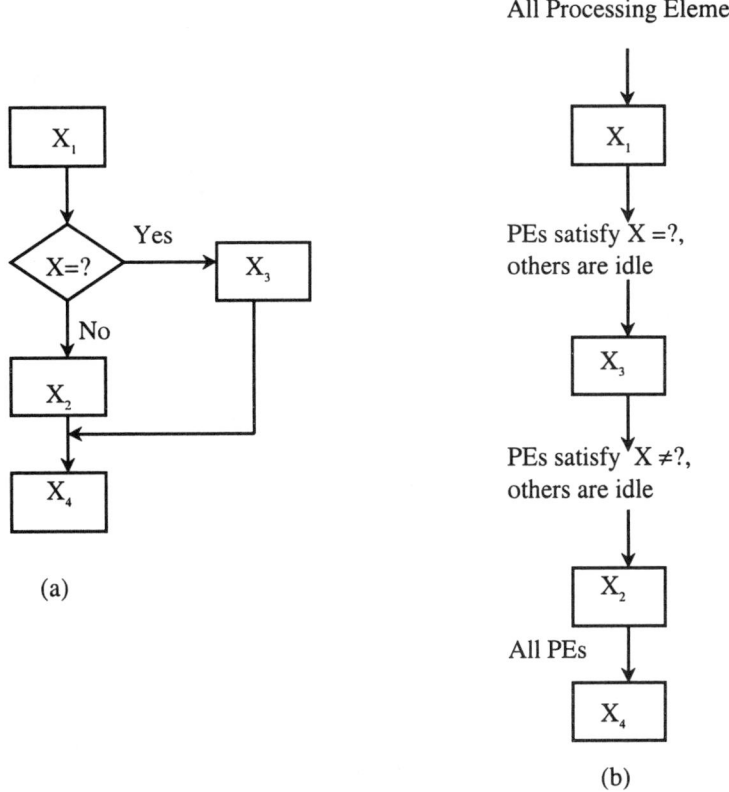

Figure 1.8. SISD and SIMD execution. (a) SISD execution. (b) SIMD execution.

A general structure of 16 processing elements and a single control unit is shown in Figure 1.9. The processor arrays may differ among themselves with regard to the following issues:

- Processing element structures
- Control unit structures
- Memory structures
- Interconnection topology
- Input and output structures

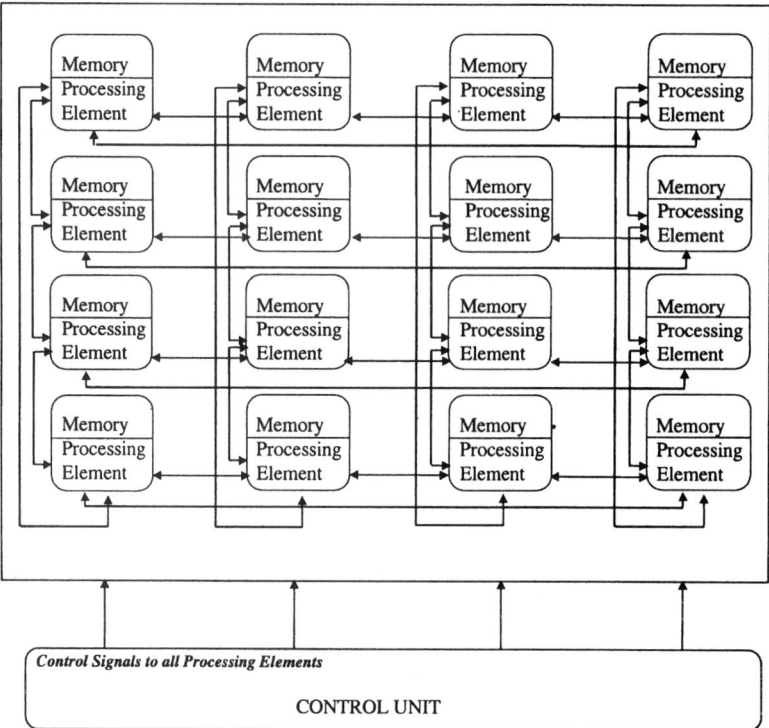

Figure 1.9. An SIMD architecture consisting of 16 processing elements and a single control unit.

Array processing was the first form of parallel processing to be studied and implemented. There are two different types of machines.

- Those that perform bit operations, such as MPP and CM-1 machines.
- Those that perform word operations, such as the ILLIAC IV machine.

The bit processor arrays operate on bit planes which is a two dimensional of bit slices. The processing elements communicate with the nearest neighbor processing element utilizing an interconnection network. Figure 1.10 shows three different array processing architectures.

Examples of SIMD computers include the ILLIAC IV, MPP, DAP, CM-2, MasPar MP-1 and MasPar MP-2.

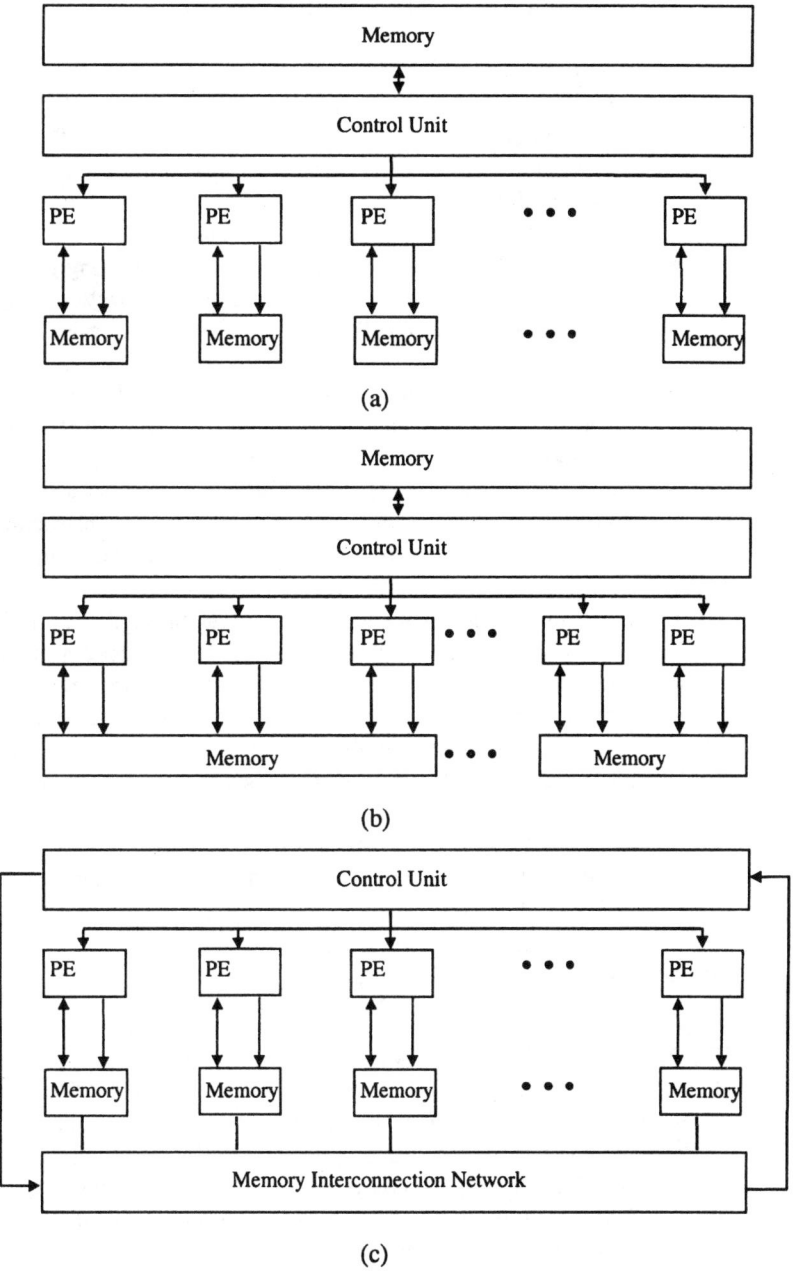

Figure 1.10. Three different SIMD processor array architectures. (a) Goodyear's Massively Parallel Processor. (b) Goodyear's STARAN. (c) ILLIAC IV.

We summarize this section by comparing some of the general features of the SIMD computers with those of the MIMD computers:

- Less hardware than MIMD because they have only one global control unit.
- Less memory than MIMD because only one copy of the instructions needs to be stored in the system memory, thus possibly reducing memory cost, allowing for more data storage, and reducing communication traffic between primary and secondary storage.
- Less startup time for communicating with neighboring processors.
- Single instruction stream and implicit synchronization of the processing elements make SIMD application easier to program, understand and debug.
- Control flow instructions and scalar operations that are common to all processing elements can be executed on the control unit, while the processors are executing the other instructions.
- Need synchronization mechanism among processors after each instruction execution cycle, meaning implicitly at the instruction level. In contrast, explicit synchronization primitives may be required in MIMD architecture, which can be regarded as overhead.
- If the processing elements communicate through messages, during a given transfer, all enabled processing elements send a message to distinct processing elements, thus implicitly synchronizing the send and receive commands and implicitly identifying the messages. In contrast, MIMD architectures involve the overhead of message identification protocols and a scheme to signal when a message has been sent or received.
- Less cost because of the need for only a single instruction decoder in the control unit versus one decoder in each processing element for MIMD architecture.

MasPar MP-1

The MasPar was formed in 1988 by a Digital Equipment Corporation Vice-President and the company retains its association with DEC. The company produces a single range of SIMD machines, the MP-1 series, which consists of five models ranging from 1024 to 16384 processors [MasPar Computer Corporation 91, Nickolls 90]. The range supports a UNIX operating system, ANSI compatible C and MasPar Fortran (MPF), which is an in-house version of Fortran 90, and an advanced graphical programming environment. In addition, MasPar has licensed a version of the Fortran conversion package VAST-2 from Pacific-Sierra Research Corporation. This product converts from scalar Fortran 77 source code to parallel MPF source. The conversion can also be done in reverse.

The machine consists of processing elements (RISC-like) grouped into clusters of 16 on the chips and connected in a 2-D lattice. Each cluster has the processing element memories and connects to the communication network. The machine is driven by a front-end computer (typically a VAX).

There are two main parts in the MasPar architecture:

1. MasPar Front End
2. Data Parallel Unit (DPU)
    *   Array Control Unit (ACU)
    *   Processor Element Array (PE Array)

The DPU executes the parallel portions of a program. The PE Array consists of a 64 × 64 array of processing elements for a total of 4096 processors. The front end is a DEC 3100 workstation. It runs DEC's version of UNIX (called ULTRIX) and provides users with a windowing programming environment. A pictorial view of the MasPar architecture is shown in Figure 1.11. The Array Control Unit (ACU) performs two tasks:

1. Executes instructions that operate on singular data.
2. Simultaneously feeds instructions which operate on parallel data to each processing element.

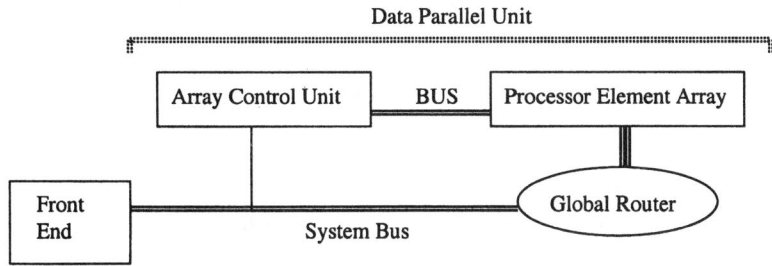

Figure 1.11. MasPar architecture.

Programs written in C and Fortran are executed on the front-end computer. The programs contain procedures written in MPL (MasPar Programming Language). When the procedures are called, they are executed inside the DPU. In general, the ACU broadcasts each instruction to all processing elements in the PE Array. Each processing element in the array then executes the instruction simultaneously. For more information about MasPar MP-1 architecture refer to [Blank 90, Christy 90].

The Connection Machines

The fundamental idea behind the Connection Machine family of SIMD machines from the Thinking Machine Corporation is that the data must be spread across the network to reduce the load on any single memory, meaning that in such machines, memory is distributed [Tucker 88]. The CM-1 is a true SIMD machine: processors execute in lock-step fashion from a single stream of instructions, meaning that it has one control unit for sequencing all processors. Generally speaking, the design of CM-1 was based on the semantic network, which is a data structure used in artificial intelligence to model the human brain's ability to manipulate unstructured data and ontract facts that are not explicitly defined in the database of knowledge. The CM-2, a fine-grain SIMD computer, can hold from 4096 to 65,536 processors. Each processor is 1 bit wide and supports from 65,536 to 262,144 bits of local memory. The CM-2 hardware consists of one to four front-end computers, a parallel processing unit (PPU), and an I/O system that supports mass storage and graphical devices [Thinking Machines Corporation]. The average speed of the CM-2 for most applications is two billion operations per second.

The front-end computer controls the processors. For example, after data are partitioned and distributed to each memory, an instruction is sent from the front-end processor to all CM-2 processors. Then each processor executes the instruction in lock-step fashion on its own data. This can be viewed as a data-parallel extension to the conventional front-end computer because control flow is handled by the front-end computer while parallel operations are executed on the PPU. A 4×4 crossbar switch connects the front-end computer to the four sections of the PPU. Each section is controlled by a *Sequencer*, which decodes the assembly language instructions and generates a series of micro-instructions for each processor. Each section of the PPU contains 1024 processor chips, 512 floating point interface chips, 512 floating point execution chip and 128 megabytes of RAM.

The 16 processors are connected by a 4×4 mesh, allowing processors to communicate with North, East, West and South (NEWS) neighbors. Interprocessor communication is handled by either a hypercube interconnection network or a faster multidimensional grid that allows processors to simultaneously transmit data. In general, CM-2 from the Thinking Machine Corporation shifted the emphasis from symbolic to numeric processing. This shift continued with subsequent products such as CM-5.

It is worth noting that the CM parallel instruction set, called PARIS (PARallel Instruction Set), provides a rich set of parallel primitives ranging from simple arithmetic and logical operations to sorting and communication operations. The high-level languages for the Connection Machines are built on top of the PARIS.

Figure 1.12. shows the general structure of the SIMD CM-2 adopted from the Thinking Machine Corporation.

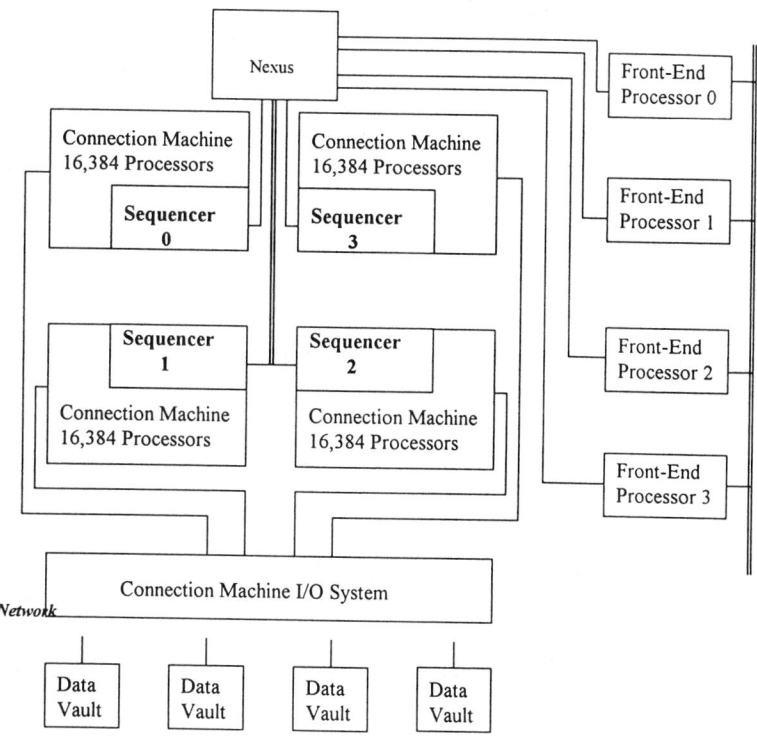

Figure 1.12. General architecture of SIMD CM-2.

1.2.2   MISD Architectures

A pipeline processor is an MISD processor that works according to the principle
of pipelining. Pipeline architecture is the fundamental form of parallel execution
of a process and is a powerful idea that can significantly improve SIMD computer performance. The pipelining principle implies the segmentation or partition of a computational process. A process can be broken down into several
stages (segments). Serial processing is concerned with the execution of all
stages of one process before starting the execution of the first stage of the next
process. Therefore, in serial processing, one process is completely finished before the next process is started. Rather than executing each stage of a process serially, a processor can speed up the execution by utilizing pipelining. In pipelining, while one stage is executing, another stage is being loaded and the input
of one stage is the output of the previous stage. This demonstrates that pipelin-

ing overlaps the execution of stages of the process; it consists of a number of successive stages separated by registers which save the results of the intermediate stages. Figure 1.13 illustrates the basic principles of pipelining for a process consisting of four stages with regard to serial and parallel execution. As a result of pipelining, the processor carries out many different computations concurrently, but at any time each computation is in a different stage of execution.

A process with 4 stages:

Serial execution of two processes consisting of 8 stages:

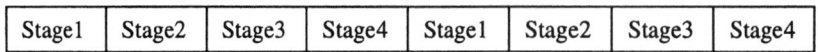

Pipelined execution of the same two processes consisting of 8 stages:

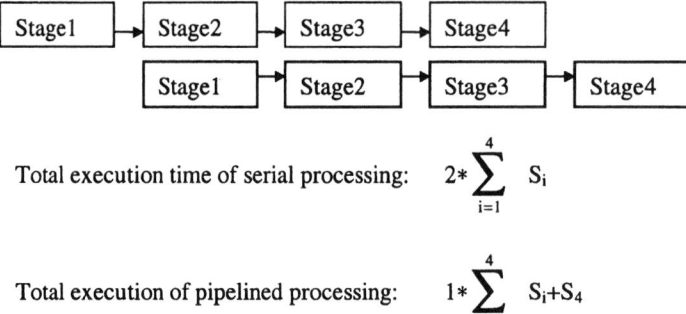

Total execution time of serial processing: $2 * \sum_{i=1}^{4} S_i$

Total execution of pipelined processing: $1 * \sum_{i=1}^{4} S_i + S_4$

where S_i is the execution time of stage i.

Figure 1.13. Serial and pipelined execution of a process consisting of four stages.

The principles of pipelining can be used at two different levels—arithmetic-unit pipelines and instruction-unit pipelines—resulting in two different design approaches. As shown in Figure 1.14, in arithmetic-unit pipelining, the arithmetic logic unit (ALU) is organized into several segments, and operations inside the ALU are pipelined. In instruction-unit pipelining, the control unit (CU) consists of several segments organized as a pipeline. For example, assume that the two floating point numbers after the operands are converted into binary as follows:

$$A = P * 2^Q \text{ and } B = R * 2^S$$

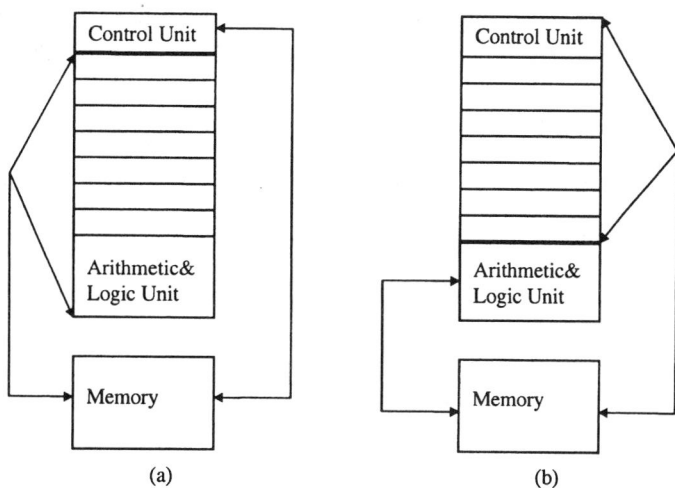

Figure 1.14. Principles of pipelining. (a) Arithmetic-unit pipelining.
(b) Control-unit pipelining.

The floating point addition operation can be divided into four distinct stages:
Stage 1. Compare the exponents to obtain the value (Q − S).
Stage 2. Align the mantissa of the smaller number. The value (Q − S) determines the number of places to shift P with respect to R to align the binary points.
Stage 3. Add the mantissas R and P.
Stage 4. The result can be normalized by shifting the result until the leading non-zero digit is next to the binary point.

In serial execution, one stage is executed after the other in the order given above. The time to execute each stage may be different, but to simplify the analysis we assume that the time to execute each stage is the same, say T seconds. Thus, the result of adding two floating point numbers can be produced in 4 *T seconds utilizing serial processing. We can generalize this idea such that there are D stages and N pairs of numbers on which the floating point operation has to be performed. In this case one pair of numbers is added before another pair is considered, resulting in N * D * T total computation time utilizing serial processing. As a result of having four stages in floating point operation addition, it is possible to have four pairs of numbers being processed in parallel with pipelining. Thus the time to process N pair of numbers utilizing pipelining is D * T + (N − 1) * T. In this example, the time taken to compute the addresses of numbers and other overheads, such as transfer between memory and pipeline unit, are ignored.

As we see, pipelining may be used to overlap phases of instruction execution and data communication. In addition to this pipelining operation, a cyclic pipeline may be formed among processors, memories and the interconnection networks, such as first used in the Burroughs Scientific processor. For example, four components, such as memory, two interconnection networks (one for writing result to memories and one for reading data from memories) and processing elements may form a cyclic pipeline architecture as shown in Figure 1.15.

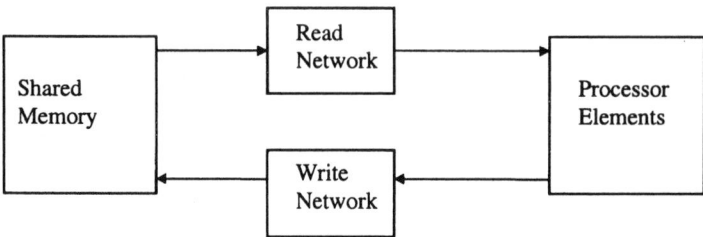

Figure 1.15. An example of a cyclic pipeline.

The operations performed by the control unit of this cyclic pipeline architecture can be broken down into five stages as follows:

Stage 1. Read operations: To read data from shared memories.

Stage 2. Transfer operations: To transfer data from memories to processing elements utilizing read network.

Stage 3. Execute operations: To execute instructions using processing elements.

Stage 4. Transfer operations: To transfer results to memories utilizing write network.

Stage 5. Store operations: To store the result in shared memories.

This architecture indicates that in addition to the parallelism achieved by concurrent execution of stages of instruction through pipelining, more speedup can be achieved by simultaneous operation of processing elements.

To design a pipeline architecture, the architect breaks down the critical processes of each operation into stages and develops special circuitry to perform each stage. Latches that are fast registers can hold the operands for each stage and the result of the previous stage. A clock performs the synchronization of all stages by informing the latches when to read the results of the current stage and pass the result to the successive stage. Figure 1.16 illustrates a pipeline consisting of three stages with all other components to connect them.

In general, the principles of pipelining, which is the overlapping of operations executed simultaneously, can be exploited in computer architecture at various levels as follows:

- *Instruction level.* This is used in the design of instruction processing units. An instruction passes through one segment during each cycle, so that after the input of instructions into the pipeline, instructions are emitted in every cycle.
- *Subsystem level.* Pipeline arithmetic units are one example. The pipelined operations ADD, MUL, DIV, and SORT are found in many computer architectures. Computers using an instruction pipeline are more common than those using pipeline arithmetic.
- *System level.* The pipeline segment need not be at the hardware level, and the pipeline can form a software structure. This also includes specialized computer networks and various types of high-reliability systems.

Pipeline
Clock

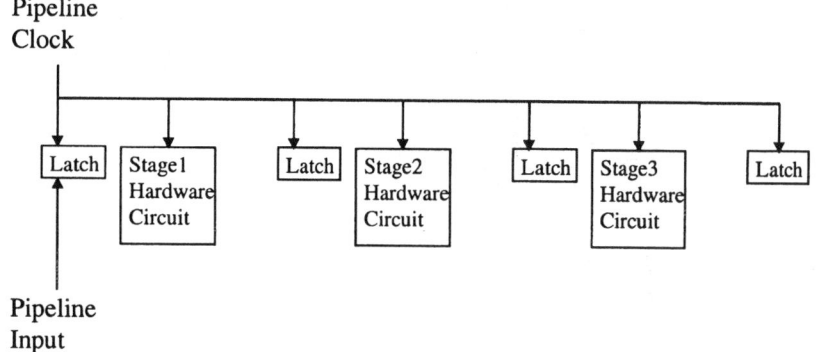

Pipeline
Input

Figure 1.16. Architecture of a pipeline.

Consequently, pipelining is in principle a concept for vector processing and can be found in most computers designed for these purposes. The architectures such as CDC STAR 100, Texas Instruments ASC, and Cray 1 are examples.

CDC STAR 100

The CDC STAR 100 computer was the first pipelined vector processor. Its design was started in 1965 and was available in 1974. A block diagram of this architecture is shown in Figure 1.17. The Central Processing Unit (CPU) consists of two pipelined floating point arithmetic units. Access Units for data access and storing provide efficient data flow. The Stream Control Unit (SCU) controls the stream of data, instructions, operand modification, buffer storage and addressing. Three address register-to-register instructions are used, two of them for source registers and one for the destination register. With continuous activity in both pipelines it is possible to generate a 64- or 32-bits floating point result every synchronization period. The vector operation start-up is slow, meaning that the pipelining is effective only if the vectors have a minimum length of 100 elements. Since 1979, a new CDC STAR 100 C vector processor has been available which has significantly reduced pipeline start-up time.

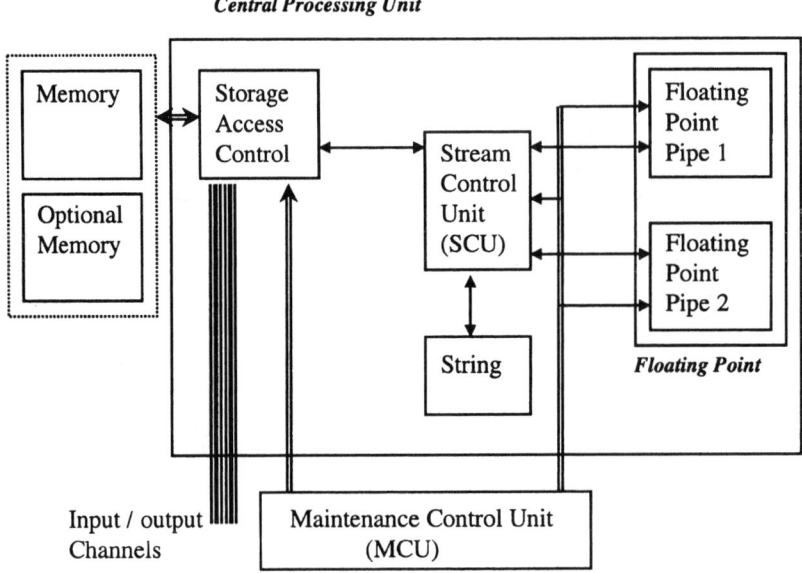

Figure 1.17. Block diagram of the CDC STAR 100 architecture.

Systolic Array Processors

In 1978, Kung and Leiserson [Kung 78] introduced systolic arrays for special purpose computing. This work was carried on at Carnegie-Mellon University when a solution for the application of VLSI technology to signal and image processing was being sought. The idea was to map a specific algorithm into a fixed architecture to provide for massive parallel computations. A systolic array is formed with a network of functional units which are locally connected. This array operates synchronously with multidimensional pipelining. As a consequence, this class of multidimensional pipelined array architectures is designed for implementing fixed algorithms. For example, the commercial machine Intel *i*Wrap system [Anaratone 86] was designed with a systolic architecture.

The systolic array design has been a popular research area since the time of its introduction. A systolic array can match the communication structure of the application by performing synchronous operations with fixed interconnection networking. It offers good performance for special applications, like signal and image processing, with simple, regular and modular layouts. The architecture favors CPU-bound computations. However, the architecture has limited applicability and can be very difficult for programming. Also, the interconnection pattern should be simple and regular, with only local connections of processing elements and without long wires. The speed of operations of these arrays is usually very high, meaning that long connections might introduce delays. Systolic array processors are already used in signal processing and appear well suited for other special applications characterized by simple control and data flow processing.

From the architecture viewpoint, each processing element (array cell) consists of a few registers, an adder, control circuits and a simple Arithmetic and Logic Unit (ALU). The data are processed in each array cell and flow out from the cell. The key feature is to schedule the computations in an array. From the programmer's point of view, the systolic arrays are similar to data flow, although they are control driven rather than data driven, since the computations are executed according to a schedule determined by the array design and not the data arrival. Figure 1.18 represents the basic operations involved in a systolic array processor system, in which the array operates under the supervision of a general controller. The controller, which is an interface with the host processor, propagates the control signals, inputs data to the processing element and collects the produced results.

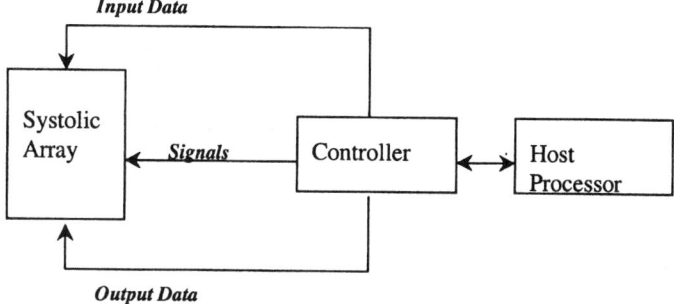

Figure 1.18. Systolic array processor architecture.

Because the performance of systolic array systems is highly dependent on the input and output characteristics of the data, these systems are recommended for those applications that are computationally intensive, meaning that once input data are fetched from memory, it is desirable to perform as many operations as possible before the output is sent back to memory. Some examples are matrix multiplication and image and signal processing. There are several topologies involved in systolic array processors design. Some of them are shown in Figure 1.19.

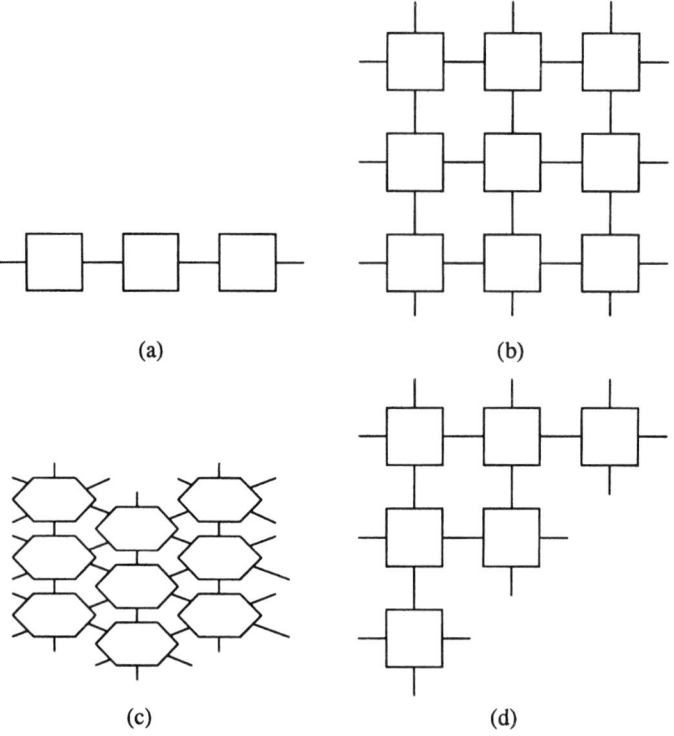

Figure 1.19. Systolic array topologies. (a) One-dimensional systolic linear array. (b) Two-dimensional systolic square array. (c) Two-dimensional systolic hexagonal array. (d) Triangular systolic array.

The first systolic array machine, called Wrap, was developed by Kung in the mid-1980s as a joint effort between Carnegie-Mellon University and Intel Corporation. It was a one-dimensional systolic array machine and proved the feasibility of the systolic computational concept. It consists of three components:

- The Wrap processor arrays, which consists of 10 or more cells
- The interface unit
- The host processor

The interface unit is a controller. It provides an input and output interface with the host processor and generates the control signals and addresses for the systolic processing element. The host processor executes the parts of the application that are not mapped to the array and receives the produced result.

The second systolic array machine, called *i*Wrap was built as a two-dimensional system in 1990. In contrast to the first design, it included more complex cells instead of large fine-grained cells. The reason was to support a broad range of applications. The *i*Wrap cell performs instruction level parallelism to allow simultaneous operations of multiple functional units and can simultaneously communicate with a number of *i*Wrap processors at very high speed. This indicates that the *i*Wrap cell provides both high-speed computation and communication capability in a single component. It addition, it supports programming models of tightly coupled and loosely coupled computing mode of systolic array machines. Each *i*Wrap cell consists of two individual components as follows:

- *i*Wrap Component, which contains *Communication Agent* and *Computation Agent*. The agents are controlled independently to allow overlapped communication and computation. As a result of this design, nonadjacent cells can communicate with each other without disturbing the computation of other cells.
- *i*Wrap Memory, which contains several local memory modules.

The computation agent consists of the Local Memory Unit (LMU), Register File Unit (RFU), Program Store Unit (PSU), Instruction Sequencing Unit (ISU), Integer Logic Unit (ILU), Floating Point Unit (FPU), and Streaming/Spooling Unit (SSU). The local memory unit provides the interface between the *i*Wrap Component and *i*Wrap Memory. The local memory unit contains data and instructions and provides a direct interface with other units for computations, to maximize computational performance. Figure 1.20 shows the *i*Wrap cell architecture, which is the basic block of the *i*Wrap systolic array computer.

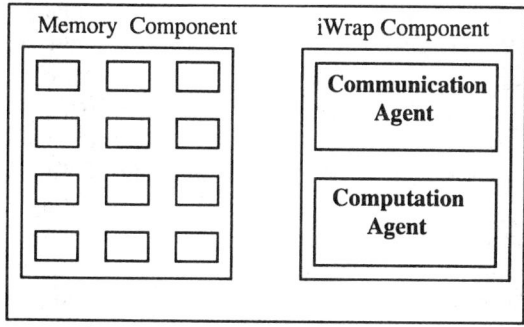

Figure 1.20. *i*Wrap systolic machine cell architecture.

A classical use for a two-dimensional systolic array system is matrix-matrix multiplication. Matrices A and B enter the systolic array such that corresponding elements that are needed to be multiplied are provided in the same cell to produce a partial result of the product matrix C. Figure 1.21 shows a systolic array specifically designed for performing matrix-matrix multiplication in which the interior node degree is 6, and $A_{2\times2} \times B_{2\times2} = C_{2\times2}$.

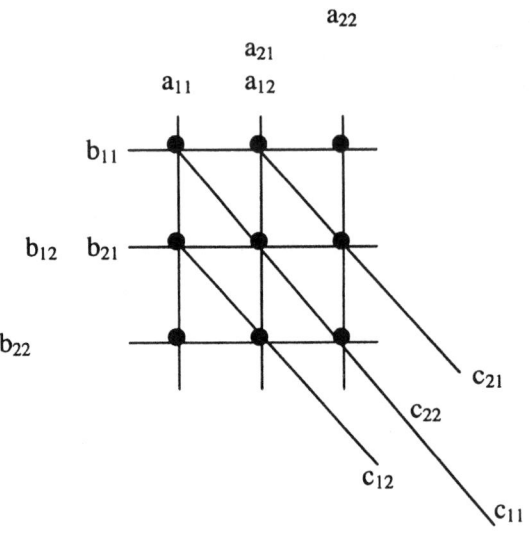

Figure 1.21. A systolic array architecture for two-dimensional matrix multiplication.

Another example is the systolic matching queue used in the Ultracomputer switch to speed the process of finding and combining memory requests with matching addresses. The CHiP (Configurable Highly Parallel) computer [Lawrence 82], which is a lattice of identical processing elements set into a lattice of identical switches. The system provides the configuration of many different systolic arrays. The number of parts per switch is usually four or eight, while the number of processing elements ports is eight or fewer. Each switch in the lattice has local memory capable of storing the switch setting for several different configurations.

In addition to the above, there are two popular vector processor architectures: The C series of mini-supercomputers from Convex Computer Corporation [Hwang 93] and the 5000 Series of attached processors from Floating-point Systems [Hamacher 96]. The Convex C Series are built from Multiple 64-bit CPUs tightly coupled through a shared memory. The C1 system was announced in 1983, C2 in 1986, and C3 in 1991. The Floating-Point Systems (PFS) series are array processors with a high-speed computational device attached to a general purpose computer as a host. The high performance of the systems are achieved through the use of multiple functional units operating in parallel and using pipelining within the individual units. The design also employs multiple memories and multiple data paths between these memories and the functional units.

1.2.3   MIMD Architectures

An MIMD system is a multiprocessor or multicomputer system in which each individual processor has its own control unit and executes its own program. MIMD computers have the following characteristics:

- They distribute processing over a number of independent processors.
- They share resources, including main memory system, among processors.
- Each processor operates independently and concurrently.
- Each processor runs its own program.

This indicates that MIMD systems execute operations in a parallel asynchronous fashion, meaning that active nodes cooperate closely but operate independently. MIMD architectures differ with regard to the interconnection networks, processors, memory addressing techniques, synchronization and control structures. The interconnection networks allow the processors to communicate and interact with each other. Examples of MIMD computers include the Cosmic Cube, nCUBE2, iPSC, Symmetry, FX-8, FX-2800, TC-2000, CM-5, KSR-1 and Paragon XP/s.

We can categorize MIMD computers as being either **tightly coupled** or **loosely coupled** systems, depending on how the processors access each other's memory. The processors in a tightly coupled multiprocessor system generally share one global memory system; thus, the system is also known as a **Shared-Memory** system. Those of a loosely coupled MIMD system may also share a memory system, but each also has its own local memory. This is also known as a **Message-Passing** system. Thus, tightly coupled and loosely coupled computers correspond to the Global-Memory MIMD **(GM-MIMD)** and Local-Memory MIMD **(LM-MIMD)** systems, respectively. MIMD message-passing computers are referred to as multicomputers in which each processor has its own memory, called the local or private memory, and is accessible only to that processor. The message-passing MIMD architecture is also referred to as a distributed-memory or private-memory architecture. A message-passing interconnection network provides point-to-point static connections among the processors. Figure 1.22 shows the structure of a shared-memory MIMD system in which any processor N can access any memory M through the interconnection network. Computation results are stored in memory by the processor that executed that task. If the results are needed by other processors, they can be easily accessed from the memory. There is no local memory associated with processors, and each processor acts as a single SISD capable of fetching instructions from its allocated memory and executing them on the data retrieved from the memory. A shared-memory

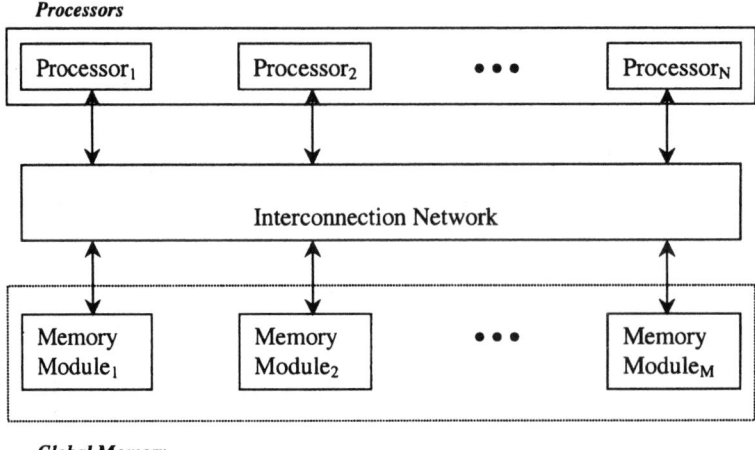

Figure 1.22. A pictorial view of tightly coupled MIMD architecture, known as shared-memory, global-memory or uniform memory access (UMA) MIMD.

MIMD system is also called a **Uniform Memory Access** (UMA) system, because the memory access time is the same for all the processors. Figure 1.23 shows the structure of a message-passing MIMD system. If data exchange is required between two processors, the requesting processor P sends a message to processor Q in whose local memory the required data are stored. In reply to this request, the processor Q reads the requested data from its local memory and passes it on to processor P through the interconnection network, meaning that the message-passing method of communication is used. In contrast to shared-memory systems, the memory access time varies between the processors; thus, this architecture is known as **Non-Uniform Memory Access** (NUMA). MIMD computers offer the following advantages:

- A high throughput can be achieved if the processing can be broken into parallel streams, thereby keeping all the processors active concurrently.
- Because the processors and memory blocks are general-purpose resources, a faulty resource can be easily removed and its work allocated to another available resource, thereby achieving a degree of fault tolerance.
- A dynamic reconfiguration of resources is possible to accommodate varying processing loads.

In the shared-memory model, processors can communicate in a simple and unconstrained fashion by sharing data using commonly known address space, meaning that undesired data sharing can be prevented by using the standard data-hiding methods of modern programming languages. Because of this ability to support a variety of programming models efficiently, a shared-memory multiprocessor system will always be the first choice of parallel programming users. In contrast, message-passing systems are easier to design but more difficult to program. In general, tightly coupled MIMD systems provide more rapid data interchange between processors than loosely coupled MIMD systems. Memory competition is not a problem in the message-passing systems because only one processor has access to a memory block associated with that processor. Examples of GM-MIMD computers are the CDC 6600 series and the Cray XM-P. Examples of LM-MIMD computers are the Carnegie-Mellon Cm* and the Tandom/16. In summary, shared memory has placed more of the burden of parallel processing on the hardware designer, whereas message passing placed it more on the programmer.

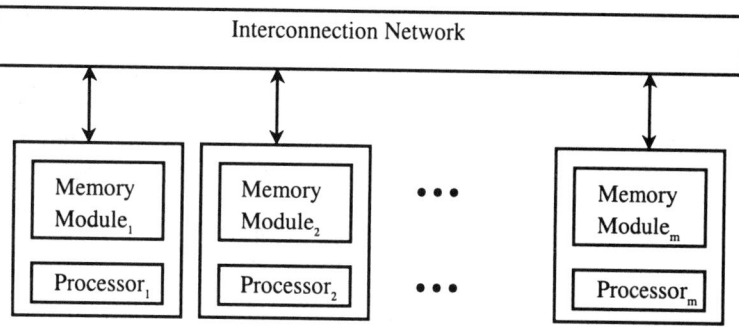

Figure 1.23. A pictorial view of loosely coupled MIMD architecture, known as message-passing, local-memory or non-uniform memory access (NUMA) MIMD.

MIMD computers can also be modeled as either private-address-space or shared-address-space computers. Both models can be implemented on GM-MIMD and LM-MIMD architectures. Private-address-space computers combine the benefits of message-passing architectures with the programming advantages of shared-memory architectures. A example of this machine is J-Machine from MIT, with a small private memory, a large number of processors, and a global address space. MIMD computers are more flexible in applications than SIMD computers but are harder to program because they are not synchronized at the instruction level as SIMD computers are. This flexibility is achieved at the cost of a considerably more difficult mode of operation. In general, the algorithm must exhibit a high degree of parallelism in which in order to be partitioned into independent tasks to be allocated to individual processors and performed concurrently.

The architecture trend for future general-purpose computers favors MIMD configurations with distributed memories involved in a global shared virtual address space. We summarize this section by comparing some of the general features of the MIMD computers with those of the SIMD computers:

- Store the program and operating system at each processor.
- Allow different operations to be performed on different processing elements simultaneously, meaning that they can support both functional parallelism (independent functions are assigned to and executed on different processors simultaneously) and data parallelism (the same set of instructions is applied to all the elements in a data set), in contrast to SIMD architectures, which are limited to data parallelism.
- More complex because each processor has its own control unit.
- No need for the SIMD instruction broadcasting mechanism.
- It is possible to use general-purpose microprocessor as processing unit.
- In the execution of a conditional statement (if-then-else) based on the available data, each processing element can independently follow either direction path. Conversely, in SIMD architecture, all of the instructions for the *then* block must be broadcast, followed by all of the *else* block with regard to the appropriate processing element enabled for each block. For example, in the following if-then-else statement

```
If (Boundary-Element)
   Do Something
Else
   Do something
End if
```

the fragment can be executed on an SIMD machine in two phases; first the processors containing the interior elements are masked out and then the processors containing the boundary elements are masked out.
- Processors may be cheaper and more powerful than SIMD.
- Consider a sequence of instructions in which the execution time is data dependent. The MIMD architecture allows each processing element to execute the sequence of instructions independently, resulting in a Max-Of-Sums. In contrast, in the SIMD a processing element must wait until all the others have finished the execution before continuing the next instruction, resulting in a Sum-Of-Max, as in the following:

$$T_{SIMD} = \sum_{instruction} Max_{PE} \, (instruction.time)$$

$$T_{MIMD} = Max_{PE} \cdot \sum_{instruction} (instruction.time)$$

as a consequence, $T_{MIMD} \leq T_{SIMD}$ holds.

- MIMD architectures are able to operate in SIMD mode as well such as DADO [Stolfo 86] and CM-5 [Thinking Machines Corporation 91].

Intel iPSC Machines

The Intel Personal SuperComputer (iPSC) is one of the first commercially available parallel computers. The first parallel computer, iPSC/1, was introduced in 1985, followed by the iPSC/2 in 1987 and the iPSC/860 in 1990. The iPSC is a message-passing MIMD machine in which all processor nodes are identical and are connected by bidirectional links in a hypercube topology. An iPSC system consists of one, two, or four computational units called the *cube* and a host processor called the *cube manager*. The cube is the hypercube interconnection of the processing nodes in which each node consists of a self-contained processor and memory. The iPSC/1 is a one unit cube message-passing system and consists of 32 nodes, a cube manager, and 16 Mbytes of unshared memory evenly divided among the nodes [Moler 86]. The nodes are Intel 80286/80287 processors (16-bit processors) with 512 Kbytes of memory allocated to each one. The peak performance of the system is about 2 MFLOPS. Ethernet channels are used for internode communication because of their availability.

The iPSC/2 is a 64-node message-passing system. Each node consists of 80386/80387 processors and 4 Mbytes of memory expandable to 16 Mbytes. In general, each node contains the 32-bit Intel 80386 microprocessor and 80387 floating point coprocessor, local memory and a routing module for high-speed message-passing within the communication network. The cube manager functions are contained in the System Resource Manager (SRM). The SRM performs systemwide support and control and provides a user entry point to the cube. The average peak performance of the system is about 5.6 MFLOPS. The latest in the iPSC systems is the iPSC/860 message-passing system with 128 nodes, in which, each node contains Intel's i860, 64-bit RISC processor. Each processor includes a floating point multiplier and adder, an 8-Kbyte instruction cache, and a 16-Kbyte data cache. Because the i860 microprocessor is like a supercomputer on a chip and is capable of 80 MFLOPS, the iPSC/860 system performance rating far exceed that of existing supercomputers. The system uses the XENIX operating system. The first generation of Intel message-passing systems (iPSC/1) was characterized by software-managed *store-and-forward message passing*. In order to send a message from one processor to a nonadjacent processor, every intermediate processor along the path must store the message and then forward it to the next processor in the path. The data can be transferred through the channel, but the CPU is interrupted when the transfer is initiated. In contrast, the second generation of Intel message-passing systems (iPSC/2 and iPSC/860), have adopted a *circuit-switched message-routing* scheme in which the message flows in a pipelined fashion from the source node to the destination node without disturbing the intermediate nodes to store the messages. In essence, a routing logic card called *Direct-Connect-Routing Module* is involved which allows a connection between sender and receiver processors and keeps the CPUs of the intermediate nodes from being interrupted when a message transfers.

The successor of the iPSC/860 is the Intel Paragon, which consists of a mesh of connected i860 processors. Figure 1.24 shows the Intel iPSC/2 node architecture. Further information on the Intel iPSC machines can be found in [Babb 88, Moler 86, Shiva 96, Hwang 93].

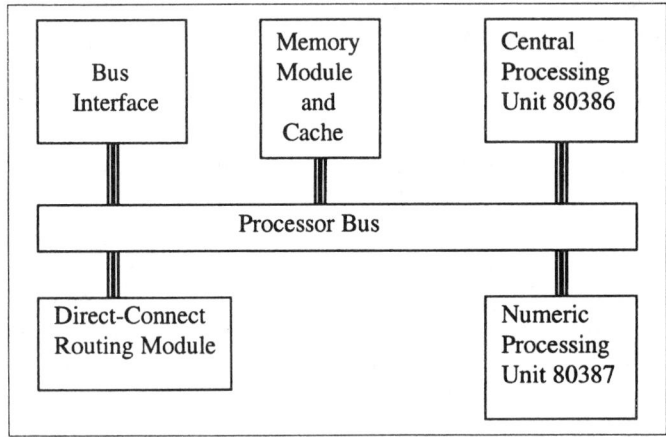

Figure 1.24. Intel iPSC/2 node architecture (courtesy of Intel Scientific Computers).

Symmetry Machine

The Sequent Balance, manufactured by Sequent Computer Systems, Inc., of Beaverton, Oregon, was a shared-memory MIMD machine consisting of 30 processors based on the National Semiconductor 32032 microprocessor. A new system, the Sequent Symmetry, employs up to 30 Intel 80386/80387 microprocessors. It is a commercial example of UMA multiprocessors and is representative of the class of bus-structured shared-memory MIMD computers. The processors, memory modules and other peripherals are interconnected via a high-speed pipelined 64-bit system bus. The Sequent System Bus (SSB) carries 32- or 64-bit data items and addresses up to 32 bits in length. The input and output operations are pipelined, which means that after the system bus has transmitted an input or output request to system memory, it can proceed with another request even before the memory has processed the first request. The processor is based on a 32-bit 80386 microprocessor and an Intel 80387 floating point coprocessor. In addition, each processor has a System Link and Interrupt Controller to manage the interaction among processors, since the Intel 80386 is not designed to be used as a multiprocessor CPU. Each processor is supported by 64-Kbyte cache memories. The cache memories in the Sequent Symmetry system have a very important role—they keep the CPUs busy and reduce competition for the System Bus, meaning that the CPU can operate at full speed. Additional hardware associated with this system includes a bus arbitrator SCED, dual-channel disk controller DCC, serial device controller MBUS, and auxiliary peripherals. An ethernet channel is used for interconnection among other components. Figure 1.25 shows a block diagram of the Sequent Symmetry multiprocessor architecture with bus arbitrator and other controllers.

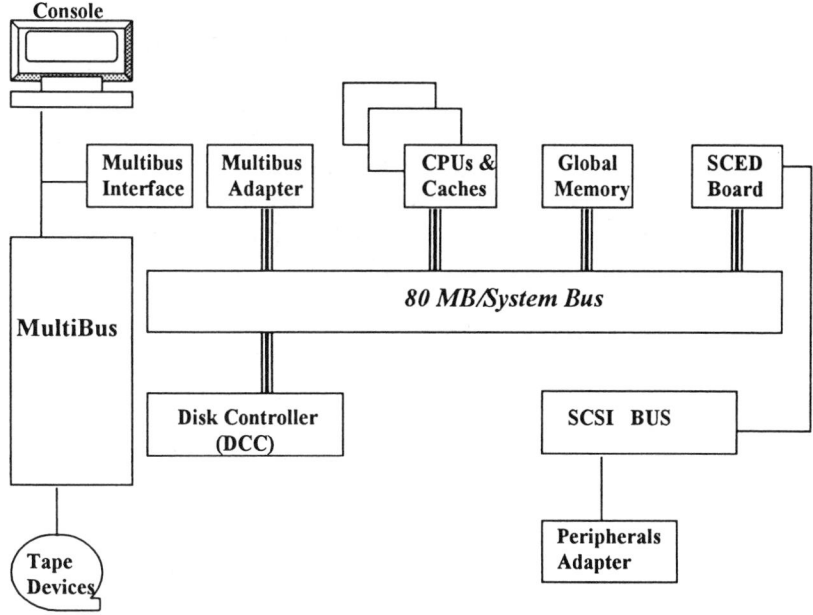

Figure 1.25. Sequent Symmetry multiprocessor architecture.

Carnegie-Mellon Multi-Mini-Processor

The C.mmp (Computer with multi-mini-processor) was a project originated in 1971 at the Carnegie-Mellon University [Wulf 72]. It consisted of 16 minicomputers connected to 16 memory modules through a multistage crossbar switch to form a shared memory MIMD system. In this architecture design, 16 memory references can be in progress simultaneously, provided that reference is to a different memory port. The Cm*, designed with multi-micro-processor, was announced in 1975 by the Carnegie-Mellon University as the successor of the C.mmp system [Kumar 94]. The basic unit of this design was a processor-memory pair called a Computer module (Cm). The memory local to each processor was also the shared memory to all other processors. The processors are

grouped into local clusters, in which clusters are organized into a tree structure
and connected via Inter-Cluster Buses. The interconnection of this shared memory MIMD system was a three level hierarchy of buses. The lowest level consists of an arbitrary number of computer modules. Each module contains five
components: a microprocessor, a bus-interface processor called a local switch, a
local bus, local memory, and local devices. The second level consists of clusters
of computer modules. Using the Map Bus, a processor can access to the memory
of the other processors in the same cluster. The third and highest level consists
of a group of clusters connected by Inter-Cluster Buses. A processor within a
cluster can access to the memory of the other clusters via this level of hierarchy.
A pictorial view of this architecture is shown in Figure 1.26. A major drawback
of these architectures is that the bandwidth of the interconnection network must
be substantial to ensure good performance. This is because, in each instruction
cycle, every processor may need to access a word from the shared memory
through the interconnection network. Furthermore, memory access through the
interconnection network can be slow, since a read or write request may have to
pass through multiple stages in the network.

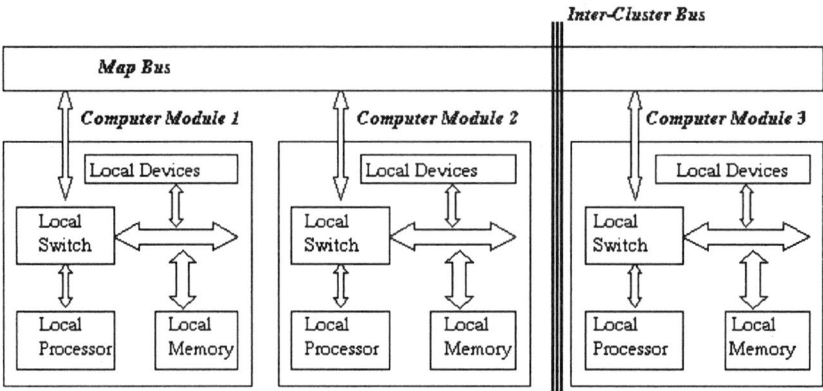

Figure 1.26. The structure of a cluster of three computer modules in C.m* architecture.

1.2.4   SIMD-MIMD Hybrid Architectures

The SIMD architecture is a set of N processors, N memories, an interconnection
network and a control unit (e.g., ILLIAC IV, STARAN, CLIPP, MPP). The
control unit broadcasts instructions to the processors and all active processors
execute the same instruction at the same time. The MIMD architecture consists
of N processors and N memories, where each processor can follow an independent instruction stream (e.g., C.mmp, and Cm* ultracomputer). A hybrid
SIMD/MIMD architecture is a parallel processing system that can be structured
as one or more independent SIMD and/or MIMD architectures of various sizes,

for example, TRAC (Texas Reconfigurable Array Computer) [Sejnowski 80]. TRAC was a dynamically partitionable mixed-mode shared-memory parallel machine developed at the University of Texas at Austin. Generally speaking, a hybrid architecture does not fit into either the SIMD or the MIMD computational model. In this section, we discuss three main categories of this architecture design:

1. **PASM:** Partitionable SIMD/MIMD systems
2. **VLIW:** Very Long Instruction Word systems
3. **MSIMD:** Multiple SIMD systems

PASM Architecture (a reconfigurable parallel system for image processing) is a hybrid SIMD/MIMD architecture designed at Purdue Universsity to be a large-scale multimicroprocessor system. It is used to exploit the parallelism of image understanding tasks and is being used for a variety of image processing and pattern recognition problems. The basic components of the PASM architecture are shown in Figure 1.27.

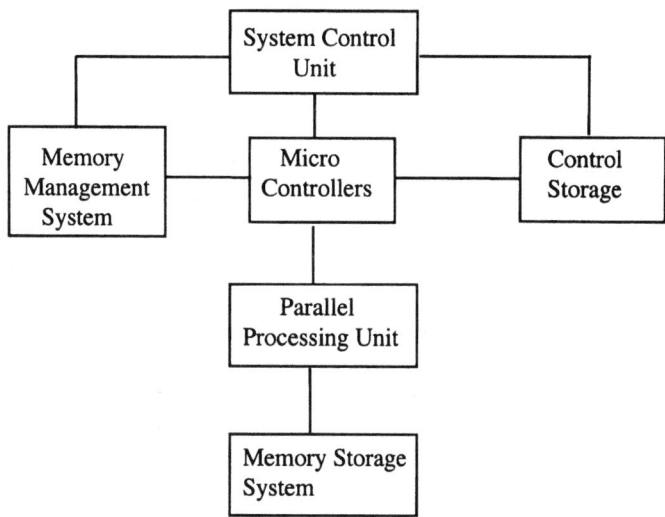

Figure 1.27. Basic components of PASM architecture.

The System Control Unit component is responsible for process scheduling, resource allocation, parallelism mode and overall coordination. Micro controllers control the activities. Each one consists of a microprocessor and two memory units to perform memory loading and computations. Microprocessors perform the SIMD and MIMD computations and the memory modules are used for data storage in SIMD mode and both data and instruction storage in MIMD mode. Each microprocessor and two memory units is called a processing element. These are numbered from 0 to N − 1. In practice, each processing element can operate in both SIMD and MIMD modes of parallelism. The interconnection network provides communication among the processing elements. Figure 1.28 shows the parallel computation unit consisting of N microprocessors and two memory modules associated with each one.

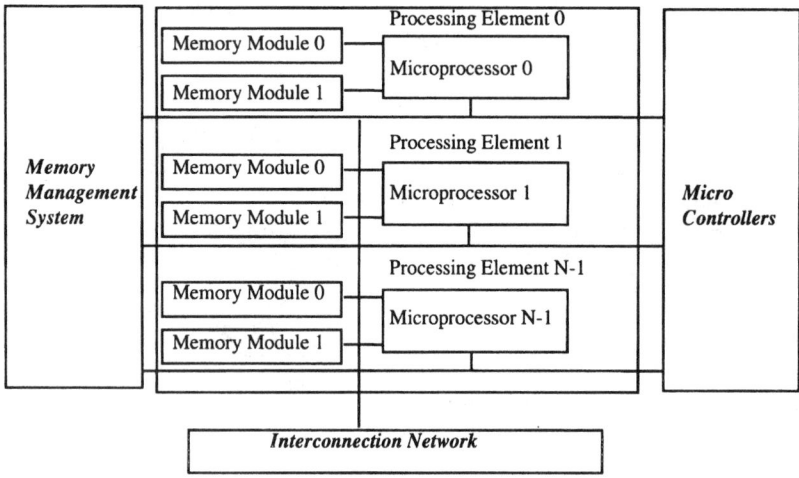

Figure 1.28. Parallel computation unit consisting of n microprocessors and two memory modules associated with each one.

A prototype of the PASM system is constructed such that all the processors are based on the Motorola MC68010 16-bit microprocessor. A CPU board containing the MC68010 microprocessor, a dynamic memory board with up to 1 megabyte of memory, an I/O board, a network interchange board and a specialized board are included in each microprocessor. The parallel computation unit consists of 16 processing elements connected by an interconnection network and controlled by four microcontrollers. Figure 1.29 shows the PASM parallel processing architecture. The memory storage units are managed by the Memory Management System, which consists of a Directory Lookup Processor, a Memory Scheduling Processor, a Command Distribution Processor and an Input/Output and Reformatting Processor.

User programs and data can be received from or sent to a local network connected to the PASM system which consists of twenty DEC VAX and PDP-11 computers at Purdue University.

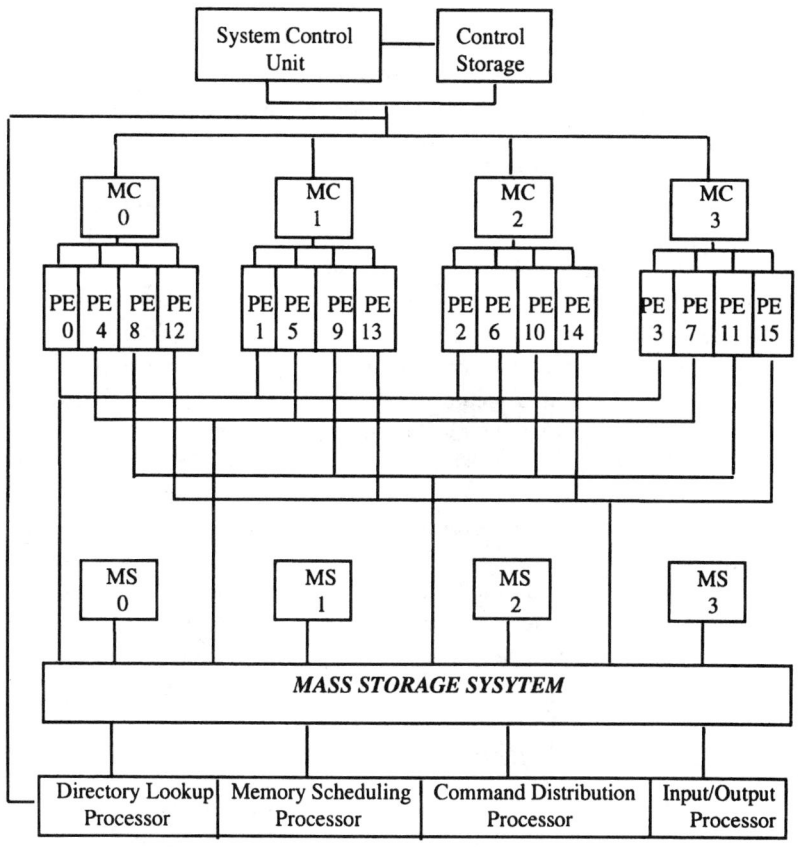

Figure 1.29. PASM parallel processing architecture.

VLIW (Very Long Instruction Word) Architecture

In VLIW architecture design, the processing elements are under centralized control, but the individual processing elements can perform a different operation on different data elements. This architecture may be regarded as a form of liberated SIMD or as specially designed MIMD with the essential difference that there is only one thread of control, meaning that there is a central controller that issues very long instructions. The VLIW idea is related to the generation of horizontal microcode, because conventional compilers operate on one basic block at a time and it is not necessary to have parallel architecture as a target design. In general, in program execution there are huge backlogs of instructions that could be performed in parallel, even though the conventional processing model performs them in sequential form. For example, the Bulldog Fortran reassembling compiler [Fisher 83, Ellis 86] is an approach to parallelize at the instruction level for programs written in Fortran. The computer architectures with the VLIW system design are used for reassembling compilers such as Bulldog.

Multiflow Computer Inc. designed a series of long instruction word computers on the Eli-512 [Fisher 83]. (The company encountered financial problems in 1990 and no longer exists.) The Multiflow TRACE 7/200 has a 256-bit instruction word and can perform up to seven operations at a time. Later, in the model 14/, the instruction length and the number of simultaneous operations doubled. The long instruction word approach has also been used in several other architectures such as CHoPP and Cydra 5 computers. In late 1970s, the CHoPP (Columbia Homogeneous Parallel Processor) project was begun as a research project based on shared-memory MIMD computers with a plan for a multistage network connecting up to a million processing elements [Sullivan 77]. The CHoPP 1 [Mankovich 87] is a shared-memory MIMD architecture with 16 processing elements in which the design was based on negotiation between running processes. High performance can be achieved by issuing multiple instructions on each clock, fast execution of individual instructions, conflict-free memory access shared by multiple processors, and fast context switching hardware. Each processing element contains nine computational functional units that can simultaneously execute nine operations under the control of a 256-bit instruction size in which each functional unit can perform one operation per clock cycle.

MSIMD Tree Machines (Multiple SIMD Systems)

MSMID consists of Multiple SIMD and several tree-connected and circuit-switched reconfigurable designs that can be partitioned into multiple sub-configurations, each one operating in SIMD mode. The main advantage of this architecture is that the interconnection of the processing elements offers simplicity and is well matched to the layout of VLSI chips and circuit boards, but it may suffer from traffic at the root if there is much communication among the processing elements located at the leaves.

The Cellular Computer [Mago 79] is a tree machine designed with 10^6 processors for parallel execution of the expressions written in a reduction language such as the FP functional programming language. The key components of a functional programming language are a set of functional forms and the application operation. The set of functional forms is used for combining functions into new ones and the application operation is a method to apply a function to an argument and produce a result value. The entire program is loaded into leaves, and execution consists of several iterations. In each iteration, called a reduction process, data from the leaves are carried toward the root of the tree, followed by a downward tree that ends up modifying the leaves. A leaf contains a CPU, several dozen registers and microprogram storage. The CPU can execute segments of microprograms and performs processing related to memory management. An internal node contains six groups of registers and four processors and can hold up to four nodes, each belonging to a different partition of the machine. One layer of tree provides input and output operations for the system.

The NON-VON architecture [Shaw 84] is designed as a massively parallel tree-connected system. The target of this architecture is rapid execution of large-scale data manipulation tasks, including relational database operations. The system consists of small processing elements, each one with an 8-bit ALU, 16 registers, 64 bytes of local memory and an I/O switch connecting to a parent and two children.

Generally speaking, the single processor architecture is the most efficient solution if the performance requirements of the application can be achieved. If not, an SIMD system might be evaluated as an alternative solution. If the application is not tailored to the SIMD system or the performance is not satisfactory, the MIMD system is the final alternative and would be appropriate. In addition to performance and cost constraints, application characteristics can dictate the architecture selection.

1.3   Data Flow Architectures

The single or multiprocessor architectures are based on the principles of the execution of a sequence of instructions by the control unit and the determination of the flow of control by the program. On the contrary, in a data flow architecture, operations can be performed by allowing an instruction to be executed immediately when its operands and computational resources are available. This means that the data flow architecture relaxes the constraints imposed by the execution order of instructions and the availability of data determines which instruction is to be executed. If the data for several instructions are available at the same time, these instructions can be executed in parallel.

A program for a data flow architecture consists of a kind of symbolic representation of the computations, which is called the data flow model of computation. The computational models that data flow architectures represent are called data flow graphs and are inherently parallel models of computation. The applications that exhibit a fine-grain parallelism, such as image processing and scene analysis, are more adopted in data flow architectures.

A programmer describes the computations by giving the data flow graph problem such that the nodes correspond to the operations and the arcs indicate where the results of the operation are to be forwarded. Arcs leaving the graph are output arcs and arcs entering the graph from outside are input arcs. Thus, the data flow graph specifies the overall design of an application and defines connections between processes, which are represented by circles in the graph, and data, which are represented by edges in the graph. After the graph is defined, every process and arc is labeled with an alphanumeric name which is used in the data graph language. It is useful to label each arc with the kind of data that is expected to be passed over the arc. Although the optimum parallelism of work utilizing processes can involve some trial and error, the structure of the problem being solved suggests a good first approximation.

For example, the execution of the expression $X = (A + B) * (C - D)$ on a conventional architecture can produce an instruction sequence as follows:

```
Add    A, B
Store  T1
Sub    C, D
Store  T2
Mult   T1, T2
Store  X
```

where A, B, C, D, X, T1 and T2 are the symbolic name of memory locations and Add, Sub, Mul, and Store are the symbolic names of the operations. This execution of the expression needs six operations to be performed. Utilizing a data flow architecture, the computation of the expression can be represented by the graph in Figure 1.30. In this example, the addition and subtraction can take place in parallel and then the multiplication can be performed.

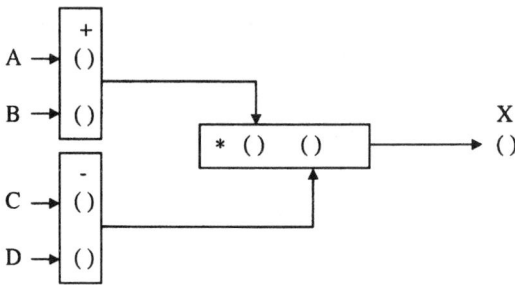

Figure 1.30. Graph representation for the expression $X = (A + B) * (C - D)$. The boxes in the graph represent vertices to perform operations and the arrows represent arcs to pass the data to the vertices.

There are many complex and interesting issues involved with the design of data flow architectures, such as:

- The architecture must reconfigure itself during execution of a series of computations.
- The nodes must perform various auxiliary functions such as queuing of data that have been received along arcs to perform a computation.

For instance, if a processing element is to add two numbers and one has arrived and the other hasn't, the processing element must hold and queue the operand that is available and wait for the second operand.

A data flow architecture has many independent processing elements, and one of them acts as a supervising processor. When the data are available, the supervising processor transfers the data and an instruction to a processing element, which performs the operation and transfers the result to memory. The data of a data flow program are contained in tokens, and tokens require storage. The method of token storage is the key feature that distinguishes data flow architectures. It is possible to regard the data flow approach as a way of expressing parallel computation which can be used with any multiprocessor architecture. These architectures need some form of dynamically connecting processor. Each processor can be viewed as executing the function specified by an individual processor. Outputs are produced and are passed as inputs for subsequent operations. Because data flow machines do not execute programs in the conventional sense and perform computations based on a data flow model, these machines are neither SIMD nor MIMD.

There are several main groups working on data flow architectures design. In Britain, the Manchester group supervised by John Gurd has developed several prototypes. Dennis and Arvind were two main working groups at MIT. The reader should refer to [Gurd 85], [Dennis 80] and [Arvind 81] for their achievements. Data flow concepts have been utilized in the design of various processors, including the CDC 6600 series of computers and some Japanese computers.

It is worth noting that a high throughput can be achieved by data flow architectures because the algorithms are represented at the finest grain parallelism, and hence the maximum degree of concurrency is possible. Data flow architectures are divided into three different categories:

1. **Static Architecture:** This architecture can evaluate only one program graph. Possibly the only interesting static architecture would be one that could evaluate and run any program. In this case, all the complexity of executing a data flow program would be transferred away from the architecture design to the compilation stage. This is an acceptable strategy although it is difficult to see what form of machine the architecture should take.

2. **Reconfigurable Static Architecture:** This architecture consists of a number of processors for which the logical interconnections between the processors are made when the program is loaded for execution. This indicates that the decisions about connections must be made by the compiler and the loaded program remain fixed throughout the execution. This approach requires two criteria:

   • Physical connections must exist.

- The number of available processors must be more than the minimum required number of processors, since it is difficult to see how is possible to use an optimal number of processors with fixed links.

3. **Dynamic Architecture:** This architecture allows programs to be evaluated dynamically. The main feature of a dynamic architecture is the logical connection between processors, which can be changed during the execution of a program.

The difference between the models depends on the number of arguments and tokens allowed to be passed on a given arc at a time.

1.3.1   Static Data Flow Architectures

In static data flow models, the arcs are restricted to one token at a time. The data flow graph problem describing the computation to be performed is held as a collection of activity templates in the specific area called activity storage. Each activity template has a unique address and can be saved in a queue called an Instruction Queue until the instruction is ready to be executed. There is a fetch operation, which takes an instruction address from the Instruction Queue and an activity template from the activity storage and changes it into a specific operation. The operation can be passed to a specific area for execution, which is called the Execution Unit.

In the Execution Unit the instruction can be processed and a result packet for the destination field of the operation is generated, which is the output of the node in the data flow graph problem. The send and receive unit connects this processor with other components in the system to make this transfer possible.

Figure 1.31 illustrates the computation of a static data flow graph problem. There is a module on checking and updating which tests whether all operands are required to activate.

The operation instruction has been received and, if so, updates the values it carries into operand fields of activity templates and enters the instruction address in the Instruction Queue. The number of instructions in the Instruction Queue can address the degree of concurrency presented in the program.

The degree of parallelism can be seen in the fact that, once the fetch unit has sent an operation packet to the execution unit, it may immediately read another entry from the instruction queue without waiting for the previous fetched instruction to be processed.

This stream of operations may be continued as long as the instruction queue is not empty. The reason that only one token is allowed to exist on an arc at one given time is that otherwise it would not be clear which set of tokens belonged to which set of inputs. The static data flow model cannot support programming constructs such as procedure calls, recurrences and arrays.

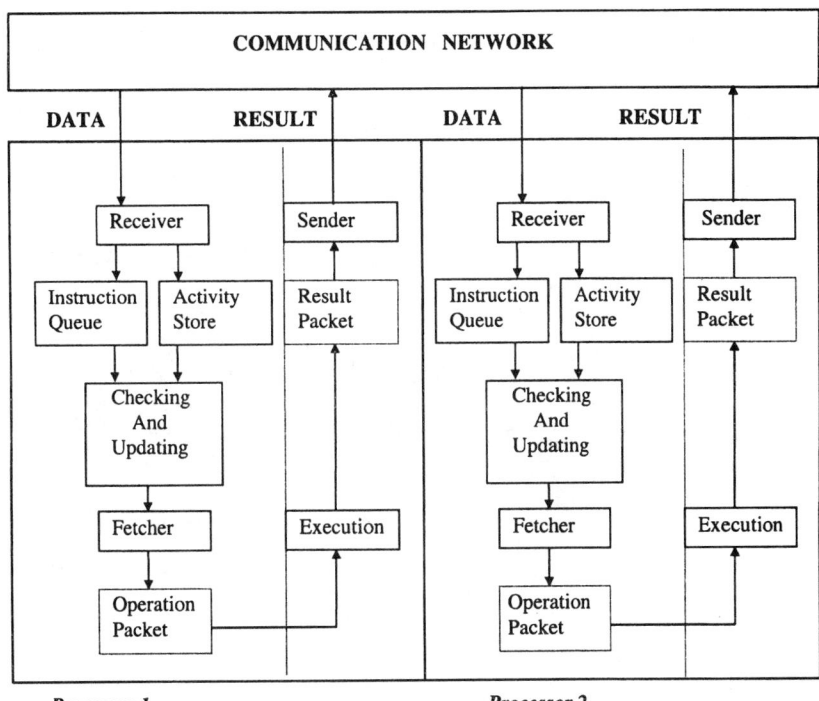

Figure 1.31. Computation of a static data-flow graph problem.

1.3.2   Reconfigurable Static Data Flow Architectures

In general, drawing a diagram of the logical structure of a data flow computation yields a tree such that control flows from the roots to the leaves and results propagate from the leaves to the roots. This suggests that the logical connection between processors in a data flow architecture might be constructed as a tree structure. Thus, an obvious architecture seems to be a physical representation of the logical tree structure.

However, such an architecture would require more processors than the minimum number required for a particular computation. In addition, it is difficult to ensure that all possible parallelism is exploited, and the tree structure would be static whereas we need a dynamic architecture. A tree architecture designed to execute Lisp programs has been developed by Keller [Keller 79] working at Utah. A pictorial view of this proposal is given in Figure 1.32.

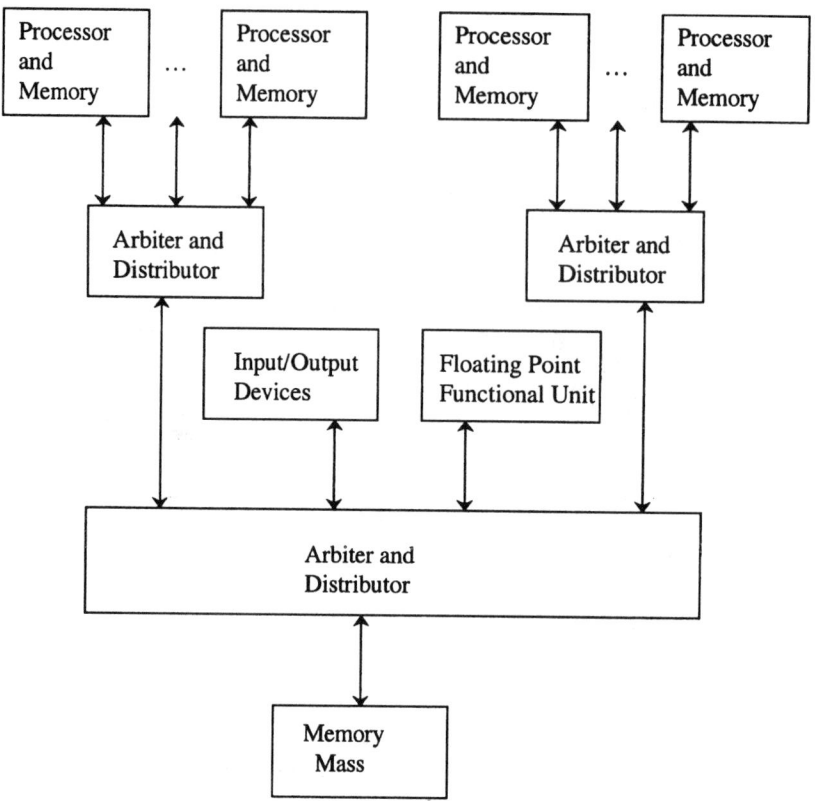

Figure 1.32. A Lisp architecture based on a tree structure.

It is worth noting that Lisp was the first real applicative functional programming language designed by McCarthy at MIT in the late 1950s, and an alternative classification of functional programming language is that of data flow language. The MIT architecture [Dennis 80], the Data Driven Processor (DDP) of Texas Instruments, Inc. (TI) [Douglas 78], and the French LAU system [Syre 77] are the popular static data flow architectures.

Static data flow computers using packet communication constitute the largest group architecture design. The prototype of the category is the family of designs started in 1971 by Jack Dennis at MIT. It was shown that it was feasible to use the technology of the day to design a data flow computer that would achieve a reasonable computation speed. The Toulouse LAU project proposed a prototype architecture containing 32 processing elements and eight 32-KB memory banks configured to hold a total of 32K 64-bit instructions. It was built at the Department of Computer Science, ONERA/CERT, France. Data Driven Machine #1 (DDM1) was completed at Burroughs in 1971 and featured the processing elements arranged as a tree [Veen 86]. In the following two static data flow architectures, MIT and DDP are introduced in detail to address the execution of data flow programs.

MIT Data Flow Architecture

Figure 1.33 represents a schematic view of the main components of the MIT static architecture [Dennis 80]. The MIT computer consists of five units connected by channels, as follows:

1. **Processing Unit**, which consists of processing elements.
2. **Memory Unit**, which consists of cells representing the nodes of a data flow graph. They are used for holding the instructions and their operands. When all the operands and control signals in a cell have arrived, the cell becomes an operation packet.
3. **Arbitration Network**, which transfers the instruction as an operation packet to the processing elements for execution.
4. **Distribution Network**, which transfers the result data from the processing elements to memory. The result is sent back through the distribution network to the destination in memory.
5. **Control Processing Unit**, which performs functional operations on data tokens and manages all other activities.

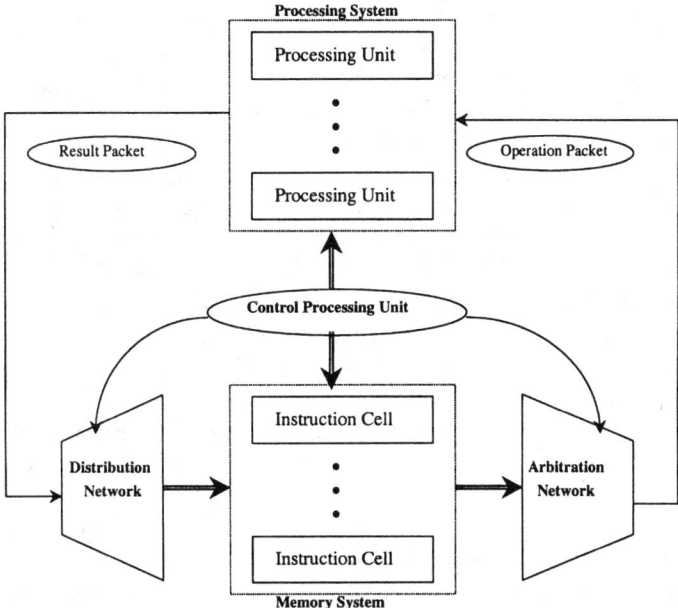

Figure 1.33. A pictorial view of MIT data flow architecture.

Data Driven Processor Data Flow Architecture (DDP)

This data flow architecture is based on the MIT design and was developed at Texas Instruments, Inc. (TI). It is a one-level (multiple processing elements) design that became operational in 1978 [Douglas 80]. It was designed to execute a Fortran program in a data flow fashion. The compiler could create additional copies of a procedure to increase parallelism, but the creation had to be done before run time, meaning that statically. A prototype was built consisting of four processing elements connected by a ring to a TI990/10 minicomputer host. The communication between processing elements is in the form of 34-bits packets over the E-bus interconnection network. The Host computer compiles Fortran programs into data flow graph program and a cluster detection algorithm is used to partition the data flow graphs into subgraphs. A component called Maintenance Controller is used to enable the loading and dumping of the contents of the memory, monitor the performance of the processor and diagnoses the problems when any fault occurs. A pictorial view of this architecture is shown in Figure 1.34. Each processing element consists of four independent components interconnected by a ring:

1. **Memory Unit**, into which the subgraphs are loaded. Each subgraph stored in the memory represents a node or an operation. A counter called the *predecessor counter* is used to determine whether a node is enabled for firing or not.
2. **Input Queue**, which is used to hold the instruction awaiting execution.
3. **Result Queue**, which is used to store the results generated from the node firing.
4. **Arithmetic and Logic Unit**, which executes an enabled node. The result will be forwarded to successor nodes in the processor's memory or to another processing element.

The static firing rule is difficult to implement in hardware. Special feedback acknowledge signals are needed to secure the correct token passing between the producing nodes and the consuming nodes. For example, the number of acknowledge signals may grow too fast to be supported by the hardware. This drawback allows only a limited amount of parallelism to be explored. Another drawback is the overhead caused by acknowledgment signals as the token propagates. Also, static rule makes it inefficient to process arrays of data. This is because consecutive iterations of loops can only partially overlap in time and they can never proceed concurrently, even in the absence of interloop dependencies. In addition, each token is assumed to carry its index and iteration number as a label. The labeling method permits the use of static code and enables maximum use of any parallelism that exists in the problem specification. This can be achieved at the cost of the extra information that must be carried by each token and extra time that must be consumed for processing labels, which is a penalty associated with static data flow architectures.

However, static data flow architectures are an inspiration for the development of dynamic data flow computers, which are being researched at MIT and in Japan.

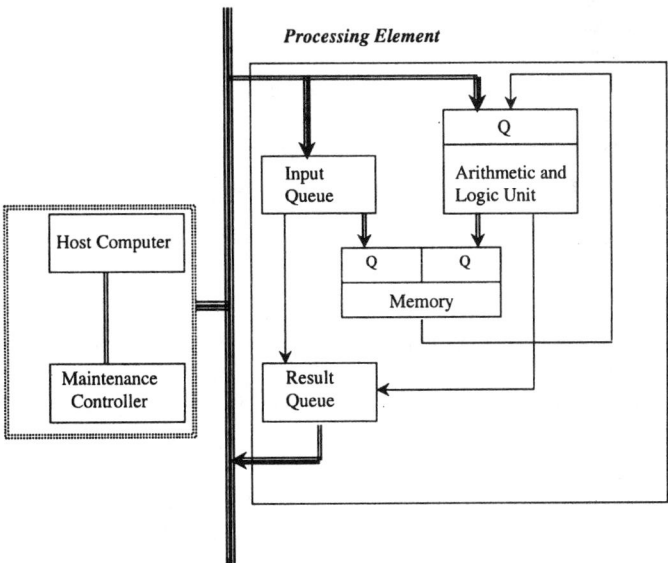

Figure 1.34. Structure of DDP data flow architecture.

1.3.3   Dynamic Data Flow Architectures

The tagged token principle is the fundamental concept of dynamic data flow architectures. This leads to a significant modification in the operation of the data flow graph. With this approach, any arc may carry several tokens, each one carrying a different tag. The execution of an operation is enabled as soon as tokens with identical tags are present at each of its input arcs. The advantage of the tagged token method is that it eliminates the need for acknowledgment signals, which decreases the amount of token traffic. With dynamic data flow architectures, the parallelism can be achieved when loop iterations are performed in parallel. To achieve this parallelism, each iteration has to be able to be executed as a separate instance of a reentrant subgraph.

To distinguish activities of different iterations, basic activity names are extended such that each one carries an iteration count and the procedure to be executed. Therefore, each node can be replicated for every loop iteration and procedure. Assume a tagged token in the form $< c, op, I, v >$ where c is the procedure to be performed; op is the operation to be executed; I is the iteration number; and v is the value carried by the token. When the node in the graph with operation as op is called, it consumes two tokens of the same iteration,

$$< c, op, I, v1 > \text{ and } < c, op, I, v2 >$$

with the produced result token as $< c, op, I, v12 >$. The contents, operation types and iteration members for operands to participate in a computation have to be matched. This is necessary for operands to constitute a pair and execute a computation.

The Irvine data flow machine developed by Arvind, the Manchester data flow machine developed by Watson and Gurd at Manchester in England, the Data Driven Machine (DDM) proposed by Davis, the Epsilon data flow processor of the Sandia National Laboratories, the Experimental system for Data Driven processor array (EDDY) of Japan and the MIT Monsoon system are examples of dynamic data flow architectures. The ETL Data Driven Machine-3 (EM-3) from the Electrotechnical Laboratory and the Data Flow Machine (DFM) from Nippon Telephone and Telegraph are Lisp machines intended for list processing. The Parallel Interface Machine based on the Data flow model (PIM-D) is a joint project of the Institute for New Generation Computer Technology and OKI Electric Industry Co. The languages to be supported include AND-parallel and OR-parallel Prolog. The Distributed Data Driven Processor (DDDP) from OKI Electric has a centralized tag manager and performs token matching using a hardware hashing mechanism consisting of four processing elements.

In the following we proceed with three prototypes of dynamic data flow architectures—Manchester, Sigma-1 and Loral (LDF 100) computers—to address the data flow program execution. The Sigma-1 is based on the MIT tagged token data flow architecture design (TTDA). The TTDA was simulated but never built.

Manchester Data Flow Machine (MDM)

One design which allows any processor to communicate with any other processor is the Manchester data flow architecture [Gurd 85], which is organized as a circular pipeline and uses a ring structure with all communication passing through a switch, as shown in Figure 1.35. This machine has been in operation at the University of Manchester since 1981. It operates asynchronously using a separate clock for each processing element with a performance similar to that of the VAX/780 and consists of four independent components:

1. **Token Queue** consists of three pipeline buffer registers surrounding a first-in-first-out circular store with a capacity of 32K tokens and an access time of 120 nanoseconds. The width of the store and the register is 96 bits, and the clock period is 37.5 nanoseconds. The maximum throughput of the queue is 2.67 million tokens per second. The *token queue* is a way of storing results in case results are produced faster than the *matching store* can process them.

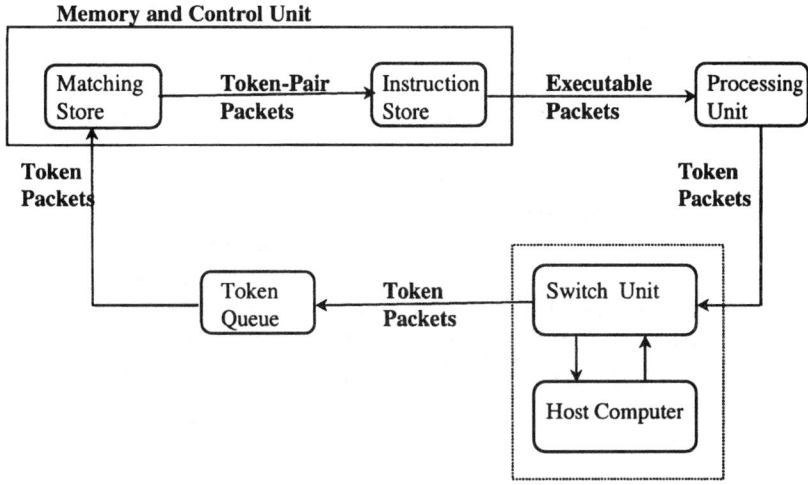

Figure 1.35. The Manchester data flow architecture.

2. **Matching Store** performs the token matching. It matches the tokens
    with the same tags, meaning that it pairs tokens that are intended for the
    same operation. The matching process utilizes a hardware mechanism
    and consists of an associative memory capable of holding up to 1.25
    million unmatched tokens. If a match is found, the two tokens are com-
    bined into a packet and sent to the instruction store. If no match is
    found, the incoming token is written at the address associated with one
    of the 20 locations. This indicates that the system can concurrently ac-
    cess 20 tokens that hash to the same address.

3. **Instruction Store** is a buffered random access memory with a capacity
    of 64K instructions with a memory access time of 150 nanoseconds and
    a clock period of 40 nanoseconds, which provides a maximum rate of 2
    million instruction fetches per second. It receives the token pair packets
    and forms executable packets by adding to them information such as the
    instruction to be performed and the destination address for the result to-
    ken. Once the data has been matched, the required instruction is selected
    from the *instruction store*. At this stage the instruction is ready for exe-
    cution and may be forwarded to the *processing unit*.

4. **Processing Unit** consists of 20 functional units, each with 51 internal
    registers and 4K words of memory with a word size of 24 bits. In this
    design each processor produces results, which are returned to a *memory
    and control unit*. This unit collects the results required by subsequent
    operations and generates new tokens, which are passed to the *input out-
    put switch*, where depending on their addresses they either leave to

pipeline for the host or continue, in which case they are placed in the token queue. Results will be produced by the *processing units* at different rates and at different stages of execution, depending upon the number and complexity of the operations. The parallel execution of instructions is provided in the *processing unit*, which performs the execution of the instructions and propagates the output results to the ring, meaning that the processing units can operate in parallel.

An important component of this architecture is the ring, which facilitates data flows consisting of four modules connected to a host system, each of which operates independently and in a pipelined fashion. The pipeline has the capacity to process about 30 token packets simultaneously. A number of rings may be connected with a switch to construct parallel layers, allowing communication between rings. The switch allows the program and data to be loaded from a host processor and the produced results to be output. In this architecture the matching store is a critical component.

Sigma-1 Data Flow Architecture

The Sigma-1 data flow computer was built in 1988 at the Electrotechnical Laboratory in Japan [Hiraki 91]. It is the most powerful data flow computer, with a performance of 200 to 400 million floating point operations per second. A pictorial view of this architecture is shown in Figure 1.36. It consists of six independent components:

1. **128 Processing Elements (PEs)**, which operate as a two-stage pipeline. The first stage is the firing stage, consisting of a FIFO input buffer, an instruction fetch unit accessing a program memory, and a matching unit with memory. The second stage contains the execution unit, which produces the addresses for the result tokens. It executes the instruction, and the destination address of the result packet is prepared by the destination unit.

2. **128 Structure Elements (SEs)** to handle complex data structures and provide input and output interfaces through the matching memory unit. Simple data structures for scalar variables are stored in the matching memory of SEs. Several functions such as array management, garbage collection, and memory allocation are provided in order to avoid a potential bottleneck in the matching unit.

3. **32 Local Networks**, each one a 10×10 packet switching crossbar interconnecting four PEs, four SEs, one port of global network and a maintenance processor.

4. **1 Global Network** which is a two-stage Omega network and connects the local networks in the system.

5. **16 Maintenance Processors**, which operate independently and in a pipelined fashion, each one interconnecting 8 PEs, 8 SEs, and 2 local networks.

6. **1 Host Computer**, which connects 16 PEs and is an interface between the user and the system.

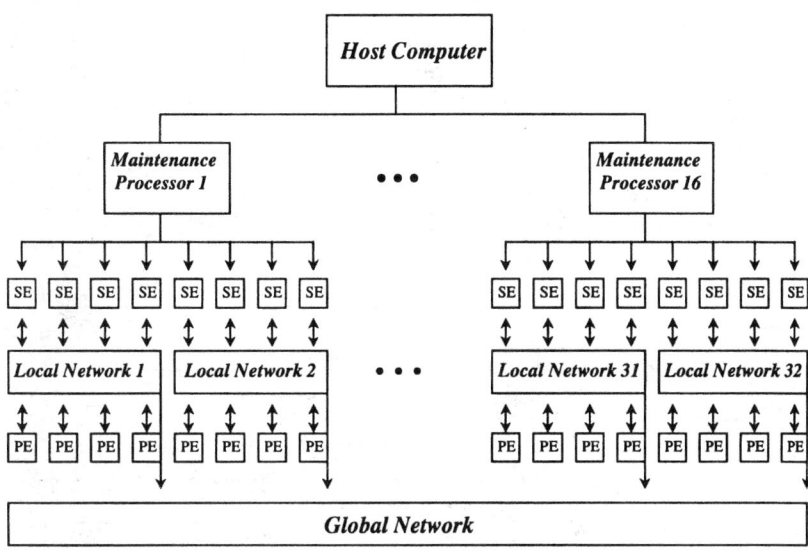

Figure 1.36. Pictorial structure of Sigma-1 (courtesy of Hiraki 91).

The EM-4 developed at the Electrotechnical Laboratory in Japan [Sakai 91] is an extension of the Sigma-1 consisting of 1024 processing elements, but only 80 PEs became operational in 1990.

Loral Data Flow Machine

The Loral Dataflo LDF 100 machine was developed by Loral Instrumentation (located in San Diego, California) to extend the capabilities of real time data collection, analysis and output devices manufactured by Loral [Babb 88, Loral Instrumentation 86]. It is also flexible enough to perform many general-purpose computational tasks. The Dataflo name describes the data flow nature of the computer, in which a process is scheduled for execution only after all its required run time input values are provided, because they have been produced as output by other processes. The Loral Dataflo LDF 100 was designed to exploit large-grain parallelism. In this case the unit of computation scheduled for computation is larger than a single machine instruction. The architecture consists of one host processor, in which an application is prepared for execution, and 1 to 256 node processors, in which the application is executed. In model LDF 100 there are only 4 node processors.) Each node processor consists of two sections:

- **Node Processing Section:** It executes the process code supplied by the user. Each section of the node processor has its own NS32016 micro-processor, 16 Kbytes of ROM, 48 Kbytes of static RAM consisting of 32 Kbytes for the TPS and 16 Kbytes for the NPS, a floating point processor as well as memory management and interrupt control units.
- **Token Processing Section:** It is invoked only in receiving and assembling messages for the processes running on the node.

The two sections communicate with each other through 16 Kbytes of communication RAM. A pictorial view of a node processor is shown in Figure 1.37, in which there are 4 node processors in model LDF 100.

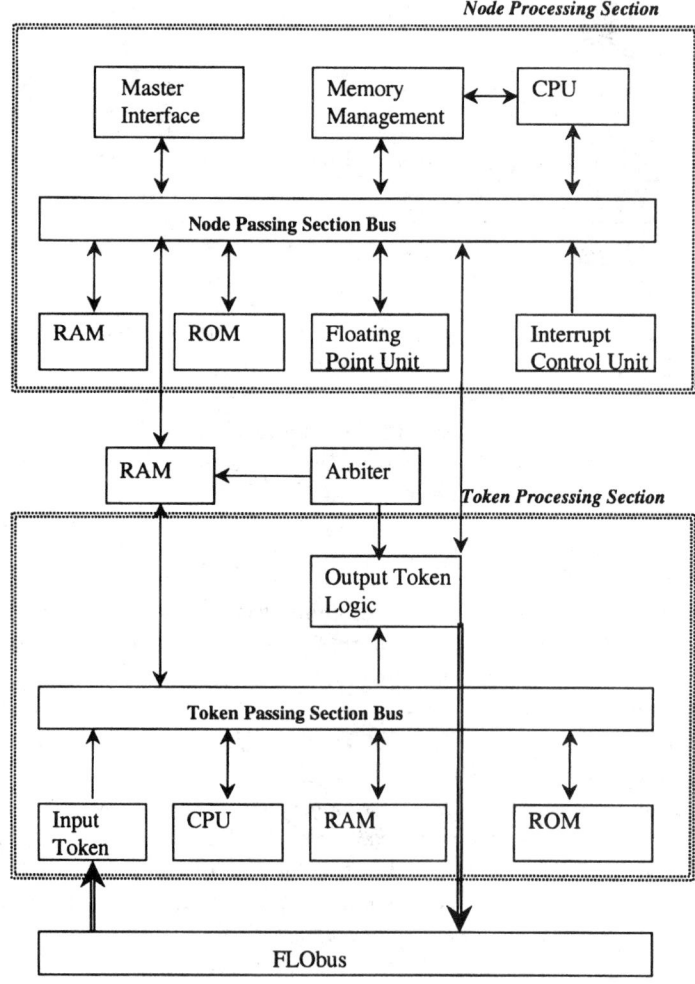

Figure 1.37. A Loral Dataflo LDF 100 node processor.

The host processor, where the program development environment resides has the same configuration as the node processor with more memory—1 Mbyte dynamic RAM and 128 Kbytes static RAM. A common bus called FLObus is used to send messages between node processors. To send a message, the application running on the RAM of the sending node processor copies data flow tokens onto the bus. Each token is 32 bits long and consists of 16 bits of data along with 16 bits of tag to identify the associated arc with the data. These tokens are copied off the FLObus by the RAM on all node processors that have processes requiring input from that arc. The receiving processors reassemble the message. The operating system on the host is GENIX and Dataflo Kernel the on node processors. All editing, preprocessing, compiling, and linking are performed on the host processor, which runs the GENIX operating system, a variant of UNIX. The supporting languages are Fortran 77 and Loral Data Graph Language (called DGL). Although parallelism is not explicitly stated in this data flow machine, it is typical for many processes to run concurrently. If more than one process is assigned to a single node processor, only one runs at a time, even though several may have their firing rules satisfied.

Table 1.1 categorizes several data flow architectures according to the communication between processing elements.

Table 1.1. Categorization of different data flow architectures.

Data Flow Machine	Project Leader	Project Started
Direct Communication Data Flow Machines		
Data Driven Machine #1 (DDM1)	Davis	1972
Microprogrammed (Micro)	Marczynski	1975
Data Driven Processor Array (DDPA)	Takahashi	1981
Static Communication Data Flow Machines		
Distributed Data Processor (DDP)	Cornish	1976
LAU System Prototype #0 (LAU)	Syre	1975
Prototype Basic Dataflow Processor (Form I)	Dennis	1971
Dataflow Image Processor (μPD7281)	Iwashita	1981
Hughes Data Flow Multiprocessor (HDFM)	Vedder	1982
Dynamic Communication Data Flow Machines		
Dataflow multiprocessor (Rump)	Rumbaugh	1974
Dynamic dataflow processor (Form IV)	Misunas	1976
Multiuser dataflow machine (Multi)	Burkowski	1977
Id Machine (Id)	Arvind	1974
Paged memory dataflow machine (Paged)	Caluwaerts	1979

Table 1.1. (cont.) Categorization of different data flow architectures.

Manchester Dataflow Machine (MDM)	Gurd	1976
Data Driven Signal Processor (DDSP)	Hogenauer	1980
List-processing oriented DataFlow Machine (DFM-1)	Amamiya	1980
ETL Data Driven Machine-3 (EM-3)	Yuba	1983
Distributed Data Driven Processor (DDDP)	Kishi	1982
Parallel Interface Machine based on Dataflow (PIM-D)	Ito	1986
Dataflow Computer for scientific computations (SIGMA-1)	Hiraki	1985

Summary

Progress in hardware technology has a tremendous impact on parallel computers. In this chapter, we introduced the notion of computer architectures. Parallel computing or high-performance computing has received considerable attention in the US, Europe and Japan. We described the major categories of computer architectures according to number of instruction streams, number of data streams, and type of memory as global or local. The chapter is not an exhaustive survey of computer architecture taxonomies, but describes the most popular taxonomy due to Flynn. Based on the Flynn taxonomy, we classified the computer architectures into four categories: SISD (Single Instruction Stream, Single Data Stream), SIMD (Single Instruction Stream, Multiple Data Stream), MISD (Multiple Instruction Stream, Single Data Stream), and MIMD (Multiple Instruction Stream, Multiple Data Stream). A taxonomy of parallel architectures can address four classifications: SIMD, MISD, MIMD and combination of SIMD and MIMD, which we described in this chapter.

SISD computers have been recognized having one CPU that executes one instruction at a time utilizing one item of data at a time. SIMD computers have a single control unit and execute a single instruction stream, but they duplicate the computation on a number of different data streams. SIMD computers are suitable for computational environments that exhibit a high degree of data parallelism. In general, they can be considered a special subset of MIMD architectures which offer the least amount of overhead. We classified SIMD computers into three different categories: associative processors computers, processor arrays computers, and hypercube computers.

Examples of SIMD computers include the ILIAC IV, MPP, DAP, CM-2, MasPar MP-1, MasPar Mp-2, Goodyear's massively parallel processor and Goodyear's STARAN. The chapter provides a description of hardware characteristics of two commercial SIMD systems (Thinking Machine Corporation's Connection Machine and MasPar Corporation's MP Series), two well-known computers.

MIMD computers have a number of independent processors, each with its own control unit, thus executing its own instruction stream. Additionally, each processor operates on its own data stream. MIMD machines are characterized as tightly coupled or loosely coupled machines. Tightly coupled machines share memory using a circuit-switched interconnection network. Loosely coupled machines share memory using a packet-switched interconnection network. Most commercial machines, including pipelined vector machines, are tightly coupled, whereas most fault-tolerant machines are loosely coupled. MIMD machines can also be categorized by the way the CPU is accessed. UMA (Uniform Memory Access) multiprocessors have a single shared memory, in which the memory access time is the same for all processors. In contrast, NUMA (Non-Uniform Memory Access) has various memory access times between processors, in which the processors interact in a message passing fashion. Examples of MIMD computers include the Cosmic Cube, nCube2, iPSC, Sequent Symmetry, FX-8, FX-2800, TC-2000, CM-5, KSR-1 and Paragon XP. Details of two commercial well-known MIMD computers, the Intel iPSC and Symmetry machines, are provided. We summarized some of the general features associated with SIMD and MIMD computers along with the advantages and disadvantages of each category. Generally speaking, MIMD computers can be operated in SIMD mode as well, such as DADO and CM-5.

Pipelining has been used to enhance the performance of serial processing structures. The chapter covers the basic principles and design methodologies for pipeline processing. We discussed pipelined processing as a class of MISD architectures, in which the process is divided into several stages to be performed in parallel fashion. This indicates that pipelining overlaps the execution of stages of the process and consists of a number of successive stages separated by registers which save the results of the intermediate stages. The principles of pipelining can be exploited at various levels, such as the instruction level, subsystem level, and system level. In addition, a cyclic pipeline may be formed among processors, memories and the interconnection networks, as in the Burroughs Scientific processor. For example, components such as memory, two interconnection networks (one for writing results and one for reading data from memories) and processing elements may form a cyclic pipeline architecture. A comparison of the serial and pipelined execution addressed the efficiency involved in this class of architectures.

Systolic Array Processors is the next category explained in MISD classification. It has been introduced for special purpose computation, which is to map a specific algorithm into a fixed architecture that provides for massive parallel computations. There are several systolic arrays topologies: one-dimensional linear array, two-dimensional square array, two-dimensional hexagonal array, and triangular array. We described in some detail the CDC star 100 machine.

A hybrid SIMD-MIMD architecture is a parallel processing system which can be structured as one or more independent SIMD and/or MIMD systems. We described three architectures—PASM architecture, VLIW architecture, and MSIMD tree machine—for parallel execution of the applications written in functional programming languages. PASM is a reconfigurable parallel system for image processing designed at Purdue University. In this system, each processing element can operate in both SIMD and MIMD modes of parallelism. The parallel computation unit consists of 16 processing elements connected by an interconnection network and controlled by four microcontrollers. In a VLIW architecture, a machine instruction corresponds to a packet of independent instructions created by the compiler, and no dynamic hardware scheduling is used. The system may be regarded as a form of liberated SIMD or as specially designed MIMD, with the essential difference that there is only one control mechanism that issues very long instructions. An example of this system is the Multiflow TRACE 7/200, which has a 256-bit instruction word and can perform up to seven operations at a time. In the model 14/200, the instruction length and the number of simultaneous operations are doubled.

Although there have been efforts to build these machines, there is no commercial architecture of this type. MSIMD architecture consists of multiple SIMD formed in a tree-connected structure. It is a reconfigurable design system that can be partitioned into multiple sub-configurations, each one operating in SIMD mode. The main advantage of this architecture is that the interconnection of the processing elements offers simplicity and is well matched to the layout of VLSI chips and circuit boards. An example of this system is the Cellular Computer designed with 10^6 processors for parallel execution of the expressions written in a reduction language such as the FP functional programming language.

Data flow and demand-driven architectures achieve parallelism by using a number of different computational components, and they execute data flow models of computation rather than executing a control flow program. Two main groups working on data flow architecture design are the Manchester group in Britain and the MIT group at MIT. We divided the data flow architectures into three categories: static, dynamic and reconfigurable static architectures. Generally speaking, the static data flow architecture is restricted to one token at a time. In this paradigm, the computation to be performed is held as a collection of activity templates. Static data flow computers using packet communication constitute the largest group of this architecture design. Details of two static dataflow architectures, MIT and DDP, are provided to address the components, interconnection and model of computation. The MIT design consists of 5 units connected by channels, known as processing unit, memory unit, arbitration network, distribution network, and control processing unit. DDP design is based on the MIT design and was developed by Texas Instruments, Inc. It was designed to execute a Fortran program in a data flow fashion. In this design, each processing element consists of four components known as memory unit, input queue, result queue and arithmetic and logic unit. Dynamic data flow or tagged token leads to a significant modification in the operation of the data flow model of computation. With this design any arc may carry several tokens such that each one is carrying a different tag. The execution of an operation is enabled as soon as tokens with identical tags are present at each of the input arcs.

Prototypes of three dynamic data flow architectures—Manchester, Sigma-1 and Loral—are detailed to address the data flow program execution. The Manchester machine consists of four components: token queue, matching store, instruction store and processing unit. An important component of this system is the ring which facilitates data flows. It consists of four modules connected to a host system which operate independently and in a pipelined fashion. The Sigma-1 developed at the Electrotechnical Laboratory in Japan is the most powerful data flow computer and consists of six components: 128 processing elements, 128 structure elements, 32 local networks, 1 global network, 16 maintenance processors, and 1 host computer. An extension of Sigma-1 is EM-4, developed in Japan and consisting of 1024 processing elements. Loral LFT 100 was developed by Loral Instrumentation. The system consists of one host computer, in which an application is prepared for execution, and 1 to 256 processing elements, each one consisting of two sections known as the node processing section and the token processing section. A Table 1.1 categorized several dataflow architectures according to the communication between processors.

As a conclusion, in this chapter we have seen that parallel computer architectures can be judged and compared on the basis of a number of factors, including ease of understanding, ease of use, generality of application, technical complexity, efficiency and performance. The following table summarizes the designated factors of the associated architectures.

Table 1.2. Summary of computer architectures.

System	Concept	Interface	Generality	Complexity	Efficiency
SIMD	Easy	Easy	Moderate	High	High
MIMD	Hard	Hard	Good	High	Moderate
Pipeline	Easy	Easy	Poor	Low	High
Systolic	Hard	Easy	Poor	Moderate	High
Associative	Moderate	Moderate	Poor	Moderate	High
Data flow	Hard	Moderate	Good	High	High

A more recent book in the architecture design area, which discusses many practical design aspects, is [Zomaya 96]. Many aspects of parallel computers and interconnection networks are presented in [Moldovan 93, Almasi 94, Hwang 93, Zargham 96, Yuen 93, Shiva 96, Leighton 92].

For details on the latest architectures and their characteristics, refer to corresponding manufacturers' manuals and magazines such as IEEE Spectrum, IEEE Computer, EDN, Computer Design, and Byte.

Exercises

1. Define the following terms:

Von Neumann machine	Computational model
SISD	Serial processing
SIMD	Parallel processing
MISD	Pipelined processing
MIMD	Uniform memory access
Shared memory	Non-uniform memory access
Tightly coupled machine	LM-MIMD,
Loosely coupled machine	GM-MIMD
Data flow machine	Systolic array processors
VLIW	MSIMD

2. Briefly describe the fundamental features of the conventional Von Neumann architecture.

3. What are the main components of an SIMD architecture? Explain two main functions of this system which a technology must provide.

4. What are the main components of a shared-memory MIMD architecture? Explain two main functions of this system that a technology must provide.

5. What are the main components of a private-memory MIMD architecture? Explain two main functions of this system which a technology must provide.

6. What are the advantages of building a parallel machine out of very powerful processors? Which kind of application is more suitable?

7. What are the advantages of building a parallel machine out of very weak processors? Which kind of application is more suitable?

8. Would you prefer to use a parallel system with ten 100-MIPS (Million Instructions Per Second) processors or one 1000-MIPS processor?

9. Why might someone argue that pipelined vector processors are MISD computers? How is this characterization applicable, and how is it misleading? What is a good example of an MISD system?

10. Describe the conditions under which an n-stage pipeline is n times faster than a serial machine.

11. How are MIMD computers different from computer networks?

12. Compare and contrast the machine designs of the ILLIAC IV, the MP-1, the iPSC and the Symmetry.

13. Discuss the relative advantages of static versus dynamic data flow architectures.

14. Read the manual for your favorite parallel processor and describe the debugging facilities provided with the applications programmer.

15. How many cycles are needed to multiply two 100×100 matrices on a 100×100 systolic array processors? What if the system is bigger, say 1000×1000 processors.

16. For a typical dynamic data flow system with a tagged-token circular pipeline which is operating at instruction level granularity.
    (a) Specify the main source of parallelism.
    (b) Specify the main obstacles for achieving high performance.

17. If a vector computer runs 10 times faster on vectorized code than on scalar code, what percentage of vectorization is required to achieve vectorization speedups by factors of 2, 4, 6 and 8? Calculate the vectorization percentage for the same speedup factors if the vector computer is 100 times faster.

18. Show how a simple systolic array would calculate the product of two matrices as

$$A = \begin{pmatrix} x_1 & x_2 \\ x_3 & x_4 \end{pmatrix} \quad \text{and} \quad B = \begin{pmatrix} y_1 & y_2 \\ y_3 & y_4 \end{pmatrix}.$$

19. Show how the instruction sequence given below can be executed on a processor that utilizes the pipeline of Figure 1.38:

LOAD	R_1	Memory$_1$
LOAD	R_2	Memory$_2$
Mul	R_3	R_1
ADD	R_4	R_2

where, R_1, R_2, R_3, and R_4 are Registers, Memory$_1$ and Memory$_2$ are Memory addresses.

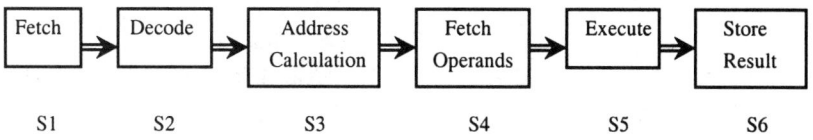

Figure 1.38. An instruction pipeline.

Reference-Needed Exercises

20. What are the advantages and disadvantages of a reconfigurable systolic array processor such as CHiP?

21. The following code segment needs to be executed on a vector processor with a five-stage floating point adder and a six-stage floating point multiplier:

$$A = B + C$$

$$D = S * A$$

$$E = D + B$$

where, A, B, C, D and E are 32 element vectors and S is a scalar. Assume that each stage of the adder and multiplier consumes one cycle, that memory load and store each consume one cycle, and that there are a required number of memory paths. Derive the computation time if chaining is not allowed and if chaining is allowed. Show the timing diagram for each case.

22. Most of the original vector supercomputers use no data cache, only an instruction cache. Give reasons for this design issue.

23. A pipeline vector processor uses a five-stage pipeline to perform vector additions. Each pipeline stage requires 10 ns, and the vectors have 48 elements each. How long does it take to compute the result vector?

Discussion Exercises

24. In large computer design projects, the technologists work on improving the performance while the architects work on decreasing the number of clock cycles per instruction and finding new ways to exploit parallelism. Historically, currently, and in the future what are the relative speedups offered by the architects and the technologists?

25. What do you think will be the ideal architecture for a parallel machine? Why?

26. What advantages do various types of pipelining provide for highly sequential computation (i.e., when a large fraction of the operations in a computation depend on other recent computations).

CHAPTER 2
Components of Parallel Computers

Parallel processing is information processing that illustrates the concurrent manipulation of data elements belonging to one or more processes solving a single computational problem. The past several years have witnessed an increasing acceptance and adoption of parallel processing both for high-performance scientific computation and for more general-purpose applications. This was a result of the demand for high performance, lower cost, and sustained productivity. The acceptance has been facilitated by multiprocessor architectures such as SIMD and MIMD computers. These machines combine a few hundred to a few thousand processors connected to hundreds of gigabytes of memory.

The most important characteristic of SIMD computers is that the arithmetic processors are synchronized at the instruction level, so the performance is influenced by the data structure used and the memory organization employed. Some issues of concern in the design of a parallel architecture are:

- **Large set of registers**, which decreases the effect of interrupts.
- **Large physical address space**, which decrease the effect of swapping.
- **Processor scheduling**, which refers to the efficient allocation of processors to individual tasks in a dynamic fashion as the computation proceeds.
- **Processor synchronization**, which refers to preventing processors from trying to change a memory location simultaneously and obeying the precedence constraints in data manipulation. Efficient primitives must be provided to handle synchronization and interrupts.
- **Interconnection network topology design**, which refers to processor-to-memory and processor-to-processor connection in the system. The interconnection network topology addresses the most expensive component of the parallel system design, and be reliable to support the inter-process communication.
- **Partitioning**, which refers to identifying parallelism in algorithms to specify the concurrent processing streams. Partitioning can be performed at different levels of concurrent processing, such as, statement, procedure and program level partitioning.
- **Reliability**, which refers to incorporating graceful degradation and better fault tolerance in the system. If any processor fails, its workload can be taken over by another processor in the system.

- **High performance**, which refers to peak performance of parallel systems compared with a single processor system, where all the processors are working on some useful computation. However, such peak performance is difficult to achieve on account of the overhead involved due to, for example, communication and waste of processor time if any processor runs out of tasks to do.

2.1   Memory

One of the most important issues involved in computer architectures is the design of the memory system. Memory units in a memory system are formed as a hierarchy of memories (memory level 1, 2,..., m) as represented in Figure 2.1.

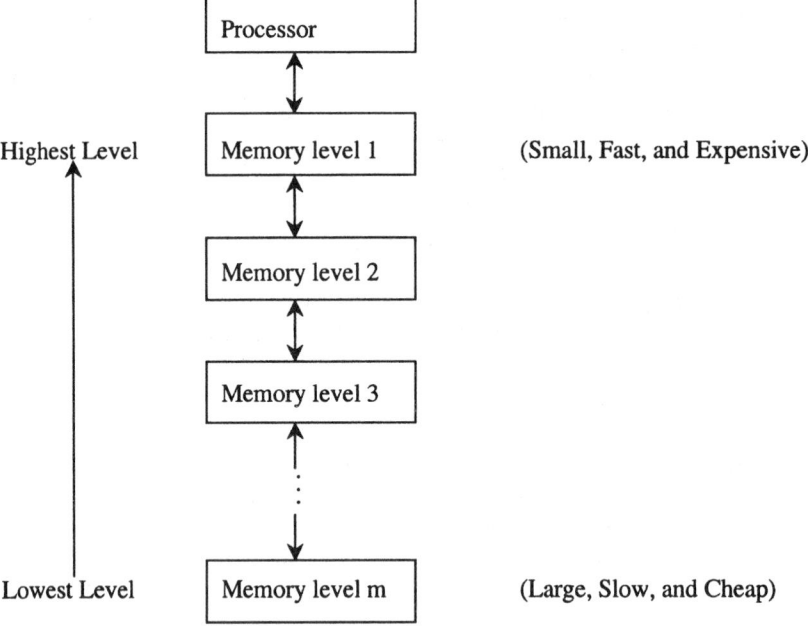

Figure 2.1. Memory system hierarchy.

From the theoretical point of view, memory level 1 is the highest level of memory, smallest, fastest, and most expensive, and is located closest to the processor. The second level of memory is larger than the first level, slower, less expensive, and not as close to the processor as the first level. The same pattern is true for other levels of memory. Consequently, as the level increases, the speed and the cost per unit increase, which indicates decreasing memory capacity. Generally, data are transfered between adjacent levels and are entirely controlled by the activity in the first level of the memory. The main advantage of this hierarchy is that the data are retrieved most of the time from the fastest level, 1. This phenomenon is known as the property of locality of reference, meaning that at any given interval of time the references to memory tend to be confined within local areas of memory. Generally speaking, in this hierarchy the average memory access time is nearly equal to the speed of the highest level, and the average unit cost of the memory approaches the cost of the lowest level. There are three terms associated with the memory hierarchy:

- **Hierarchical Level** is an index beginning with 1 for the level closest to the processor.
- **Multilevel Inclusion** is the property that the content of each level is always found at the next level; for example, the content of level ℓ is found in $\ell + 1$.
- **Main Memory** is the largest random access memory in the system.

Memory Models for Random Access Machines

A memory unit in which any particular word can be accessed independently is known as Random Access Memory (RAM). This indicates that the stored data are identified by means of a unique address assigned to each data item [Cragon 96]. It is worth noting that this RAM is different from the standard computational model for serial computers, which is Random Access Machine (RAM), which captures the behavior of the traditional machines quite well. In a random access memory, the time required for accessing a word is the same for all words. In general, there are two types of memories:

- Static Random Access Memory (SRAM), which retains the data when a word is read from it. Thus this type of memory is said to have a non-destructive-read property, meaning that the data are not destroyed after reading.
- Dynamic Random Access Memory (DRAM), in which data need to be written back into the corresponding memory location after every read operation. Thus, dynamic memories are characterized by a destructive-read property. Dynamic memories need to be periodically refreshed, and a refreshing circuit is considered an acceptable and unavoidable cost of DRAM.

Associative Memory

Associative Memory (AM) or Content Addressable Memory (CAM) consists of memory locations and an associated logic known as data gathering logic [Baron 92, Hayes 78, Hanlon 66]. The associative memory system locates data by searching its memory cells for a specific bit pattern. In general, each memory location has sufficient logic to determine whether or not it holds data that match some pattern that is broadcast from the central control unit. The user supplies the bit pattern by giving two values: an argument and a mask; the argument holds the value being searched and the mask specifies which argument bits to use when comparing the argument to the value in each cell. This indicates that the memory location is addressed on the basis of its content rather than on the basis of its memory location, which is the basic difference between RAM and AM. As we can see, because of the nature of data access in associative memories, this is also known as content addressable memories (CAM).

Each memory cell has four inputs and two outputs, as shown in Figure 2.2. The inputs are the argument bit a, the read/write (R/W) bit to specify the appropriate operation to be performed, the key bit k, and the select bit s to select the particular memory cell for read or write operation. The outputs are the match bit m, which specifies if the data stored in the location match with the argument bit, and the output bit q. Associative memories can be categorized into two basic types:

- **Exact** match associative memories, in which data are tested for equality with certain key data. This type is referred to as **exact match CAM**.
- **Comparison** associative memories, in which the search is based on a general comparison rather than on a search for equality. This is an enhancement of the exact match and supports different relational operators, such as greater than and less than.

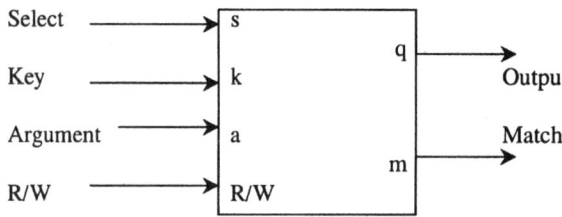

Figure 2.2. An associative memory cell structure.

All associative memories are organized by words and are made up of an array of similar cells. Figure 2.3 shows a block diagram of an associative memory having m words and n bits within each word. Each of these $m{\times}n$ memory locations has circuitry for comparing the argument with the value the location holds, and each memory location has circuitry to indicate a successful search. The argument register holds the argument for an associative search, the mask register specifies the fields of each word that the memory should match, and the bits of the match register (called match bits) indicate which words match the search criterion. An example of an associative search might be:

Search for all words whose 8 highest order bits contain the value $(1101\ 1110)_2$ and return the value of the first word that matches.

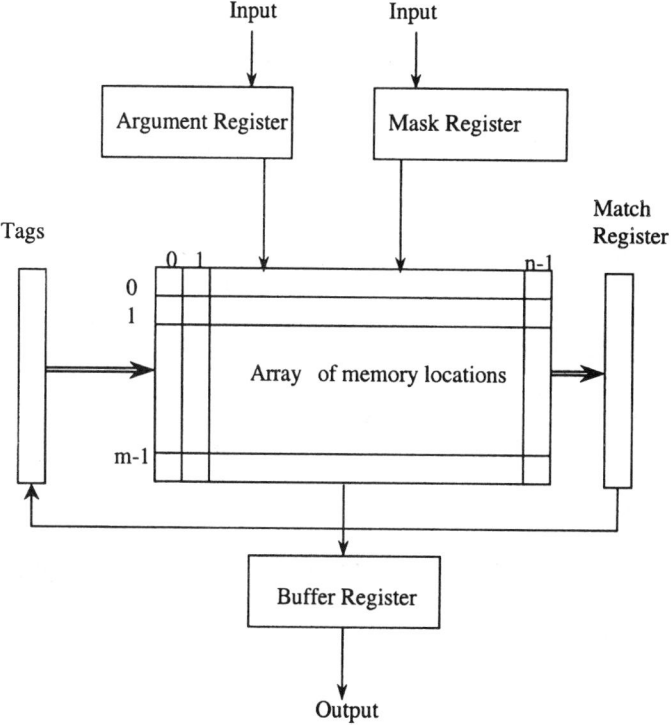

Figure 2.3. Associative memory structure.

The value $(1101\ 1110)_2$ is the argument of this search, the specification **8 highest order bits** is the mask, and the specification **return the value of the first word that matches** is the directive when several words satisfy the search criteria. The search process follows:

1. The word to be searched $(1101\ 1110)_2$ is loaded into the argument register.

2. The segment of interest in the word, the **8 highest order bits**, is specified by the bit positions having ones in the mask register.
3. Each word in memory is compared in parallel with the content of the argument register.
   - If a word matches the argument, the corresponding bit in the matching register is set to 1.
   - If more than one bit is set to 1 in the matching register, the circuitry determines which word is to be accessed for read or write purposes.

Compared with random access memories, associative memories are very expensive but have much faster response times in searching. In view of this cost disparity, associative memories might be used only in applications for which the search time is vital to the proper implementation of the task under execution.

Memory Models for Parallel Random Access Machines

The parallel computation model known as PRAM (Parallel Random Access Machine) consists of a common memory of type RAM (Random Access Memory) with M locations where M is large but finite and is shared by the P processors. The global memory stores data and serves as the communication area for the processors. It also allows processors to access data and operate in an asynchronous fashion. For example, P_i writes data to a memory location, and the data can be accessed by P_j, meaning that P_i and P_j can use the shared memory to communicate with each other.

Access Memory Primitives

There are different forms to overlap read or write accesses of several data by processors. These instructions for reading and writing memory locations are:

- **Concurrent Read** (CR), in which two or more processors read from the same memory location at the same time.
- **Exclusive Read** (ER), in which p processors can simultaneously read p distinct memory locations. Each one reads from exactly one memory location, and each memory location is read by exactly one processor.
- **Concurrent Write** CW), in which two or more processors can write to the same memory location at the same time.
- **Exclusive Write** (EW), in which p processors can simultaneously write to p distinct memory locations. Each one writes to exactly one memory location, and each memory location is written to by exactly one processor.

It is worth noting that ER and EW are special cases of CR and CW, respectively. The concurrent write instructions can be characterized as follows:

- **Priority CW**, in which the processors are assigned certain priorities and the one with the highest priority is allowed to write to a given memory location. The priority can be static or dynamic according to a specific rule during the execution.
- **Common CW**, in which the processors are allowed to write to a memory location only if they write the same value. In this case, one processor is selected to perform the operation.
- **Arbitrary CW**, in which several processors attempt to write simultaneously to a memory location, but one is allowed to change the value in that memory location. In this case, we need to specify exactly how the processor is to be selected.
- **Random CW**, in which the processor that succeeds in writing to a memory location is chosen by a random process.
- **Combining CW**, in which all the values that several processors are attempting to write simultaneously to a memory location are combined into a single value. This value is written in that memory location.

Multiport Memory

These devices contain multiple ports and individual port controls that allow simultaneous access to data stored in the memory. This indicates that one port can be reading from a memory location while the other can be writing to another location, or several ports can be reading from the same location. In general, when multiple ports try to write to the same location, only one of the ports (the one with the highest priority among them) will be successful. Multiple port memories are useful in building multiple processor systems because the memory subsystem resolves the memory competition problem associated with multiple processors accessing the memory simultaneously. Thus, the availability of multiport memories make it possible to construct interconnection networks in which multiple processors communicate via memories instead of buses. Figure 2.4 shows a four-port memory accessed simultaneously by four processors.

Note that large-capacity multiport memories are not generally a viable option because of the packing costs and pin-bandwidth limitation, but complex interconnection networks may be built using multiport memories. In addition to the cost issue, access to the same memory location in reading and writing must be prevented through some priority primitives (i.e., concurrent and exclusive read and write operations). One of the advantages of this memory organization is that the communication protocol is reduced because the transferred data can be temporarily stored in the memory. For example, the Univac 1100/94 multiprocessor consists of four CPUs, four I/O processors, and two vector processors connected to four shared memory modules, each of which has a 10-way port. Access to these 10 ports is prioritized under operating system control. One of the disadvantages of this scheme is the need for a large number of interconnection cables and connectors when the configuration becomes large. In addition, a multiport memory system cannot be expanded with more processors without redesigning the memory controller.

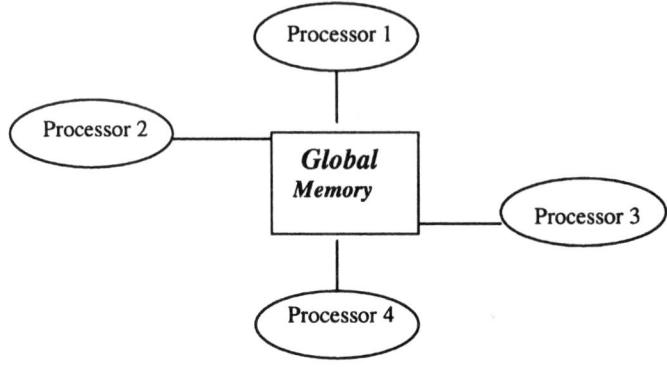

Figure 2.4. Four-port memory.

Multiprocessor Memory

The processors in a multiprocessor system communicate with each other through shared variables in a common memory. A shared-memory machine must have a fast network with high bandwidth, because processor modules frequently access the remote memory modules that constitute the global shared memory. A slow network would quickly become a bottleneck and performance would severely degrade. The shared memory of a multiprocessor system might be organized in three distinct categories:

1. Uniform Memory Access model (UMA), in which the shared memory is centralized.
2. Non-Uniform Memory Access model (NUMA), in which the shared memory is distributed.
3. Cache-Only Memory Architecture (COMA), in which the distributed main memories are converted to caches.

Uniform Memory Access of Shared Memory

In this scheme all the processors work through a central switching mechanism to access shared memory. The physical memory is uniformly shared by all the processors, meaning that all processors have equal access time to all memory words. There are a variety of ways to implement this switching mechanism such as a common bus, a crossbar switch, a packet-switched network, and a multi-stage network.

When all processors have equal access to all peripheral devices, the system is called a *symmetric* multiprocessor system. The Encore Multimax and the Sequent Symmetry S81 are examples of this structure. In a symmetric system, all processors are equally capable of running programs such as OS kernel and I/O service routines. If only one processor executes the OS and I/O service routines and the remaining processors (called attached processors) have no I/O capabilities, the system is called an *asymmetric* multiprocessor. The attached processors execute user programs under the master processor's supervision.

Non-Uniform Memory Access of Shared Memory

Unlike uniform memory access organization, memory is distributed and partitioned into a number of independent memory modules. The shared memory is physically distributed to all processors, called local memory modules, and the collection of all memory modules forms a global memory accessible by all processors. The processors are allowed simultaneous access to one or more memory modules and operate more or less independently of each other utilizing the memory modules. The TC2000 machine manufactured by BBN Systems and Technologies of Cambridge, Massachusetts, and the Cedar System at the University of Illinois are examples of this structure. The TC2000 system consists of 128 processors in which each processor has 19 Mbytes of primary memory. The memory system on each processor converts every 32-bit virtual address into a 34-bit physical address. This address may be in cache memory, in the processors' memory modules, or in another processor's memory. Data from another processor's memory can be retrieved by sending a request through the butterfly switching network.

Cache-Only Memory Architecture

In this memory access organization, the distributed main memories are converted to caches and all the caches form a global address space. The Swedish Institute of Computer Science's Data Diffusion Machine (DDM) [Hagersten 90, 92] and Kendall Square Research's KSR-1 machine [Burkhardt 92] are examples of this organization.

Multicomputer Memory

Each processing node in a multicomputer system is a self-contained computer with a local memory unshared with other processors. It communicates with other processing nodes by sending messages over the network. Systems of this type are often called message-passing systems. In multicomputer systems, the demand on the interconnection network is less restricted than in shared-memory multiprocessor systems. In a multicomputer system, messages are sent much less frequently, resulting in less traffic. Therefore, a simpler and less expensive network can be used. The message-passing network provides point-to-point static connections among the processors, whose local memories are private and accessible only by local processors. Hence, the memory management system is similar to that of the single processor systems. For this reason, the traditional multicomputer systems are called no-remote-memory-access. However, this restriction might be removed with distributed shared memory in the design of multicomputer systems. Taking the memory of the parallel systems into account, the data are distributed among the memories such that each processing element can access the data it operates on. The control processor system accesses the memory for instruction retrieval, and processing elements access the memory for data retrieval and storage.

Generally speaking, there are two parameters of interest in memory design of parallel systems—**bandwidth** and **latency**. For a parallel system, the memory bandwidth must be high enough to provide for simultaneous operation of all processors. When memory modules are shared, memory competition must be minimized. Also, the memory latency, which is defined as the time elapsed between a processor's request for data from the memory and its receipt, must be minimized. In general, the memory latency can be reduced by increasing the memory bandwidth, which can be accomplished by one or both of the following mechanisms:

1. By building the memory system with multiple independent memory modules, thus providing for concurrent access of the modules. Memory banked and memory interleaved are alternatives used in such systems.
2. By reducing the memory access and cycle times utilizing memory devices (cache memories or memory-mapped I/O) from the highest speed technology available.

2.2   Interconnection Networks

In most parallel architectures, such as multiprocessor shared memory, multiprocessor multi-memory and distributed memory systems, one key design issue is the interconnection network. The interconnection networks refer to connecting the processors and memories together in a parallel architecture. Ideally, one wants each processor to be connected to any other processor. For example, a parallel processor organization can be represented by the graph in Figure 2.5, in which the vertices represent processors and the edges represent communication paths between pairs of processors. This fully connected graph is the simplest form of parallel processor organization and requires $P \times (P - 1)$ links. Figure 2.5 represents a complete graph interconnection network of 6 processors, with each processor having 5 links. Clearly, this becomes expensive when P is large.

There are two groups of interconnection network topologies, static and dynamic. Static networks provide fixed connections between components, processors or memories, and connections between components are not changeable. In contrast, a dynamic network is reconfigurable. In this interconnection network, the connection can be established by setting a set of interconnected switch boxes. Researchers have done a tremendous amount of theoretical work in this field. In the following sections, we present a variety of types and topologies of processor organizations, such as linear and ring, shuffle exchange, hypercube, star, De Bruijn, binary tree, delta, butterfly, mesh, omega and pyramid.

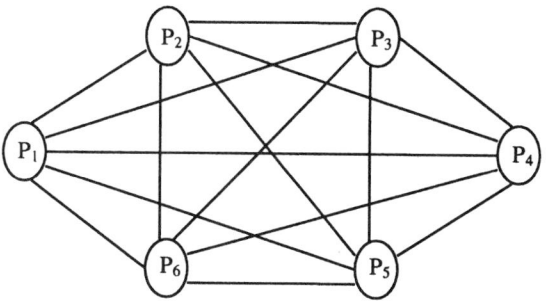

Figure 2.5. A complete graph interconnection network (G_6).

2.2.1   Linear and Ring

Linear and ring interconnection topologies (one-dimensional mesh) were very popular in terms of simplicity and theoretical work. In a Linear interconnection network, processors are organized in ascending order from 0 to p − 1. Excluded the first and the last processors, each processor has two neighbors, its predecessor and its successor. For example, processor x for x = 1,2,...,p − 2 has two neighbors, {x − 1, x + 1}. The neighbors of the first and last processors are {1} and {p − 2}, respectively. Figure 2.6 represents a linear interconnection network with 6 processors. Although the topology is simple, the data must pass through a number of processors in order to reach the destination, resulting in long communication delays, especially between the first and last processors.

Figure 2.6. A linear interconnection network with 6 processors.

A ring interconnection network can be organized by connecting the first and the last processors to each other as shown in Figure 2.7. A ring can be unidirectional or bidirectional. In a unidirectional ring topology, the communication is established in only one direction, clockwise or counter-clockwise. However, in a bidirectional topology, the communication is established in both directions. The ring structure can still cause long communication delays between components.

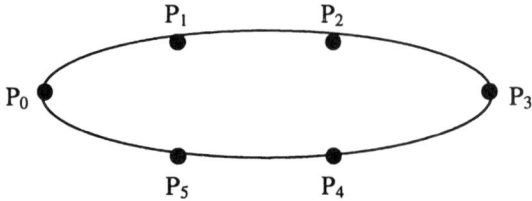

Figure 2.7. A ring interconnection network with 6 processors.

2.2.2   Shuffle Exchange

Assume that N processors P_0, P_1,....P_{N-1} are available where N is a power of 2. In the perfect shuffle interconnection network, a one-way communication line links P_i to P_j, where

$$j = \begin{cases} 2i & for\ 0 \leq i \leq N/_2 - 1 \\ 2i+1-N & for\ N/_2 \leq i \leq N-1 \end{cases}$$

Figure 2.8 shows a perfect shuffle interconnection network for N = 8 processors, in which shuffle connections are illustrated by the solid arrow lines and the exchange links are represented by the solid lines. In general, the perfect shuffle interconnection network connects node i with {2i modulo (N – 1)}, with the exception that node N – 1 is connected to itself. An alternative representation of the perfect shuffle can be obtained by a binary representation of the processor such that the binary representation of j is obtained by cyclically shifting that of i one position to the left, meaning that P_i and P_j are connected.

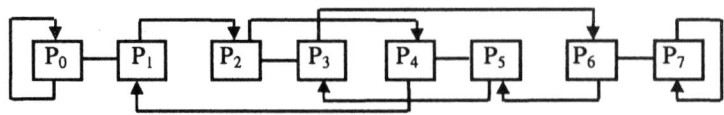

Figure 2.8. A perfect shuffle interconnection network with 8 connected processors.

This is illustrated in Figure 2.9 in which an alternative representation of the interconnection is given by mapping the set of processors onto itself. As we can see, the processor P_{001} is connected to P_{010}, meaning that 001 is shifted one position to the left to make 010. If the direction of the links is reversed, the perfect unshuffle interconnection is obtained. A network such as that shown in Figure 2.10 is known as the perfect unshuffle interconnection network because the links are undirected or are two-way connected. The exchange links, shown as solid lines, are achieved by connecting every even-numbered processor to its successor. Any network with the shuffle, unshuffle or exchange links is called a shuffle exchange network.

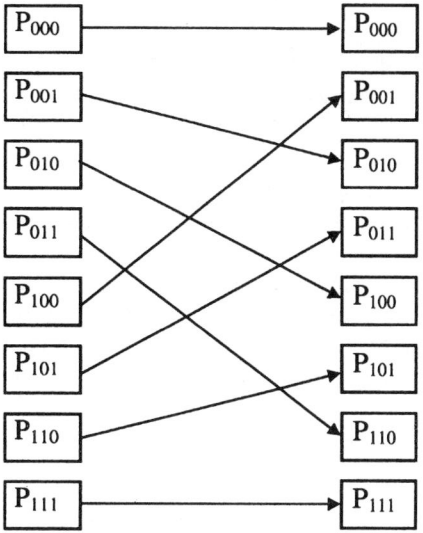

Figure 2.9. Alternative representation of the perfect shuffle interconnection network.

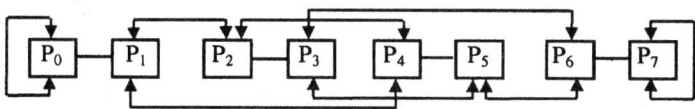

Figure 2.10. A perfect unshuffle interconnection network.

2.2.3   Two-Dimensional Mesh

The two-dimensional mesh interconnection network used by ILLIAC IV, Goodyear's Massively Parallel Processor (MPP), the ICL Distributed Array Processor (DAP), and the IBM Wire Routing Machine (WRM) is a topology in which the processors are arranged in a two-dimensional matrix. Each processor is connected to four of its neighbors (top, down, left and right). There is no general consensus on boundary connections, and they depend on the parallel architecture. For example, in the WRM the boundary and corner processors have degree 3 and 2, respectively. In contrast, in the ILLIAC machine, all processors have degree 4, and the bottom processors are connected to the top processor in the same column and the rightmost processors in a row are connected to the leftmost processors in the next row. Some variants of 2-dimensional mesh allow wrap-around connections between processors on the edge of the mesh; for example, between processors in the same row or column.

The mesh topology can be generalized to more than two dimensions. In a q-dimensional mesh, each processor is connected to two neighbors in each dimension, with processors on the boundary having fewer connections. In addition, a mesh can be categorized by number of rows and columns. For example, a mesh of size $q_1 q_2$ consists of q_1 rows and q_2 processors in each row. Each processor has four neighbors, except those on the first and last rows and columns.

Figure 2.11 (a) shows a two-dimensional mesh with no wrap-around connections, and Figure 2.11 (b) presents a 2-D mesh with wrap-around connections between processors in the same row or column.

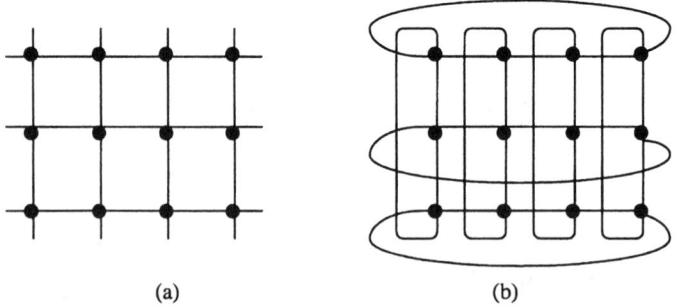

(a)   (b)

Figure 2.11. Two-dimensional mesh. (a) Mesh with no wrap-around connections. (b) Mesh with wrap-around connections between processors in same row or column.

2.2.4   Hypercube or n-Cube

Assume N processors $P_0, P_1, \ldots, P_{N-1}$ are available such that N is a power of 2; $N = 2^q$ for some $q \geq 0$. If each processor is connected to exactly q neighbors, a q-dimensional hypercube can be obtained, meaning that each processor has a degree of q. Note that the hypercube in dimension q can be obtained by connecting corresponding processors in two q/2-dimensional hypercubes. Formally, the network of N processors is called a binary n-cube network, such that the N processors are labeled from 0 to N−1 and two processors of this network are adjacent if their labels differ by exact one bit position. The indices of the processors are given in binary notation. Generally speaking, the neighboring processors differ by a power of 2. The hypercube was the most popular processor organization used by several companies, such as Intel Corporation, NCUBE Corporation, Thinking Machine Corporation and FPS. Figure 2.12 represent two hypercube interconnection networks with $2^3 = 8$ (called three-cube) and $2^4 = 16$ (called four-cube) connected processors.

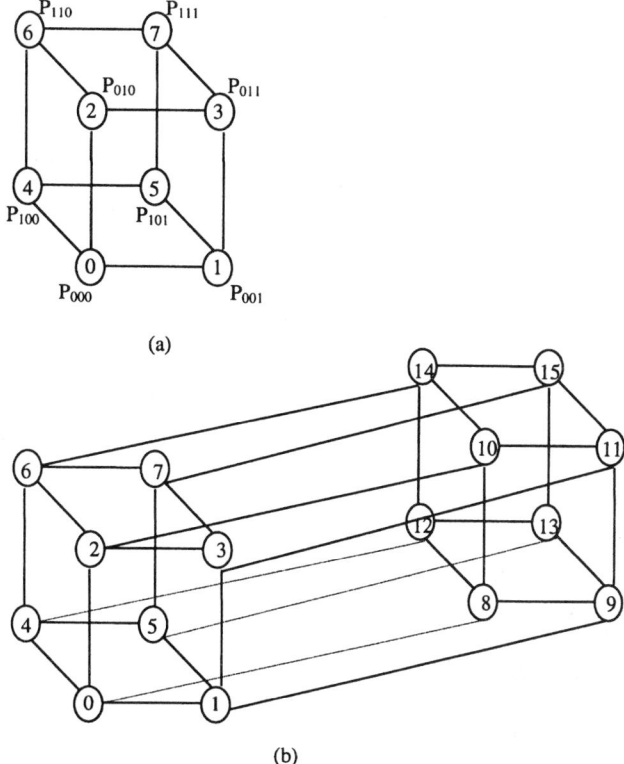

Figure 2.12. A hypercube interconnection network. (a) With 8 connected processors and q = 3. (b) With 16 connected processors and q = 4.

The routing algorithm for the hypercube topology is very simple. For example, for a q-dimensional hypercube, the algorithm uses at most q steps. During step x (for x = 1,2,...,q) the messages are transferred to the adjacent processor in dimension x if the i_{th} bit of the processor is 1; otherwise, the messages remain in the sending processor. After q steps, all the q adjacent processors have received the messages. In the 1980s, hypercube-based interconnection networks were most popular. Such networks were used in several message-passing multiprocessor systems, typically using bit-serial transmission. Examples of such machines are Intel's iPSC, NCUBE's NCUBE/ten, and Thinking Machine's CM-2.

2.2.5   Star

A star interconnection network of processors has the property that for any integer n, each processor corresponds to a distinct permutation of n symbols; i.e., {1, 2, 3, ... ,n}. This indicates that the network connects P = n! processors where n! = n * (n − 1) * (n − 2) * ... * 3 * 2 * 1.

Each processor is labeled with a permutation to which it corresponds. For example, for n = 4 a processor may have label 3124 or 1234. In a star interconnection network denoted by S_n, a processor P_i is connected to a processor P_j if and only if the index j can be obtained from i by exchanging the first symbol with the x_{th} symbol where $2 \leq x \leq n$.

Thus, for n = 4, if P_i = 2134 and P_j = 3124 then P_j and P_i are connected by two arc links in S_4 since 3124 and 2134 can be obtained from each other by exchanging the first and the third symbols. A star interconnection network with S_4 = 4! = 24 processors is shown in Figure 2.13.

2.2.6   De Bruijn

A De Bruijn network of processors consists of $N = d^k$ processors, each one represented with a k-digit word as $(a_{k-1}a_{k-2}...a_1a_0)$, where $a_j \in \{0,1,...,d-1\}$ for j = 0,1,...,k − 1. The processors reachable by $(a_{k-1}a_{k-2}...a_1a_0)$ are

$(a_{k-2}a_{k-3}...a_0q)$ and $(qa_{k-1}a_{k-2}...a_2a_1)$

where q = 0,1,...,d − 1. A De Bruijn network with d = 2 and k = 3 is shown in Figure 2.14. Compared with the shuffle exchange interconnection network, the De Bruijn network contains shuffle connections, but the diameter is about half the diameter of a shuffle exchange network. The processors of the Triton-1, which has a hybrid SIMD/MIMD parallel architecture, are connected with a De Bruijn network.

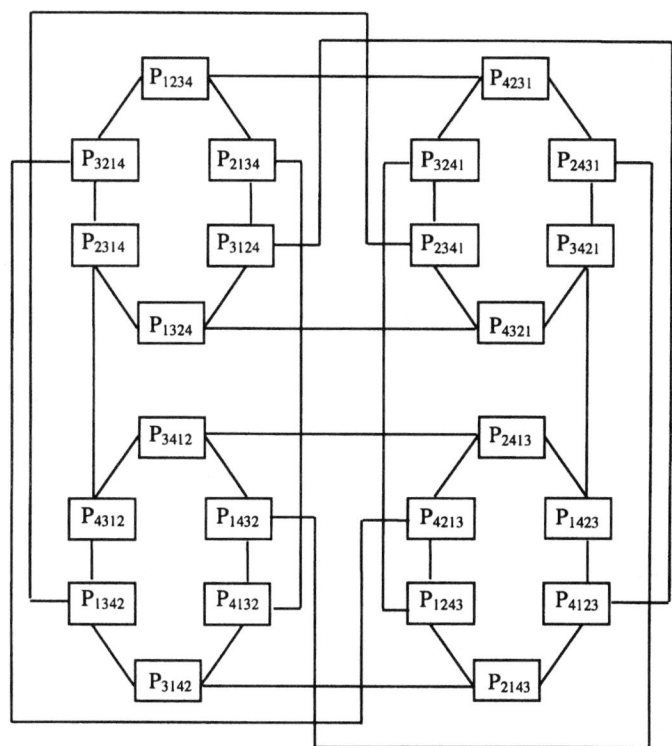

Figure 2.13. A star interconnection network with 24 processors.

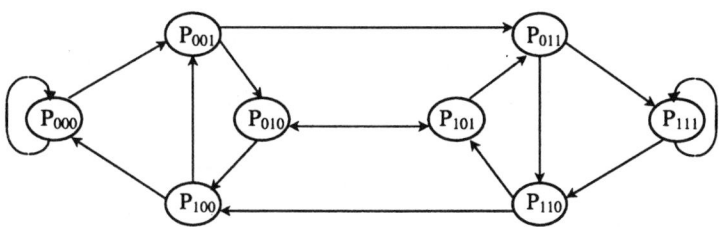

Figure 2.14. A De Bruijn interconnection network with 8 connected Processors.

2.2.7   Binary Tree

In a binary tree interconnection network, the connection forms a complete binary tree with $N = 2^d - 1$ vertices in which d is the number of levels in the tree and the levels are numbered from 0 to $d - 1$. Figure 2.15 shows a binary tree interconnection network for $d = 3$ with $N = 2^3 - 1 = 7$ connected processors.

Each processor at level i is connected to its parent at level $i + 1$ and to its two children at level $i - 1$, meaning that every interior processor can communicate with its two children and every processor except the root processor can communicate with its parent.

In general, in a binary tree interconnection network, each interior processor has a degree 3 (two children and one parent), terminal processors have degree 1 (parent), and the root processor has degree 2 (two children). The processors are typically numbered consecutively, starting with the root processor as 1. The left and right children of processor x are numbered 2x and 2x + 1, respectively.

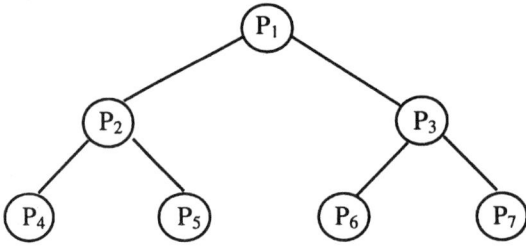

Figure 2.15. A binary tree interconnection network with 7 connected processors.

Another alternative in a tree interconnection network is a mesh of trees. In a mesh interconnection network, the N processors are arranged in a square with $N^{1/2}$ rows and $N^{1/2}$ columns.

Communication is allowed only between neighboring processors. The processors in each row are interconnected to form a binary tree, as are the processors in each column. Figure 2.16 shows a mesh of trees for $N = 16$ connected processors with $16^{1/2} = 4$ rows and $16^{1/2} = 4$ columns. Thinking Machine's CM-5 is an example of a message-passing machine that uses a fat tree network with a link width of four. Intel's Paragon uses a mesh network with a link width of 16. To facilitate message passing, it is common to include a special communication unit at each node of the tree. For example, the Paragon machine has a message processor that essentially frees the application processor from having to be involved in the details of message handling.

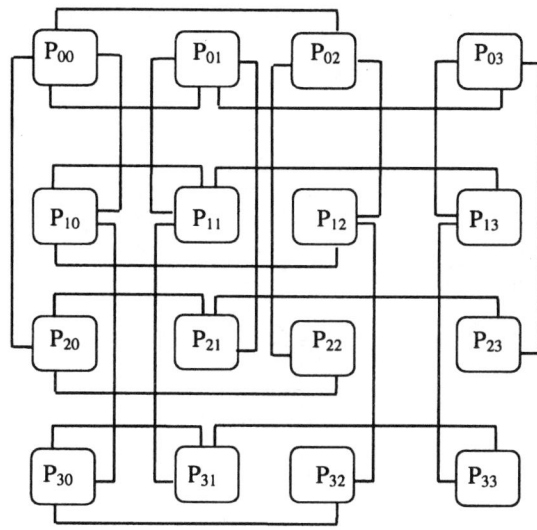

Figure 2.16. A mesh of trees with 16 connected processors.

2.2.8   Delta

A delta interconnection network is a staged network with the following properties:

1. There are k stages.
2. Each stage consists of crossbars having m inputs and n outputs totaling m*n crossbars.
3. The network consists of m^k inputs and n^k outputs; thus it is a network consisting of $m^k * n^k$ switching.
4. The switching connections allow exactly one path from any input to any output.
5. If A is the destination address of a desired connection in the base of n, then the digits of A express the crossbar settings to establish the desired connection.

In Figure 2.17, a three-stage $2^3 * 2^3$ delta interconnection network utilizing 2 * 2 crossbars is shown.

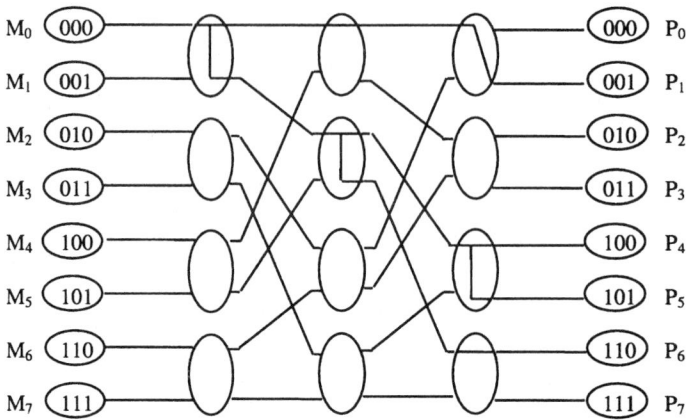

Figure 2.17. A delta interconnection network.

2.2.9   Butterfly

A butterfly interconnection network of processors consists of $(n + 1)2^n$ processors divided into $n + 1$ rows, each containing $P = 2^n$ processors.

The rows are labeled from 0 to n and are combined in a way that gives each processor four connections to other processors.

Assume that processor (i, j) refers to processor number j in row number i, where $0 \le i \le n$ and $0 \le j < P$. Then processor (i, j) on row $i > 0$ is connected to two other processors on row $(i - 1)$, processor $(i - 1, j)$ and processor $(i - 1, m)$, where m is the integer formed by inverting the i_{th} most significant bit in the binary representation of j. It is noted that if (i, j) is connected to processor $(i - 1, m)$, then processor (i, m) is connected to processor (i, j).

In a butterfly interconnection network, the length of the longest network edge increases as the number of network nodes increases. Figure 2.18 represents a butterfly interconnection network consisting of 32 processors arranged in 4 rows.

The processors of BBN's TC2000 MIMD parallel architecture are connected with a butterfly interconnection network.

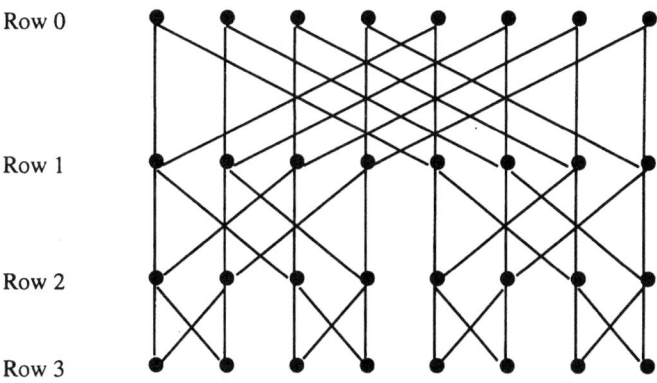

Row 0

Row 1

Row 2

Row 3

Figure 2.18. A butterfly interconnection network with 4 rows and 32 processors.

2.2.10 Omega

The omega interconnection network was proposed by Lawrie [Lawrie 75] as an interconnection network between processors and memories. The omega interconnection network provides one unique connection network between processors and memories. This network has n = log_2N stages of N/2 switching boxes, where N is the number of inputs (outputs). The network uses 4 different switching boxes, as shown in Figure 2.19, and the switching boxes in each stage are under independent control. Figure 2.20 presents the interconnection topology when N = 8. As we can see, between two adjacent stages there is a perfect shuffle interconnection. In other words, each stage in the network consists of a shuffle pattern of links followed by a column of N/2 switches.

straight-through   criss-cross   upper broadcast   lower broadcast

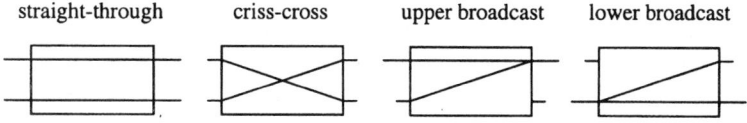

Figure 2.19. The four switching boxes for the omega network.

In addition to one-to-one connections, the omega network also supports broadcasting messages. For example, the network can be used to broadcast data from one source to many destinations by setting some of the switching boxes to the upper or lower broadcast state. This indicates that more internal interconnections are possible on this network regarding each switching box that can be represented as a four function switching box.

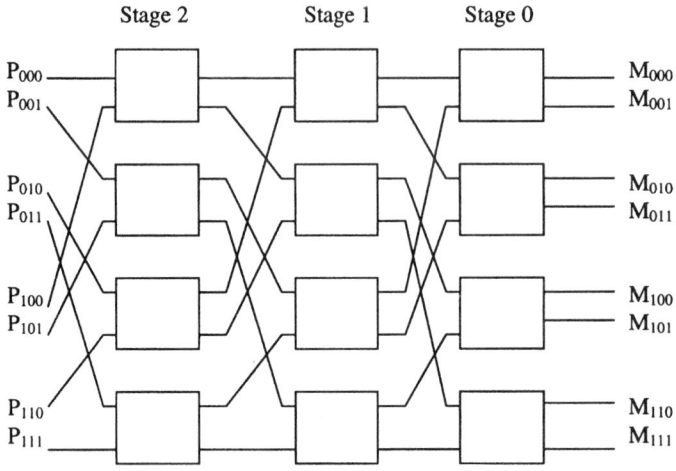

Figure 2.20. Omega interconnection network with 8 inputs.

There is an efficient routing algorithm for setting the stages of the switching boxes in the omega network. The algorithm uses a distributed control scheme that takes advantage of a simple message-routing algorithm suitable for both SIMD synchronous operations and MIMD asynchronous operations.

Assume that an input with address $I_{n-1}I_{n-2} \ldots I_0$ has to be connected to a certain output with address $O_{n-1}O_{n-2} \ldots O_0$. Starting with the input address, each bit of the input address determines the appropriate output port of the switching box with regard to the stage. For example, if the I_{n-1} bit of the input address is 0 and the input is connected to the $(n-1)_{th}$ stage, then the upper output of the switch is selected; otherwise, the lower output of the switch is selected. In the same way, bit I_{n-2} determines the output of the switch located on the next stage. If $I_{n-2} = 0$, then select upper output port; if $I_{n-2} = 1$, then select the lower output port. Generally speaking, if the bit of the input address is zero, the message is sent out to the upper output port of the switch; if the bit is 1, the message can be transferred to the lower output port of the switch. Figure 2.21 illustrates a connection between input P_{010} and output M_{110}. The bold line shows the path of this connection for a message leaving processor 2 to be connected to memory 6. The omega interconnection network is perfect for matrix multiplication because it allows conflict-free access to rows, columns, diagonal elements and square blocks of matrices [Lawrie 75].

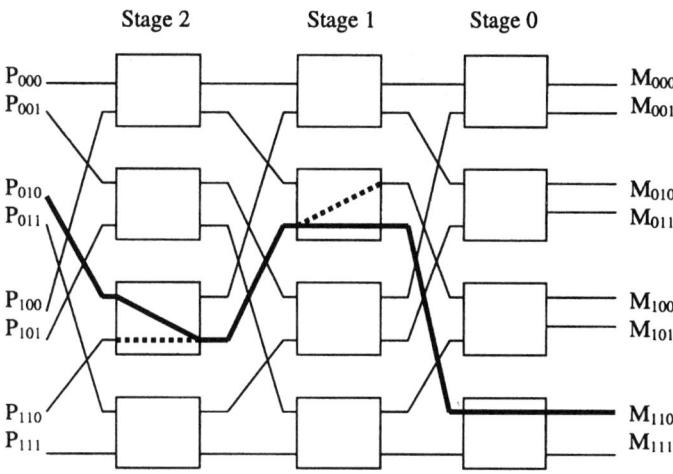

Figure 2.21. Message routing in an omega network.

2.2.11 Pyramid

A two-dimensional pyramid consists of $(4^{d+1} - 1)/3$ processors distributed in $d + 1$ levels with the following properties:

- There is 4^{d-2} processor at level d,
- There are 4^{d-1} processors at level $d - 1$, and
- There are 4^d processors at level $d - 2$.

As we can see, there is only one processor at level d. In general, any processor at level x:

- Is connected to its four neighboring processors at the same level if $x < d$,
- Is connected to four children at level $x - 1$ if $x \geq 1$, and
- Is connected to one parent at level $x + 1$ if $x \leq d - 1$.

A pyramid with 21 processors $\{(4^{d+1} - 1)/3 = 21\}$ and 3 levels $(d + 1 = 3)$ is shown in Figure 2.22. As we can see, a pyramid has at its base a two-dimensional mesh containing d^2 processors. In general, a pyramid interconnection network is a generalization of the ring-binary tree and provides another possible solution for combining meshes and trees. As we can see, this pyramid consists of a 4-array tree with meshes on each level. In a pyramid interconnection network, the message travels up and down the tree rather than across the mesh, meaning that fewer link traversals are required compared with a two-dimensional mesh network. Table 2.1 presents the number of processors and the interconnection topology used in some of the parallel architectures, including vector processors.

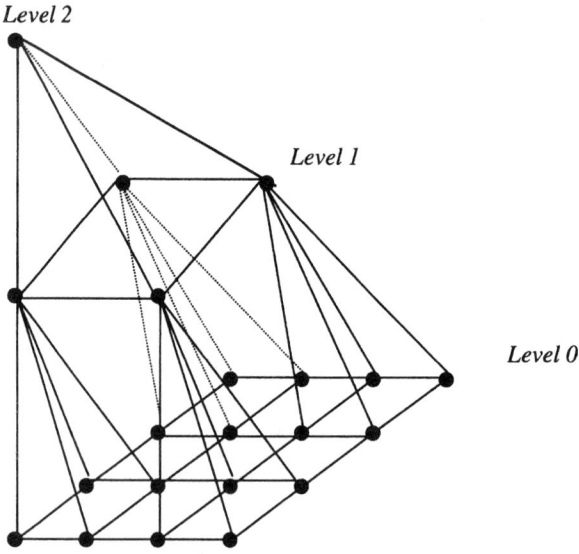

Figure 2.22. A pyramid network with 21 processors in 3 levels, 0, 1 and 2.
$d + 1 = 3 \Rightarrow d = 2$
$4^{d-2} = 1$ processor at level 2
$4^{d-1} = 4$ processors at level 1
$4^{d-0} = 16$ processors at level 0

Table 2.1. A spectrum of parallel architectures showing the number of processors and the interconnection topology.

Parallel Architecture	Year	Class of Machine	Number of Processors and Interconnection Topology
ILLIAC IV	1972	SIMD	64, Linear
DAP	1974	SIMD	4096, Lattice
MPP	1980	SIMD	16384, Hypercube

Table 2.1. (cont.) A spectrum of parallel architectures showing the number of processors and the interconnection topology.

CM-1	1983	SIMD	4096, Hypercube
CM-2	1985	SIMD	65536, Hypercube
MasPar MP-1	1988	SIMD	16384, Hypercube
MasPar MP-2	1990	SIMD	16384, Hypercube
C.mmp	1971	MIMD	16, Multistage Crossbar
Cm*	1977	MIMD	50, Bus
BBN Butterfly	1981	MIMD	256, Butterfly
Cyber	1983	MIMD	16, Ring
Cosmic Cube	1983	MIMD	64, Hypercube
Grip	1984	MIMD	120, Bus
Field Analysis	1984	MIMD	64, Multistage Crossbar
Ncube	1985	MIMD	1024, Hypercube
IPSC/1	1985	MIMD	128, Hypercube
Meiko Surface	1986	MIMD	40, Reconfigurable
Sequent Symmetry	1986	MIMD	30, Bus
Encore MultiMax	1987	MIMD	11, Bus
IPSC/2	1987	MIMD	256, Hypercube
DADO	1987	MIMD	8191, Tree
Cray Y-MP	1988	MIMD	16, Multiport
FPS T/2000	1988	MIMD	16384, Hypercube
Ultracomputer	1988	MIMD	4096, Omega
Alice	1988	MIMD	64, Shuffle-Exchange
Cedar	1989	MIMD	32, Multistage Crossbar
IPSC/860	1990	MIMD	512, Hypercube
CM-5	1991	MIMD	1024, Tree
Paragon XP/s	1991	MIMD	4096, Mesh
KSR-1	1992	MIMD	1088, Ring
J-Machine	1992	MIMD	1024, 3-D Mesh
STAR 100	1971	Vector	4
Cray 1	1976	Vector	1
Cyber 205	1980	Vector	1
Wrap	1980	Vector	10
Fujitsu VP-200	1982	Vector	1
Cray X-MP 2	1982	Vector	1, 2, 4
Cray 2	1985	Vector	4
Eta 10	1987	Vector	2, 4, 6, 8
Cray 3	1988	Vector	16
Intel Wrap	1990	Vector	50

2.3   Goodness Measures for Interconnection Networks

Given an interconnection network model M, there are three basic goodness measures of M that are related to communication and complexity within that network. These three measures are:

1. Diameter of the network
2. Degree of the processor
3. Bisection width of the network

Assume that an arbitrary pair of processors P_1 and P_2 are in M. Given any algorithm, sometime during the execution, the local memories of P_1 and P_2 must be combined. Assume that the shortest path connecting P_1 and P_2 is $Dist(P_1, P_2)$, which is the number of links in that path. The minimum number of communication steps required for information to be shared by P_1 and P_2 will then be $Dist(P_1, P_2)/2$. Thus the first goodness measure can be defined as:

$$Diameter(M) = Max\{Dist(P_i, P_j); P_i, P_j \in M \}$$

It is worth noting that keeping the diameter of a network small provides a lower bound for the communication complexity of algorithms implemented on the network, which requires information sharing among the processors. In general, to keep the diameter of a network small requires a large number of links to each processor in that interconnection network. The second goodness measure is based on the degree of the processor, which is defined as the number of links to the processor. Because the current state of technology requires intercommunication networks with small degrees, the second goodness measure can be defined as:

$$Maximum\text{-}Degree(M) = Max\{Degree(P); P \in M\}$$

Given a bipartition of the processors of M as two sets, X and Y, the third goodness measure can be defined. Assume All-links(X, Y) is the set of all links joining a processor in X to a processor in Y. Clearly, any path joining a processor in X to a processor in Y must contain at least one link from All-links(X, Y). If the size of the X set is large compared with the size of Y, then All-links(X, Y) must be small in size. Thus, communication between processors in X with processors in Y will result in congestion, because of the large number of ratings that will have to use the small number of links in All-links(X, Y). The size of the smallest link in All-links(X, Y) is defined as the bisection width of the network. Thus the third goodness measure can be defined as:

$$Bisection\text{-}Width(M) = Min\{|All\text{-}links(X,Y)|; Abs(|X| - |Y|) < 1\}$$

Generally speaking, one network topology is more desirable than another if it is more efficient, more convenient, and more extendable than the other. One particular criterion of interest is the length of the longest link in the network. For example, in the linear and mesh networks, all links have a constant length regardless of the number of elements used. On the other hand, the hypercube has a smaller diameter than the mesh, and the tree appears to be better than either the mesh or the hypercube, but its link length is a function of the number of processors. A corollary follows that beside of these criteria listed, there are other features to take into consideration; for example, potential bottleneck (in a tree network the root is a potential bottleneck), regularity (is the network easy to implement) and modularity (is the network easy to extend by a row or a column if required). Clearly, there is no interconnection network that maintains and optimizes all these three goodness measures. This indicates that sometimes trade-offs between these three goodness measures are necessary. Table 2.2 compares the characteristics of various interconnection topologies with regard to the number of nodes and degrees. The interconnection networks in the table are undirected; that is, there are single connections between one element and another.

Table 2.2. Comparison of the characteristics of various interconnection networks.

Network topology	Number of Nodes	Degree
Linear and ring	d	2
Shuffle-exchange	2^d	3
2-D mesh	d^2	4
Hypercube	2^d	d
Star*	$m!$	$m - 1$
De Bruijn	2^d	4
Binary tree	$2^d - 1$	3
Delta	2^d	2
Butterfly	$(d + 1)2^d$	$d + 1$
Omega	2^d	2
Pyramid	$(4d^2 - 1/3)$	9

*For m as a given integer, $N = m!$ is the number of processors in the star interconnection network.

2.4   Compilers

Once a program has been written in one of the conventional programming languages, it must be translated into terms that the hardware understands, which is machine language. Compilers and interpreters are used to perform this translation. Interpreters execute one statement at a time. There are some advantages to using interpreters: programs are smaller and easier to write, execution starts more quickly, and debugging is easy. However, memory has to be allocated for the source program as well as for the interpreter, and in addition there is a performance penalty. In contrast, the compiler generates a complete machine code of the program before the execution starts.

One of the most essential components of parallel computers is parallel compilers. Generally speaking, parallel compilers decrease the execution time of the program by breaking it up into blocks that may be processed simultaneously by the multiple processing units. Some progress has been made in the area of vectorizing compilers, which generate code suitable for execution on pipelined vector processors. Some compilers perform only parallelism detection and partitioning functions, whereas more sophisticated compilers perform even scheduling problems. The parallel architecture raises questions for the compiler about what kind of blocks the program should be divided into and how these parts may be rearranged. In general, these questions involve the granularity, the level of the parallelism, an analysis of the dependencies and run time scheduling.

There are three approaches involved in compiler construction for parallel computers:

1. **Run Time Partitioning and Run Time Scheduling.** This approach is practical for specific applications. There is significant overhead when partitioning and scheduling are performed at run time thus, decreasing performance.

2. **Compile Time Partitioning and Run Time Scheduling.** This approach is the most common model of compiler construction in multiprocessor systems. The scheduling is performed at the run time phase, but the program must be partitioned into blocks by the programmer or compiler. Synchronization and communication have to be provided.

3. **Compile Time Partitioning and Compile Time Scheduling.** This approach requires the most sophisticated compiler construction. There is no overhead involved at run time. In general, it is difficult to estimate the program execution time, thus the scheduling may be far from the optimum.

Generally speaking, most of the work in compiler construction for parallel computers has been done for Fortran programs. For example, the **Paraphrase** compiler [Kuck 84] used by the Cedar multiprocessor, developed at the University of Illinois, is a source to source constructing compiler that utilizes a data dependence graph to transform a Fortran program from its original sequential form into a suitable form for parallel execution. This compiler performs two phases:

1. In the first phase, it performs machine-independent transformations and changes the program into an intermediate form that express the parallelism form of the program code.

2. In the second phase, it performs a mapping to change the intermediate form into a specific architecture, such as simple execution of array instructions or multiple execution of array instructions.

In general, the most exploited form of parallelism in Fortran programs is associated with loops, for example, when working with vector and array elements. This indicates that the parallelism is typically present at the innermost level. Vector parallel systems use parallelism in innermost loops only. Figure 2.23 presents the translation done by the Paraphrase parallel compiler to produce an executable code for pipelined vector processors. The Paraphrase compiler was successful in extracting parallelism in Fortran programs for execution on vector processor machines such as the Cray X/MP.

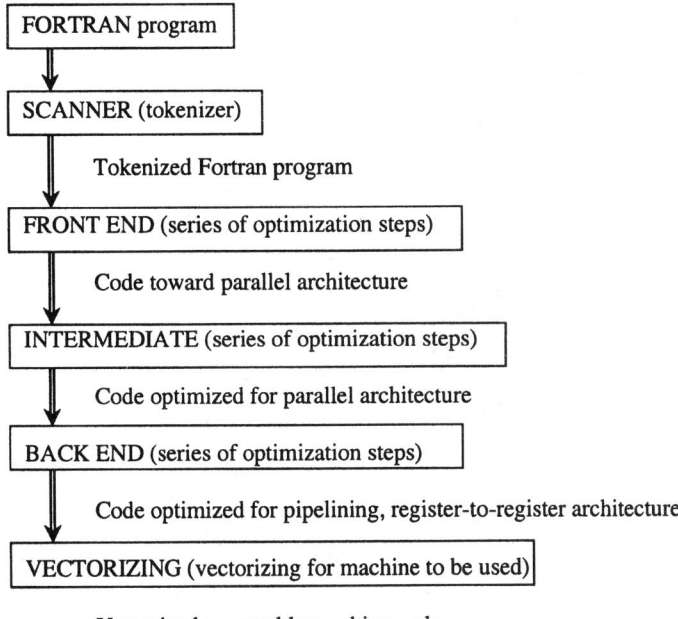

Figure 2.23. Paraphrase source to source constructing parallel compiler.

The **Bulldog** reassembling compiler developed at Yale University [Ellis 86] is designed to detect parallelism at the instruction level. It aims for automatic parallelism detection for scientific programs written in Fortran. The central ideas are **VLIW** (Very Long Instruction Word) architecture design and the **trace** scheduling compilation techniques. In general, sequences of code blocks might be grouped together into much larger blocks, called traces, with a high probability of being executed from beginning to end without interruption. The VLIW architecture is designed with very long instructions. For example, the ELI-512 machine consists of sixteen 32-bit RISC processors with an overall instruction word length of 512 bits. The VLIW architecture can provide the increased parallelism found within the traces. Bulldog takes advantage of the fact that most of the time, a conditional branch proceeds in the same direction. This indicates that sequences of code segments are linked together in a trace, and these can be executed from beginning to end without interruption, providing parallelism. In addition, Bulldog does not perform the loop dependencies analysis; it relies on the formation of traces. However, the traces can be formed only for blocks inside the loops. Figure 2.24 shows a pictorial view of the Bulldog compiler design.

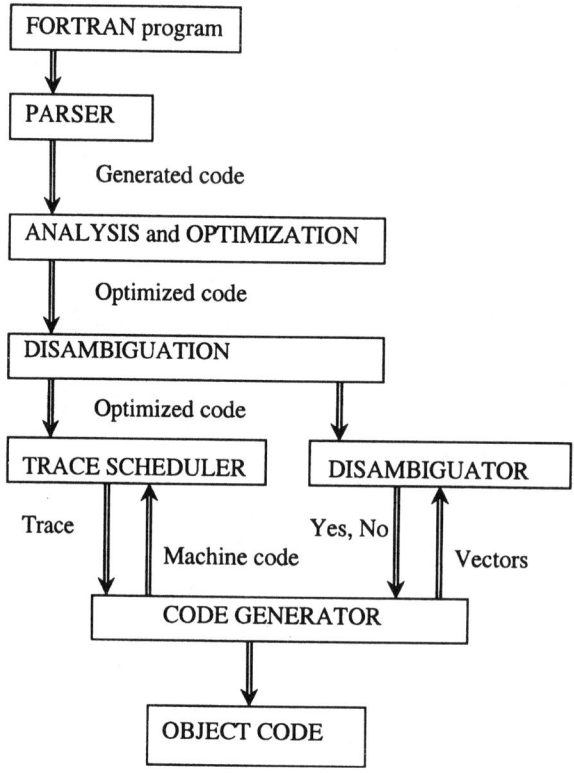

Figure 2.24. Pictorial view of the Bulldog compiler organization.

The organization indicates that a parallelizing compiler converts the program into parallel executable code. In that case, the compiler establishes which statements can be executed simultaneously. It might rearrange the compiled code to achieve concurrency.

Another example of parallel compiler construction concerns data parallel programming language called **Fortran D** [Fox 91, Hiranandani 92, 93]. A version of this language is also called **High Performance Fortran (HPF)**. Fortran D is an extension of Fortran which enables the programmer to specify the desired decomposition of the data. It provides efficient means of both problem mapping using array alignments and machine mapping using data distribution and decomposition. This enhancement can be applied to Fortran 77 producing Fortran 77D, or to Fortran 90, producing Fortran 90D.

Problem mapping is concerned with aligning arrays with respect to one another. For example, given two 20×20 two dimensional arrays, you may wish to have row I of the first array aligned with column I of the second array.

In Fortran D this can be accomplished in two steps:

1. Decomposition: Define a decomposition which syntactically looks like an array but occupies no storage. Arrays are aligned in this phase, meaning that it assures that corresponding elements would require no communication.

2. Distribution: Decide how to distribute the elements of a decomposition across the processors.

The following example is helpful in understanding this process.

```
REAL X(N), Y(N, N), Z(N, N), W(N, N), A1(N, N), A2(N, N)
DECOMPOSITION D1(N), D2(N, N)
ALIGN A1, A2 with D2
ALIGN Y(I, J) with D2(J, I)
ALIGN Z(I, J), W(J, I) with D1(I)
```

The first align statement assures that corresponding elements of A1 and A2 are aligned. It is worth noting that A1 and A2 do not share storage. The second align assures that if Y is set equal to the transpose of either A1 or A2, no communication will be required. This can be compared with the nested loop in Fortran 77, as illustrated by the following code:

```
      DO 20 I = 1, N, 1
         DO 10 J = 1, N, 1
            Y(I, J) = A1(I, J)
10          CONTINUE
20    CONTINUE
```

Again note that since Y and A1 do not share storage, interprocessor data communication and synchronization are required. In the first example above, the last align places all of row I of Z and all of column I of W in the same processor. Thus, the diagonal elements of the matrix product of Z and W can be computed without communication. In other words, row I and column J are aligned with the I_{th} element of the decomposition. Consequently, when we know where D1(I) is stored, all the array elements aligned with it might be stored there as well. For simplicity, we begin with one-dimensional distribution and assume that the number of processors can be divided by N. Then there are two possibilities, **block** distribution and **cyclic** distribution. In a block distribution, D1, which is of size N, is divided into p contiguous blocks of size N/P in which each block k is assigned to processor k. In a cyclic distribution, D1 is divided into N blocks of size 1 in which each block k, $k+P$, $k+2P$, ... is assigned to processor k. This indicates that cyclic distribution propagates the decomposition across the processors in a round-robin manner. The rationale behind this distribution is that block distribution is stored sequentially, whereas cyclic distribution is stored interleaved. Figure 2.25 illustrates the array partitioning in memory with regard to the block and cyclic approaches.

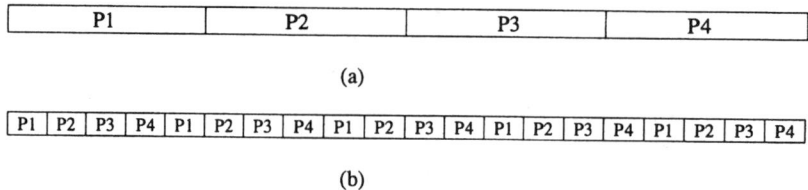

Figure 2.25. Array partitioning between processors. (a) Block partitioning. (b) Cyclic partitioning.

For multidimensional decomposition, one can choose a distribution for each dimension. Fortran D supports a FORALL loop with semantics different from those of the DOALL loop. In the DOALL primitive, the programmer assumes that the different iterations will not interfere with each other. In contrast, the FORALL primitive instructs the compiler to make sure that the iterations do not interfere. For example, if one iteration writes a variable that the other iteration reads, the value read is guaranteed to be the old value. Another feature of Fortran D is the ability to specify the destination processor in which the iteration can be performed. This can be illustrated by the following code:

```
FORALL   I = 1, 25 on HOME (X(I))
       X(I + 25) = F(X(I))
ENDFOR
```

which performs the computation where the input data are stored rather than where the result is to be stored.

HPF, proposed by Loveman [Loveman 93], provides additional parallel constructs which allow many Fortran programs to be compiled with reasonable efficiency for a range of parallel computers. Typically, the programmer is responsible for specifying the domain decomposition, but the compiler partitions the computation automatically. Many of these ideas also apply to other data-parallel languages, such as C* [Thinking Machine Corporation 90], data-parallel C [Hatcher 91] and pC++ [Bodin 91]. Compilers for HPF and related data-parallel languages generally proceed as follows. Data decomposition statements are analyzed to determine the decomposition of each array in a program. Computation is then partitioned across processors in the parallel architecture. This process allows global access to reference of data. We illustrates the HPF compiler operation with a program presented in Figure 2.26. The program illustrates a sequential array assignment by performing a four point finite difference stencil to the array X to obtain the array NEW and then computes the maximum difference between the two arrays. Two functions, ABS and MAXVAL, are used. The program presented in Figure 2.27 is an HPF version (parallel version) of the sequential program. Three different directives, PROCESSORS, DISTRIBUTE and ALIGN, have been utilized to partition each of the two arrays by row, thus allocating 25 rows to each of four processors. Figure 2.28 presents the compiler-generated code that has been produced by the HPF compiler to be executed in a parallel architecture with 4 processors.

```
PROGRAM DIFFERENCE
REAL X(100,100), NEW(100,100)
NEW(2:99,2:99) = (X(1:98,2:99)+X(3:100,2:99)+X(2:99,1:98)
+ X(2:99,3:100))/4
DIFFMAX = MAXVAL(ABS(NEW−X))
STOP
END
```

Figure 2.26. A sequential version of two-dimensional finite difference program.

```
!HPF$  PROCESSORS p(32)
       REAL D(1024), E(1024)
!HPF$  DISTRIBUTE D(BLOCK)
!HPF$  DISTRIBUTE E(BLOCK) ONTO p
       PROGRAM DIFFERENCE
!HPF$  PROCESSOR pr(4)/* Four processors are utilized
       */REAL X(100, 100), NEW(100, 100)/* Data   */
!HPF$  ALIGN NEW(: , :) WITH X(: , :)/* Array is
       decomposed in one dimension */
!HPF$  DISTRIBUTE X(BLOCK, *) ONTO pr
       NEW(2:99,2:99) = (X(1:98,2:99)+X(3:100,2:99) +
       X(2:99,1:98)+X(2:99,3:100))/4
       DIFFMAX = MAXVAL(ABS(NEW - X) )
       STOP
       END
```

Figure 2.27. An HPF version of two-dimensional finite difference program.

In this example, two library routines that perform communication operations, called as STENCIL_EXCHANGE_1D and REDUCE_REAL, are utilized. The first routine exchanges data with the neighboring processors, and the second routine performs the reduction operation required to compute the maximum difference.

```
PROGRAM COMPILER_GENERATED
REAL X(100, 0:26), NEW(100,25)
REAL DIFFLOCAL, DIFFMAX
MY_P = MYNODE() /* Processor number, 0,1,2,3 */
```

```
*      Exchange data with the neighbors
       CALL STENCIL_EXCHANGE_1D(X,MY_P,4,100,25,1)
       LB = MAX( (MY_P*25) + 1,2) - (MY_P*25)
       UB = MIN( (MY_P + 1)*25,99) - (MY_P*25)
       NEW(2:99,1:25) = (X(1:98,LB:UB) + X(3:100,LB:UB) +
       $     X(2:99,LB - 1:UB - 1) + X(2:99,LB + 1:UB + 1))/4
       DIFFLOCAL = MAXVAL(ABS(NEW(2:99,1:25)-X(2:99,1:25)))
*      Obtain the diffmax
       CALL REDUCE_REAL("MAX", DIFFLOCAL, DIFFMAX)
       STOP
       END
```

Figure 2.28. The code generated by the HPF compiler for parallel execution.

2.5   Operating Systems

An Operating System (OS) is a program that is designed to coordinate computer operations. Operating systems perform functions such as system initialization, program partitioning and scheduling, interprocess communication and synchronization, system managing and monitoring. In a centralized operating system, decisions are made based on total and accurate knowledge of the state of the system. In contrast, a multiprocessing operating system does not have up-to-date consistent knowledge about the state of a distributed system. The primary goal of a multiprocessing operating system is to integrate the computing resources and processors connected by a communication network into one unified system. This goal should be achieved in the presence of some restrictions imposed by users or computer systems, such as transparency, failure conditions and security.

Consequently, a multiprocessing operating system must contain the same management components as a centralized operating system—process management, memory management, resource management and file management. From the complexity point of view, the operating systems for parallel architectures can be classified into three categories:

1. Operating systems that are a simple modification of a single processor operating system, such as VMS and UNIX. The modified operating system can be run on some parallel architectures. Usually, these architectures are adopted in a master/slave configuration.

2. Operating systems that are designed for specific parallel architecture, such as Hydra OS for the C.mmp multiprocessor or Medusa OS for the Cm* multiprocessor, both designed at Carnegie-Mellon University.

3. General-purpose operating systems that are designed to be implemented on different parallel architectures, such as the MACH multiprocessor operating system.

Most modern versions of UNIX will run on multiprocessor systems. This includes System V Release 4 from AT&T, Solaris from SUN, HP UNIX from HP, Digital UNIX from Digital, AIX from IBM and IRIX from SGI. Any operating system can be converted to work on multiprocessors by protecting all the shared data structures from simultaneous access by two or more processors. Newer operating systems like Windows NT and MACH were designed from the beginning to work on multiprocessor systems. Research in the area of parallel architectures operating system design has been directed towards achieving the following properties:

1. **Resource sharing:** The operating system should provide the mechanism for sharing resources among various processors of a multiprocessor system (for example, in SIMD systems with global memory).

2. **Extensibility:** It would be beneficial if the operating system allowed the addition of new processors (and thus new services) to a system, either statically or dynamically.

3. **Availability:** The operating system should be constructed in such a way that it maintains the functionality of the system in the event of the loss of components and failure of the processors in the system.

From a user's point of view, the parallel architecture operating system must make management decisions oriented towards all resources and all the processors on the system, meaning that it has to be constructed on top of the system to allow it to see all resources without interference from any component of the system.

Multiprocessor Operating System Organization

In general, three basic organizations are used in the design of multiprocessor operating systems:

- Master/slave organization
- Separate executive organization
- Symmetric organization

Master/Slave Organization

In a master/slave multiprocessor architecture, one processor is designated as the master and the others are the slaves. The master performs input/output and necessary computations. The slaves can run CPU-bound jobs effectively, but I/O-bound jobs running on the slaves cause frequent calls for services only the master can perform. Only the master may execute the operating system. A slave processor can execute only user programs. When a process execution on a slave requires the attention of the operating system, it generates an interrupt and waits for the master to handle the interrupt. In other words, all components of the operating system are dependent on the master component. If the master fails, the system cannot perform input and output operations.

The master/slave design has been used for many multiprocessor architectures. It is easy to implement, it can be designed by making simple extensions to a single-processor operating system, and it requires very simple software and hardware structures. But it is very poor from the graceful degradation and failure points of view. Generally speaking, the operating system with master and slave structure is effective for special applications in which the workload is well defined and relatively static. It is a poor operating system for systems that execute a dynamic changing workload. It is worth noting that the operating system does not have to be reentrant, since it can be used by only one processor at a time, and on behalf of only one user at a time. In corollary, the overall system is not flexible. Computational functions are permanently assigned to various processors, which can lead to poor use of resources and an increase in the number of interrupts, since each slave processor must interrupt the master every time it needs operating system intervention. Figure 2.29 shows a typical master/slave configuration.

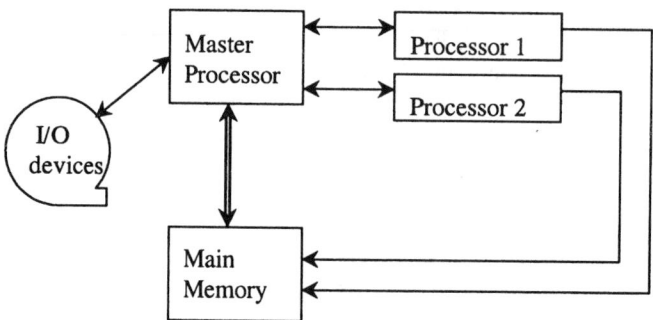

Figure 2.29. A typical master/slave multiprocessor configuration.

Separate Executive Organization

In the separate executive structure, each processor has its own identical copy of the operating system and responds to interrupts from that processor. In this organization, a task assigned to run on a particular processor proceeds to completion on that processor, meaning that each processor can service its own needs and its own dedicated resources, such as files and input/output devices. The processors do not cooperate on the execution of an individual task, and some of the processors may remain idle while one processor executes a time-consuming computation. If there is a failure in a single processor, it is unlikely to cause general system failure, which eliminates a major bottleneck problem of the master/slave organization. However, restarting an individual failed processor can be difficult. In general, this organization is more reliable than the master/slave structure.

In the overall system, some information tables contain global data, and access to this information has to be controlled with mutual exclusion methods. An alternative solution is to replicate tables in each local processor memory that requires them, meaning that each processor has its own executive.

Symmetric Organization

The symmetrical configuration is one of the most powerful and complex multiprocessing operating systems. The structure is based on a master that floats from one processor to another. The operating system can manage several identical processors, any one of which may be used to control the I/O devices or to reference any memory unit. This processor is called the executive processor. However, several processors may be executing the supervisor services at once.

Because many processors may be executing the operating system at once, reentrant code and mutual exclusion are provided. But only one processor at a time may be the executive, and this prevents conflicts over global system information. In this organization, conflict resolution hardware and software are provided. Conflicts between processors regarding access to the same memory location may be resolved by hardware, and conflicts in accessing global data are resolved by software. This organization is the most reliable system, in that a failure in one processor causes the operating system to remove that faulty processor from the system. In general, the operating system floats from one processor to the next, and a task running may be executed at different times by any of the equivalent processors. Because several processors may be in the supervisor state at once, severe conflict may result. An alternative approach to minimize conflict in the system is to divide the system data structure into separate and independent entities that may be locked individually. It is worth noting that the addition of processors does not cause the system throughput to be increased, due to additional operating system overhead, increased competition for system resources, hardware delays in switching between components, and table access conflicts and lockout delays. Generally speaking, this organization is the most difficult method to use from both the design and the operating points of view. Some of the advantages of this operating system configuration are:

- Better graceful degradation capability
- Flexibility to use fewer processors
- Better system recovery in case of single processor failure
- Effective use of resources.

Distributed Operating System Organization

A distributed operating system governs the operation of a distributed computer. It provides a virtual machine abstraction of the distributed system and offers a unified interface for resource access and manipulation of resources regardless of its location. The key objective of a distributed operating system is transparency. It looks to its users like an ordinary centralized operating system but provides the user with transparent access to the resources of different computer systems. It uses a communication network for basic services. Ideally, the components and resources that are distributed should be hidden from users and application programs unless they are explicitly demanded.

Generally speaking, a distributed operating system varies in the type of functions performed in each processor. For example, the various operating system utilities and functions are distributed among the various processors, and each processor is dedicated to process a particular utility or function. This indicates that a given processor is allowed to execute functions if that code segment is present in the processors's local memory. Consequently, this approach avoids the need for global memory access, reentrant code and interprocess synchronization. The interprocess communication (message passing) has to be provided in this system, utilizing a message/mailbox mechanism. The operating system is illustrated in Figure 2.30. This figure shows that there are two very important parts of the system:

- A communication subsystem, which links all computer systems and servers and provides an effective communication service.
- An interprocess communication mechanism, which allows remote processors to exchange messages.

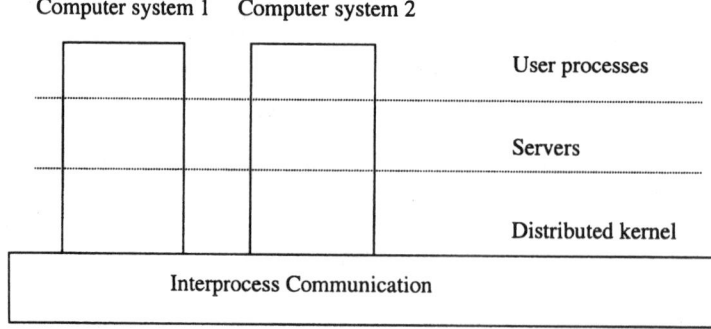

Figure 2.30. Distributed operating system organization.

In the following sections, we survey a number of operating systems to identify their basic research and design issues and features. In deciding which operating system to be studied, the following selection criteria are considered:

- The system should have good documentation.
- The system should have been implemented.
- The system should possess features to influence the design and implementation of the other systems.
- The system should be representative of a specific category, such as UNIX-based, process-based, or object-based.

The representative operating systems from the research and application point of view discussed in this section are:

- UNIX-based: MACH
- Object-based: Amoeba
- Process-based: Accent

MACH Operating System

The MACH operating system was developed at Carnegie-Mellon University [Accetta 86]. It is the successor of two previous projects, RIG [Rashid 86] and Accent [Rashid 81]. RIG was developed at the University of Rochester in 1970 and Accent was developed at Carnegie-Mellon University during the first half of the 1980s. The MACH was developed to provide direct compatibility with UNIX (by emulating the UNIX operating system). It was designed to allow a UNIX implementation to be spread across a network of multiprocessor and single processor systems [Boykin 93]. Version 2.5 of MACH includes all the UNIX compatibility codes inside the kernel and runs on the Sun-3, the IBM RT PC, multiprocessor and single processor VAX systems, and the Encore Multimax and Sequent multiprocessors. An older version of MACH was used as a basis for the operating system for the NeXT workstations.

The UNIX code was removed from version 3.0 of MACH. It runs on Intel 386 and 486 based PCs, DEC stations 3100 and 5000 series computers, some Motorola 88000 based computers and SUN SPARCS workstations. In general, it is an extension of UNIX and supports several languages. It runs with small changes on the Sequent Balance, the Encore Multimax, the BBN Butterfly and other machines.

MACH structure principles

MACH consists of a kernel that provides the following services:

- Interprocess communication
- Virtual memory management with paging and sharing of memory between tasks
- Resource management
- Controlled access to physical devices

In addition to the kernel, there is a nonkernel for user level services. System functions such as synchronization, semaphores and file servers are performed in user level server programs. This arrangement provides a separation of functions in a multiprocessor system. Individual components of MACH can run on different processors. The operating system emulations that have been produced include UNIX, OS/2, MS-DOS and VMS. MACH was designed to execute on shared memory-multiprocessors, meaning that both kernel and nonkernel could be executed by any processor. A general structure of MACH is shown in Figure 2.31.

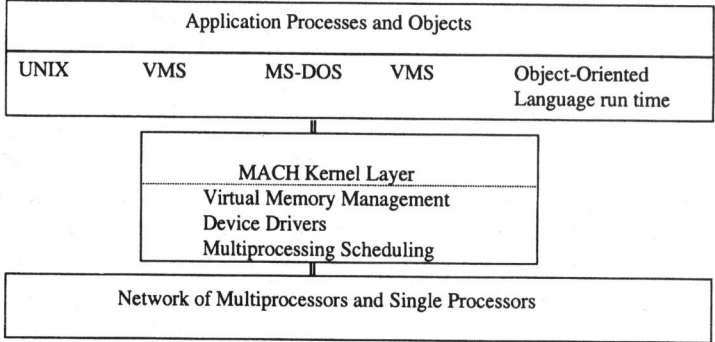

Figure 2.31. The MACH organization.

MACH design principles

The main MACH design goals and features are:

Process: A process was split into two new concepts, **task** and **thread**:

- A task is a basic unit of resource allocation which includes a page address space and protected access to system resources.
- A thread is a basic unit of CPU utilization.

In general, these concepts give users the ability to execute multiple threads simultaneously within a single process.

Portability: MACH was designed to be portable to a variety of hardware platforms.

Operating system emulation: To support different operating systems and handle user level operating system servers.

Flexible virtual memory management: To support large virtual address space memory, read/write memory sharing between processes, memory-mapped files, backing stored objects, paging and sharing of memory between tasks.

User level servers: MACH supports an object-based model such that resources are managed by the kernel or by the user level servers.

Language support: To support and handle the remote procedure calls between tasks written in C, Pascal, Ada, and Common Lisp.

Transparent extension to network operation: In order to allow for distributed programs that extend transparently between single processors and multiprocessors across a network, the MACH kernel supports a location-independent communication model involving ports as destinations.

Data transferring: The interprocess communication facility is integrated with the virtual memory system to enable transferring large amounts of data.

Amoeba Operating System

Amoeba is a distributed operating system which was designed at the Vrije University in Amsterdam under the supervision of Andrew Tanenbaum, where its design and implementation were begun in 1981 [Tanenbaum 90, Tanenbaum and Renesse 85]. The major goal was to include all the basic facilities that one would expect from a conventional operating system.

Amoeba structure principles

Amoeba uses the object-oriented model for distributed computing, remote procedure calls and lightweight processes. It supports different CPUs, such as the Motorola 68020, 8088, VAX and PDP-11. A number of utilities, including compilers, editors and shells, are operational and UNIX can be supported. The main components making up the Amoeba distributed system are the processor pool, workstations (SUN and VAX), X-terminal, servers and gateways. The gateways are used for connecting different sites over the interconnection network. Figure 2.32 shows the Amoeba organization.

The central idea of this architecture is that memory and processors will become cheap such that each user will be allocated multiple processors and each processor will have plenty of memory to run applications. This indicates that rather than allocating a multiprocessor to each user, processing power may be concentrated in the processor pool, where it can be shared among users.

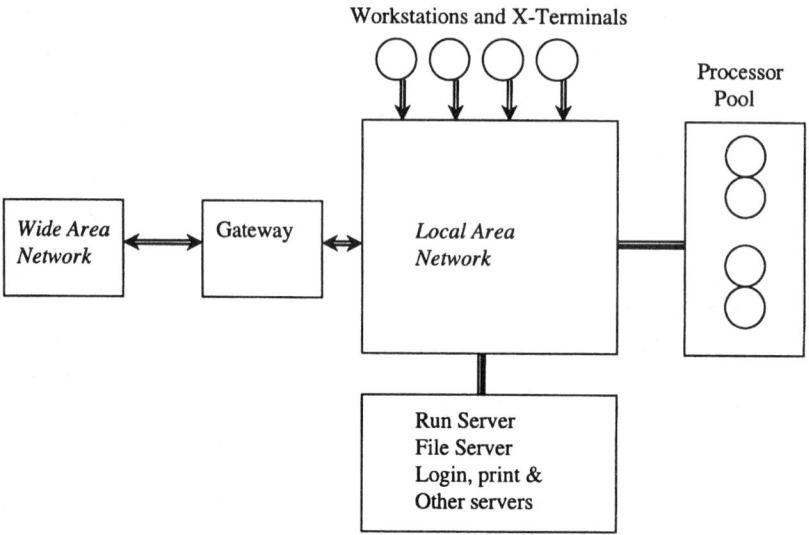

Figure 2.32. The Amoeba organization.

Amoeba design principles

The main Amoeba design goals are:

Network transparency: In this system all resource access is network transparent. This indicates that without the user's knowledge the processes are assigned to one of the processors from the *processor pool*.

Object-oriented environment: All resources, such as files, directories, disk blocks, processes and devices are objects. Each object is defined by its particular service and is under the supervision of particular server processes. All objects are accessed by a uniform naming scheme. In general, objects are managed by servers and they can be accessed only by sending messages to the servers.

Capability: All objects in this system are named and protected by secure capabilities. The system provides a uniform interface to all objects. In general, users view the system as a collection of objects named by capabilities in which they can perform operations.

Remote procedure calls: RPC protocol (communication between processes) is implemented by assembling an operation code and its arguments in a request message, which is sent to the appropriate server. The sender process is blocked while the receiver is working, whereas the receiver is blocked while it is waiting for a request. The operation is performed by the receiver. The result of that operation is returned to the sender by a response message.

Kernel server: The Amoeba micro-kernel supports a uniform model for accessing resources using capabilities. The micro-kernel is running at all computers in the system, regardless of their role. The basic abstractions supported by the micro-kernel are processes, threads and ports for communication. The characteristics are all as existing conventional operating systems. In particular, Amoeba took precedence over any issues of compatibility with existing operating systems.

Accent Operating System

The Accent operating system was developed as part of the Carnegie-Mellon Spice project [Fitzgerald 86]. It was designed to support a large network of computers and was used at Carnegie-Mellon University in a network of over 150 workstations. Accent is a communication-oriented operating system. It is designed in a way that memory management can be effectively integrated with the interprocess communication system. Thus, access to all services and resources is provided through communication facilities.

Accent structure principles

The Accent operating system is organized as a protected interprocess communication system which allows processes to be bound together and provides a uniform interface at the system level. The operating system consists of a number of layers. The bottom layer of each workstation is the kernel, which supports a collection of processes. The kernel provides an execution environment for processes running on its workstation, such as interprocess communication, virtual memory management and process management. All resources, services and functions are accessible through an interprocess communication facility provided by the system. The Accent operating system organization is shown in Figure 2.33.

Accent design principles

The main Accent design goals are:

Fork and terminate primitives: The system supports the fork and terminate primitives for process creation and destruction.

Protection: Because it is a large network of uniprocessor scientific personal computers, their interactions should be predictable to avoid conflicts.

Programming language support: The system should support many programming languages.

Network transparency: The system should support network transparency, meaning that all resources should be accessible.

Fault recovery, debugging and monitoring: The system should support tools for process monitoring and debugging to make a reliable system.

Problem decomposition: The system should support modular decomposition of a large problem into smaller units. This can be performed concurrently by a single processor or distributed between several processors.

Micro-kernel: The system supports a micro-kernel, which consists of language-independent microcode support, low-level scheduling, input and output interrupt support and virtual address translation mechanism.

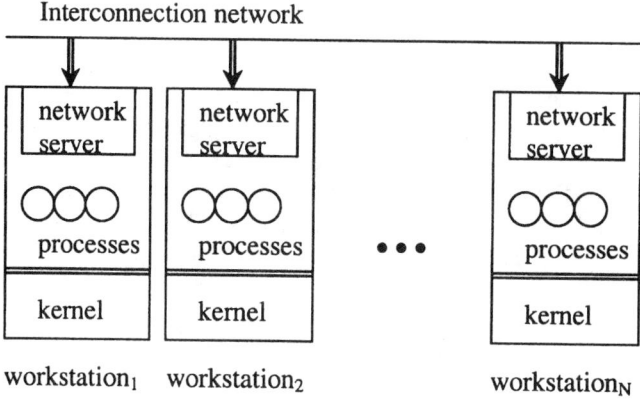

Figure 2.33. The Accent organization.

2.6   Input and Output Constraints

Any parallel machine must have some mechanism to read data from external input devices into the processor's local memory, as well as to write data from its memory to external output devices. Practical constraints will prevent some parallel computations from being executed truly simultaneously. For example, the implications are not obvious if we choose a model that allows several processors to assign new values to the same variable in parallel. In corollary, if simultaneous assignment is possible, what is the result of assigning different values simultaneously to the same variable? For these and similar reasons, there is no general consensus regarding which model of computation is the best. In this text we adopt a high-level approach in which we leave the exact nature of the input and output mechanism unspecified. Similar to serial (single-processor) computers, we simply assume that suitable parallel versions of read and write statements are available.

In fact, we always assume that the central processing unit has already placed input data into shared memory, so that little effort is needed to read or write statements. Also, in interconnection network models, we often assume that input data for algorithms have already been distributed to the local memory of the relevant processors without specifying the mechanism for accomplishing it. However, we make more use of read and write statements for interconnection network models, since it is important to specify how data are distributed to the processors' local memories. In addition, in interconnection network models, when a procedure is called or a function is invoked, we have to specify those processors that receive the input data and those that receive the provided output data. For example, if an algorithm for an interconnection network is supposed to sort a list of array elements, we have to specify precisely which processors receive the list on input, as well as a linear ordering of those processors that contain the sorted list on output. Each local processor manages parameters, local and global variables, in a manner similar to single-processor computers.

The PRAM computation model (Parallel Random Access Machine) consists of P autonomous processors, executing synchronously and all having access to a common shared memory. At each step, each processor performs one operation from its instruction stream. Instructions accessing shared memory are also assumed to be accomplished in one cycle. In a shared-memory parallel architecture such as PRAM, more than one processor can try to read from or write to the same memory location simultaneously, meaning the possibility of conflict arises. In general, there are four variants of the PRAM computational models for dealing with such conflict, depending upon how concurrent memory accesses are allowed. These are shown in Figure 2.34.

1. EREW (*Exclusive Read, Exclusive Write*) model of computation: A memory location cannot be simultaneously accessed by more than one processor, meaning no concurrent reads or writes are allowed.

2. CREW (*Concurrent Read, Exclusive Write*) model of computation: Several processors may simultaneously read the value of a memory location, but exclusive access is required for write.

3. ERCW (*Exclusive Read, Concurrent Write*) model of computation: Simultaneous write operations are allowed, but not simultaneous read operations.

4. CRCW (*Concurrent Read, Concurrent Write*) model of computation: Processors may simultaneously access the same memory location to perform read or write operations.

Parallel algorithms for EREW are assumed to be in error if a read or write conflict ever arises and are the most realistic computational model in practice. Parallel algorithms for CRCW allow multiple processing elements to read from and write to the same memory location concurrently.

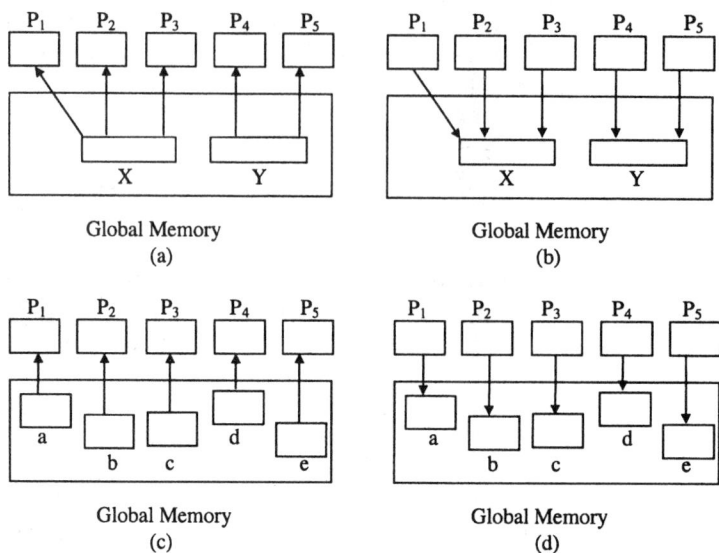

Figure 2.34. Computational models for accessing the memory locations regarding read and write operations. (a) Concurrent read. (b) Concurrent write. (c) Exclusive read. (d) Exclusive write.

Summary

The focus in this chapter was on the use of parallelism to speed up a computer. The chapter focused on processor parallelism. We briefly addressed the issues that are involved in the design of parallel computers: register sets, address space, scheduling, synchronization, network topology, partitioning, reliability, and performance. Having dealt with the question of how a user interacts with parallel systems, we considered how the various elements of a parallel system, such as memory and processing elements, are connected together. Memory system technology has changed quickly, and large main memories are becoming commonplace. We briefly discussed the memory system as a hierarchy of memory levels to emphasize the cost and speed of the associated memory levels in the design of parallel computers. We discussed different types of memory organization: random access memory, associative memory, parallel random access machines memory, multiport memory, and multiprocessor memory. A memory unit in which any particular word can be accessed independently is known as a random access memory (RAM). Two types of RAM are recognized: static and dynamic.

Associative memory or content addressable memory (CAM) consists of memory locations and an associated logic known as the data gathering logic. The memory system with the associative memory organization locates data by searching its memory cells for a specific bit pattern. Each memory cell has four inputs and two outputs which are used for particular operations such as read or write.

The PRAM is a parallel execution of the RAM model of serial computation and consists of a common memory of type RAM shared by the processors. A PRAM allows operations to be performed simultaneously on a large data set. PRAM models provide four categories indicating whether multiple processors are or are not allowed to access the same memory location simultaneously. The categories are: EREW (exclusive read, exclusive write), CREW (concurrent read, exclusive write), CRCW (concurrent read, concurrent write), and ERCW (exclusive read, concurrent write). Access memory primitives were briefly discussed to address access to the memory location regarding reading and writing. Multiport memory parallel systems allow simultaneous access to data stored in the memory. Thus while one port is reading from a memory cell, the other would write to another location. We discussed three categories of the multiprocessor memory system, known as the uniform memory access model, the non-uniform memory access model, and the cache-only memory model. The cache-only memory systems are the most efficient type of memory organization, of which the Swedish Institute of Computer Science's Data Diffusion Machine and Kendall Square Research's KSR-1 machine are two examples. Then we continued our discussion by describing and classifying various interconnection networks, their control characteristics, and their topologies. The chapter has discussed several processor organizations for different parallel computer architectures. Processor organizations include the linear and ring, shuffle exchange, mesh, hypercube, star, De Bruijin, tree, delta, butterfly, omega, and pyramid networks. We have compared these organizations according to several criteria: architecture, number of processors, topology, number of nodes and degrees. These criteria can be used to determine both the suitability of the processor organization for supporting the parallel algorithms, and the practicality of the organization from a production point of view. There are clearly a number of points which should be noted concerning communication in parallel computers. The most important one is that systems should be coherent and should map properly in all respects to the desired area of application. For a detailed discussion about interconnection networks, interested readers can refer to [Almasi 94, Shiva 96, Zomaya 96, Foster 94].

Goodness measures for the interconnection networks was the next topic in this chapter. We discussed three measures: diameter of the network, degree of the processor, and bisection width of the network. Generally speaking, one network topology is more desirable than another one if it is more efficient, more convenient, and more extendable than the others. A table compared the topologies with regard to the number of nodes in the network and the degree of each processor in the system.

There are three approaches in compiler construction of parallel systems: run time partitioning and run time scheduling, compile time partitioning and run time scheduling, and compile time partitioning and compile time scheduling. An example is the Paraphrase compiler developed at the University of Illinois, which performs a two phase operation to transform a Fortran program from its original sequential form into a suitable form for parallel execution. In the first phase, it performs a machine-independent transformation to produce an intermediate form, in which it expresses the parallelism form of the program. The second phase performs a mapping to change the intermediate form into a specific parallel system for execution. The compiler was used on vector processor machines such as the Cray X/MP. Bulldog is another example of a compiler that detects parallelism at the instruction level. The central idea was to use the VLIW architecture design along with the trace scheduling compilation technique. Another example of parallel compiler construction refers to HPF (high performance fortran), proceeds as follows. Data decomposition statements are analyzed to determine the decomposition of each structure in the program. Computation is then partitioned across processors in the parallel architecture.

We classified the operating systems for parallel computers into three different categories: simple modification of the single-processor operating systems such as VMS OS and UNIX OS, operating systems designed for specific parallel computers, such as Hydra OS and Medusa OS, and adopted general-purpose operating systems for parallel computers, such as MACH OS. Generally speaking, the area of parallel architecture operating system design has been directed toward achieving the properties known: resource sharing, extensibility, portability, and availability. Four different organizations were suggested to achieve these criteria in the operating system: master/slave, separate executive, symmetrical, and floating control organizations. We detailed the design principles of MACH OS, developed at Carnegie-Mellon University, Amoeba OS, designed at the Vrije University in Amsterdam, and Accent OS, developed at Carnegie-Mellon University.

We discussed the input and output constraints imposed in any parallel system regarding reading data from external input devices into processor local memory and writing data from its memory to external output devices. We classified four variants of the PRAM computational model for dealing with the potential conflict, depending upon how concurrent memory accesses are allowed. The computational models are: EREW, CREW, ERCW, and CRCW.

Many aspects of distributed systems design including interconnection networks are discussed in [Coulouris 96, Sloman 97, Umar 93]. Much attention has been given to designing distributed operating systems. A representative set of references includes [Boykin 93, Tanenbaum 92, Chow 97,Goscinski 91]. Aho [Aho 86] provides a good reference for compiler design.

Exercises

1. Define the following terms:

Linear	PRAM
Ring	EREW
Shuffle exchange	CREW
Mesh	ERCW
Hypercube	CRCW
Star	De Brujin
Tree	Delta
Butterfly	Omega
Pyramid	Compiler

2. What are the advantages of a dynamic network?

3. Typical interconnection networks delay the signals passing through them by a time that is proportional to the number of stages. What are the delays (number of stages) of the interconnection topologies described in this chapter?

4. How many steps can be required for routing a signal datum on a 64×64 processor array? How many for a 4096-node hypercube? As usual, state your assumption carefully.

5. For a centrally controlled $n \times n$ crossbar, give an algorithm for setting the switches. Assume there are n processors and n banks of memory, and the n processors request different banks of memory. You may assume n is a power of 2.

6. What types of conflicts must a compiler detect for SIMD parallelism, MIMD parallelism and vectorization?

7. In what ways is the PRAM model of computation unrealistic? Is a PRAM an MIMD or an SIMD model? Is PRAM a synchronous or asynchronous computation model?

8. Consider an 8×8 crossbar that interconnects eight processing elements. Show the active crosspoints needed in this crossbar if the following interconnections are needed:

   (a) A ring
   (b) Two-dimensional nearest-neighbor
   (c) Three-dimensional hypercube
   (d) Shuffle exchange

9. List the desired characteristics of a compiler that performs parallelization of the sequential codes for an SIMD system.

10. List the detailed characteristics of an operating system needed for static and dynamic dataflow machines.

11. Describe different techniques a compiler can use to optimize code for a parallel system.

12. A memory system has two access speeds, A and B. A holds for 20% of the accesses, while B holds for the remaining 80%. What is the average access speed?

13. What types of conflicts must a compiler detect for SIMD and MIMD parallelism?

14. Show that the processing element addresses of a 4-cube can be arranged in a 4×4 array whose adjacent elements differ by exactly one bit position. Also show that the right and left addresses on each row differ by exactly one bit position, and the same for the top and bottom addresses in each column.

15. Explain the difference between the SRAM and DRAM memories.

16. Summarize the similarities and differences between the RAM model of serial computation and the PRAM model of parallel computation.

17. Given a shuffle-exchange network, prove that if a shuffle link connects nodes i and j, then j is a single bit left cyclic rotation of i.

18. Consider mapping a 4×8 mesh into a 32-node hypercube. Two bit positions are reserved for the row and three bit positions for the column. Let us assume that the first two bit positions are used for the row. The 2-bit code {00,01,11,10} corresponds to a traversal through rows 0, 1, 2 and 3. The 3-bit code {000,001,011,010,110,111,101,100} corresponds to a traversal through columns 0, 1, 2, 3, 4, 5, 6 and 7. What is the mapping of this 4×8 mesh into a 32-node hypercube system?

19. A hypercube multiprocessor consists of two processors numbered with binary integers using a string of n bits. Each processor is connected to every other processor whose binary number differs from its own by exactly one bit. This connection scheme places the processors at the vertices of an n-dimensional cube. Devise a hypercube interconnection network for n varying from 1 to 4.

20. Assume eight processors are available. Construct a Butterfly interconnection network such that pairs of processes synchronize at each stage in the following manner:

First Stage	$P_0 \Leftrightarrow P_1$,	$P_2 \Leftrightarrow P_3$,	$P_4 \Leftrightarrow P_5$,	$P_6 \Leftrightarrow P_7$.
Second Stage	$P_0 \Leftrightarrow P_2$,	$P_1 \Leftrightarrow P_3$,	$P_4 \Leftrightarrow P_6$,	$P_5 \Leftrightarrow P_7$.
Third Stage	$P_0 \Leftrightarrow P_4$,	$P_1 \Leftrightarrow P_5$,	$P_2 \Leftrightarrow P_6$,	$P_3 \Leftrightarrow P_7$.

21. A three-dimensional binary cube network is shown in Figure 2.35. Assume the vertex address is defined as $C_2C_1C_0$. A routing pattern can be defined by exchanging the data between adjacent vertices which differ in the least significant bit C_0, as shown in Figure 2.35 (a). Specify two other routing patterns:

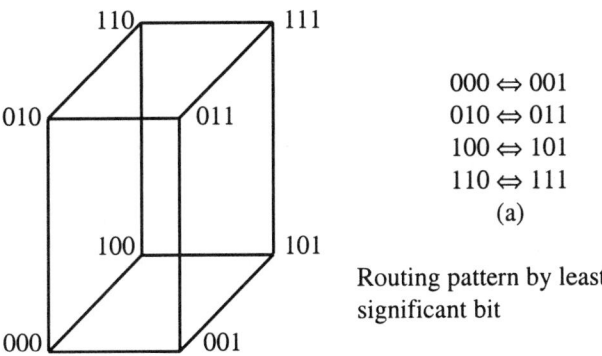

$000 \Leftrightarrow 001$
$010 \Leftrightarrow 011$
$100 \Leftrightarrow 101$
$110 \Leftrightarrow 111$
(a)

Routing pattern by least significant bit

Figure 2.35. A 3-cube network with nodes denoted as $C_2C_1C_0$ in binary.

22. The perfect shuffle interconnection network can be represented with 2^m processors. Show the interconnection network for $m = 3$ and $m = 4$.

Reference-Needed Exercises

23. Using the goodness measures studies, evaluate a number of computers against the criteria given in Section 2.3.

24. Three types of networks are described: WANs, LANs and interconnection networks. WANs are characterized by large and unpredetermined transmission times and multiple routing possibilities. Usually LANs are conceptually a single cable linking a number of nodes. Interconnection networks are those described here for interconnecting the components of a multiprocessor computer system. Listed below are some alternatives that are used for communication protocols on networks. Which one is appropriate for each type of interconnection network discussed in Chapter 2?

   • Circuit switching or packet switching
   • Packets of a fixed size, or variable in size
   • Message header defines sender and destination
   • Messages are acknowledged by receiver

25. Associative memory is still expensive. Discuss ways to use a large conventional memory to back up the contents of an associative memory in order to make a large associative processor practical.

CHAPTER 3
Principles of Parallel Programming

We assume that our readers are computer literate, meaning that they can write programs in a high-level programming language and that they have at least a basic understanding of what a computer does in the execution of a program.

The term **process** can be used to describe a sequence of program instructions that can be performed in sequence or in parallel with other program instructions. Therefore, a program can be viewed as a number of processes which are executed sequentially or concurrently. The point at which a processor is interrupted from one process and given to another process is dependent on the progress of the processes and the algorithm used to determine the available processor. This means that the user is allowed to execute the program using more than one process at a time.

In a sequential programming environment, each time a program is submitted for execution with the same data, identical results will be obtained. Each executing program makes up a process inside the system which is invisible to the user, and each instruction is executed without interference from the other instructions of the program.

In a multiprogramming environment the processing unit is switched from one program to another, causing their instructions to be interleaved at stages in their execution. Also, in a multiprogramming multiprocessor environment, more than one program can be active at the same time, meaning that each program proceeds autonomously with its execution process. In such systems the programs will interact and affect each other's progress.

The net effect is that processes are capable of interacting in a time-dependent manner. As a result of this time-dependent interaction, the series of states the system passes through is not identical when the same program and data are presented in different execution.

Thus, in a parallel programming environment, a programmer provides not only program and data, as in a sequential programming environment, but also the tools to control the synchronization and interaction among the processes. In this case, the user needs to create and schedule processes for execution; thus program execution needs to be visible to the programmer.

Two approaches have been used in providing programming facilities for parallel processors:

1. Development of languages that can express the parallelism inherent in the algorithm [Doeppner 87, Geist 94, Foster 92].

2. Development of compilers that recognize the portions of sequential code and parallelise them [Benerjee 93, Kuck 84, Fox 91].

These two approaches complement each other, and using only one of them may not result in the most efficient parallelized code. In general, concurrency may be implicit or it may be expressed by using explicit parallel constructs. For example, the following array assignment statement (in Fortran 90) is an explicitly parallel construct:

$$A = B * C$$

It specifies that each element of array A is to be assigned to the product of the corresponding elements of arrays B and C. The statement also implies *conformity*, meaning that the three arrays have the same size and shape. In contrast, the following do-loop is implicitly parallel, and a compiler may be able to detect that the various do-loop iterations are independent, meaning that one iteration does not write a variable read or written by another. Hence the iterations can be performed in parallel. Thus, a parallel program is a sequence of explicitly and/or implicitly parallel statements.

```
do I = 1,m
    do J = 1,n
        A(I,J) = B(I,J) * C(I,J)
    enddo
enddo
```

As a consequence, parallel programming is not a simple extension of the sequential programming. In order to exploit the possibilities offered by parallelism, programmers need to look at the problem from a different point of view and reconsider the solution process. A programming language that contains explicit mechanisms for parallel processing must have a construct for creating new processes. Some of the distinct parallel programming approaches are:

- Shared-memory SIMD parallel programming, in which memory access is synchronous.
- Shared-memory MIMD parallel programming, in which memory access is asynchronous.
- Distributed-memory MIMD parallel programming, in which memory access is asynchronous.
- Shared-memory SPMD parallel programming, in which memory access is asynchronous.
- Distributed-memory SPMD parallel programming, in which memory access is asynchronous.
- Shared-memory MPMD parallel programming, in which memory access is asynchronous.

- Distributed-memory MPMD parallel programming, in which memory access is asynchronous.

In shared-memory SIMD parallel programming, all processing elements operate in a lock-step fashion, meaning that the processors are synchronized at the instruction level. This indicates that in SIMD systems the interprocessing element communication is directly controlled by hardware in a lock-step fashion and at the instruction level. As a result, there is no need to associate mutual exclusion or synchronization problems with this parallel programming paradigm.

MIMD parallel programming can be classified into two categories: *centralized asynchronous MIMD parallel programming* and *distributed asynchronous MIMD parallel programming*. In centralized asynchronous parallel programming, also known as shared-memory MIMD parallel programming, the control process must select for initiation fragments whose execution is enabled. In this paradigm, each processor executes a serial program independently. This indicates that processors execute different instructions asynchronously. As a result, we need to include mutual exclusion and synchronization problems in this parallel programming scheme. Some of the instructions in these programs may be for load, store, or read-modify-write operations that access a shared memory location. We call the code executed by each processor a sequential program segment, and the union of all these segments is the parallel code executed by the machine as a whole.

In distributed asynchronous parallel programming, also known as distributed-memory MIMD parallel programming, the exchange of information and control data is performed through isolated or controlled direct communication paths which are a dynamic memory structure (message-passing scheme). Control is decentralized with each statement determining independently its degree of readiness to initiate computations.

We can split the current process into two or more processes that continue to execute copies of the same subprogram (or a segment of code) simultaneously. In general, the basic subprogram is the same for all processes. This method of parallel programming resembles the SIMD programming model and is called SPMD (Single Program Multiple Data) programming. In contrast to SIMD, the synchronization is performed at the subprogram level rather than at the instruction level. In practice, there is a need for process synchronization in the programming scheme. Compilation typically translates the statements into an SPMD program in which each processor executes the same code on a subset of the data structure. SPMD parallel programming can be used in both shared-memory and distributed-memory MIMD systems.

In an MPMD programming scheme, a segment of code is explicitly associated with each new process. Thus, different processes have different code. This method is called MPMD (Multiple Program Multiple Data) programming. In a typical example of this method, a process creates several child processes, each with its own code.

A corollary follows that asynchronous parallel programming schemes are most flexible in the sense of describing or defining *maximum parallelism*, meaning that they model sequentially parallel programs fairly easily. All this stems from the fact that fragment parallelism and independence are emphasized. The technique is conceptually simple and corresponds to the parallelism in the problem and the asynchronous organization of the computer system. Various modifications of asynchronous programming involve the organization of the data exchange between program fragments and the nature of control. The facilities provided by a programming language to control process execution and interaction in the source program are known as the *language support* for parallel programming. In this chapter, the general requirements of parallel programming with regard to data and control parallelism, shared memory versus private memory, mapping and granularity are discussed. Many aspects of parallel programming design are discussed in [Best 96, Hanse 95, Burns 93, Hatcher 91].

3.1   Programming Languages for Parallel Processing

Programming languages are like operating systems, meaning that they need to provide programmers with mechanisms for process creation, synchronization and communication. However, a programming language has stricter requirements than an operating system, which means that its facilities must be machine independent and must adhere to language design principles such as readability, writability, maintainability, and portability. In general, most programming languages have provided a particular model of parallel organization in providing parallel facilities. Thus they are extensions of languages used for a single-processor machine. Some languages use the shared-memory model and provide facilities for mutual exclusion, whereas others assume the distributed model and provide communication facilities. A few languages have included both models, because different models are preferable in particular situations. In general, the current parallel programming languages lack essential constructs for parallel processors such as synchronization, communication protocols, granularity, network control, masking and others.

In a parallel programming environment, the actions of the program which can conceptually proceed in parallel must be identified. Such actions are usually referred to as processes, or more recently as tasks. Each individual process can be specified by using the features that are recognized for parallel programming. In addition, the language features are necessary to regulate the situations in which the processes are required to interact. The need to control such interaction is raised when information has to be exchanged or the progress of one process depends on the progress of another. The situations in which processes interact with each other can be divided into two possibilities:

1.   When processes wish to update a shared variable or a resource at the same time. At any one time, only one process can access the resource.

Once the process has obtained access to the resource, it must be able to use the resource without interference from another process.

2. When processes are cooperating to perform operations with regard to their activities. This needs scheduling among processes to represent each other's existence and purpose.

Two methods have been introduced to solve these problems. In the first one, all the processes use a common structure to update information and to communicate with each other. In the second one, all the processes use a common approach called wait and pass, in which one waits for a signal from each other and then passes information directly. Generally speaking, there are two approaches to developing parallel programs:

- To extend existing languages or define new notations to include specific constructs to express the parallelism and deal with the potential access conflicts.
- To define a language which does not include specific parallel constructs, but rather omits the implicit sequencing constructs of existing notations.

3.2   Precedence Graph of a Process

The study of the precedence relations of computations is essential for parallel processing. Dependencies can be studied at several levels of computation, such as block computation level, statement level, variable level and even bit level. Thus, the precedence relation of computations needs to be satisfied in order to process a computation correctly. In the following, we concentrate on dependencies between statements and variables.

Example 3.1: Consider the execution of a simple sequence of statements:

$$S_1: A = B + C$$
$$S_2: B = A + E$$
$$S_3: A = A + B$$

A careful analysis of this example indicates several dependencies, and one must become aware of the dependencies among the statements. Parallel execution of these three statements is an alternative to sequential execution. The Data Dependency Graph (DDG) of this example is presented in Figure 3.1.

The possible scenario of this execution can be illustrated as follows:

1. Statement S_1 produces the variable A used in statement S_2 and S_3. This results in dependencies d_1 and d_2.
2. Statement S_2 produces the variable B used in statement S_3. This results in dependency d_3.
3. The previous value of variable B was used in statement S_1. This results in dependency d_4.

4. Both statements S_1 and S_3 produce the same variable A. This results in dependency d_5.
5. Statement S_3 produces variable A, which was previously used in statements S_2 and S_3. This can be viewed as dependencies d_6 and d_7.

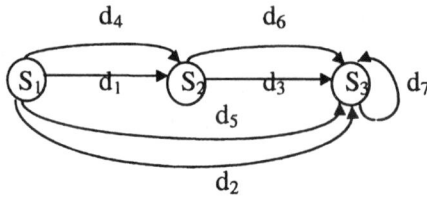

Figure 3.1. Data dependency graph for Example 3.1.

All these dependencies must be taken into consideration when parallelism is involved. Five different types of dependencies can be identified when parallelism is analyzed.

Data flow dependency: The most fundamental form of dependency is data flow dependency, in which one statement cannot be executed until after another, because the second statement requires a value computed by the first statement. This means that these statements cannot be executed in parallel. In the previous example, d_1, d_2 and d_3 represent the data flow dependencies of the statements.

Data anti-dependency: A related form of dependency is data anti-dependency, in which a statement cannot be executed before another statement because doing so would delete a value which is required by the earlier statement. In other words, data anti-dependency occurs when the value of a variable produced in one statement has been used previously in another statement or in the same statement. This dependency prevents parallelism, because it is possible to overwrite some variables before they are used. Dependencies d_4, d_6, and d_7 represent data anti-dependencies of the statements in Example 3.1. Renaming allows this form of dependency to be removed. The two dependencies discussed above are related to the use of values. Two more dependencies can be defined which are related to the production and use of values: data input dependency and data output dependency.

Data output dependency: Data output dependency occurs when two statements produce the same values. Clearly, if statements are executed simultaneously, they overwrite the same variable of memory location. Dependency d_5 addresses the data output dependency between S_1 and S_3 in Example 3.1. In other words, these statements must be executed in the correct order to prevent the wrong value being used.

Data input dependency: Data input dependency occurs when two statements both use the same value. Once again, renaming can remove this form of dependency. It is worth noting that in a sense, data input dependency is not a true dependency, since the statements can be executed in any order, but it does illustrate a relationship between the statements.

Data control dependency: Data control dependency occurs when the execution of a statement depends on a value produced by another statement.

Now, the data dependency graph can be defined as a directed graph G = (V,E) with vertices V corresponding to statements in the program and edges E representing data dependencies among statements. Clearly, parallel execution of the statements can be achieved with the elimination of the anti-dependencies and output dependencies among the statements. For example, it is typical for programmers to use a scalar variable repeatedly, as shown in the following fragment:

```
for    i = 1, n, 1
    x = A[i] + B[i]
    Y[i] = 2 * x
    x = C[i] * D[i]
    P = x + 15
endfor
```

where x is an ordinary variable. If the second instance of x is renamed xx as shown below, the code segment becomes data independent, thus allowing a better parallelization.

```
for    i = 1, n, 1
    x = A[i] + B[i]
    Y[i] = 2 * x
    xx =C[i] * D[i]
    P = xx + 15
endfor
```

Example 3.2: Consider the following pseudocode and basic forms of dependency between statements:

```
S₁  A = B + C
S₂  B = A * 3
S₃  A = 2 * C
S₄  P = B ≥ 0
    if       (P is TRUE)
S₅  then   D = 1
S₆  else   D = 2
    endif
```

Figure 3.2 presents the dependencies between statements using the basic forms of dependencies. To allow for parallel processing, it is necessary to remove some of these dependencies. For example, simple renaming can remove output and anti-dependencies, as illustrated in Figure 3.3.

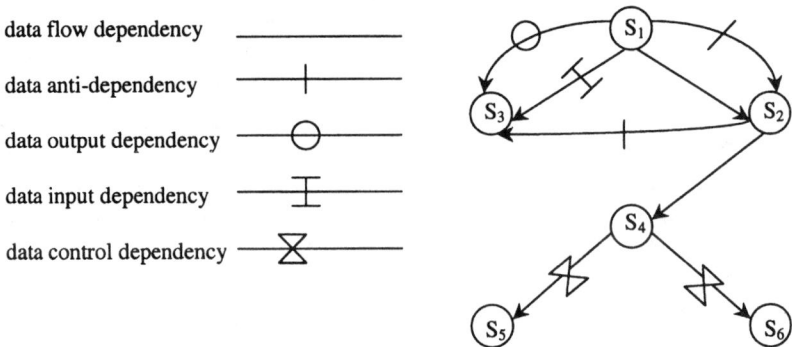

data flow dependency

data anti-dependency

data output dependency

data input dependency

data control dependency

Figure 3.2. Dependency graph and basic forms of dependencies for Example 3.2.

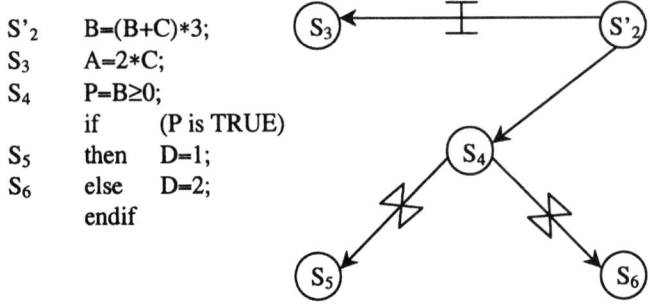

S'_2 B=(B+C)*3;
S_3 A=2*C;
S_4 P=B≥0;
        if   (P is TRUE)
S_5 then   D=1;
S_6 else   D=2;
        endif

Figure 3.3. Removing output and anti-dependencies for Example 3.2.

A more complicated problem is removing the cyclic dependencies associated with the loops in a program. For example, if the scalar is expanded into a vector as shown below, the statements are independent, thus allowing a better parallelization

```
for   i = 1, n, 1          for   i = 1, n, 1
      x = A[i] + B[i]             X[i] = A[i] + B[i]
      Y[i] = 2 * x               Y[i] = 2 * X[i]
endfor                     endfor
```

Example 3.3: Consider the following pseudocode consisting of a loop:

```
Loop  I = 1, 20
        S₁:    A(I) = X(I) + 3
```

```
S₂:    B(I + 1) = A(I) * C(I + 1)
S₃:    C(I + 4) = B(I) + A(I + 1)
S₄:    D(I + 2) = D(I) + D(I + 1)
S₅:    C(I + 3) = X(I)
Endloop
```

The dependency graph of this program is shown in Figure 3.4. There are dependencies between statements within the same iteration. Programs with nested loops involve as many indices as loops, and there are dependencies between iterations. Table 3.1 indicates the dependencies between the statements and iterations of this example.

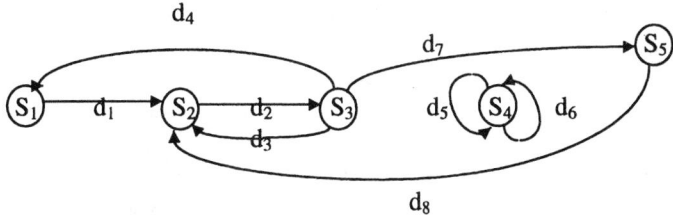

Figure 3.4. Dependency graph for Example 3.3.

Table 3.1. Dependencies between statements and different iterations.

Variable	Statement	Dependence	Description
A	S_1, S_2	d_1	flow dependency
B	S_2, S_3	d_2	flow dependency
C	S_3, S_2	d_3	flow dependency
A	S_3, S_1	d_4	data anti-dependency
D	S_4, S_4	d_5	flow dependency
D	S_4, S_4	d_6	flow dependency
C	S_3, S_5	d_7	output dependency
C	S_5, S_2	d_8	flow dependency

3.3   Data Parallelism Versus Control Parallelism

Parallelism can be achieved in many forms:

- Concurrent processing of input and output operations using independent processors.

- Concurrent memory accesses using multiported storage systems and interleaved memory.
- Concurrent execution of instructions using pipelined functional units.
- Concurrent decoding of instructions using pipelined control unit.
- Concurrent execution of instructions using multiple functional units.
- Concurrent transmission of data between devices using multiple buses.

Data parallelism can be achieved by assigning data elements to multiple processors, each of which performs the identical operation simultaneously on its data. A k-fold increase in the number of processing elements may lead to a k-fold increase in the throughput of the results, if there is limited overhead associated with this increase of parallelism. An example of data parallelism is matrix multiplication. When multiplying, two n×n matrices A and B produce matrix C, for which each element $C_{i,j}$ can be computed by performing a dot product of the i_{th} row of A with the j_{th} column of B. This indicates that each element $C_{i,j}$ is computed by performing the identical operation on a different data item, meaning data parallelism.

The programming languages supporting data parallelism are called data parallel programming languages, and the programs are called data-parallel programs. Thus, a data-parallel program consists of single sequences of instructions, or instruction streams, each of which is applied to the different data elements. Data parallel programs can be executed on both SIMD and MIMD computers but are naturally suited to SIMD computers, in which a global control unit broadcasts the instructions to the processing elements which contain the data item and execute the instructions synchronously. The following example illustrates the difference between sequential data processing and data parallelism and provides a demonstration of the speedup factor.

Assume that a specific computation consists of the execution of three instructions, S_1, S_2 and S_3, and that each instruction requires one unit of execution time, meaning it takes three units of execution time to perform the required computation. A single processing element spends one unit of execution time performing the S_1 instruction followed by one unit of execution time performing S_2 and one unit of execution time performing S_3. Clearly, a single processing element performs this computation in three units of time, two computations in six units of time and so on, as illustrated in Figure 3.5 (a). Of course, we are assuming that the computations are uniform with regard to the execution of the instructions, meaning that each computation consists of three instructions to be executed.

Now, assume a three parallel processing element system such that each processing element performs every instruction as does the single processing element system. Throughput can be increased by replicating processing elements. Another three computations appear every three time units. Figure 3.5 (b) shows a three data-parallel processor system.

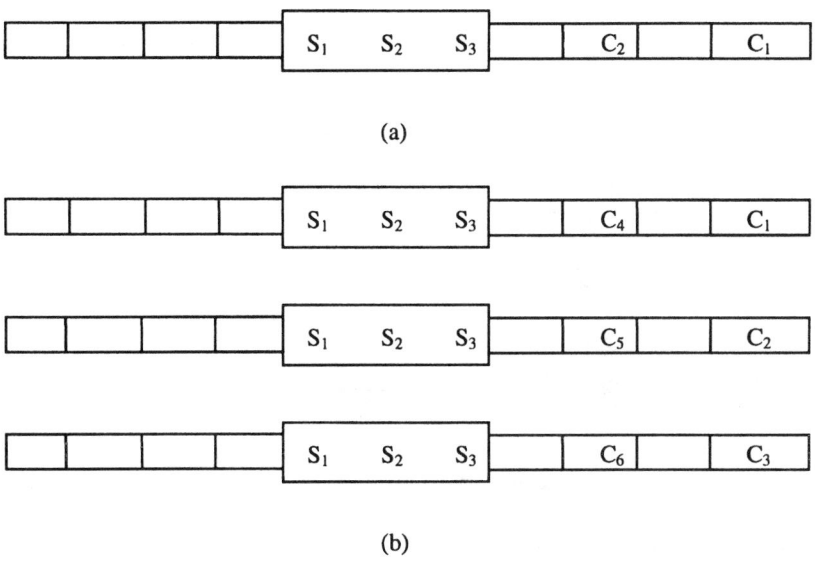

(a)

(b)

Figure 3.5. Two models for performing a computation. (a) A single processing element system performs each computation in three units of execution time. (b) A three parallel processor system performs three computations in three units of execution time.

Figure 3.6 shows the speedup factor achieved by the data-parallel system. The x axis represents the number of computations and the y axis represents the speedup factor achieved. The speedup factor may be computed by dividing the time needed for the single processing element to perform p computations by the time needed for the data-parallel system, of course with regard to the same result.

In contrast to data parallelism, in which parallelism can be achieved by performing a single operation on a data set, control parallelism is achieved by performing different operations on different data elements simultaneously. In other words, control parallelism refers to simultaneous execution of different instruction streams. An example of control parallelism is pipelining. If the data flow graph forms a simple directed path, then we say the problem is pipelined. In pipelining, the operation can be parallelized by executing a different program at each processor and sending intermediate results to the next processor, meaning the result is a pipeline of data flowing between processing elements. Problems suitable for control parallelism usually map into MIMD architectures, because control parallelism require multiple instruction streams. The amount of control parallelism in a problem is usually independent of the size of the problem. In contrast, the amount of data parallelism in a problem depends on the size of the problem. Thus, in order to achieve good efficiency with a large number of processors, it is necessary to explore the data parallelism of a problem.

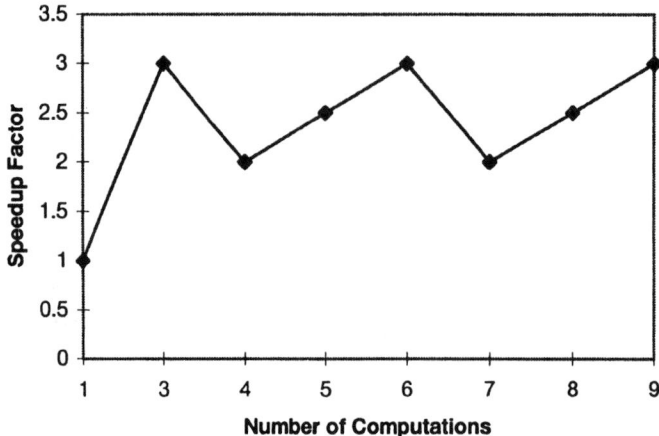

Figure 3.6. Speedup factor achieved by three data-parallel processor system compared with a single-processor system.

3.4   Message Passing Versus Shared Address Space

Two distinct possibilities exist regarding the way processors communicate with each other:

1. Message passing communication: processors communicate via communication links.
2. Shared memory communication: processors communicate via common memory.

Single message passing can be supported by two message communication primitives: Send and receive operations, defined in terms of destination and messages. In order for one process to communicate with another, one process sends a message (a sequence of data items) to a destination and another process at the destination receives the message. This activity involves the communication of data from the sending process to the receiving and may involve the synchronization of the two processes. Send and receive primitives that can be made to wait are said to be blocking and those that never wait are said to be nonblocking.

Message-passing systems are separated into two different categories, synchronous and asynchronous. In a synchronous message-passing system, the send and receive primitives are executed simultaneously and are defined as blocking send and blocking receive operations. Thus, the sender and receiver are synchronized when information is exchanged. If the send operation is executed before the corresponding receive operation, the sending process waits until the receiving process executes the receive operation and vice versa. When information is exchanged, the processes continue their asynchronous execution.

In an asynchronous message-passing system, the message are buffered and the sending process proceeds without delay. The system is defined as a nonblocking send and a blocking receive operation. Later, when the receive operation is executed, the message is delivered. In general, in a synchronous system, the sender knows that the message has been received but does not know if it has been processed, whereas in an asynchronous system, the sender does not know if the receiver has received the message. A simplified diagram of a message-passing system is represented in Figure 3.7, in which several computers and an interconnection network are connected together. Each computer system has a processing element, a memory, and an input/output interface. In a message-passing system, communication of shared data can be carried out through messages exchanged directly between processing elements, and each message consists of a number of fixed-size packets. The processes may be executing on different processors that do not share a common memory or they may be on the same processor but executing in different address spaces. In message-passing systems, the memory is distributed among the processing elements such that each processing element has its own program and its own data memory. This model of operation affects the architecture design as well as the type of problems suitable for message-passing multiprocessors.

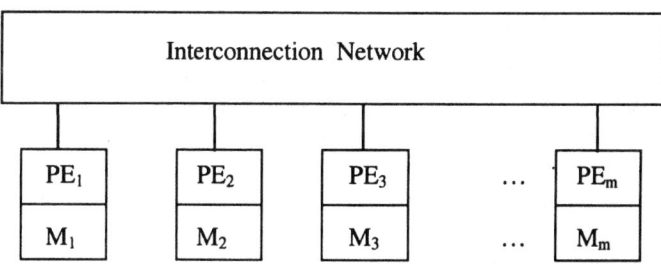

Figure 3.7. A message-passing architecture.

A communication protocol has to be established for interprocess communication. The performance of message-passing systems is more difficult to determine, because the performance depends directly on the communication patterns specified in the implementation of the algorithms.

An important problem in implementing shared memory is how to achieve good performance that is retained as support large numbers of computers. Accesses to shared memory involve potential underlying network communication. Processes competing for the same or neighboring data items may cause large amounts of communication to occur. The amount of communication is strongly related to the consistency model of a shared memory, which is the model that determines which written values may be returned when a process reads from a memory location. In shared-memory communication, there is a complete connectivity between processing elements and memory modules. A simplified diagram of a shared-memory system is shown in Figure 3.8. It consists of a set of M processing elements, a set of N memory modules and an interconnection network.

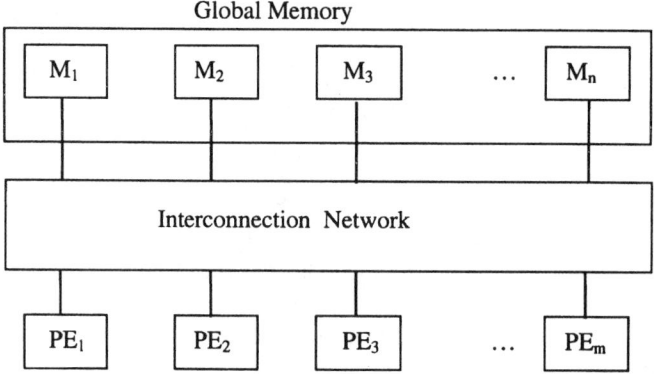

Figure 3.8. A shared-memory architecture.

The interconnection network is a potential of data exchange between processing elements and memories. In shared-memory systems, each processing element operates on its own instruction stream, which can be accessed either from the local memory or from the shared memory. The shared memory is composed of independent modules, each one connected to a port of the interconnection network. This results in the operation of processors more or less independently of each other. In a shared-memory system, a single common operating system can control and coordinate the interaction between processing elements and running processes. Processors are provided with an interprocess communication mechanism such that an individual processor can directly interrupt other processors. Synchronization between processors is needed and has to be provided by the operating system primitives. Based on the need of many processors to simultaneously access the same memory locations, memory access conflict has become an important factor in the performance of shared-memory systems. This can create an upper limit to the number of processors in the system.

To decrease the communication traffic in the network, several alternative solutions are presented, including:

- Reducing the number of memory requests through the interconnection network. This can be achieved by placing a local memory (LM) directly accessed by the processor.
- A cache memory can be provided in order to increase the memory bandwidth.

A possible scheme for these alternatives is shown in Figure 3.9. In general, shared-memory systems are efficient for small to medium size multiprocessors. The Cedar multiprocessor, the Ultracomputer, the Alliant, the Encore Sequent, and the Cray Y-MP are some examples of shared-memory systems.

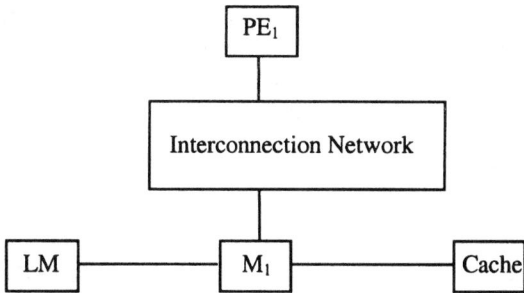

Figure 3.9. An alternative scheme to reduce the interconnection network traffic.

3.5   Mapping

There are a number of approaches to the mapping of parallel algorithms to parallel architectures. The work by Li et al. [Li 85] provides examples of language-based approaches to the problem of relating algorithms to architectures. One of the powerful approaches that has been applied to a variety of architectures is mapping based on graph transformations [Bokhari 81], [Berman 84], [Chiang 83]. The strength of this method is that it employs the formalisms of graphs to address specific aspects of the mapping problem, such as process-to-processor assignment, minimizing the communication, and breaking large problems into small tasks allocated to the processors. Therefore, in addition to a program and data, a programmer also determines a particular implementation, called mapping. Mapping is not necessary for programs executing on single-processor architecture because the execution can be performed in a sequential manner. In general, the mapping of a program specifies the sequence in which each processor executes the instructions assigned to it. Related to the mapping problem is the transformation of the computational problem from one form to another form more suitable for the parallel architecture. This transformation consists of the following steps:

- A description of how the operations of each instruction can be executed by the processors,
- An allocation of each variable of the program to a memory, and
- A specification of the single flow of control, common to all processors.

Mapping is involved in two different communication schemes: synchronous and asynchronous. In the synchronous form of communication, the sending and receiving processes synchronize at every message transformation. In this case, both the send and receive operations are blocking primitives whenever a send is issued. The sending process is blocked until the corresponding receive is issued. Whenever a receive is issued, the process blocks until a message arrives. In the asynchronous form of communication, the use of the send operation is nonblocking such that the sending process is allowed to proceed as soon as the message has been copied to a local buffer, and the transmission of the message proceeds in parallel with the sending process.

In asynchronous communication, the receive operation can have blocking and nonblocking variants. In the nonblocking variant, the receiving process proceeds with its program after issuing a receive operation which provides a buffer to be filled in the background, but it must separately receive notification that its buffer has been filled, by polling of the interrupt. Nonblocking communication appears to be more efficient, but it involves extra complexity in the receiving process associated with the need to acquire the incoming message out of its flow of control. A simple blocking receive could wait forever for the arrival of a message, but for many purposes a time out is required. A time out specifies an interval of time after which the operation will give up its action. Choosing an appropriate time out interval is difficult, but it should be fairly large in comparison to the time required to transmit a message. Table 3.2 shows the variations of synchronous and asynchronous communication with examples of languages and operating systems that are associated with them. In practice, the synchronous architectures focus on the computation each processor may perform, and in asynchronous architectures the focus is on the synchronization between processors in addition to the computational purpose.

Table 3.2. Synchronous and asynchronous communication with examples of languages and operating systems.

Communication Type	Blocking Send	Blocking Receive	Languages and Operating System
Synchronous	Yes	Yes	OCCAM
Asynchronous	No	Yes	Mach, Chorus, UNIX
Asynchronous	No	No	Charlotte

In the following sections, mapping to three different environments -- synchronous, asynchronous and distributed systems -- is examined.

3.5.1   Mapping to Asynchronous Architecture

An asynchronous shared-memory computer consists of a fixed set of processors and a fixed set of memories. Associated with each memory is the set of processors that can read from it and the set of processors that can write to it. Mapping a program to an asynchronous shared-memory computer has the following steps:

1.   Allocate each statement in the program to a processor.
2.   Allocate each variable to a memory.
3.   Specify the control flow for each processor.

In asynchronous communication the exchange of a message is an atomatic action requiring the participation of both the sending process (the sender) and the receiving process (the receiver). If the sender is ready to send but the receiver is not ready to receive, the sender is blocked, and similarly, if the receiver is the first process ready to communicate, it is blocked. In other words, the act of communication synchronizes the execution sequence of the two processes.

Alternatively, the sender is allowed to send a message and continue without blocking. The communication is called asynchronous because there is no time connection between the execution sequences of the two processes. The receiver could be executing any instructions when a message is sent and then, at a later time, check the communications channel for messages. The important difference between the two schemes is the need for buffering messages. In asynchronous communication the sender may send many messages without the receiver removing them from the channel. Thus, the channel must be prepared to buffer a potentially unlimited number of messages. If the number of messages in the channel is limited, eventually the sender will be blocked. The problem with an asynchronous system is that we have to specify the buffering system at the time the distributed primitives are being designed rather than leaving it as the responsibility of the programmer.

3.5.2   Mapping to Synchronous Architecture

A parallel synchronous architecture has the same processor memory structure as an asynchronous shared-memory architecture. In addition, processors in a synchronous architecture have a common clock for synchronization purposes. At each step (at each clock tick) each processor executes an instruction. In synchronous communication, only one message exists at any one time on the channel, thus no buffering is needed. More than one processor may write to the same memory cell at the same step, which means that all of them write the same value. An arbitrary number of processors may read a memory cell at the same step. Concurrent reading and writing of the same memory location is not permitted. For example, a program with multiple assignments, such as x = x + 1; y = x + 2, can be executed concurrently by two processors in the following scenario:

1. Both processors read the value of x.
2. One processor computes x + 1 while the other computes x + 2.
3. One processor assigns x + 1 to x while the other assigns x + 2 to y.

3.5.3   Mapping to Distributed Architecture

A distributed system consists of a fixed set of processors, a fixed set of channels and a local memory for each processor. A local memory of a processor is a memory that only that processor can access for reading or writing. The channels are error free and deliver messages in the order in which they arrive. For each channel, there is exactly one processor that sends messages along that channel and exactly one processor that receives messages along that channel. Associated with each channel is a buffer. For each channel, the only action that can be taken by the sending processor is to send a message if the buffer is not full, and the only action that can be taken by the receiving processor is to receive a message if the buffer is not empty. Mapping a program to a distributed system is the same as in the asynchronous shared-memory architecture, except that each variable is allocated either to a processor or to a channel. In addition to the constraints involved in shared-memory architecture, the mapping has to satisfy the following constraints:

1. At most one variable is allocated to each channel, and this variable represents the sequence of messages in transit along it.
2. A variable allocated to a channel is called by statements of exactly two processors, and these statements are of the following format and cannot be accessed in any other way. The instructions in one of the processors modifies the variable by appending an item of data to the rear of the sequence, if the size of the sequence does not exceed a constant which is the buffer size. The instructions in the other processor modify the variable by deleting the item at the head of the sequence, if the sequence is not null.

3.6   Granularity

The granularity of a parallel algorithm and its implementation relates to the ratio of the amount of computation to the amount of communication. We use the terms fine, medium and coarse granularity to describe the computation-to-communication ratio in a parallel algorithm. If a large amount of computation is performed for each communication, then coarse granularity has been achieved, and if only a small amount of computation is performed for each communication, then the algorithm is fine grained.

SIMD computers are built for efficient communication, and fine-grained solutions can perform well on these machines. MIMD computers involve more overhead for moving information from one processing element to another. For example, in a shared-memory system, the time for interprocess synchronization of memory access is the overhead, whereas in a message-passing system, the overhead refers to the sending and receiving of messages among the processing elements. Consequently, medium granularity is a good result on an MIMD machine.

Finally, a group of workstations communicating in a local area network have slow communications among processors, because the local area network bandwidth is more restricted. Thus, a network of workstations used for parallel processing is appropriate for coarse-grained problems, meaning there is a great deal of computation for each communication. When a problem involves regular structure, it is possible to change the granularity to increase the speedup factor of computation or to reduce the communication overhead factor. The idea is to use the locality, so related computations of the problem are grouped together and executed. To illustrate the concept of the granularity problem, let us consider the matrix multiplication A * B = C, where the matrix B is partitioned in columns to produce the columns of matrix C as follows:

Here the basic unit of computation is involved in the calculation of a single column of the result matrix C. To achieve this computation, all rows of the A matrix must be communicated to the location of a B matrix column. To change the granularity of this matrix computation, one may determine some number m of columns to be passed together to a single processing element to compute the m columns of the result matrix C, as represented in Figure 3.10. As we see, the communication -- transferring the rows of the A matrix -- has remained constant. However, the computation factor is m times greater, since m columns of the result matrix may now be computed.

The granularity of an algorithm for a problem is one important criterion for determining what kind of parallel architecture is appropriate for that computational problem. The granularity, the number of processing elements, the size of the physical memory, and the type of interconnection network differ from one implementation to another. Several factors may affect the granularity of a solution for a given problem. For instance, if a solution requires communication with a central process for each small piece of computation, then the solution is fine grained.

However, if the computation requires communication only at the end of each step, depending on how data are assigned to each process, this approach can range from fine to coarse grained. From the computational point of view, in some computational problems, individual statements can each become a separate process. Another possibility is for procedures to be assigned to processes. Another alternative is for processes to represent whole programs. The different size of the code assignable to individual processes is referred to as the module granularity of the processes. There are three choices of module granularity for parallel execution:

1. Statement level parallelism: fine grained
2. Procedure level parallelism: medium grained
3. Program level parallelism: large grained

Granularity is an issue in computational efficiency, depending on the kind of machine. In general, module granularity refers to the number of computations contained in a typical module. The module may be a program, a procedure or an instruction, depending on the level at which the parallelism is expressed. This is the topics of the following sections.

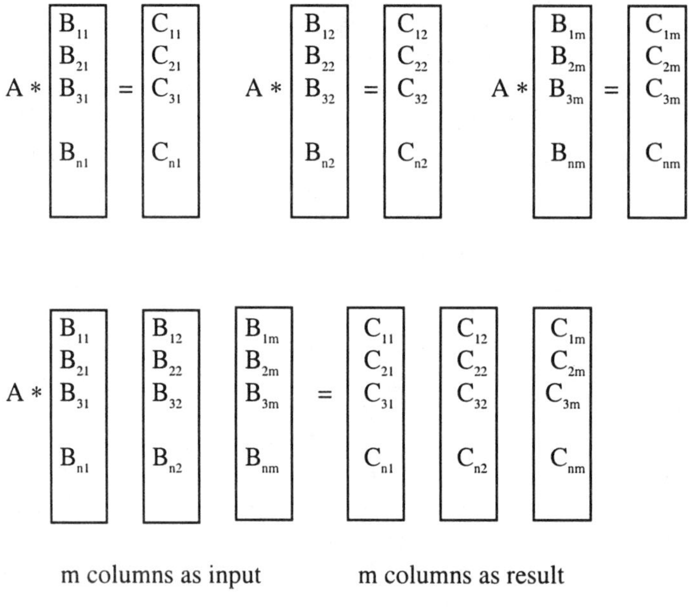

$$A * \begin{bmatrix} B_{11} \\ B_{21} \\ B_{31} \\ \\ B_{n1} \end{bmatrix} = \begin{bmatrix} C_{11} \\ C_{21} \\ C_{31} \\ \\ C_{n1} \end{bmatrix} \quad A * \begin{bmatrix} B_{12} \\ B_{22} \\ B_{32} \\ \\ B_{n2} \end{bmatrix} = \begin{bmatrix} C_{12} \\ C_{22} \\ C_{32} \\ \\ C_{n2} \end{bmatrix} \quad A * \begin{bmatrix} B_{1m} \\ B_{2m} \\ B_{3m} \\ \\ B_{nm} \end{bmatrix} = \begin{bmatrix} C_{1m} \\ C_{2m} \\ C_{3m} \\ \\ C_{nm} \end{bmatrix}$$

$$A * \begin{bmatrix} B_{11} \\ B_{21} \\ B_{31} \\ \\ B_{n1} \end{bmatrix} \begin{bmatrix} B_{12} \\ B_{22} \\ B_{32} \\ \\ B_{n2} \end{bmatrix} \begin{bmatrix} B_{1m} \\ B_{2m} \\ B_{3m} \\ \\ B_{nm} \end{bmatrix} = \begin{bmatrix} C_{11} \\ C_{21} \\ C_{31} \\ \\ C_{n1} \end{bmatrix} \begin{bmatrix} C_{12} \\ C_{22} \\ C_{32} \\ \\ C_{n2} \end{bmatrix} \begin{bmatrix} C_{1m} \\ C_{2m} \\ C_{3m} \\ \\ C_{nm} \end{bmatrix}$$

m columns as input   m columns as result

Figure 3.10. Increased granularity of matrix multiplication problem.

3.6.1   Program Level Parallelism

In this method of process creation, the whole program can become a process. This indicates that a program creates a new process by creating a complete copy of itself. The typical example of this method of process creation is the Fork primitive in the UNIX operating system, which simply replicates the process executing the Fork. It has the following form:

```
Proc-id = Fork()
```

where the Proc-id is the identification number of the newly created process. Execution of this statement causes the current process, called the parent, to be replicated. The only distinction between the parent and the newly created process, called the child, is the variable Proc-id. In the parent it has the process number of the child as its value, whereas in the child its value is zero. This permits each of the two processors to determine its identity and to proceed accordingly. Typically, the next statement following Fork is of the form

```
if Proc-id = 0
then do
    {child processing}
else do
    {parent processing}
```

Clearly, such primitives are incorporated directly in a programming language suitable for parallel processing. After a call to Fork, a process can be terminated by a call to Exit. Process synchronization can be achieved by calls to Wait, which causes a parent to suspend its execution until a child terminates.

3.6.2   Procedure Level Parallelism

In this form of process creation, a procedure is associated with a process and the process executes the code of that procedure. This process creation mechanism has the form:

```
Proc-id = new process (Q)
kill process (Q)
```

where Q is a declared procedure and Proc-id is the process designator. One example of such a language is Mesa [Lampson 80], which permits the procedure Q to be invoked as a separate process. The statement used to spawn a new process has the following form:

```
P ← Fork Q(...)
```

where the Fork statement creates a new process that begins executing the procedure Q concurrently with the parent process. In Mesa, each process is treated as an object and may be assigned to a variable. In the preceding statement, the variable P represents the child process. It is worth noting that the variable P contains not only a process identifier, but also the process object itself. This permits a process to be treated as any other variable; for instance, it may be passed to another procedure as a new parameter.

3.6.3   Statement Level Parallelism

A typical construct to indicate that a number of statements can be executed in parallel is the Parbegin-Parend block::

```
Par-begin
    Statement₁
    Statement₂

    Statementₙ
Par-end
```

In this mechanism, the statements Statement₁,...Statementₙ are executed in parallel. It is assumed that the main process is suspended during their execution. Assume an expression $(a + b) * (c + d) - (e/f)$. The following code performs the parallel evaluation of the expression:

```
Par-begin
    Par-begin
        t₁ = a + b
        t₂ = c + d
    Par-end
    t₄ = t₁ * t₂
    t₃ = e/f
Par-end
t₅ = t₄ - t₃
```

The primitives **fork, join** and **quit** provide a more general means for describing parallel activity in the statement level of a program.

Fork Primitive

Execution of the following instruction by a process P causes a new process Q to be created and to start executing at the instruction labeled x.

```
Fork x
```

Thus, P and Q perform execution simultaneously from different locations in the program.

Quit Primitive

If a process P executes the instruction "Quit," then the process P terminates.

Join Primitive

The instruction "Join t, y" has the following effect:

```
t = t - 1
if t = 0 then go to y
```

A program segment for parallel evaluation of the expression is given below:

```
            n = 2
            m = 2
            Fork P₂
            Fork P₃
P₁:         t₁ = a + b;  Join m, P₄;  Quit;
P₂:         t₂ = c + d;  Join m, P₄;  Quit;
P₄:         t₄ = t₁*t₂;  Join n, P₅;  Quit;
P₃:         t₃ = e / f;  Join n, P₅;  Quit;
P₅:         t₅ = t₄ - t₃
```

This is certainly less transparent than the par-begin par-end method.

Summary

There are many papers, survey articles, and books in the general area of programming languages [Appleby 97, Carricro 92, Chandy 88, Chandy 92, Ghezzi 82]. In this chapter we have given a brief outline of the state of the art in the field of parallel programming. Parallel programming can be categorized as either data-parallel or control-parallel programming. Data parallelism is the use of multiple functional units to apply the same operation to different elements of data. Control parallelism is achieved through the simultaneous execution of different operations to different data elements. With the present generation of parallel computers, attention has focused on the problem of parallel programming, which can be separated into two categories:

- Asynchronous parallel programming, in which independent parts of a program are competed and cooperate with each other to improve the efficiency of the execution.
- Synchronous parallel programming, in which the same operation can be performed in parallel by forcing all processes to act in unison.

Further, we classified parallel programming into four categories: synchronous SIMD, asynchronous SIMD, synchronous SPMD, and asynchronous MPMD parallel programming. We briefly discussed the classifications and the supporting environments. In general, specialized programming schemes are needed to efficiently utilize the computational power offered by parallel computers. In order to make valid judgements about parallel computing, it is necessary to understand how particular problems will map onto specific implementations of parallelism.

We discussed the precedence graph of a process to address the dependencies at several levels of computation, such as block level, statement level, variable level and bit level. The data dependency graph illustrated five different dependencies among the individual computations: data flow dependency, data anti-dependency, data output dependency, data input dependency, and data control dependency. We discussed these dependencies along with examples and suggested how to remove the dependencies to utilize the efficiency associated with parallel execution of the constructs. Briefly we discussed the message-passing and shared address space communication paradigms to provide the necessary information for the next sections.

We also discussed different aspects of the problem of matching parallel algorithms to parallel architectures. The fundamental issue in parallel programming is how to distribute the data structures among the memories of the individual processors. For this reason, we discussed the mapping problem, the problem of changing a graph representing the interaction of data into a graph representing the topology of the underlying architecture. We outlined three mapping paradigms: mapping to asynchronous architecture, mapping to synchronous architecture, and mapping to distributed systems. Wijshoff [Wijshoff 89] has studied the effect of data distribution on the performance of parallel systems. We have observed that a parallel program depends on a number of parameters, including the programming notation, the computational model supported by the notation, and the level of parallelism. Further, the latter can be defined by means of three features: program level parallelism, called large grained, procedure level parallelism, called medium grained, and statement level parallelism, called fine grained.

Generally speaking, we characterized the computation and communication requirements for our parallel algorithms by considering mapping and granularity. One of the important problems facing parallel computing is the granularity, the problem of optimally partitioning applications into modules and then scheduling these modules onto parallel or distributed environments. Mapping and granularity decisions are particularly subject to modification, which indicates that we may postpone these decisions until they can be most easily changed. Although we did not concentrate on how algorithms are represented in programs, it is worth pointing out some trends in programming languages intended for large-grain parallelism. At the least, a reasonable language provides ordinary sequential operations and a way to send messages between processes. Interprocess communication can be abstracted as a form of message-passing paradigm. As a consequence, we can claim that the programming schemes of distributed-memory parallel computers is much different from that of shared-memory computers because distributed-memory computers have no global address space containing shared data. Processors interact by message-passing paradigms among themselves. A good source on design and principles of parallel computing can be found in [Fountain 94, Lipovski 87, Miklosko 84].

Exercises

1. Define the following terms:

   Data parallelism   Control parallelism
   Shared-memory parallelism   Message-passing parallelism
   Dependency analysis   Data flow graph
   Granularity   Fine-grained granularity
   Medium-grained granularity   Large-grained granularity
   Synchronous mapping   Asynchronous mapping
   Pipelining   Overlapped processing
   Multiprogramming   Multiprocessing

2. Match each of the terms on the left with its attributes on the right.

   Data dependency   a) Reassembling compiler for VLIW trace scheduling

   Anti-dependency   b) Reconstructing FORTRAN compiler

   Output dependency   c) Two statements produce the same variable

   Bulldog compiler   d) Variable assigned in one statement used in a preceding statement

   Paraphrase compiler   e) Variable assigned in one statement used in a succeeding statement

3. What is the advantage of using fine-grained granularity?

4. What is the advantage of using medium-grained granularity?

5. What is the advantage of using large-grained granularity?

6. Compare and contrast the programming environments for the shared-memory SIMD and shared-memory MIMD systems.

7. Compare and contrast the programming environments for the shared-memory MIMD and private-memory MIMD systems.

8. Show how to compute the conditional expression below using the data flow graph of computation.

   ```
   If X > Y then
       X - Y
   Else
       X + Y
   ```

9. Draw the data flow graph for the solution of $AX^2+BX+C=0$.

10. Devise an algorithm to increase the granularity of a matrix multiplication problem.

11. Two concurrent processes P1 and P2 each have their own local variables A and B, respectively. The values of these variables are to be exchanged using the following sequence of indivisible machine-level operations:
    Load A into register R1
    Load B into register R2
    Store value from register R1 in B
    Store value from register R2 in A.
    What is the effect of concurrent execution if P1 and P2 do not execute the exchange of the values under mutual exclusion conditions?

12. Differentiate between SIMD programming, SPMD programming, MIMD programming and MPMD programming.

13. The following segment is devised to calculate the roots of a quadratic equation. Write a program to extract the parallelism using fork and join primitives.

```
begin
input(A,B,C);
 A := 2 * A;
 C := B↑2 - 2 * A *C;
 C := sqrt(C);
 C := C/A;
 B := -B/A;
 A := B + C;
 B := B - C;
Output(A,B);
end
```

14. Consider the following program fragment. Rewrite the program in equivalent form with regard to dependency between the statements and draw the dependency graph.

```
if A > 1 then   goto  X;
endif
   if B > 0 then   D = 3 goto  X;
   else            goto  Y;
   endif
   X: E = 5
   Y: B = E + D
```

15. Consider the operation $P = (A \times B) + (C \times D)$ where P, A, B, C and D are memory operands. This can be performed by the following sequence:
$$R_1 \Leftarrow A$$
$$R_2 \Leftarrow (R_1) \times (B)$$
$$R_3 \Leftarrow (C)$$

$R_4 \Leftarrow (R_3) \times (D)$

$P \Leftarrow (R_4) + (R_2)$

Show the data flow graph for these operations.

16. Consider the following statements. Specify the dependencies between the statements and draw the dependency graph.

```
A = B + C
DO 5   I = 1,N,1
     D(I)  = A * E(I)
     S = E(I) * 5
     T = T + S
A = D(N) - 7
```

17. For the graph shown below, write the control flow using fork and join primitives. Can this be executed by statement level parallelism?

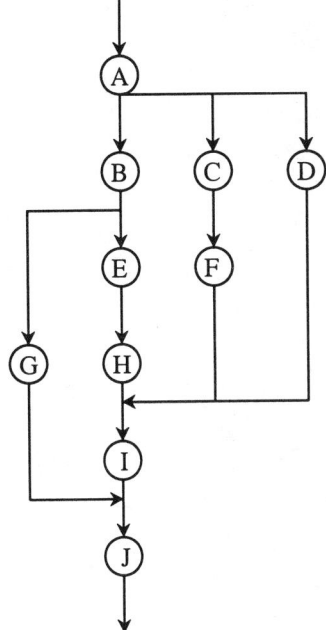

18. The following program indicates that 24 instructions are to be executed (8 division, 8 multiplication, and 8 addition):
    (a) Show the data flow graph of the program.
    (b) Assume that each add, multiply, and divide requires 1, 2, and 3 cycles to complete, respectively. Show the sequential execution of the 24 instructions on a control flow uniprocessor and determine the number of cycles to complete.

(c) Assume a 4-processor data flow computer. Show the data-driven execution of the 24 instructions and determine the number of cycles to complete.

```
Input D, E, F
For   I  from 1  to  8  do
   Begin
       A[I]=D[I]+E[I]
       B[I]=A[I]*F[I]
       C[I]=B[I]+C[I]-1
   End
Output   A, B, C
```

CHAPTER 4
Parallel Programming Approaches

Scientific and engineering computations focus on theories, methods and applications in such areas as large-scale simulations, time-critical computing, computer-aided design and engineering, computer-aided manufacturing, visualization of scientific data and human-machine interface technology. Parallelism offers one way to solve these computational problems quickly by creating and coordinating multiple execution processes. However, until recently parallelism has been extremely difficult to use because of the lack of suitable parallel programming approaches. In general, the acceptance of parallel computation has been facilitated by two major developments: massively parallel processors and the widespread use of distributed computing. A good parallel programming environment must fulfill a number of objectives:

1. It must augment the sequential programming language that is most appropriate for whatever the computational problem is.
2. It must support both process creation and interprocess communication as extensions of the high-level base programming language.
3. It must be able to be run on any parallel architecture or on any collection of networked computers.
4. It must be easy to use with regard to parallelism implementation, meaning that it must offer simple operations to create and coordinate parallel processes.

Common parallel programming paradigms can be divided into two categories:

- The master-slave model, in which a separate control process termed the master is responsible for process spawning, initialization, collection and display of results, and perhaps timing of functions. The slave processes perform the actual computation involved. Either they are allocated their workloads by the master (statically or dynamically) or perform the allocations themselves.
- The node-only model, in which multiple instances of a single program execute, with one process taking over the noncomputational responsibilities in addition to contributing to the computation itself.

In practice, the execution of a parallel program forms a set of concurrently executing processes, sometimes called threads, which communicate and synchronize by reading and writing shared variables. There must be a way to create parallel processes, and there must be a way to coordinate the activities of these processes. Sometimes the processes work on their own data and do not interact. But processes must communicate and synchronize with each other when they exchange results of the execution. In general, there are two methods of synchronization:

- Synchronization for precedence
- Synchronization for mutual exclusion

Synchronization for precedence guarantees that one event does not begin until another event has been finished. In contrast, the mutual exclusion synchronization guarantees that only one process can access the critical section where the data are shared and must be manipulated. It is often desirable that the number of processes be larger than the number of processors, meaning the parallel programming approach has to adopt flexible scheduling methods that overlap computation and communication, thus improving parallel efficiency. An examination of parallel programming approaches reveals that they represent virtually every possible answer to the fundamental design questions:

- Should the parallelism be implicit or explicit?
- Should the parallel programming approach be based on imperative, functional or logic programming languages?
- Should the processes execute synchronously or asynchronously?
- Should the level of parallelism be fixed at compile time or chosen at run time, or should they be dynamic?
- Should the programmer view memory as distributed or shared?

In general, in designing a parallel programming language one often faces a dilemma involving compatibility, expressiveness, ease of use, efficiency and portability. Parallel programming approaches are developed either by introducing new paradigms such as Linda and Occam or by extending existing sequential languages such as C and Fortran, in which the special language constructs and data array expressions must be supported for exploiting parallelism in programs. We can categorize the parallel programming languages into four classifications:

- **SIMD programming languages** should have a global address space, which obviates the need for explicit data routing between processing elements. SIMD programs can be recompiled for shared-memory MIMD systems. The most important characteristic of this paradigm is that the processors are synchronized at the instruction level, meaning that they execute programs in a lock-step fashion in which each processor has its own data stream. Hence, this paradigm is also called data-parallel programming.

- **SPMD programming languages** (single program multiple data) are a special class of SIMD programs which emphasize medium-grain parallelism and synchronization at the subprogram level rather than at the instruction level. In this sense, the programming paradigm applies to both synchronous SIMD and loosely coupled MIMD systems.
- **MIMD programming languages** are involved when each processor has its own program to execute. Message passing is the popular parallel programming language scheme. It consists of two categories: synchronous and asynchronous. The concept behind asynchronous message passing is simple: the sender initiates the message and then continues with its processing. The message is accepted by the underlying system, and some time later it will be delivered to its destination. A process waiting for a message will be delayed until the message arrives. Synchronous message passing requires both the sender and the receiver of a message to be delayed until its correspondent is ready. Once the message has been exchanged, both processes can continue.
- **MPMD programming languages** can be described as a multiple program multiple data paradigm. This programming model is a popular subset of MIMD. Of course, some of the program to be executed could be copies of the same program, and typically only two source programs are written, one for a designated master processor and one for the remaining processors, which are called slave processors.

The parallel programming approaches we discuss are useful on many kinds of parallel architectures, and each can be expressed in several different parallel programming languages (for example, C and Fortran). Each parallel programming approach involves a different view of the role of the processes and the distribution of data in a parallel program.

Execution is deterministic, unless specialized primitives are invoked to make nondeterministic choices. The basic conceptual approaches and programming languages we have mentioned are not provably the only ones possible. But empirically they cover all examples we have encountered in the research literature and in our own programming experience. Our goal here is to explain the conceptual classes and programming methods, and the mapping among them. In the following sections we describe six parallel programming approaches developed for the SISD, SIMD and MIMD systems under the supervision of the UNIX operating system. The parallel programming paradigms can be viewed as synchronous MIMD parallel programming approaches, in which they use the shared variables for synchronization purposes.

4.1   Parallel Programming with UNIX

Most of the vendors of parallel architectures provide their machines with versions of the UNIX operating system extended with libraries for parallel programming environment [Robbins 96]. Therefore, the UNIX operating system allows users to access process management through system calls. These facilities allow a user to create, schedule and control processes in a parallel processing environment. In this section, the parallel programming approach provided on the Encore Multimax System utilizing the UNIX operating system is discussed. A parallel program written in C that uses the parallel library must include the **parallel.h** header file, which contains the functions provided in the parallel library. The programs must be complied with the command:

```
cc program.c -lpp
```

where the option **-lpp** informs the loader that the parallel library is used.

Process Creation

A process can be created by the **fork()** system call. It differs from its parent only in the value returned by the call. Consequently, when more processes are created, the values returned by the **fork()** system call at each process creation are guaranteed to be different for each call, but there are no formal relations between these values. This indicates that these values cannot be used for scheduling purposes or other disciplines established by the programmer. Assume that **ppid** is an integer variable initialized in the parent process to 0. The following C code, called **Makeprocess()** function, takes as its argument a number n of processes to be created. It creates n processes and returns in each process created an integer $i \leq n$ that can be used as the programmer process identification number, or **ppid**.

```
Makeprocess(n)
   int n;
   {
   int i;
   for (i = 0; i<n; i++)
      {
      switch (fork())
         {
         case 0: /* PROCESS CREATED */
            return(i + 1);
         case -1: /* PROCESS CANNOT BE CREATED */
            {
```

```
            printf("Cannot create process %d\n",i);
            return - 1;    }
      default: /* CREATE NEXT PROCESS */
      }
   }
   return 0;
   }
```

The rationale behind this function for process creation is that the variable **ppid** is defined as:

$$
ppid = \begin{cases}
0 \text{ in parent process} \\
1 \text{ in child 1 of the parent process} \\
.... \\
n \text{ in child n of the parent proces}
\end{cases}
$$

In the sequel, it will be convenient to create a number of processes in the program and schedule them according to specific computation needs. In this respect, consider the following scheme of a parallel program:

```
main   (argc, argv)
   int argc;
   char * argv[];
   {
   int ppid, procs;
   scanf(argv[1], "%d", &procs);
   ppid = makeprocs(procs);
/* All PROCESSES ARE CREATED HERE */
   switch    (ppid)
      {
      case 0:   {code to be executed by parent}
      case 1:   {code to be executed by child 1}
      case 2:   {code to be executed by child 2}
      ...
      case n:   {code to be executed by child n}
      default:
         {
         printf("Something is wrong");
         break;
         }
      }
/* All PROCESSES ARRIVE HERE FOR TERMINATION */
   if (ppid ! = 0)
```

```
            {
            printf("Child number %d terminates\n", ppid);
            exit (ppid);
            }
      }
```

Process Interaction

There is no mechanism in UNIX that allows user-created processes to interact by sharing resources. Thus, in order to perform parallel programming and user-process interaction, UNIX allows the user to define and declare shared data. The following rules are used to declare and define shared data and code in parallel programs:

- Shared data are defined using the type of constructors available in the programming language in use. For example, in C, shared data (called **Shared**) and a pointer to it (called **ToShared**) can be defined as the following:

```
struct   SharedData
          {
          int x, y, z;
          float a, b;
          } Shared, *ToShared;
```

where **Shared** is a variable of type struct SharedData and **ToShared** is a pointer variable that points to a variable of type struct SharedData.

- Data can be declared as shared by a call to a function that tells the C compiler to collect it into a shared segment and return a pointer to it. For example, to make a copy of the **Shared** variable of type structure to be shared, we need to use the **Share()** system call, which has the following syntax:

```
ToShared = Share(0, sizeof(Shared));
```

where **Toshared** is a pointer variable and **Shared** is a variable of type structure **SharedData**.

As a consequence of these rules, the parent process and all its children share a piece of shared data as declared above, and shared data must be declared prior to process creation.

Timing of Process Execution

By timing the process execution, programmers can observe the behavior of the sequential components of their parallel programs. Alternatively, programmers can achieve high efficiency by balancing computation loads. To allow process execution timing, a clock that can be accessed from the program by function calls is provided in a parallel library. This clock ticks continuously, and each tick records a microsecond. A call to the function timer-init() starts the clock and a call to the system function timer-get() returns a number that represents the time in microseconds elapsed from the call to timer-init(). Therefore, the difference between the numbers returned by two system calls represents the execution time spent by the process in performing the execution of that piece of code. The net effect of this issue is:

- Set the process clock by performing the timer-init() system call
- Issue the timer-get() system call to get the consumed execution time of a section of code by calculating the time difference between these calls.

An example of this process execution timing is illustrated in the following:

```
main    (argc, argv)
        int argc;
        char *argv[];
        {
        double ProcessTime;
        long timer;
        int ppid, procs;
        scanf(argv[1], "%d", &procs);
        ppid = Makeprocs(procs);
        switch (ppid)
            {
            case 0: /* {code to be executed by parent} */
                    {
                    timer - init();       /* Set the clock */
                    timer = timer - get();/* calculate the
                        execution time of parent */
                    ProcessTime =
                        (timer - get() - timer)/1000000.0;
                    break;
                    }
            case 1:   /* {code to be executed by child 1} */
                    {
                    timer - init(); /* Set the clock */
                    timer = timer - get();/* calculate the
                        execution time of child 1 */
                    ProcessTime =
                        (timer - get() - timer)/1000000.0;
                    break;
```

```
                              }
              ...
              case n:    /* {code to be executed by child n} */
                         {
                         timer - init(); /* Set the clock */
                         timer = timer - get();/* calculate the
                             execution time of child n */
                         ProcessTime =
                             (timer - get() - timer)/1000000.0;
                         break;
                         }
              default:
                         {
                         printf("Something is wrong");
                         break;
                         }
              }
/* All PROCESSES ARRIVE HERE FOR TERMINATION */
       if (ppid ! = 0)
          {
          printf("Child Process %d Computation Time is %lf
              \n", ppid, ProcessTime);
          exit (ppid);
          }
          else
          printf("Parent Process %d Computation Time is %lf
              \n", ppid, ProcessTime);
       }
```

The invocation of these function calls in the program guarantees that the clock is set and obtained in the code associated with the process and that each process uses its own copy of the variable ProcessTime, meaning that the time of one process does not interfere with the time of another process.

Scheduling created processes

The actions of the created processes need to be synchronized in the parallel programs. This mechanism of process synchronization in parallel programs is provided by an appropriate *lock data type* variable. This indicates that once an operation on a variable of type lock is started, it is guaranteed that it will be terminated without interference with the operations issued by other processes on the same variable.

There are two operations provided with each lock data type, *lockname_create* and *lockname_init* where

```
lockname∈{LOCK, BARRIER, SEMAPHORE, EVENT}.
```

In this respect, some of the *LOCK data types* provided in parallel programs are as follows:

- LOCK: It is a data type whose objects have two values denoted by PAR_LOCKED and PAR_UNLOCKED. It allows mutual exclusion implementation of processes that operate on shared variables.
- BARRIER: It is a data type whose objects are tuples of the form *(count, flag)*. The *count* object is of type BARRIER and indicates the number of processes that are expected to arrive at the barrier before it opens. The *flag* objects represent the choices of the process waiting at the barrier and are defined as follows:
- *flag* = SPIN_BLOCK locks the process in a busy waiting loop.
- *flag* = PROCESS_BLOCK, meaning locks the process in the process data structure.
- EVENT: It is a data type whose objects are tuples of the form *(event, flag)*. The *event* object is of type EVENT and indicates that the event is expected to occur before all processes waiting for it can proceed. The *flag* object can be treated as the BARRIER data type *flag*.
- SEMAPHORE: It is a data type whose objects are tuples of the form *(count, flag)*. The *count* object is of type SEMAPHORE and indicates how many processes can access the semaphore variable before it is locked. The *flag* object can be defined in the same way as the BARRIER data type.

The SEMAPHORE data type allows the semaphore variable *"count"* to be set to a given positive integer by semaphore_set. At least two automatic operations are associated with each lock data type, called *lockname_lock* and *lockname_unlock*, which allow processes to check the lock and perform an appropriate action.

Examples: In the following, some examples are presented to address declaration, initialization and synchronization of created processes using the LOCK data type.

- Declare variables of LOCK data type associated with a shared-memory area.
```
Tolock = spin_create(state);
Tobarr = barrier_create(count,flag);
Tosemaph = semaphore_create(flag);
Toevent = event_create(flag);
```

- Declare pointer variables of LOCK data type. The variables are not initialized, meaning they must be initialized before being used.

```
LOCK lock, *Tolock;
BARRIER barr, *Tobarr;
SEMAPHORE semaph, *Tosemaph;
EVENT event, *Toevent;
```

- The created objects must be initialized by calls to lockname_init function.

```
spin_init(&lock, PAR_UNLOCKED);
Tolock = &lock;
spin_init(Tolock, PAR_UNLOCKED);
/* Set Barrier for 5 processes to be created */
barrier_init(&barr,5,PROCESS_BLOCK);
Tobarr = &barr;
barrier_init(Tobarr, 5, PROCESS_BLOCK);
/* Set Semaphore for 2 processes to be created */
semaphore_init(&semaph, SPIN_BLOCK);
Tosemaph = &semaph;
semaphore_init(Tosemaph, SPIN_BLOCK);
semaphore_set(semaph, SPIN_BLOCK,2);
Tosemph = $semaph;
semaphore_set(Tosemaph, SPIN_BLOCK,2);
event_init(&event, PROCESS_BLOCK);
Toevent = &event;
event_init(Toevent, PROCESS_BLOCK);
```

Process synchronization is provided and depends on the lock data type used. In the following, the synchronization between processes is explained with regard to the BARRIER and SEMAPHORE data types.

- **BARRIER:** The synchronization can be explained as follows:

barrier(Tobarr);

If the number of processes waiting at the barrier Tobarr is less than Tobarr = count − 1, then the number of waiting processes is increased by 1. Otherwise, the barrier is available and all processes waiting can resume execution. The number of processes waiting at the barrier is set to zero.

- **SEMAPHORE:** The synchronization can be explained as follows:

semaphore_signal(Tosemaph);

If a process is waiting for the semaphore variable, then the process will be released and Tosemaph = count + 1, meaning that the semaphore variable is increased by 1.

semaphore_wait(Tosemaph);

Depending on the value of the Tosemaph variable, this call can be executed as follows: If Tosemaph > 0, then the shared resource is available and Tosemaph = count = count − 1. Otherwise, the process is suspended and has to wait for the semaphore variable Tosemaph = count to become positive, meaning the shared resource has to be available.

A Sample Parallel Program

The program accepts an integer as the number of processes and performs vector-matrix multiplication by reading a vector and a matrix from a file:

```
#include <parallel.h>
#include <stdio.h>
#define lines 10
#define cols 100
        struct     SharedData     {
                   int m, n, k, State;
                   double mat[lines][cols];
                   double v1[cols], v2[lines];
                   int count, jobs, procs;
                   LOCK lock;
                   };
        int upid = 0;
main    (argc, argv)
        int argc; char *argv[];
        {
        int i; long t1; double t2;
        FILE    *In, *Out;
        glob = share(0, sizeof(*glob));
        scanf(argv[1], "%d", &glob->procs);
        In = fopen(argv[2], "r");
        ReadMatrix(glob->mat, In);
        ReadVector(glob->v1, In);
        glob->count = 0;
        glob->jobs = glob->n;
        glob->State = PAR_UNLOCKED;
        spin_init(&glob->lock, glob->State);
```

```
timer_init();
t1 = timer_get();
upid = Makeprocs(glob->procs - 1);
i=GetNextProcess(glob->lock,glob->count,glob->jobs);
while  (i < glob->n)
        {
  glob->v2[i]=Scalar(i,glob->m,glob->mat,glob->v1);
   i=GetNextProcess(glob->lock,glob->count,glob->jobs);
        }
if      (upid != 0)
        exit (0);
t2 = (timer_get() - t1)/1000000.0;
printf("\n Execution Time: %lf\n", t2);
Out = fopen(argv[3], "w");
PrintVector(glob->n, glob->v2, Out);
fclose(Out);
}
```

The processes are scheduled by calling the following function:

```
GetNextProcess(lock, count, jobs)
      int *count, jobs;
      LOCK *lock;
      {
      int which;
      spin_lock(lock);
          which = *count;
          *count = *count + 1;
      spin_unlock(lock);
      if (which > jobs)
          which = - 1;
      return which;
      }
```

The following functions are used to read a two-dimensional matrix from a file and to print a vector to a file:

```
ReadVector(v, data)
   double v[];   FILE *data;
   {
   int i;
   fscanf(data, "%d", &glob -> k);
   for (i = 0;   i < glob->k; i++)
       scanf(data, "%lf", &v[i]);
   }
```

```
ReadMatrix(a, data)
    double a[][cols];    FILE *data;
    {
    int i, j, k;
    fscanf(data, "%d", &glob -> n);
    fscanf(data, "%d", &glob -> m);
    for    (j = 0; j < glob -> n; j++)
            for    (i = 0; i <glob -> m; i++)
                    fscanf(data, "%lf", &a[j][i]);
    }
PrintVector(m, v, data)
    int m; double v[];    FILE *data;
    {
    int i;
    for (i = 0;    i < m; i++)
        fprintf(data, "%lf\n",v[i]);
    }
```

Finally, the function scalar is defined as the following:

```
double    Scalar(i, length, a, v)
            int i, length;    double a[][cols], v[];
            {
            int j, k; double s = 0;
            for (j = 0; j < length; j++)
                s = s + a[i][j]*v[j];
            return s;
            }
```

4.2   Parallel Programming with PCN

Program Composition Notation (PCN) [Foster 91, 92], developed by Argonne National Laboratory, the California Institute of Technology and the Aerospace Corporation, is both a parallel programming approach and a parallel programming system. It is based on program composition, and the focus of attention is the technique used to compose the components. PCN can be used to express concurrent algorithms and to compose programs written in sequential programming languages. Like any programming language, it has a distinct syntax that must be considered in order to write parallel programs. PCN is in the public domain. The latest version of both the software and the manual can be obtained by anonymous ftp from Argonne National Laboratory in the directory pub/pcn at info.mcs.anl.gov. Figure 4.1 illustrates a combining form used to compose three programs.

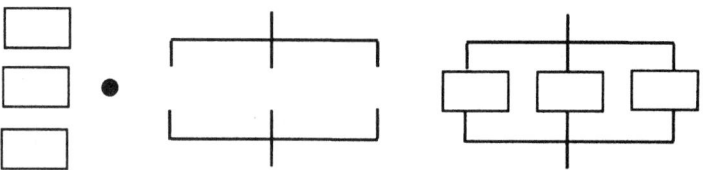

Figure 4.1. Combining form used to compose three programs.

Parallel programs can be developed by composing existing modules written in programming languages such as Fortran and C. An interface to the C preprocessor allows macros, conditional compilation features, and file inclusion constructs to be used in PCN programs. In other words, the PCN compiler applies the C language preprocessor (cpp) to each component before compiling it. Command line arguments can be passed to PCN programs as they would be to a C program, as the arguments of the main function. This indicates that PCN programs can make use of cpp's capabilities, including files, macros, and conditional compilation.

PCN simplifies development, debugging and optimization by exposing the basic structure of parallel programs. PCN provides extensive use of recursion and supports both numeric and symbolic computing as well as an interface to sequential languages such as Fortran and C. The syntax of PCN is similar to that of the C programming language. The facilities provided by PCN are machine independent and may be performed on a wide variety of uniprocessors, multiprocessors, and multicomputers. A set of standard libraries provides access to UNIX facilities and input and output capabilities. The compiler translates a PCN program to a machine-independent PCN object code. The PCN linker creates an executable program by combining PCN object code, other codes that are called by PCN, libraries and the PCN run time system. The PCN system structure consists of three components, as shown in Figure 4.2. The core PCN programming notation is a high level-language that provides three basic composition primitives:

1. Parallel composition primitive
2. Sequential composition primitive
3. Choice composition primitive

The PCN toolkit consists of a compiler, a linker, a language interface, standard libraries, process mapping tools, a programmable transformation system, a symbolic debugger, an execution profiler and a trace analyzer. They are supported by a run time system that provides basic machine-dependent facilities.

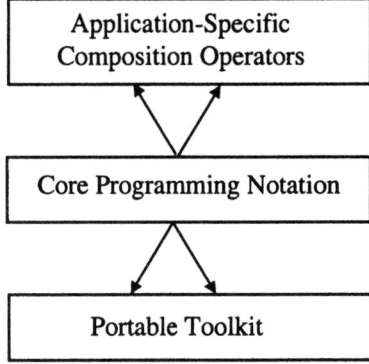

Figure 4.2. The PCN system structure.

A Simple Program

A PCN program consists of one or more modules, each is contained in a separate file with a .pcn extension. For example, assume a single module contained in a file as **myprogram.pcn** with the following code:

```
module myprogram.pcn
      main(argc, argv, exit - code)
      {;
      stdio:printf("HELLO WORLD.\n", {}, d),
      exit - code = 0
      }
```

Every program must have an entry point, which is the procedure that is initially called when the program is executed. By default, the following PCN procedure is called when a PCN program is executed:

```
      main(argc, argv, exit - code)
```

where
- argc is the argument count, meaning the number of parameters in the calling command
- argv is a list of arguments, meaning an array of strings

- Exit-code is undefined, meaning it can be set to an integer number, exit status, before terminating. As with C programs, exit-code = 0 means successful execution and exit-code ≠ 0 means failure to execute.

In other words, the default entry point to a PCN program is the main() function in the main module. The procedure calls the printf function in the stdio library to display "HELLO WORLD." in which is distributed with the PCN system. The PCN compiler, **pcncomp**, is used to compile a PCN module, and a separate file with a .pam extension as PCN object code may be produced. To compile myprogram.pcn, we issue the command

```
pcncomp  -c myprogram.pcn
```

where the result is myprogram.pam as the object code of this compilation process. The PCN object code, .pam files, is analogous to the .o files that are produced by C compiler. However, PCN object codes are completely machine independent, meaning the PCN object code that is compiled for one machine will execute on any other machine without recompilation.

After the compilation, the linking has to be performed to produce an executable version of the program under consideration. The PCN linker will be called by pcncomp when the -c option is not coded in the pcncomp command. For instance, in the following command, an executable program produced by the linker will be named myprogram utilizing PCN object code, or myprogram.pam:

```
pcncomp  myprogram.pam  -o myprogram
```

To execute a PCN program, we can just call the executable file produced by the linker. For instance, to run myprogram.pcn, you would type the following commands at the UNIX shell prompt:

```
%pcncomp -c myprogram.pcn
%pcncomp myprogram.pam  -o myprogram
%myprogram
HELLO WORLD.
%
```

Composition

The PCN provides three composition primitives which provide three fundamental methods of putting program components together.

Sequential composition

The sequential composition primitive is used to specify that a set of statements should be executed sequentially, meaning in the order that they are written in the program. In conventional programming languages, for instance C, this is the normal mode of the execution.

A sequential composition has the following syntax:

$$\{ ;\ block_1, block_2, ..., block_n \}$$

where ";" is the sequential composition primitive and $block_1, ..., block_n$ are other components.

Example of sequential composition

Assume it is required to swap the value of the array elements as the following program illustrates:

```
Swapelement()
int a[2],  i,  j;
{;
a[0]  := 0,    a[1]  := 1,
i := 0,        j := 1,
stdio:printf("Before swapping the array elements:%d
    %d\n", {a[0],a[1]},_),
swap(a,i,j),
stdio:printf("After swapping the array elements:%d
    %d\n", {a[0],a[1]},_)
}

Swap(array,i,j)
int array[],  i,  j,  temp;
{;
temp := array[j],
array[j] := array[i],
array[i] := temp
}
```

The procedure Swapelement is used to call the Swap function in order to exchange the values stored at the i_{th} and j_{th} positions of an integer array. In the Swap function the assignment statements are placed in a sequential composition, utilizing the sequential composition primitive, to ensure that they are executed in the correct sequence. The procedure Swapelement calls the function stdio:printf to display the contents of the array elements before and after modification. Note also that in Swapelement the sequential composition primitive ensures that the swap and display array elements occur in the correct order.

Parallel Composition

The parallel composition primitive, which specifies that a set of statements is to be executed concurrently, has the following syntax:

$$\{|| \quad \text{block}_1, \text{block}_2, ..., \text{block}_n\}$$

where $||$ is the parallel composition operator and $\text{block}_1, \text{block}_2, ..., \text{block}_n$ is a group of statements. Execution of a parallel composition terminates when all of its related blocks are executed. A mechanism is provided for communication and synchronization between processes and program components, called definitional variables.

Definitional variables are declared in the same way as other ordinary variables, except that an underscore character "_" is used to represent an anonymous value, meaning that a definitional variable is initially undefined and can be assigned at most a single value, which subsequently cannot be changed. A process that requires the value of a definitional variable is suspended until the variable is defined. The definition statement of a definitional variable is represented as

```
variable = expression
```

where variable is a definitional variable and expression is used to specify a defined value of that variable. Definitional variables can be used to communicate values and to synchronize operations. For example, if two concurrent processes share a variable to perform a specific operation, then a value provided by one process for the variable is communicated to the other process, and the execution of each process is suspended until the value of the variable is provided to the other process, meaning the execution is permitted.

Example of parallel composition

The following program illustrates concurrent execution of a parallel composition containing four procedures. The procedures execute concurrently, with the execution order constrained by the availability of definitional variables. Variable Product is the input and Consume is the output. Procedure Producer needs Product and is blocked until an input value is available. Similarly, the Consumer procedures are blocked until Product_1 and Product_2 are defined by Producer. The Combine procedure can proceed to generate the output, which is Consume, where Consume_1 and Consume_2 are defined by the execution of the Consumer process.

```
Producer-and-Consumer(Product,Consume)
  {||
  Producer(Product,Product_1,Product_2),
  Consumer(Product_1,Consume_1),
  Consumer(Product_2,Consume_2),
  Combine(Consume_1,Consume_2,Consume)
  }
```

Choice Composition

A choice composition provides a mechanism for choosing between alternatives with the following syntax:

```
{? guard₁->block₁,  guard₂->block₂,…,  guardₙ->blockₙ}
```

where "?" is the choice composition operator, $guard_i$ is a sequence of one or more tests and $block_i$ is a sequence of statements. A single guard->block is called an implication. In general, the choice composition may be regarded as a parallel if-then-else, switch, or guard command. Each guard specifies the conditions that must be satisfied for the associated block to be executed, meaning that at most one of these blocks will be executed.

Example of choice composition

The following module illustrates the choice composition such that if the value of x is greater than the value of y then z is assigned the value of x; otherwise, if the value of x is less than the value of y then z is assigned the value of y.

```
Module Greater.pcn
  greater  (x,y,z)
    {?
    X > y -> z = x,
    X < y -> z = y
    }
```

Tuples

PCN provides another sort of data structure called the tuple. Similar data structures are used in symbolic languages such as Prolog and Lisp. A tuple is a definitional data structure used to group together other definitional data structures in the general form:

```
{term₀, …, termₖ₋₁}
```

where $term_0$, ..., $term_{k-1}$ are definitional data structures and $k \geq 0$.
Example: the following are some valid tuples:

```
{a,b}, {"abc"}, {}, {12,{13,{}}}, {5.2,"ABC"}.
```

Tuples can be represented as trees. For example, a tuple such as {a,b} can be represented as a tree with a root and two children as follows:

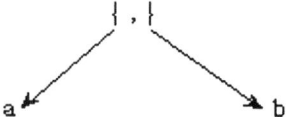

Figure 4.3. Representation of a tuple as {a,b}.

In general, a tuple such as {$term_0$, ..., $term_{k-1}$} can be represented as a tree with a root and k children.

Building tuples

The primitive operation make-tuple can be used to build a tuple of specified size with each argument a definitional variable. For example,

```
Make-tuple(3, tup)
```

defines tup as a three-tuple {_, _, _}. Tuples can be written as arguments to a procedure call. For example,

```
{|| proc(1,{x,y,{z}}), x = "abc", y = {456}}
```

invokes a procedure call with the tuple {"abc",{456},{z}} as the second argument.

Accessing tuples

Tuple elements can be accessed in the same way as array elements, where t[i] is the element i of a tuple t, for $0 \leq i <$ length(t). For example, the statement

```
Make-tuple(3,tup), tup[0] ="abc", tup[1] ={456}, tup[2] ={z}.
```

produces the tuple as the input to procedure proc as previously defined.

Lists

A list is a two-tuple in which the first element represents the head and the second element the tail of the list. For example, [1,2,3] is the list containing the elements 1, 2, and 3. The function listlen returns the length of a list as the value of len. A call listlen([1,2,3,4,5], len) returns the result as len = 5, which is the length of the list.

Building lists

The procedure buildlist forms a list of length len. A call buildlist (5, ls) gives the result as ls = [5,4,3,2,1], a list containing of 5 elements.

Communication Between Processes

Two processes can use the shared variable to communicate with each other, simply by performing read and write operations on the shared variable. The shared definitional variable can be used both to communicate a value and to synchronize the actions of the processes and can be thought of as a *communication channel*. The use of a definitional variable to specify communication has two results:

1. No special "packing" or "unpacking" operations need be performed when processes are communicating, which is the advantage of retargeting programs to different parallel computers.
2. It is possible to include variables in data structures and to establish dynamic communication mechanisms.

Example of communication between processes

Consider two processes, a Producer and a Consumer, which share a definitional variable x as follows:

```
Producer (x) and Consumer (x)
```

Assume that the producer is defined to write the variable, as follows:

```
Producer (x)
{|| x = "Hello World"}
```

This indicates the effect of communicating the message "Hello World" to the consumer. The consumer receives this value by reading (examining) the variable. For example, the following procedure checks o see whether x has the value "Hello World".

```
Consumer (x)
{? x == "Hello World" → stdio:printf("Hello World", {}, _),
 default → stdio:printf("sorry", {},_)
}
```

We illustrate the communication protocol with the following program module, named Module sumsquares.pcn, which computes the sum of the squares of the integers from 1 to N. We decompose the problem into two subproblems: constructing a stream of squares and summing a stream of numbers. The first subproblem is solved by the procedure **squares**, which recursively produces a stream of messages N^2, $(N - 1)^2$, ..., 1. The second subproblem is solved by the procedures **sum** and **sumx**, which recursively consume this stream. The procedure **sumx** accumulates the sum produced so far and returns the final result as sum. The structure of the producer (squares) and consumer (sumx) are listed in the following program. In producer, a list **sqs** of squares recursively is constructed by defining sqs = [n * n|sqs1] and calling squares to compute sqs1. In consumer, a list **ints** of integer numbers is separated recursively by matching **ins** ? = [i|ints1] and calling **sumx** to consume the rest of the message.

```
sum_squares(N, sum)
{| | squares(N, sqs), sum(sqs,sum)}
squares(n, sqs)                              /* Producer    */
{? n > 0 -> {| | sqs = [n*n | sqs1], squares(n-1, sqs1) },
                                  /* Produce element */
    n == 0 -> sqs = [ ]                   /* Close list */
}


sum(ints, sum)
{| | sum1(ints, 0, sum)}

sum1(ints, sofar, sum)                         /* Consumer */
{? ints ? = [i|ints1] -> sum1(ints1, sofar + i, sum),
                                /* Consume elements */
    ints ? = [ ] -> sum = sofar      /* End of list: Stop */
}
```

PCN provides a compositional approach to parallel programming, in which complex programs are built by the parallel composition of simpler components. Program components composed in parallel are executed concurrently, and they communicate by reading and writing definitional variables. Read and write operations on definitional variables can be implemented efficiently on both shared-memory and distributed-memory parallel computers. Thus, parallel composition and definitional variables address three important issues involved in parallel computation: concurrency, compositionality and mapping independence. The sequential composition operator and mutable variables together provide a method for integrating state change into definitional programs. We present an implementation of the QuickSort algorithm to address the definitional program. The program, qsortd, uses two definitional variables as input arguments, x and e, and one output argument, b. Definitional variables are not defined by the program, and b is a definitional variable that is defined by the program. All three are lists of numbers. The output list b is defined as a sorted list, list x, sorted in increasing order concatenated with list e. For example, if e = [5, 4] and x = [2,1], then b = [1, 2, 5,4].

The **qsortd** procedure works as follows:

If x is nonempty, mid is defined as the first element and xs is defined as the remaining elements. The call **part(mid, xs, left, right)** defines left as the list of values of xs that are at most mid, and right as the list of values of xs that exceed mid. The call **qsortd(right, m, e)** defines m as the sorted list of right appended to e. The call **qsortd(left, b, [mid | m])** defines b as the sorted list of left followed by mid followed by m. The last statement indicates that if x is an empty list, define b to be e.

The **part** procedure works as follows:

If xs is not empty, hd is defined as the head and tl is defined as the tail of xs. If hd is at most mid, define ls and right by **part(mid, xs, left, right)**, and define left as hd followed by ls. If hd exceeds mid, define left and rs by **part(mid, t1, left, rs)**, and define right as hd followed by rs. The last statement indicates that if xs is an empty list, defined left and right to be empty lists.

```
qsortd(x, b, e)
{? x ? = [mid | xs] ->
      {| | part(mid, xs, left, right),qsortd(left, b,
[mid | m]), qsortd(right, m, e)}, x ? = [ ] -> b = e }
part(mid, xs, left, right)
{?     xs ? = [hd | t1] ->
          {? hd <= mid -> {| | left = [hd | ls],
             part(mid, t1, ls, right) },
             hd > mid ->   {| | right = [hd | rs],
             part(mid,  t1, left, rs) }
          },
       xs ? = [ ] -> {| | left = [ ], right = [ ]}    }
```

Matrix-Vector Multiplication Program

This programming example is a solution to a general problem that arises when solving the system of linear equations or matrix vector multiplication which typically has application in the linear boundary value problem in ordinary differential equations defined as:

$$y' = M(t)y + q(t) \qquad t \in [a, b], y \in R^n$$

such that $B_a y(a) + B_b y(b) = d$ and represented as:

$$
\begin{pmatrix}
B_a & & & & & B_b \\
A_1 & C_1 & & & & \\
& A_2 & C_2 & & & \\
\dots & \dots & \dots & \dots & \dots & \\
& & & A_k & C_k
\end{pmatrix}
*
\begin{pmatrix}
y_1 \\
y_2 \\
y_3 \\
\dots \\
y_{k+1}
\end{pmatrix}
=
\begin{pmatrix}
d \\
f_1 \\
f_2 \\
\dots \\
f_k
\end{pmatrix}
$$

A more substantial challenge is to solve it in a parallel computing environment. The algorithm uses a factorization technique, in which transformations are used to compress each two successive rows of the linear system into a single row. This produces a reduced system that has the same structure as the original system but is half the size. The compression process can be applied recursively until a small system such as

$$
\begin{pmatrix}
B_a & B_b \\
A_1 & C_1
\end{pmatrix}
*
\begin{pmatrix}
y_1 \\
y_{n+1}
\end{pmatrix}
=
\begin{pmatrix}
d \\
f_1
\end{pmatrix}
$$

remains. The PCN program creates a set of k processes connected in a tree structure. The computation starts at the k/2 leaves of the tree and proceeds up the tree to the root.

The leaves perform the initial compression, while at the higher levels of the tree, the compression is applied recursively, and at the root the small system is solved. Finally, the computation propagates down the tree to recover the remaining elements of the solution vector. Input to the program is provided at each leaf i $(0 \le I < k / 2)$ as two $n \times n$ blocks (A_i and C_i) and one n vector (f_i), and at the root as two $n \times n$ blocks (B_a and B_b) and one n vector (d). the program consists of two main parts. The first part creates the process tree by creating a root process and calling a doubly recursive tree procedure to create k / 2 leaf processes and (k / 2 − 1) nonleaf processes.

Shared definitional variables (strm, left, right) establish communication channels between the nodes in the tree. The second part of the program defines the actions performed by the leaf, nonleaf and root processes. The leaf process initializes two sets of blocks and calls the compress procedure to produce a, c, and f. It sends a message to its parent containing the computed values and slots for return values (ybot, ytop) which will be computed by its parent. The recover procedure delays until values for ybot and ytop are received, then it computes the solution y. The nonleaf procedure receives messages from left and right children and calls compress to perform the compress operation to produce a, c, and f. The new values are communicated to the parent in the process tree. The parent produces the values for ytop and ybot. Then the recover operation proceeds to produce ymid. These values are returned to the left and right children by the four definitional statements. The root process receives a single message containing the completely reduced blocks. It call comp_root to perform the final computation to produce ybot1 and ytop1, which are returned to its children.

```
solve(k, t0, t1)
{| |   root(strm)    tree(strm, {t0, t1}, 1, k/2)   }

tree(strm, as, from, to)
{? from == to -> leaf(from * 2, strm, as),
   from < to -> {| |   mid = from + (to - from)/2,
nonleaf(left, right, strm),
   tree(left, as, from, mid), (tree(right, as, mid+1, to) }
}

leaf(id, parent, as)
double
a[MM],a1[MM],a2[MM],c[MM],c1[MM],c2[MM],f[M],f1[M],f2[M],
y[M],r[MM]
{? as ? =    {t0, t1} ->
   {; init_(id-1, a1, c1, f1, t0, t1),
init_(id, a2, c2, f2, t0, t1),
      compress_(a1, c1, f1, a2, c2, f2, a, c, f, r),
      parent = {a, c, f, ybot, ytop},
      recover(a1, c1, f1, r, ybot, ytop, y)   }   }

nonleaf(left, right, parent)
double ymid[M], a[MM], c[MM], f[M], r[MM];
{? left   ? =    {a1, c1, f1, ybot1, ytop1},
   right   ? =    {a2, c2, f2, ybot2, ytop2} ->
   {; compress_(a1, c1, f1, a2, c2, f2, a, c, f, r),
      parent = {a, c, f, ybot, ytop},
      recover_(a1, c1, f1, r, ybot, ytop, ymid),
      ybot1 = ymid, ytop2 = ymid, ytop1 = ytop, ybot2 = ybot }   }
```

```
root(child)
double ybot1[M], ytop1[M], ba[MM], bb[MM], brhs[M];
{? child ? =    {a, c, f, ybot, ytop}   ->
   {; init_root_(m, ba, bb, brhs),
comp_root_(a, c, f, ba, bb, brhs, ybot1, ytop1),
       ytop = ytop1, ybot = ybot1 }
}
```

Process Mapping

Parallel compositions define concurrent processes, and shared definitional variables define how these processes are communicated and synchronized. In a parallel program we must specify how these processes are to be mapped to the processors of a parallel computer. In PCN this mapping can be performed by the programmer, meaning that the choice of mapping process applied in an application can change performance. In general, developing a PCN program consists of two phases:

1. Develop and debug the program on a workstation without concern for process mapping.
2. A process mapping method can be specified and the efficiency evaluated on a parallel computer.

In the mapping process, we require information about the parallel computer on which the process is executing. The information is provided by the primitive functions as follows:

Topology(): Returns a tuple describing the type of parallel computer, for example {"array", 512}.

Nodes(): Returns the number of processors in the parallel architecture.

Location(): Returns the location of the process on the computer.

Mapping is specified by invoking procedure calls with system- or user-defined location functions utilizing the operator @. These functions are evaluated to identify the node on which an associated call is to execute. For example, the following two functions implement the location node(i) and mesh_node(i,j), which compute the location of a procedure that is to be mapped to the i_{th} node of an array and the $(i, j)_{th}$ node of a mesh:

```
function node(i)
{| |   return( i%nodes( ) ) }

function mesh_node(i, j)
{? topology()   ? = {"mesh", rows, cols} -> return((i
* rows + j)%nodes()),
 default -> error()
}
```

The following composition primitive utilizes the function node(i) to locate the procedure calls P(x) and C(x);

```
{| |  P(x) @ node(10), C(x) @ node(20) }
```

Using Multiple Processors

A PCN program with process-mapping primitives can be executed on a single-processor machine. However, to improve the performance, we can run the program on a multiple-processor machine. The syntax used to start PCN on multiple processors varies according to the type of parallel processor computer. On multicomputers, it is required first to allocate a number of nodes and then to load the program in these nodes. For example, on the Intel iPSC/860, we must log into the host computer (System Resource Manager) and type the following commands to allocate 64 nodes, then run the program and finally free the allocated nodes as follows:

```
% getcube -t 64
% load program ; waitcube
% killcube
% relcube
```

On multiprocessors (a shared-memory Sun multiprocessor) we need only add a –n flag to the command line when running the program. For example, to run on 4 processors we normally type the following command:

```
% program myargs -pcn -n 4
```

When running on a network of computer systems, we need to list the names of the computers on which to run nodes, or provide a configuration file indicating the names of the computers on which PCN is to run. Table 4.1 shows the machines on which PCN is supported.

Table 4.1. The computers that support PCN.

Architecture	Computer
Delta	Intel Touchstone Delta
IPSC860	Intel iPSC/860
Iris	Silicon Graphics Iris
NeXT040	NeXT
RS6000	IBM RS/6000
Sun4	Sun 4 (SPARC based)

Standard Libraries

The **sys** and **stdio** modules are distributed with PCN and may be called from within user programs to invoke a variety of useful functions. This indicates that the standard input and output functions may be used in the PCN programs. For example, the following program opens a file **test** for writing and writes the character TEST to this file, then close the file.

```
#include <pcn_stdio.h>
putc_test()
FILE *fp;
{; stdio:fopen("ptest", "w", fp, _),
   stdio:putc("T", fp, _),
   stdio:putc("E", fp, _),
   stdio:putc("S", fp, _),
   stdio:putc("T", fp, _),
   stdio:fclose(fp,_)
}
```

The following program writes the character TEST on the screen (default output stream).

```
#include <pcn_stdio.h>
putchar_test()
{; stdio:putchar("T", _),
   stdio:putchar("E", _),
   stdio:putchar("S", _),
   stdio:putchar("T", _)
}
```

Support for detection of logical errors is provided by the debugging version of the PCN run time system. To use this version, the user must add a **–pdb** argument to the **pcncomp** command line. Use of these features is recommended during program development. In addition, two tools are provided to assist in the detection of performance errors: **gauge**, which collects information about the amount of time that each processor spends in different parts of a program, and **upshot**, which is a low-level tool to provide insights into the fine-grained operation of parallel programs. Upshot requires that the programmer support a program with calls to event logging primitives. Other distinctive supported features of PCN, including, extensive use of recursion, integrating foreign codes (compiling with foreign codes, linking with foreign codes), detection of logical errors, debugging PCN programs, opening and closing files and cross compiling can be obtained from [Chandy 91, 88] and [Foster 91, 92, 89].

4.3   Parallel Programming with PVM

This section presents a system for developing parallel programs executable on networked UNIX computers. The system called Parallel Virtual Machine (PVM) allows a heterogeneous collection of workstations and computers to construct a parallel processing environment. PVM is portable and runs on a wide variety of modern systems. PVM was a collaborative project between Oak Ridge National Laboratory, the University of Tennessee, Emory University, and Carnegie-Mellon University and was started in 1989 at Oak Ridge National Laboratory by Vaidy Sunderam and Al Geist. The latest version of PVM 3 was completed in 1993 [Geist 94]. The PVM system permits a heterogeneous collection of UNIX computers networked together to be viewed by a user program as a single parallel environment with some distinctive features:

- Explicit message-passing model: For a collection of computational tasks, each one performs computations.
- Heterogeneity support: PVM supports heterogeneity in terms of machines, networks and applications.
- Multiprocessor support: PVM uses the native message-passing facilities on multiprocessors to take advantage of the underlying hardware.
- Process-based computation: The unit of parallelism in PVM is a task, which is an independent sequential thread of control that transfers between communication and computation. PVM tasks are identified by an integer task identifier. The task identifiers are supplied by the PVM system and are not user chosen, because they must be unique across the entire virtual system.
- User-configured host pool: The computational tasks execute on a set of machines that are selected by the user for program execution. Both single-processor and multiprocessor computers may be part of the host pool. The host pool may be altered by adding and deleting machines during operation.

The PVM approach uses the message-passing model of execution to allow programmers to exploit distributed computing across a wide range of architectures, including high-performance workstations, 386/486 PC computers, shared-memory multiprocessors, vector supercomputers, mini-computers, mainframe computers and Massively Parallel Processors (an SIMD processor built by Goodyear Aerospace Corporation which had up to 16,384 1-bit processing elements). A key concept in PVM is that it makes a collection of computers appear as one large virtual machine.

PVM handles all message routing, data conversion and task scheduling across a network of computers. With regard to message passing, PVM permits messages containing more than one data type to be exchanged between machines having different data representations.

The PVM system is composed of two major parts:

1. A daemon called **pvmd** or "**pvm3**" which resides on all the computers making up the virtual machine. For example, a mail program that runs in the background and handles all the incoming and outgoing messages on a computer is a daemon program.

2. A library of pvm **interface routines**. It contains a set of primitives that are needed for cooperation between tasks of an application. This library contains routines for message passing, spawning processes, coordinating tasks, and modifying the virtual machines.

The PVM message-passing primitives are oriented towards heterogeneous operations involving strongly typed constructs for buffering and transmission. Any process may communicate and/or synchronize with any other. Any specific control and dependency structure may be implemented under the PVM system by appropriate use of PVM constructs and language control statements.

The PVM computing model is based on the notion that an application consists of several tasks. Each task is responsible for a part of the computational program. Depending on the function, tasks may execute in parallel and may need to synchronize or exchange data. In general, PVM tasks may possess arbitrary control and dependency structures. This indicates that at any point in the execution of a concurrent application, any task may start or stop other tasks or add or delete computers from the virtual machine. In PVM there is no restriction on which task may communicate with which other tasks.

A PVM computing model is shown in Figure 4.4, and an architecture view of the PVM system represented in Figure 4.5. The dashed arrows indicate inter-component communication and synchronization, and the solid lines represent the inter-instance communication and synchronization. A general paradigm for program execution in the PVM system has the following steps:

- A user writes one or more sequential programs in C, C++ or Fortran 77, which are programming languages that are supported by PVM. The programs contain embedded calls to the PVM system libraries.
- The programs are compiled for each architecture in the host pool, and the resulting object files are placed in a location accessible to all computers in the host pool.
- The user starts one copy of one task called **master** or an initial task by hand from a machine within the host pool. This process subsequently starts other PVM tasks called **slaves**, eventually resulting in a collection of active tasks that compute locally and exchange messages with each other to solve the problem.

In general, a user who wishes to run a PVM application first creates a virtual machine by starting up PVM. The PVM application can then be started from a UNIX prompt on any of the hosts. Multiple users can configure overlapping virtual machines and can execute several PVM applications simultaneously.

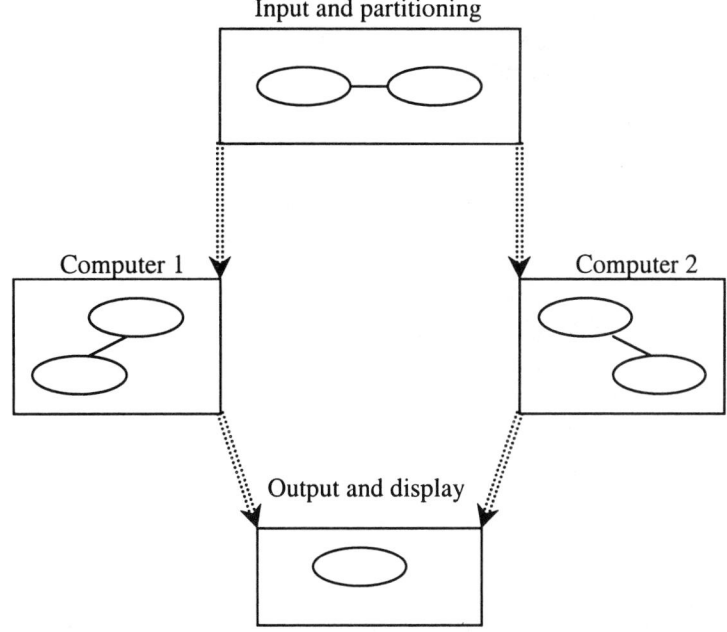

Figure 4.4. PVM computational model.

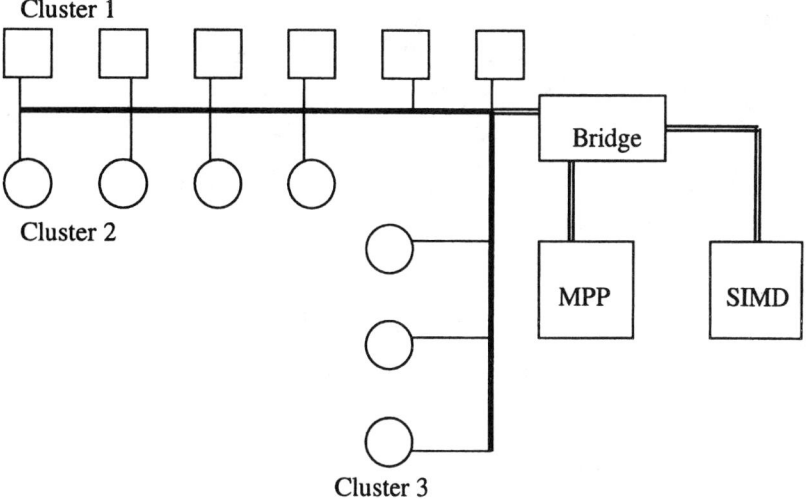

Figure 4.5. PVM architecture.

This indicates that each user has to write an application as a collection of standard interface routines. These routines allow the initiation and termination of tasks across the network as well as communication and synchronization between tasks. The PVM system and documentation are available through **netlib**, which is a software distribution service set up on the Internet which contains a wide range of computer software. The PVM system can be obtained by anonymous **ftp** from **netlib2.cs.utk.edu**. Using a worldwide web browser, the PVM files can be accessed at **http://www.netlib.org/pvm3/index.html**. The PVM system is distributed as a compressed file, meaning that it has to be uncompressed before using. The documentation is distributed as postscript files and include a User's Guide, reference manual, and quick reference card. The PVM system can be requested by sending an email to **netlib@ornl.gov** with the message: **send index from pvm3**. A list of available files and further instructions will be returned.

A Simple Program

The program prints its task ID which is obtained by **pvm_mytid()**, and then it initiates a copy of another program called **hello_other** using the **pvm_spawn()** function. A successful spawn causes the program to execute a blocking receive using **pvm_recv**. The final **pvm_exit** call terminates the program from the PVM system. In the slave program, the first PVM action is to obtain the task ID of the master using the **pvm_parent** call. The program then obtains its host name and transmits it to the master using the three function calls:

- **pvm_initsend:** To initialize the send buffer
- **pvm_pkstr:** To place a string into the send buffer
- **pvm_send:** To transmit it to the destination process specified by **ptid**

```
/*The main program "master" named hello.c   */
#include  "pvm3.h"
main() {
    int cc, tid,   msgtag;
    char    buf[100];
    printf("master ID number %x\n",   pvm_mytid());
    cc = pvm_spawn("hello_other", (char**)0, 0, "", 1,&tid);
    if (cc == 1)
        {
        msgtag = 1;
        pvm_recv(tid, msgtag);
        pvm_upkstr(buf);
        printf("from master %x: %s\n", tid, buf);
        }
```

```
        else
        printf("cannot start hello_other\n");
     pvm_exit();
}    /* end of the main program "master" */

/* The other program "slave" named hello_other.c */
#include  "pvm3.h"
main()
{
    int ptid,  msgtag;
    char   buf[100];
    ptid = pvm_parent();
    strcpy(buf, "hello world from ");
    gethostname(buf + strlen(buf), 64);
    msgtag = 1;
    pvm_initsend(PvmDataDfault);
    pvm_pkstr(buf);
    pvm_send(ptid, msgtag);
    pvm_exit();
}    /* end of the other program "slave" */
```

PVM System Setup

The following steps are required to set up the PVM system. It is worth noting that only one person at an organization needs to get and install the PVM system and everyone at that organization can use it.

- Set PVM_ROOT and PVM_ARCH environment variables in your **.cshrc** file.
- PVM_ROOT is a variable which is set to the location of the installed pvm3 directory.
- PVM_ARCH is a variable which tells PVM the architecture of this host.
- Build PVM for each architecture type.
- Create a .rhosts file on each host listing all the hosts you wish to use.
- Create a $HOME/.xpvm_hosts file listing all the hosts you wish to use appended by an "&".

Some of the machines supported by the PVM system are as follows:

- BBN Butterfly TC2000
- 80386/486 PC running UNIX
- Thinking Machine's CM-2 and CM-5

- Cray-2 and Cray 5-MP
- Encore 88000
- HP-9000 PA-RISC
- MIPS
- NeXT
- Intel Paragon
- Silicon Graphics IRIS
- SGI Multiprocessor
- Sun 4, SPARC stations
- SPARC Multiprocessor
- Sequent Symmetry
- DEC MicroVAX

Process Control

Any PVM system call will enroll a task in PVM if the task is not enrolled before the call, but it is common practice to call **pvm_mytid** first to perform the enrolling. For example, the following **pvm_mytid()** call returns the **TID** of this process and can be called multiple times.

```
int    tid = pvm_mytid(void)
call pvmfmytid(tid)
```

To start up **ntasks** copies of an executable task on the virtual machine pvm_spawn() function can be used with the following syntax:

```
int numt = pvm_spawn(char *task, char **argv, int
   flag, char * where int ntask, int *tid)
call  pvmfspawn(task, flag, where ntask, tids, numt)
```

where

argv is a pointer to an array of arguments to **task** with the end of the array specified by NULL.

flag is used to specify options as represented in Table 4.2.

Table 4.2. The flags that are used in the PVM system.

Value	Option	Description
0	PvmTaskDefault	PVM chooses where to spawn processes
1	PvmTaskHost	**where** argument is a particular host to spawn on
2	PvmTaskArch	**where** argument is a PVM_ARCH to spawn on
4	PvmTaskDebug	starts task under a debugger
8	PvmTaskTrace	traces data that are generated
16	PvmMppFront	starts task on MPP front-end
32	PvmHostCompl	complements host set in **where**

Signaling

The **pvm_sendsig()** function is used with the following syntax to send a signal **signum** to another PVM task identified by **TID**:

```
int    info = pvm_sendsig(int tid, int signum)
call   pvmfsendsig(tid, signum, info)
int    info = pvm_notify(int what, int msgtag, int cnt, int
       tids)
call   pvmfnotify(what, msgtag, cnt, tids, info)
```

The **pvm_notify()** function requests PVM to notify the caller on detecting certain events:

```
PvmTaskExit:    notify if a task exits
PvmHostDelete:  notify if a host is deleted
PvmHostAdd:     notify if a host is added
```

The names are predefined in pvm3/include/pvm3.h.

Message Passing

Sending a message consists of three steps in the PVM system, as follows:

1. A send buffer must be initialized by a call to pvm_initsend() or pvm_mkbuf().
2. The message must be packed into the buffer by pvm_pk* () function calls.
3. The message can be transmitted to another process by pvm_send() or multicast by pvm_mcast() function calls.

```
int     bufid = pvm_initsend(int    encoding)
call    pvmfinitsend(encoding,  bufid)

int     bufid = pvm_mkbuf(int     encoding)
call    pvmfmkbuf(encoding,     bufid)
```

where **bufid** is the buffer identifier. Some of the packing data functions that pack an array of the given data type into the active send buffer are as follows:

```
int info = pvm_pkbyte(char * cp, int nitem, int stride)
int info = pvm_pkint (char * np, int nitem, int stride)
int info = pvm_pklong(long * np, int nitem, int stride)
```

```
int info = pvm_pkshort(short * np, int nitem, int stride)
int info = pvm_pkfloat(float * fp, int nitem, int stride)
```

Sending and receiving data can be accomplished by the following function calls:

```
int info = pvm_send( int tid, int msgtag)
call   pvmfsend(tid, msgtag, info)
int info = pvm_mcast( int * tids, int ntask, int msgtag)
call   pvmfmcast(ntask, tids, msgtag, info)

int bufid = pvm_recv( int tid, int msgtag)
call   pvmfrecv(tid, msgtag, bufido)
```

This communication is a blocking receive function and will wait until a message with label **msgtag** has arrived from **TID**. A value of −1 in **msgtag** matches anything.

```
int   bufid = pvm_nrecv( int tid, int msgtag)
call   pvmfnrecv(tid, msgtag, bufido)
```

This communication is a nonblocking receive function and returns **bufid** = 0. We summarize this section with a PVM program. In addition, for the other distictive features of the PVM system, such as dynamic process group, synchronization primitives, resource manager, PVM communication supporting protocols, task environment, supporting architectures, windows interfaces and debugging interested readers can refer to the PVM manual and User's Guide.

Matrix Multiplication Program

The PVM program is based on the matrix multiplication algorithm described by Fox [Fox 87] which is adapted from the PVM manual. The program calculates C = AB, where C, A, and B are all square matrices. For simplicity, we assume that n×n tasks are used to calculate the product matrix C. Each task calculates a sub-block of the matrix C. The block size and the value of n are given as command line arguments to the program. The matrices A and B are stored as blocks distributed over the n^2 tasks. Initially, each task t_{ij}, where $0 \leq i,j < n$, contains blocks C_{ij}, A_{ij} and B_{ij}. The algorithm works as follows:

1.   The tasks on the diagonal elements (t_{ij} where i = j) send their block A_{ij} to all the other tasks in row i.
2.   All tasks calculate $A_{ii} \times B_{ij}$ and add the result to C_{ij}.
3.   The column blocks of matrix B are rotated such that t_{ij} sends its block of B to $t_{(i-1)j}$.

4.   The tasks now return to the first step, meaning that A $_{i(i+1)}$ is propagated
      to all other tasks in row i, and the algorithm continues with step 1.

After n iterations, the C matrix contains A×B, and the B matrix has been rotated back into place. In this program we look at the tasks as a two-dimensional
matrix such that each task joins the group **Mat_Mult**. Group IDs are used to
map tasks. In general, the first task to join a group is given the group ID of zero.
It spawns the other tasks and sends the parameters for the matrix multiplication
to those tasks. The parameters are **n** (the square root of the number of blocks)
and **blksize** (the size of a block). After all tasks have been spawned and the parameters transmitted, the **pvm_barrier()** function is called to make sure that all
the tasks have joined the group. The **InitBlock()** function initializes A to random values, B to the identity matrix and C to zeros. This enables the verification
of the calculation at the end of the program by checking that A = C. The main
function is used to calculate the matrix multiplication such that first the tasks on
the diagonal broadcast their block of A to the other tasks in their row. Then,
both the broadcasting task and the tasks receiving the block calculate AB for the
diagonal block and the block of B residing in the task. Different message tags
are used for sending the A blocks and the B blocks as well as for different iterations of the loop. Once the computation is completed, the calculation is verified
by checking A = C to see that the product is correctly calculated.

```
#include   "pvm3.h"
#include   "stdio.h"
/*Maximum number of children this program will spawn*/
#define    MAXNTIDS   100
#define    MAXROW 10
/*Message Tags*/
#define    ATAG       2
#define    BTAG       3
#define    DIMTAG 5
void   InitBlock(float *a, float *b, float *c, int blk, int
row, int col)
{
   int len,   ind;
   int i, j;
   srand(pvm_mytid());
   len = blk * blk;
   for (ind = 0;      ind <len; id++)
       { a[ind] = (float)(rand()%1000) / 100.0; c[ind] = 0.0; }
   for (i = 0;        i < blk   ;   i++)
       {
       for (j = 0;        j < blk   ;   j++)
           {
           if (row == col)
```

```
            b[j * blk + i] = (I == j)? 1.0 :   0.0;
        else
        b[j * blk + i] = 0.0;
        }
    }
}
void  BlockMult(float *a, float *b, float *c, int blk)
{
    int i, j, k;
    for (i = 0;      i < blk   ; i++)
        for (j = 0;      j < blk   ;  j++)
            for (k = 0;       k < blk   ;  k++)
    c[i * blk + j] = c[i * blk + j] + (a[i * blk + k] * b[k
        * blk + j]);
}
main(int argc,   char *argv[])
{
/* Number of tasks to spawn*/
    int ntask = 2;   /* number of tasks to spawn */
    int info;      /* return code from pvm calls */
    int mytid, mygid; /* my task and group id */
    int child[MAXNTIDS - 1]; /* children task id array */
    int i, n, blksize;
    int myrow[MAXROW];       /* array of the tids in my row */
    int row,   col,   up, down;
    float *a, *b, *c, *atmp;
    mytid = pvm_mytid();        /* to find my task id number */
    pvm_setopt(PvmRoute,    PvmRouteDirect);
    if (mytid < 0)           /* check for error */
        {
        pvm_perror(argv[0]);
        return -1;
        }
        /* join the Mat_Mult to the group */
    mygid = pvm_joingroup("Mat_Mult");
    if (mygid < 0)
        {
        pvm_perror(argv[0]);
        pvm_exit();
        return -1;
        }
    if (mygid == 0)      /* spawn the other task */
        {
        if (argc == 3)   /* how many tasks to spawn */
            {
```

```
            m = atoi(argv[1]);
            blksize = atoi(argv[2]);
            }
        if (argc < 3)
            {
            fprintf(stderr, "USAGE: Mat_Mult n blk\n");
            pvm_lvgroup("Mat_Mult");   pvm_exit();return -1;
            }
    ntask = nxn;           /* tasks are legal */
    if ( (ntask < 1) || (ntask >= MAXNTIDS) )
        {
        fprintf(stderr, "ntask = %d not valid. \n", ntask);
        pvm_lvgroup("Mat_Mult");   pvm_exit();return -1;
        }
        /* do not spawn if only one task */
    if (ntask == 1) goto  barrier;
/* spawn the child tasks */
info = pvm_spawn("Mat_Mult", (char **)0, PvmTaskDefault,
(char *)0, ntask-1, child);
    if (info ! =    ntask-1)     /* spawn is successful */
        {
        pvm_lvgroup("Mat_Mult");   pvm_exit();return -1;
        }
        pvm_initsend(PvmDataDefault);    /* send the matrix */
        pvm_pkint(&n, 1, 1);
        pvm_pkint(&blksize, 1, 1);
        pvm_mcast(child, ntask-1, DIMTAG);
        }
    else                         /* receive the matrix */
        {
        pvm_recv(pvm_gettid("Mat_Mult", 0),  DIMTAG);
        pvm_upkint(&n, 1, 1);
        pvm_upkint(&blksize, 1, 1);
        ntask = nxn;
        }
barrier:                 /* all tasks joined the group */
    info = pvm_barrier("Mat_Mult", ntask);
    if (info < 0)pvm(perror(argv[0]);
    for (i = 0;  i < n; i++)
        myrow[i] = pvm_gettid("Mat_Mult", (mygid/n) * n + i);
    /* memory allocation for local blocks */
    a = (float*)malloc(sizeof(float) * blksize * blksize);
    b = (float*)malloc(sizeof(float) * blksize * blksize);
    c = (float*)malloc(sizeof(float) * blksize * blksize);
    atmp = (float*)malloc(sizeof(float) * blksize * blksize);
```

```
    if (! (a && b && c && atmp) )
        {
        fprintf(stderr, "%s: out of memory.\n", argv[0]);
        free(a);      free(b);      free(c);      free(atmp);
        pvm_lvgroup("Mat_Mult");   pvm_exit();return -1;
        }
    row = mygid/n;   col = mygid%n;
    up  = pvm_gettid("Mat_Mult",
((row)?(row-1): (n-1)) * n + col);
    down   = pvm_gettid("Mat_Mult",
((row == (n-1))?col: (row + 1) * n + col));
    /* initialize the blocks */
    InitBlock(a, b, c, blksize, row, col);
    /* matrix multiplication */
    for(i = 0; i < n;   i++)
        {
        if (col == (row + i)%n)
            {
            pvm_initsend(PvmDataDefault);
            pvm_pkfloat(a, blksize * blksize, 1);
            pvm_mcast(myrow, n, (I + 1) *ATAG);
            BlockMult(c, a, b, blksize);
            }
        else  {
        pvm_recv(pvm_gettid("Mat_Mult",
row * n + (row + i)%n), (i + 1) *ATAG);
        pvm_upkfloat(atmp, blksize * blksize, 1);
        BlockMult(c, atmp, b, blksize);
            }
    pvm_initsend(PvmDataDefault);
/* rotate the B columns */
    pvm_pkfloat(b, blksize * blksize, 1);
    pvm_send(up, (i + 1) *BTAG);
    pvm_recv(down, (i + 1) *BTAG);
    pvm_upkfloat(b, blksize * blksize, 1);
        }  /* check to verify that A = C for correctness */
    for(i = 0;   i < blksize * blksize; i++)
        if (a[i] ! =   c[i])
    printf("Error a[%d] (%g) ! = c[%d] (%g) \n", i, a[i], i, c[i]);
    printf("Done.\n"0;
    free(a);      free(b);      free(c);      free(atmp);
    pvm_lvgroup("Mat_Mult");
    pvm_exit();
    return 0;
}/* End of the main program */
```

4.4   Parallel Programming with C-Linda

Linda is a registered trademark of Scientific Computing Associates, Inc., and is a language-independent set of operations which when integrated into a base language yields a high-level parallel dialect. C-Linda uses the C programming language; Fortran-Linda exists as well. This section describes C-Linda, which is a parallel programming approach based on the C programming language. It enables users to conceptually create the parallel programming environment. C-Linda uses four operations and two variant forms of operations to extend the C programming language to a complete parallel programming language. The underlying philosophy of Linda is that parallel programming requires the use of both a computing language such as C and a coordination language such as Linda. Coordination refers to the process of allowing active programs (also called processes, tasks, threads, etc.) representing independent activities to communicate and synchronize with each other. In most cases, active pieces that make up a coordinated program may be expressed in many different languages (language-heterogeneous program), may be separated by space (the active pieces are running on different machines), or may even be separated by time (like file systems or databases). The Linda coordination language approach differs from standalone integrated parallel languages, distributed programming languages and operating systems that support parallel or distributed programming. To date, Linda has been implemented on shared- and disjointed-memory architectures, as well as on local area networks. The Linda paradigm seems appropriate for platforms such as parallel workstations, shared parallel computers and even a network of autonomous machines.

In addition, the C-Linda compiler supports syntax, compile time error checking, and high-level run time debugging. Most distributed operating systems make excellent C-Linda hosts. Of course, C-Linda is available on a large number of shared-memory and distributed-memory computers, meaning it is a portable parallel programming environment. Conceptually, C-Linda implements parallelism with a small number of simple operations to create and coordinate parallel processes. The key features of the Linda paradigm are:

- Processes are decoupled, meaning they do not communicate directly.
- Processes create, look at and destroy objects that are called tuples.
- An attempt to read a nonexistent object causes a wait.
- Objects are stored in a shared space called tuple space.
- Objects are identified by their contents rather than their location, meaning tuple space can be viewed as an associative memory.

Linda Principles

C-Linda provides a mechanism to create and coordinate multiple execution·processes with a small number of simple operations. The operations are added to the language and are able to create and coordinate multiple processes as required. The C-Linda operations implement the tuple space model of parallel programming, which consists of a collection of data sets called tuples, as follows:

1. Process tuples, which perform the execution utilizing data tuples
2. Data tuples

A tuple is simply a series of typed values. The word "tuple" designates the argument to an operation. Example of tuples are:

```
("Hello World", 12, 1.58, val)
(2, 5)
```

There are four basic tuple space operations in C-Linda:

- out
- in
- rd
- eval

Example:

```
out(x)
```

A new tuple x is added to tuple space and the invoking process continues immediately.

```
in(x)
```

An arbitrary in(x) tuple x, which matches the argument y, is withdrawn from tuple space. This indicates that y is the anti-tuple of x and both have the same number of operands. The types of operands match pairwise, and each actual value in y matches the value of the corresponding operand in x. After this matching and assigning of corresponding operands in y, the invoking process continues to execute. In the case of no matching tuple for y, the invoking process is suspended until one is available.

```
rd(y)
```

This operation is identical to in(y) except that the matched tuple remains in tuple space to be used by other processes.

```
eval(x)
```

This operation is identical to out(x) except that the new tuple x is evaluated after it is added in tuple space. In other words, eval(x) creates a new process to evaluate each operand of x. In addition to these four operations, two variant forms, in(p) and rd(p), are provided which are predicate forms of in(y) and rd(y). The only difference is that they do not suspend the process if no matching tuple exists. They attempt to determine a matching tuple and return 0 if there is none, otherwise they return 1 and perform the assignment as described before.

Tuple Matching

Tuples have lives that are completely independent of their creating processes. This in important, for it means that tuples can be used to create data structures in tuple space that persist even after the creating process terminates. Since tuples can be referenced associatively, they are convenient building blocks for many types of data structures. First, we need to distinguish between tuples, which are arguments of out and eval operations and are inserted into tuple space, and anti-tuples, which are arguments of in, inp, rd, and rdp operations and are used as templates for searching purposes. Second, we need to know that a tuple is a sequence of **typed values**, such as:

```
("Hello World", 25, 17, a)
```

and an anti-tuple is a sequence of typed values or formal fields, such as:

```
("Hello World", ?a, ?b, c).
```

Here, the first and last fields are typed values and the middle two fields are formals. The in and rd operations provide a mechanism for retrieving data from tuple space. As an example, consider the following statement executing the **in** operation:

```
in("Hello world", ?f, ?i, y)
```

Execution of this operation performs a search in tuple space for each data tuple having four elements. This means matching any tuple with the first element equal to the string "Hello world", the second element with the same types as the variable f, the third element with the same types as the variable i, and the last element equal to the value bound to the y variable. If there is a matching tuple, it will be removed and the values of the second and third elements will be assigned to f and i, respectively.

Tuples are withdrawn from tuple space atomically, meaning a tuple can be grabbed by only one process. If no matching tuple exists in tuple space, the process executing the in operation suspends until one tuple becomes available. If many tuples satisfy the matching criteria, then one of them is chosen arbitrary.

Example: Consider the following statement as executing the **rd** operation:

```
rd("Hello world", ?f, ?i, y)
```

Executing this statement causes the same results as for the in operation except that the matched tuple would not be removed from the tuple space, meaning the tuple would remain in tuple space to be used by other processes.

Example: Consider the statements executing the **out** operation:

```
for(i = 0; i<100; i++)
   out("Square Root", i, sqrt(i));
```

Execution of the out operation causes a tuple to be evaluated and to be added to the tuple space, meaning the first 100 integers and their square roots as 100 tuples are added to the tuple space. There is no assumption for the case that the tuple space is full. In practice, such events must be addressed by the programmer to specify the action in situations when stack overflow occurs. The alternative is to rebuild the system with a larger tuple space.

Example: Consider the statements executing the **eval** operation:

```
for(i = 0; i<100; i++)
   eval("Worker", i, sqrt(i));
```

Execution of the eval operation causes each field of the tuple argument to be evaluated independently and asynchronously with the eval executing process and each other, meaning the fields of an eval tuple are evaluated concurrently. When every field has been evaluated completely, then the tuple appears in the tuple space, which consists of the values evaluated by each field. In the above example, execution of the eval operation creates 100 parallel processes to perform the sqrt function on the 100 integer numbers. We can look at the inp and rdp operations from two points of view. First, they attempt to locate a matching tuple, return 1 and perform an actual-to-formal assignment if they succeed, or return 0 otherwise. Second, the inp and rdp operations do not suspend the executing process if no matching tuple is found. In practice, the inp and rdp operations correspond to the in and rd operations, meaning they are alternative mechanisms that provide equivalent functionality and performance. Note that the rd statement will cause its executing process to block if the processes created by the eval have not completed and there is no other matching data tuple in tuple space. One significant detail of eval concerns inherited bindings for its argument expressions. For example, the statement

```
eval("Q",f(x, y))
```

implicitly creates two new processes to evaluate "Q" and f(x, y). The process evaluating f(x, y) does so in a context in which the names f, x and y have the same values they had in the environment of the eval executing process.

Tuple Matching Rules

Tuple matching is performed as a field by field comparison and is defined as follows:

1. A tuple generated by **out** or **eval** matches an anti-tuple generated by **in** or **rd** precisely when the tuple and the anti-tuple have the same number of fields and the i_{th} field of the tuple matches the i_{th} field of the anti-tuple.

2. A formal field and an actual field match precisely when their types and their sizes are the same.
   - For matching purposes, the type of an aggregate field is its "base type." The base type of an array is the type of the array's elements. The base type of a pointer is the type of the object to which it points.
   - For matching purposes, the type of a **struct** or **union** field is extended to include the structure or union name.
   - Scalar type fields do not match aggregate type fields. For example, if x's data type is int *, then *x and x:1 do not match.
   - Fixed aggregate type fields match other fixed aggregate fields of the same length only.

3. Two actual fields match exactly when their types are the same and their values are the same. Scalar actuals must have equal values. Aggregate actuals require agreement in number and value of elements.

Example: The following are all valid statements.

```
int   i, *pi;  /* i as an integer and pi as a
pointer to integer data type variables */
pi = &i; /* pi points to I variable */

out("integer", i);
out("integer", 7);
out("integer", *pi);
```

The following operations all consume the tuple("integer", 2).

```
in("integer", i);
in("integer", * pi);
in("integer", 2);
```

A Simple Program

The C-Linda program is a parallel program such that a loop is used to create a number of parallel processes and each one prints a message in the form:

"Hello world From Process number i"

where $1 \leq i \leq N$, and N is the number of created processes.

```
/* Program name: hello.cl        */
#include <stdio.h>
#define Num_Procs 5
real_main( )
    {
    int i, Hello_World( );
    out("count", 0);
    for(i = 1; i< = Num_Procs; i++)
        eval(Hello_World(i));
    in("count", Num_Procs);
    printf("All Processes Are Done Execution.");
    }
Hello_World(i)
    int i;
    {
    int j;
    printf("Hello World From Process %d.\n", i);
    int("count" ?j);
    out("count", j + 1);
    }
```

As we see, the statements are in C and only the coordination activities involve Linda operations. In this program, the eval operation creates 5 processes and the in and out operations are used to process a counter variable in tuple space that controls the termination of the program. A possible output of this program execution is as follows:

```
Hello World From Process 1.
Hello World From Process 3.
Hello World From Process 2.
Hello World From Process 5.
Hello World Form Process 4.
All Processes Are Done Execution.
```

The output indicates that C-Linda programs are asynchronous and any particular process may execute before any other process unless a synchronization mechanism is explicitly imposed by the programmer.

Array Fields

The general form of a varying array field is the following:

```
array:length:limit
```

where **array** is a pointer, **length** is the number of elements, and **limit** specifies a maximum number of elements. Both **length** and **limit** are optional for formal varying arrays, but if present, the length must be an integer variable to which is assigned the number of elements. The ":" notation may be used with data structure in order to specify a structure size in bytes. In general, an array or some part of an array can be added or removed from tuple space. In an **out** operation, the length is used to determine how many elements should be added to tuple space. An integer constant or variable or an expression can be used to specify a length for an **out** operation.

Example: An array is retrieved using both explicit and implicit lengths.

```
Int *pa, a[20],   len,  lim; pa = a;
out("array", a:20);  out("array", a:);
out("array", pa:20);
```

In out("array", a:), omitting a length, indicates a varying aggregate whose length is the declared length of the array. In an **in** operation, the return value of **len** in both cases is 20.

```
in("array", ?pa:len);
in("array", ?a:len);
```

Multidimensional arrays match only if the types of the referenced components are in agreement.

```
int a[3][5][2], b[4][6][2];
/* match succeeds */
out("array", a[0][0]);  in("array", ?b[0][0]);
/* match fails */
out("array", a[0]); in("array", ?b[0]);
```

Ping-Pong Program

This C-Linda program demonstrates interprocess communication via tuple space. Two concurrent processes play a ping-pong game by sending tuples back and forth, using the in() operator to receive a tuple (ball) and out() to send a tuple (ball). The two processes are created using eval().

```
real_main(argc, argv)
    int argc;
    char **argv[];
    {
    int start_ping(), start_pong();
    long total_loops;
    if (argc ! = 2)
        {
        printf("Usage: %s <Loops>", *argv);
        exit(1);
        }
    total_loops = atol(*++argv);
    start_timer();
    /* Create the Player */
    eval(start_ping(total_loops));
    eval(start_pong(total_loops));
    timer_split("eval done.");
    /* signal the players to start the game */
    out("START");
    timer_split("out done.");
    /* wait for the players to finish */
    in("DONE");
    timer_split("in done.");
    in("DONE");
    timer_split("done.");
    print_times();
    }/* End of the MAIN Program */

start_ping(loops)
    register long loops;
    {
    register long i;
    /* wait for the start signal from the control program */
    rd("START");
    for(i = 0; i < loops; i++)
        {
        out("ping"); /* hit the ball */
        in("pong");  /* receive the ball */
        }
    /* tell the control program that I am done */
    out("DONE");
    }

start_pong(loops)
    register long loops;
```

```
{
register long i;
/* wait for the start signal from the control program */
rd("START");
for (i = 0; i < loops; i++)
    {
    in("ping");   /* receive the ball */
    out("pong"); /* return the ball */
    }
/* tell the control program that I am done */
out("DONE");
}
```

The C-Linda Compiler

The C-Linda compiler is invoked with the **clc** command to compile a C-Linda program. The compiler performs the following operations:

1. A C-Linda program (a program with the extension **.cl**) is parsed such that the Linda operations are transformed into normal C operations, and data are collected about the operations.
2. The generated C program is compiled using the C compiler (**cc**).
3. The object code of the program and the descriptive information from the Linda operations are combined to form a Linda object file with the extension **.lo**. At link time, this object code is analyzed as a program. The Linda object code is similar to the C object code, but it contains additional information about the Linda operations which is used by the linker.

For example, the following command compiles a program with the name **hello.cl** and specifies the output file name as **hello** rather than **a.out**.

```
%clc  hello.cl -o hello
```

In general, the **clc** command has the following syntax.

```
clc [-c]   [-Dname[ = def] ]   [-g]   [-help]   [-Ipathname]
    [-Ldirectory] [-llibrary]
    [-linda   [compile-args "args"] | [info] |
        [link_args "args"] | [ts integer] |
        [tuple_scope] | [t_scope] [tuple_dump] ]
    [-O[level] ] [-o oututfile] [-v] [-w] filename
```

Each of the filenames in the command line may be one of the following types:

name.cl	C-Linda source file name which is processed by clc.
name.c	C source file name which is passed to the C compiler.
name.lo	Linda object file name which is passed to the clc linker.
name.o	C object code name which is passed to the linker.
name	An object routine library which is passed to the linker.

The following options are available in the C-Linda compiler and are interpreted by clc.

-c

    Compile the specified files but do not link them.

-Dname or -Dname = def

    Defines the symbol name for the preprocessor.

-g

    The compiler produce the symbol table information for debugging. The E_{max} loader will include appropriate debugging libraries.

-help

    Display help information about clc.

-Ipathname

    Add the directory "pathname" to the list of directories.

-Ldirectory

    Add the directory "directory" to the list of directories.

-llibrary

    Direct the linker to link library named "liblibrary.a".

-linda directive

    Add C-Linda compiler directives.

compile_args "args"

    Pass args as an option in each invocation of C compiler.

Info

    Print the pathname of the "Linda directory" that is being used by clc.

link_args "args"

    Pass args as an option to the C compiler used to link the executable file.

ts integer

    Cause the run time system to initialize a tuple space as 200 byte blocks.

tuple_scope or t_scope or tuple_dump

    Generate the information required by the X-based debugging tool.

-o outputfile

    Use "outputfile" for clc output.

-v

    Display the subcommands used in each step of the compilation.

-w

    Suppress the warning messages.

Debugger

Linda provides a parallel program debugging tool that helps users to list and monitor the correctness of their programs. There are two types of tools provided with C-Linda:

1. Generic monitoring tools that can be used in any UNIX environment.
2. Graphical debugger and program monitor that runs only in the X windows-based environment.

As stated before, Linda's processes do not communicate directly and they produce data structures called tuples which are stored in a common shared space called the tuple space. The Tuplescope run time debugging tool allows tuple space to be visualized. This tool is called a coordination debugger, since it shows the coordination state of the C-Linda program. To use the Tuplescope debugger, simply compile your C-Linda program with the Linda Tuplescope compiler option in clc command. This option causes the linker to link in the Tuplescope library and changes your program to an X windows-based client application. The Tuplescope display consists of a main window used to control program execution and a number of tuple space partition windows used to display information about tuples and processes. In other words, by providing a window onto tuple space, Tuplescope permits visualization of the multiplicity of processes and data objects that constitute a running C-Linda program. The main window, which is labeled with the name of the program is made up of two distinct regions as follows.

1. The button region contains labeled buttons (Modes, Aggregates, Run, Break, Continue, Debug, Save, Quit) and a speed control bar.
2. The icon region displays process icons (which appear when a process is created and terminated) and tuple space partition icons (used to iconify a partition window).

The tuple space partition windows appear beneath the main window. Each has a label at the top, which identifies it by means of a template of the tuples it contains. The nested square icon on the left of each of these labels is a resize button, which responds differently to the left, middle, and right mouse buttons. The tuple space partition window is made up of data tuples and live tuples called processes. A data tuple is represented by a round ball. Whenever a tuple is output to the tuple space (through the out operation), a new round ball appears, and whenever a tuple is removed (through the in operation) a round ball disappears. A live tuple is represented by a square icon which is labeled with the process's ID. By clicking on a round ball, you can see the value of that tuple. By clicking on a square icon, you can see the source code for the last Linda operation executed by a live tuple.

Generally speaking, the Tuplescope provides a variety of techniques, from simple visual inspection to the formulation of complex breakpoints, for the user to verify the logical correctness of a C-Linda program. The run time debugger is used in C-Linda on shared-memory parallel computers on which the Tuplescope can efficiently interact with and control the C-Linda program as it is executing. The use interfaces of these two tools are mostly similar to each other.

Process Displays

Each C-Linda process is represented by a process icon and is numbered to indicate the relative order in which processes were created. The shape of the process icon changes during execution to indicate the most tuple space operation performed by that process. The process icon forms are as follows:

↓   An **out** or **eval** was the most recently used operation.

↑   An **in** was the most recently used operation.

◆   The process is blocked on an **in** operation.

✧   The process is blocked on a **rd** operation.

⇧   A **rd** operation was the most recently used operation.

■   The process has not performed any operation, or it has completed all of its operations and is ready to be terminated.

More detailed information regarding the state of a process can be obtained by clicking on the process icon.

Timing Facilities

Three functions in the C-Linda parallel programming environment are provided for timing options, as follows:

starttimer()	Initializes and starts the stopwatch.
Timersplit(string)	It takes a time split when invoked and labels the time split with the specified string. The maximum string size and the maximum number of timer splits is 32.
printtimes()	Prints all time splits executed in a tabular format with strings.

Linda has been implemented on networks where every processor is connected to a single high-speed bus. There are two approaches to a network implementation. The tuple space can be replicated on each processor or it can be distributed among the processors. In the first case, Output broadcasts each tuple. When a processor tries to input or read a tuple, the tuple space exists locally and the search is efficient. If no matching tuple exists, the process suspends until some incoming tuple matches. Some mechanism must exist to ensure that the tuple is not removed by two different processors.

Matrix Multiplication in Linda

The main process of matrix multiplication is presented in the following program. First the program initializes the tuple space with the rows of the first matrix and the columns of the second matrix. Then the process adds to the tuple space a "Next job counter" called Next with initial value 1. Finally it loops on an Input statement and the result tuples are added to the tuple space.

```
Output("A", 1, (1,2,3));   /* Row 1 of the first matrix */
Output("A", 2, (4,5,6));   /* Row 2 of the first matrix */
Output("A", 3, (7,8,9));   /* Row 3 of the first matrix */

Output("B", 1, (1,0,2));/* Column 1 of the second matrix */
Output("B", 2, (1,2,1));/* Column 2 of the second matrix */
Output("B", 3, (1,1,1));/* Column 3 of the second matrix */

Output("Next", 1);            Next Job Counter

    for I in 1..3 loop
       for J in 1..3 loop
          Input("C", I, J: Integer, C: Integer);
          /* PRINT THE PRODUCT MATRIX C */
       end loop;
    end loop;
```

The actual work of this matrix multiplication is done by the worker processes such that each worker process takes the job counter from the tuple space and returns it to the tuple space after incrementing the value. The value of the counter is the element of the result array that needs to be computed. The row and column whose multiplication gives this result element can easily be computed. For example, the fourth element needs the first column and the second row. The equation for an array element is element = (row − 1) * 3 + col which produces 4 = (2 − 1) * 3 + 1 in this example. The row and column of the two input matrices are obtained from the tuple space using READ rather than Input, since the data must remain for computing the other elements. Finally, the result tuple is added to the tuple space.

Consequently, this program remains identical no matter how many worker processes are computing concurrently. There are nine multiplications to be performed and it does not matter whether there are nine worker processes or just one.

This part of the program is presented as follows.

```
/* WORKER PROCESS */
/* Local Data Declaration */
begin
   loop
      Input ("Next", Element);    /* Get job number */
      Output("Next", Element + 1); /* Put next job number */
      Exit when Element > 3 * 3;  /* Check for termination */
      I : = (Element - 1) / 3 + 1;/* Compute row number */
      J : = (Element - 1) mod 3 + 1;/* Compute column number */
      Row_Tuple : = Read("A", I, V1);   /* Get row */
      Col_Tuple : = Read("B", J, V2);   /* Get column */
      X : = Inner_Product(V1, V2);   /* Compute product */
      Output("C", I, J, X);          /* Save result */
   end loop;
end Workers;
```

One of the advantages of the Linda solution is that the solution is robust even if the processes execute on several different processors with different performances. We may have two fast processors and two slow processors. This indicates that two parts of the job will be done by the fast processors and one part of the job by the slow ones.

The C-Linda paradigm provides a limited tuple tracing facility which allows the experienced C-Linda programmer to monitor tuple traffic during the execution of a C-Linda parallel program. In order to use the tracing facilities, the file linda.h must be included using the standard C preprocessor as follows:

```
#include <linda.h>
```

To summarize, the C-Linda parallel programming approach uses extremely powerful, but very simple, primitives to construct a parallel programming environment. The Linda paradigm is suitable not only for a network of linked machines, but also for shared-memory computers (i.e., the Encore Multimax, which is a shared-memory multiprocessor system). Other distinctive features of C-Linda may be obtained from [Gelernter 85] and [Ahuja 86].

4.5   Parallel Programming with EPT

A thread is an independent unit of execution that can be performed concurrently with other threads. The **Encore Parallel Threads** (EPT) is based on the Thread Package that has been developed by Thomas Doeppner at Brown University [Doeppner 87] and is a set of functions implementing the threads abstraction.

Encore parallel threads run on Encore Multimax parallel computers no matter how many processors are available for use, meaning that EPT is completely independent of the number of processors. The Encore Multimax system is a multiprocessor system in which a number of concurrent threads of control are executing in a single shared address space. Threads communicate through this shared memory and all threads can participate in input/output operations. Setting up a threads environment has some overhead, but initialization takes place only at startup and does not affect the performance of the threads program. The initialization can be performed by

- Forking the number of processes specified.
- Creating a shared memory area to be accessed by all processes.
- Creating a small amount of process private data.

The Encore Parallel Threads library has a set of functions supporting Microthreads which are intended for applications such as parallelization of loops [Brawer 89].

Thread Creation

Threads can be created by calling the THREADgo function with the following syntax:

```
int    THREADgo(Num-Procs, data-size, function, args,
argsize, stacksize, priority)
```

where the data types of the arguments are defined as follows.

```
int    Num-Procs;
int    data-size;
int    args;
int    argsize;
int    stacksize;
int    piority;
void   (* function) ( );
```

Calling the THREADgo function creates Num-Procs processors for use by EPT. The data size is an upper bound in bytes for representing the shared address space. The initial thread starts execution by calling the THREADgo function. It is passed a single argument args which might be either a value, a pointer to a value or set of values. The value of argsize is checked as follows:

if   argzise = 0,   args is passed to the thread unchanged,
     argsize ≠ 0,   argsize bytes of data pointed to by args are placed on the
                     new thread's stack and the thread is passed a pointer to
                     this location.

Therefore, if arguments are copied to the thread's stack, they are private to that thread; otherwise, they are accessible from other threads. Stacksize and priority are the maximum size of stack and run time priority given to the newly created thread, respectively. Priority ranges from 0 through 31 with 0 being the highest priority. The newly created thread can create a new thread by calling the THREADcreate function with the following syntax:

```
THREAD    THREADcreate(function, args, argsize,
          detached, stacksize, priority)
```

and the data types of the arguments are defined as:

```
int    * args;
int    argsize;
int    stacksize;
int    priority;
int    (*function) ( );
char   detached;
```

Calling the TREADcreate function creates a new thread of type THREAD. The detached argument determines the termination situation of the created thread with regard to the parent with regard to the synchronization as follows:

if   detached = DETACHED,   there is no relation between child and its
                              parent,
     detached = ATTACHED,   the child and parent relationship is main-
                              tained, meaning the parent is not able to
                              terminate until the child terminates and
                              the parent can wait until the child termi-
                              nates.

When the child terminates, it can return a value to its parent, and after the return value has been obtained, the allocated storage of the child can be released by the parent utilizing a call to the THREADfree function. The following syntax can be used to synchronize a parent and an attached terminating child:

```
THREAD    child;
int    Returnvalue;

       .

       .

child = THREADjoin();
Returnvalue = THREADreturnvalue(child);
THREADfree(child);
```

A thread terminates when it returns from its first function. THREADkill can be used to kill off a thread.

Matrix Multiplication

The following program uses multiple threads for matrix multiplication.

```
#include <thread.h>
#include <stdio.h>
int A[9] =    { 1, 2, 3,
              4, 5, 6,
              7, 8, 9};
int B[9] =    { 9, 8, 7,
              6, 5, 4,
              3, 2, 1};
int C[9];
main(argc, argv)
int argc;
char *argv[ ];
{
    extern void startup( );
    if (argc ! = 2)
    { fprintf(stderr, "usage : tst #processors"); exit(1);}
    THREADgo(atol(argv[1], 2 * 1024 * 1024, startup, 0, 0,
20 * 1024, 2);
}

Void startup( )
{
extern void mult( );
/* We need a structure to pass multiple parameters because
of the way EPT works */
```

```
struct {
    int i;
    int j;
    } ij;
for (ij.i = 0; ij.i < 3; ij.i++)
    for (ij.j = 0; ij.j < 3; ij.j++)
THREADcreate(mult, &ij, sizeof(ij), ATTACHED, 20 * 1024, 2);
    while (THREADjoin( ) );
    printf("%3d %3d %3d\n %3d %3d %3d\n %3d %3d %3d\n",
    C[0], C[1], C[2], C[3], C[4], C[5], C[6], C[7], C[8]);
}

void mult (ij)
    struct {
    int i;
    int j;
        } *ij;
{
    register int i;
    register int t = 0;
    register int col = 3 * ij -> i;   /* row i and col 0    */
    register int row = ij -> j;       /* row 0 and col j    */
    for (i = 0; i < 3; i++)
        {
        t = t + A[col] *B[row];
        col = col + 1;
        row = row + 3;
        }
    C[3 * ij -> + ij -> j] = t;
}
```

Synchronization

The synchronization mechanism in Encore Parallel Thread can be implemented utilizing the following methods:

- Barrier
- Semaphore
- Monitor
- THREADjoin

Here, the semaphore and monitor synchronization primitives are discussed.

Semaphores

The semaphore mechanism is very efficient and is useful when simple mutual exclusion is required. To create a semaphore we need to use the following syntax:

```
SEMAPHORE
THREADseminit(initialvalue)
int    initialvalue;
```

where initialvalue is the initial value given to the semaphore, and the value returned is the mean for referencing the semaphore and is of type SEMAPHORE. The wait and signal primitives on semaphore are performed utilizing THREADpsem and THREADvsem with the following syntax:

```
void   THREADpsem(sem);
       SEMAPHORE sem;
void   THREADvsem(sem);
       SEMAPHORE sem;
```

where sem parameter is the name of the semaphore variable. THREADpsem and THREADvsem might be implemented as follows:

```
THREADpsem: while (sem ≤ 0)
                  {
                  Keeptesting;
                  }
            sem = sem - 1;
```

meaning that THREADpsem decrements the value of the semaphore variable by 1 if the thread is eligible to access to the critical section; otherwise, the thread is suspended and appended at the end of an associated queue of the semaphore variable.

```
THREADvsem: sem = sem + 1;
```

This indicates that the first suspended thread on the semaphore's queue is released, if there is any. Also, the value of the semaphore variable is increased by 1.

Monitors

A monitor must be created by a thread before any thread can use it. This can be done by a call to THREADmonitorinit with the following syntax:

```
THREAD_MONITOR
THREADmonitorinit(conditions, resetfunc)
int conditions;
void (*resetfunc) ( );
```

The **conditions** argument specifies the number of condition queues to be created inside the monitor and **resetfunc** is called if an exception is raised in a thread that is active in the monitor. The THREADmonitorinit function returns a handle for the newly created monitor which is of type THREAD_MONITOR and is used to identify the monitor. For example, a monitor can be used to provide mutually exclusive access to the shared data by a thread call THREADmonitorentry before accessing data and THREADmonitorexit after accessing data with the following syntax:

```
void THREADmonitorentry(monitor, &manager)
THREAD_MONITOR monitor;
THREAD_MANAGER manager;

void THREADmonitorexit(monitor)
THREAD_MONITOR monitor;
```

Here, the **manager** is the address of the data structure of type THREAD_MANAGER and **monitor** is the handler of the monitor that has been created to protect the data structure. It is often necessary for a thread to modify the monitor-protected data only if certain conditions are true, when the condition itself must be checked inside the monitor. This can be accomplished by using a condition queue. If the condition is true, the thread continues; otherwise, the thread suspends itself by calling THREADmonitorwait. Then, after some time the second thread can wake up the suspended thread by calling THREAD-monitorsignalexit.

```
int THREADmonitorwait(monitor, condition)
THREAD_MONITOR monitor;
int condition;

int THREADmonitorsignalandexit(monitor, condition)
THREAD_MONITOR monitor;
int condition;
```

```
int THREADmonitorsignalandwait(monitor, signalcondition,
   waitcondition)
THREAD_MONITOR monitor;
int signalcondition, waitcondition;
```

The **condition** (numbering from 0) identifies the condition queue to which the thread is referring. A thread calling THREADmonitorwait is suspended and placed at the end of the associated queue. It is resumed when it is first in that queue and a signal is sent for that condition by THREADsignalandexit or THREADsignalandwait. A thread calling THREADsignalandwait signals signalcondition and then is suspended and placed on the associated condition queue specified by waitcondition. Input and output can be safely performed in EPT by utilizing the appropriate system call or standard Input/Output calls. If a computation must access one of several files, for example, read from the keyboard, there are two approaches available:

- Create a separate thread to deal with each Input/Output device
- Use UNIX system calls to access the device

In the second approach, a single thread can wait for any one of many I/O devices to be ready to transfer and then perform the appropriate transfer request. To avoid any possible race conditions, this is all done within the domain of a monitor using an additional monitor call THREADmonitorwaitevent with the following syntax:

```
int THREADmonitorwaitevent(monitor, condition, limit, rmask,
   wmask, timeout)
THREAD_MONITOR   monitor;
int condition;
int limit;
fd_set  *rmask;
fd_set  *wmask;
fd_set  *xmask;
struct timeval    *timeout;
```

The typedef fd_set provides a bit vector to represent the file names.

Producer-Consumer

This example illustrates the producer-consumer problem in which the producer can supply more than the buffer can hold and the consumer can request more than the buffer can hold, so the transfer might be incremental. The monitors are used to ensure that the consumer consumes only the produced amount of data.

```
#include <thread.h>

char   buffers[5][80], fgets_ret = 1;
int    firstbuf, lastbuf, totalbuf, fullbuf;
int    stacksize = 10 * 1024;

extern void producer(), consumer(), produce(), consume(),
master();

THREAD_MONITOR mon;

main()
{
   int    processes = 2;
   int    datasize = 2 * 1024 * 1024;
   firstbuf = 0;
   lastbuf = 0;
   totalbuf = 4;
   fullbuf = 0;
   THREADgo(processes, datasize, master, 0, 0, stacksize, 0);
}

void   master()
{
   mon = THREADmonitorinit(2, NULL);
   THREADcreate (producer, 0, 0, ATTACHED, stacksize, 0);
   THREADcreate (consumer, 0, 0, ATTACHED, stacksize, 0);
}

void   producer()
{
     FILE *file;
     char *fgets(), string[80];
     file = fopen("procon.c", "r");
     while (fgets_ret = fgets(string, 78, file) ! = NULL)
        {
        produce(string);
        }
     string[0] = ' ';
     produce(string);
}

void   produc(string)
   char string[];
{
```

```
    THREAD_MANAGER_BLOCK man;
    THREADmonitorentry (mon, &man);
    if (fullbuf == totalbuf)
        {
        THREADmonitorwait( mon , 0);
        }
    strcpy(buffers[lastbuf], string);
    lastbuf = lastbuf%totalbuf + 1;
    fullbuf = fullbuf + 1;
    THREADmonitorsignaland exit(mon, 1);
}

void   consumer()
{
    char   string[80];
    string[0] = '*';
    while (string[0] ! = ' ')
        {
        consume(string);
        printf("%s", string);
        }
}

void   consume(string)
    char string[80]
{
        THREAD_MANAGER_BLOCK man;
        THREADmonitorentry (mon, &man);
    if (fullbuf == 0)
        {
        THREADmonitorwait( mon , 1);
        }
    strcpy(string, buffers[firstbuf]);
    firstbuf = firstbuf%totalbuf + 1;
    fullbuf = fullbuf - 1;
    THREADmonitorsignaland exit(mon, 0);
}
```

Microthreads

Microthreads have low overhead because they are intended strictly for computation. They are used in **for** or **do loop** structures, where one wants to utilize all available processors with a minimum amount of overhead. The synchronization is limited to a **barrier** function, which holds each thread of a group until all the threads have completed a call to the barrier function. Microthreads are created in groups with the following syntax:

```
UTHREAD_CONTROL
UTHREADcreate(number, stacksize)
int number;
int stacksize;
```

where UTHREAD_CONTROL identifies this group of microthreads. A group of microthreads can be used any number of times and there are two steps associated with microthreads, as follows:

Ready state: Each microthread grabs a processor. This can be achieved by:

```
void  uTHREADready(control)
UTHREAD_CONTROL control;
```

where control is the microthread group identifier.

Busy state: Until the microthread changes to the **go** state to start executing. This can be achieved by:

```
void  uTHREADgo(control, function, arg)
UTHREAD_CONTROL control;
void  (*function) ();
int arg;
```

where each microthread in the control group calls function **function** as follows:

```
func(control, index, arg)
UTHREAD_CONTROL control;
int index;
int arg;
```

where index is the identifier of the individual microthread. The calling thread has an index 0, and the microthreads have indices between 1 and the number of microthreads in the group. The intent of the microthread index is to determine the range of data values on which to operate. For example, assume nine microthreads are being used to parallelize a for loop structure whose index is from 0 to 99. Thus, each microthread might compute a range of 10 values of the loop index. Once returned from the routine **function**, each microthread and the calling thread wait at a barrier until all return. The microthreads are put back into the ready state and the calling thread returns from uTHREADgo. The microthreads are put into the quiescent state with the following call, if they are not supposed to consume processor resources:

```
void  uTHREADpark(control)
UTHREAD_CONTROL control;
```

The following call can be used to clean up a group of microthreads and free all the storage associated with them:

```
void  uTHREADkill(control)
UTHREAD_CONTROL control;
```

All active microthreads are synchronized by the following call:

```
void  uTHREADjoin(index, control)
int   index;
UTHREAD_CONTROL control;
```

This can be performed by each microthread to ensure synchronization. No microthread returns from this call until all microthreads of the group **control** have called it, forming a barrier synchronization primitive.

Threads and Concurrency

Generally speaking, the programmer is concerned not with the processors but with what we call threads. This notion of threads is independent of the processors, meaning that we may have the concurrent execution of many threads on one processor or on many processors. The execution of a thread causes local variables and a run time stack to be allocated, but these are considered not a part of the thread itself but rather a part of the program being executed. A number of issues must be dealt with in the design of a concurrent programming environment, such as thread synchronization, scheduling, exceptions, interrupts and I/O. Scheduling entails the assignment of processors to threads. Since the notion of processor does not exist in the thread abstraction, this is really an implementation concern. In general, this is an assignment of the world of threads to the world of processors.

Exceptions are a call for a thread to retreat, meaning that an unexpected event has occurred and the thread must cancel what it is doing and attempt to recover. An interrupt is part of the processor abstraction. It indicates that some sort of event has occurred, whether generated externally or by the program. This event requires immediate attention. Thus, we need to provide services for this immediate attention at the level of the threads. For example, clicking a mouse might cause an interrupt, and to have a new thread be created in response to the mouse click is one way of dealing with this external event. The thread would execute the code associated with the mouse click.

I/O must be provided in some fashion to allow communication with the input and output devices. In EPT the technique we use is to have threads make synchronous requests of I/O devices. A thread performing a read or write request is suspended until the request has been completed.

Matrix Multiplication with Microthreads

The following program solves a matrix multiplication problem using micro-threads.

```
#include <thread.h>

extern   void  run();
int    isize;
int    nprocs = 10;
float a[1000][1000], b[1000][1000], c[1000][1000];

main()
{
    THREAD_go(nprocs, run, 0, 0);
}

void  run()
{
extern   void  mm();
int    i, j;
UTHREAD_CONTROL control;

    control = uTHREADcreate(nprocs - 1, 12 * 1024);
    uTHREADready(control);
    isize = 1000;
    for   (i = 0; i < isize; i++)
       for   (j = 0; j < isize; j++)
          {
          a[i][j] = 0;
          b[i][j] = i+j;
          b[i][j] = i - j;
          }
uTHREADgo(control, mm, 0);
uTHREADkill(control);
}

void  mm(control, index, arg)
```

```
UTHREAD_CONTROL    control;
int    index;
int    arg;
{
   int    i, j, k;
   extern    int    isize;

for    (i = index; i < isize;      i = i + nprocs)
    for    (j = 0;      j < isize;      j = j + 1)
       for    (k = 0;      k < isize;      k = k + 1)
       a[i][j] = a[i][j] + b[i][k] * c[k][j];
}
```

Example of Thread Concepts

Assume that we have a windows-based application and each window is represented by a data structure which contains the attributes of that window, including a monitor which is used for synchronization purposes. The following procedure is used for interacting with a window by outputing a prompt to the window and then reading a response:

```
promptwndow(window, prompt, response, length)
   WINDOW window;
   char  *prompt, *response;
   int    length;        {
   MANAGER manager;
   monitorentry(window.monitor, &manager);
   write(window.out, prompt, strlen(prompt));
   read(window.in, response, length);
   monitorexit(window.monitor);
   }
```

where **window** represents a data structure describing the window. The **monitor** member is used for synchronization and **in** and **out** members are used to identify the read and write system calls in which I/O operations are performed. Now, suppose when an interrupt occurs we would like a thread to be created which will pop up a window. In order to do this, we need to tell the thread system how to respond to this interrupt:

```
   SIGHANDLER  response = {CREATETHREAD, 0, popup};
   registersignal(SIGINT, &response, NULL);
```

Whenever an interrupt of type SIGINT occurs, the response should be to create a new thread which executes the procedure popup, as follows:

```
popup()  {
WINDOW    newwindow = create_window(…);
char    request[80];
promptandread(newwindow, "yes?", request, 80);
handle_request(request);
}
```

This creates a new window by calling create_window and allocates a new monitor to synchronize the window. It calls promptandread to prompt for a command name, and finally it calls handle_request to carry out the command. Other distinctive features of the Encore Parallel Threads, such as preemptive scheduling functions, signal handling functions, microthread functions, monitor support functions, semaphore support functions and exception handling functions may be obtained from the Encore Parallel Thread manual and [Doeppner 87].

4.6   Parallel Programming with CHARM

CHARM is a parallel programming system that supports an explicitly C-based language [Kale 94, Intrepid Group 94]. It is a language designed for portable parallel programming with two major objectives:

- It should be portable across various MIMD machines.
- It should make the task of programming easier for the programmer.

The system is suitable for programming in both shared-memory and non-shared-memory parallel machines. It is completely portable and the source code need only be recompiled for it to run on a different machine. CHARM reduces the complexity of parallel programming significantly such that the programmer is responsible for the creation of parallel tasks and the system decides when and where to execute them.

CHARM Principles

CHARM uses a message-driven model of execution as illustrated in Figure 4.6. CHARM forms a workpool of messages for all the processing that needs to be done. Syntactically, a message is defined to be a collection of data, and in CHARM it has the same syntax as a C structure declaration defined as follows:

```
struct    tag_name
          {
          /* {declaration of the members of the structure} */
          } variable_list;
```

where variable_list is the name of variables of type structure tag_name. In general, the system keeps extra information about messages to facilitate their handling by system routines. An example of a message declaration appears below:

```
message    msg_type
           {
           /*{declaration of variables, message structure}*/
           };
```

where the following code defines two pointers **msg1** and **msg2** to messages of type msg_type:

```
msg_type    *msg1,    *msg2;
```

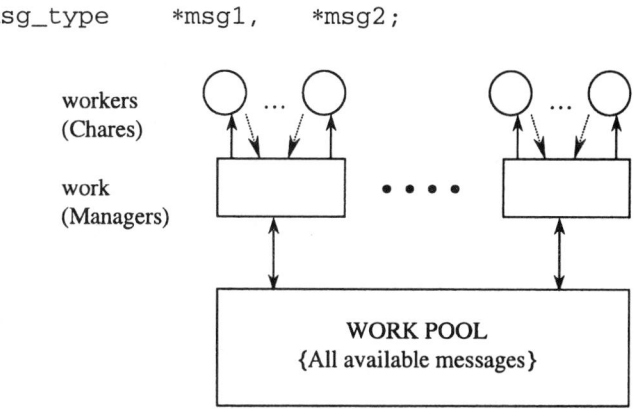

Figure 4.6. CHARM message-driven system.

There are multiple workers located on multiple CPUs which are assigning tasks by the work managers or the run time system. Processing of a message may lead to the creation of new messages which are placed in the workpool, as represented by the dashed line in the figure. Workers are created and destroyed as needed by the run time system during execution. CHARM can support the following machines:

- Uniprocessor
- Multimax
- Symmetry
- FX2800
- network of workstations
- NCUBE
- i860
- iPSC

Chares

A CHARM program consists of objects called chares. The chare is the basic unit of work within a CHARM program. During the execution of a program, chares may create new chares or communicate with existing chares by sending messages. Within a chare are entry points. When a message is sent, its destination is an entry point. Each entry point has an associated block of C code which is executed upon receiving a message. Messages are one of three basic types:

1. A new chare message, which requests a new instance of a chare to be created on a single processor.
2. A for-chare message, which is delivered to an existing chare.
3. A branch office chare message, which requests one instance of a chare to be created on every processor of the parallel machine.

When a message is created, it is placed in the pool of available messages maintained by the CHARM kernel. The kernel is continually running a loop, which consists of picking a message from the pool and delivering it to the correct instance of chare to be processed, resulting in the execution of C code associated with the entry code. When the execution has finished, control is returned to the kernel which continues looping and picking the next message. Chares have only private functions that may be called only from within the same chare. In contrast, branch office chares can have public functions that may be called from other chares. This indicates that branch office chares provide a facility to distribute data abstractions across processors in the system. In addition, the chares could request data from a branch office chare, which would communicate with its children on other processors to collect the data.

CHARM Program

A CHARM program is similar to a C program and consists of modules such that all code must be within a module. A CHARM program syntax is presented in Figure 4.7. A module can have messages, chares, variable declarations and information sharing abstraction declarations. Only one module is permitted in a given source file, meaning that every CHARM program consists of at least one module. A chare definition starts with the name of the chare, a declaration of local variables of the chare, entry_point definitions and the definition of private functions. Each entry_point definition consists of an entry_point name followed by a declaration of the message associated with it, and a block of C code. This block may contain arbitrary C code, function calls, or calls to CHARM primitives. To run any program, there must exist at least one initial chare instance, which can then create other chare instances at run time. Thus there is a special chare in a CHARM program named **main**. The **main** chare must have an entry_point named **ChareInit**. In other words, execution of a CHARM program begins with the creation of an instance of the **main** chare and execution of the code associated with the ChareInit entry_point.

Creating Chares

The CreateChare call permits a user to create a new instance of a chare with the following syntax:

```
ChareIDType   CreateChare(entry_name, msg [, anchored, destPE])
              EntryPointType   entry_name;
              void     *msg;
              boolean    anchored;
              PeNumType destPE;
```

If we need the address of the new chare instance, the following code can be used to assign the ID of the new chare as the value of **chare_id**:

```
chare_id = CreateChare(entry_name,   msg [, anchored, destPE])
```

where **chare_id** is a variable of type ChareIDType. The **entry_name** is the entry_point in the chare from which the execution is to start. An entry_name is a variable of type EntrypointType. It can be specified as **modulename :: charename@entry_name**, which refers to the entry_point **entry_name** in the chare **charename** defined in module **modulename**. If the CreateChare call is made inside **modulename**, then the entry_point could be specified as **charename@entry_name**. The **msg** is a pointer to the message of the type associated with the entry point. The **anchored** is a boolean specifying whether the chare is anchored on the processor where it was instantiated; otherwise, it can not be migrated. The **destPE** is a parameter to enforce creation of the chare on a specific processor, which overrides the system's dynamic mapping.

Sending Messages

Chares can communicate with each other using the SendMsg call with the following syntax:

```
SendMsg (entry_name,   msgpointer, chare_id)
        EntryPointType entry;
        void    *msgptr;
        ChareIDType chare_id;
```

where the **entry_name** is an entry_point in the chare to which the message is addressed.

The **msgpointer** is a pointer to the message of the type associated with the entry point, and the **chare_id** is the address of the chare to which the message is to be sent.

```
module Module
      {
      type declarations
      Message definitions, information sharing abstractions

      chare  main
         {
         local variable declarations
         entry  CharmInit: C code block
         other entry points
         }
      chare  sample
         {
         local variable declarations
         /* Entry Point Definitions */
         entry  EP1:    (message  MessageType1 *msgptr)
         C code block

         ...

         entry  EPn:    (message  MessageTypen *msgptr)
         C code block

         /*Local Function Definitions*/

         private ExampleFunction1(int ........)
         C code block

         ...

         private ExampleFunctionn(int ........)
         C code block
         }   /* End of Chare Sample */

      BranchOffice Chares and other function declarations

      }
```

Figure 4.7. Syntax of a CHARM program.

CHARM Program Compilation

The CHARM language compiler is called ICC (Intrepid Charm Compiler). ICC translates the CHARM code into C code and then produces an executable code by compiling the C code. The internal working of ICC is transparent to the user. For example, to compile a program named as sample_program.p and to create an executable code, we can issue the following command:

```
ICC sample_program.p
```

where ICC creates an executable code called sample_program in the current directory. The following command creates an executable code called outputname in which the CHARM program is named somename.p:

```
ICC   -o outputname   somename.p
```

To execute the program, just type **outputname**.

Sum of the Integer Numbers

The following program computes the sum of all integers up to a user-specified limit. Generally speaking, when the program is executed, control passes to the CharmInit entry point of the main chare. The CkScanf function is used to get the user-specified limit. The main chare creates two instances of the **Compute** chare such that each is responsible for adding half the numbers. This can be achieved by creating a message of type **JobMsg** using the CreateChare call. The message contains the range of numbers that have to be added up and the ID (address) of the main chare. The StartQuiescence function is then called to let the system know the entry point to which control should pass on quiescence detection. A private function **AddUp** is called by the Compute chares to add up the range of numbers specified in the **JobMsg** message they received. They then send a message of type **DoneMsg** to the **Result** entry point of the main chare, where the partial sums are added. On reaching Quiescence, control passes to the **Final** entry point which prints out the sum and then calls CkExit to terminate the program.

```
#include  "charm.int"
module Sample
{
message   JobMsg {int   low;   int high;   ChareIDType MainID;}
message   DoneMsg   {int   PartialSum;}

chare  main
```

```
{
int limit;
int FinalSum;
int midlimit;
entry  CharmInit:
        {
        JobMsg *msg1, *msg2;
        CkPrintf("Enter limit: ");
        CkScanf("%d", &limit);
        midlimit = limit / 2;
        msg1 = (JobMsg *)CkAllocMsg(JobMsg);
        msg1->low = 1;
        msg1->high = midlimit;
        msg1->MainID = MyChareID();
        CreateChare(Compute@first, msg1);
        msg2 = (JobMsg *)CkAllocMsg(JobMsg);
        msg2->low = midlimit + 1;
        msg2->high = limit;
        msg2->MainID = MyChareID();
        CreateChare(Compute@first, msg2);
        StartQuiescence(main@Final, MyChareID());
        }  /* end of entry CharmInit */
 entry  Reslt: (message DoneMsg *dmsg)
        {
        FinalSum = FinalSum + dmsg -> PartialSum;
        }  /* end of entry Result */
 entry  Final: (message DoneMsg *nmsg)
        {
        CkPrintf("The Final Sum is: %d ", FinalSum);
        CkExit();
        }  /* end of entry Final */
  }  /* end of main chare */

chare  Compute
    {
    entry  first: (message JobMsg *msg)
        {
        int partsum;
        DoneMsg *donemsg;
        Partsum = AddUp(msg -> low, msg -> high);
        Doneptr = (DoneMsg *)CkAllocMsg(DoneMsg);
        Doneptr -> PartialSum = partsum;
        SendMsg(main@Result, doneptr, msg -> MainID);
        }  /* end of entry first */
```

```
Private        int AddUp(int lo, int    hi)
   {
   int i;
   int sum = 0;
   for (i = lo; i ≤ hi; i++)
      sum = sum + i;
   return (sum);
   }   /* end of Private */


}   /* end of Compute chare */

}  /* end of module */
```

The program begins by executing the code contained in the CharmInit entry point of the main chare. The first CreateChare call creates an instance of the **Compute** chare and sends the message msg1 to the **result** entry point. The second CreateChare call similarly creates an instance of the **Compute** chare and sends the message msg2 to the **result** entry point. Finally at the end of the CharmInit code StartQuiescence is called to inform the system that the code in the **Final** entry point of the main chare should be executed on Quiescence detection. The **Result** entry point receives two messages, each containing a partial sum of the range of numbers specified by the user. It computes the actual sum by adding the two partial sums. It is very important to realize that no assumptions can be made about the order in which chares are created and executed or about the order in which messages arrive. For example, the second CreateChare call could create an instance of the **Compute** chare before the first CreateChare call created one. It would be much more efficient to decide the number of chares to be created dynamically depending on the computation required.

Memory Allocation

Dynamic memory allocation is essential for managing memory efficiency. The CHARM system calls support allocating and de-allocating of memory and are similar to **malloc** and related routines which are available in C. The memory allocation routines in the CHARM system are CkAlloc and CkAllocMsg, and are used for variable and message memory allocation, respectively.

Allocating Memory for Messages and Variables

The CkAllocMsg call allocates space for a message of message type **msg_type** with the following syntax. If successful, then a pointer to the allocated space is returned; otherwise, it returns NULL. Any data to be used as a message and passed to system routines must be allocated using CkAllocMsg.

```
void   *CkAllocMsg(msg_type [, size_array])
       MSG_TYPE msg_type;
       int    *sizes_array;
```

The CkAlloc call allocates space for a variable with the following syntax. It allocates size bytes of memory and returns a pointer to the allocated space if successful. If not, it returns NULL.

```
void   *CkAlloc(size)
       int    size;
```

There is one call for freeing memory allocated to messages and variables with the following syntax. It frees the space allocated by CKAlloc or CkAllocMsg function calls.

```
void   CkFree(pointer)
       void   *pointer;
```

Chare Addresses

We need to determine the address ID of the chare in order to send the message to the other chare. The address of a chare can be obtained by two system calls as follows:

MyChareID() with the following syntax:
                ChareIDType MyChareID()

MainChareID() with the following syntax:
                ChareIDType MainChareID()

where MyChareID() returns the ID (address) of the currently executing chare, and MainChareID() returns the address of the main chare.

CHARM encourages a programming style that counters the unpredictability of available work by creating many small chares in the hope of being able to distribute them as needed. Thus, in a message passing version of CHARM, many chares that are created are not sent to any other processors, but are used locally. Figure 4.8 illustrates a program which creates a user-specified number of chares.

For more distinctive features available in the CHARM parallel programming approach the reader can refer to [Intrepid Group 94].

```
#include   "charm.int"
module     MsgSample {
message    CreateMsg {int   number};
message    DoneMsg   {int   chare_number, ChareIDType
           chare_id};
chare main    {
      CreateMsg *msgptr;
      entry CharmInit:    {
          int num_chares;
          int i;
          CkPrintf("Number of Chares to be created: ");
          CkScanf("%d", &num_chares);
          Msgptr = (CreateMsg *)CkAllocMsg(CreateMsg);
          for (i = 1;   i ≤ num_chares;      i++)   {
              msgptr -> number = i;
    CkPrintf("msgptr -> number = %d ", ,msgptr -> number);
              CreateChare(Compute@first, msgptr);
              }
          StartQuiescence(main@Final, MyChareID());
          }
      entry Result: (message DoneMsg    *doneptr){
      CkPrintf("Created Chare Number %d having ChareID = %u",
              doneptr -> chare_number, doneptr -> chare_id);
          }
      entry Final: (message DoneMsg     *nmsg)    {
          CkPrintf("Program exits after creating user
                  specified number of chares");
          CkExit();
          }
      }  /* end of main chare */
chare Compute    {
    entry first: (message     CreateMsg *cmsg)        {
        DoneMsg    *replymsg;
        CkPrintf("cmsg -> number = %d", ,cmsg -> number);
        replymsg = (DoneMsg *)CkAllocMsg(DoneMsg);
        replymsg -> chare_number = cmsg -> number;
        replymsg -> chare_id = MyChareID();
CkPrintf("replymsg -> chare_number = %d", replymsg -> chare_number);
        SendMsg(main@Result, replymsg, MainChareID());
        }
    }  /* end of Compute chare */
}  /* end of MsgSample module */
```

Figure 4.8. A program to create a user-specified number of chares.

Summary

It is now possible to construct parallel systems that are both efficient and reliable. However, it is the software that has proved to be the most difficult to master and the use of parallel computing will not occur if this problem is not solved. In addition, there is no widely acceptable single model of parallel computation which software and algorithm designers can use as the fundamental approach for their applications. This results in a range of different types of languages being proposed or used to efficiently exploit the underlying parallel hardware. In this chapter, we have discussed several parallel programming approaches that provide a direct and complete implementation of the process programming model described in Chapter 3. In keeping with the design methodology discussed in Chapter 3, these approaches allow mapping and granularity decisions to be changed independently of our algorithm design aspects. We outlined the parallel programming approaches as:

- Parallel programming with UNIX which is an augmented version of the UNIX OS with libraries for a parallel programming environment.
- Parallel programming with PCN, which is based on program decomposition. Parallel programs can be developed by composing existing modules written in languages such as Fortran and C. The PCN compiler applies the C language preprocessor to each component before compiling it, and translates the program to a machine-independent object code. The linker creates an executable program in which may be performed on a wide variety of uniprocessors, multiprocessors and multicomputers.
- Parallel programming with PVM, which is used for developing parallel programs executable on networked UNIX computers. PVM uses the message-passing model of execution to allow the programmers to exploit distributed computing across a wide range of architectures including workstations, PC computers, multiprocessor systems, minicomputer systems, mainframe systems and supercomputer systems. The system consists of two components: a Daemon, which resides on all the computers, and a Library, which consists of a set of primitives needed for cooperation between tasks of an application.
- Parallel programming with C-Linda, which is a language-independent set of operations which, when integrated into a language, provide a parallel programming environment. Linda is a set of primitives that can be used to transform a sequential language into a parallel language. The Linda parallel programming approach assumes a shared associative memory called tuple space, through which a collection of MIMD processes interact. There are four basic tuple space operations in C-Linda: out, in, rd and eval. The C-Linda compiler transforms Linda operations into normal C operations that are used by the C compiler to generate an

object code. The object code and the descriptive information from Linda are combined to form a Linda object file which can be used by the linker to the executable version of the program.

- Parallel programming with EPT is based on the Thread package, which is a set of functions implementing the threads abstraction. It runs on Encore's Multimax system, an SIMD computer, such that a number of concurrent threads of control are executing in a single shared address space. The synchronization among the concurrent threads can be implemented utilizing the primitives: barrier, semaphore, monitor and THREADjoin. There are several distinctive features associated with the EPT: preemptive scheduling, signal handling, microthread functions, monitor support, semaphore support and exception handling.

- Parallel programming with CHARM, which is a parallel programming system that supports an explicitly C-based language. It is a portable system across various MIMD computers and supports both shared and nonshared memory models. A CHARM program consists of objects called chares which are the basic unit of work within a program. The system uses a message-driven model of execution along with a work-pool of messages for all the computation that needs to be done. The compiler converts the CHARM program into C code, in which the executable code can be produced by compiling the C code. Some of the systems supported by CHARM are: uniprocessor, Multimax, Symmetry, FX-2800, NCUBE, i860 and iPSC systems.

Generally speaking, this chapter concerned the implementation of parallel algorithms. We compared the performance of the parallel programs with regard to requirements. Doing this can help to improve the quality of the parallel algorithms. A parallel programming language gives information about one aspect of a parallel algorithm: its expected parallel performance. We can use this information, when it is combined with the estimated cost of implementation, to make a reasonable judgement between different parallel programming languages.

Although the details vary according to the languages used, the solutions do not differ greatly. Much of the difficulty of constructing a parallel program lies in the design of the structure and the choice of processes. In the following we summarized the parallel programming paradigms used along with the supporting environment and operating system.

Table 4.3. A representation of parallel programming paradigms.

Approach	Environment	Operating System
Parallel Programming with UNIX	SIMD MIMD shared memory	UNIX
Parallel Programming with PCN	SISD, SIMD MIMD shared memory	UNIX
Parallel Programming with PVM	SISD, SIMD, MIMD	UNIX
Parallel Programming with C-Linda	MIMD shared memory	UNIX
Parallel Programming with EPT	SIMD MIMD shared memory	UNIX
Parallel Programming with CHARM	SIMD MIMD shared-memory	UNIX

Further information on parallel programming languages can be found in [Nevison 94, Perrott 87, Brawer 89, Snow 92].

CHAPTER 5
Principles of Parallel Algorithm Design

The innovation of parallel computing has added a new dimension to the design of algorithms. Thus, parallel processing consists of parallel architectures and parallel algorithms, and recent interests in parallel computers has motivated the development of parallel algorithms to solve many types of problems. Many aspects of parallel algorithm design are presented in [Smith 93, Cosnard 95, Miller 96]. Algorithms in which several operations may be executed simultaneously are referred to as parallel algorithms. In general, a parallel algorithm can be defined as a set of processes or tasks that may be executed simultaneously and may communicate with each other in order to solve a given problem. The term task or process may be defined as a part of a program that can be executed on a processor.

In both parallel architectures and parallel algorithms, there are many design choices for which there are no direct counterparts in conventional sequential processing. In parallel architectures, examples of such choices include the number of processors, local versus global memory organization, synchronous versus asynchronous execution, and interconnection network topologies. In parallel algorithms, issues that do not arise in sequential algorithms include determination of the number of processors needed for a computation, data allocation across memories, whether synchronization is beneficial or necessary, and interprocess communication requirements.

In general, parallelism has introduced new degrees of freedom to both the architecture and algorithm design approaches. For effective use of parallel systems, it is essential to obtain a good match between algorithm requirements and architecture capabilities. A parallel algorithm can be viewed as a collection of independent task modules, some of which can be executed concurrently utilizing the parallel computer. Information that captures the relationship between sequential algorithms and parallel algorithms can be of use in a number of different ways. In general, sequential algorithms may have several parallel versions, depending on

- how data can be accessed.
- how data can be partitioned into tasks.
- how those tasks are allocated to processes.
- how the processes are synchronized.

In practice, there are several principles in the design of parallel algorithms:

The Brent Scheduling Principle: This principle makes it possible to reduce the number of processors used in existing parallel algorithms, without increasing the total execution time. In general, the execution time of the algorithms increases somewhat when the number of processors is reduced, but not by an amount that increases the total execution time. In other words, if an algorithm has an execution time of O(log n), then the total execution time might increase by a constant factor.

The Pipelining Principle: Pipelining can be used in situations in which we want to perform several operations in a sequence $\{P_1,...,P_n\}$, where those operations have the property that some steps of P_{i+1} can be carried out before operation P_i is finished. In a parallel algorithm, it is often possible to overlap these steps and decrease total execution time. Although this technique is most often used in MIMD algorithms, many SIMD algorithms are also able to take the advantage of this principle. Several algorithms in this book illustrate this principle.

The Divide and Conquer Principle: This is the principle of splitting a problem into several small independent components and solving them in parallel. There are many examples of this technique in this book: the parallel prefix, the cycles in a graph, the shortest paths, and matrix multiplication. One of the most basic principles in MIMD algorithm design is to analyze the computations to be performed and determine the parallelism, meaning the dependency graph of the computation.

The Dependency Graph Principle: We create a directed graph in which the nodes represent blocks of independent operations and the edges represent situations in which one block of operation depends on the outcome of performing other blocks. To design an MIMD algorithm sometimes involves the conversion of a good SIMD algorithm. This conversion requires the computations to be synchronized, which is the principle that arises in the design of MIMD algorithms. This principle is identical to those involved in concurrent programming and is called the race condition principle.

It is worth noting that the main difference between MIMD algorithm design and concurrent algorithm design involves questions of when and why one creates multiple processes. When designing concurrent algorithms to run on a single-processor computer, we create processes in order to handle asynchronous events, because we expect little real concurrency to occur. An example is input and output operations, because there is no real concurrency on a single-processor computer. In contrast, when designing MIMD algorithms to run on a parallel computer, we try to maximize the amount of concurrency, and we look for operations that can be carried out simultaneously and try to create multiple processes to handle this situation.

The Race Condition Principle: If two processes try to access the same shared data, they may interfere with each other.

Example: Suppose two processes update a shared linked list simultaneously such that the head of the list is pointed to by a pointer variable named **head** and each entry has a **next** pointer to the next entry. For instance, this linkedlist in C can be defined as the following:

```
struct    Node
          {
          <Members of the node in the linkedlist >
          struct Node *Next;
          };
struct    Node   *head;
```

There are two processes involved:

Process P wants to add a record to the beginning of the linked list by:

P.1 Making the new record's next pointer variable equal to the head pointer variable.

P.2 Making the head pointer variable point to the new record.

Process Q wants to delete the first record of the linked list by:

Q.1 Making the head pointer variable equal to the next pointer variable.

Q.2 Deleting the record that was originally the target of the head pointer variable.

With the execution sequence P.1, P.2, Q.1, and Q.2 the result of that computation is correct, but through unlucky timing these operations could be carried out in the sequence, P.1, Q.1, P.2 and Q.2. The result would be that the head would point to the new record added by process P, but the next pointer of the new record would point to the record deleted by process Q. This can render the result of the concurrent processing completely inaccessible. This is an example of the race condition principle. Two processes are in the race with each other, and the outcome of the computation depends completely on which process accesses the shared data first. This discussion of parallel algorithm design illustrates a number of important points:

- The algorithms for parallel computation are different from those for sequential computation, and in order to measure real performance on parallel systems, rewriting must be permitted.
- Performance can be a function of problem size. If the problem size is not chosen to be optimal then one is not measuring the true performance of that parallel computation.
- For similar parallel architectures, the performance can vary significantly. With regard to this, the crucial factor is the interconnection network topology. For example, DAP is an SIMD computer with 64×64 processors and MPP with 128×128. The DAP matrix multiplication time is linear according to the matrix size, which depends on the existence of row and column highways for fast transmission of data. In

contrast, MPP does not possess such an interconnection, and the computation time becomes proportional to matrix size.

- In addition to demanding new techniques of algorithm design, parallel processing also requires us to rethink what we know about computer system, parallel languages and computational methods.

5.1   Design Approaches

There are three approaches dealing with parallel algorithms design:

1.   Parallelize the existing sequential algorithms or modify an existing sequential algorithm exploiting those parts of the algorithm that are naturally parallelizable.
2.   Design a completely new parallel algorithm that might be adapted to parallel architectures.
3.   Design a new parallel algorithm from the existing parallel algorithm.

This indicates that from the theory point of view, algorithms can be transformed from sequential to parallel form or from one parallel form to another. An algorithm transformation is valid only when it maintains algorithm equivalence. As a result of performing this transformation, one can answer questions such as:

- Which architecture is more suitable for a given computational problem?
- What efficiency can a computational problem achieve on a given parallel architecture?

In practice, some parallel versions of sequential algorithms may be better adapted to the structure of the computer than others. For instance, SIMD computers are not suitable to execute asynchronous algorithms. In contrast, MIMD computers do not have enough potential for synchronous algorithms.

Since the parallel algorithms are executing on parallel architectures, the relation between algorithm space and architecture space has to be considered. All three approaches must take the particular architecture of the parallel machine into consideration. For example, in designing MIMD algorithms to run on a parallel computer, we try to maximize the amount of concurrency. We look for operations that can be carried out simultaneously and try to create multiple processes to handle these operations. This can raise the issue in MIMD computations not to create more processes than the number of processors to execute them. This is in contrast to SIMD algorithms, in which there is little overhead involved in creating parallel threads of data and computations. The more we know about the interaction between these two computational models, the better we can design parallel algorithms and parallel processing environments. Some of the features of parallel algorithm designs and parallel architectures and their correlation are summarized in Table 5.1.

Table 5.1. Relation between parallel architectures and parallel algorithms.

Parallel Algorithm	Parallel Architecture
Granularity	Complexity
Concurrency	Operation Mode
Data Structure	Memory Structure
Communication Environment	Interconnection Network
Algorithm Size	Number of Processing Elements
Programming Approach	Architecture Category

We assume a target parallel architecture with the general attributes listed below. The purpose is to define a very general architecture framework, so that no undesirable restrictions are imposed on the architecture by the assumptions. Some of the existing hybrid parallel architectures, such as the Ultracomputer, Butterfly, Connection Machine and MPP, can be characterized in terms of the subsets of these attributes:

- The computer system consists of a large number of homogeneous processors. This indicates that in mapping the algorithm to an ideal parallel architecture, the number of processors available is considered to be unlimited.
- The system can be organized with processors accessing a shared global memory or with each processor having an associated local memory, or a hybrid of the two approaches.
- The system is partitionable into independent subsystems of various sizes. The partitioning can be changed dynamically at execution time.
- Each partition of the computer system is capable both of SIMD and MIMD operations and can dynamically switch between modes during execution.
- The computer system has a flexible interconnection network that can provide a wide variety of communication patterns within each partition. In any specific instance of mapping a particular algorithm onto a particular architecture, details of the interconnection network will be of importance. For example, in a multistage network, any single point-to-point data transfer can be done in one pass through the network, regardless of the distance between the source and the destination. In such a network, communication distance is not concern, but the size of the message transfers is a factor in the algorithm's performance. In contrast, in systems in which communication time is proportional to communication distance, both distance and data transfer are important.

Given the above assumptions, the problem of matching the attributes of the algorithm involves selecting the architecture configuration, memory organization, partition size, mode of operation and network configuration.

5.2   Design Issues

In this section, we show how a problem specification might be translated into an algorithm that displays concurrency, scalability, locality and modularity. With regard to these issues, one should be able to design simple parallel algorithms in a methodical fashion (a sequence of phases) and recognize design flows that compromise the efficiency of the algorithms. The design issues that we describe are intended to present an exploratory approach to the design process in which machine-independent issues such as concurrency and decomposition are considered first and machine-specific aspects of design such as communication cost and number of processors are delayed until later in the design process. This methodology structures the design process issues into four distinct phases: partitioning, communication, agglomerations and mapping.

In the first and second issues of design, concurrency and scalability are involved, and in the third and fourth issues of the design process, performance and communication costs are involved. These four phases are presented in Figure 5.1, and a brief description of each one follows.

Partitioning: The partitioning phase is intended to expose opportunities for parallel execution by decomposing computations into small tasks. Issues such as the number of processors in the target parallel architecture are ignored and attention is focused on defining a large number of small tasks in order to get a fine-grained decomposition of the problem. In general, a good partitioning method divides both the computation and the data associated with a problem into small pieces. The partitioning methods are based on two approaches:

1. Domain decomposition, which first focuses on the data associated with a problem and then determines an appropriate computation with those data (i.e., decomposing the data associated with a problem).
2. Functional decomposition, which first focuses on decomposing the computation and then works on the associated data (i.e., dividing the computation into disjoint tasks).

These techniques may be applied to different components of a single problem or even to the same problem to obtain alternative parallel algorithms. Consequently, in the first phase of a design process, replicating computation and data is avoided and we define tasks that partition both computation and data into disjoint sets.

Communication: The communication phase is intended to establish an appropriate communication structure and algorithms to coordinate task execution. To allow computation to proceed, the data must be transferred between tasks, which is the outcome of the communication phase of a design. To establish the associated approach we focus on two issues involved: channel structure and message-passing structure. In channel structure, we link (directly or indirectly) tasks that require data with tasks that possess those data. In message passing-structure, we specify the message that must be sent and received on these channels. In general, we seek to optimize performance by distributing communication operations over many tasks and by organizing communication operations in a way that permits concurrent execution. Nevertheless, thinking in terms of channel structures might help us to evaluate the algorithms from the viewpoint of communication cost.

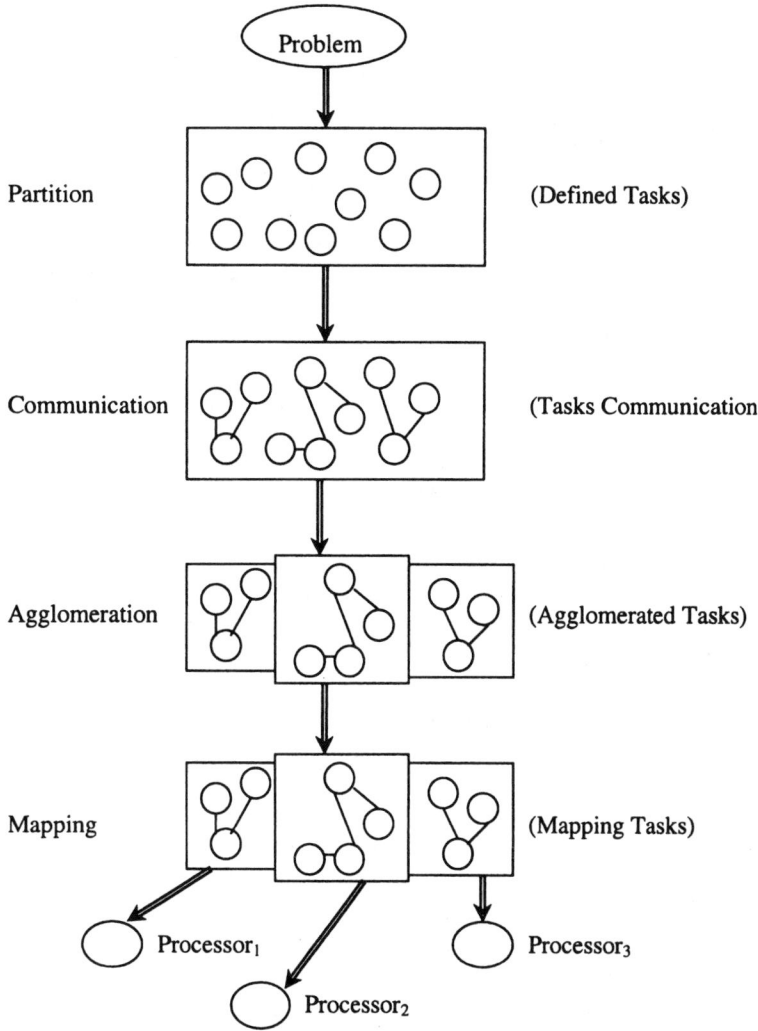

Figure 5.1. Different phases in designing a parallel algorithm.

Agglomeration: The first two phases of the design process can address dividing the computations into a set of tasks and communication to provide data required by these tasks. The agglomeration phase is intended to evaluate the tasks and required communication with respect to performance and implementation costs. For example, it might be inefficient to create many more tasks than there are processors on the target parallel architecture. Thus, we must review the partitioning and communication phases to answer issues involved in the agglomeration phase:

- To combine or agglomerate tasks identified.
- To replicate data and computations.
- To retain flexibility with regard to scalability.
- To reduce software engineering cost.
- To define mapping of tasks to processors.

In general, in the agglomeration phase we move from abstract to concrete. We revisit the last two phases of design to make the appropriate decisions with regard to the issues that are involved. For example, one critical issue influencing parallel performance is the communication cost. The performance might be improved by reducing the amount of time spent communicating, meaning sending less data. In addition to communication cost, we might be concerned with task creation cost to reduce the communication requirements or execution time.

Mapping: The mapping phase is intended to specify where each task has to be executed. In other words, each task is assigned to a processor in a manner that attempts to maximize processor utilization and minimize communication costs. Mapping can be performed statically or dynamically, meaning before the execution process or at the run time phase. Mapping is not an issue on uniprocessors or on shared-memory parallel computers that provide task scheduling in which the operating system or hardware mechanisms can schedule executable tasks to available processors.

When measuring the efficiency of mapping, we classify a parallel computer into three categories regarding the number of processors [Miller 84, Akl 97, Ben-Ari 90]:

1. A fine-grain parallel system, where the system is composed of a large number of relatively less powerful processors. Examples are CM-2, MPP, MasPar Mp-1, and MasPar MP-2.
2. A coarse-grain parallel system, where the system is composed of a small number of very powerful processors. Examples are Cray Y-MP, Cyber, iPSC/1, and BBN butterfly.
3. A medium-grain parallel system, where the system is composed of a few thousand processors (systems between fine-grain and coarse-grain systems). Examples are CM-5, nCUBE, Paragon XP/S, iPSC/860, and J-machine.

In general, there are two important issues involved in the mapping phase: enhancing concurrency and increasing locality. Enhancing concurrency deals with placing tasks that can be executed simultaneously on different processors, and increasing locality refers to placing tasks that likely communicate frequently on the same processor. Generally speaking, the mapping process is a difficult issue in parallel algorithm design and is known as an NP-Complete problem, meaning that there is no general computational algorithm for the evaluation of that mapping method.

Consequently, the outcome of this design process is a program that creates tasks and performs the mapping of tasks to individual processors. The central idea of these issues involved in the design process is to target a design with general attributes as follows:

Data parallelism: This involves dividing the data among the processors by decomposing the data into tasks that can be assigned to different processors. Data parallelism will often be amenable to SIMD implementation.

Functional parallelism: This refers to decomposing the algorithm into segments that can be assigned to different processors. Functional parallelism will always imply MIMD execution.

Module granularity: This deals with the amount of processing that can be done independently, with either processes or operations being performed on other processors. It is a measure of the synchronization issue and will affect the choice of SIMD versus MIMD architectures, the assignment of processes to processors, the memory organization, the communication requirements and the execution time of the algorithm. Algorithms characterized by fine-grain granularity will require frequent synchronization and will often be suitable for SIMD execution. Algorithms with large-grain granularity typically have less need for efficient communications and thus often suggest MIMD operations.

Data granularity: This quantifies the size of the data to be processed. It provides an indication of the measure needed to communicate a single data item. Some of the issues involved in data granularity are data allocation, communication requirements, processor capability and memory requirements.

Degree of parallelism: This is related to both data granularity and module granularity and affects the choice of machine size and the maximum speedup attainable. In addition, it is often related to the mode of operation and the memory organization.

Uniformity of the operations: Uniformity will generally be associated with data parallelism. In general, if the operations to be performed are uniform, then SIMD or pipelining may be feasible; otherwise, MIMD processing will be chosen. It is possible to construct different level of uniformity, depending on the granularity or resolution at which operations are examined.

Synchronization: It will affect the assignment of processes to processors and the scheduling of various components of the algorithm. In addition, the precedence constraints are an important issue in characterizing the synchronization requirements.

Data dependency: This specifies the data allocation patterns, communication characteristics and memory organization (local versus global). It plays the largest role in dictating data allocation patterns and communication characteristics.

Process generation and termination: These affect the processor utilization, scheduling of subprocesses, the mode of processing, the memory organization, and the communication requirements.

5.3   Performance Measures and Analysis

A sequential algorithm can be evaluated in terms of its execution time, which can be expressed as a function of the size of its input. The execution time of a parallel algorithm depends not only on the input size of the problem but also on the architecture of the parallel computer and the number of available processing elements. Mapping parallel algorithms to parallel computers and balancing parallel processors is indeed a very difficult task and the state of knowledge in this area is quite poor. Sometimes, a small change in problem size while using different algorithms or different applications may cause undesirable effects and can lead to performance degradation. Hence, a parallel algorithm cannot be evaluated in isolation from a parallel architecture.

The study of performance evaluation is motivated by the degree of parallelism which is the maximum number of independent operations that can be executed simultaneously at any time in a parallel algorithm. The degree of parallelism is a measure of the number of operations that an algorithm can perform in parallel for a problem of size W, and it is independent of the parallel architecture. If P(W) is the degree of parallelism of a parallel algorithm, then for a problem of size W, no more than P(W) processors can be employed effectively. In general, the following is a list of major characteristics that effect parallel system performance [Levesque 89, Chaudhuri 92, Fortes 85, Gibbons 88]:

- Clock speed.
- Size and number of registers.
- Number of concurrent paths to memory.
- Instruction issue rate.
- Memory size.
- Ability to fetch/store vectors efficiently.
- Number of duplicate arithmetic functional units.
- Whether function calls can be chained together.
- Indirect addressing capabilities.
- Handling of conditional blocks of code.

Vector processor performance is usually identified based on the following criteria:

- Peak rate can be obtained under the most ideal circumstances, and it does not reflect the true operating environment [Shiva 96].

- Sustained rate can be obtained in terms of MFLOPS (Million Floating-Point Operations Per Second) which is more valid.

In general, the sustained rate performance is more difficult to obtain regarding a number of factors such as:

- Level of vectorization which refers to the fraction part of the application applicable to parallelization.
- Average vector length.
- Possibility of vector chaining.
- Overlap of scalar, vector, and memory operations.
- Memory contention resolution procedure.

Because of the complexity level involved in parallel computation, in this section we study various indices for evaluating global measurements of the performance of parallel computations. We briefly discuss indices such as; execution rate, speedup factor, efficiency of execution, redundancy of computation, and utilization factors that are proposed to specify a parallel computer system's performance measure.

5.3.1   Amdahl's and Gustafson's Laws

Amdahl's law [Amdahl 67] is a mathematical model to address the limits of parallel computation and works as follows:
  1. Two different rates, R_H as high execution rate and R_L as low execution rate, are introduced.
  2. Two different fractions, f as a fraction of generated results at a high execution rate and $(1 - f)$ as a fraction of generated results at a low execution rate, are proposed.
Then the Amdahl's law formula becomes:

$$R(f) = \frac{1}{f / R_H + (1 - f) / R_L}$$

where f is the sequential execution part and $(1 - f)$ is the parallel execution part of the program. If f is 1, the speedup equals R_H, and for f = 0, the speedup equals R_L. This indicates that, a significant increase in speedup might be obtained only when f is close to 1. This means that, unless a program is heavily parallelized, the slower scalar mode of operation dominates the performance.

This formula is useful to analyze the system performance that results from two different individual rates of execution, such as parallel and serial operations (that is, when the program is divided into two parts such that one part can be executed in serial form and the other part in parallel form). On a shared-memory architecture, memory size is not relevant. Thus, with either one or p processors the same instance of the problem can be solved by applying Amdahl's law. This does not hold for distributed-memory architectures. The result expresses the fact that speed-up is bounded by a constant that is independent of the number of processors and the computer architecture. Amdahl's law led those involved in researching parallel computing to deduce that substantial increases in performance could not be achieved by implementing parallelism and that the number of processors has to be restricted. The performance evaluation of the parallel computation can be derived utilizing the Amdahl's law formula.

Gustafson's law [Gustafson 88] came up with a solution for a class of problems whose execution time increases with the size of the instance under consideration. Distributed-memory architectures are the basis of Gustafson's discussion that with a distributed memory-computer, larger size problems can be solved. This model proves to be adapted to distributed-memory architectures and explains the high performance achieved with these problems. Gustafson's law is based on the following assumptions:

1. The execution time of a parallel algorithm written for p processors is S + P, since all the processors will compute simultaneously.
2. The execution time of a sequential algorithm written for p processors is S + pP.

where S is the sequential execution part and P is the parallel execution part of the program, meaning that S + P = 1. Thus, the Gustafson's law formula becomes

$$G_p = \frac{S + pP}{S + P} = S + pP \le pP$$

which indicates that the speedup increases linearly with p, the number of available processors.

5.3.2 Speedup Factor and Efficiency

The speedup factor is a measure that captures the relative benefit of solving a computational problem in parallel. The speedup factor of a parallel computation utilizing p processors is derived as the following ratio:

$$S_p = \frac{Ts}{Tp}$$

where T_s is the execution time taken to perform the computation on one processor and T_p is the execution time needed to perform the same computation using p processors. Of course, it is assumed that the processor used in parallel computation is identical to the one used by the sequential algorithm. We denote speedup by the symbol S_p utilizing p processing elements in parallel computation. Therefore, S_p can be defined as the ratio of the sequential processing time to the parallel processing time. As a consequence of this comparison, the sequential algorithm has to be the best algorithm known for a particular computational problem. This means that it is fair to judge the performance of parallel computation with respect to the farthest sequential algorithm for solving the same problem in a single-processing-element architecture. Several issues such as synchronization, communication, and other overhead factors are involved in the parallel computation. The speedup factor is normally less than the number of processors, meaning that

$$1 \leq S_p \leq p$$

A speedup factor greater than p is possible only if each processor spends less than $\dfrac{T_S}{P}$ time solving the problem. In practice, a speedup factor greater than p is observed and is known as superlinear speedup. This is usually due to a nonoptimal sequential algorithm or a disadvantage of the sequential algorithm due to hardware characteristics. For instance, if data of a problem are large enough to fill the main memory of a single processor machine (i.e., AI applications), performance will be degraded due to the use of secondary storage. But when data are partitioned among several processing elements, the individual data would be small enough to be fitted into the processors' main memories. In these circumstances the p processor can execute a parallel algorithm more than p times faster than a single processor executing the best sequential algorithms. The reader may favor either side of the argument, but we disregard the superlinear speedup phenomenon in the performance evaluation of parallel algorithms. The efficiency of a parallel computation can be defined as the ratio between the speedup factor and the number of processing elements in a parallel system as follows:

$$E_p = \frac{S_P}{P} = \frac{T_S}{PT_P}$$

Indeed, efficiency is a measure of the fraction of time for which a processing element is usefully employed in a computation. In a ideal parallel system, the speedup factor is equal to p and efficiency is equal to one. But in practice, ideal behavior is not achieved because the processors involved in parallel computation cannot devote 100 percent of their time to the computation of the algorithm.

In general, every parallel program has certain overhead factors, such as creating processes, input/output operations and process synchronization, for which the rate might be changed with the problem size. This indicates that in practice the speedup factor is less than p and efficiency is between zero and one, depending on the degree of effectiveness with which the processing elements are utilized. The following example illustrates speedup and efficiency as functions of the number of processors that are involved in parallel algorithms. Consider the problem of adding n numbers on a p processor hypercube system. Assume it takes one unit of execution time for two directly connected processors to add two numbers and to communicate to each other. Then, adding the n/p numbers local in each processor takes $\dfrac{n}{p-1}$ units of execution time. After the local addition, the p partial sums may be added in log p steps, each consisting of one addition and one communication. Thus, the total parallel computation time T_p is $\dfrac{n}{p-1} + 2\log p$. For large values of p and n this computation time can be approximated by

$$T_p = \frac{n}{P} + 2\log p$$

The serial computation time can be approximated by n, meaning the expressions for speedup and efficiency are as follows:

$$S_p = \frac{T_S}{T_P} \qquad S = \frac{n}{n/P + 2\log P} \qquad S = \frac{nP}{n + 2P\log P}$$

$$E = \frac{S}{P} \qquad\qquad E = \frac{n}{n + 2P\log P}$$

As a consequence of these two expressions, the speedup and efficiency for any pair of n and p can be calculated as shown in Figure 5.2, which gives s versus p for different values of n and p, and Table 5.2, which illustrates the corresponding efficiency of these values. A corollary follows immediately from this example that for a given parallel program instance, both speedup and efficiency continue to drop with increasing p. This is a natural phenomenon for a large class of parallel problems.

5.3.3   Cost and Utilization

The serial computation run time is defined as the time elapsed between the beginning and the end of program execution on a sequential computer. The parallel computation time is the time that elapses from the moment a parallel program starts to the moment that the last processor terminates execution. The cost of solving a problem on a parallel system is defined as the product of parallel computation time and the number of processors used. This cost reflects the sum of the time that each processor spends solving the problem. Let T_p denote the time of a parallel computation for solving a given problem using p processors.

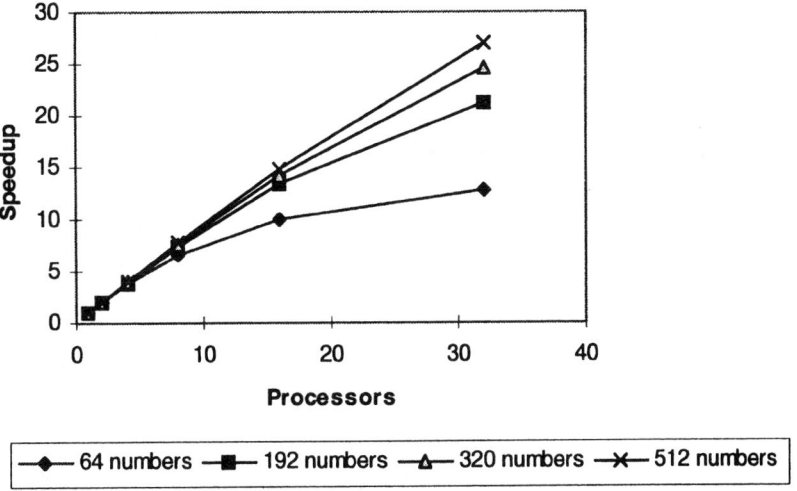

Figure 5.2. Computational speedup of n versus p for adding n numbers utilizing p processors.

Table 5.2. Computational efficiency of n versus p for adding n numbers utilizing p processors.

	Processors					
Number	1	2	4	8	16	32
64	1	0.980	0.930	0.815	0.623	0.399
192	1	0.990	0.975	0.930	0.832	0.665
320	1	0.995	0.985	0.956	0.892	0.768
512	1	0.995	0.990	0.972	0.930	0.841

The cost C_p of parallel computation is then defined as

$$C_p = p * T_p$$

where C_p is the number of operations that could have been performed with p processors in T_p time units. The utilization measure can be defined as the ratio between the actual number of operations O_p and the cost of that parallel computation C_p with the following form:

$$U_p = \frac{O_p}{p\,T_p} \qquad\qquad U_p = \frac{O_p}{C_p}$$

It is worth noting that cost is sometimes referred to as work or processor time product.

5.3.4 Execution Rate and Redundancy

The machine output per unit of time is defined as the execution rate and depends on the definition of the machine output with the following notations:

- Millions of instructions per second (MIPS)
- Millions of floating point operations per second (MFLOPS)
- Millions of operations per second (MOPS)
- Number of logic inferences per second (LIPS)

Depending on the specific architecture, the appropriate execution rate can be applied. For instance, the MIPS measurement is meaningful for uniprocessors and multiprocessors but is not appropriate for SIMD computers, in which one instruction operates on a large number of operands. Also, while the MFLOPS measure is appropriate for many numeric applications, it is not very useful for general-purpose programs. The peak throughput performance of representative supercomputers is shown in Table 5.3, where the performance measure ignores the overhead and is dependent entirely on cycle time. In addition to this, sometimes the type of application can address the specific execution rate to be used as the performance evaluation. For example, the LIPS measurement can be used for AI and logic applications, but not for scientific programs.

Table 5.3. throughput performance rate of representative supercomputers.

Processor	MFLOPS	Cycle Times(ns)
Cray X-MP/4	1100	8.5
Cray-2	1800	4.1
Cyber-205	800	20.0
Hitachi S-810	630	4.5
Fujitsu VP-200	533	15.0
NEC SX-2	1300	6.0

In one class of computational problems, overhead increases with the number of processors rather than with the size of the problem. In another class of computational problems, the number of synchronization operations grows with the problem size, but more slowly. In practice, the redundancy R_p is related to the time lost because of overhead and is always larger than 1. The ratio between the total number of operations O_p executed to perform some computation with p processors and the number of operations O_s required to execute the same computation with single processor is defined as the redundancy of a parallel computation. The redundancy can be represented as R_p and is one of the important factors in a performance analysis of any parallel computations, as shown in the following:

$$R_p = \frac{O_p}{O_s}$$

5.4   Complexities

In this section we discuss the concepts related to the complexity of parallel algorithms underlying the design of efficient parallel algorithms. A program can be implemented on different architectures. The correctness of a program is independent of the target architecture and the manner in which the program is executed. In contrast, the efficiency of a program's execution depends on the architecture and the manner of execution. Thus, we adopt as the complexity of a computation the measures of efficiency that are associated with the program and with a mapping to a target architecture.

In other words, the complexity of a computation measures the space and time requirements of that computation. The time complexity is measured by the number of required execution time units, and the space complexity is measured as one unit of space for every register required for an individual computation. In serial algorithms the performance is measured in terms of time and space complexities. A serial algorithm has a complexity of $f(n)$, where n depends on the problems size. In parallel algorithms a number of additional measures of performance are often used. Generally speaking, the time complexity of a parallel algorithm cannot be determined simply by counting the number of operations involved in the computation, as is the case with serial algorithms. Instead, it depends on how these operations can be implemented on a p-processor computer architecture, where $p > 1$. Further, the complexity of a parallel algorithm is a function $f(n,p)$, of not only the problem size n, but also the parallel processor size p, where p is defined as the number of processors available. This indicates that the parallel algorithm can be constructed by dividing the n data points into P groups, each of approximately size n/P. Again, the situation varies depending on whether the number of available processors is bounded by an integer p or is unbounded, for example unlimited.

In the analysis of algorithms the basic quantities to be examined are the upper and lower bounds of the time and space complexity in which it is possible to solve a given problem by some algorithm from a given class of algorithms. The fastest known algorithm determines the upper bounds of the time and space required for the computation of a given problem. After these have been determined, there arises a question whether for the solution of this problem it is possible to find a faster algorithm or whether an algorithm with minimal complexity is known. Thus, the lower bound determines the complexity of the problem under examination; i.e. the minimum time and space needed for its solution by an arbitrary algorithm.

In general, for every problem solved on a computer, there exists a parameter *n* which is the measure of its size, such as the order of a matrix, number of elements, degree of the polynomial, number of graph vertices, and the like. In analyzing the complexity of the algorithms, it is necessary to define their complexity as a function of the parameter *n*. This indicates that we measure the complexity of an algorithm as a function of the size of the input of the algorithm. In the following we introduce the complexity of sequential and parallel computations with regard to the size of the problem under consideration.

5.4.1 Sequential Computation Complexity

The complexity measures of a program written in conventional sequential languages are the amounts of required resources such as time and space to execute the program on a conventional architecture (i.e., SISD computers). In practice, the complexity of a sequential computation is the function T(n) which is the maximum time taken by the program to execute over all inputs of size n. The expected time complexity of a sequential computation is the average of the execution times over all inputs of size n. Analogous definitions hold for space complexity and expected space complexity by substituting the word space for time in the appropriate definition. In particular, we can measure the time complexity in time units, meaning that one time unit is needed to execute each instruction, and space complexity in space units, meaning that one space unit is needed for every register required.

5.4.2 Parallel Computation Complexity

Time complexity is the most important measure of the performance of a parallel algorithm, since the primary motivation for parallel computation is to achieve a speedup in the computation. We can assume that the computation model consists of p processors only, where p > 1. This is referred to as *bounded parallelism*. In contrast, *unbounded parallelism* refers to the situation in which it is assumed that we have an unlimited number of processors. Parallel algorithms are executed by a set of processors and usually require interprocessor data transfer to complete execution successfully. As with serial complexity, we are not able to determine exact values for the parallel complexity and must settle for asymptotic results. The time complexity of a parallel algorithm to solve a problem of size n is a function T(n,p) which is the maximum time that elapses between the start of the algorithm's execution by one processor and its termination by one or more processors with regard to any arbitrary input data. There are two different kinds of operations associated with parallel algorithms:

- Elementary operations
- Data routing operations

Elementary operation is an arithmetic or logical operation performed locally by a processor. In a parallel algorithm an *elementary step* refers to the set of elementary operations which can be executed simultaneously by a set of processors, in which the time complexity of an elementary step is referred to as constant or $O(1)$. Data routing operations refer to the routing of data among processors for exchanging the information. A *data routing step* refers to the set of data routing operations which can be executed among a set of processors, which depends on the interconnection pattern used in the parallel system. The time complexity of a parallel algorithm is determined by counting both elementary steps and data routing steps. A corollary follows that the time complexity of a parallel algorithm depends on the type of computational model being used as well as on the number of processors available. Thus, when giving the time complexity of a parallel algorithm it is important to give the maximum number of processors used by the algorithm as a function of the problem size n. This new notation is referred to as the *processor complexity* of a parallel computation and is identified by $O(n)$.

In general, a parallel computation begins with the input stored in memory modules and a single active processing element. At each step of computation, the processing element may read a value from the memory locations, perform a single operation and write the generated result into one local or global memory location. Alternatively, during a computation step a processing element may activate another processing element performing the same instruction, albeit on different memory locations. Therefore, a parallel algorithm begins with a single processing element actively performing two phases. In the first phase a sufficient number of processing elements are activated, and in the second phase the activated processing elements perform the computation in parallel. Given a single active processing element, $\lceil \log p \rceil$ activation steps are sufficient for p processing elements to become active, since the number of active processes can be doubled by executing a single instruction at each step of this expansion.

For example, a serial algorithm to find the maximum number of a set of n numbers has the time complexity $O(n)$, since it requires $(n-1)$ comparisons. In contrast, a trivial parallel algorithm for the same problem has the time complexity $O(log\ n)$ and processor complexity $O(n)$. By finding the maximum of every disjoint pair of elements simultaneously, the number of elements remaining to be compared can be reduced by half at each comparison step. This guarantees that the largest number can be obtained after $\lceil \log n \rceil$ parallel steps. From a practical point of view algorithms for bounded parallelism are preferable. It is more realistic to assume that the number of processors available is limited and is no more than the problem size. Parallel algorithms for unbounded parallelism use a polynomially bounded number of processors (for example, $O(n^2)$, $O(n^3)$, and so on). This indicates that for very large problem sizes the processor requirement may become impractically large. Sometimes the unbounded parallelism reflects an undesirable situation. For example, if we assume the algorithm can use as many processors as it wants and there are no communication and memory access restrictions, the computational time cannot be reduced below a certain limit. This is due to the fact that some intermediate results must be known before other parts of the computation proceed. The unbounded parallel time complexity of a problem reflects this characteristic of a problem and is referred to as *anomalies*. If the model is message-passing, the initial distribution of data items to the processing elements is important. We can assume that in a balanced distribution each processor contains either $\lfloor n/p \rfloor$ or $\lceil n/p \rceil$ data items. For example, in a balanced distribution of an identity-size problem, each processor contains one datum.

In general, the number of processors on a real parallel architecture is limited, and algorithms for unbounded parallelism become practically useful only if they can be transformed to bounded parallel algorithms. As a consequence of the fact that a parallel algorithm that solves a given problem in $O(T)$ time with P processors yields a serial algorithm that solves the problem in time $O(TP)$, we provide three definitions:

> **Definition 1.** Any parallel algorithm of time complexity $O(T)$ with P processors must have at most $O(TP)$ elementary operations. This definition is known as Brent's theorem.
>
> **Definition 2.** Any parallel algorithm of time complexity $O(T)$ using a large number of processors that consists of $O(e)$ elementary operations can be implemented by P processors with a time complexity of $O(\lceil e/P \rceil + T)$. This definition indicates that if the number of available processors decreases within a given range, the algorithm still works but the running time increases in such a manner that the product of time and the number of processors remains the same and vice-versa.
>
> **Definition 3.** Any parallel algorithm A of time complexity $O(T)$ with P processors can be implemented by $\lceil P/p \rceil$, where $1 \le p \le P$ processors in time $O(pT)$. This definition provides a way to make algorithms adaptive when the number of available processors decreases.

Generally speaking, the time complexity for an algorithm expresses its time requirements by giving, for each possible input length, the largest amount of time needed by the algorithm to solve a problem of that size. Of course, this function is not well defined until one fixes the encoding scheme to be used for determining execution time by the computer model. Hence, in what follows, the reader is advised to keep in mind a particular encoding and computer model for each problem in terms of time complexity as determined from the corresponding input lengths and execution times.

5.5   Anomalies in Parallel Algorithms

We can observe the effect of parallelizing algorithms by performing several computations simultaneously. It is shown that it is quite possible for a parallel algorithm using n_2 processors to take more time than one using n_1 processors even though $n_1 < n_2$. This indicates that the problem actually takes longer to solve as more processor are added. Furthermore, it is also possible to achieve speedup that is in excess of the ratio $\dfrac{n_2}{n_1}$. For any given problem instance, let I(n) denote the number of iterations required when n processors are available.

Intuition suggests that the following might be true about I(n):

1. $I(n_1) \geq I(n_2)$ whenever $n_1 < n_2$

2. $\dfrac{I(n_1)}{I(n_2)} \leq \dfrac{n_2}{n_1}$

Lai and Sahni [Lai 84] claimed that neither of these two relations is valid. They considered the effects of parallelizing branch-and-bound algorithms by expanding several vertices simultaneously. In general, the graph theory is a popular algorithm design method which has been used successfully in the solution of problems that arise in various fields, such as combinatorial optimization problems and artificial intelligence applications. For instance, assume in a combinatorial optimization problem that it is required to find a vector $X = \{x_1, x_2, \ldots, x_n\}$ that optimizes some function f(n) subject to a set C of constraints. The constraints may be partitioned into two subsets as explicit and implicit subsets. Implicit constraints specify how the x_i's are related to each other. Two examples are:

$$\sum_{i=1}^{n} a_i x_i \leq B$$

$$ax^2 - axy + az^4 = 6$$

Explicit constraints specify the range of values each x_i can take; for example $x_i \in \{0,1\}$, and $x_1 \geq 0$. The set of vectors that satisfy the explicit constraints defines the solution space and can be organized as a graph, which is usually a tree. In other words, this resulting organization is called a state space graph (tree). For example, we can construct a state space graph for the case n = 3 and $x_i \in \{0,1\}$ as shown in Figure 5.3, such that the path from root to terminal vertices (leaves) determines an element of the solution space. Vertices that satisfy the implicit constraints are called feasible solutions and are associated with the solution space.

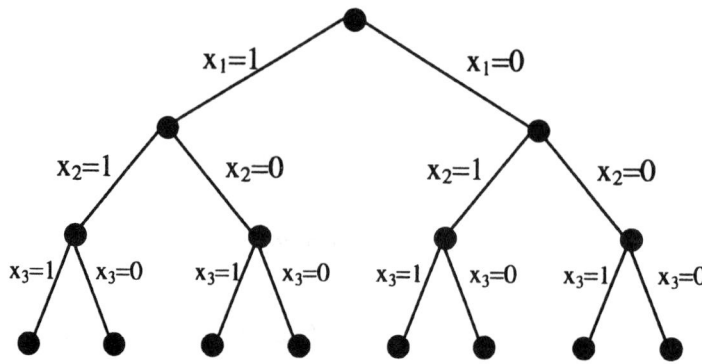

Figure 5.3. A state space tree for n = 3 and $x_i \in \{0,1\}$.

The branch-and-bound method is used in the solution of the problems associated with state space tree examinations. In this method a heuristic function $g()$
known as a bonding function is used. The branch-and-bound method generates
the vertices in a state space tree using $g()$. A list of vertices for expansion is
maintained such that in each iteration of the algorithm a vertex, N, with the least
$g()$ value is selected. If N is an answer solution, it must be a least cost value. If
N is not an answer solution, its children are generated and added to the list of
vertices for the next examination. The problem of parallelizing the branch-and-
bound method has been widely studied. For example, one of the possible
sources of parallelism is to expand more than one vertex of this state space tree
during each iteration. The number of vertices and number of processors can address this parallelism paradigm. For example, if P processors are available, then

$$k = Min\{P, \text{ number of vertices for expansion}\}$$

available vertices may be selected as the next step of expansion. If any of these
vertices is an answer, then there is a path from the root to that vertex. Otherwise,
all of k vertices are expanded and their children added to the list of candidates
for the next step of parallel computation. As remarked earlier, Lai and Sahni
claimed that several anomalies can occur when one parallelizes the branch-and-
bound algorithms using several vertices at each iteration. For example, they established that it is quite possible for a parallel branch-and-bound method using
n_2 processors to perform much worse than one using a smaller number n_1 of
processors. In order to determine the frequency of anomalies associated with
branch-and-bound, they simulated a parallel branch-and-bound with $p = 2^k$
processors for $0 \le k \le 9$. They used two test problems: the 0/1 Knapsack problem
and the Traveling Salesman problem. For example, they realized that when n =
50 (number of objects to be placed into the Knapsack), I(1) / I(p) was significantly less than p for p > 2. This indicates that the improvement in performance

was not as high as one might expect, but it does not indicate anomalous behavior. When n = 100, the ratio I(1) / I(p) was significantly less than p for p > 8, but six of the instances exhibited anomalous behavior, in which there was at least one p for which I(p) > 2I(2p).

Generally speaking, referring to the ideal model solution technique, there is some value of p such that executing the local phase, in which one processor solves a subproblem of the size (problem-size / p), takes time comparable to executing the second global phase, in which the p partial results are combined to make the final result. Thus, the time for the entire task is equal to the time for each of the two phases. At this point, the amounts of local and global work are in balance. Further increasing p will lower the time for the first phase and raise the time for the second phase, which can increase the total execution time. In summary, for some executions the parallel version provides a solution after examining more alternatives, resulting in sublinear speedups. This is referred to as *deceleration anomalies*. Execution yielding speedups greater than p by using p processors (superlinear speedup) is referred to as ***acceleration anomalies***.

As a consequence, there is little advantage to expand more than *k* vertices in parallel, where *k* depends on both the problem and the problem size being solved. If p (number of processors) is larger than *k*, then more effective use of the processors might be taken into consideration. For example, they can be divided into *k* groups, in which each group is used to expand a single vertex in parallel.

5.6   Pseudocode Conventions for Parallel Algorithms

In this section we look at how we might add the concept of parallel execution to a conventional sequential language. There are many formal models of parallel computation and there is no general consensus as to which one is best. We use the following natural convention for the parallel computation:

- Any number of processors may simultaneously read from the same memory location.
- No two processors may write simultaneously into the same memory location.

The parallelism in the algorithmic description is accomplished by the use of the following formal statements.

Syntax

The syntax for a procedure written for a parallel computation is of the following form:

> Procedure: <name> ({list of parameters})
> Model: <model name> with P = F(n) processors
> Input: <input variables>
> Output: <output variables>
> Declare: <declaration of local and global variables>

The syntax is identical to the sequential execution except for the model specification and the number of processes. We can define the syntax for a function as the following form:

> Function: <name> ({list of parameters})
> Model: <model name> with P = F(n) processors
> Input: <input variables>
> Output: <output value returned>

In the syntax the output statement describes the values returned by the function.

Parbegin and Parend Statement

The most obvious approach is to introduce an alternative to the sequential execution by introducing a semicolon. Usually blocks are bracketed by symbols such as parbegin and parend or cobegin and coend. The simple parbegin and parend model allows us to introduce the concept of concurrent processes. Each statement within the block is a separate process. If the concurrent processes use no common data they are called disjoint or independent. A simple example of this method is the program fragment below:

```
Cobegin
    Statement - 1
    Statement - 2
      .
      .
      .
    Statement - k
Coend
```

FORALL Statement

This command can be used to imitate parallel execution of code segments when there is a single statement to be performed in asynchronous or synchronous parallel execution, meaning for SIMD of MIMD parallel computation environments. The basic syntax is:

```
FORALL identifier: Range Type IN {PARALL or SYNC}
    <Statement 1>
    <Statement 2>
            .
            .
            .
    <Statement k>
END
```

where

- Identifier is a variable that becomes available inside the block code and its scope is the FORALL block. This identifier has a unique value in each of the processes that are created by FORALL statements.
- Range Type is a data type that defines a range of values and specifies the number of parallel processes created by the FORALL statement. One process is created for each value in the range type and in each process the identifier takes on the corresponding value.
- Statements are the code segments that are executed in parallel.

Example :
```
FORALL x : [1, 8] IN PARALLEL
    y = f(x) + 1;
END
```

The FORALL statement creates 8 processes with the corresponding numbers from 1 to 8, and the process P_i takes the value i for the variable x. All the 8 processes perform the computation simultaneously. The synchronization primitives, PARALL and SYNC, determine how the processes are executed with regard to the following definitions:

- PARALL primitive specifies asynchronous execution of processes, meaning MIMD parallel processing.
- SYNC primitive specifies synchronous execution of processes, meaning SIMD parallel processing.

In practice, in the synchronous case the statements are executed synchronously, where as in the asynchronous case no assumptions are made about the order of execution of the statements. An equivalent version of the FORALL statement is the following:

```
FORALL x∈X In parallel do instruction(x)
```

where x is an element of the set X and execution consists of the following two steps:
1. Assigning a processor to each element $x \in X$.
2. Executing all those operations involved in instruction(x) in parallel by the assigned processor.

The execution stops when all the processors involved complete their computation, meaning synchronous communication of this parallel processing.

In Parallel Statement

An In Parallel statement allows operations to be performed on more than one statement simultaneously; for example, on more than one component of an array. The basic syntax is:

```
For < expression involving array indices> do In Parallel
    <Statement 1>
    <Statement 2>
        . . .
    <Statement k>
End In Parallel
```

In general, the for loop involves array indices. Only those array elements whose indices satisfy the Boolean expression involve the execution of the statements in the body of the In Parallel statement. Each of these statements is performed simultaneously by a set of active processes. In this pseudocode notation, we do not specify those processors that are active. However, by convention, we need to assume that there are enough processors to perform the task. In the following example, the processors that each one is as powerful as a processor of serial machine, can read the array element and perform the required computation:

```
for i = 1  to   n   do In Parallel
    read   (A[i], B[i])
    if   A[i] > B[i]
        then   write A[i]
        else   write B[i]
    endif
end In Parallel
```

In Parallel Processor Statement

This pseudocode notation is similar to the In Parallel Statement, except that the "for loop" contains a processor index instead of an array index. For a one-dimensional mesh, the processor index is a single index, a pair of indices for a two-dimensional mesh, and a bit string in the case of the hypercube. In this sense, the active processors execute the body of the loop simultaneously while the processors, whose index does not satisfy the conditional expression, become idle. The general syntax is as follows:

```
for  <ProcessorP>,<Boolean expression involving
processor index>  do In Parallel
        <Statement 1>
        <Statement 2>
        ...
        <Statement k>
end In Parallel
```

In the following example all the processors with odd indices are idle during the execution of the body of the loop:

```
for Pi, i=1  to   n  .and.  even(i)      do In Parallel
    read   (A, B)
    if   A > B
        then    write A
        else    write B
    endif
end In Parallel
```

Par Statement

Several parallel languages offer the possibility of specifying concurrent statements, as in the Par construct:

```
Par    {
        <Statement 1>
        <Statement 2>
         .
         .
         .
        <Statement k>
        {
```

The keyword Par indicates that statements in the body are to be executed concurrently. This is instruction level parallelism. In general, in instruction level parallelism, concurrent processes could be as short as a single statement. Single statements might cause an unacceptable overhead in many systems, although the construct allows this possibility. Multiple concurrent processes or threads could be specified by listing the routines that are to be executed concurrently:

```
Par    {
          <Proc 1>
          < Proc 2>
             .
             .
             .
          < Proc k>
          {
```

Here, <Proc 1>; <Proc 2>; ... ;<Proc k>; are executed simultaneously if possible. The Par {.......} construction can be found in various parallel languages; for example, CC++ [Foster 95].

5.7   Comparison of SIMD and MIMD Algorithms

Many computational problems will naturally lend themselves to an SIMD or MIMD implementation, and another implementation may turn out to be substantially different. The only parallelism we can exploit on an SIMD algorithm, also called a synchronous algorithm, is data parallelism. This data mechanism refers to the way in which instruction operands are used. In an SIMD parallel architecture a single control unit dispatches instructions to each processor and the same instruction is executed synchronously by all processors. A drawback of this mechanism is that different processors cannot execute different instructions in the same clock cycle. The following example can address this drawback. For instance, in a conditional statement, as below, the instructions for each condition must be executed sequentially by all eligible processors:

```
if (X == Y)
     then  Sum = X + Y
     else  Sum = X - Y
```

The execution of this conditional statement can be explained in the following two steps:

1. All processors are ready to execute the instruction Sum = X + Y when the value of X variable is equal to the value of Y variable, meaning the condition is satisfied for this group of processors. These processors are called active processors in this step.

    All other processors are idle as long as the active processors in this step are executing the instruction Sum = X + Y.

2. All processors are ready to execute the instruction Sum = X - Y when the value of X variable is not equal to the value of Y variable, meaning the condition is not satisfied for this group of processors. These processors are called active processors in this step. All other processors are

idle as long as the active processors in this step are executing the instruction Sum = X − Y.

As we see, the processors that were active in the first step now become idle in the second step and the processors that were idle in the first step become active in the second step, all performing the execution in one clock cycle. In other words, some of the processors can be selectively idle during an instruction cycle. Figure 5.4 illustrates the execution of a conditional statement on an SIMD computer. Generally speaking, the most important characteristic of SIMD algorithms is that the processors are synchronized at the instruction level; that is, they execute programs in a lock-step fashion, where each processor has its own data stream, and the algorithm maintains a global address space. As a result, there is no need to have the synchronization problems associated with MIMD algorithms. In general, the number of processors is a function of the problem size rather than a function of the target machine. A corollary follows immediately after this illustration that data parallel programs in which a significant part of the program involves conditional statements are not suited to SIMD architectures.

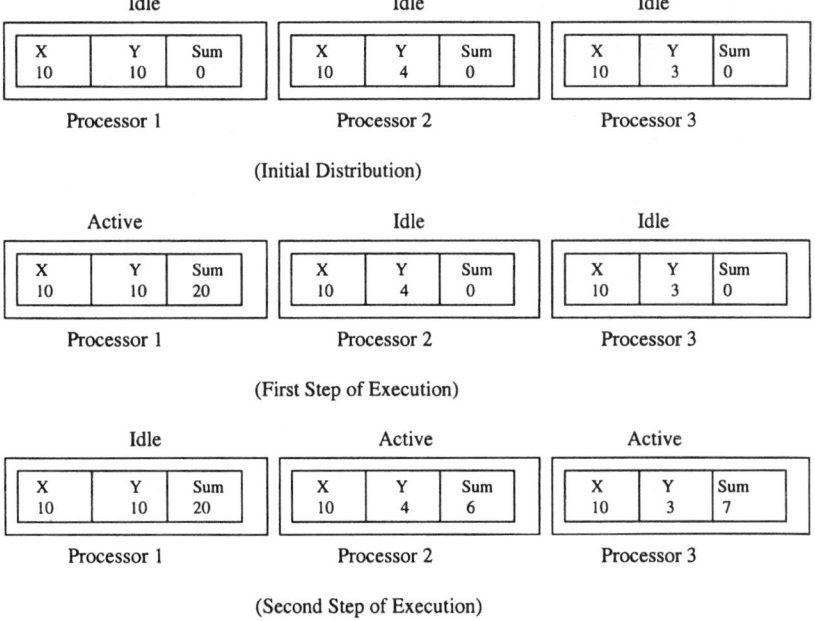

Figure 5.4. The execution sequences of a conditional statement on an SIMD computer.

SPMD algorithms, also called asynchronous algorithms, are a special class of SIMD algorithms which emphasize medium-grain parallelism and synchronization at the subprogram level rather than at the instruction level. For example, consider this simple fragment of code running on two processors at the same time:

```
if X
    then   S1
    else   S2
```

where the value of X will be determined by the particular values of data at each processor. Suppose the first processor finds X true and executes S1. Also, suppose the second processor finds X false. In an SIMD algorithm the second processor does nothing, based on the synchronization at the instruction level. In contrast, in the SPMD paradigm the second processor executes statement S2, while the first processor executes S1. In this sense, the data parallelism can be applied to asynchronous MIMD algorithms at the subprogram level. SPMD algorithms are different than SIMD algorithms, because processors are not tightly synchronized; rather they are synchronized at the beginning and end of a subprogram (procedure) or section of code that is duplicated on all processors. The processors execute asynchronously within each procedure or identical section of code, to yield a form of pseudo-SIMD operation.

MIMD algorithms, also called asynchronous algorithms, are the most general form of parallel algorithms, whereby processors operate freely on tasks, without regard for global synchronization. MIMD algorithms are best suited to large-grained problems because of the overhead in passing data and control from task to task. With regard to the various forms of synchronization, the asynchronous MIMD algorithms rely on locks and explicit control flow, meaning that synchronization is achieved explicitly and locally rather than through a global synchronization mechanism. MIMD algorithms are classified into two categories: shared-memory MIMD algorithms and distributed-memory MIMD algorithms.

The shared-memory MIMD algorithm uses a simple synchronization mechanism called *mutual exclusion*. This means the necessity of enforcing strict sequential use of a resource by competing or cooperating processes until the task is finished. This mechanism is usually implemented by a *lock* which prevents all but one access to data at any instant in time. All other accesses must wait until the mutual exclusion lock is removed by the process that originally issued the lock. The distributed-memory MIMD algorithms are much different from the shared-memory algorithms because distributed-memory processors have no global address space containing shared data. Instead, each processor has its own private address space, and processors interact by passing messages among themselves. Unlike synchronization in asynchronous shared-memory algorithms, the synchronization is a byproduct of message passing, in which a processor sends a message to all processors to inform them about the action that must be performed. This indicates that in MIMD algorithms we can look for ways to exploit both data parallelism and control parallelism.

A synchronization mechanism is classified as either a shared-variable or a message-passing mechanism, in which the shared-variable mechanism is involved in the execution of SPMD algorithms and shared-memory MIMD algorithms to make the communication among the processors possible. Message-passing synchronization mechanism is involved in the distributed-memory MIMD algorithms. The synchronization schemes can be divided into *access control* (semaphore and monitor) and *sequence control* (barrier). In the following we describe semaphore and barrier as two synchronization primitives. The first synchronization scheme is referred to as the **Semaphore** variable, in which the instruction steps required to perform the synchronization are:

- Check a semaphore
- Suspend a process
- Awaken a suspended process

We attach a single semaphore variable to each shared-memory location and each time step. When a processor attempts to read the data that are needed for a given computation step, it checks the semaphore variable for that data item at the required time step and issues a **Wait** operation on the corresponding semaphore variable. When a processor completes a computation in the given time step, it performs a **Signal** operation on the corresponding semaphore variable, meaning that the shared data have been released. Generally speaking, entrance to and exit from the critical region (the region in which shared data are accessed) are controlled by a semaphore variable. The synchronization primitives Wait and Signal based on the semaphore variable S are defined as:

Wait(S)
> If $S = 0$, then process invoking Wait is delayed until $S > 0$. If $S > 0$, then $S = S - 1$, and the process invoking Wait enters critical section.

Signal(S)
> $S = S + 1$, meaning that S is initialized to 1.

The following pseudocode shows the use of Wait and Signal to synchronize processors P_1 and P_2.

```
P₁: Wait(S)
    {Critical Section}
    Signal(S)

P₂: Wait(S)
    {Critical Section}
    Signal(S)
```

Monitor is another common choice as a shared-variable synchronization concept. The abstraction exhibited in the monitor concept makes it a suitable model for a data object and resource sharing. The **Barrier** primitive ensures data dependencies among cooperating processes. All the processes that synchronize at the barrier must reach the barrier before any of them can continue. In other words, the processes must wait for the slowest process to reach the barrier before continuing. There are a queue and a counter associated with a barrier primitive, in which the queue holds the processes and the counter keeps track of the number of processes in the queue. For example, consider the following subprogram implemented on a shared-memory MIMD algorithm:

```
For    I = 1 to N do
       {
       S₁: A = A + 5;
       S₂: B = B + 5;
       S₃: C = A + B;
       }
```

Assume this subprogram is divided into 3 processes, in which each process takes care of one statement of each iteration of the for loop in a parallel processing environment. Also, suppose the algorithm requires that the results of all iterations of S_1 and S_2 (in this case N) are needed in the execution of S_3 for the calculation of C. This indicates that S_3 in each iteration must be executed after S_1 and S_2 in each iteration. On account of the nature of MIMD algorithms, nothing can be predicted about the order of the statements on various processors. For instance, S_3 may be executed before S_1 or S_2 in each iteration. In other words, in MIMD algorithms, it is possible to ensure this order if and only if all the processes execute their statements S_1 and S_2 before any process starts statement S_3. The safety of the execution can be ensured by the inclusion of a BARRIER primitive after statement S_2 in the algorithm, as shown below:

```
For    I = 1 to N do
       {
       S₁: A = A + 5;
       S₂: B = B + 5;
       BARRIER(2);
       S₃: C = A + B;
       }
```

The **BARRIER(N)** primitive can be illustrated as:

```
{
Counter = Counter + 1;
If     (Counter < N)       then
       {place the process in BARRIER queue}
else
       {resume all processes and reset the Counter}
}
```

A **Monitor** is a concurrency primitive that contains both the data and procedures needed to perform allocation of a particular reusable shared resource or a group of reusable shared resources. The notion of a monitor was suggested by Dijkstra, then by Hansen, and then refined by Hoare [Goscinski 91]. To accomplish a resource allocation, a process must call a particular monitor entry. Because mutual exclusion is enforced at the monitor boundary, only one process at a time is allowed to enter. A process desiring to enter the monitor when it is in use must wait. This waiting period is automatically managed by the monitor. Since mutual exclusion is guaranteed by the monitor structure, the concurrency problems are avoided. The notion of a *conditional variable* is introduced in **Wait** and **Signal** operations as: Wait(Condition-Variable-Name) and Signal(Condition-Variable-Name).

In general, when a conditional variable is defined, a queue is established, in which a process calling wait is suspended and appended into the queue, and a process calling signal causes a waiting process to be removed from the associated queue and to enter the monitor. A simple monitor for handling the assignment and deassignment of resources can be constructed as follows:

```
Monitor  Resource-Allocator
Var   Resource-in-use: Boolean;
   Resource-is-free: Condition;
Procedure   Get-Resource
   begin
      if Resource-in-use   then
         Wait(Resource-is-free)
      Resource-in-use = True
   end
Procedure   Release-Resource
   begin
      Resource-in-use = False
      Signal(Resource-is-free)
   end
   begin
      Resource-in-use = False
   end
End Monitor
```

Other synchronization mechanisms used for access and sequence control are: Test-and-set, Fetch-and-add and Compare-and-swap. Asynchronous synchronization can also be implemented via the message-passing mechanism used for distributed-memory MIMD algorithms. In this method, the processes send and receive messages to each other. The synchronization can be accomplished because the received message can address the actions to be performed.

Generally speaking, the following steps can be applied to convert an algorithm from the SIMD to the MIMD form:

1. Trace the algorithm to generate understanding.
2. Locate the critical synchronization points.
3. Eliminate recursions, if any.
4. Draw a communication diagram.
5. Focus on the SIMD algorithm from the viewpoint of an MIMD computer with a single processor.
6. Rewrite the algorithm using communication and synchronization schemes.

After this conversion, it is possible to execute an SIMD algorithm on an MIMD computer with n processors using synchronization primitives.

Summary

In general, an efficient algorithm for an SISD system is not efficient on parallel systems. New algorithms and corresponding specialized programming languages are required to efficiently utilize the computational power offered by parallel computers. The wide variety of parallel architectures available presents the fundamental problem of determining the portability of an algorithm written for a specific architecture. The PRAM model is a natural extension of the sequential model of computation, RAM. This makes the PRAM model conceptually easy to work with when developing parallel algorithms. Furthermore, algorithms developed for the PRAM model can be translated into algorithms for many of the more practical computers. As a consequence, the PRAM model serves as a good introduction to parallel algorithms. We introduced the principles of parallel algorithm design which are commonly used for the design of efficient parallel algorithms. We discussed several principles: the Brent scheduling principle, the pipeline principle, the divide-and-conquer principle, the dependency graph principle, and the race condition principle.

Efficiency in parallel processing comes both from the performance of computer architectures and from communication between parallel processors. The problem of gaining an understanding of the relationship between algorithms and architectures is a critical one. Toward this end, we discussed the design approaches of parallel algorithms and architecture-dependent algorithms. The model allows us to specify the point at which architectural considerations enter into the algorithm design process, and therefore allows us to trace the relationship between parallel algorithm characteristics and architecture features that support these characteristics. For example, we can parallelize the existing sequential algorithms, design a completely new parallel algorithm or design a new parallel algorithm from the existing parallel algorithm. We summarized the relationship between parallel architectures and algorithms to address the important criteria of the algorithm design.

We detailed the design features that are intended to specify the machine-independent issues such as concurrency and decomposition and the machine aspects of design such as communication cost and number of processors. There are four distinct phases in the design process: partitioning, communication, agglomeration, and mapping. Generally speaking, the central idea of these issues involved in the design process is to target a design with the general attributes of data parallelism, functional parallelism, module granularity, data granularity, degree of parallelism, synchronization, data dependencies, and process generation and termination.

We described different important measures of the quality of a particular parallel algorithm implementation, including speedup, efficiency, cost, utilization, execution rate and redundancy. These desirable attributes refer to the performance, complexity, and modularity of the parallel algorithms. These topics are necessarily brief. Interested readers may refer to the books listed as references for further details.

We discussed our performance models and conducted simple experiments to determine unknown parameters such as performance measures. In these systems, processors act independently, either sharing a common memory or with their own local memory. In either case performance can be improved over that of a single processor system. The refined models can be used to increase our confidence in the quality of our design before implementation. Amdahl's law expresses maximum speedup as a function of the inherently sequential component and the number of processors executing a parallel algorithm. This indicates that Amdahl's law assumes that parallel processing is used to reduce the time needed to solve a problem of a fixed size. However, parallel computers are often useful to increase the size of a problem that can be solved in a fixed amount of time. Gustafson's law introduced a solution for a class of problems whose execution time increases with the size of the instance under consideration. The law proved to be adapted to distributed-memory architectures, and high performance was achieved with the problems associated with these architectures. In general, an important issue is that as the size of the problem increases, inherently the sequential operations constitute a smaller fraction of the total computation, making the problem more applicable to parallelization.

The speedup factor of a parallel computation utilizing p processors can be derived as $S_p = T_s / T_p$, where T_s is the execution time taken to perform the computation on one processor and T_p is the execution time needed to perform the same computation using p processors. The speedup factor is normally less than the number of processors, meaning that $1 \leq S_p \leq P$. It is worth noting that a speedup factor greater than P is possible only if each processor spends less than T_s / P time solving the problem. The efficiency of a parallel computation can be defined as $E_p = S_p / P$, which is the ratio between the speedup factor and the number of processing elements.

Many of the factors associated with processor design are modified or controlled by the question of cost effectiveness. The cost of solving a problem on a parallel system is defined as the product of parallel computation time and the number of processors used, $C_p=P*T_p$. While it is relatively easy to estimate the costs associated with a particular implementation, the other side of the equation, performance, is a much more difficult problem. We explained different measures for execution rate: millions of instructions per second, millions of operations per second, millions of logic inferences per second, and millions of floating point operations per second.

Generally speaking, the performance measures and analysis of algorithm design depend on the load balancing. Applications must be analyzed to make sure that the work load is divided evenly among parallel processors to address efficiency with regard to the performance measures and analysis. As a consequence of load balancing, data parallel algorithms are more scalable than control parallel algorithms, because the level of control parallelism is usually a constant, independent of the problem size, whereas the level of data parallelism is an increasing function of the problem size.

We introduced the complexity of sequential and parallel computations with regard to time and space requirements. Wyllie [Wyllie 79] has studied the effect of complexity on the performance of parallel systems. We claimed that it is quite possible for a parallel algorithm using P number of processors to take more computation time than one algorithm using Q number of processors where Q < P. This is called an anomaly in parallel algorithms. We outlined several pseudocode conventions for parallel algorithms in which the concept of parallel execution can be added to a conventional sequential algorithm. We discussed Parbegin and Parend, Forall, In Parallel, and Par structures as the prototypes of the pseudocode conventions for parallel algorithms. Finally we compared the SIMD and MIMD algorithms with regard to data and control parallelism. We claimed that the only parallelism we can exploit in SIMD architectures is data parallelism, in contrast to MIMD architectures, in which we can look for ways to exploit both data and control parallelism. As a conclusion to this section, it seems intuitively likely that a data parallel solution should be sought first and a control parallel implementation considered next.

Many aspects of sequential algorithm designs are presented in [Sedgewick 88 and 96, Cormen 97, Neopolitan 98, Drozdek 96, Berman 96, Standish 94].

Many aspects of the parallel algorithms are discussed in the books by [Leighton 92] and [JaJa 92]. For further reading on parallelism for graph algorithms refer to [Quinn 84]. An edited book by Jamieson, Gannon and Douglass [Jamieson 87] contains a wealth of information on the characteristics of parallel algorithms. Jeong and Lee [Jeong 90] have discussed the parallel algorithms on mesh connected computers. A number of particular application areas can be identified in which many problems suitable for the application of parallel computing are to be found. These areas include image processing, mathematical modeling, scientific computation and artificial intelligence.

Exercises

1. Define the following terms:

Complexity of a problem	Efficiency
Bounded parallelism	Anomalies in parallel processing
Unbounded parallelism	Time complexity
Speedup factor	Utilization
Amdahl's law	Gustafson's law
Synchronization primitives	Semaphore
Execution rate	Degree of parallelism
Mutual exclusion	Monitor

2. Explain the relationship between the computing speed and physical size of a serial computer. Is this relationship likely to hold for a parallel system?

3. Design a parallel algorithm to compute

    $$F(x) = x^{32} + x^{16} + x^8 + x^4 + x^2 + x^1$$

    (a) Express your algorithm as a computational graph.
    (b) Express the speedup of your parallel algorithm over the sequential algorithm.

4. Consider element by element the addition of two N-element vectors A and B to create the sum vector C; that is

    $$C[i] = A[i] + B[i] \qquad 1 \leq i \leq N$$

    This computation requires N add times plus the loop control overhead on an SISD system. Show the SIMD implementation of this computation using N processing elements. Specify the throughput enhancement over the SISD system.

5. Consider the calculation of one root of a quadratic equation as follows:

    $$X = (-b + (b ** 2 - 4 * a * c) ** .5) / (2 * a)$$

    This assignment might be evaluated on a sequential processor as follows:

    ```
    1   b ** 2
    2   4 * a
    3   (4 * a) * c
    4   (b ** 2) - (4 * a * c)
    5   (b ** 2 - 4 * a * c) ** .5
    6   -b
    7   (-b) + ( ( b ** 2 - 4 * a * c) ** .5 )
    8   2 * a
    9   (-b + ( b ** 2 - 4 * a * c) ** .5) / (2 * a)
    ```

Here, each of the nine operations is executed one at a time in a sequence determined by the system. Write a high-level program for a system that supports parallel processing using parbegin and parend primitives. Hint: four operations can be evaluated in parallel.

6. Consider the following computation:

$$X_i = A_i * B_i + C_i * D_i \qquad \text{for} \qquad 1 \le i \le N$$

Write a high-level program for this computation using
(a) FORALL Primitive
(b) Parbegin/Parend Primitives
(c) In Parallel Primitive

7. Consider the program segment depicted by the following flowchart which has a conditional branch and is executing on an SISD system. Convert the branch operation into a sequential operation and depict the execution of the program for an SIMD system.

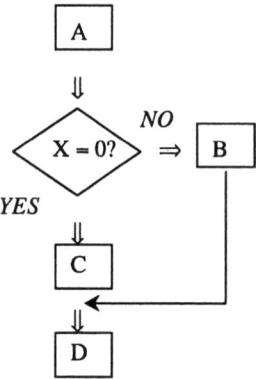

8. Consider the matrix multiplication algorithm for an SISD system depicted by the following program.

```
For   k = 1 to N
    For   i = 1 to N
        C[i,k] = 0
        For   j = 1 to N
            C[i,k] = C[i,k]+A[i,j] * B[j,k]
        Endfor
    Endfor
Endfor
```

To implement the algorithm on an SIMD system, one attempt would be to store A by column and B by row, so that the appropriate row and column could be accessed simultaneously. This allows the generation of the N products simultaneously. Assume matrices A and B are stored by column. Implement the algorithm for an SIMD computation.

9. Estimate the time needed to perform the multiplication of two (N × N) matrices on an (N × N) systolic array.
   Rewrite the following parallel computation as a simple sequence of calculations.

   ```
   A = B+ C
       Parbegin
           D = B * C - X
           E = A/6 + N ** 2
       Parend
   ```

10. Describe in detail w hat happens if the following incorrect program is written to ensure mutual exclusion.

    ```
    P(MUTEX)
        CRITICAL SECTION
    P(MUTEX)
    ```

11. Assuming that (1 / N)th of the time to execute an algorithm involves operations that must be performed sequentially, prove that an upper limit on the speedup achievable by executing the algorithm on a parallel system is N.

12. Is it possible for the average speedup exhibited by a parallel algorithm to be superlinear? Why?

13. Design an algorithm for finding the Sum of N integers on a $\sqrt{N} \times \sqrt{N}$ mesh with the property that, at the end of the computation, every processing element contains the sum.

14. Given a 2-D mesh SIMD model with wraparound connections, devise an algorithm that uses N^2 processors to multiply two N × N arrays in O(N) time.

15. Given a particular branch-and-bound problem to be solved and a particular lower bounding function g, define I(P) to be the number of iterations required to find a solution node where P processors are involved. Prove that increasing the number of processors can increase the number of iterations required to find a solution. What problem does this refer to?

16. Given A as a parallel algorithm with computation time T, if parallel algorithm A performs M computational operations, prove that P processors can execute algorithm A in time T + (M − T) / P.

17. Devise an algorithm to implement a binary semaphore expressed by means of the monitor.

18. The Dot Product of $A = (a_1, a_2, \ldots, a_n)$ and $B = (b_1, b_2, \ldots, b_n)$ is defined by

$$A \circ B = a_1 b_1 + a_2 b_2 + \ldots + a_n b_n$$

Develop an algorithm for this problem and implement it on a two-dimensional mesh system.

19. Consider the following example involving an if-then-else statement for an SIMD system. Adopt the corresponding version of this example for an MIMD system.

For $1 \leq i \leq 10$ do   in parallel
     $A[i] = 2 * A[i]$
End in parallel

For $11 \leq i \leq N$ do   in parallel
     $A[i] = A[i] + 1$
End in parallel

20. Let P_1 and P_2 be two fragments of an algorithm and let T_1 and T_2 be the times taken by P_1 and P_2, respectively. The sequence rule says that the time required to compute "$P_1;P_2$" that is first P_1 and then P_2, is simply $T_1 + T_2$. Consider the following segment and analyze the time taken by the loop.

$I \Leftarrow 1$
While $I \leq M$ do
     $P(I)$
     $I \Leftarrow I + 1$

21. To illustrate a race condition, consider the following two pieces of code written in an imperative language:

$X = 2$	$X = 107$
$X = X + 13$	$X = X + 1381$
Print X	Print X

Now consider the effects of running the code fragments in parallel processors. If we assume that the two processes share X, how many different pairs of values can appear?

22. Consider the problem of exhaustively generating all the permutations of n things. Suppose $A[1..n]$ contains n distinct values. The following algorithm generates all the permutations of $A[1..n]$ in the following sense: A call to procedure Permute(n) will result in procedure process(A) being called once, with $A[1..n]$ containing each permutation of its content:

Procedure   Permute(n)
     if   n = 1   then   process(A)
                        else   B = A
                                Permute(n − 1)
                    for   i = 1 to n − 1 do
                                swap A[n] with A[1]

Permute(n − 1)

A = {B cyclically shifted one place right}

What is the worst-case complexity of this algorithm?

23. For the following loop:

Do   10   I = 1 + ID, N, Processes

{WORK}

10   Continue

What is the ideal speed if Processes = 10 and N = 10, 20, and 100?

What about $N = 9$, 19, and 109?

What about $N = 11$, 21, and 101?

24. Consider the following parallel code. Specify the action of an In Parallel statement for sample arrays.

For   I = 1 to (2K − 1) .and. Odd(I) do In Parallel

A[I] = A[I] + B[i]

B[I] = 2 ∗ B[I]

If   I Mod 4 = 3   then

B[I] = B[I] − 6

Endif

End In Parallel

A = {23, 2, 108, 7, 55, 1, 2, 0, 17, 6},

B = {55, 300, 123, 11, 0, 1, 2, 0, 19, 99}.

25. Specify the action of the following parallel code for the sample arrays

For   PI, I = 1 to (2K − 1) .and. Odd(I)   do In Parallel

A = A + B

B = 2 ∗B

If   I mod 4 = 3   then

B = B − 6

Endif

End In Parallel

A={23, 2, 108, 7, 55, 1, 2, 0, 17, 6},

B={55, 300, 123, 11, 0, 1, 2, 0, 19, 99}.

Reference-Needed Exercises

26. Consider a family of parallel computers that implements both scalar and vector operations. Plot the speed ratios of two computers with vector accelerators as a function of the percent of vectorization. One vector accelerator performs vector operations 4 times faster than scalar operations and the other 20 times faster.

27. Design a benchmark program to address the anomalies in parallel processing. Your benchmark should document the machine's slowdown as more and more processors are used to solve the test program. In other words, for n > 2 the solution time for n processors is greater than for n1 processors.

CHAPTER 6
Parallel Graph Algorithms

One area in which a great deal of work has been done in the development of parallel algorithms is that of graph algorithms. An undirected graph G is a pair of (V,E), where V is a finite set of points called vertices and E is a finite set of arcs called edges. An edge $e \in E$ is an unordered pair (v,u) where $v, u \in V$ and vertices v and u are connected. Similarly, a directed graph G is a pair of (V,E) where V is a finite set of points called vertices and $e = (v,u) \in E$ is an ordered pair of vertices, meaning that there is a connection from v to u. Throughout this chapter the term graph refer to both directed and undirected graphs. Figure 6.1 illustrates a directed and an undirected graph. Many definitions are common to directed and undirected graphs, and in the following some of these definitions are presented. In addition, there are many introductory texts, for example [Sahni 85], which may be consulted.

Definitions

- If (v,u) is an edge in an undirected graph, then (v,u) is **incident on** vertices v and u.
- If (v,u) is an edge in a directed graph, then (v,u) is **incident from** vertex v and **incident to** vertex u.

For example, in Figure 6.1 (a), edge e_1 is incident from vertex 1 and incident to vertex 4, but in Figure 6.1 (b), edge e_2 is incident on vertices 1 and 4.

- If $(v,u) \in E$ is an edge in an undirected graph G, then v and u are said to be adjacent, and if the graph is directed, then vertex v is said to be adjacent to vertex u.
- A path in graph G from vertex v_1 can be defined as a sequence of vertices $\{v_1, v_2, \ldots, v_k\}$ such that $(v_i, v_{i+1}) \in E$ for all $1 \leq i \leq k$.
- A cycle is a path in which the start vertex and the end vertex are the same, and a graph with no cycle is called an acyclic graph.
- A simple cycle in a graph is a cycle in which no vertex occurs more than once in the cycle.

For example, in Figure 6.1 (a) there is a path from vertex 1 to vertex 4 shown as $\{1,3,5,4\}$, and there is a directed simple cycle shown as $\{2,5,4,3,2\}$.

- An undirected graph G is connected if every pair of vertices is connected by a path.
- A graph G' = (V',E') is a subgraph of graph G = (V,E) if V'⊆V and E'⊆E.
- A complete graph is a graph such that each pair of vertices is adjacent.
- A tree is a connected acyclic graph in which $|E| = |V| - 1$, and a forest is an acyclic graph.

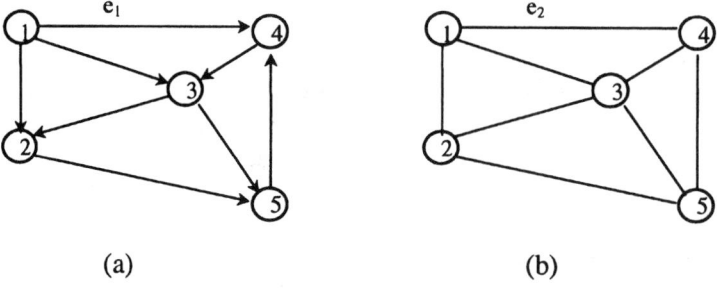

(a)   (b)

Figure 6.1. (a) A directed graph. (b) An undirected graph.

The following statements about a graph G are equivalent:

- G is a tree.
- G is connected with n vertices and n – 1 edges.
- G has n vertices, n – 1 edges, and no cycles.
- G is such that each pair of vertices is connected by a unique chain.

Sometimes a weight can be associated with each edge in E of the graph G = (V,E). These are real numbers representing the measure of performance of that associated edge, i.e., the cost or benefit of traversing that edge.

- A graph with the associated weight of each edge is called a weighted graph and can be represented as G = (V,E,W), where W:E ⟹ R is a real-valued function defined on E, and V and E are defined as before. The weight of the graph is defined as the total of the weights of its edges. Similarly, the weight of a path is the sum of the weights of its edges.

Representing a graph in an algorithm may be accomplished via two different methods: adjacency matrix and linked lists.

- Consider a graph with n vertices that are numbered 1,2,...,n. The adjacency matrix of this graph can be defined as an n × n matrix A = (a_{ij}) with the following properties:

$$a_{ij} = \begin{cases} 1 & if\,(v_i, v_j) \in E \\ 0 & otherwise. \end{cases}$$

Figure 6.2 (a) represents the adjacency matrix of the directed graph 6.1 (a) and Figure 6.2 (b) represents the adjacency matrix of the undirected graph 6.1 (b).

- A graph G = (V,E) can be represented with an adjacency list consisting of an array Adjacency[1...|V|] of lists. For each vertex v∈ V a linked list called Adjacency[v] can be defined with all vertices containing an edge (v,u)∈ E, meaning that the Adjacency[v] is a list of all vertices adjacent to v.

$$A = \begin{bmatrix} 0 1 1 1 0 \\ 0 0 0 0 1 \\ 0 1 0 0 1 \\ 0 0 1 0 0 \\ 0 0 0 1 0 \end{bmatrix} \qquad A = \begin{bmatrix} 0 1 1 1 0 \\ 1 0 1 0 1 \\ 1 1 0 1 1 \\ 1 0 1 0 1 \\ 0 1 1 1 0 \end{bmatrix}$$

(a)   (b)

Figure 6.2. (a) Adjacency matrix of the directed graph 6.1 (b) Adjacency matrix of the undirected graph 6.1 (b).

Figure 6.3 (b) illustrates the adjacency list representation of the graph 6.3 (a), which is a directed graph.

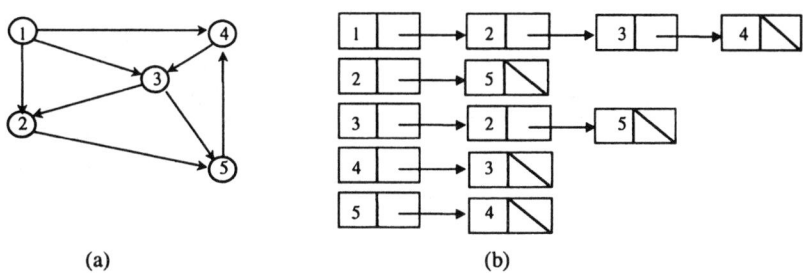

(a)   (b)

Figure 6.3. (a) A directed graph. (b) Adjacency list of the graph.

It is worth noting that the last member of each adjacency list points to the NULL, indicating the end of that adjacency list. If G is a weighted graph, the weight matrix of G is defined by

$$w_{ij} = \begin{cases} 0 & if \ \ i = j \\ w(i,j) & if \ \ there \ is \ an \ edge \ from \ vertex \ i \ to \ vertex \ j \\ \infty & otherwise \end{cases}$$

where w(i,j) is the weight of the edge connecting vertices i and j, if this edge exists. Note that the diagonal element of this matrix is 0.

- The connectivity matrix of a directed or undirected graph G with n vertices is an n × n matrix C with the following properties for the elements of matrix C:

$$C = \begin{cases} 1 & if \ there \ is \ a \ path \ of \ length \ 0 \ or \ more \ from \\ & v_j \ to \ v_k \ such \ that \ no \ vertex \ appears \ more \ than \ once \\ 0 & otherwise \end{cases}$$

where $0 \le j,k \le n - 1$. Here the length of the path is defined as the number of edges on the path. A path of length 0 begins and ends at a vertex without using any edges, whereas a path of length 1 consists of one edge. The matrix C is also known as the reflexive or transitive closure matrix of the graph G.

- A bipartite graph is a graph G = (V,E) for which it is possible to partition the vertices into two subsets V_1 and V_2, where $V_1 \cup V_2 = V$ and $V_1 \cap V_2 = \emptyset$, such that there is no edge with both endpoints in V_1 or both endpoints in V_2.

In practice, the nature of the graph determines which representation should be used. This chapter examines a number of parallel algorithms developed to solve problems in graph theory. These problems relate to searching graphs and finding connected components: minimum spanning trees, shortest paths in graphs, cycles in graphs, and traveling salesman problem utilizing the defined definitions.

6.1   Connected Components

Let G = (V, E) be an undirected graph such that V is the set of vertices and E is the set of edges of the graph as shown in Figure 6.4(a). This graph is represented by an n × n adjacency matrix A whose entries a_{ij}, $0 \le i,j \le n - 1$ are defined as follows and which is shown in Figure 6.4 (b):

$$a_{ij} = \begin{cases} 1 & \textit{if } v_i \textit{ is connected to } v_j \\ 0 & \textit{otherwise} \end{cases}$$

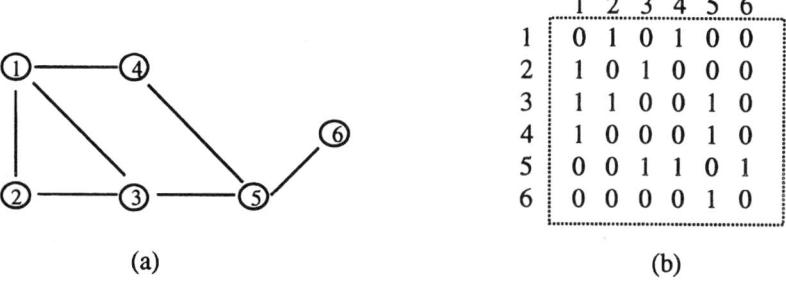

(a)   (b)

Figure 6.4. (a) An undirected graph. (b) Its adjacency matrix.

Since this graph is undirected, the adjacency matrix is symmetric. A subgraph $G' = (V', E')$ of G is connected if there is a path between every pair of its vertices where $V' \subseteq V$ is the set of vertices and $E' \subseteq E$ is the set of edges. A connected component of an undirected graph in G is a connected subgraph G^* of G of maximum size, meaning the maximal disjoint sets $C_1, C_2, \ldots, C_k$ such that $V = C_1 \cup C_2 \cup \ldots \cup C_k$ and $(u,v) \in C_i$ if and only if u is reachable from v and v is reachable from u. Figure 6.5 shows graphs G_1 and G_2 with connected components G'_1 and G'_2 respectively. We are interested in identifying the connected components of G. This problem occupies a central place in the parallel computation of algorithmic graph theory.

There are three approaches to find the connected components of an undirected graph. The first approach uses some form of search, such as depth-first or breadth-first search methods. The second approach finds the transitive closure of the graph using the adjacency matrix of graph. The third approach separates vertices into larger and larger sets of vertices until each set corresponds to a single subgraph component. In a sequential computation the problem may be solved by a search method and labeling approach. The search method, depth first or breadth first, begins at an arbitrary vertex $v \in V$ of G. All vertices that can be reached from v are given label v to identify them as connected components of v. When no more vertices can be reached from v, a new search begins from an unlabeled vertex w, and all vertices that can be reached from w are given the label w. This continues until all connected components are found. Assuming $|V| = n$ and $|E| = m$, the number of vertices and edges of graph G, respectively, the required computation time of sequentially computing connected components is O(n + m).

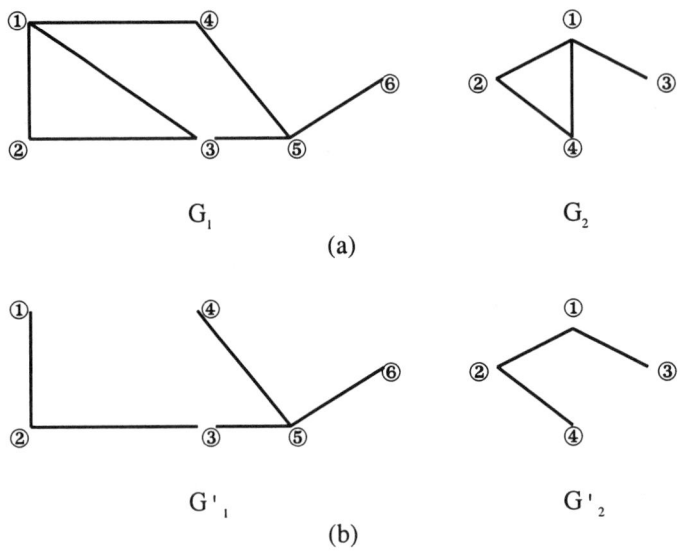

Figure 6.5. Graphs and connected components. (a) Two graphs G_1 and G_2. (b) Two connected components of G_1 and G_2, as G'_1 and G'_2.

There are four approaches to compute the connected components of a graph in parallel form:
1. Pointer-jumping method utilizing one form of the search methods.
2. Transitive closure method utilizing the adjacency matrix of the graph.
3. Supervertex method, which collapses vertices into larger and larger sets of vertices until each set corresponds to a single connected component.
4. Adjacency matrix partitioning method, in which the graph is partitioned into subgraphs and each subgraph is assigned to one processor.

Pointer-Jumping Method

This method is based on building rooted directed trees from the vertices of G such that each vertex points to its parent in the rooted tree. The pointer-jumping algorithm is an efficient method of determining the root vertex of the tree containing a given vertex in a forest of trees implemented with parent pointers. At any time during execution of the algorithm, all the vertices in a rooted tree belong to a connected component of G. Initially, the algorithm begins with the set of vertices V such that each vertex $v \in$ V represents a separate tree and maintains a pointer parent[v] to a parent. Initially parent[v] = v, meaning that vertex points to itself with no children. These trees are then merged to form larger trees and the process is repeated several times until the trees can no longer be merged. At this point, the vertices in each tree represent one connected component of G, and for any two vertices u, $v \in$ V, we have parent[v] = parent[u] if and only if $u \Rightarrow v$ in G. Generally, the pointer-jumping method is used after each merge to reduce the depth of the trees, and at the termination of the algorithm each tree has depth 1 and all of its vertices point to the root.

The algorithm assumes that each edge $(u,v) \in$ E appears twice in the tree, as (u,v) and (v,u), and works as follows. There is a rooted tree G with n vertices. We denote the vertices by 1,2,…,n, and for a given vertex v in the tree, R[v] denotes the root of the tree containing the vertex v, v = 1,2,…,n. R[1:n] is an array such that R[v] is the root of the tree G containing v, v = 1,2,…,n, and we are interested in forming this array. The following pseudocode presents the sequential pointer-jumping algorithm in which for any particular vertex v in G (it can be also called forest F) we follow the path up the tree from v to form R[v].

Algorithm: Pointer-Jumping(G)

```
for each v between 1 and n
    current_vertex = v
    while    current_vertex ≠ parent[current_vertex] do
                current_vertex = parent[current_vertex]
    endwhile
R[v] = current_vertex
endfor
```

In general, when G consists of a single tree and the tree is a path with v as a leaf, then the algorithm performs n assignments. As we can see, the algorithm repeats this process for each vertex in G between 1 and n to compute R[1:n]. Thus, the overall worst-case time complexity of the algorithm is $O(n^2)$. The pseudocode of the parallel algorithm is illustrated as follows. At each step the number of levels is doubled until the root is reached. The algorithm uses two basic operations, LINK and JUMP, such that it performs an initial LINK and then performs LINK, JUMP, LINK, JUMP and so on, until no pointer is changed by a JUMP operation. The parallel algorithm computes the array R[1:n] on the CREW PRAM model of computation.

Algorithm: Connected Components(G)
LINK

```
for each edge (u,v) ∈ E(G) do in parallel
    if        parent[u] > parent[v] then
                parent[parent[u]] = parent[v]
end inparallel
```

```
            for each edge (u,v)∈ E(G) do in parallel
                if      parent[u] ≠ parent[v] then
                        parent[parent[u]] = parent[v]
            end inparallel
            JUMP
            for each vertex v∈ V(G) do in parallel
                        parent[v] = parent[parent[v]]
            end inparallel
            R[v] = parent[v]
```

The key idea in the design of a parallel algorithm is based on the notion of the pointer-jumping method. The jumping is accomplished by replacing parent[v] with parent[parent[v]] exactly n times. Once we reach a root vertex we remain at the root R[v].

Transitive Closure Method

The key structure in this method is the computation of the connectivity matrix of the graph. The approach is boolean matrix multiplication utilizing the following properties:

- The matrix to be multiplied is binary, each entry is either 0 or 1
- The Boolean "and" operation is used; that is,

$$0 \text{ and } 0 = 0$$
$$0 \text{ and } 1 = 0$$
$$1 \text{ and } 0 = 0$$
$$1 \text{ and } 1 = 1$$

- The boolean "or" operation is used; that is,

$$0 \text{ or } 0 = 0$$
$$0 \text{ or } 1 = 1$$
$$1 \text{ or } 0 = 1$$
$$1 \text{ or } 1 = 1$$

Assume X and Y are $n \times n$ boolean matrices. Then Z can be defined as the boolean product of X and Y such that:

$$Z_{ij} = (x_{i1} \text{ and } y_{1j}) \text{ or } (x_{i2} \text{ and } y_{2j}) \text{ or } \ldots \text{ or } (x_{in} \text{ and } y_{nj})$$

where $i,j = 0,1,\ldots,n-1$ and Z is an $n \times n$ boolean matrix. The first step for the computation of the connectivity matrix C is to obtain an $n \times n$ matrix B from A as follows:

$$b_{jk} = \begin{cases} a_{jk} & \text{if } j \neq k \\ 0 & \text{otherwise} \end{cases}$$

where $j,k = 0,1,\ldots,n - 1$. This indicates that matrix B is the augmented matrix A with 1's as the diagonal elements, meaning $b_{jj} = 1$ for all j. Thus, matrix B represents

$$b_{jk} = \begin{cases} 1 & \text{if there is a path of length 0 or 1 from } v_j \text{ to} \\ & v_k \text{ in which no vertex appears more than once} \\ 0 & \text{otherwise} \end{cases}$$

We use the boolean product of B to obtain the connectivity matrix C. The matrix B^2, the boolean product of B with itself, represents all the paths of length 2 or less.

$$\begin{bmatrix} 1 & 0 \\ 1 & 1 \end{bmatrix} \quad \times \quad \begin{bmatrix} 1 & 0 \\ 1 & 1 \end{bmatrix} \quad = \quad \begin{bmatrix} 1 & 0 \\ 1 & 1 \end{bmatrix}$$

$$\text{B} \qquad\qquad \text{B} \qquad\qquad \text{B}^2$$

Figure 6.6. Computation of matrix B^2 from B.

For example, Figure 6.6 illustrates the computation of matrix B^2 utilizing matrix B. Any entries of B^2 represent a path of length 2 or less. Similarly, B^3 represents all the paths of length 3 or less, B^4 represents all the paths of length 4 or less and B^n represents all the paths of length n or less. For example, if $b_{ij} = 1$ and $b_{jk} = 1$ are entries of matrix B, then matrix B^2 can be produced by product B×B such that $b^2_{ik} = 1$, representing a path of length 2 or less. In general, if $b_{ij} = 1$ and $b_{jk} = 1$ are entries of matrix B^m, then in matrix $B^m \times B^m$, the boolean product of B^m with itself, $b^{2m}_{ik} = 1$ represents a path of length 2m from v_i to v_k through v_j. This is illustrated in Figure 6.7. We observe that if there is a path from v_i to v_j it cannot have length more than $n - 1$, because G has n vertices. Thus, $C = B^{n-1}$ is computed by successive boolean products; for instance B^2, B^4,…,B^m,B^n, when m $= (n - 1) / 2$. This indicates that the connectivity matrix C is obtained after $\lceil \log(n - 1) \rceil$ boolean matrix multiplication. It is worth noting that when $n - 1$ is not a power of 2, C may be obtained from B^m where m is the smallest power of 2 larger than $n - 1$, since $B^m = B^{n-1}$. For example, if matrix A is 7×7, then matrix B is 7×7 and matrix C may be obtained from B^8, because $n - 1 = 6$ is not a power of 2 and the smallest power of 2 larger than 6 is 8, meaning that $C = B^8$.

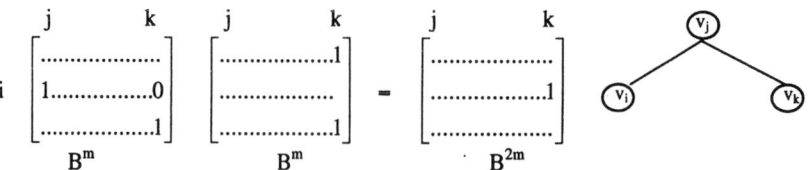

Figure 6.7. Boolean product of B^m. B^{2m} indicates a path from v_i to v_k through v_j.

Example: A directed graph with 3 vertices and its adjacency matrix A are shown in Figures 6.8 (a) and (b), respectively.

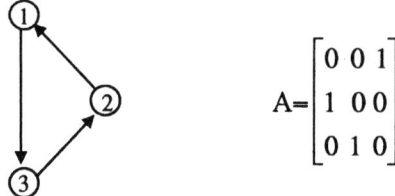

$$A = \begin{bmatrix} 0 & 0 & 1 \\ 1 & 0 & 0 \\ 0 & 1 & 0 \end{bmatrix}$$

Figure 6.8. (a) A directed graph. (b) Its adjacency matrix.

The matrix B is obtained from matrix A with 1 as the diagonal elements as follows:

$$A = \begin{bmatrix} 0 & 0 & 1 \\ 1 & 0 & 0 \\ 0 & 1 & 0 \end{bmatrix} \qquad B = \begin{bmatrix} 1 & 0 & 1 \\ 1 & 1 & 0 \\ 0 & 1 & 1 \end{bmatrix}$$

and the connectivity matrix C may be obtained as $C = B^{3-1} = B^2$ as shown in Figure 6.9 (a). Since $b_{13} = 1$ and $b_{32} = 1$, it follows that $b^2_{12} = 1$, representing a path of length 2 from v_1 to v_2 through v_3 as shown in Figure 6.9 (b).

The following pseudocode represents a parallel algorithm to compute the connectivity matrix of a graph in which the adjacency matrix A is the input and the connectivity matrix C is the output. The architecture is a hypercube with $N = n^3$ processors as $P_0, P_1, \ldots, P_{N-1}$ in each dimension of $n \times n \times n$ array of processors. In this array of processors, P_x occupies position (i,j,k), where $x = in^2 + jn + k$ and $0 \le i,j,k \le n-1$ with three assigned registers $A(i,j,k)$, $B(i,j,k)$ and $C(i,j,k)$. The adjacency matrix A as input is defined in the processor in position $(0,j,k)$; that is, $A(0,j,k) = a_{jk}$.

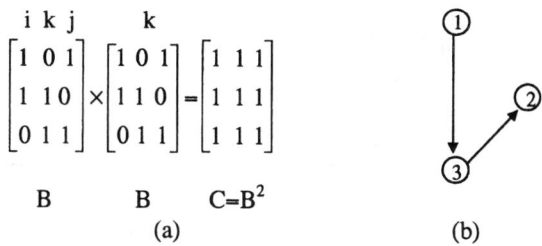

$$\begin{matrix} i & k & j & & k \\ \begin{bmatrix} 1 & 0 & 1 \\ 1 & 1 & 0 \\ 0 & 1 & 1 \end{bmatrix} & \times & \begin{bmatrix} 1 & 0 & 1 \\ 1 & 1 & 0 \\ 0 & 1 & 1 \end{bmatrix} & = & \begin{bmatrix} 1 & 1 & 1 \\ 1 & 1 & 1 \\ 1 & 1 & 1 \end{bmatrix} \\ B & & B & & C=B^2 \end{matrix}$$

          B   B   C=B²

                      (a)   (b)

Figure 6.9. (a) The connectivity matrix C. (b) A path from v_1 to v_2 through v_3.

Algorithm: Connectivity Matrix(A,C)

    for j = 0 to n−1 do in parallel

        A(0,i,j) = 1

    endfor

    for j = 0 to n−1 do in parallel

        for k = 0 to n−1 do in parallel

            B(0,j,k) = A(0,j,k)

        endfor

    endfor

    for i = 0 to $\lceil \log(n-1) \rceil$ do

Algorithm: Hypercube Matrix Multiplication(A,B,C)

    for j = 0 to n−1 do in parallel

        for k = 0 to n−1 do in parallel

            A(0,j,k) = C(0,j,k)

            B(0,j,k) = C(0,j,k)

        endfor

        endfor

    endfor

Matrix multiplication is a parallel algorithm to multiply two n × n matrices A and B utilizing a hypercube with $N = n^3$ processors to construct a matrix C. After the construction of the connectivity matrix C of the graph G, we can obtain the connected components, matrix D, with the following properties:

$$d_{jk} = \begin{cases} v_k & if\ c_{jk} = 1 \\ 0 & otherwise \end{cases}$$

where $0 \le j,k \le n - 1$. This indicates that row j of matrix D contains the name of vertices to which v_j is connected and forms a path, meaning a connected component. Thus, the connected components of G are obtained by each row of the matrix D such that v_j is assigned to a connected component x if x is the smallest index for which $d_{jx} \neq 0$.

The time complexity of the last loop can address the worst-case time complexity of the connectivity matrix computation, since it dominates the initialization time. The parallel Hypercube Matrix Multiplication is iterated $\log(n - 1)$ times and each one requires $O(\log n)$ time, thus yielding the running time as $O(\log^2 n)$. Since n^3 processors are used, the cost of the connectivity matrix computation is $O(n^3 \log^2 n)$.

The following pseudocode represents a parallel algorithm to compute connected components of a graph G in which the connectivity matrix C is the input and the connected components are the output. The architecture is a hypercube with $N = n^3$ processors, each provided with three registers, A, B, and C. Initially, $A(0,j,k) = C_{jk}$ for $0 \leq j,k \leq n - 1$ contains the connectivity matrix, meaning the processors in position $(0,j,k)$ contain the connectivity matrix of G. When the algorithm terminates, $C(0,j,0)$ contains the component number for vertex v_j where $j = 0,1,\ldots,n - 1$.

Algorithm: Connected Components(C)
```
        for  j = 0 to n−1 do in parallel
              for  k = 0 to n−1 do in parallel
                    if    C(0,j,k) = 1
                            then      C(0,j,k) = v_k
                    end if
              endfor
        endfor
              for  j = 0 to n−1 do in parallel
              n processors in row j determine the
                    smallest x for which
              C(0,j,x) ≠ 0
              C(0,j,0) = x
        endfor
```

The implementation of the algorithm indicates that first the matrix D is created and stored in the C registers of the processors. Second, the elements of the component to which v_j belongs overwrite the contents of register $C(0,j,0)$. Finally, the contents of the C registers are the component numbers, meaning $C(0,0,0)$ gives the component number v_0 and $C(0,1,0)$ gives the component number v_1, etc. Since the initialization takes constant time, the overall cost of the Connected-Components algorithm is bounded by that of the Connectivity Matrix algorithm. Thus, the overall cost of the Connected Components algorithm is $O(n^3 \log^2 n)$.

Supervertex Method

Hirschberg [Hirschberg 1976, Hirschberg et al. 1979] has used the supervertex method to develop a connected-components algorithm for processor arrays based on the CREW PRAM model of parallel computation. The algorithm collapses the vertices of a graph G into larger and larger sets of vertices until each set of vertices corresponds to a single connected component.

Summary of the Algorithm. Vertices are combined into supervertices which are themselves combined until each remaining supervertex represents a connected component of the graph. Each vertex is a member of exactly one supervertex and every supervertex is identified by its lowest numbered vertex, which is the root. The parallel algorithm iterates through three phases as follows:

1. The lowest numbered neighboring supervertex of each vertex is found.
2. Each supervertex root is connected to the root of the lowest numbered neighboring supervertex.
3. All newly connected supervertices are collapsed into larger supervertices.

One immediate implication of this method is that each vertex is always a member of exactly one supervertex and each supervertex can be identified by its lowest numbered member vertex, which is known as its root. This algorithm has a complexity of $O(\log^2 n)$ and requires n^2 processors. Nassimi [Nassimi 80] has adopted Hirschberg's algorithm to a mesh SIMD model of computation to compute the connected components of a graph G with $n = 2^k$ vertices.

We present Nassimi's algorithm for a two-dimensional mesh model such that different procedures are involved, as follows: The procedure **READ**(*variable*, [*index*]*value*) indicates that the value of the variable *variable* of every processor is identical to the value of variable *value* of the processor which is indexed by the value of the variable *index*. The procedure **WRITE**(*variable*, [*index*]*value*) indicates that the second argument specifies the address to which the value of the first argument has to be written. For example, the value of variable *variable* of each processor is written to variable *value* of the processor which is indexed by the value of the variable *index*. The algorithm uses a function called **BITS**(i, j, k), which returns the value of bits j of integer value i through k, where there are $p = 2^k$ processing elements and they are numbered in shuffled row-major order. If $j < k$ the function returns 0, otherwise it returns the corresponding value. In the **UPDATE-SUPERVERTEX**(*candidate*, *root*) subroutine, each supervertex *root* gets the minimum of the root numbers of neighboring supervertices. The procedure **COLLAPSE**(*root*, *number*) collapses vertices such that every vertex in a supervertex points to the *root*. This algorithm has a worst-case time complexity of $T(n) = O(\log^2 n)$ on the PRAM model with n^2 processors [Hirschberg 79].

Algorithm: Connected Components(G)
Assume adjacent(i, j) where $1 \leq i \leq n$ and $1 \leq j \leq degree$ and *degree* is the maximum degree of any vertex in G.
When vertex i has $degree_i < degree$, then adjacent(i, j) = ∞ for $degree + i + 1 \leq j \leq$ degree.
Each processing element has a local variable *root* which is a pointer to the supervertex *root*.

```
for all       P_i   where 1 ≤ i ≤ n   do
        root = i
endfor
for  count=0 to ⌈log n⌉−1 do
        for all       P_i   where 1 ≤ i ≤ n   do
        candidate = ∞
        endfor
        for  edge = 1 to degree   do
                for all       P_i   where 1 ≤ i ≤ n   do
        FETCH-AND-COMPARE(adjacent[edge], root, candidate)
                endfor
        endfor
        for all       P_i   where 1 ≤ i ≤ n   do
                UPDATE-SUPERVERTEX(candidate, root, i)
        endfor
COLLAPSE(root, n)
endfor
```

FETCH-AND-COMPARE(vertex, root, candidate)
```
    READ(temp,[vertex]root)
        if   temp = root   then
            temp = ∞
        endif
        candidate = min(candidate, temp)
```

UPDATE-SUPERVERTEX(candidate, root, i)
```
    WRITE(candidate, [root]root)
        if   root = ∞     then
            root = i
        endif
        if   root > i      then
            READ(root,[root]root)
        endif
```

COLLAPSE(root, number)
```
    for  count = 1    to ⌈log number⌉  do
        for all       P_i   where 1 ≤ i ≤ number do
```

if BITS(root,log(number−1),count)
        = BITS(i,log(number−1),count)
    then**READ**(root, [root]root)
        endif
    endfor
endfor

Adjacency Matrix Partitioning Method

The primary data structure of this method is the adjacency matrix. The method is based on partitioning the adjacency matrix of G into p parts as $\{G_1,G_2,...,G_p\}$. Each part corresponds to a subgraph, and each subgraph is assigned to one of p processors. Each processor P_i has a subgraph G_i of G, where $G_i = (V,E_i)$ and E_i are the edges that correspond to the portion of the adjacency matrix assigned to this processor. In the first step of this parallel formulation each processor P_i computes the depth-first tree of the graph G_i. At the end of this step, p trees have been constructed. In the second step, trees are merged until only one tree remains. The remaining tree has the property that two vertices are in the same connected components of G if they are in the same tree.

Figures 6.10 (a) and (b) represent a graph and the adjacency matrix of the graph, respectively. The adjacency matrix can be partitioned, for example, into two parts P_1 and P_2, in which each part corresponds to a subgraph and can be assigned to one processor. Figures 6.10 (c) and (d) represent these two subgraphs. Each processor gets the corresponding partition of the adjacency matrix and computes the spanning tree of the subgraph utilizing a search method. For example, using the depth-first search method, the spanning trees of the subgraphs are shown in figures 6.10 (e) and (f), respectively. Finally, the spanning trees are merged to form the connected components of the graph which is the solution.

The algorithm can be outlined in the following steps.

Algorithm: Connected Components(A)

Step1: Partition the adjacency matrix A of graph G into *p* parts as $\{G_1,G_2,...,G_p\}$, where $G_i = (V,E_i)$ and E_i are the edges of the subgraph.

Step2: Assign each subgraph Gi to processor pi and the corresponding adjacency matrix of the subgraph.

Step3: Processor pi computes a spanning tree of the subgraph Gi using the depth-first search method.

Step4: Generated spanning trees of Step 3 are merged pairwise until one spanning tree remains.

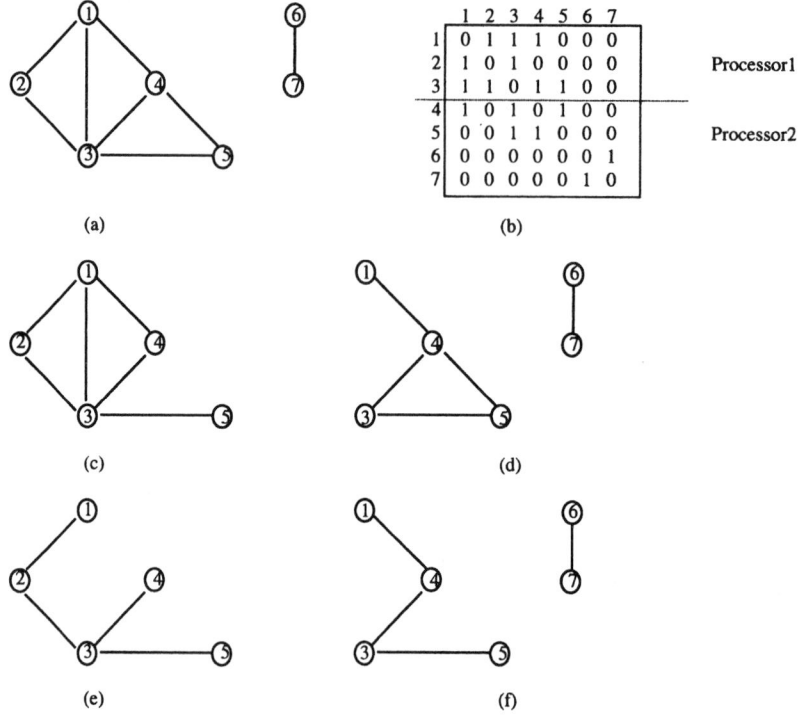

Figure 6.10. Construction of the connected components in parallel.

We can merge the pairs of spanning trees as follows. Assume S_1 and S_2 are the two spanning trees to be merged. At most $(n-1)$ edges of one tree are merged with the edges of the other tree, because S_1 and S_2 are spanning trees. If we want to merge tree S_1 into tree S_2, then for each edge $(u,v) \in S_1$, a search operation might be performed for each vertex to determine if the two vertices are already in the same tree of S_2. If not, then the two trees of S_2 containing u and v are united; otherwise, the union operation can be ignored.

With the provided data structure, Step 3 and Step 4 dominate the time complexity of the algorithm. Step 3 for computing the spanning trees, based on the $(n/p) \times n$ adjacency matrix assigned to each processor, requires $O(n^2/p)$ time. Step 4 of the algorithm is performed by $(\log p)$ merging stages, in which each stage takes $O(n)$ time, thus yielding time complexity as $O(n \log p)$. Hence, the parallel time of the algorithm utilizing p processors and n vertices is:

$$T(p) = O(n^2/p) + O(n \log p).$$

6.2   Paths and All-Pairs Shortest Paths

A graph consisting of vertices and edges in which each edge is associated with a positive number, called its weight, is called a weighted graph. A weighted graph may be directed or undirected. The meaning of an edge's weight depends on the application. It may represent distance, cost, time, probability or any other quantity that accumulates along a path to be minimized. The graph can be represented by an adjacency matrix W, called the weighted matrix, in which the elements of W represent the weight of the edge between vertices, meaning w_{ij} of W represents the weight of edge (v_i, v_j). If v_i and v_j are not connected by an edge, then w_{ij} may be equal to zero, infinity, or any appropriate value depending on the application to address disconnectivity between these two vertices.

Suppose that we are given a directed and weighted graph G = (V,E,W) with n vertices as shown in Figure 6.11 (a). The graph is defined by its weighted matrix W as shown in Figure 6.11 (b).

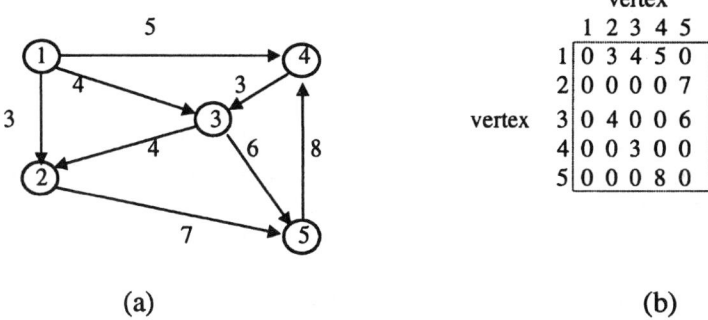

Figure 6.11. (a) A directed graph. (b) Its weighted matrix.

Since each edge of the graph has a length represented by its weight, it makes sense to speak of the length of a path through the graph. One natural question is whether it is possible to travel through the graph from one vertex to another and, if so, what the path between the vertices is. Concerning the paths between vertices, we are most interested in finding the shortest paths, either in terms of the number of edges that have to be traversed or in terms of the sum of the edge weight of edges to be traversed in the case of weighted graphs. In this section, we show how to solve such problems efficiently. In a shortest-paths problem we are given a weighted directed graph G = (V,E), with weight function $W:E \Rightarrow w$ mapping edges to real valued weights (positive or negative). The weight of path $p = (v_1, v_2, \ldots, v_k)$ is the sum of the weights associated with edges:

$$W(p) = \sum_{i=1}^{k} W(v_{i-1}, v_i).$$

We define the shortest-path weight from s to t as:

$$\text{Path}(s,t) = \begin{cases} \text{Min}\{W(P) \mid s \xrightarrow{p} t \text{ where there is a path from s to t}\} \\ \infty \quad \text{otherwise} \end{cases}$$

Many other problems can be solved by the invariant of the shortest-paths algorithm:

- Single-Destination Shortest-Paths problem: Find a shortest path to a given destination vertex d from every vertex s.
- Single-Pair Shortest-Paths problem: Find a shortest path from v_i to v_j for given vertices v_i and v_j.
- All-Pair Shortest-Paths problem: Find a shortest path from v_i to v_j for every pair of vertices v_i and v_j.

The problem that we address here is known as the all-pairs shortest path problem and is stated as follows. For every pair of vertices v_i and v_j in graph G = (V,E), it is required to find the length of the shortest path from v_i and v_j along edges in E. The solution is based on the construction of a matrix D such that each element of this matrix, d_{ij}, is the length of the shortest path from v_i to v_j in G, for all i and j. Generally speaking, the shortest-paths algorithms exploit the property that a shortest path between two vertices contains other shortest paths within it. This property can address the applicability of both dynamic programming and the greedy method. In fact, Dijkstra's algorithm is a greedy algorithm, and Floyd's algorithm, which finds shortest paths between all pairs of vertices, is a dynamic programming algorithm.

Dijkstra's Labeling Algorithm

Dijkstra presented an algorithm to solve the single-source shortest-paths problem on a directed graph with no negative weight associated with edges. Dijkstra's algorithm is similar to Prim's algorithm to find the minimum spanning tree, which incrementally finds the shortest paths from a source s to all the other vertices of G, differing only in the way the next edge is selected. In this algorithm, to find the shortest path from vertex s to each of the other vertices, we label each vertex j with two labels:

d(j) = length of shortest path from vertex s to vertex j passing through permanently labeled vertices only

p(j) = immediate predecessor to vertex j in the path from vertex s

This labeling algorithm indicates that at any stage of the algorithm the label of each vertex is either temporary or permanent. The complexity of this algorithm is $O(n^2)$, the same running time as a proper version of Prim's algorithm for the minimum spanning tree; indeed, except for the extension condition it is the same as Prim's algorithm.

Dijkstra's shortest-path algorithm can be described by the following steps.

Dijkstra's Shortest-Path Algorithm

Step 0: Initially give vertex s permanent labels,

$d(s) = 0$ and $p(s) = \varnothing$

and give all other vertices temporary labels,

$d(j) = + \infty$ and $p(j) = \varnothing$

Step 1: Let k = vertex whose labels were most recently made permanent.

For every vertex j linked to vertex k and having temporary labels, update the labels:

$d(j) = \text{Minimum}\{d(j), d(k) + d_{kj}\}$, and

if $d(j) = d(k) + d_{kj}$, then $p(j) = k$

Step 2: Make permanent the label of the vertex having the smallest $d(j)$.

If some labels are still temporary, return to Step 1; otherwise, stop.

Justification for Dijkstra's Algorithm

Suppose vertex x has the smallest temporary label, meaning that $d(x)$ = shortest length of any path from vertex s to vertex x using only intermediate vertices with permanent labels. The shortest path from vertex s to vertex x which includes some vertex y with a temporary label must be $\geq d(y) + d_{xy} \geq d(x)$. Therefore, we can make the labels of node x permanent.

The following psuedocode is a high-level description of Dijkstra's shortest-paths algorithm.

Algorithm: Dijkstra's Shortest Path

$V_p = \{s\}$

for all $v \in (V - V_p)$ do

        if (s,v) exists   then $d(v) = w_{su}$

                              else $d(v) = \infty$

endfor

while $(V_p \neq V)$ do

    select a vertex u such that

        $d(u) = \min\{d(v) \mid v \in (V - V_p)\}$

    $V_p = V_p \cup \{u\}$

$$\text{for all } v \in (V - V_p) \text{ do}$$
$$d(v) = \min\{d(v), d(u) + w_{uv}\}$$
$$\text{endfor}$$
$$\text{end while}$$

If we want to find the length of the shortest path among all pairs of n vertices in a graph, we could perform Dijkstra's algorithm n times, once from each possible starting vertex. This yields a cubic time algorithm for all the pairs shortest path, meaning $O(n^3) = n \times O(n^2)$.

Example: The execution of Dijkstra's algorithm is illustrated in Figure 6.12, in which it is required to find the shortest paths from vertex 1 to all other vertices. The initial graph is represented in Figure 6.12 (a). We start by assigning the initial labels (0 for vertex 1 and $+\infty$ otherwise), as shown in Figure 6.12 (b). Next, we update the labels on vertices 2 and 3 as follows:

$$d(2) = \text{minimum}\{+\infty, 0 + 10\} = 10$$
$$d(3) = \text{minimum}\{+\infty, 0 + 5\} = 5$$

as shown in Figure 6.12 (c). In each case, the predecessor label will indicate vertex 1. Next, we select a temporary label to be made permanent. This will be the label of vertex 3, since it has the smallest temporary label as represented in Figure 6.12 (d). Next, we update the labels of vertices 2 and 4 (neighbors of vertex 3) as follows:

$$d(2) = \text{minimum}\{10, 5 + 3\} = 8$$
$$d(4) = \text{minimum}\{+\infty, 5 + 2\} = 7$$

as shown in Figure 6.12 (e). The next step is to choose the temporary label to be made permanent. This will be the label of vertex 4, which is the smallest temporary label as shown in Figure 6.12 (f). Next we update the temporary label of the neighbor of vertex 4 as follows:

$$d(5) = \text{minimum}\{+\infty, 7 + 4\} = 11$$

where the next temporary label to be permanent is vertex 2 as shown in Figure 6.12 (g). Next we update the label of vertex 5:

$$d(5) = \text{minimum}\{11, 8 + 1\} = 9.$$

Finally, we select the label of vertex 5 to be permanent as represented in Figure 6.12 (h). Since no temporary labels remain, the algorithm terminates and the graph represents the shortest paths from vertex 1 to all other vertices. The predecessor labels (indicated by the bold arrows) allow us to trace the shortest path. For example, the shortest path to vertex 5 is: 1→3→2→5.

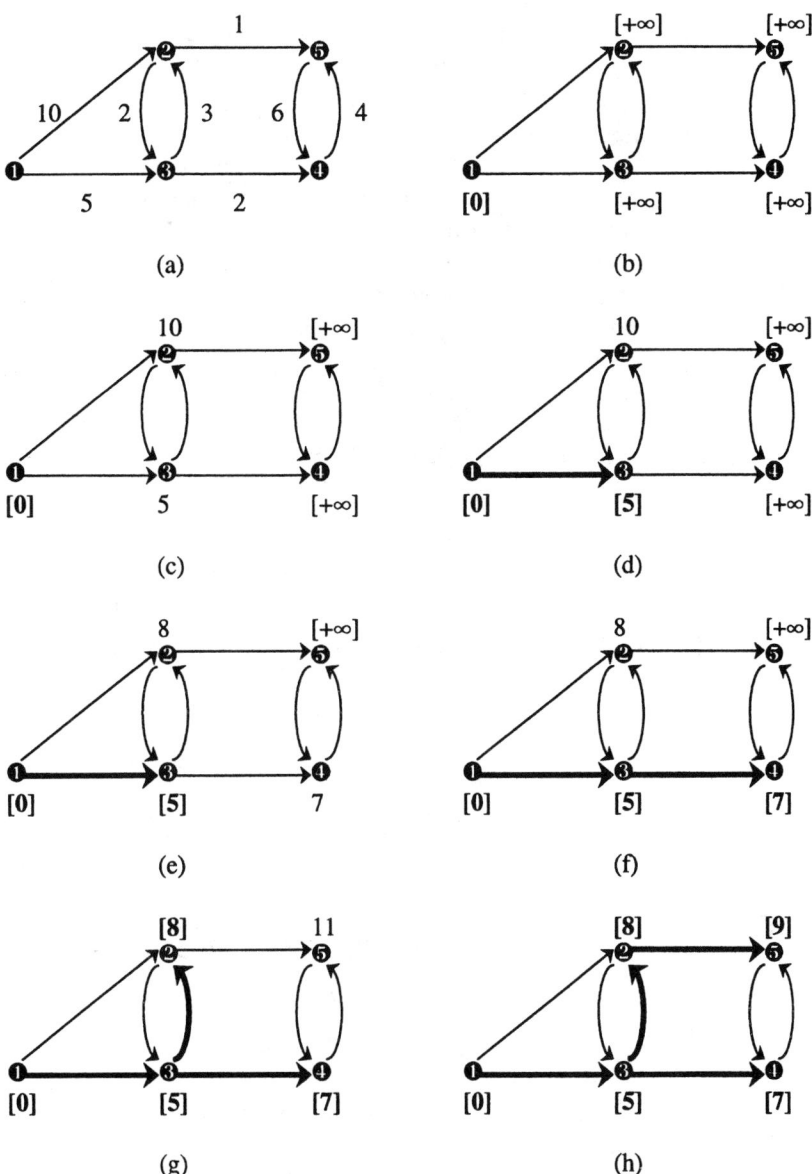

Figure 6.12. The execution of Dijkstra's algorithm.

Floyd's Shortest-Path Algorithm

We use Floyd's algorithm [Floyd 62] for finding a shortest path between every pair of vertices of a weighted directed graph G. Unlike Dijkstra's all-pairs shortest-path algorithm, Floyd's algorithm works even if some of the edges have negative weights, provided that there is a nonnegative path, meaning that some of the weights of the edges in the path are negative. The cost of a path is the sum of the weights of the edges in the path. Assume no negative length cycles exist in the weighted graph G with vertex set $V = \{1,2,\ldots,n\}$ and edge set E, and that the matrix W represents the associated weight of the edges. Floyd's algorithm is based on the Triangle Operation between each pair of vertices in the graph G.

Assume P is a path joining two vertices i and j of V, and suppose there is a vertex k which is an interior vertex in P. The Principle of Optimality indicates that the subpath P_1 from i to k is a shortest path from i to k and the subpath P_2 from k to j is a shortest path from k to j. Since P is a shortest path from i to j, it follows that the length of P_1 and P_2 are equal to the minimum lengths, which is the base of the triangle operation between three vertices, meaning that P is the shortest path. Given an $n \times n$ weighted matrix $W = \{w_{ij}\}$, a triangle operation for a fixed vertex k is defined as:

$$w_{ij} = \text{Minimum}\{w_{ij}, w_{ik} + w_{kj}\} \text{ for all } i,j = 1,\ldots,n \text{ but } i,j \neq k.$$

Theorem: If we perform a triangle operation on the weighted matrix for successive values of $k = 1,2,\ldots,n$, then each entry w_{ij} of the final matrix becomes equal to the length of the shortest path from v_i to v_j.

Justification for Floyd's Algorithm

In particular,

$$w_{ij}^1 = \begin{cases} w_{ij} & \text{if there is an edge from } v_i \text{ to } v_j, \text{ the length of the path} \\ \infty & \text{if there is no edge from } v_i \text{ to } v_j, \text{ where } i \neq j \\ 0 & \text{if } v_i = v_j, w_{ii} = 0, \text{ the length of the path from } v_i \text{ to } v_j \end{cases}$$

The algorithm consists of n passes. In the first pass, the edge from i to j (for $1 \leq i,j \leq n$) is replaced with the minimum cost path from i to j that is allowed to pass through only vertex 1. This can be accomplished by $\text{Min}\{w_{ij}, w_{i1}+w_{1j}\}$, selecting the smaller value. The result matrix after the first pass is called $W_{ij}^{(1)}$. In the second pass, the path from i to j computed from the first pass is replaced with the minimum cost path from i to j passing through only vertices 1 and 2.

The path is found by $w_{ij}^{(2)} = \mathrm{Min}\{w_{ij}^{(1)}, w_{i2}^{(1)} + w_{2j}^{(1)}\}$, in which the result matrix

is called $W_{ij}^{(2)}$. In order to compute $w_{ij}^{(k)}$, which is the minimum cost of a path

from vertex i to vertex j using only vertices $v_1, v_2, \dots, v_{(k-1)}$, we can use the recurrence formula:

$$
w_{ij}^{(k)} = \begin{cases} w_{ij} & k = 0 \\ \mathrm{Min}\{w_{ij}^{(k-1)}, (w_{ik}^{(k-1)} + w_{kj}^{(k-1)})\} & 0 \le k \le n-1 \end{cases}
$$

This identifies the minimum cost path between i and j that passes through only vertices 1,2, ... ,k. In general, the minimum cost path between each pair of vertices is computed after the nth pass. The validity of this relation is established by induction proof as follows. After performing the triangle operation for step k_0, w_{ij} is the length of the shortest path from v_i to v_j with only intermediate vertices $k \le k_0$. Assume this relation is true for $k_0 - 1$. Consider the triangle operation for k_0 which is:

$$
w_{ij} = \mathrm{Min}\{w_{ij}, (w_{ik_0} + w_{k_0 j})\}.
$$

If the shortest path from v_i to v_j, using only intermediate vertices $1,2,\dots,k_0$, does not pass through k_0, then w_{ij} is unchanged by this operation, and w_{ij} will still satisfy the above property for k_0; otherwise, $\{w_{ij}, (w_{ik_0} + w_{k_0 j})\}$, and since w_{ik_0} and $w_{k_0 j}$ each satisfy the property $(w_{ik_0} + w_{k_0 j})$, will satisfy the property. This indicates that to obtain $w_{ij}^{(k)}$ we can compute all combinations of subpaths whose concatenation is a path from v_i to v_j and then choose the shortest one. In accordance with this discussion, the matrix D, all-pairs shortest-path matrix, can be computed from W, the weighted adjacency matrix, by evaluating $W^2, W^4, \dots, W^m$ where m is the smallest power of 2 larger than or equal to $n-1$, meaning that $D = W^m$. In order to obtain W^k from $W^{k/2}$ we can the matrix multiplication utilizing standard operations of matrix multiplication that are 'x' and '+' operations.

The sequential Floyd's shortest-path algorithm can be described as the following procedure:

Procedure   sequential-shortest-path(W[n,n])
    array D[n,n], W[n,n]
    for i,j = (1,2, ... ,n) D[i,j] $\Leftarrow$ W[i,j]
        for k = (1,2, ..., n)
            for i = (1,2, ... ,n)

$$\text{for } j = (1,2, \dots ,n)$$
$$D[i, j] \Leftarrow \min\{D[i, \quad j], (D[i, k] + D[k, j])\}$$

return D

End   sequential-shortest-path

The sequential formulation requires n iterations, and each iteration requires $O(n^2)$ time. Thus, the overall run time of the sequential all-pairs shortest-path Floyd's algorithm is $O(n^3)$, which asymptotically is no better than n times running Dijkstra's algorithm. However, the loops are so tight and the program so short that it runs better in practice. The parallel algorithm is a variation of Floyd's algorithm which calculates the length of the shortest path between each pair of vertices. The parallel algorithm constructs a matrix D that provides the length of the shortest path between each pair of vertices. D is initialized to the direct weight between vertices as follows:

$$\begin{cases} W(i,i) = 0 \\ W(i,j) \geq 0 \; if \, i \neq j \\ W(i,j) = \infty \; if \, the \, edge \, (k, j) \, does \, not \, exits. \end{cases}$$

The algorithm uses n^2 processors and is organized into a two-dimensional array. Processor P_{ij} computes the value $w_{ij}^{(k)}$ for $k = 1,2, \dots ,n$. The algorithm performs $\lceil \log_n \rceil$ iterations, in which after iteration k, matrix D provides the length of the shortest path that consumes not more than 2^k edges, or, in other words, not more than $2^k - 1$ intermediate vertices. The calculated matrix after $\lceil \log_n \rceil$ iterations provides the shortest path between each pair of vertices, which is the result that we are looking for. In each iteration k, processor P_{ij} needs the values $w_{ij}^{(k-1)}$, $w_{ik}^{(k-1)}$, and $w_{kj}^{(k-1)}$. The outline of the algorithm is presented below.

Procedure   parallel-shortest-path(W[n,n])
    array D[n,n], W[n,n], T[n,n]
    for all   i,j = (1,2, \dots ,n) **in parallel do** D[i,j] $\Leftarrow$ W[i,j]
    repeat $\lceil \log_n \rceil$ times
        for all i,j,x = (1,2, \dots ,n) **in parallel do**
            T[i, x, j] $\Leftarrow$ D[i, x] + D[x, j]
        for all i, j = (1,2, \dots ,n)   **in parallel do**
            D[i, j] $\Leftarrow$ min(D[i, j], T[i, 1, j], T[i, 2, j], \dots , T[i, n, j])
    return D
End   parallel-shortest-path

The array T stores the intermediate path lengths to avoid conflicts between reading and writing in the last for statement.

In general, at each iteration, for instance k, the algorithm checks for each pair of vertices (i,j) whether or not there exists a new path from i to j using more than 2^{k-1} and no more than 2^k edges which is better that the current best path that uses no more than 2^{k-1} edges. If there is any such path, it has an intermediate vertex x such that neither the part of the path from i to x, nor the part from x to j, uses more than 2^{k-1} edges. The shortest path length is the current value of D[i,x] + D[x,j]. Since the principle of optimality is considered by checking whether a best new path from i to j exists, we can compare the length of the shortest path (best one so far) with D[i,x] + D[x,j] for each possible value of x to simply choose the minimum length. This new path ensures the path with the shortest length. Since each iteration of the last for statement is performed by one processor, there is no conflict regarding the old value of D[i,j] and its new value in this statement.

The execution of the parallel algorithm is illustrated in Figure 6.13, in which D_k is the matrix D after the k-th iteration for k = 1,2,3,4,5. Matrix D_s can address to the solution which identifies the length of the shortest path between every pair of vertices. For example, the first row of the D_s identifies the shortest path from vertex 1 to all the other vertices which, is the same as the Dijkstra's solution represented in Figure 6.12(h). The algorithm can be implemented in parallel systems such as hypercubes to achieve efficient parallel solutions.

$$W = \begin{pmatrix} 1 & 10 & 5 & \infty & \infty \\ \infty & 0 & 2 & \infty & 1 \\ \infty & 3 & 0 & 2 & \infty \\ \infty & \infty & \infty & 0 & 4 \\ \infty & \infty & \infty & 6 & 0 \end{pmatrix} \quad D_1 = \begin{pmatrix} 1 & 10 & 5 & \infty & \infty \\ \infty & 0 & 2 & \infty & 1 \\ \infty & 3 & 0 & 2 & \infty \\ \infty & \infty & \infty & 0 & 4 \\ \infty & \infty & \infty & 6 & 0 \end{pmatrix} \quad D_2 = \begin{pmatrix} 1 & 10 & 5 & \infty & 11 \\ \infty & 0 & 2 & \infty & 1 \\ \infty & 3 & 0 & 2 & 4 \\ \infty & \infty & \infty & 0 & 4 \\ \infty & \infty & \infty & 6 & 0 \end{pmatrix}$$

$$D_3 = \begin{pmatrix} 1 & 8 & 5 & 7 & 9 \\ \infty & 0 & 2 & 4 & 1 \\ \infty & 3 & 0 & 2 & 4 \\ \infty & \infty & \infty & 0 & 4 \\ \infty & \infty & \infty & 6 & 0 \end{pmatrix} \quad D_4 = \begin{pmatrix} 1 & 8 & 5 & 7 & 9 \\ \infty & 0 & 2 & 4 & 1 \\ \infty & 3 & 0 & 2 & 4 \\ \infty & \infty & \infty & 0 & 4 \\ \infty & \infty & \infty & 6 & 0 \end{pmatrix} \quad D_5 = \begin{pmatrix} 1 & 8 & 5 & 7 & 9 \\ \infty & 0 & 2 & 4 & 1 \\ \infty & 3 & 0 & 2 & 4 \\ \infty & \infty & \infty & 0 & 4 \\ \infty & \infty & \infty & 6 & 0 \end{pmatrix}$$

Figure 6.13. The parallel execution of Floyd's algorithm.

6.3   Minimum Spanning Trees and Forests

Let G = (V,E) be a connected undirected graph. Figure 6.14 (a) shows an example of such a graph in which the number on each edge represents a measure of performance of that edge, for example cost or benefit. For instance, the cost of the edge (1,6) is 10 and that of (5,7) is 24. This graph could represent the links in a proposed communication network between 7 cities represented by 7 vertices. For example, the goal is to install links between pairs of cities so that communication can be routed in the resulting network. Each edge of G represents a link that can be installed. A spanning tree of G is defined as a subgraph T such that:

1.   All of the vertices of G are in T
2.   T is a tree which means that T has no cycles

Since T is acyclic and connects all of the vertices, it must form a tree, which is called a spanning tree since it spans the graph G. This indicates that a spanning tree of an undirected connected graph G is a subgraph of G as T, which is a tree containing all the vertices in G. If G is not connected and consists of components $\{G_1,...,G_k\}$, then a spanning forest of G is a set of trees $\{ T_1,...,T_k \}$, where T_i is a spanning tree of G_i. Figure 6.14 (b) represents a spanning tree with a total cost of 110 and Figure 6.14 (c) shows another spanning tree with a total cost of 129 for the same graph of Figure 6.14 (a).

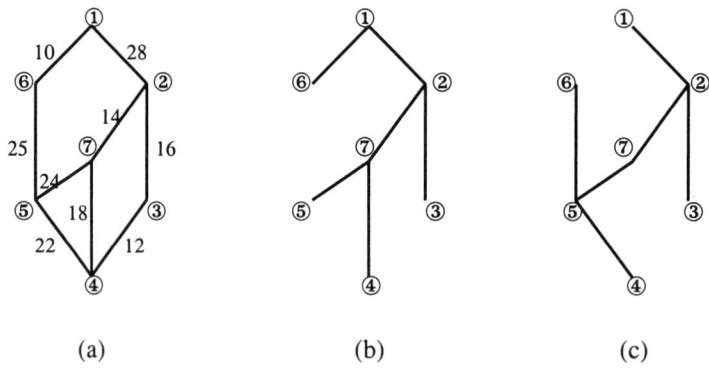

(a)   (b)   (c)

Figure 6.14. (a) An undirected connected graph. (b) Spanning tree with total cost of 110. (c) Spanning tree with total cost of 129.

Suppose that we are interested in building a least cost communication network T and that we are given a weighted graph G that contains an edge for each feasible link. The network T to be built is a subgraph of G. Further, this subgraph must be connected and must include every vertex in G, meaning that T is a spanning tree of G. To be more precise, for each edge $(u,v) \in E$, we associate a weight $w(u,v)$ specifying the cost to connect u and v. We then wish to find an acyclic subset $T \subseteq E$ which connects all of the vertices and whose total weight is

$$w(T) = \sum_{(u,v) \in T} w(u,v)$$

In general, we are interested in finding a spanning tree with the minimum total cost. Thus, a minimum spanning tree for a weighted undirected graph G is a spanning tree with minimum length. We present a weighted graph by its adjacency matrix. That is, we represent it by $n \times n$ array w of numbers where

$$w_{ij} = \begin{cases} weight\ on\ edge & if\ there\ is\ an\ edge\ between\ v_i\ and\ v_j \\ \infty & if\ there\ is\ no\ edge\ between\ v_i\ and\ v_j \\ 0 & if\ i = j. \end{cases}$$

The graph in Figure 6.14 (a) is represented in this manner in Figure 6.15.

	1	2	3	4	5	6	7
1	0	28	∞	∞	∞	10	∞
2	28	0	16	∞	∞	∞	14
3	∞	16	0	12	∞	∞	∞
4	∞	∞	12	0	22	∞	18
5	∞	∞	∞	22	0	25	24
6	10	∞	∞	∞	25	0	∞
7	∞	14	∞	18	24	∞	0

Figure 6.15. The weighted matrix representation of the graph in Figure 6.14 (a).

This problem has many applications. For instance, suppose the vertices of graph G represent the town and let the length of an edge $\{a,b\}$ be the cost of laying a telephone line from a to b. Then a minimum spanning tree of G corresponds to the cheapest possible network serving all the towns. Examples of such physical networks include telecommunication networks, transportation networks, energy pipelines, VLSI chips and so forth. In all of these examples, the weight of a minimum spanning tree provides a lower bound on the cost of building the network. The minimum spanning tree problem has many solutions and only a handful of them are presented here. For a review of these methods, see Graham [Graham 85]. Efforts to find the minimum cost spanning tree of a weighted connected undirected graph have focused on the following categories:

1. Creating and expanding at the same time many trees to be merged into larger trees is known as Boruvka's algorithm [Boruvka 26]. This was the first algorithm for finding the MST which was devised by Otakar Boruvka in 1926. We start with $|V|$ one vertex trees, and for each vertex v we look for an edge (vw) of minimum weight among all edges outgoing from v, in which it creates small trees by including these edges. Then we look for edges of minimum weight that can connect the resulting trees into larger trees.

2. Expanding a set of trees to form one spanning tree is known as Kruskal's algorithm [Kruskal 56].

3. Creating and expanding only one tree by adding new branches to it is known as Jarnik's algorithm [Jarnik 30] and Prim's algorithm [Prim 57].

4. Creating and expanding only one tree by adding new branches to it and possibly removing branches from it is known as Dijkstra's algorithm [Dijkstra 59].

5. Creating and expanding connected components by choosing a smallest-weight edge joining that connected component to another component is known as Sollin's algorithm [Sollin 77].

The rationale behind the algorithms is that there are two possible lines of attack to this problem:

- Choosing a vertex and building a tree from there by selecting at every step the shortest available edge that can extend the tree to an additional vertex.

- Choosing an edge and building the tree by selecting at every stage the shortest edge that has not yet been chosen or rejected regardless of where this edge is positioned in the graph G.

In this section, we introduce Prim's and Kruskal's algorithms for the minimum spanning tree problem. They each use a specific rule to determine a safe edge. In Kruskal's algorithm, the set T is a forest and the safe edge added to T is always a least-weighted edge in the graph which connects two distinct components. In Prim's algorithm, the set T forms a single tree, and the safe edge added to T is always a least-weighted edge connecting the tree to a vertex not in the tree.

Prim's Algorithm

In Prim's algorithm the minimum spanning tree grows by starting from an arbitrary vertex. At each stage, a new branch, vertex and edge are added to the tree that is already constructed, and the algorithm terminates when all the vertices have been selected. Clearly, the Prim's algorithm produces a spanning tree. However, is it necessarily minimal? Because at each step we select the vertex nearest to the created tree, intuitively it seems that the tree should be minimal (for proof of this claim, interested readers can refer to the graph theory text books).

Prim's algorithm for finding a minimum spanning tree (MST) of a network is represented in the following steps and is based on the vertex selection.

Prim's Algorithm

Step 1: (Setup)

Select any arbitrary starting vertex to begin the tree.

Step 2: (Addition)

Find a vertex not currently in the tree which is nearest to the set of vertices in the tree. Add that vertex and the connecting edge to the tree.

Step 3: (Stopping criterion)

If all vertices are in the tree, stop; otherwise return to Step 2.

End Prim's Algorithm

Let B be a set of vertices and T a set of edges. The following psuedocode represents a Prim's sequential minimum spanning tree algorithm in which the first step initializes B with an arbitrary vertex and T as empty.

Algorithm: Prim{G = (V,E)}

Step 1: $T \Leftarrow \varnothing$

$B \Leftarrow \{$ an arbitrary vertex of V $\}$

Step 2: while($\{B\} \neq \{V\}$) do

find   e = {u, v} of minimum length such that

$u \in B$ and $v \in \{V - B\}$

$T \Leftarrow \{T\} \cup \{e\}$

$B \Leftarrow \{B\} \cup \{v\}$

return {T}

At Step 2, Prim's algorithm looks for the shortest possible edge {u,v} such that $u \in B$ and $v \in \{V - B\}$. Then v is added to B and {u,v} to T to form a tree. At each stage, the edges in T form a minimum spanning tree for the vertices in B. To illustrate the algorithm, consider the graph represented in Figure 6.16 (a). We arbitrary choose vertex A as the starting vertex. Now the algorithm might progress as follows:

Step	Edge Considered	B
Initialization		{A}
1	{A,G}	{A,G}
2	{A,C}	{A,C,G}
3	{B,C}	{A,B,C,G}
4	{F,G}	{A,B,C,F,G}
5	{E,F}	{A,B,C,E,F,G}
6	{D,E}	{A,B,C,D,E,F,G}

Since all vertices are in the tree, the algorithm stops. T contains the chosen edges as:

$$({A,G},{A,C},{B,C},{F,G},{E,F},{D,E})$$

and B contains all vertices as B = {A,B,C,D,E,F,G}. Figure 6.16 (b) shows the minimum spanning tree of the graph G represented in Figure 6.16 (a). The main loop of the Prim algorithm is executed $(n-1)$ times. In each n iteration it scans through all the m edges and tests whether the current edge joins a tree with a nontree vertex and whether this is the smallest edge found so far. Thus, the enclosed loop takes time $O(n)$, yielding the worst-case time complexity of the Prim algorithm as $O(n^2)$.

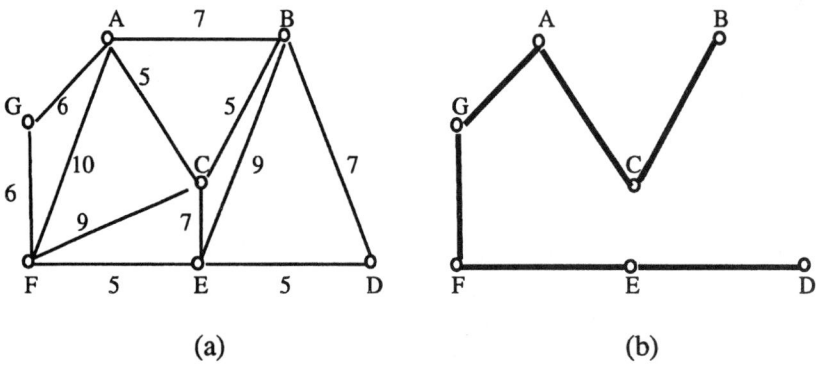

(a)   (b)

Figure 6.16. (a) An undirected connected graph. (b) Minimum spanning tree.

Kruskal's Algorithm

Kruskal's algorithm for the minimum spanning tree problem starts by creating disjoint subsets of V, one for each vertex and containing only that vertex. It then inspects the edges according to non-decreasing weight. If an edge connects two vertices in disjoint subsets, the edge is added and the subsets are merged into one set. The process continues until all the subsets are merged into one set. In other words, at each step an edge (u,v) is determined which can be added to T without violating this invariant, in the sense that $T \cup \{u,v\}$ is also a subset of a minimum spanning tree. We call such an edge a safe edge for T, since it can be safely added to T without destroying the invariant. The Kruskal's algorithm for finding a minimum spanning tree (MST) of a network is represented as following and is based on the edge selection.

Kruskal's Algorithm
Step 1: (Setup)
  Let $G_0 = (V, \varnothing)$ and $i = 0$
Step 2: (Addition of edge)
  Find (x,y) which minimizes w(x,y), and set w(x,y) = +∞
Step 3: (Test for cycle)
  If the addition of edge (x,y) to the graph G_i would form a cycle, then go to Step 2; otherwise, add edge (x,y) to graph G_i and increment i.
Step 4: (Test for termination)
  if $i \leq n - 1$, then return to Step 2; otherwise, stop with G_{n-1} = MST.
End Kruskal's Algorithm

The following psuedocode represents Kruskal's sequential MST algorithm:
Algorithm: Kruskal{G = (V,E)}
  Step 1 $i \Leftarrow 0$
    $N \Leftarrow$ number of vertices in V
    $T \Leftarrow \varnothing$ {edges of the minimum spanning tree}
  Step 2 while($i \leq n - 1$) do
    find   e = {u,v} shortest edge not yet considered
        if there is no cycle by adding e to T then
          $T \Leftarrow \{T\} \cup \{e\}$ and $i \Leftarrow i + 1$
    return {T}

At Step 2, Kruskal's algorithm performs a loop such that each iteration finds a shortest edge e = {u,v}. If the addition of the edge e would not form a cycle with regard to all the edges in T, then it will be added to T to form a minimum spanning tree. The algorithm can be performed in the following steps utilizing the graph G shown in Figure 6.16 (a).

Step	Edge Considered	Edges in G_i
Initialization		$(V, \varnothing)$
1	{A,G}	$(V, \{A,G\})$
2	{B,C}	$(V, \{A,G\}, \{B,C\})$
3	{D,E}	$(V, \{A,G\}, \{B,C\}, \{D,E\})$
4	{E,F}	$(V, \{A,G\}, \{B,C\}, \{D,E\}, \{E,F\})$
5	{F,G}	$(V, \{A,G\}, \{B,C\}, \{D,E\}, \{E,F\}, \{F,G\})$
6	{A,C}	$(V, \{A,G\}, \{B,C\}, \{D,E\}, \{E,F\}, \{F,G\}, \{A,C\})$

Since i = 6, meaning that n − 1 = 6, the algorithm terminates and G_6 represents the minimum spanning tree of the graph G as shown in Figure 6.16 (b). It is worth noting that the constructed trees of both Prim's and Kruskal's algorithms are equivalent with regard to the length of the tree.

We can evaluate the time complexity of the Kruskal's algorithm in a graph with *n* vertices and *m* edges as follows:

1. The time to sort the edges. We assume that the edges are sorted in non-decreasing order of their weights, thus presorting can be done in time $O(m \log m)$.

2. The time in the *while* loop. The while loop makes at most *m* iterations, each testing the connectivity of two trees plus an edge, yielding the time complexity as $O(m \log m)$.

3. The time to initialize *n* disjoint sets. It is given by $O(n)$.

With this data structure, the sorting and manipulation of disjoint sets dominates the initialization time, thus resulting in an $O(m \log m)$ algorithm, which is faster than the Prim algorithm for sparse graphs.

Parallel Minimum Spanning Tree Algorithm

Parallel algorithms for finding the minimum spanning tree on a linear systolic array of processors were presented by Savage [Savage 84] in which for a graph of n vertices and m edges the minimum spanning tree can be computed using m processors. Bentley [Bentley 80] proposed an algorithm for finding the minimum spanning forest on a linear array and a binary tree of p processors.

Leighton [Leighton 83] and Nath [Nath 83] presented algorithms for finding the minimum spanning forest using an n × n mesh of tree processors. In general, there are several considerations which have a strong influence on how we can write parallel solutions for the minimum spanning tree problem. For example, one of them is the synchronization problem that occurs when we perform some of the operations in parallel. For instance, in Prim's algorithm each iteration in Step 2 adds a new vertex to the minimum spanning tree, and the length of the tree may change every time a new vertex is added. Both vertices on an edge might have that edge as their minimum cost edge. Once one vertex claims that edge, the second vertex cannot use that edge too. Neither can it simply use its next best edge, because the second best edge from that vertex might or might not be in the spanning tree.

Unfortunately, we cannot make the while loop parallel, because there are precedence constraints between iterations. In other words, each of the trees existing on iteration I must be joined with the nearest tree before iteration I + 1 can begin. This indicates that different iterations of the while loop cannot be performed in parallel. Consequently, once two vertices share a common minimum edge, they must cooperate to find a new edge. Thus, parallelization must be done inside the while loop. For example, the loop can be made parallel through the prescheduling method, meaning that each processor is responsible for one part of the graph. This is most efficiently done by assigning each processor its fair share of vertices, then allowing it to examine every outgoing edge from this set.

Given a connected undirected graph $G = (V,E)$ with a weight w_{ij} associated with every edge (i,j), we outline a parallel algorithm to find a spanning tree T such that the sum of the edge weights of the tree is minimum. The input for this algorithm is an $n \times n$ weight matrix W such that element $w_{ij} \in W$, and $1 \le i,j \le n$ denotes the weight of the undirected edge (i,j). If there is no edge between vertices i and j then $w_{ij} = \infty$. The parallel computation model is a linear array of p processors such that $|E| = m$ edges are initially distributed equally among the processors. The algorithm is an adaptation of the connected components algorithm and the algorithm to find a spanning tree in which the minimum spanning tree is found by successively enlarging components of the tree. The algorithm can be outlined in the following steps and works by iterating $log_2 n$ times, where n is the number of vertices in the graph:

Step 1: For every connected component of T, choose a smallest weight edge of G joining that component to another component of T.

Step 2: Add to T the edges chosen in Step 1.

Step 3: Steps 1 and 2 are iterated until T becomes a single connected component.

Algorithm: Minimum-Spanning-Tree(A,W)
{The parallel computation model is a linear array of p processors}
{C is a vector of connected components of length n }
{ such that C(i)=C(j)}
{if and only if vertex i is in the same connected component as vertex j}
{let the iteration number be k}
{T(k) consists of sets of vertices generated at each iteration}

Initialization:

        for all   vertices i $1 \le i \le n$ in parallel   do
                $C(i) = i$
        for $k = 1$ to $log_2 n$ do

Step 1:

        for all   vertices i   in parallel   do
                $T(i) = Min_j \{W_{ij} \mid A(i,j) = 1 \text{ and } C(j) \ne C(i)\}$
        endfor
        for all   vertices i   in parallel   do
                $T(i) = Min_j \{T(j) \mid C(j) = i \text{ and } T(j) \ne i\}$
        endfor

{the input to Step 2 is the connected components induced by the set}
{of vertices output from Step 1, with regard to the presented graph}
{the set $T = (T_1, T_2) = ([1,4,5],[2,3,6,7,8,9])$}
{B is an auxiliary vector}

Step 2:

for all   vertices i   in parallel   do
                    B(i) = T(i)
           endfor

           repeat log_2n   times
                    for all   vertices i   in parallel   do
                             T(i) = T(T(i))
                    endfor

           for all   vertices i   in parallel   do
                    C(i) = Min{B(T(i)), T(i)}
           endfor
      endfor
End   Minimum Spanning Tree

We can observe that the number of connected components of T decreases by a factor of 2 after each iteration (Steps 1 and 2), and this number is $\leq n/2^{k-1}$ prior to the k_{th} iteration. Note that this indicates the total number of iterations is no more than log_2n. The input to each iteration, described by the following steps, is the vector C. In Step 1, we choose an edge from each vertex to the neighboring vertices which has least weight. The net effect of Step 1 is to merge vertices recursively into larger and larger components. In other words, T(i) is assigned the vertices of least weight which are adjacent to vertex i but which are in different connected components.

In Step 2, we merge vertices in the same component: specifically we merge them into the vertex with the least vertex number. The auxiliary vector B is used to keep a copy of connected vertices in Step 1. Finally, the vector C describes a set of connected vertices which forms the input for the next iteration. Consequently, after each iteration we can discard all the edges of G whose endpoints are in the same connected component of T, and if there is more than one edge of G joining two connected components of T, we can consider only the lowest weight edge. In general, at the k_{th} iteration we wish to determine the minimum of T(k) sets of vertices. The total number of elements in the T(k) sets is m, which is the total number of edges and the algorithm uses p processors. Step 1 and 2 are iterated for log_2n times to produce the minimum spanning tree of the input graph.

The rationale behind this algorithm is that we can effectively collapse in G the vertices that belong to the same connected components of T into a single vertex, remove all the loops from the resulting graph and keep only a smallest weighted edge between any pair of the vertices. For the purpose of illustrating the algorithm, we take the input weighted graph of Figure 6.17. For our example, Figure 6.18 provides the digraph consisting of two connected components after the first iteration. It shows the set of weighted tree edges added at the end of the first iteration to the minimum weighted tree under construction. The input to the second iteration is the graph induced by the set of vertices output from the previous iteration, in this example the set T=(T_1,T_2) in which T_1 = {1,4,5} and T_2 = {2,3,6,7,8,9}.

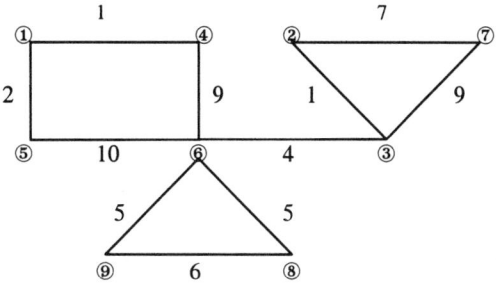

Figure 6.17. Input graph of minimum spanning tree algorithm.

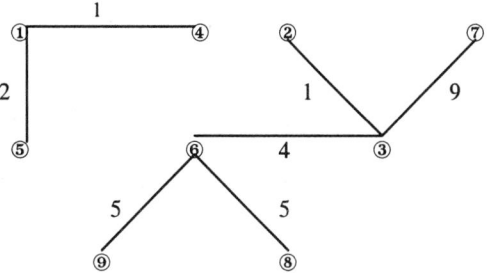

Figure 6.18. Two sets of vertices {1,4,5} and {2,3,6,7,8,9} after the first iteration.

In the second iteration an edge chosen between sets of vertices {1,4,5} and {2,3,6,7,8,9} is an edge of minimum weight. In this case, there are two edges between sets of vertices, namely $w_{4,6}$ = 9, and $w_{5,6}$ = 10, and of these $w_{4,6}$ has minimum weight. Thus, edge (4,6) is chosen to provide an endpoint for the vertices connecting two components. The edge is added in the final iteration to form the minimum weighted spanning tree of the example graph represented in Figure 6.19.

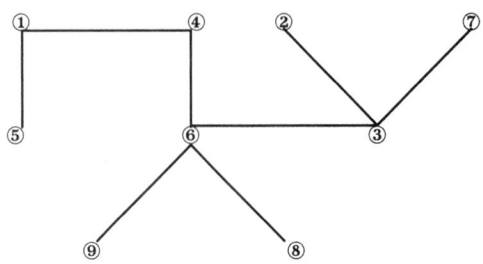

Figure 6.19. Minimum spanning tree of the sample graph.

6.4   Traveling Salesman Problem

Let G = (V,E) be a graph and let P = $V_1, V_2, ..., V_k$ be a path in G. This path is called a Hamiltonian path if and only if P is containing every vertex in V. P is a Hamiltonian cycle if and only if $V_1 = V_k$ and P is a Hamiltonian path. When G is a directed graph, the terms directed Hamiltonian path and directed Hamiltonian cycle are used. The problem of determining a shortest directed Hamiltonian cycle in a weighted directed graph G is called the Traveling Salesman Problem (TSP).

In other words, the Traveling Salesman Problem is stated as: given a set of vertices and a non-negative cost C_{ij} associated with each pair of vertices i and j, find a circuit containing every vertex in the graph so that the cost of the entire path is minimized. This circuit is called a Hamiltonian circuit and is defined as a path which visits each vertex exactly once and terminates at the initial vertex. A traveling salesman problem in a complete network can be further classified as:

- Symmetric Salesman Problem such that

$$C_{ij} = C_{ji} \text{ for all i and j}$$

- Asymmetric Traveling Salesman Problem such that

$$C_{ij} \neq C_{ji} \text{ for all i and j}$$

where C_{ij} is the associated value, cost or distance, of the edges. The problem can be represented as a complete undirected graph with n vertices and we assume that the distance between vertices is always positive.

Our problem therefore requires us to find the shortest Hamiltonian cycle in a given graph. For example, Figure 6.20 (a) represents a graph consisting of seven vertices with the associated weight of each edge, and the traveling salesman tour, the Hamiltonian cycle of the graph, is given in Figure 6.20 (b), which is:

Traveling Salesman Path = $1 \Rightarrow 3 \Rightarrow 6 \Rightarrow 7 \Rightarrow 5 \Rightarrow 4 \Rightarrow 2 \Rightarrow 1$.

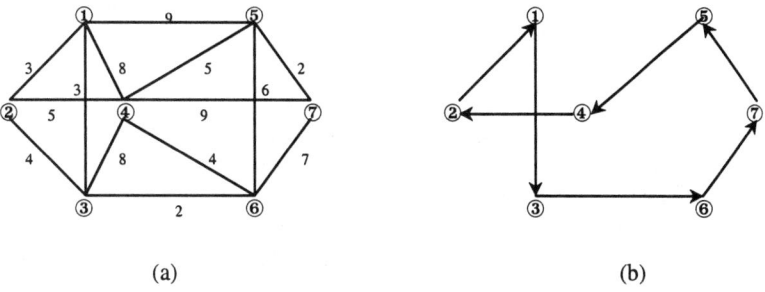

(a)   (b)

Figure 6.20. (a) An undirected graph. (b) Traveling salesman tour.

Generally speaking, in the traveling salesman problem, the goal is to find the shortest route that starts at one city and visits each of a list of other cities exactly once before returning to the first city. For n cities, there are (n − 1)! different paths starting and ending in city 1. Unless n is small, this number is very large. Thus, we need to look for ways to cut down on the amount of computation that has to be performed and for ways to use parallelism to speed up the computation. In practice, the traveling salesman problem may be formulated as a Mathematical Programming Model or as the Integer Programming Model to be used by classical algorithms. Some of algorithms used to solve the TSP problems are:

- Vertex Penalty Algorithm
- Nearest Neighbor Algorithm
- Nearest Insertion Algorithm
- Farthest Insertion Algorithm
- Space-Filling Curve Algorithm
- Branch-and-Bound Algorithm

In practice, finding an exact solution, one that finds a minimum cost tour, is infeasible except for small values of n. Consequently, many heuristic algorithms have been developed to generate approximate solutions to the traveling salesman problem. In this section, two sequential algorithms and one parallel algorithm are explained. The sequential algorithms are based on the minimum spanning tree method, explained in Section 3 of Chapter 6, and the depth-first search method, explained in Section 2 of Chapter 7. The parallel solution uses the bag-of-tasks paradigm and is based on the depth-search method.

Sequential Solution

Consider an n × n distance matrix D with positive entries; for example, the distances between the cities the traveling salesman is visiting. We assume D is symmetric, meaning that $d_{ij} = d_{ji}$ for all i and j and $d_{ii} = 0$ for i = 1,2, ... ,n. We claim that $[d_{ij}]$ satisfies the triangle inequality if

$$d_{ij} + d_{jk} \geq d_{ik} \qquad \text{for all } 1 \leq i, j, k \leq n,$$

What the triangle inequality constraint essentially says is that going from city i to city k through city j can not be cheaper than going directly from city i to city k. This is a reasonable assumption, since the imposed visit to city j appears to be an additional constraint, meaning that can only increase the cost. As a rule of thumb, whenever the entries of the distance matrix represent cost, the triangle inequality is satisfied.

Notice that the graph in this variant of the problem is undirected. If we remove any edge from an optimal path for such a graph, we have a spanning tree for the graph. Thus, we can use an algorithm to obtain a minimum spanning tree, then by going twice around the spanning tree, we can convert it to a path that visits every city. Recalling the transformation from Hamiltonian circuit to traveling salesman problem, Christofides [Christofides 76] introduced a heuristic algorithm based on the minimum spanning tree for this problem.

Christofides' Traveling Salesman Problem Algorithm
Step 1: Find the minimum spanning tree T using the distance matrix D.
Step 2: Find the nodes of T having odd degree and find the shortest complete matching M in the completed graph consisting of these nodes only. Let G' be the graph with nodes {1,2,...,n} and edges in T and M.
Step 3: Find a Hamiltonian circuit in G'.

Finding a shortest complete matching in a complete graph is a version of the *minimal weight matching* problem, in which the total weight of the edges obtained from the matching is minimal. Christofides' algorithm is illustrated in Figure 6.21, in which the graph is represented in (a) and the minimum spanning tree T with the odd-degree vertices encircled is shown in (b). Figure 6.21 (c) shows the shortest matching of these odd-degree vertices, and a corresponding traveling salesman tour is shown in (d) which is {1,2,4,5,7,9,10,8,6,3,1}.

Recalling the depth-first search method, one sequential solution is to examine all feasible paths. A path is feasible if it is not longer than the best complete path that has been determined so far. To find the shortest path that visits all cities exactly once, we must consider every possible tour. In general, if we start in city 1, there are n − 1 possible cities we could visit next. From each of these, there are n − 2 possible cities to visit, and so on. Thus, we can represent all possible paths by a tree in which city 1 is the root. In general, we need to find a permutation of integers 1 to n such that the sum of the distances between adjacent pairs of cities (plus the distance back to city 1) is minimized. Figure 6.22 illustrates a search tree for four cities in which there are 6 = (n − 1)! paths. If we search from left to right in the tree, corresponding to the depth-first search method, we would visit the four cities in the following order:

$$\{(1,2,3,4), (1,2,4,3), (1,3,2,4), (1,3,4,2), (1,4,2,3), (1,4,3,2)\}$$

The standard method to examine all paths in a tree such as this is to use the depth-first search method, which is realized by a recursive and backtracking algorithm. With regard to the traveling salesman, whose goal is to find the shortest path, it is not necessary to consider a path that is known to be longer than the shortest completed path that has been found so far. This fact can help to prune infeasible paths from further consideration. The larger the number of cities, the more dramatic the effect pruning can have.

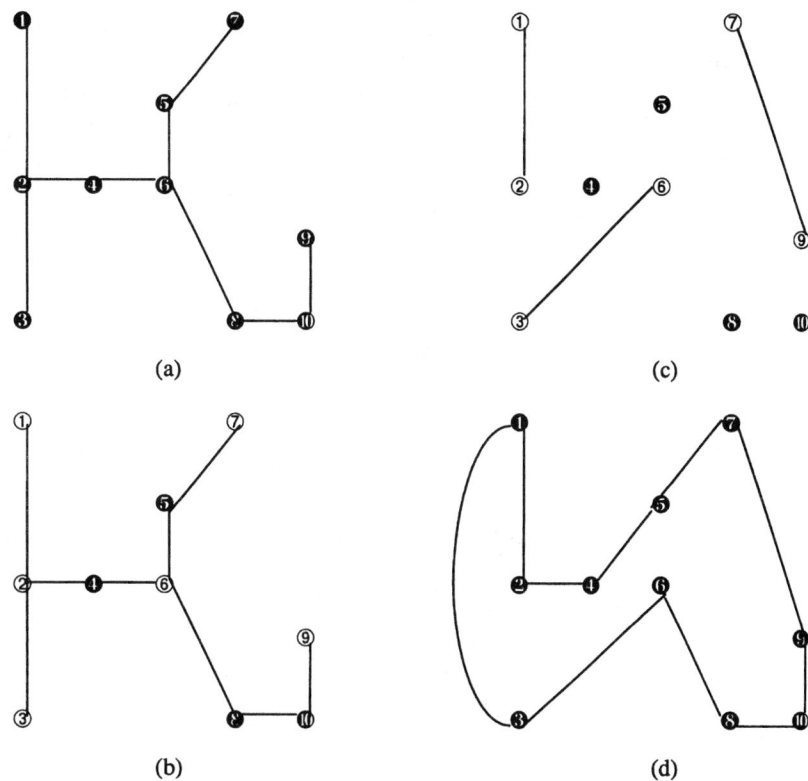

Figure 6.21. Christofides' algorithm for traveling salesman problem.

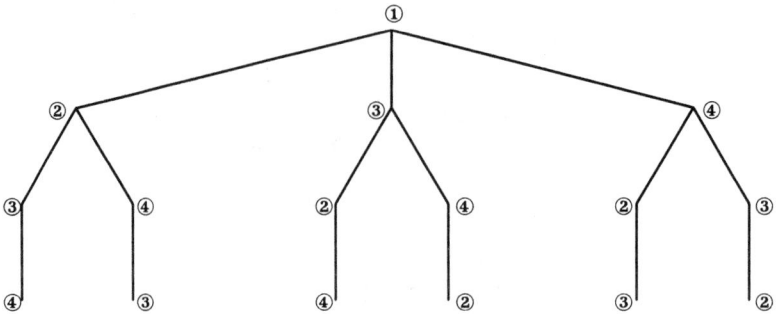

Figure 6.22. Search tree for four cities.

Determining whether a graph contains a Hamiltonian cycle is a computationally difficult problem. In fact, the fastest algorithm known has a worst-case time complexity of $O(n^2 2^n)$ in the case of n points. We can evaluate the time complexity of the Christofides' algorithm as follows:

1. The time to find the minimum spanning tree. This time is bounded by $O(n \log n)$ in the case of n points in the plane (see Section 6.3).
2. The time to find a Hamiltonian cycle. In general, for each set A of k vertices, we need to consider $(n - 1 - k)$ vertices, in which for each of these vertices the basic operations are done k times.

Since the number of sets of size k is $\begin{pmatrix} n-1 \\ k \end{pmatrix}$, the total number of assignments that are performed is given by

$$\sum_{k-1}^{n-2} k(n-1-k)\begin{pmatrix} n-1 \\ k \end{pmatrix} = \sum_{k=1}^{n-2} k(n-1)\begin{pmatrix} n-2 \\ k \end{pmatrix} = (n-1)\sum_{k=1}^{n-2} k\begin{pmatrix} n-2 \\ k \end{pmatrix} = (n-1)(n-2)2^{n-3}$$

Hence, the traveling salesman problem has an exponential worst-case complexity of $O(n^2 2^n)$.

Below we present a sequential program to solve the traveling salesman problem. The positive distance entries are stored in the matrix **dist**, and **shortest** variable contains the length of the shortest path so far. The matrix **shortest_path** contains the cities in the shortest path. The final code prints the result once the program terminates.

```
/*depth-first-search sequential program to solve traveling salesman problem */
shortest: integer = 2**20          /* best path so far, any large number */
dist[1:n, 1:n] : integer           /* distance matrix */
shortest_path[1:n] : integer       /* shortest path cities */
```

```
for       i = 1 to n, and j = 1 to n
          read(dist[i,j])
endfor
```

Main Program

```
TSP: /* the computation is carried out by tsp procedure once for each partial */
     /* path of length 2 and recursively examines all other feasible paths */
         proc    tsp(path[1:*], length)
                 number − cities = path
                 if number − cities = n
                         length + = dist[path[n], 1]
                         update(path, length)
                 else
                         for city = 2 to n
                                 visit(path, city)
                                 newpath[1:number_cities] = path
                                 newpath[number_cities + 1] = city
                                 newlength = length +
                                         dist[newpath[number_cities],
                                             newpath[number_cities + 1]]
                                 if newlength < shortest
                                         tsp(newpath, newlength)
                                 endif
                         endfor
                 endif
         end
         for     i = 2 to n
                 path[2] = i
                 tsp(path, dist[1,i])
         endfor
Update: /* update the shortest length and path if necessary */
         proc    update(path, length)
      if     length < shortest
             shortest = length
             shortest_path = path
    endif
         end
Visit: /* to extend a path by a city, if that city has not been visited */
     /* add it and return true */
         proc    visit(path[1:*], city)
                 for i = 2 to n
                         if       path[i] = city
                         flag = false
                         endif
                 flag = true
```

```
            endfor
      return flag
      end
Report: /* report the length of the shortest path and included cities */
      write("The shortest path has length:", shortest)
      write("The cities on the shortest path are:")
      for     i = 1 to n
            write (shortest_path[i])
      endfor
End Main Program
```

Parallel Solution

Recalling the search tree, in the traveling salesman problem the paths are independent; thus, we could evaluate all of them in parallel. An alternative approach is to provide a fixed number of slave processes that share a pool of tasks. Each task consists of a partial path, the number of cities visited on the path, and the path's length. In this approach, there are $n - 1$ tasks representing the $n - 1$ paths starting at city 1. Each process takes a partial path and extends the path with every city that has not been considered. If the length of the new generated path is longer than the shortest completed path that has been found so far, it is discarded. If the path does not include all cities and it is valid with regard to length, the process appends the new path and its length into the pool of the tasks. Consequently, if the path includes all cities and it might be shorter than the shortest path found so far, the shortest path length is updated by the process. The synchronization is performed using a semaphore variable which prevents access to the shared variables by more than one process at the same time. The parallel traveling salesman algorithm can be illustrated as follows.

Parallel Traveling Salesman Problem Algorithm
Step 1: Create a pool with $n - 1$ partial tasks.
Step 2: Create k number of processes.
Step 3: Take a partial path from the pool and extend the path with regard to the unvisited cities.
Step 4: If all the cities are not included and the length is not longer than the shortest competed path, this path is appended to the pool of tasks; otherwise, it is discarded. If there are any more tasks, then return to Step 3; otherwise, report the progress.

```
/*depth-first-search parallel program to solve traveling salesman problem */
shortest: integer = 2**20        /* best path so far, any large number */
dist[1:n, 1:n] : integer         /* distance matrix */
shortest_path[1:n] : integer     /* shortest path cities */
```

path[1:n] : integer
semaphore Mutex =1

    for i = 1 to n, and j = 1 to n
        read(dist[i,j])
    endfor

Update: /* is executed as a critical section by a semaphore variable to */
    /* alter the shared variables, shortest and shortest_path */

    proc   **update**(path, length)
      P(Mutex)   /* block shared variables */
        if   length < shortest
            shortest = length
            shortest_path = path
        endif
      V(Mutex)   /* release shared variables */
    end

Visit: /* to extend a path by a city, the city is added if it is not visited */
    proc   **visit**(city, path[1:*], number_cities, length)
        for i = 2 to number_cities
            path[i] = city
            newlength = 0
            return newlength
        endfor
      newlength = length + dist[path[number_cities], city]
      path[number_cities + 1] = city
    end

Main Program
/* put the first set of partial paths into the pool */
    for   i = 2 to n
        path[2] = i
        send pool(path, 2, dist[1,i])
    endfor

/* create k number of slave processes */
    for   i = 1 to k
        create slave()
    endfor

Process Slave
    while(pool ≠ φ)
    receive pool (path, number_cities, ength)
    for   city = 2 to n
        newlength = **visit**(city, path, number_cities, length)
        if   newlength ≠ 0   then
            if   number_cities + 1 < n and new
                length < shortest then

```
                                    send pool(path, number_cities + 1,
                                            newlength)
                        endif
                        if       number_cities + 1 = n then
                        newlength = newlength + dist[path[n], 1]
                                    if  newlength < shortest   then
                                            update(path, newlength)
                                    endif
                        endif
                endif
            endfor
        endwhile
    end
    End Main
```

Paths are computed by instances of the slave process. On each iteration, the slave process receives a new task from the pool of tasks which is a partial path. Each process calls two procedures, *visit* and *update*, in which *visit* extends the partial path by each city that has not been visited. The *update* is a shared procedure and is called by the process when a complete path is found that might be better than the best completed path. In general, the size of the pool could become very large with regard to the number of tasks. This can cause to the program to run out of memory. In this approach, we do not need to communicate with instances of processes or to destroy them.

6.5   Cycles in a Graph

A **cycle** in a graph $G = (V,E)$ is a sequence of edges:

$$(v_1,v_2),(v_2,v_3),(v_3,v_4), \ldots ,(v_{i-1},v_i),(v_i,v_1)$$

where every vertex of this sequence is in V and every edge of this sequence is in E, and only the first and last vertices in the sequence of edges are identical. Generally speaking, a path from a vertex to itself is called a cycle. The paths $((v_1,v_4),(v_4,v_5),(v_5,v_1))$ and $((v_1,v_2),(v_2,v_3),(v_3,v_4),(v_4,v_5),(v_5,v_1))$ in Figure 6.23 are cycles of the graph. If a graph contains a cycle, it is called cyclic, otherwise; it is called acyclic.

To be more precise, if the graph is not a tree, it must contain a cycle, and such a cycle can be identified as soon as the first back edge is detected. If (v_1,v_2) is a back edge, then there must be a path in the tree from v_2 to v_1, or else there is a cycle from v_2 to v_1. Deadlock detection in distributed systems is one of the applications of the cycles. Given a finite graph G as the interconnection of the processors, the problem is to detect whether there is a cycle in the graph from some vertex root to itself. This can address the reachability of that vertex. In reachability, a vertex receives a message only if there is a path (of at least one edge) from the root to that vertex. In particular, the root receives a message only if the root is in a cycle.

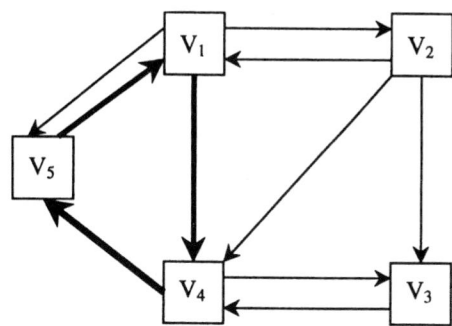

Figure 6.23. A directed graph.

Alternatively, a **Complete** cycle or an **Eulerian** cycle of a graph is a cycle which traverses every edge of the graph precisely once. A graph containing an Eulerian cycle is called an Eulerian graph. As is well known, an undirected graph G is Eulerian if and only if the degree of every vertex of G is even.

Suppose you are given map of a city and are required to find paths for garbage collection, snow plows, or postman. In all of these applications, every road in the city must be completely traversed at least once in order to ensure that all deliveries or pickups are made. Such applications are examples of the Eulerian cycle problem. For efficiency, we seek to minimize total drive time, or equivalently the total distance or number of edges traversed. In general, we seek a path or cycle through a graph that visits each edge exactly once. There are well-known conditions for determining whether a graph contains an Eulerian cycle or path, as follows:

1. An undirected graph contains an Eulerian cycle if and only if
   - It is connected, and
   - Each vertex is of even degree, or
   - Each vertex has the same in-degree as out-degree.
2. An undirected graph contains an Eulerian path if and only if
   - It is connected, and
   - All vertices have even degree except the start and end points of the path, or
   - All vertices have the same in-degree as out-degree except the start and end points, whose in-degree and out-degree differ by one.

In view of this characterization of Eulerian graphs, it is easy to test whether such a cycle exists or whether the graph is connected using a search method (i.e., depth-first or breadth-first search). For example, use depth-first search to find a cycle in the graph, then delete this cycle and repeat the process until the entire set of edges has been partitioned into a set of edge disjoint cycles. Since deleting a cycle reduces each vertex degree by an even number, the remaining graph satisfies the same Eulerian graph characteristics. The Eulerian cycle, if one exists, solves the stated problems, since any tour that visits each edge only once must have a minimum length. In many situations, it is useful to designate a special vertex of a graph as the root and then seek an Eulerian cycle or path asociated with that vertex. In this case, an Euler tour can be made by choosing an edge leaving the root as the first edge and performing the depth-first search traversal. Atallah and Vishkin [Atallah 84] developed a parallel algorithm to find the Euler tour in a graph.

We describe a parallel algorithm to find an Eulerian cycle of a directed graph. The algorithm presumes that the input graph is an Eulerian directed graph. Assuming a directed graph $G = (V,E)$ with n vertices, then the input to the algorithm is n linked lists, one for each vertex of the graph G. Each element (e_{ij}) of the associated linked list with vertex v_i, consists of two fields, a field **edge** containing edge (v_i,v_j) and a field **next** containing a pointer to the next element of that linked list. There is a pointer associated with each linked list which points to the first element of that linked list. For example, the directed graph of Figure 6.24 (a) can be represented by the data structure of Figure 6.24 (b). The presented algorithm rearranges all the edges of the linked lists to construct a single linked list such that each edge (v_i,v_j) is followed by an edge (v_j,v_k). We obtain a lexicographic ordering of the elements of the linked lists utilizing the following procedures.

> **Successor(v_i,v_j)**
>   if next(ji) = jk
>   then   Successor(i) $\Leftarrow$ jk
>   else   Successor(i) $\Leftarrow$ head(v_j)
>   endif
> **end**

> **Successor(v_j,v_i)**
>   if next(ij) = im
>   then   Successor(j) $\Leftarrow$ im
>   else   Successor(j) $\Leftarrow$ head(v_i)
>   endif
> **end**

The result of this process is a copy of edges into a vector called **Successor** with their reorder according to the lexicographic order defined as $(i,j) < (k,l)$ if $i = k$ and $j < l$. To be more precise, on any cycle, the edge following the edge $e_{ij} = (v_i, v_j)$ is to be found in successor(i).

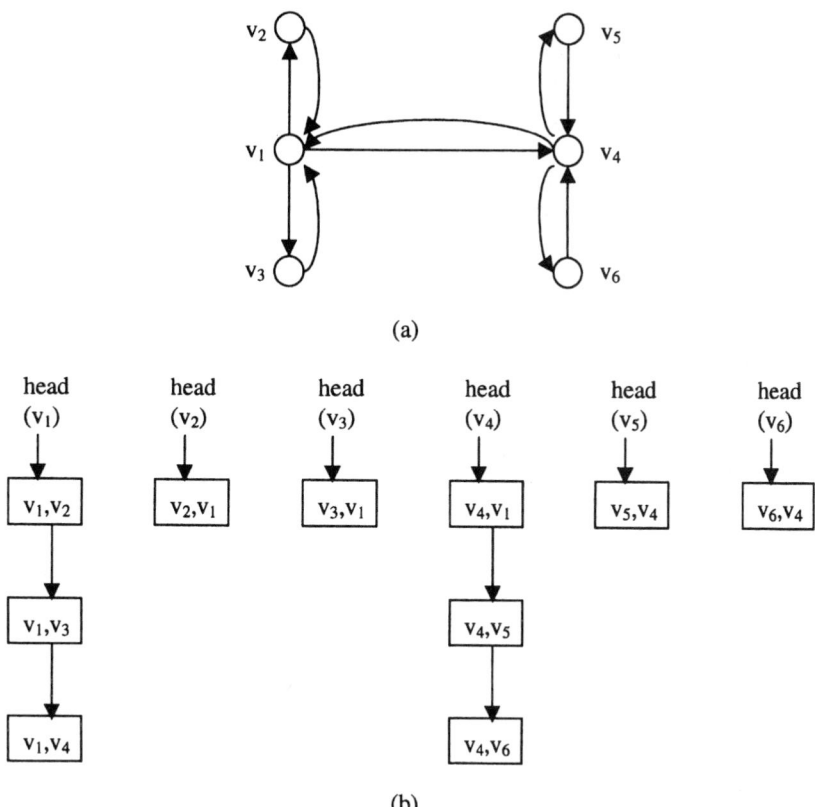

(a)

(b)

Figure 6.24. A directed graph and its data structure represented by linked lists.

We assume there are n processors such that each processor P_{ij} is in charge of two edges, (v_i,v_j) and (v_j,v_i). The processor P_{ij} determines the position of the two elements holding (v_i,v_j) and (v_j,v_i), denoted by e_{ij} and e_{ji}. This can be done as follows. If, in the linked list for v_j, edge (v_j,v_i) is followed by some edge (v_j,v_k), then the successor of (v_i,v_j) is (v_j,v_k). The successor of (v_j,v_i) is determined by the processor P_{ij} in a similar way. The algorithm is now as follows:

Procedure   Cycle(E)
    for all   i, $1 \le i \le n$, in parallel do
    Cycle(v_i) $\Leftarrow$ Successor(v_i)
    endfor
End Cycle

where Cycle(v_i) represents the Eulerian cycle of the graph from vertex v_i to itself, meaning that there is a tour starting from vertex v_i and traversing all the edges. The time complexity of the algorithm can be evaluated as follows:

1. The successor of each edge is found in constant time.
2. The loop is iterated (log n) times and each one requires a constant time.

This results in the running time of O(log n). Since n processors are used, the total cost of the algorithm is O(n log n). The Eulerian cycle of graph G is represented in Figure 6.25.

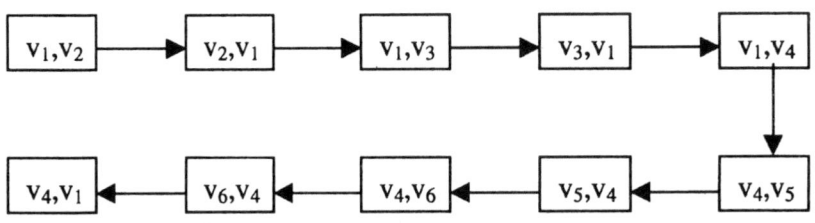

Figure 6.25. The Eulerian cycle of graph G represented as a linked list.

6.6   Coloring of Graphs

Let G be an undirected graph and let c be an integer. A coloring of graph G is an assignment of colors to the vertices or edges such that no two adjacent vertices (edges) are to be similarly colored. Within this constraint we are concerned to minimize the number of colors used. It is a c-coloring problem if it uses no more than c distinct colors. The smallest c such that a c-coloring exists is called the graph's chromatic number and any such c-coloring is an optimal coloring, meaning it uses the minimum number of colors. In general, the goal is to use as few colors as possible. The following two problems are defined in the area of graph coloring.

1. **The Graph Coloring Optimization Problem:** Given a graph G, it is required to determine the minimum number of colors needed to color the graph so that no two adjacent vertices are colored the same color. This number is called the **chromatic** number of the graph.
2. **The Graph Coloring Decision Problem:** Given a graph G, it is required to determine for an integer m whether there is a coloring that uses at most m colors and no two adjacent vertices are the same color. The Graph Coloring Decision Problem has the same parameters as the Graph Coloring Optimization Problem plus the additional parameter m.

Example: The graph of Figure 6.26 can be colored using two colors, say blue for vertices 2 and 3 and red for vertices 1 and 4. We can augment either breadth-first or depth-first search methods so that whenever we discover a new vertex, we color it the opposite of its parent. For each edge not discovered, we check whether it links two vertices of the same color. Assume the graph represented in Figure 6.27. There is no solution to the 2-coloring problem of this graph because, if we can use at most two different colors, there is no way to color the vertices such that all adjacent vertices are different colors.

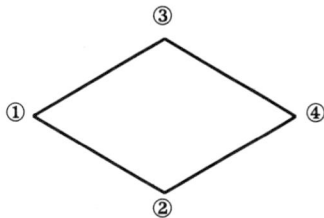

Figure 6.26. A graph with 4 vertices to be colored with 2 colors, red and blue.

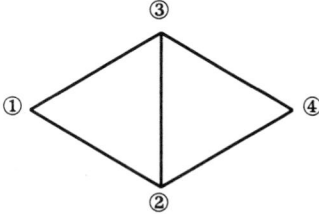

Figure 6.27. A graph with 4 vertices for which there is no solution using only 2 colors.

The problem of finding a proper vertex c-coloring of a graph for a given c has many practical applications, such as scheduling, time-tabling, register allocation for compilers and coloring of maps. A simple graph-coloring algorithm works by choosing a color and an arbitrary starting vertex and then considering each vertex in turn. If a vertex can be colored with the first color, we color the vertex, and if no more vertices can be colored, we choose a new color and a new starting vertex that has not yet been colored. We color as many vertices as we can with this second color. This time, we color a vertex if none of its neighbors has already been colored.

For example, consider graph G in Figure 6.26 with 4 vertices. If vertex 1 is colored red, we are not allowed to color vertices 2 and 3 with the same color. However, vertex 4 can be colored red. If we start again at vertex 2 using blue, we can color vertex 3 blue and finish the graph coloring utilizing only two colors. In practice, the graph-coloring problems are divided into different categories:

1. Vertex Coloring
2. Map Coloring
3. Edge Coloring
4. Total Coloring

A map is a connected plane (possibly with multiple edges and loops) with no bridges. If M is a map, we define its chromatic number to be the minimum number of colors needed to color its faces so that no two neighboring faces are assigned the same color. It is easy to see that a map is 2-colorable if and only if the map is an Eulerian graph.

Total coloring deals with the total chromatic number of a graph. If G is a graph, we define its total chromatic number to be the minimum number of colors needed to color the vertices and edges of G such that no adjacent vertices, adjacent edges, or incident edges and vertices are assigned the same color. In this section, we deal with vertex-coloring and edge-coloring problems. We present parallel algorithms for finding a proper c-coloring of a graph G with regard to the vertex-coloring and edge-coloring problems.

Vertex Coloring of Graphs

We examine the vertex graph-coloring problem for the particular case of a 2-dimensional mesh SIMD model. The parallel computation model is a concurrent-read and exclusive-write parallel random access machine (CREW PRAM). The central idea of this algorithm is that in a graph with n vertices, 2^n processors are created and each processor indicates a different coloring of the graph. Then each processor checks to see if that represented coloring is valid or not. If the coloring is valid it will be considered as a coloring solution; otherwise, it will be discarded from the set of possible solutions. For example, assume a graph $G = (V,E)$ with an $n \times n$ adjacency matrix W:

$$W[i,j] = \begin{cases} 1 \ if \ vertix \ i \ and \ j \ are \ adjacent, \\ 0 \ otherwise. \end{cases}$$

We create a processor for every possible coloring of graph G utilizing different colors. For example, processor $p_i(c_1,c_2,...,c_n)$ corresponds to a coloring of graph G as the following:

> vertex v_1 is colored with color c_1
> vertex v_2 is colored with color c_2
> vertex v_3 is colored with color c_3
> ....
> ....
> ....
> ....
> ....
> vertex v_n is colored with color c_n

Then a checking for the validity of that coloring can be performed with regard to the adjacency matrix and colors used such that if $W[j,k] = 1$ and $c_j = c_k$, then the coloring is not valid, meaning that vertices j and k are adjacent and have the same color.

Consequently, if a processor detects an invalid coloring, that coloring of the graph will be discarded from the set of the candidates for the solution. For example, assume it is required to color the following graph with 4 vertices using only two colors. There are 4 vertices, indicating 16 processors to be created such that each processor sets its value in the 4-dimensional possible-solution array to 1.

If a processor detects an invalid coloring with regard to the adjacency matrix and colors used, it sets the corresponding element of the possible-solution array to 0, otherwise; the possible solution remains 1. Finally, if any element in the possible-solution array is still 1, then that coloring is valid as a solution to the vertex-coloring problem.

Figure 6.28 illustrates this example, in which the solutions are highlighted with the corresponding values of 1 in the possible-solution array. There are two solutions to this graph-coloring problem using two colors.

The psuedocode of the algorithm is outlined as follows.

Algorithm: Vertex-Coloring Graph(W)
{create 2^n processors one for each possible coloring solution, where n is the number of vertices in the graph}
{initially there are 2^n possible candidate solutions}
for all $p_i(c_1, c_2, \ldots, c_n)$ do; where $1 \leq i \leq 2^n$
possible-solution$[c_1, c_2, \ldots, c_n] = 1$

    begin
    for   j = 1 to n do
        for   k = 1 to n do
            if $w[j,k] = 1$ and $c_j = c_k$
            then
                possible-solution$[c_1, c_2, \ldots, c_n] = 0$
        endfor
    endfor
endfor

Report all coloring solutions of the graph with regard to each element of the possible-solution array as 1.
End   **Vertex-Coloring**

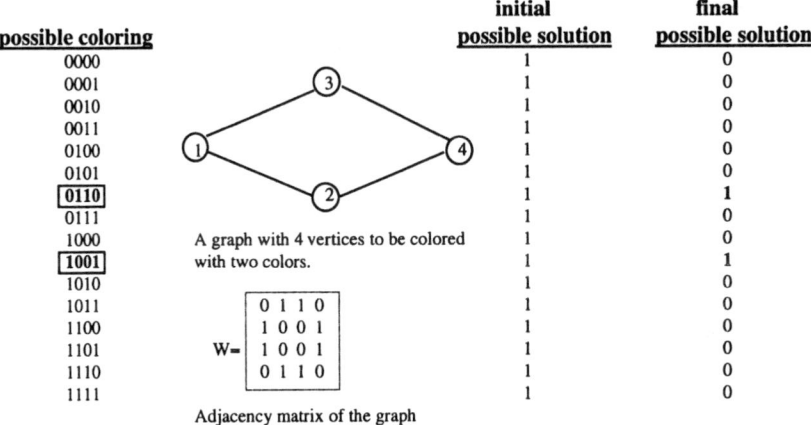

possible coloring		initial possible solution	final possible solution
0000		1	0
0001		1	0
0010		1	0
0011		1	0
0100		1	0
0101		1	0
0110		1	1
0111		1	0
1000	A graph with 4 vertices to be colored	1	0
1001	with two colors.	1	1
1010		1	0
1011		1	0
1100		1	0
1101		1	0
1110		1	0
1111		1	0

$$W = \begin{bmatrix} 0 & 1 & 1 & 0 \\ 1 & 0 & 0 & 1 \\ 1 & 0 & 0 & 1 \\ 0 & 1 & 1 & 0 \end{bmatrix}$$

Adjacency matrix of the graph

Figure 6.28. Example of a vertex-coloring of a graph.

Edge Coloring of Graphs

In this section we deal with the edge-coloring problem, which asks that all edges of a given graph G be colored using the minimum number of colors so that no two adjacent edges are colored with the same color. The minimum number is called the *chromatic* index of graph G. In general, the edge-coloring problem belongs to the edge-partitioning problem. Gabow and Kariv [Gabow 82] have developed an optimal edge-coloring algorithm for any bipartite graph. A graph is bipartite if it can be colored without conflicts using only two colors. Bipartite graphs are important because they arise often in practice and have more structure than arbitrary graphs. In general, the bipartite graphs can be colored exactly by finding a forest of rooted spanning trees using the Euler tour technique (discussed in Section 6.4). The idea is to compute the depth of each vertex using list ranking and then assign vertices of odd depth one color and vertices of even depth the other color.

Gibbons and Rytter [Gibbons 87, 88] have adopted Gabow's algorithm to develop an optimal edge-coloring parallel algorithm for any bipartite graph. The central idea of the algorithm is that a bipartite graph G may be recursively divided into two bipartite graphs G_1 and G_2 both of which have maximum degrees of power 2. In one such decomposition, the maximum degree of the input graph is exactly halved in the two graphs which are output. This can be achieved using an Euler partition of a graph. The Euler partition of a graph is a partition of the edges of the graph into edge disjoint paths and cycles so that each vertex of odd degree is the endpoint of exactly one path. In general, if G is Eulerian we can employ the method to find an Eulerian circuit by partitioning the edges into edge disjoint cycles. If G is not Eulerian, we add a dummy vertex v and an edge from v to each vertex of odd degree to get a new graph G^+. Then, we can obtain a partitioning of the edges of G^+ into edge disjoint cycles. If we drop the edges added in constructing G^+ from G, these cycles become paths. The Euler-coloring algorithm, which produces an optimal edge coloring of a bipartite graph, is outlined as follows.

Algorithm   Euler-Color(G)
　　　{G has maximum degree *degree* as a power of 2}
　　if　　*degree* = 1　　　then
　　　　　{color all edges of G with the color 1}
　　else
　　　　　{find an Euler Partition of G, then using the Euler Partition
　　　　　　　divide G into}
　　　　　{two graphs G_1 and G_2 with maximum degree *degree*/2}
　　　　　for　　$G = G_1$ and $G = G_2$　　　in parallel　　　do
　　　　　　　Euler-color(G)
　　　　　{reconstruct G from G_1 and G_2 renaming colors in G_1 so that}
　　　　　　　{G_1 and G_2 use disjoint color sets}
　　　　　endfor
　　endif
End Euler-Color

Gibbons and Rytter used the procedure Euler-Color to optimally edge color any bipartite graph. Figure 6.29 illustrates the Euler-Color algorithm for an example graph G with maximum degree 4 which is a power of 2. All edges labeled dashed lines constitute graph G_1 and those solid lines form graph G_2. Consequently, G_1 and G_2 are colored and each uses the degree / 2 colors denoted by {1,2,...,(degree / 2)}. We obtain an edge coloring of graph G when renaming the colors of graph G_2 by adding the number (degree / 2) to the colors assigned to each of its edges. For example, graph G_2 uses the color set {1,2}. The colors in G_2 are renamed 3 and 4 in reconstructing graph G, meaning that the number of colors used is {1,2,3,4}.

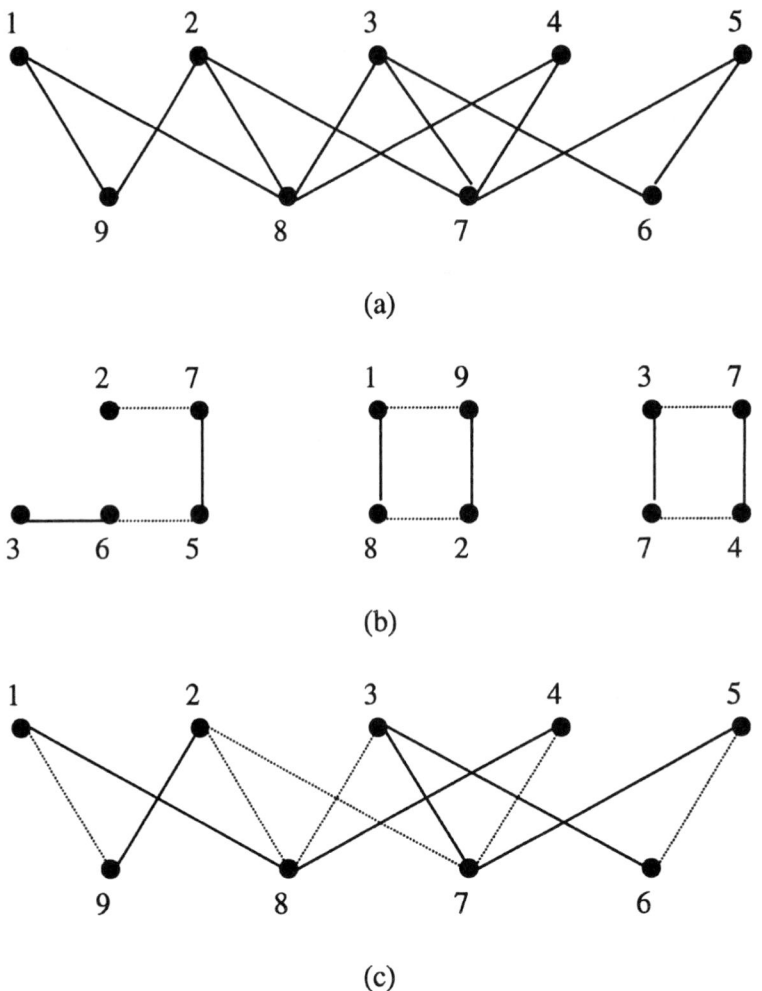

Figure 6.29. Edge coloring of graph G with 4 different colors. (a) Graph G with degree 4. (b) Euler partition of graph G. (c) Partitioning of G into graph G_1 and graph G_2.

Summary

One area in which a great deal of work has been done in the development of parallel algorithms is that of graph algorithms. After a brief discussion of the definitions we illustrated two methods to represent the graphs: adjacency matrix and adjacency lists.

Several graph algorithms have been presented in this chapter. We examined the connected components of an undirected graph. We outlined four different approaches to compute the connected components of a graph in parallel form: the pointer-jumping method utilizing one form of search algorithms, the transitive closure method utilizing the adjacency matrix, the supervertex method which follows collapsing vertices and the adjacency matrix partitioning method. We discussed paths and all-pairs shortest paths associated with directed weighted graphs. In this sense, we explained two methods: Dijkstra's labeling algorithm and Floyd's shortest-path algorithm. In Dijkstra's algorithm we found the shortest path from vertex s to each of the other vertices in the graph. In general, Dijkstra's algorithm is the same as Prim's algorithm to find the minimum spanning tree, which incrementally finds the shortest paths from a source to all the other vertices. We outlined the steps of the algorithm along with justification. We used Floyd's algorithm for finding a shortest path between every pair of vertices of a weighted directed graph. Unlike Dijkstra's algorithm, Floyd's algorithm works even if some of the edges have negative weights. The algorithms is based on triangle operations between each pair of vertices in the graph. For example, a triangle operation for a fixed vertex k is defined as:

$$w_{ij} = \text{Minimum}\{w_{ij}, w_{ik} + w_{kj}\} \text{ for all } i,j = 1,\ldots,n \text{ but } i,j \neq k$$

We outlined the steps of the algorithm along with justification. The next topic was minimum spanning trees and forests of a weighted graph. We defined a spanning tree of graph G as a subgraph T such that all of the vertices of G are in T and T is a tree, meaning that T has no cycle. This indicates that a spanning tree of an undirected connected graph G is a subgraph of G as T that is a tree containing all the vertices in G. If G is not connected and consists of components $\{G_1,\ldots,G_k\}$, then a spanning forest of G is a set of trees $\{T_1,\ldots,T_k\}$, where T_i is a spanning tree of G_i.

We introduced two algorithms to find the minimum spanning trees: Prim's algorithm and Kruskal's algorithm. In Prim's algorithm the minimum spanning tree grows by starting from an arbitrary vertex. At each stage a new branch, vertex and edge are added to the tree that is already constructed and the algorithm terminates when all the vertices have been selected. Because at each step we select the vertex nearest to the created tree, intuitively it seems that the tree should be minimal. Kruskal's algorithm is an alternative approach to finding minimum spanning trees which is more efficient on sparse graphs. Unlike Prim's algorithm, it does not start with a particular vertex. It works by creating disjoint subsets of vertices, one for each vertex and containing only that vertex. This indicates that each vertex forms its own separate component in the tree to be. The algorithm repeatedly considers the lightest remaining edge and tests whether the two endpoints lie within the same connected component. If so, the edge will be discarded; if not, we insert the edge and merge the components. We discussed the parallel versions along with examples to illustrate the implementation of the algorithms. For example, the parallel minimum spanning tree was presented by Savage utilizing a linear systolic array of processors, in which for a graph of n vertices and m edges, the minimum spanning tree can be constructed using m processors. The binary tree of processors is another alternative that has been used by Bentley. We discussed the traveling salesman problem, which is the problem of determining a shortest directed Hamiltonian cycle in a weighted directed graph. There are several algorithms used to solve the TSP problem: the vertex penalty algorithm, the nearest neighbor algorithm, the nearest insertion algorithm, the farthest insertion algorithm, the space-filling curve algorithm and the branch-and-bound algorithm. We presented a sequential solution of this problem based on the triangle inequality, which essentially says that going from city i to city k through city j cannot be cheaper than going directly from city i to city k. As a consequence of this assumption, we used an algorithm to obtain a minimum spanning tree, then by going twice around the spanning tree, we converted it to a path that visits every city. This approach was introduced in Christofides' traveling salesman problem algorithm to construct a Hamiltonian circuit as the solution. A parallel alternative solution was to provide a fixed number of slave processes that share a pool of tasks. Each task consisted of a partial path, the number of cities visited on the path, and the path's length. For example, in this approach there were n − 1 tasks representing the n − 1 paths starting at city 1. Each process took a partial path and extended the path with every city that had not been considered. We performed the synchronization utilizing the semaphore primitive to ensure that the length and shortest path were not manipulated by more than one process at a time.

In a directed graph, a path $(v_1, v_2, \ldots, v_k)$ forms a cycle if $v_1 = v_k$ and the path contains at least one edge. We introduced the cycles in a directed graph in which there are well-known conditions for determining whether a graph contains a cycle or path, which are: the graph is connected, each vertex has even degree and each vertex has the same in-degree as out-degree. We presented an algorithm that rearranged all the edges of the graph represented in the linked lists to construct a single linked list. The linked list represented a cycle of the graph from vertex v_1 to itself. We assumed there are n processors such that each processor is in charge of two edges and determines the position of the two elements holding the two edges. We discussed the coloring of graphs as an assignment of colors to the vertices or edges of a graph such that no two adjacent vertices or edges were similarly colored, and within this constraint we were concerned to minimize the number of colors used. We divided the graph-coloring problem into two categories: the *graph-coloring optimization problem*, in which it was required to determine the minimum number of colors needed to color the graph, and the *graph-coloring decision problem*, in which it was required to determine for an integer k whether there was a coloring that uses at most k colors. We outlined parallel vertex-coloring and edge-coloring algorithms along with examples. In the parallel vertex-coloring problem, 2^n processors were involved where n was the number of vertices and each processor was assigned one possible coloring solution. The processors used the adjacency matrix to determine the valid solution among all possible coloring solutions. In the edge-coloring problem we outlined an Euler-coloring algorithm to produce an optimal edge coloring of a bipartite graph. We divided the graph G into Euler graphs, G_1 and G_2, then reconstructed the graph G from the Euler graphs G_1 and G_2 by renaming colors in graphs such that they used disjoint color sets. The algorithm found the optimal edge coloring of graph G.

Exercises

1. Define the following terms:
    Directed graph   Undirected graph
    Adjacency matrix   Adjacency list
    Weighted graph   Spanning tree
    Connected component   Cycle in a graph
    Connectivity matrix   Path in a graph

2. Devise a PRAM algorithm to solve the graph-coloring problem that has lower time complexity than the algorithm presented in this chapter. You may use a more powerful PRAM model.

3. Design a parallel algorithm for the connected components problem on a cube-connected SIMD computer with N^3 processors. What is the time complexity of your algorithm?

4. Design a parallel algorithm to find all triangles of a directed graph (a triangle is a directed cycle of length three) on the CREW PRAM model. Analyze its complexity. What will be the time complexity of your algorithm if implemented on the CRCW PRAM model of computation?

5. Design a parallel algorithm for a minimum spanning tree on a CRCW PRAM model. What is its time complexity?

6. Dijkstra's single-source shortes- paths algorithm requires non-negative edge weight. Show how Dijkstra's algorithm can be modified to work on graphs with negative weights but no negative cycles. Analyze the performance of the parallel formulation of the modified algorithm on a P-processor hypercube.

7. Consider the following graph whose weighted matrix W is shown. By setting $D^1 = W$, compute the matrices D^2, D^4 and D^8. What is D^8?

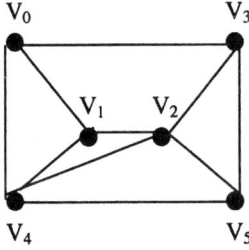

	0	1	2	3	4	5
0	0	1	∞	∞	∞	∞
1	∞	0	2	∞	9	∞
2	∞	∞	0	∞	3	∞
3	-2	∞	7	0	∞	∞
4	-1	∞	∞	∞	0	4
5	∞	∞	6	5	∞	0

8. Explain the difference between Dijkstra's and Floyd's algorithms for the shortest-path problems.

9. Explain the difference between Prim's and Kruskal's algorithms for the minimum spanning tree problem.

10. Draw the spanning tree of the following graph.

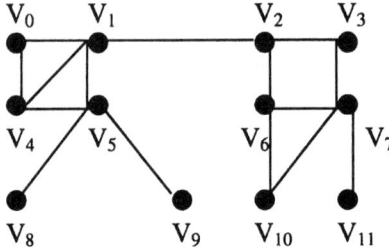

11. Illustrate the parallel Floyd algorithm utilizing a sample digraph D and weighted function W.

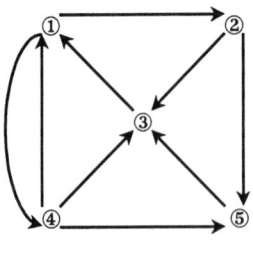

$$\begin{array}{ccccc} 0 & 4 & \infty & 3 & \infty \\ \infty & 0 & 6 & \infty & 2 \\ 1 & \infty & 0 & \infty & \infty \\ 4 & \infty & 2 & 0 & 3 \\ \infty & \infty & 1 & \infty & 0 \end{array}$$

D   W

12. Consider the following weighted graph G.
(a) Devise a parallel minimum spanning tree utilizing the Prim algorithm.
  (b) Devise a parallel minimum spanning tree utilizing the Kruskal algorithm.

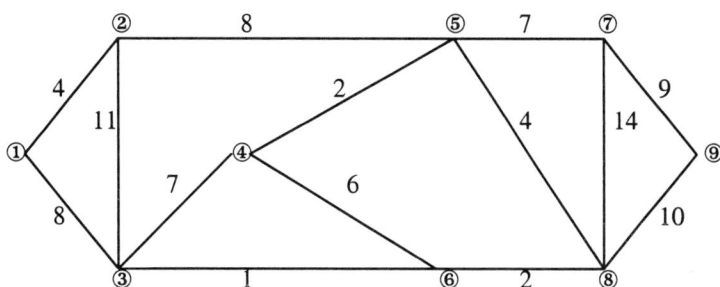

13. Devise a parallel algorithm that, given a directed graph G with *n* vertices, prints all the Hamiltonian cycles in G. What is the time complexity of this algorithm?

14. Specify the paths and cycles in the following graph utilizing a parallel algorithm.

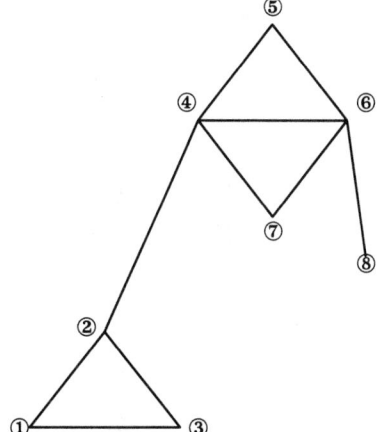

15. The notion of a strongly connected component in a digraph $G=(V, E)$ is a generalization of the notion of a component in a graph. Two vertices u and v in a digraph G are strongly connected if there is a directed path from u to v and a directed path from v to u:
(a) Specify the strongly connected components of the following graph.
(b) Devise a parallel algorithm to identify the strongly connected components of graph G.

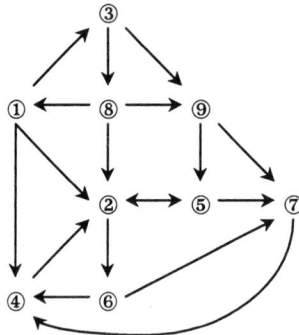

Reference-Needed Exercises

16. Write a PRAM algorithm to solve the vertex cover problem. The problem is: given a graph with n vertices and a positive integer k, determine whether there is a set of k vertices such that every edge in the graph is incident upon at least one of the vertices. Assume the inputs to your algorithm are n, k, and an n × n adjacency matrix A representing an undirected graph.

17. Prove that given an N-vertex weighted graph, the all-pairs shortest-path problem can be solved in $O(\log^2 N)$ time on the hypercube SIMD and shuffle-exchange SIMD models, in which $N^3 = 2^{3Q}$ processors are involved [Dekel 81].

18. Prove that the minimum cost spanning tree of a weighted, undirected, connected graph with m edges can be found in time $O(m)$ on a UMA multiprocessor system with $\lceil \log m \rceil$ processors [Yoo 83].

CHAPTER 7
Parallel Search Algorithms

A graph is a mathematical object naturally formulated in terms of objects and connections between them. Graphs are important because they can be used to represent any relationship. Graph theory provides a language for talking about the properties of graphs, and several problems have simple descriptions and solutions in terms of graph properties. A graph can be used to represent the optimization problems, a class of computationally expensive problems with significant theoretical and practical interest.

The optimal solution to a problem is based on an exploration of all possible solutions, but in the worst case it can be exponential in complexity. This, however, can be considerably reduced by using appropriate strategies in graph theory. There are many possibilities. We can use the classical methods of graph theory such as maximum flow, minimal cuts, or the mathematical programming techniques such as linear programming or dynamic programming, or search methods such as depth first, breadth first, branch and bound, and alpha beta. For many of these inherently difficult problems, only small instances can be solved in a reasonable amount of time on sequential architectures. In contrast, parallel architectures strongly influence the design of parallel search algorithms for solving these optimization problems.

This chapter examines a number of parallel algorithms developed to solve problems in graph theory. These problems are related to searching graphs and finding a feasible solution. With regard to the design of parallel search algorithms for solving a given problem on a particular parallel architecture, we can draw the following conclusions:

1. Implementation on SIMD architecture is appropriate only for problems with operations performed in constant time.
2. Synchronization appears unnecessary in most cases.
3. Some of the search methods are more amenable to parallelism.
4. Some of the search methods can be implemented with different approaches; i.e., breadth-first search.
5. The type of parallel architecture has a significant effect on the performance of the search methods; i.e., SIMD compared with MIMD parallel architectures.
6. The computational efficiency of the algorithms depends on the data structure and the search strategies.

7.1   Divide and Conquer

The divide-and-conquer method is patterned after the French emperor Napoleon in the Battle of Austerlitz on December 2, 1805. A combined army of Austrians and Russians outnumbered Napoleon's army by about 15,000 soldiers. The Austrian and Russian forces launched a massive attack against the French army. Anticipating their attack, Napoleon drove against their center and split their forces in two. Because the two smaller armies were individually no match for Napoleon, they each suffered heavy losses. By dividing the large army into two smaller armies and individually conquering these two smaller armies, Napoleon was able to conquer the large army. The divide-and-conquer approach employs this strategy and involves partitioning a problem into a number of independent subproblems. This is the divide step. The subproblems are then solved independently. This is the conquer step. The last step is to combine the obtained solutions of the subproblems to form a solution for the original problem. Therefore, strictly speaking, the method should be called divide, conquer, and combine.

The methodology is recursive, and subproblems themselves may be solved by the divide-and-conquer technique, meaning the subproblems are recursively subdivided into smaller problems until their size becomes manageable. The net effect is that the divide-and-conquer approach is a top-down method, meaning that the solution to the top level can be obtained by combining the solutions to the lower levels. Binary search tree is the simplest method to implement the divide-and-conquer algorithm because the instance is broken down into subinstances. The problem solution can be represented by a binary AND tree, since the solution to any problem represented by an interior vertex requires the solution of all its subproblems represented by the children of that vertex. In other words, every vertex in the tree must be examined and the solution for a problem at one level of the tree has to be formed by the solutions of its subproblems. The divide-and-conquer method is widely applicable in sequential computations and is a design approach with many important algorithms to its credit, including mergesort, quicksort, the fast Fourier transform and Strassen's matrix multiplication algorithm. However, with the exception of the binary-search approach, divide and conquer is a difficult technique to apply in practice.

In the sequential processing, the subproblems are solved serially, but in parallel processing, these subproblems can be solved at the same time given sufficient parallelism. Some processing is required either to split the original problem into subproblems or to combine the results of the subproblems for the final solution. For example, we can look at Batcher's bitonic merge sort [Batcher 68] as the first example of the divide-and-conquer approach. It is required to sort n data elements using n processors. For the sake of simplicity, we assume $n = 2^k$ for some k and that each processor initially contains one data element. The result should leave the smallest data element in the processor labeled 1, the next smallest data element in the processor labeled 2, and so forth. The divide-and-conquer algorithm divides the sequence of elements into two subsequences, performing an increasing sort on the first half and a decreasing sort on the second half. The result of this process is a bitonic sequence.

We can look at matrix multiplication as another example of the divide-and-conquer approach, in which we multiply two n × n matrices utilizing n^2 processors. The processors are viewed as an n × n array where the processors are labeled PE_{ij} for $0 \le i,j \le n - 1$. The input matrices A and B are initially distributed in the n^2 processors such that a_{ij} and b_{ij} are contained in processor PE_{ij}. When the algorithm terminates, c_{ij} is stored in PE_{ij}. Consider the 2 × 2 case such that PE_{00} stores a_{00} and b_{00}, PE_{01} stores a_{01} and b_{01} and so forth. To compute c_{00} by PE_{00}, two other elements a_{01} and b_{10} are needed. Similarly, all other processors need only two other elements that are not stored at that processor. To provide the required elements for each processor to compute the element of the product, each processor sends its a_{ij} value to the other processor in the same row and its b_{ij} value to the other processor in the same column. After this communication process, each processor PE_{ij} has all the required elements to compute c_{ij}. The approach can be expanded for the n × n case. Figure 7.1 illustrates the multiplication of two 2 × 2 matrices and shows the communication between the processors.

$$\begin{bmatrix} a_{00} & a_{01} \\ a_{10} & a_{11} \end{bmatrix} * \begin{bmatrix} b_{00} & b_{01} \\ b_{10} & b_{11} \end{bmatrix} = \begin{bmatrix} c_{00} & c_{01} \\ c_{10} & c_{11} \end{bmatrix} = \begin{bmatrix} a_{00}b_{00} + a_{01}b_{10} & a_{00}b_{01} + a_{01}b_{11} \\ a_{10}b_{00} + a_{11}b_{10} & a_{10}b_{01} + a_{11}b_{11} \end{bmatrix}$$

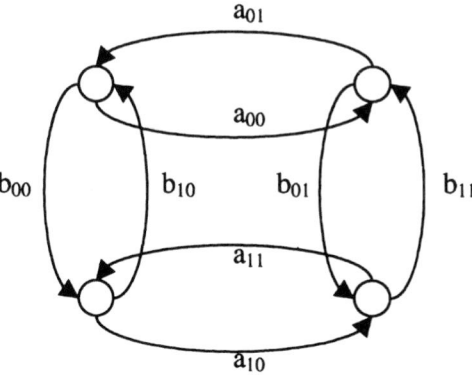

Figure 7.1. Computation of element c_{ij} by PE_{ij}.

Example and Implementation: Assume it is required to determine whether the number x is in the list S of n numbers. The algorithm compares x with the middle number in the input sequence. If they are equal, the algorithm terminates, meaning x is in the list located at the middle. Otherwise, depending on the outcome of the comparison, the left or right half of the input sequence is discarded from further consideration and the algorithm is applied recursively to the other half. The procedure is repeated until x is found or until it is determined that x is not in the input sequences. Suppose x = 18 and it is required to determine whether x is present in the sorted sequence of elements as follows:

$$S = \{10, 11, 12, 13, 14, 18, 20, 25, 26, 28, 30, 35, 45, 48, 54\}$$

The algorithm works as follows:
1. Compare x with 25, which is the middle number. Because x < 25 choose the left subsequence which is (10 11 12 13 14 18 20).
2. Divide the left subsequence into subsequences (10 11 12) and (14 18 20) with the middle number as 13.
3. Compare x with 13, which is the middle number. Because x > 13 choose the right subsequence which is (14 18 20).
4. Divide the right subsequence into two subsequences (14) and (20) with the middle element as 18.
5. Compare x with 18, which is the middle number. Because x = 18 then report that x is present in S.

The recursive algorithm is now as follows.

location(index low, index high)
```
{
middle = ⌊(low + high) / 2⌋
if   (x = = S[middle])
     return middle
     else if (x < S[middle])
             return location(low, mid-1)
             else
             return location(mid + 1, high)
}
```

In general, we can formulate the sequential divide-and-conquer algorithm as the following recursive procedure calls:

Procedure   Divide-and-Conquer(Input, Output)
Divide(Input, Input$_1$, Input$_2$, ...,Input$_m$)
for i = 1 to m do
        Divide-and-Conquer(Input$_i$, Output$_j$)
endfor
Combine(Output$_1$, Output$_2$, ...,Output$_m$, Output)
End   Divide-and-Conquer

where **Input** is an input given to the problem and **Output** is a solution to the problem. Alternatively, $Input_1$, $Input_2$, ...,$Input_m$ are the subinputs corresponding to **Input**, and $Output_1$, $Output_2$, ...,$Output_m$ are the corresponding outputs of the subinputs. Combine is the process for obtaining a solution **Output** to the problem by combining obtained solutions. As we see, in the sequential algorithm each of the subproblems is solved using a sequence of recursive calls.

In a parallel setting the method requires that the subproblems at the same level of recursion be computed independently, assuming that a sufficient number of processors are available. In this section we provide a number of examples demonstrating the effectiveness and efficiency of the divide-and-conquer approach in deriving parallel algorithms. In general, there are three ways of executing divide-and-conquer algorithms on parallel architectures:

1. To build a tree of processors that corresponds to the search tree.
2. To use a virtual tree machine that has an interconnection network with a hypercubic processor organization. In this approach we need a good algorithm to map subproblems to processors in order to minimize communication time.
3. To use multicomputer architecture to execute divide-and-conquer algorithms. In this approach the shared global memory facilitates access to subproblems by the various processors.

Example and Implementation: Assume the sequence of n elements is stored in the shared memory of a parallel architecture with N processors P_1, P_2, ..., P_N where $1 \leq N \leq n$. Assume further that one processor reads x and stores it in shared memory and initializes index to 0, which indicates the location of x as the processor number.

1. All processors read x.
2. Processor P_i compares x to S[i], where $1 \leq i \leq n$.
3. Those processors P_j for which x = S[j] update index = j.

We can assume that several numbers satisfy the condition, meaning that possibly many indices j are found which satisfy x = S[j]. Since all such j are found simultaneously, choosing the smallest is one way to break the tie. We need to select one Concurrent Write (CW) instruction, **MIN CW** or **ARBITRARY CW**, to set the value in **index**. If the number of processors is less than the number of elements in S, meaning N < n, the sequence $S = \{E_1, E_2, ..., E_n\}$ is subdivided into N subsequences of length n / N each and processor P_i is assigned the subsequence

$$\{E_{(i-1)(n/N)+1}, E_{(i-1)(n/N)+2}, E_{(i-1)(n/N)+3, ...}\}.$$

The algorithm now works as follows:

1. All processors read x.
2. Those processors P_i for which $E_{(i-1)(n/N)+1} \leq x \leq E_{i(n/N)}$ perform.
   2.1. Compare x with input elements of the processor.
   2.2. Set j as the subscript of the input element P_i if there is any.

3.   Those processor P_k for which $x = E_{(k-1)(n/N)+j}$ update index$=(k-1)(n/N)+j$.

In general, the parallel algorithm can be represented as follows to address the speedup over the sequential version.

Procedure   **Parallel-Divide-and-Conquer(Input, Output)**
Divide(Input, Input$_1$, Input$_2$, …,Input$_m$)
for i = 1 to m do in parallel
Parallel-Divide-and-Conquer(Input$_1$, Output$_1$|,
Input$_2$, Output$_2$|,
………
Input$_m$, Output$_m$)
endfor
Combine(Output$_1$, Output$_2$, …,Output$_m$, Output)
End   **Parallel-Divide-and-Conquer**

7.2   Depth-First Search

Sequential graph algorithms often employ some form of graph traversal, which is equivalent to tracing the edges of a spanning tree of the graph. Perhaps, from the sequential complexity point of view, the most successful and commonly used form of graph traversal is the Depth-First Search (DFS). The importance of the depth-first search is that many efficient sequential algorithms on graphs use DFS as the basic procedure. The graph G is represented by its adjacency list and for each vertex v there is a list of all vertices adjacent to v. Depth-first search is the process of searching a graph in such a way that the search moves forward until it reaches a vertex whose neighbors have all been examined. At this point it backtracks a minimum distance and continues in a new direction. In other words, in a depth-first search, if v is the vertex being searched from (starting vertex), (v,w) is the edge being examined and w is unvisited, w will be the next vertex searched from (the new starting point). The DFS is called recursively.

However, if v is the starting vertex and (v,w) is the edge being examined and w is already visited, v remains the vertex being searched from, and another vertex adjacent to v which has not been visited, is chosen as the vertex to be examined. This indicates that in the DFS strategy the vertices are examined in order of decreasing depth in the tree.

Although in a depth-first search it is not required the children of a vertex be visited in any particular order, we follow the convention that the children of a vertex are visited from left to right. The depth-first search algorithm assigns a number to each vertex v which specifies the order in which the vertex is visited during the graph traversal. This number is called the depth-first index of the vertex. Formally, the DFS is described as follows.

Depth-First-Search   (DFS)

Input: A directed connected graph G and a specified starting vertex v.

Output: The depth-first indices of the vertices of G starting with v = 1.

Figure 7.2 shows a depth-first search of a tree performed in this manner such that the vertices are numbered in the order they are visited, with the starting vertex being A. The sequential DFS can be represented in terms of the following recursive procedure. The algorithm is called a depth-first search because it initiates as many recursive calls as possible before it ever returns from a call. The recursion stops only when exploration of the graph is blocked and can go no further. At this point the recursion stops so alternate possibilities at higher levels can be explored.

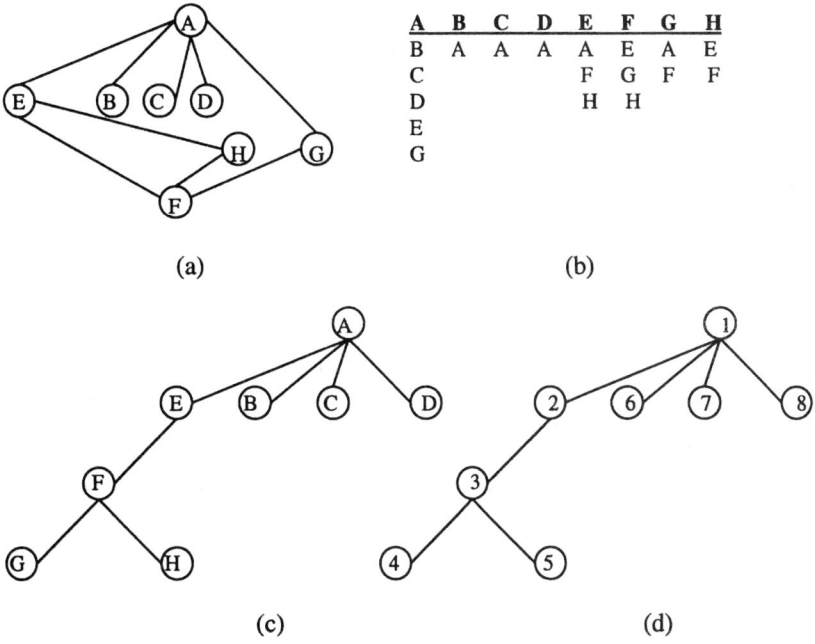

A	B	C	D	E	F	G	H
B	A	A	A	A	E	A	E
C				F	G	F	F
D				H	H		
E							
G							

(a)   (b)

(c)   (d)

Figure 7.2. A graph and its corresponding depth-first tree. (a) Graph G. (b) Adjacency of graph G. (c) Depth-first tree obtained from depth-first traversal. (d) Depth-first index tree obtained from depth-first traversal.

Procedure   Depth-First(A)

```
begin
        mark every vertex "unvisited"
        v⇐start vertex
        /* v is the vertex being searched from */
        Call Depth-First-Search(v)
```

Procedure   Depth-First-Search(v)
        begin
        mark v "visited"
        for each vertex w adjacent to v do
                if w is marked "unvisited"
                    then Call Depth-First-Search(w)
            endfor
    End Depth-First-Search
        end
End   Depth-First

We analyze the time complexity of DFS in a graph with n vertices and m edges, with respect to two basic operations, visiting a vertex and examining a vertex, to determine if it has been visited. The worst-case complexity for both operations occurs when the graph is connected. If the graph is connected, we can verify that every vertex is visited exactly once with a total of n vertex visits. Each edge in the graph addresses exactly two vertex examinations, thus yielding the number of vertices to be examined as $2m$. Therefore, the total number of operations by DFS in the worst-case is $n + 2m$, resulting in a complexity of $O(n + m)$.

In general, parallel processing is a major approach to enhance the efficiency of search algorithms. We focus entirely on bounded parallelism, which corresponds to the more realistic assumption that a given computing system has only a fixed number of processors functioning in parallel. The computational efficiency of the algorithms depends on the data structure and the search strategies. Alton and Eckstein [Alton 77] proposed a parallel algorithm for a depth-first search. Reghbati and Corneil [Reghbati 78] conjectured that a depth-first search was inherently sequential. It is generally assumed that the use of DFS is incompatible with efforts to process the search space in parallel, meaning it seems that the problem of finding a depth-first search tree is hardly parallelizable. Hence, many fast parallel computations in graph theory avoid depth-first search computations. For the moment, consider the instructions of the depth-first search procedure given earlier. The crucial issue in an effort to parallelize the algorithm are the lines

```
for each vertex w adjacent to v do
        if w is marked "unvisited"
        then ...,
```

which mean to find the next unvisited vertex on the adjacency list of v. Alternatively, instead of an adjacency list representation of the adjacent vertices to each vertex, we consider an "adjacency list matrix" such that every row represents all the adjacent vertices to each vertex. With this assumption, different processors can simultaneously examine successive vertices to identify whether they are visited or unvisited. We also define an "unvisited adjacency list" U(v) which

lists all vertices that are adjacent to v and are still labeled "unvisited." As soon
as a vertex w is "visited," it will be removed from the lists U(v) for all v adjacent to w. Of course, the problem of finding an "unvisited" vertex adjacent to v
now becomes trivial, by taking the first element of U(v) if U(v) is not empty.
Such an approach of deleting elements from "unvisited" adjacent lists is compatible with DFS, since the flow of control of DFS-based algorithms, the order
in which the various recursive calls are performed, depends only on the vertices
which remain "unvisited." In this approach the need for communication between
processors is eliminated.

Two lists, ARC_LIST and FROND_LIST, as the output of the DFS are defined such that the final FROND_LIST(v) is a list of vertices w such that there is
a frond from v to w, and the final ARC_LIST is a list of vertices w such that
there is an arc from v to w. Figure 7.3 illustrates the representation of a graph in
the adjacency list matrix, adjacency list, associated end-marker vector, and unvisited adjacency matrix forms.

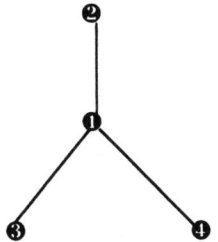

The Adjacency List

L(1): 2→ 3→ 4→ null

L(2): 1→ null

L(3): 1→ null

L(4): 1→ null

The Adjacency List Matrix

1 →2 →3 →1

2 →1 →0 →0

3 →1 →0 →0

4 →1 →0 →0

The Unvisited Adjacency Matrix

U(1): null →2→ 3→ 4→ null

U(2): null → 1→ null

U(3): null →1 → null

U(4): null →1 → null

The End-Marker Vector

1 →3

2 →1

3 →1

4 →1

Figure 7.3. Representation of graph regarding different forms.

A parallel depth-first search algorithm is now defined follows.

Input: Adjacency list matrix, ALM(1:n,1:n − 1), the associated end-marker vector EM(1:n), the initial unvisited adjacency list, U(i), $1 \leq i \leq n$

Output: ARC_LIST(v) and FROND_LIST(v), $1 \leq v \leq n$

Machine: Classical k-bounded parallel architecture with k processors

The parallel depth-first search can be represented in terms of the following procedure:

Procedure   Parallel-Depth-First(ALM, EM, U)

begin

for each v∈ V do initialize ARC_LIST(v) as null list

mark every vertex "unvisited"

/* v is the vertex being searched from */

$v \Leftarrow$ start vertex and   father(v) $\Leftarrow 0$

numb_vertices_visited $\Leftarrow 0$

CallParallel-Depth-First-Search(v)

Procedure Parallel-Depth-First-Search(v)

begin

        mark v "visited"

        numb_vertices_visited $\Leftarrow$ numb_vertices_visited +1

        number(v) $\Leftarrow$ numb_vertices_visited

        instruct processor(i)   where $1 \leq i \leq k$

        for j = 1 to k do

                if $(k * (j - 1) + i) \leq EM(v)$

                then   begin

                        w(i)$\Leftarrow$ALM(v, k * (j − 1) + i)

                        delete v from U(w(i))

                        if w(i) is "unvisited"

                              then   add v to FROND_LIST(w(i))

                        end

                endif

        endfor

        for   w∈ U(v) do

                begin

                father(w) $\Leftarrow$ v

                add w to ARC_LIST(v)

                remove v from the end of FROND_LIST(w)

                Call Parallel-Depth-First-Search(w)

                end

        endfor

end

EndParallel-Depth-First

The parallel depth-first search discussed is applicable to SIMD and MIMD architectures. However, it is not recommended to implement a parallel DFS on SIMD computers because the following two problems.

1. Since all processors execute identical instructions, all must be in the same stage of the search tree. It is possible that only some of the processors are busy and others are idle, which will reduce the overall execution rate compared with the MIMD computers.

2. Due to the architectural constraints of SIMD computers, load balancing must be performed globally at the beginning of the search tree or at the end of each stage of the search. When some of the processors are idle, busy processors can share the work with the idle processors. This requires a mechanism that determines when load balancing is appropriate as well as the load mechanism itself. This is in contrast to MIMD computers, which can handle load balancing in an appropriate form.

7.3   Breadth-First Search

A breadth-first search (BFS) starts from a vertex, the start vertex or root, and searches all vertices at a distance of one level from the root. Next all the vertices at a distance of two levels from the root will be examined, and so forth, until the entire graph is examined. Once we start searching from a vertex v, we continue to search from v until all edges involving v have been examined. Vertices are searched from in the order in which they are labeled as visited, so this search technique can be implemented via a queue. In other words, the vertices are examined in order of increasing depth. This indicates that a breadth-first tree of graph G is a spanning tree for which every path from a vertex to the root is a shortest path in graph G. As with a depth-first search, we examine the children of a vertex in the order from left to right. The breadth-first search algorithm assigns a number to each vertex v. The number is called the breadth-first index and specifies the order in which the vertex is examined during the graph traversal. Formally, the BFS is described as follows.

Breadth-First-Search (BFS)
Input: A directed connected graph G and a specified starting vertex v
Output: The breadth-first indices of the vertices of G starting with $v = 1$

As with a depth-first search, we can associate a search tree with a breadth-first strategy. Figure 7.4 shows the tree generated by the breadth-first search method associated with the graph G of the previous section, with A as the starting vertex.

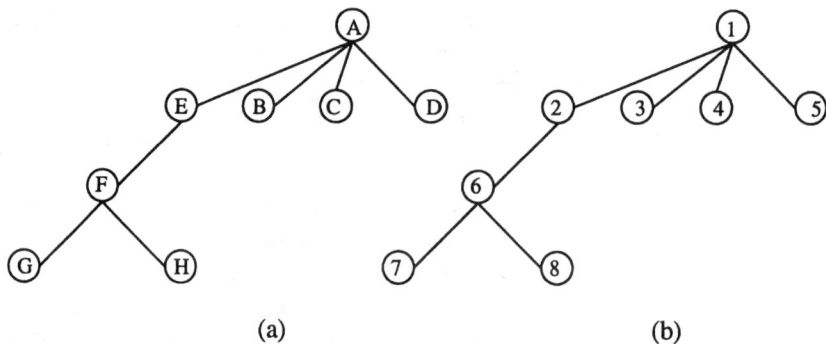

Figure 7.4. A graph and its corresponding breadth-first tree. (a) Breadth-first tree obtained from breadth-first traversal. (b) Breadth-first-index tree obtained from breadth-first traversal.

As we see, the strategy underlying the breadth-first search is to visit all unexamined vertices adjacent to a given starting vertex before moving forward. This strategy can be implemented by placing the visited vertices on a queue and removing the next vertex to be started from the top of the queue.

The sequential BFS can be represented by the following procedure:

Procedure   Breadth-First-Search:
    begin
    mark every vertex "unvisited"
    initialize "queue" with the start vertex v
       while "queue" is not empty do
            begin
            v $\Leftarrow$ remove the first vertex from the queue
            /* v is the vertex being searched from */
            for each vertex w adjacent to v do
                if w is marked "unvisited"
                thenbegin
                      mark w "visited"
                      place w on queue
                      end
                endfor
      endwhile
  end

EndBreadth-First-Search

Clearly, BFS has the same O(n + m) time complexity as DFS.

The breadth-first search is one of the search methods most amenable to parallelism. In general there are two approaches which can be used to parallelize a BFS:

1. **Vertex-by-Vertex Parallel Breadth-First Search (VPBFS)**
2. **Level-by-Level Parallel-Breadth-First Search (LPBFS)**

Vertex-by-Vertex Parallel Breadth-First Search

We can use the approach described for a parallel depth-first search to perform a parallel breadth-first search with the classical k-bounded parallel model. In this approach, as soon as a vertex w is "visited" it will be removed from the "unvisited" adjacency list, U(x), for x adjacent to w. A parallel algorithm to perform a BFS can be outlined as follows:

Input: Adjacency list matrix, ALM(1:n,1:n − 1), the associated end-marker vector EM(1:n), the initial unvisited adjacency list, U(i), 1 ≤ i ≤ n.

Output: List of all visited vertices with respect to each vertex.

Machine: Classical k-bounded parallel model with k number of processors.

The vertex-by-vertex parallel breadth-first search can now be represented in terms of the following procedure.

Procedure   Parallel-Breadth-First-Search-Vertex(ALM, EM, U)
begin
      mark every vertex "unvisited"
      v ⇐ start vertex
      mark v "visited"
      instruct processor(i) where $1 \le i \le k$
          for j = 1 to k do
              if $(k * (j - 1) + i) \le EM(v)$
              then delete v from $U(ALM(v, k * (j - 1) + i))$
              endif
          endfor
      end-instruction
      initialize queue with v
      while queue is not empty do
          begin
          v ⇐ first vertex from the queue
          for each w∈ U(v) do
              begin
              mark w "visited"
              instruct processor (i) where $1 \le i \le k$
                  for   j = 1 to k do
                      if $(k * (j - 1) + i) \le EM(w)$

```
                    then delete w from U(ALM(w, k * (j – 1) + i))
                    endif
            endfor
        end-instruction
        add w to queue
        end
    endfor
  endwhile
end
```

End   **Parallel-Breadth-First-Search-Vertex**

It seems intuitively likely that the parallel breadth-first search requires fewer branching steps, because processors examine all vertices at level x of the search tree before moving forward to level x + 1.

Level-by-Level Parallel Breadth-First Search

If the degree of a vertex is less than k (the number of available processors), then by assigning processors to the edge of that vertex, we are not efficiently utilizing all the processors. In this case the maximum number of processors being used is equal to the degree of the vertex from which the search is being performed. Based on the nature of the breadth-first search, it is possible to simultaneously search from different vertices on the same level and still maintain the integrity of the BFS. If we list the vertices belonging to level ρ in the vector $V_\rho(1:n_\rho)$ where n_ρ is the number of vertices on level ρ, then we can create an array $E_\rho(1:m_\rho)$ with respect to the vertices on level ρ such that m_ρ is the number of edges incident to the vertices. Based on the E_ρ vector, each processor will search some specific number of edges to find the "unvisited" vertices, which form level $\rho + 1$.

A parallel algorithm to perform a level-by-level BFS can be outlined as follows:

Input: Adjacency list matrix, ALM(1:n,1:n – 1), the associated end-marker vector EM(1:n), the initial unvisited adjacency list, U(i), $1 \leq i \leq n$.

Output: List of all visited vertices with respect to each vertex.

Machine: Classical k-bounded parallel model with k number of processors.

The level-by-level parallel breadth-first search can now be represented in terms of the following procedure.

Procedure Parallel-Breadth-First-Search-Level(ALM, EM, U)
```
begin
    mark every vertex "unvisited"
    instruct processor(i) where    1 ≤ i ≤ k
        for j = 1 to k do
```

$$\text{if } k * (j(i) - 1) + i \leq n$$
$$\text{then mark vertex } k * (j(i) - 1) + i \text{ "unvisited"}$$
endif
endfor
end-instruction
$v \Leftarrow$ start vertex and $\text{level}(v) \Leftarrow 0$
mark v "visited"
create the vector v_1 for the search from level one
instruct processor(i) where $1 \leq i \leq k$
    for $j(i) = 1$ to k do
        if $(k * (j(i) - 1) + i) \leq EM(v)$
        then $V(1, (k * (j(i) - 1) + i)) \Leftarrow ALM(v, k * (j(i) - 1) + i)$
        endif
    endfor
end-instruction

$n(1) \Leftarrow EM(v)$
for $\rho = 1$ to n while $n(\rho)$ is not empty do
    begin
    create vector E_ρ
    create vector $V_{\rho+1}$ with $n_{\rho+1}$ distinct vertices
        instruct processor (i) where $1 \leq i \leq k$
        for $j(i) = 1$ to k do
            if $(k * (j(i) - 1) + i) \leq n(\rho + 1)$
            then mark vertex $(V(\rho + 1), k*(j(i) - 1) + i) \Leftarrow \rho + 1$
            endif
        endfor
        end-instruction
    end
endfor
end
End   **Parallel-Breadth-First-Search-Level**

7.4   Best-First Search

In this section, we discuss a new method called best-first search, which is a way
of combining the advantages of both the depth-first and the breadth-first search
into a single method. The Best-First Search (BFS) strategy uses a heuristic
function to direct the traversing of the search tree. The expansion of a vertex v is
estimated numerically by a heuristic evaluation function $f(v)$ which may depend
on the description of v, the description of the goal, the information gathered by
the search up to this point and any extra knowledge about the problem domain.
The vertex selected for consideration is the one having the best value of this

evaluation function. If the selected vertex is a solution, we can quit; otherwise, all those new vertices are added to the set of vertices generated so far for the next step of examination. For example, this value should be the associated cost of the element at that level with respect to the objective function.

The chosen evaluation function in this search strategy is the most important factor in the performance of this strategy. The sequential best-first search can be presented as follows:

Procedure   Best-First-Search
    begin
    mark every vertex "unvisited"
    initialize queue with the start vertex
        compute the evaluation value for start vertex on
            queue
        while queue is not empty do
            sort the queue in ascending order with regard to
                evaluation values
            $v \Leftarrow$ remove the vertex from top of the queue
            v is the vertex being searched from as the best
                value of evaluation
            for each vertex w adjacent to v do
                if w is marked "unvisited"
                    then   begin
                  mark w "visited"
                      compute evaluation value for w
                        if w is a solution then stop
                        else place w on queue
                    end
                endif
            endfor
        endwhile
    end
End   Best-First-Search

The main disadvantage of BFS is its memory requirement, which is linear in the size of the search space explored. For problems with a large search space tree, providing the required memory becomes a problem. Figure 7.5 illustrates the best-first search method, in which initially there is only one vertex ①, which will be expanded as shown in Step 2. Expanding ① generates three new vertices. The heuristic function, which in this example is an estimate of the cost of getting to a solution from a given vertex, is applied to each of these new vertices. Since vertex ④ is the most promising, it is expanded next, producing two successor vertices, ⑤ and ⑥. Again, the heuristic function is applied to them. Now another path that goes through vertex ② looks most promising, so it is pursued, resulting in vertices ⑦ and ⑧. Again when these new vertices are evaluated they look less promising than another path, meaning that attention is returned to the path through ④ to ⑤. Vertex ⑤ is then expanded, yielding vertices ⑨ and ⑩. At the next step, ⑩ is examined as the most promising vertex, and the search indicates this vertex as the solution, resulting in the termination of the algorithm. In general, the process continues until a solution is found.

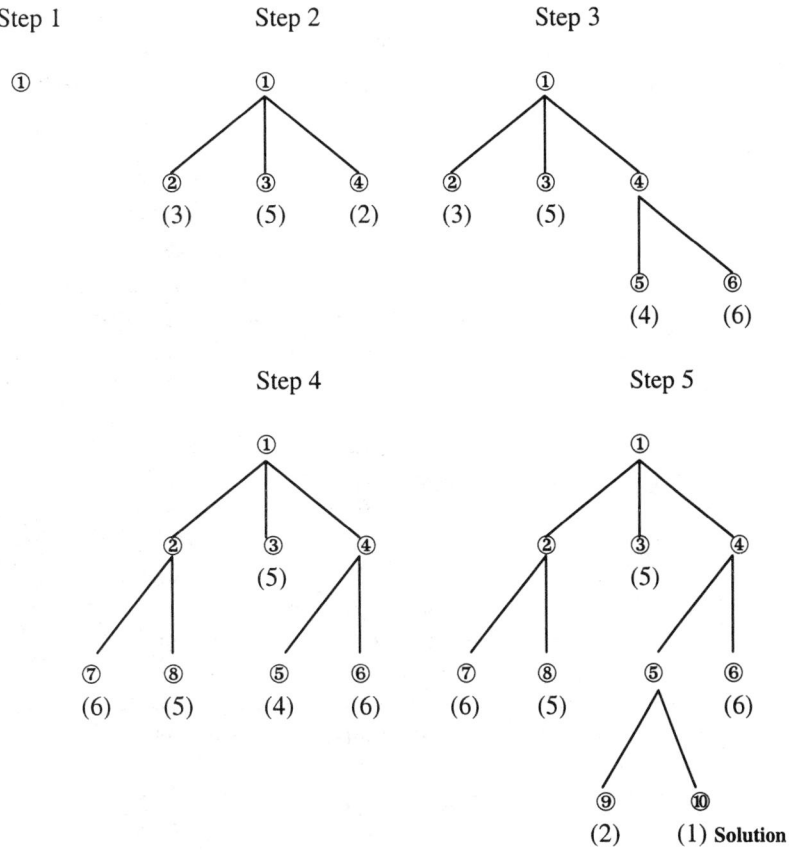

Figure 7.5. Best-first search execution method.

Parallelism in a best-first search can be introduced by expanding the vertices in parallel. Suppose n processors are available. At each time t, instead of expanding a single vertex with the best value of the evaluation, n vertices are considered for expansion as the n best values of the evaluation. After each iteration, each processor needs only to place the generated vertices on queue. The new vertices are evaluated and placed on queue for the next step of the examination. Using the sequential best-first algorithm, the parallel version can be illustrated as follows:

Procedure   Best&First
    begin
        for k = 1 to # of processors
        status[k] = waiting
        Run **Best-First** on processor 1
        while (status[processor] = busy for some processors)
            Run **Best-First** on W of the waiting processors
        endwhile
    end
End   Best&First

7.5   Branch-and-Bound Search

Several important classes of optimization problems are amenable to solution using the Branch-and-Bound (BB) algorithms. Such algorithms are employed both to solve general optimization problems, such as $0 - 1$ and mixed-integer programs, and for problems in which some special structure can be exploited.

For many of these inherently difficult problems, only small instances can be solved in a reasonable amount of time on sequential computers. Consequently, the use of parallelism to speed up the execution of BB algorithms has emerged as a way to solve larger problem instances in this group of problems. Suppose that we are given a problem for which it is desired to find a least-cost solution from among N feasible solutions. Each vertex on a path from root to leaf represents a partial solution, obtained by expanding the partial solution represented by its parent. In branch-and-bound algorithms we think of the N feasible solutions as the leaves of a BB tree, starting with the empty solution at the root.

A BB algorithm exhaustively searches through a state space, visualized as a tree, seeking an optimal solution, meaning that it continues to search even after finding a solution path. Which vertex is selected for inspection at any moment is decided by a strategy, such as the depth-first, breadth-first and best-first search methods. Branch-and-bound algorithms using these three search methods are called LIFO (Last-In, First-Out) branch-and-bound, FIFO (First-In, First-Out) branch-and-bound, and least-cost branch-and-bound, respectively. In general terms we may say that a depth-first search finishes exploring vertices in inverse order of their creation, using a stack to hold vertices that have been generated but not yet fully explored. A breadth-first search finishes exploring vertices in the order of their creation, using a queue to hold those that have been generated but not yet explored. A best-first search uses a priority list to hold those vertices that have been generated but not yet explored. We assume that best-first is the chosen strategy. Least-cost branch-and-bound applies to problems involving minimizing an objective function. We assume that all processors have access to the same list of vertices. BB discards inferior partial solution paths, the paths whose extensions are guaranteed to be worse than the current best solution path.

It has been noted that it is possible for branch-and-bound algorithms using n processors to spend longer searching a state space than a single processor requires. More generally speaking, it is possible for n_2 processors to use more time than n_1 processors where $n_2 > n_1$. This can occur when a processor which is about to evaluate a vertex of the optimal subtree is preempted in priority by a bound generated by one of the added processors. (For details refer to [Kindevater 1988]).

Backtracking is a systematic way to go through all the possible configurations of the state space search. These configurations may be all possible arrangements of vertices or all possible ways of building a collection of them. The search algorithm works by forming solutions one vertex at a time. At each step in the search, we construct a partial solution. From this partial solution we form the set of possible candidates. We will then try to extend the partial solution by adding the best vertex from the set of possible candidates. However, at some point the partial solution might be invalid with regard to some criteria, meaning that there is no legal way to extend the current partial solution. If so, we must backtrack and replace the last vertex in the solution path with the next best candidate vertex. Both backtracking and branch-and-bound are based on a search of an associated state space tree, modeling all possible sequences of solutions that are quite widely applicable as general problem-solving techniques. Thus, backtracking might be one of the fundamental issues involved in BB algorithms.

Example: Sum of Subset Problem

The problem can be stated as: There is an input set $A = \{x_1, x_2, \ldots, x_n\}$ of n positive integer numbers, and a positive integer Sum. A solution can be defined as a subset of elements of A such that:

$$x_1 + x_2 +, \ldots, + x_k = \text{Sum}$$

where $1 \le k \le n$. It is required to determine all the solutions of this problem. For instance, if $A = \{2,5,7,11,5\}$ and Sum = 12, there are three goal states:

$$x_1 + x_2 + x_5 = 12$$
$$x_2 + x_3 = 12$$
$$x_3 + x_5 = 12$$

The state space tree for this instance is shown in Figure 7.6, with three goal states highlighted. Consider the problem state $(x_1 + x_2 + x_3)$ in the state space tree corresponding to Sum = 14 > 12. Since there is no path in the state space tree from this state to a goal state, we can discard this state from further consideration. Now we can use the definition of a bounding function for the problem states by:

$$\text{Bounded}(x_1 + x_2 +, \ldots, + x_k) = \begin{cases} .True. & if\ x_1 + x_2 +, \ldots, + x_k > Sum, \\ .False. & Otherwise. \end{cases}$$

In other words, if the elements corresponding to $(x_1 + x_2 + , ..., + x_k)$ have a sum greater than Sum, then any extension of $(x_1 + x_2 + , ..., + x_k)$ corresponds to a set of elements whose sum is greater than Bound, in this case Sum. Thus, if Bounded$(x_1 + x_2 + , ..., + x_k)$ is True, then no descendant of $(x_1 + x_2 + , ..., + x_k)$ can drive to a goal state. Figure 7.7 shows the state space tree after it has been pruned with regard to the defined Bound as 12. The bounded states and goals are highlighted by B and G, respectively.

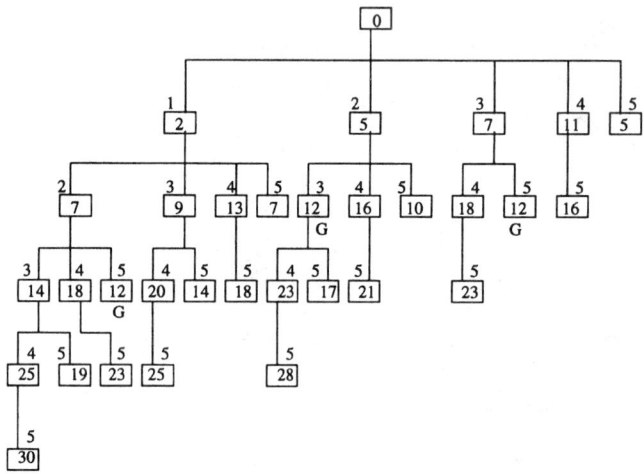

Figure 7.6. The state space tree of the subset problem.

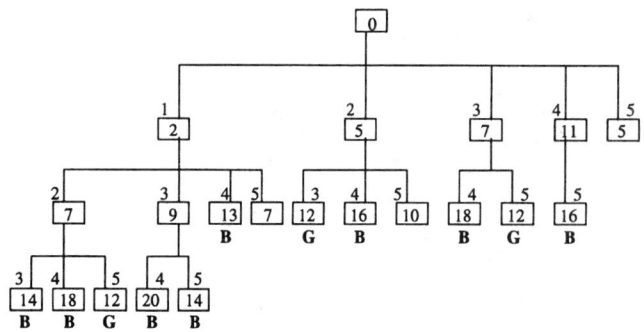

Figure 7.7. Pruned state space tree of the subset problem.

The setting for the BB algorithm is as follows: There is a finite tree T and a set of vertices S for which the vertices in S are called the solution vertices. With each solution vertex x there is an associated real number $f(x)$, known as the cost of that vertex. The objective is to find a least cost solution vertex, meaning to find x_0 in S having

$$f(x_0) \leq f(x)$$

for all $x \in S$. One may define a function f_{opt} on the vertices of tree T such that $f_{opt}(x) = \infty$ if x is not a solution vertex. Therefore, for every solution vertex x, $f_{opt}(x) \leq f(x)$.

To help the searching, a function g is available which associates a real number to each vertex x of T defined as $g(x)$. The function g is called as a bounding function with two properties defined as:

- g is nondecreasing on T, meaning that if y is a child of x, then $g(y) \geq g(x)$
- $g(x) \leq f_{opt}(x)$ for every vertex x of T

A tree T equipped with S, f, and g is called a BB-tree. Sequential processing of the branch-and-bound algorithm searches the BB-tree by expanding "live" vertices one at a time to find a least-cost solution. It must also maintain an "incumbent," which is a record of the cheapest solution vertex found so far. Initially, the root is the only live vertex. To expand vertex x means that for every child y of x,

- Check if y is a solution vertex, and if so, update the incumbent.
- Add y to the live set of vertices if $g(y) < z$, where z is the value of the incumbent and y is not a leaf.

The algorithm continues until $g(y) \geq z$ for every live vertex y. Figure 7.8 shows the outline of the branch-and-bound algorithm to find a least-cost solution in BB-tree T. Since it is unnecessary to expand the terminal vertices, we do not add leaves to the live set for further consideration.

Procedure   Branch-and-Bound(S, f, g)
```
        begin
            live-set={root}
            if root is a solution vertex
                then z=f(root) /* z is incumbent value */
                else z = ∞
            endif
            while live-set contains a vertex x with g(x)< z do
            begin
            x=vertex in live-set with minimum g()
            delete x from the live-set
            /* expand vertex x */
                for each child y of x do
```

```
            begin
            if y is a solution ∧ f(y)<z then z=f(y)
            if y is not a leaf ∧ g(y)<z then add y to
                  live-set
            end
            endfor
        end
    end
End    Branch-and-Bound
```

Figure 7.8. A sequential branch-and-bound algorithm.

Parallelism can be introduced into a branch-and-bound algorithm by expanding vertices in parallel. The main distinction is certainly the existence of one unique live set. Suppose n processors are available. At each time t, instead of expanding a single vertex in the live set, the number of vertices expanded is n, unless the live set contains fewer vertices than n, in which case all live vertices are considered for expansion. Generally speaking, in a typical parallel processing approach, individual processors are assigned to search specific areas of the search tree more or less independently. After every iteration, each processor needs to check only its current upper bound, which is used in pruning the tree, against a temporary overall problem upper bound, referred to as the incumbent.

Some of the features of the BB algorithms are:

- It is easy to keep track of unexamined vertices and reassign processors when appropriate.
- The interprocess communication and shared-memory requirements are minimal.
- Communication is highly asynchronous.

The branch-and-bound algorithm has been implemented on shared-memory computers as well as on distributed computers. On shared-memory computers the parallelization of the best-first BB algorithm is straightforward. All of the processors access the live set, retrieve vertices from it and insert newly generated vertices into it. This technique presents the problem of having all the processors access one single data structure, which leads to the mutual exclusion problem. On distributed-memory computers, the implementation might be realized by a master-slave scheme. One distinguished processor keeps the live set, distributes the vertices to the slave processors and collects from them the vertices to be inserted into the live set, addressing the bottleneck problem. Using the sequential branch-and-bound procedure, the parallel version of BB can be illustrated in the following procedure. The algorithm uses a divide-and-conquer approach that implicitly enumerates a live set utilizing k available processors.

Procedure   Branch&Bound
    begin
        for k = 1 to # of processors
        status[k] = waiting
        Run **Branch-and-Bound** on processor 1
        while (status[processor] = busy for some processors)
            begin
            I = # of unsolved vertices in live-set
            J = # of processors with status[processor] = waiting
            W = Min(I,J)
            Run **Branch-and-Bound** on W of the waiting processors
            end
        endwhile
    end
    Output(z)
End   Branch&Bound

7.6   Alpha-Beta Minimax Search

Searching for the global maximum or minimum of a function is a problem of unconstrained optimization. For example, several game-playing programs search for the best move to make next by using the alpha-beta minimax search, which is an exhaustive search of the possible moves using a variation of back-tracking. The minimax search method is a depth-first, depth-limited search strategy. The idea is to start at the current position and determine the set of all possible successor positions. We can apply an evaluation function to those positions and simply choose the best one for the next move. After doing so, we can propagate that value of the best move to the starting position to represent our evaluation of it. We can assume that the evaluation function returns large values to indicate good positions, so our goal is to maximize the value of the evaluation function of the next position. For example, Figure 7.9 shows this operation such that an evaluation function can return values ranging from −10 to 10, with 10 indicating a win for us and −10 a win for the opponent. Since our goal is to maximize the value of the evaluation function, we choose to move to B, and after updating A's value to 8 we can conclude the operation. After our move, the situation would appear to be very good at this level. But, if we look one move ahead (one more level down), maybe the situation is not as favorable as it seems. So, we would like to look ahead and to see what will happen to each of the new positions after the next move by the opponent. Thus, we apply the evaluation function to each of the positions that we just generated. This operation is shown in Figure 7.10.

    Now we must take into consideration that the opponent gets to choose which successor moves to make, thus what value should be assigned to the next level.

Since the opponent's goal is to minimize the value of the evaluation function, the expected move is to chose F. The net effect is that if we make move B, the opponent's move is F and the actual position in which we will end up in a two-level search tree is very bad for us. Alternatively, a possible situation that is represented by E is very favorable for us. Since at this level we are not the ones to move, we will not get the chance to choose E.

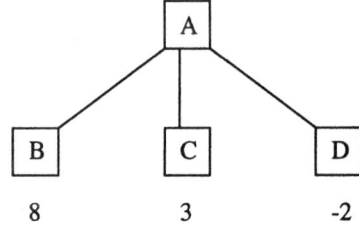

Figure 7.9. One-level search.

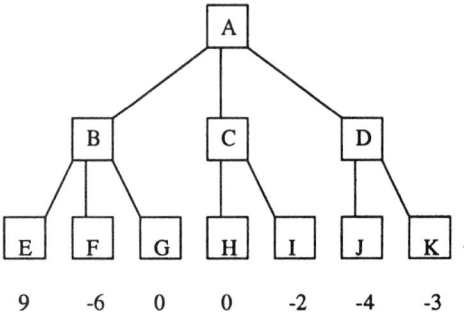

Figure 7.10. Two-level search.

Generally speaking, at the level representing the opponent the minimum value and at the level representing our choice the maximum value of all possible successor positions can be chosen and propagated up. Figure 7.11 illustrates the result of propagating the new values up the tree. After propagating the values up, the correct move for us can be chosen. For example, given the information, the correct move for us is C, since there is nothing the opponent can do from that level to produce a value worse than –2. With regard to the number of search levels, this process can be repeated and the propagation can be used to choose the correct move at the top level. In what follows, we denote that one player looks for a move that leads to a large positive number and assumes that the other player will try to force that play toward situations with large negative numbers.

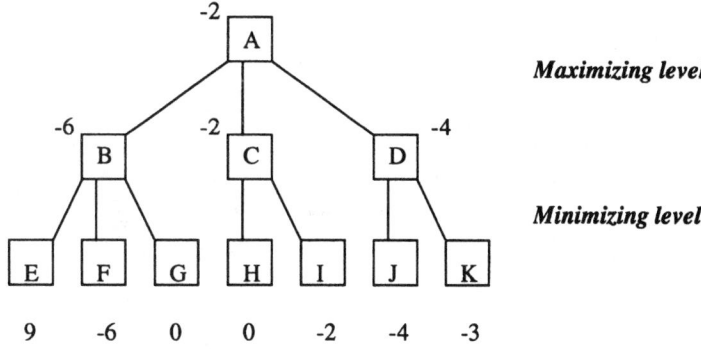

Figure 7.11. Propagating up the values in a two-level search.

To be more precise, the minimax strategy is a recursive procedure with the following properties:

- **Move Generator:** This returns a list of all possible successor moves that can be made by a Player.
- **Players:** The player hoping for positive numbers is called the maximizing player or the **maximizer**. The other player is called the **minimizer** or minimizing player.
- **Evaluation Function:** This returns a value representing the effectiveness of a move from the player's point of view. The process is called the static evaluation, the function is called the static evaluator, and the values are called the static evaluation values.
- **Termination:** This indicates when to stop the recursion and call the evaluation function. Some of the stopping criteria are the number of levels and how much time is left.

Procedure   **MINIMAX(Position, Level, Player)**
                Position indicates the current position.
                Level indicates number of moves ahead from that position.
                Player specifies which player is to move first.

if Player = Player-One
    then   player-one(Position, Level)
    else   player-two(Position, Level)

function player-one(w,n)
    if n = 0 or w has no successor
            then   return evaluate(w)

           else   return Min{player-two(x, n − 1) | x is a successor of w}
       endif
   end player-one

   function player-two(w,n)
      if n = 0 or w has no successor
         then   return evaluate(w)
         else   return Max{player-one(x, n − 1) | x is a successor of w}
       endif
   end player-two
End   MINIMAX

As we can see, in minimax strategy, one path is explored as far as time allows, then the evaluation function is applied to the terminal positions at the last level and the value can be passed one level up, meaning that minimaxing can be expensive, because the generation of either paths or evaluation values can require a lot of computation. There is a heuristic strategy called alpha-beta pruning that can result in a significant reduction in the amount of computation required during an n-level minimax search and still correctly compute the value of a given solution. An alpha-beta search is essentially a depth-first branch-and-bound search method that searches for an optimal solution in an AND/OR graph. The alpha-beta strategy requires two threshold values, a lower bound called alpha value and an upper bound called beta value. Alpha value represents the lower bound value that a maximizing vertex may ultimately be assigned, and beta value represents the upper bound value that a minimizing vertex may be assigned. In general, the alpha-beta pruning strategy avoids searching sub-trees whose evaluation cannot influence the outcome of the search. Two rules for terminating a search based on alpha and beta values are:

1.   A search can be stopped below any minimizer having a beta value less than or equal to the alpha value of any of its maximizers.
2.   A search can be stopped below any maximizer having an alpha value greater than or equal to the beta value of any of its minimizers.

As an example, Figure 7.13 takes the search space of Figure 7.12 and applies the alpha-beta pruning strategy. Note that the resulting backed-up value is identical to the minimax result and the search savings is considerable.

From this example, we see that at maximizing levels, we can rule out a move early if it becomes clear that its value will be less than the current threshold, while at minimizing levels, a search will be terminated if values that are greater than the current threshold are discovered. In general, ruling out a possible move by a maximizer actually means cutting off the search at a minimizing level.

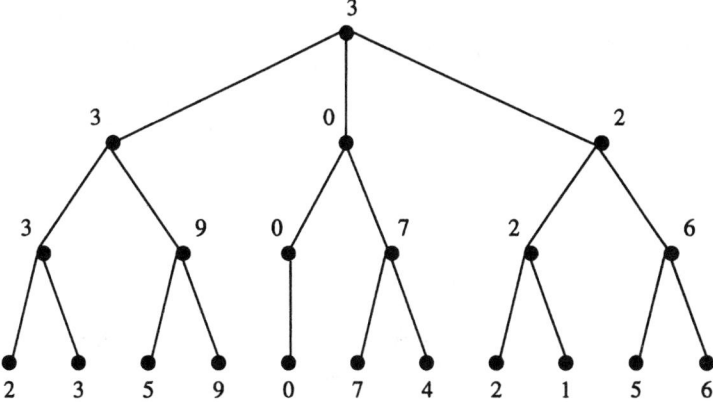

Figure 7.12. Minimax method applied to state space search. Terminal positions show the evaluation values, internal positions show the propagated values.

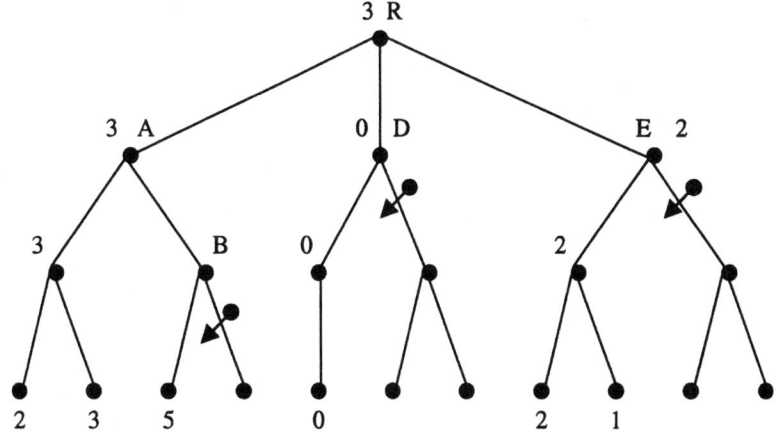

Figure 7.13. Alpha-beta strategy applied to state space search. Positions without numbers are not evaluated.

So the way alpha and beta are actually used is that a search at a minimizing level can be terminated when a value less than alpha is discovered, while a search at a maximizing level can be terminated when a value greater than beta has been found. The alpha-beta algorithm is invoked with four parameters: the current position of the player, the level of the search that is to be made, the alpha value, and the beta value. The recursive function returns a value which is the minimax value of the current position. The sequential algorithm is illustrated in Figure 7.14, and generally speaking, the quantity of interest is the number of evaluations cut off from the minimax search strategy.

A has $\beta = 3$, meaning that A will be no greater than 3.

B is β pruned, since $5 > 3$.

R has $\alpha = 3$, meaning that R will be no smaller than 3.

D is α pruned, since $0 < 3$.

E is α pruned, since $2 < 3$.

Procedure   ALPHA-BETA(Position, Levels, α, β)

α is the lower cutoff value and β is the upper cutoff value.

Successors is number of possible moves with regard to this position.

Cutoff is a flag to address pruning when it is set to TRUE.

X[1,...,k] is the array representing the children of Position.

begin

    if Levels ≤ 0

        then return (Evaluation(Position))

    endif

Successors $\Leftarrow$ Move-Generator(Position)

if Successors = 0

        then return (Evaluation(Position))   /*there is no possible move */

endif

Cutoff $\Leftarrow$ False

i $\Leftarrow 1$

while (i $\leq$ Successors && Cutoff = FLASE) do

    value$\Leftarrow$ALPHA-BETA(X[i], Levels-1, α, β)

    if   (Position = Maximizer && value$>\alpha$)

        then $\alpha \Leftarrow$ value

        else if   (Position = Minimizer && value$<\beta$)

                then $\beta \Leftarrow$ value

            endif

    endif

if $(\alpha > \beta)$ then   Cutoff $\Leftarrow$ TRUE

endif

i = i + 1

endwhile

if   (Position = Maximizer)

    then return α;   else return β

endif

end

End   ALPHA-BETA

Figure 7.14. The sequential alpha-beta algorithm.

Much research has been done in the area of parallel formulation of the alpha-beta search [Akl 82, Ferguson 88, Monien 90, Powley 90]. Some of these techniques have shown reasonable speedup. However, in most cases the speedups are typically limited to a factor of a small number of processors, meaning that alpha-beta can be parallelized, but not easily. An alpha-beta minimax search has several opportunities for parallel execution. Some of the approaches are:

- Parallelize the move generation and position evaluation.
- Praallelize the search process.
- Parallelize the search of independent sub-trees.

For example, the Custom Chess Machine HITECH with 64 processors, organized as an 8×8 array, has taken the move generation and position evaluation approach [Luger 93]. However, the speedup that is achieved is limited by the parallelism inherent in those activities. More improvement in speedup might be achieved through parallelizing the search process.

Finkel and Fishburn [Finkel 82] have developed a distributed parallel algorithm for implementing an α–β search on a tree of processors. Each processor is an independent computer and is connected by communication links to each of its nearest neighbors. The algorithm is called *tree-splitting* and can also be implemented in message-passing or shared-memory parallel architectures. The processors are built as a tree in which a processor's parent is its master and its child is its slave. At various points in the parallel algorithm the root processor evaluates the root position and each interior processor evaluates its assigned position by generating the successors and queuing them for parallel assignment to its slave processors. Thus, a processor at level k in the tree always evaluates positions at level k in the look ahead tree. When an interior process receives responses from its slaves, it tells working slaves about the improved α and β values. And, when all successors have been evaluated, the interior processor is able to compute the value of its position. Each leaf processor evaluates its assigned position with the serial α–β search algorithm. Finally, when a processor finishes, it reports the computed value to its master. The algorithm consists of two parts:

1. The leaf algorithm
2. The interior algorithm

The **leaf** algorithm runs at terminal processors of the tree. The master calls the procedure **Leaf$\alpha\beta$** and can interrupt a search in progress to tell its slaves of new α, β values by invoking the **Update** procedure in the slave. The leaf processor communicates with its master by means of remote procedure calls. The **interior** algorithm runs on interior processors of the tree and generates all successors of the position to be evaluated. Each of the slaves is requested to evaluate one of these positions and the remaining positions are queued for later evaluation. A separate process is created for each successor. If the returned value from a slave causes α value to increase, then the algorithm sends -α as an updated β value to all active slaves. When all successors have been evaluated, the algorithm returns the final value to its master. Generally speaking, the significant speedups can be achieved by allowing processors to examine independent subtrees in parallel. There are two important overheads to be considered. **Search overhead** refers to the increase in the number of nodes that must be examined and **communication overhead** which refers to the time spent coordinating the processes performing the searching. Search overhead can be reduced at the expense of communication overhead by keeping every processor aware of the current search window. The leaf algorithm is as follows.

Algorithm: Leaf(depth, α, β)
{slave is informed of the new α and β values}
[successor specifies the successor of this processor}
{succno specifies the successor processor}
{succlimit specifies how many successor processors}
{the α and β values are global variables in order to facilitate updating their values}
{depth is the depth of the processor tree}

Update(newα, newβ)
for   k = 1   to   depth   do
$\alpha[k] = \max(\alpha[k], \text{new}\alpha)$
$\beta[k] = \min(\beta[k], \text{new}\beta)$
temp = newα
newα = $-$ newβ
newβ = temp
endfor

Leaf$\alpha\beta$(position, α ,β)
$\alpha[1] = \alpha$
$\beta[1] = \beta$
return   **AlphaBeta**(position, 1)

AlphaBeta(position, depth)
if   succlimit=0   then return   (position)
endif
for   succno=1 to   succlimit do
$\alpha[\text{depth}+1] = -\beta[\text{depth}]$
$\beta[\text{depth}+1] = -\alpha[\text{depth}]$
$\alpha[\text{depth}]=\max\{\alpha[\text{depth}], \text{AlphaBeta(successor[succno],depth+1)}\}$
if $\alpha[\text{depth}] \leq \beta[\text{depth}]$
then return   ($\alpha[\text{depth}]$)
endfor
return   ($\alpha[\text{depth}]$)
End   Leaf-Algorithm

The interior algorithm is as follows.

Algorithm: Interior(globalα, globalβ)

    Update(newα, newβ)

        globalα = max(globalα, newα)

        globalβ = min(globalβ, newβ)

        for   all   [slave_id]   do

                [slave_id].Update(-globalβ, -globalα)

        endfor

    Interiorαβ(position, α, β)

        globalα = α

        globalβ = β

        if   succlimit = 0   then return   (position)

        endif

        if   depth(successor[1]) < q then

                g = interiorαβ

        else g = leafαβ

        endif

        for   all   succno = 1   to   succlimit do

        if   globalα < globalβ   then

            temp[succno] = -[slave_id].g(successor[succno],

                -globalα, -globalβ)

            if   temp[succno] > globalα then

                globalα = max(temp[succno], globalα)

                for all   [slave_id] do [slave_id]**Update**

                    (-globalβ,-globalα)

            endif

        endif

        endfor

        return(globalα)

End   **Interior-Algorithm**

Summary

This chapter has described parallel algorithms to implement searching methods. All algorithms associate processes with particular operations to be performed. In general, the optimization problems are subject to an exploration of all possible solutions. We discussed algorithms for graph problems, including divide-and-conquer, depth-first, breadth-first, best-first, branch-and-bound and alpha-beta minimax search algorithms. These search methods are the basis of many classical optimization problems adopted to graph theory. We discussed the divide-and-conquer method as strategy to partition a problem into a number of independent subproblems, known as the divide step. The subproblems are solved independently of each other, which is known as the conquer step. Then we combine the obtained solution of the subproblems to form a final solution for the original problem. An example of this strategy was the bitonic merge sort, in which it was required to sort n data elements using n processors. We looked at matrix multiplication as another example of divide-and-conquer, in which it was required to multiply two n × n matrices utilizing n^2 processors. The processors were viewed as an n × n array where the processors were labeled as PE_{ij} for $0 \leq i,j \leq n - 1$. We outlined the parallel algorithm along with the implementation as a recursive method.

The depth-first search has a host of applications. It is the process of searching a graph in such a way that the search moves forward until it reaches a vertex whose neighbors have all been examined. At this point it backtracks a minimum distance and continues in a new direction. The literature in graph theory is very rich, and interested readers can refer to different books in the list of references. Although in the depth-first search it was not required that the children of a vertex be visited in any particular order, we followed the convention that the children of a vertex are visited from left to right. We used a graph in the form of an adjacency list matrix and outlined a parallel depth-first search algorithm. The parallel algorithm was applicable to SIMD and MIMD systems; however, the parallel depth-first search was not recommended on SIMD systems with regard to processor utilization.

In contrast to the depth-first search, the breadth-first search proceeds by visiting all the neighbors of the examined vertex. This indicates that we continue to search from a vertex until all edges involving that vertex have been examined. We discussed two classification of the parallel breadth-first search: vertex-by-vertex parallel breadth-first search and level-by-level parallel breadth-first search. We used the classical parallel model with k processors to illustrate the vertex-by-vertex breadth-first search algorithm, in which each processor examined one of the neighbors of the current vertex. In this case the maximum number of processors being used is equal to the degree of the vertex from which the search is performing. In the level-by-level breadth-first search we examined different vertices on the same level simultaneously. We presented the classical parallel model with k processors to illustrate the level-by-level breadth-first search algorithm. We discussed the best-first method as an approach to direct the traversing of the search tree. We claimed that the expansion of a vertex could be estimated numerically by a heuristic evaluation function depending on the criteria used. The vertex selected for expansion was the one having the best value of this evaluation function.

We discussed the branch-and-bound search as a method for exploring an implicit directed graph. At each node we calculated a bound on the possible value of any solution that might proceed further on in the graph. If the bound indicated that any such solution must be worse than the best solution found so far, then this part of the graph was not explored. In this way, we pruned certain branches of a tree in the graph. In general, we can combine the calculation of the bounds with a depth-first or breadth-first search. Which vertex was selected for inspection at any moment was decided by a search strategy such as depth-first, breadth-first or best-first. Branch-and-bound algorithms utilizing these three search methods were called LIFO branch-and-bound, FIFO branch-and-bound and least-cost branch-and-bound, respectively. We outlined examples to illustrate the state space tree traversing and pruning used in the branch-and-bound search method. The parallel algorithm used a divide-and-conquer approach that enumerated a live set of vertices utilizing k available processors. We claimed some of the features associated with the branch-and-bound search method as: easy tracking of unexamined vertices, minimal interprocess communication and required memory, and asynchronous communication.

The alpha-beta minimax search method has proven to be an efficient method for evaluating game trees, in which the global maximum or minimum of a function is the problem to be solved. The method is a depth-first and depth-limited strategy. The idea was to start from the current vertex and determine the set of all possible successor positions. We evaluated the successor positions and simply chose the best one for the next move. After doing so, we propagated that value of the best move to the start position to reevaluate it. After this propagation the next move could be determined. In general, the strategy is a recursive procedure with the following properties: move generation, evaluation function, maximizer, minimizer and termination criteria. We outlined the sequential alpha-beta minimax search method along with an example to address the efficiency with regard to the number of branches that were not evaluated.

Several methods have been proposed to parallelize the alpha-beta search, such as parallelize move generation, parallelize the search process and parallelize search sub-trees. The methods seem to have enough parallelism to scale to massively parallel machines. We outlined a parallel algorithm on a tree of processors developed by Finkel. The algorithm consisted of two parts: the leaf procedure and the interior procedure. The leaf procedure runs at terminal processors of the tree, whereas the interior procedure runs on interior processors of the tree and generates all successors of the position to be evaluated. Generally speaking, at various points in the parallel algorithm the root processor evaluates the root position and each interior processor evaluates its assigned position by generating the successors and queuing them for parallel assignment to its slave processors. The algorithm is outlined with comments.

Exercises

1. Define the following terms:

Depth-first search	Breadth-first search
Best-first search	Branch-and-bound
Alpha-beta search	Divide-and-conquer

2. Explain how to calculate a factorial number N! using the divide-and-conquer method.

3. Let n denote the number of vertices, d_i denote the degree of vertex i, and m denote the number of edges in a graph. Prove that an upper bound for a sequential algorithm to search a graph (depth-first or breadth-first) is

$$T = \sum_{i=1}^{n} (d_i + 1) = 2m + n$$

where d_i is the maximum number of times that vertex i can be chosen as the vertex from which searching is to be done.

4. Use the minimax algorithm to evaluate the game tree of the following:

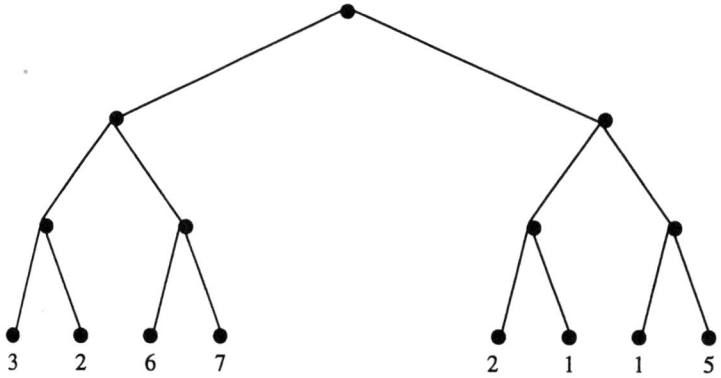

5. Devise a parallel algorithm for the depth-first search method. Analyze the complexity of your algorithm.

6. Show the states resulting from the first three steps of a depth-first search applied to an instance of the 8-puzzle problem below.

7	2	3
4	6	5
1	8	●

7. The alpha-beta search method has a number of opportunities for parallel execution. One approach is to parallelize move generation. Devise a parallel algorithm for this approach.

8. Explain the best-first search method. What is the main drawback of this algorithm?

9. Analyze the speedup in the parallel DFS.

10. Most of the parallel DFS formulations are suited only for MIMD computers. Why?

11. Devise the states generated by a breadth-first search in finding a path from the given initial state to the goal state in the 8-puzzle game.
    Devise a parallel algorithm to perform the search process.

Initial

	2	3
1	4	6
7	5	8

Goal

1	2	3
4	5	6
7	8	

Reference-Needed Exercises

12. Prove that given a perfectly ordered uniform game tree of depth D and branching factor B, the number of node examinations performed by an alpha-beta search in the first branch's subtree is as follows: [Hyatt 89].

$$B^{\lceil (D-1)/2 \rceil} + B^{\lfloor (D-1)/2 \rfloor} - 1$$

13. Given $P \geq 2$ processors on the CREW PRAM model of computation, prove that the number of active operations required by a parallel breadth-first search is

$$T_p = \sum_{i=1}^{n} \left(\left\lceil \frac{d_i}{P} \right\rceil + 1 \right) + L \lceil \log P \rceil$$

where L is the distance of the vertex farthest from the start vertex [Raghbati 78].

14. A common best-first search method is the A* algorithm. Explain the structure of this algorithm.

15. Consider a parallel formulation of DFS using a nearest neighbor search space distribution. This method works as follows: when a processor runs out of work, it sends a work request to its immediate neighbors in a round-robin fashion. For example, on a hypercube, a processor sends requests only to its (log P) neighbors. For networks in which the distance between all pairs of processors is the same, this scheme is identical to the asynchronous round-robin scheme. The nearest neighbor scheme ensures the locality of communication for both work requests and actual work transfers. A potential drawback of the scheme is that any localized concentration of work takes longer to be distributed to distant processors. Analyze the performance and scalability of this parallel formulation for a hypercube, a mesh and a ring [Kumar 87].

CHAPTER 8
Parallel Computational Algorithms

As parallel processing computers have proliferated, interest in developing parallel computational algorithms has increased. Indeed, parallel algorithms have been developed for many of the ordinary serial computational algorithms. Some algorithms are highly parallel in their formulation although they were designed for serial computation, since most of their operators can be implemented as parallel algorithms without any modification. An algorithm containing such a natural parallelism consists of mutually independent operators which require for their execution the results of only a few other operators.

Ideally, a set of characteristics would describe parallel algorithms and a corresponding set of characteristics would describe parallel architectures with a mapping from one to the other. Research in the area of parallel algorithms is so active that it would be unrealistic to try to mention all the areas where parallel techniques are being studied. Thus, we present only an introductory selection of parallel algorithms that illustrate some fundamental techniques of parallel computational algorithms. Using the application areas of prefix, transitive, matrix, expression and sorting processing as our frame of reference in this chapter, we have identified a set of characteristics that appear to capture the attributes of parallel algorithms in their relationship with parallel architectures.

Apart from the wish to be representative of the main stream of this chapter, our choice in problem selection was influenced both by the desire to illustrate commonly used methods and by the convenience of making some algorithms that contribute to the solutions of other problems. We present a number of basic parallel computational algorithms associated with prefix computation, transitive closure, matrix and vector computations, expression evaluation and sorting. Since loops represent a source of parallelism, parallel loop transformations are some of the most important techniques presented in the parallel algorithms of this chapter. In the parallel computations, we present several forms of parallel loops and identify transformations for achieving these forms. For example, many scientific and engineering problems can take the form of a system of linear equations. Because systems are often quite large, there is good reason to solve these systems efficiently on parallel computers. Natural parallelism is also present in algorithms that are based on the iterative computation of the same operator over different data. In this sense, the maximum number of processors required for their implementation is a function of the size of the problem to be solved.

The parallel algorithms in this chapter are presented in terms of one popular theoretical model, called the PRAM (Parallel Random Access Machine, pronounced "P-RAM") model of parallel computation, which consists of P autonomous processors executing synchronously and all having access to a common shared memory. The PRAM model was formalized in 1978 by Fortune and Wyllie [Fortune 1978], although many other authors had previously discussed essentially similar models. At each step, each processor performs one operation from its instruction stream. Instructions accessing shared memory are also assumed to be accomplished in one cycle. Throughout this chapter, we have assumed that the designed algorithms are to be executed on a CREW PRAM model of computation, which is an architecture that allows several processors to read the same memory location simultaneously but does not permit simultaneous writing to the same memory location. It seems intuitively likely that such an architecture should be more powerful than a EREW PRAM and less powerful than a CRCW PRAM. When analyzing parallel algorithms in the following sections, we make the crucial assumption that an access to memory in our hypothetical CREW PRAM, whether for reading or writing, can be made in constant time, regardless of the number of processors in use. This assumption is not true in practice, since it is not feasible to provide direct links in hardware from all processors to all storage locations.

It is worth noting that there is a linear algebra package called LINPACK that contains a variety of Fortran routines and can be obtained from Netlib. Netlib is an on-line repository of mathematical software which contains a large number of interesting codes, tables and papers. Netlib is a compilation of resources from a variety of places, with fairly detailed indices and search mechanisms to help you find what is there. Whenever you need a specialized piece of mathematical software, you should look here first. There are three ways to access netlib—e-mail, ftp and the www—as follows:

E-mail: Netlib provides an e-mail server to send indices and sources on demand. To get an index, send an e-mail to netlib@netlib.org with the words *send index* on its own line in the message. The index will provide a list of other files you can send for.

FTP: Connect by ftp to ftp.Netlib.org. You can log in as anonymous and use your e-mail address as your password. Use "ls" to see the contents of a directory, "cd" to move to a different directory and "get" to fetch the desire file. Type "binary" before "get" in order to ensure uncorrupted transmission, and "quit" to quit the ftp mode.

WWW: With your favorite browser, open the URL address http://www.netlib.org/. There is a forms index that permits searching based on keywords.

In addition, LEDA (Library of Efficient Data types and Algorithms) [Mehlhorn 95] is another resource available to support combinatorial computing. It has been under development since 1988 by a group at the Max Planck Institute in Saarbrücken, Germany, including Kurt Mehlhorn, Stefan Näher, Stefan Schirra, Christian Uhrig and Christoph Burnikel. LEDA is implemented in C++ using templates and it should compile on most compilers. LEDA is available by anonymous ftp from ftp.Mpi-sb.Mpg.de in directory /pub/LEDA, or at http://www.mpi-sb.de/LEDA/leda.html. The distribution contains all sources, installation procedures and a substantial users manual. LEDA is not in the public domain, but it can be used freely for research and teaching purposes. The algorithms presented in this chapter are available in the resources mentioned by establishing the required communications.

8.1   Prefix Computation

Suppose a set $\Re$ is given and an operation $\oplus$ is defined on the elements of $\Re$ such that:

- The $\oplus$ operation is binary such that $\oplus$ applies to pairs of elements of $\Re$.
- The set $\Re$ is closed under the binary operation $\oplus$, meaning if x and y are elements of $\Re$, then x$\oplus$y is an element of $\Re$, too.
- The binary operation $\oplus$ is associative, meaning if x, y, and z are elements of $\Re$, then

$$(x\oplus y)\oplus z = x\oplus(y\oplus z) = x\oplus y\oplus z.$$

Examples of such an operation include addition, multiplication, minimum of two numbers, maximum of two numbers, concatenation of strings, and logical operations such as **and, or** or **exclusive-or** for Boolean operators. We also assume the existence of an element 0, called the identity element in $\Re$, having the property that $0\oplus x = x\oplus 0$ for all $x \in \Re$.

Prefix Sums

Given the sequence of elements $\Re = \{x_1, x_2, ..., x_n\}$ and an associative operation $\oplus$, assume S_j is defined as:

$$S_j = x_i \oplus x_{i+1} \oplus ... \oplus x_j$$

where $i = 1$, $j = 1, 2, ..., n$ and $i \leq j$.

The sums $S_j = x_i \oplus x_{i+1} \oplus ... \oplus x_j$ are called the prefix sums in which $j = 1, 2, ..., n$. In other words, $S_j = S_{j-1} \oplus x_i$ for $i = 2, ..., n$ with $S_1 = x_1$. In general, the prefix sums problem is to compute the n quantities with the following properties:

$$S_1 = x_1$$
$$S_2 = x_1 \oplus x_2$$
$$S_3 = x_1 \oplus x_2 \oplus x_3$$
$$...$$
$$S_n = x_1 \oplus x_2 \oplus x_3 \oplus ... \oplus x_n$$

The process of obtaining $S = \{s_1, s_2, ..., s_n\}$ from $\Re = \{x_1, x_2, ..., x_n\}$ is known as prefix computation. Although prefix computation might seem inherently sequential, in fact it is highly parallelizable.

Example: Given the operation + and the set $\Re = \{3,2,1,4,5,6,0\}$ the prefix sums of $\Re$ will be $S = \{3,5,6,10,15,21,21\}$ as illustrated in Figure 8.1. This represents the process of carrying out 7 additions.

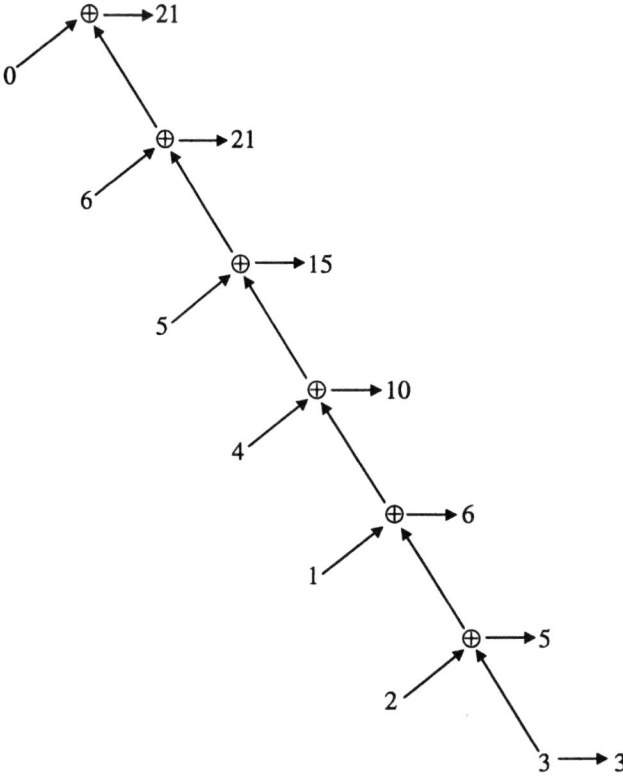

Figure 8.1. Prefix sums of $\Re = \{3,2,1,4,5,6,0\}$ computed as $S = \{3,5,6,10,15,21,21\}$.

A corollary follows immediately from this example that we are interested not only in the sum of the numbers but also in cumulative partial sums. Prefix computation has many important applications, including carry lookahead addition, polynomial evaluation, various circuit design problems, solving linear recurrence, scheduling problems, rank computation, merging two lists, broadcasting and a variety of graph problems. Prefix computation is regarded as a primitive operation in parallel algorithms and has been implemented in the instruction set of some existing parallel architectures.

Parallel Prefix Sums Algorithm

The problem of computing prefix sums in parallel can be solved on any binary tree in 2d + 1 steps where d is the depth of the tree. To construct the tree, we count the vertices from left to right along the natural linear order of the terminal vertices. For example, Figure 8.2 represents the created tree of the set $\Re$ = {3,2,1,4,5,6,0} in which the leaves of the tree correspond to the elements of the set.

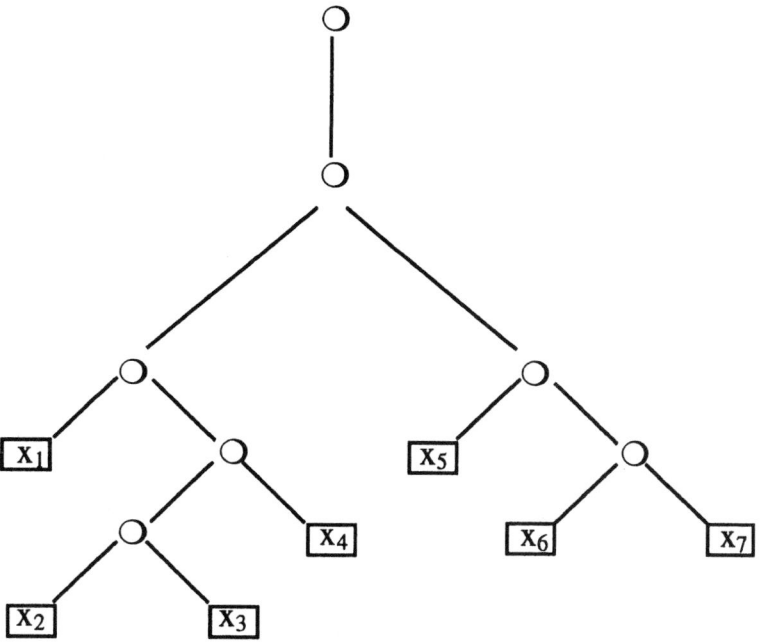

Figure 8.2. Generated tree of the set $\Re$ = {3,2,1,4,5,6,0}.

Utilizing the created tree, the parallel prefix sums algorithm consists of three phases:

1. In phase one, each internal vertex of the tree computes the sum of the entries in the leaves spanned by the vertex.
2. In phase two, each internal vertex of the tree passes the value computed by the vertex to its right child.
3. In phase three, these results are passed downward in the tree, so that the i_{th} leaf can form the i_{th} prefix.

During the first step, x_i is input to the i_{th} terminal vertex for $1 \leq i \leq n$, where n is the number of elements in the set. This value is stored in the vertex as well as passed upward to the parent of the vertex, meaning to the vertex one level up.

As a consequence of this, each internal, nonleaf vertex receives its inputs from the vertices in one level down and performs the defined operation by the vertex, meaning that each internal vertex computes a partial prefix of the terminal vertex as illustrated in Figure 8.3.

Alternatively, each internal vertex passes the value computed by the vertex to its right child vertex. Thus, each terminal vertex x_i receives its input from its parent, meaning the i_{th} terminal vertex has obtained $S_n = x_1 \oplus x_2 \oplus \ldots \oplus x_n$, for $1 \leq i \leq n$, which is the prefix sum of x_i as illustrated in Figure 8.4. In general, the value computed by the left sibling is passed to the right sibling.

It is worth noting that each vertex performs phase 2 on its own as soon as it receives all inputs from its children. In general, the parallel prefix sums algorithm takes $2d + 1$ steps, where d is the depth of the tree. For example, the depth of the tree in Figure 8.2 for the set $\Re = \{3,2,1,4,5,6,0\}$ is 4.

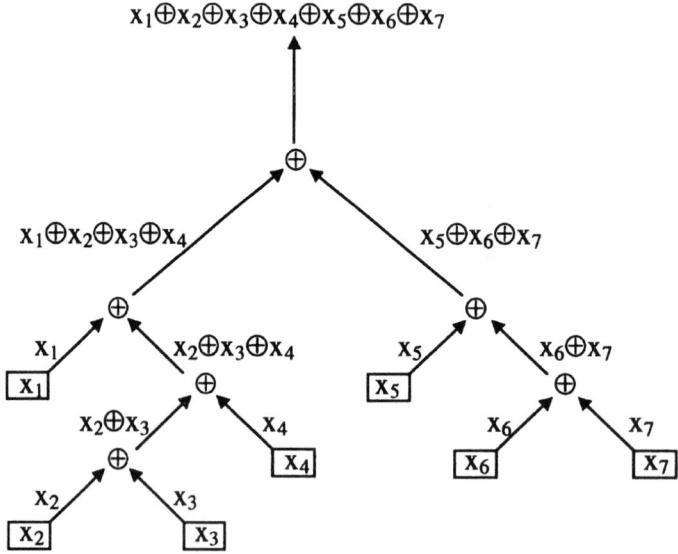

Figure 8.3. Parallel prefix sums computation. Each vertex computes the sum of the inputs and passes the computed result to its right child.

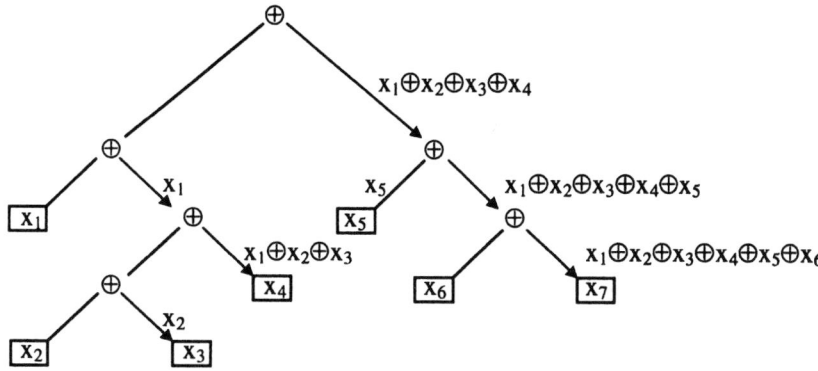

Figure 8.4. Parallel prefix sums computation. Each terminal vertex has received the computed value $S_n = x_1 \oplus x_2 \oplus \ldots \oplus x_n$ which is the prefix sum of x_n.

Parallel Prefix Computation on a Hypercube

Given n elements as $x_1, x_2, \ldots, x_n$ and n processors as $p_1, p_2, \ldots, p_n$ such that x_i resides on the processor labeled p_i, when the algorithm terminates, the same processor holds s_i which is the prefix sum of x_i. In the first step, p_i reads x_{i-1} and x_i, computes $x_{i-1} \oplus x_i$ and assigns the computed value to s_i for all $1 \le i \le n$. In the second step, p_i reads s_{i-2} and s_i computes $s_{i-2} \oplus s_i$ and assigns the result to s_i for all $3 \le i \le n$. Consequently, at the termination of the algorithm, p_i contains s_i, which is the prefix sum of x_i. The net effect is that the processor with label k uses information from only the k-processor subset of those processors whose labels are less than or equal to k.

The following pseudocode illustrates the parallel prefix sums algorithm implemented on a hypercube utilizing n processors such that $n = 2^m$.

Algorithm: Parallel Prefix Computation(X,$\oplus$,S)
Step 0:   (Initialization)
        A set of n elements $x_1, x_2, \ldots, x_n$
        A set of n processors $p_1, p_2, \ldots, p_n$, such that $p_i = x_i$ and $s_i = p_i$
        for all $1 \le i \le n$
Step 1:   for i = 1 to n do **in parallel**
            $s_i = x_{i-1} \oplus x_i$
        endfor
Step 2:   k = 2
        while k < n do

for i = k + 1 to n do **in parallel**

$$s_i = s_{i-k} \oplus s_i$$

endfor

k = k + k

endwhile

End_Parallel_Prefix

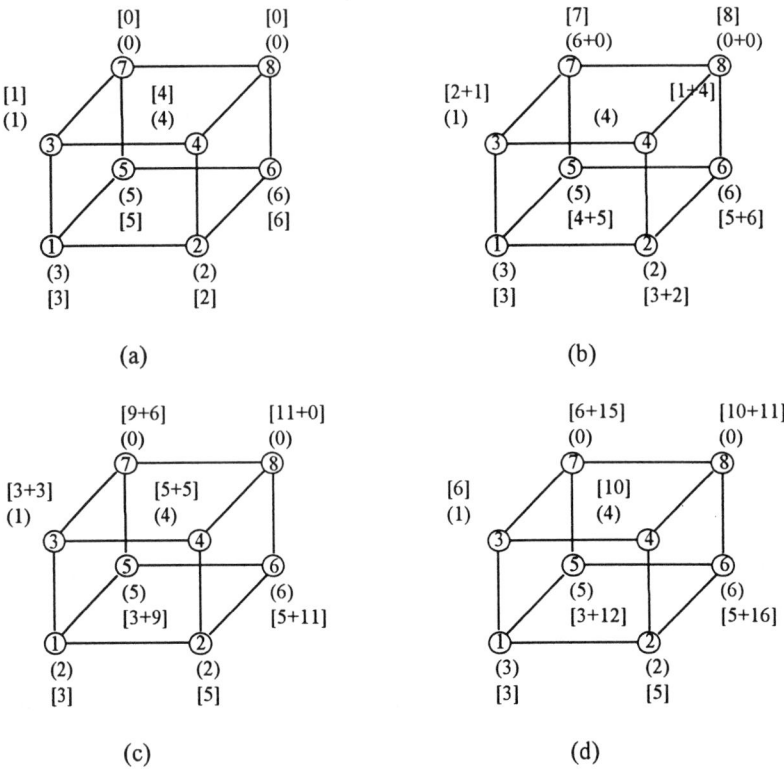

Figure 8.5. Prefix sums computation on an eight-processor hypercube. (a) Initial distribution of numbers to processors. (b) Partial prefix sums after first iteration. (c) Partial prefix sums after second iteration. (d) Final prefix sum value in each processor such that $p_i = s_i$ which is the prefix sum of x_i for all $1 \le i \le n$.

Figure 8.5 illustrates the prefix sums algorithm for an eight-processor hypercube with the set of X = {3,2,1,4,5,6,0,0} as the input. To represent the prefix sums after each step, every processor maintains an additional result buffer. This result buffer is denoted by square brackets in the figure, and the initial value of each processor is represented in parentheses. At the end of each iteration of Step 2 of the algorithm, the result buffer of each processor is updated with every incoming message just as explained. This indicates that the content of an incoming input from each processor is added to the recipient processor's result buffer only if the processor identification is valid regarding the algorithm definition. For instance, after the first iteration of Step 2, processors 2, 3, 4, 5, 6, 7 and 8 add the data received from processors 1, 2, 3, 4, 5, 6, and 7 to their result buffers. Thus, the new value of the result buffer is obtained as the content of the outgoing inputs for the next iteration of Step 2.

8.2   Transitive Closure

Given a directed graph $G = (V,E)$ such that V is the set of vertices and E is the set of edges, we are often interested in the set of vertices that can be reached from a given vertex by traversing the edges of the graph in the indicated direction. In other words, is there a connecting path between any two vertices. This is usually done by finding the transitive closure of the graph. Let $G = (V,E)$ be a graph represented by an $n \times n$ adjacency matrix A whose elements are defined as follows:

$$a_{ij} = \begin{cases} 1 & \textit{if } v_i \text{ is connected to } v_j \\ 0 & \textit{otherwise} \end{cases}$$

The connectivity matrix of G can be defined as an $n \times n$ matrix $C = [C_{ij}]$ whose elements are defined as follows:

$$c_{ij} = \begin{cases} 1 & \textit{if } \text{there is a path from } v_i \text{ to } v_j \\ 0 & \textit{otherwise} \end{cases}$$

In other words, C is an $n \times n$ matrix whose element c_{ij} is 1 if one can reach vertex j from vertex i by following the edges in E for graph G, meaning that there is a chain from i to j. If no chain exists, the entry is 0. Formally, if $G = (V,E)$ is a graph, then the transitive closure of G is defined as the graph $G^* = (V,E^*)$, where $E^* = \{(v_i,v_j) \mid$ there is a path from v_i to v_j in G$\}$. This indicates that we need to compute the connectivity matrix $A^* = [A^*_{ij}]$ defined by:

$$a^*_{ij} = \begin{cases} 1 & \textit{if } \text{there is a path in G from } v_i \text{ to } v_j \\ 0 & \textit{otherwise} \end{cases}$$

A^* is the **connectivity** matrix for the graph $G = (V,E)$, in which E^* is the **transitive closure** of the binary relation E. The matrix A^* is also known as the **reflexive** and transitive closure, or the **reachability** matrix of graph G. A graph G with its adjacency matrix A and the transitive closure G^* with its connectivity matrix A* are presented in Figure 8.6. A and A* are the adjacency matrices of G and G*, respectively. The squared elements in A* represent paths that are in G* but not in G. The loops at the vertices of G and G* are omitted for simplicity, even though $a_{ii} = a^*_{ii} = 1$ for i = 1, 2, 3, and 4.

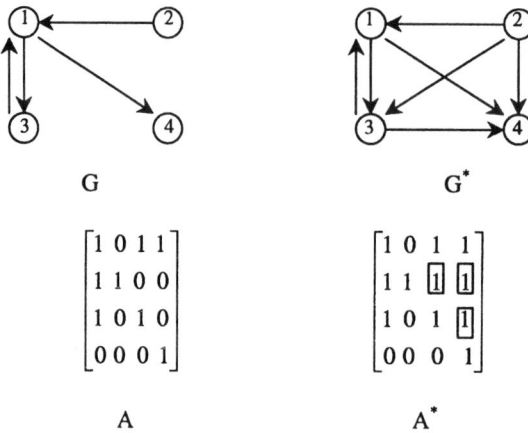

$$\begin{bmatrix} 1 & 0 & 1 & 1 \\ 1 & 1 & 0 & 0 \\ 1 & 0 & 1 & 0 \\ 0 & 0 & 0 & 1 \end{bmatrix} \qquad \begin{bmatrix} 1 & 0 & 1 & 1 \\ 1 & 1 & \boxed{1} & \boxed{1} \\ 1 & 0 & 1 & \boxed{1} \\ 0 & 0 & 0 & 1 \end{bmatrix}$$

A   A*

Figure 8.6. A graph G and its transitive closure G* along with adjacency matrices.

There are several methods to compute the connectivity matrix C:

- All-pairs shortest-path algorithms
- Floyd's algorithm
- Boolean matrix multiplication
- Identity matrix
- Edge insertion
- Warshall's algorithm

One of the solutions of the transitive closure is based on the all-pairs shortest-paths algorithm such that a matrix A* can be obtained from matrix D, where D is the solution to the all-pairs shortest-paths problem as follows:

$$a^*_{ij} = \begin{cases} 1 & \text{if } d_{ij} > 0 \text{ or } i = j \\ 0 & \text{if } d_{ij} = \infty \end{cases}$$

We assign a weight of 1 to each edge of E, and on this weighted graph we use any of the all-pairs shortest-paths algorithms.

Another method for computing matrix A* is to use Floyd's algorithm on the adjacency matrix of G. In the Boolean matrix multiplication method, matrix elements as well as the product matrix are in binary, meaning that each of their elements is either 0 or 1. The Boolean **and** operation and Boolean **or** operation are replaced as regular multiplication and addition operations, respectively. The algorithm is explained in Chapter 6 as one of the approaches for computing the connected components of the graph. The following method is based on the adjacency and identity matrix. Given the graph G with n vertices and its adjacency matrix A, the connectivity matrix C can be computed as:

$$C = (I + A)^{n-1}$$

where I is the identity matrix. The algorithm can be illustrated by the following steps:

- Add the identity matrix to the adjacency matrix A, giving matrix C.
- Raise C to the n − 1 power, yielding C^{n-1}.

Matrix C^{n-1} corresponds to the connectivity matrix or transitive closure of G. Some elementary analysis of this algorithm indicates that it will require a great number of computations for large graphs. There are n − 1 matrix multiplications, each of which requires n × n × n computations. The matrix C^{n-1} represents all paths of length n − 1 or less in the graph. Since the graph has n vertices, the longest path between any two vertices has length n − 1. The attraction of this algorithm for the connectivity matrix is that it has possibilities for parallel implementation by parallel matrix-matrix multiplication, as will be explained in this chapter. For example, we have illustrated the algorithm in Figure 8.7.

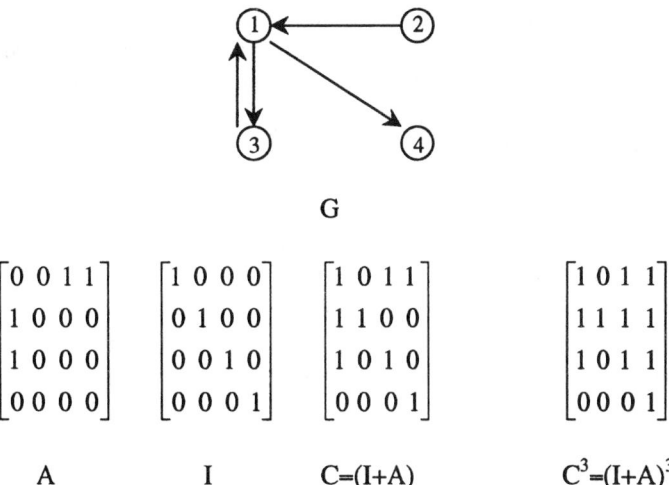

Figure 8.7. Computation of the connectivity matrix of the graph G.

The edge insertion algorithm consists of N phases where N is the number of vertices in the graph G. In the first phase, we insert the edge (v_i, v_j) into the graph for $1 \leq i,j \leq N$ if and only if $(v_i, 1)$ and $(1, v_j)$ are already in the graph. In the second phase, we insert the edge (v_i, v_j) into the graph if and only if $(v_i, 2)$ and $(2, v_j)$ are in the graph formed during the first phase.

In general, we insert (v_i, v_j) into the graph during the k_{th} phase if and only if (v_i, k) and (k, v_j) were in the graph formed during the $(k-1)$ phase. At the end of the N phases, the resulting graph will be G*, meaning a transitive closure graph of G. The rationale behind this algorithm is that the graph formed at the end of the k_{th} phase contains the edge (v_i, v_j) if and only if G has a path from v_i to v_j which contains only vertices from $\{1,2,...,k\}$.

A well-known algorithm for computing the transitive closure is Warshall's algorithm, presented as follows.

procedure   Transitive-Closure(A,A˙)
                begin
                        for k = 0 to n − 1 do
                            for i = 0 to n − 1 do
                                for j = 0 to n − 1 do
                                $a_{ij}^{k} \Leftarrow a_{ij}^{k-1} \cup (a_{ik}^{k-1} \cap a_{kj}^{k-1})$
                                endfor
                        endfor
                endfor
end Transitive-Closure

The worst-case time complexity of computing the transitive closure is $O(n^3)$. The algorithm can be implemented on a mesh SIMD architecture. In particular, we assume that each processor is capable of broadcasting a single value to every other processor in the same row of processors at each step. We conclude that all operations on the (i,j) plane can be performed in parallel and the k coordinate becomes the parallel time coordinate. The adjacency matrix of the graph is stored in the processors from the top, each element of each row in one processor of each row. Each row passes downward over the previously entered row.

In particular, as row i passes over row j, the value a_{ij} is set to 1 if $a_{i1} = a_{1j} = 1$, meaning that the edge (i,j) is inserted if and only if the edges (i,1) and (1,j) are present. If $a_{i1} = 0$ or $a_{1j} = 0$ the value of a_{ij} is left unchanged.

Figure 8.8 illustrates the flow of data for a 4x4 adjacency matrix A of graph G. For more information regarding the parallel transitive closure algorithm refer to Chapter 6, Section 6.1.

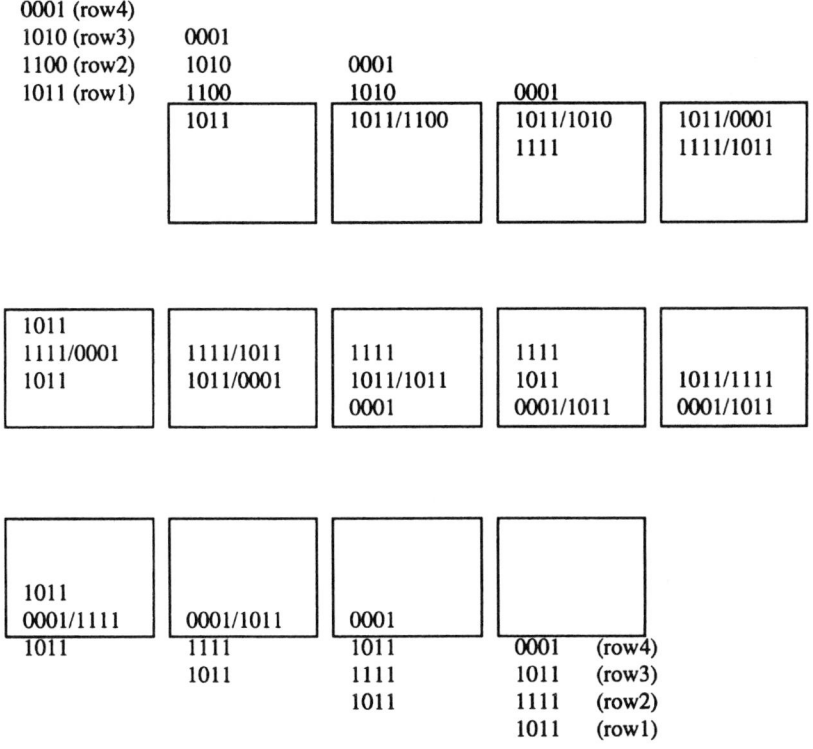

Figure 8.8. Computation of transitive closure of graph G utilizing two-dimensional mesh SIMD. The k_{th} element of each row of the adjacency matrix is stored in the k_{th} processor of the corresponding row of processors.

8.3   Matrix Computation

Matrix computation is an important problem and a fundamental component of linear algebra problems. Linear algebra problems, including systems of linear equations, linear least squares problems, and algebraic eigenvalue problems, are fundamental to the computational solutions of differential equations and optimization problems as well as to the analysis of various discrete structures. Thus, the development of parallel algorithms for matrix computations has received strong emphasis from researchers in parallel computing, both as a tool and as a paradigm for scientific computing. Its main significance for combinatorial algorithms is its equivalence to a variety of other problems such as transitive closure and reduction, solving linear systems and matrix inversion. Thus, a faster algorithm for matrix multiplication implies faster algorithms for all of these problems. Matrix multiplication also arises in computing the coordinate transformation for robotics and computer graphics. The matrices are classified into two categories:

1. Dense or full matrices with few or no zero entries
2. Sparse matrices with a majority of elements as zero

In this chapter, we deal with algorithms for dense matrices and we assume that all matrices are square (n × n) to simplify description, unless otherwise stated. It will be straightforward to generalize these problems to non-square matrices where applicable. As we know from analyzing the algorithms, it is important to determine which data mapping scheme is more appropriate and significantly affects the performance of a parallel computation. Parallel matrix computation can be performed in two different forms:

1. Block partitioning
2. Checkerboard partitioning

Block Partitioning

In block partitioning, the matrix can be divided into different groups consisting of rows or columns in which each group of rows or columns is assigned to one single processor. Each group contains an equal number of rows or columns. For example, Figure 8.9 represents distribution and propagation of data among the 4 processors utilizing row and column partitioning. Figure 8.9 (a) and Figure 8.9 (b) represent two columns per processor and two rows per processor block partitioning, respectively.

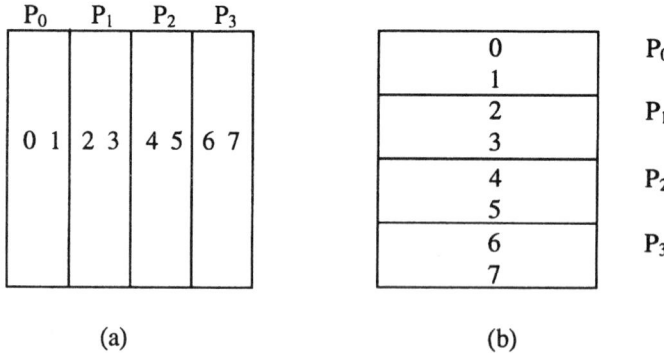

(a)   (b)

Figure 8.9. Block partitioning of 8 × 8 matrix on 4 processors. (a) Column partitioning. (b) Row partitioning.

0 4	P_0
1 5	P_1
2 6	P_2
3 7	P_3

Figure 8.10. A cyclic-block partitioning of 8×8 matrix on 4 processors.

Alternatively, the matrix can be distributed among the processors in a cyclic form. For instance, an $n \times n$ matrix can be distributed on p processors such that each processor p_i contains rows

$$i, i+p, i+2p, \dots, i+n - p$$

where $i = 0, 1, \dots, n - 1$. This partitioning is called cyclic-block partitioning, as shown in Figure 8.10, in which an 8×8 matrix is distributed among 4 processors. The rows 0 and 4 are assigned to the processor p_0, rows 1 and 5 to processor p_1 and so on.

Checkerboard Partitioning

In checkerboard partitioning the matrix can be divided into smaller submatrices that are distributed among processors. In a uniform checkerboard partitioning all submatrices are of the same size and partitioning can be applied to both rows and columns. For instance, Figure 8.11 illustrates checkerboard partitioning of an 8×8 matrix among 16 processors such that two sequences of rows of the matrix are as signed to each processor. It is worth noting that no processor is assigned any complete row or column. In general, a checkerboard partitioning maps the matrix onto a two-dimensional square mesh of processors.

In this chapter, we address two problems, matrix-vector multiplication and matrix-matrix multiplication, in which an $n \times n$ matrix and $n \times 1$ column vector are involved. In general, there are three situations that will determine how to calculate this product on a parallel architecture with N processors:

1. $N > n^3$
2. $N \geq \max(n^2)$
3. $N < \max(n^2)$

If $N > n^3$, then all multiplications can be performed by multiple positioning of the data entries. This indicates that n successive copies of the matrix are placed in adjacent positions and the columns of the vector are repeated n times. Various additions are performed and the sums assigned to the correct element of the product. If $N \geq max(n^2)$, it may be possible to perform n^2 of these multiplications in parallel by termwise multiplication. In general, one of the following three methods can be used to compute the product.

1. Each column of the product is formed in parallel at each step and in n such steps the result can be formed.
2. Each row of the product is formed in parallel at each step and in n such steps the result can be formed.
3. An n × n array is formed in parallel at each step and in n steps the result can be formed.

If $N < max(n^2)$, the matrix needs to be partitioned into smaller blocks, where each block is dealt with in parallel. The blocks correspond to the submatrices that are distributed among processors.

A_{00} A_{01} P_0 A_{10} A_{11}	A_{02} A_{03} P_1 A_{12} A_{13}	A_{04} A_{05} P_2 A_{14} A_{15}	A_{06} A_{07} P_3 A_{16} A_{17}
A_{20} A_{21} P_4 A_{30} A_{31}	A_{22} A_{23} P_5 A_{32} A_{33}	A_{24} A_{25} P_6 A_{34} A_{35}	A_{26} A_{27} P_7 A_{36} A_{37}
A_{40} A_{41} P_8 A_{50} A_{51}	A_{42} A_{43} P_9 A_{52} A_{53}	A_{44} A_{45} P_{10} A_{54} A_{55}	A_{46} A_{47} P_{11} A_{56} A_{57}
A_{60} A_{61} P_{12} A_{70} A_{71}	A_{62} A_{63} P_{13} A_{72} A_{73}	A_{64} A_{65} P_{14} A_{74} A_{75}	A_{66} A_{67} P_{15} A_{76} A_{77}

Figure 8.11. Checkerboard partitioning of 8 × 8 matrix on 16 processors.

8.3.1   Matrix-Vector Multiplication

The problem of multiplying an n×n matrix $A=[a_{ij}]_{n \times n}$ with an n×1 column vector $B=[b_0, b_1, ..., b_{n-1}]^T_{1 \times n}$ yields an n×1 result column vector $C=[c_0, c_1, ... , c_{n-1}]^T_{1 \times n}$ defined by

$$C_i = \sum_{j=0}^{n-1} A_{ij} B_j$$

where $i = 0,1,2,\ldots,n-1$. In general, in analyzing matrix-vector multiplication performances, we choose addition as the basic operation. For example, the following serial algorithm represents matrix A to be multiplied by vector B to give result vector $C = A * B$. This sequential algorithm requires n^2 multiplications and additions, meaning the sequential run time is $O(n^2)$ if a multiplication and addition pair takes unit time.

Procedure   Matrix_Vector(A,B,C)
　　　　　begin
　　　　　　　　for i = 0 to n − 1 do
　　　　　　　　　　begin
　　　　　　　　　　C[i] = 0
　　　　　　　　　　for j = 0 to n − 1 do
　　　　　　　　　　　　C[i] = C[i] + A[i,j] * B[j]
　　　　　　　　　　endfor
　　　　　　　　endfor
End Matrix_Vector

There are two possible parallel formulations for matrix-vector multiplication: block partitioning (either row partitioning or column partitioning) or checkerboard partitioning.

One Row Per Processor

Consider a shared-memory architecture such that an $n \times n$ matrix A and an $n \times 1$ vector B are distributed among n processors. Processor p_i $(0 \le i \le n-1)$ initially stores one complete row of the matrix A and the vector B. For example, A[i,0], A[i,1],…,A[i,n − 1] and B[0], B[1],…,B[n − 1] are stored in processor p_i and p_i is responsible for computing C[i], where $i = 0,1,\ldots,n-1$. Since the i_{th} element of $C = A * B$ is simply the product of the i_{th} row of A and the vector B, all the elements of the product C, C[0], C[1],…,C[n − 1] can be computed simultaneously, as the following parallel algorithm illustrates.

Procedure   Parallel_Matrix_Vector(A,B,C)
　　　　　begin
　　　　　　　　for i = 0 to n−1 do in parallel
　　　　　　　　　　C[i] = A[i,0:n−1] * B[0:n−1]
　　　　　　　　endfor in parallel
End Parallel_Matrix_Vector

The output is C[0:n − 1], where $C[i] = A_{i0}B_0 + A_{i1}B_1 + ,\ldots,A_{in-1}B_{n-1}$ and $i = 0,1,\ldots,n-1$. The multiplication of a single row of matrix A with vector B can be performed by each processor in $O(n)$ time. Thus, the algorithm can be completed by n processors in $O(n)$ time, resulting in a cost of $O(n^2)$. This indicates that the parallel algorithm is cost optimal, since the complexity of the serial algorithm is $O(n^2)$.

One Element Per Processor

Consider a shared-memory architecture such that an $n \times n$ matrix A and an $n \times 1$ vector B are distributed among n^2 processors. We create a two-dimensional mesh SIMD model such that processor p_i ($0 \leq i \leq n^2 - 1$) initially stores one element of the matrix A and the elements of vector B are distributed only in the first n processors, each of which stores one element of the vector B. Figure 8.12 illustrates the distribution of a 3×3 matrix and 3×1 vector on 9 processors such that B[0], B[1] and B[2] are stored in P_{00}, P_{01} and P_{02}, respectively. In general, the processor in row i and column j position stores A[i,j] and the processor in row 1 and column j position stores B[j].

P_{00} A_{00} B_0	P_{01} A_{01} B_1	P_{02} A_{02} B_2
P_{10} A_{10}	P_{11} A_{11}	P_{12} A_{12}
P_{20} A_{20}	P_{21} A_{21}	P_{22} A_{22}

Figure 8.12. Initial data distribution of the matrix and vector for one-element-per-processor case with 9 processors if the matrix size is 3×3 and vector size is 3×1.

The parallel algorithm consists of three steps with the following explanations. Since each element of the product $C = A * B$ can be computed by multiplying the elements of the vector B with the corresponding elements in each row of the matrix, the vector B must be distributed such that the i_{th} element of the vector is available to the i_{th} element of each row, which is the first step of the algorithm. In the second step, the product $A * B$ is computed with regard to the available data of each row of processors. Finally, we sum the stored values across each row of processors to compute the final value of the elements of the product. The result is stored in the diagonal elements of the two-dimensional mesh SIMD model.

      Procedure   Parallel_Matrix_Vector(A,B,C)
          begin
               for i = 0 to n−1 do

for P_{ij} do in parallel, $0 \le j \le n-1$

$P_{(i+1)j} \Leftarrow P_{ij} : B[j]$

endfor in parallel

endfor

/* compute A[i,j] * B[j] in parallel */

for P_{ij} do in parallel, $0 \le i \le n-1$ and

$0 \le j \le n-1$

$P_{ij} : B[j] = A[i,j] * B[j]$

endfor in parallel

/* sum the stored value of each row of processors in parallel */

for i = 0 to n−1 do

for P_{ij} do in parallel, $0 \le j \le n-1$

Sum $\Leftarrow$ Sum + $P_{ij} : B[j]$

endfor in parallel

$P_{ii} : B[i]$ = Sum

Sum $\Leftarrow$ 0

endfor

end

End Parallel_Matrix_Vector

2	-1	10
P_{00}	P_{01}	P_{02}
-2	5	3
0	6	1
P_{10}	P_{11}	P_{12}
4	1	5
P_{20}	P_{21}	P_{22}

(a)

2	-1	10
P_{00}	P_{01}	P_{02}
-2	5	3
0	6	1
P_{10}	P_{11}	P_{12}
-2	5	3
4	1	5
P_{20}	P_{21}	P_{22}
-2	5	3

(b)

2	-1	10
P_{00}	P_{01}	P_{02}
-4	-5	30
0	6	1
P_{10}	P_{11}	P_{12}
0	30	3
4	1	5
P_{20}	P_{21}	P_{22}
-8	5	15

(c)

2	-1	10
P_{00}	P_{01}	P_{02}
21	-5	30
0	6	1
P_{10}	P_{11}	P_{12}
0	33	3
4	1	5
P_{20}	P_{21}	P_{22}
-8	5	12

(d)

Figure 8.13. (a) Initial distribution of matrix and vector on two-dimensional mesh. (b) Broadcast values of vector to second and third rows. (c) Compute the product of the vector elements in each row of processors. (d) Product resides in the diagonal elements of two-dimensional mesh.

The output of this algorithm is C[0:n − 1], where C[i] is stored in P_{ii} for i = 0,1,...,n − 1, meaning in the diagonal elements of the two-dimensional mesh SIMD model architecture. The overall parallel run time of the algorithm is $O(n)$ on an $n \times n$ mesh and $O(\log n)$ on a hypercube with n^2 processors. Since the algorithm can be completed by n^2 processors, the overall running costs are $O(n^3)$ and $O(n^2 \log n)$ on mesh and hypercube, respectively. The algorithm is illustrated in Figure 8.13 utilizing a 3×3 matrix and 3×1 vector.

8.3.2 Matrix-Matrix Multiplication

The product of an n×n matrix A = $[a_{ij}]_{n \times n}$ and an $n \times n$ matrix B = $[b_{ij}]_{n \times n}$ yields an n×n matrix C = $[c_{ij}]_{n \times n}$ whose elements are defined by

$$C_{ij} = \sum_{k=0}^{n-1} A_{ik} B_{kj}$$

for $0 \le i \le n − 1$ and $o \le j \le n − 1$. The following sequential matrix multiplication algorithm requires $n \times n \times n$ additions and $n \times n \times n$ multiplications, where the addition and multiplication of n terms are done sequentially.

Procedure   Matrix_Matrix_Multiplication(A,B,C)
```
        begin
            for i = 0 to n − 1 do
                for j = 0 to n − 1 do
                t = 0
                    for k = 0 to n − 1 do
                    t = t + A[i,k] * B[k,j]
                    endfor k
                C[i,j] = t
                endfor
            endfor
```
End Matrix_Matrix_Multiplication

Suppose now we want to calculate the product of more than two matrices. Matrix multiplication is associative, so we can compute the matrix product

$$C = C_1 C_2 C_3 \ldots C_n$$

in a number of ways, which all give the same product:

$$C = (\ldots((C_1 C_2) \, C_3) \ldots C_n)$$
$$= (C_1 (C_2 (C_3 \ldots (C_{n-1} \, C_n) \ldots)))$$
$$= (\ldots((C_1 C_2)(C_3)) \ldots C_n), \ldots$$

and so on. However, matrix multiplication is not commutative, so we are not allowed to change the order of the matrices in these arrangements. In this chapter, we deal specifically with the product of two matrices for pedagogical reasons, but the algorithms in this chapter, wherever applicable, are readily adaptable for multiple matrices as well. Figure 8.14 illustrates the multiplication of two 2×2 matrices to yield the product as one 2×2 matrix.

$$
\begin{bmatrix} a_{00} & a_{01} \\ a_{10} & a_{11} \end{bmatrix} * \begin{bmatrix} b_{00} & b_{01} \\ b_{10} & b_{11} \end{bmatrix} = \begin{bmatrix} c_{00} & c_{01} \\ c_{10} & c_{11} \end{bmatrix} = \begin{bmatrix} a_{00}b_{00} + a_{01}b_{10} & a_{00}b_{01} + a_{01}b_{11} \\ a_{10}b_{00} + a_{11}b_{10} & a_{10}b_{01} + a_{11}b_{11} \end{bmatrix}
$$

Figure 8.14. Computation of element C_{ij} of $C = A * B$.

Without loss of generality we can express this matrix multiplication algorithm as a nested loop program as follows:

```
for i = 0 to n – 1 do
        for j = 0 to n – 1 do
                for k = 0 to n – 1 do
                        C_ij^k = C_ij^{k-1} + A_ik*B_kj
                        endfor
                endfor
        endfor
```

The rationale behind this algorithm is to identify the dependencies between matrix elements. For this, we rewrite the algorithm into an equivalent form to represent the flow of A's and B's data as follows:

```
for i = 0 to n – 1 do
        for j = 0 to n – 1 do
                for k = 0 to n – 1 do
                A[i,j,k] = A[i,j – 1,k]
                B[i,j,k] = B[i – 1,j,k]
                C[i,j,k] = C[i,j,k – 1] + A[i,j,k]*B[i,j,k]
                endfor
        endfor
endfor
```

The invocation of statements A[i,j,k] = A[i,j – 1,k] and B[i,j,k] = B[i – 1,j,k] indicates that variables A_{ik}^{j} and B_{kj}^{i} have the same value for all j indices and i indices, respectively. In the following sections, two parallel processor architectures, two-dimensional mesh SIMD and three-dimensional mesh SIMD, are presented for the matrix-matrix multiplication problem.

Two-Dimensional Mesh SIMD Model

Given a two-dimensional mesh SIMD architecture with wraparound connection, there is an algorithm that uses n^2 processors to perform matrix-matrix multiplication. Consider an arbitrary element $C[i,j]$ of the product matrix. If B_j denotes the j_{th} column vector of B and A_i denotes the i_{th} row vector of A, then $C[i,j]$ is the product of row i of matrix A and column j of matrix B. The parallel algorithm computes the product in three phases. Initially, the processor P_{ij} located at position (i,j), row i and column j, stores $A[i,j]$ and $B[i,j]$ elements of the matrices. In this distribution, only n processors contain a pair of elements of A and B. However, it is possible to broadcast elements so that every processor has appropriate elements to produce the specific element of the product $C = A * B$. This can be done by an upward rotation of the element of B and a leftward rotation of the element of A stored in each processor. This initial distribution of the elements of the matrices is phase one of the algorithm. In phase two of the algorithm the dot product of the stored elements of each processor is computed. In phase three, the result of phase two is broadcast to the neighboring processors in the leftward and upward direction for the elements of A and B, respectively. After n iterations of phase three of the algorithm, the element $C[i,j]$ of the product is present in the processor P_{ij}.

Procedure   Parallel_Matrix_Matrix(A,B,C)
    Phase1
        for k = 0 to n − 1 do
                for P_{ij} where $0 \le i,j \le n - 1$ do in parallel
                    if i > k
                        then $A[i - 1,j] \Leftarrow A[i,j]$
                    endif
                    if j > k
                        then $B[i - 1,j] \Leftarrow B[i,j]$
                    endif
                endfor P_{ij}
        endfor
    Phase2
        for P_{ij} where $0 \le i,j \le n - 1$ do in parallel
        $C[i,j] = A[i,j] * B[i,j]$
        endfor P_{ij}
    Phase3
        for k = 0 to n − 1 do
                for P_{ij} where $0 \le i,j \le n - 1$ do in parallel
                    $A:P_{ij} \Leftarrow (move\text{-}left)A:P_{ij}$
                    $B:P_{ij} \Leftarrow (move\text{-}up)B:P_{ij}$
                    $C[i,j] = C[i,j] + A[i,j] * B[i,j]$
                    endfor P_{ij}
        endfor
    End Parallel_Matrix_Matrix

Figure 8.15 illustrates the algorithm for two matrices $A = \begin{pmatrix} 1 & 2 \\ 3 & 4 \end{pmatrix}$ and $B = \begin{pmatrix} -1 & -2 \\ -3 & -4 \end{pmatrix}$ with the product as $C = \begin{pmatrix} -7 & -10 \\ -15 & -22 \end{pmatrix}$.

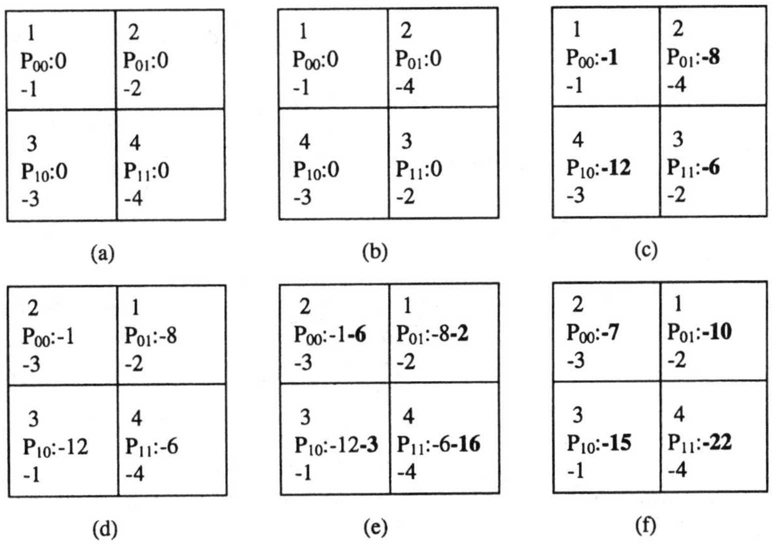

Figure 8.15. Matrix multiplication on the two-dimensional mesh SIMD model. (a) Initial distribution of the matrix elements to processors such that in P_{ij} the elements $A[i,j]$ and $B[i,j]$ are stored. (b) Broadcast the initial elements to the neighboring processors leftward and upward for A and B elements, respectively, if the processor is eligible to receive the element, meaning broadcast each column j of matrix B upward by j row positions and broadcast each row i of matrix A to the left by i column positions. (c) Each processor computes the partial result of the product utilizing the stored matrix elements of A and B. (d) Distribution of the stored matrix elements of A and B of each processor to neighboring processors leftward and upward for A and B elements, respectively, meaning each processor has a pair of elements to multiply. (e) Each processor computes the product of the stored elements of A and B which corresponds to the second partial result of the element of C matrix. (f) At this point each processor P_{ij} has computed the element $C[i,j]$ of the product.

Three-Dimensional Mesh SIMD Model

In the two-dimensional mesh SIMD model, there are various difficulties in managing the product $C = A * B$. However, the three-dimensional mesh SIMD model is ideally suited for matrix-matrix multiplication. In order to multiply the two $n \times n$ matrices A and B where $n = 2^q$, we use a three-dimensional SIMD model or a hypercube with $N = n^3 = 2^{3q}$ processors. We assume that processors are arranged in an $n \times n \times n$ array such that for each 3-tuple (i,j,k) where $0 \le i,j,k \le n - 1$ there is an associated processor $P_{ijk} = P_{(x)}$ where $x = in^2 + jn + k$ and $0 \le x \le 2^{3q} - 1$ is the position of the processor. A corollary follows immediately from this arrangement that all processors are positioned on one or two of the co-ordinates (i,j,k) to form a hypercube of processors. For example, a three-dimensional mesh SIMD is shown in Figure 8.16 in which $n = 2$ and there are $N = 8$ processors.

Initially, matrix elements $A[i,j]$ and $B[i,j]$ are stored in processor $(ni + j)$ for $0 \le i,j \le n - 1$, as illustrated in Figure 8.17 (a) for $A = \begin{pmatrix} 1 & 2 \\ 3 & 4 \end{pmatrix}$

and $B = \begin{pmatrix} -1 & -2 \\ -3 & -4 \end{pmatrix}$.

The parallel algorithm performs n^3 multiplication to compute n^2 elements of the product simultaneously. It proceeds in four phases such that in each phase the computations are performed for the appropriate range of active processors, as follows:

Phase 1. The matrices A and B are distributed over the processors such that $P_{(x)}$ stores $A[i,j]$ and $B[i,j]$ where $x = ni + j$ and $0 \le i,j \le n - 1$.

Phase 2. The $A[i,j]$ and $B[i,j]$ elements of phase 1 must be broadcast to the rest of the processors.

Phase 3. Processor P_{ijk} computes the product $C[i,j,k]=A[i,j,k] * B[i,j,k]$ which is $C_{ijk} = A_{ji} * B_{ik}$ for $0 \le i,j,k \le n - 1$.

Phase 4. The sum $C[0,j,k] = \sum_{i=0}^{n-1} C[i,j,k]$ is computed for $0 \le j,k \le n - 1$.

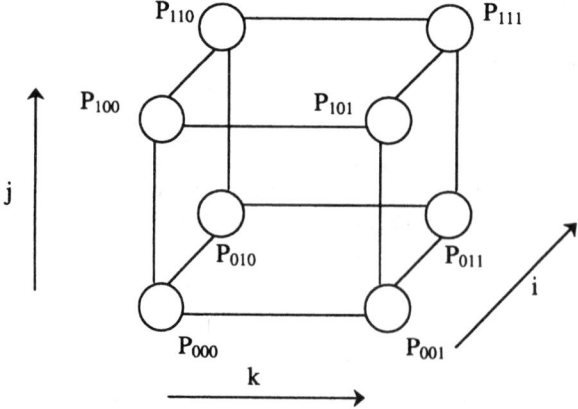

Figure 8.16. A three-dimensional mesh SIMD with 8 processors.

Figure 8.17 illustrates the phases of the algorithm as it multiplies two 2×2 matrices on an eight-processor hypercube SIMD architecture. After the parallel algorithm terminates, the product elements $C[i,j]$ for $0 \leq i,j \leq n-1$ are stored in processors $P_{(x)}$ where $x = ni + j$. The parallel algorithm is as follows:

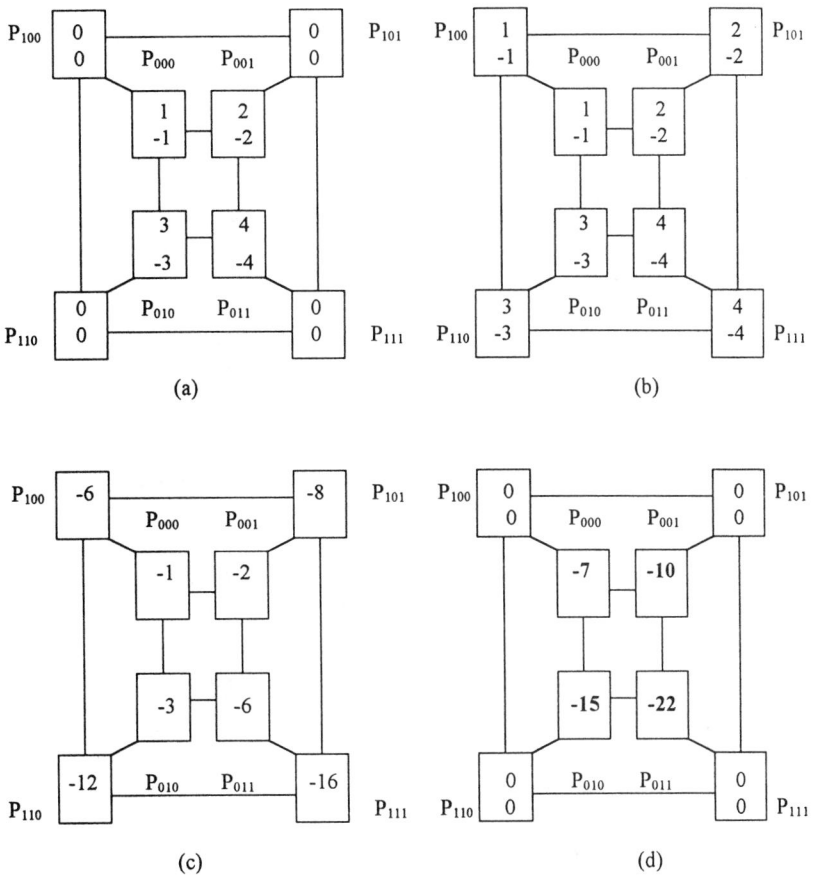

Figure 8.17. Matrix-matrix multiplication on the three-dimensional mesh. (a) Initial distribution of the matrix elements to processors. (b) Broadcasting the matrix elements to the rest of the processors. (c) Stored value in each processor after phase 3. (d) Stored element of the product in each processor after phase 4.

Procedure   **Parallel_Matrix_Matrix(A,B,C)**
  begin
  Phase 1. Initial distribution of the matrix elements
  Phase 2. Broadcast the matrix element

Phase 3. Perform the multiplication in parallel
Phase 4. Sum the products in parallel
end
End Parallel-Matrix-Matrix

8.4   System of Linear Equations

A linear equation can be expressed as:

$$a_1 x_1 + a_2 x_2 + a_3 x_3 + \ldots + a_n x_n = b$$

where a_1, a_2, a_3, ..., a_n and b are constants and x_1, x_2, x_3, ... , x_n are variables. A finite set of linear equations is called a system of linear equations. A system of n linear equations in n variables can be defined as:

$$a_{11} x_1 + a_{12} x_2 + a_{13} x_3 + \ldots + a_{1n} x_n = b_1$$
$$a_{21} x_1 + a_{22} x_2 + a_{23} x_3 + \ldots + a_{2n} x_n = b_2$$
$$a_{31} x_1 + a_{32} x_2 + a_{33} x_3 + \ldots + a_{3n} x_n = b_3$$
$$\ldots \qquad \ldots \qquad \ldots \qquad \ldots \qquad \ldots$$
$$a_{n1} x_1 + a_{n2} x_2 + a_{n3} x_3 + \ldots + a_{nn} x_n = b_n.$$

Alternatively, the system can be written as the following single matrix equation:

$$
\begin{pmatrix}
a_{11} & a_{12} & a_{13} & \ldots & a_{1n} \\
a_{21} & a_{22} & a_{23} & \ldots & a_{2n} \\
a_{31} & a_{32} & a_{33} & \ldots & a_{3n} \\
\ldots & \ldots & \ldots & \ldots & \ldots \\
a_{n1} & a_{n2} & a_{n3} & \ldots & a_{nn}
\end{pmatrix}
*
\begin{pmatrix}
x_1 \\ x_2 \\ x_3 \\ \ldots \\ x_n
\end{pmatrix}
=
\begin{pmatrix}
b_1 \\ b_2 \\ b_3 \\ \ldots \\ b_n
\end{pmatrix}
$$

A set of numbers $(s_1, s_2, s_3, \ldots, s_n)$ is a solution to the above system of linear equations if and only if making the substitutions $x_1 = s_1$, $x_2 = s_2$, $x_3 = s_3$, ..., $x_n = s_n$ satisfies all equations in the linear system. The system of linear equations can be expressed as $\mathbf{Ax = b}$, where A is an n × n matrix containing a_{ij} elements, and x and b are n-element vectors containing x_i and b_i elements, respectively. Solving a set of linear equations is a fundamental problem involved in many computational applications. This section discusses how to solve a system of linear equations using diverse methods such as elimination and factorization.

Definition: An n × n matrix A is an echelon matrix with the following properties:
- Each of the first k ($0 \le k \le n$) rows has some nonzero entries, and the remaining n − k rows consist only of zeroes.
- The first nonzero entry in each of the first k rows is a 1.

- In each of the first k rows, the number of zeroes preceding the leading 1 is smaller than it is in the next row.

Example of an echelon matrix, $A = \begin{bmatrix} 1 & 5 & 0 & 3 & 1 & 2 & 8 \\ 0 & 0 & 1 & 3 & 2 & 4 & 0 \\ 0 & 0 & 0 & 1 & 3 & 1 & 9 \\ 0 & 0 & 0 & 0 & 0 & 0 & 0 \\ 0 & 0 & 0 & 0 & 0 & 0 & 0 \end{bmatrix}$ where $k = 3$.

Definition: An $n \times n$ matrix A is upper triangular such that $a_{ij} = 0$ if and only if $i > j$.

Definition: An $n \times n$ matrix A is lower triangular such that $a_{ij} = 0$ if and only if $i < j$.

Definition: An $n \times n$ matrix A is tridiagonal such that $a_{ij} = 0$ if and only if $|i - j| > 1$.

Definition: Matrix A is equivalent to matrix B, A~B, if B is the result of a sequence of elementary row and/or column operations on A.

If only row operations are used, then A is **row-equivalent** to B.

If only column operations are used, then A is **column-equivalent** to B.

Definition: If A is nonsingular, it possesses an inverse A^{-1}, and $x = A^{-1}b$ is the solution vector.

In this section, we are concerned with the case in which A is nonsingular or the rank of A is equal to the number of linear equations which is n. If the number of equations is less than the number n, then the system is called under-determined. An under-determined system has infinitely many solutions. If the number of equations exceeds the number n, the system is over-determined and there may not be any solution. One approach is to compute A^{-1} and then multiply both sides by A^{-1}, yielding $A^{-1}Ax = A^{-1}b$ or $x = A^{-1}b$, which is the solution vector. This method suffers from the numerical instability caused by round-off when floating point numbers are used instead of integer numbers. There is another approach called LUP decomposition that is more stable and about 3 times faster. The advantage of computing an LUP decomposition for the matrix A is that linear systems can be solved more readily when they are triangular.

LUP Decomposition

The central idea of LUP decomposition is to find three $n \times n$ matrices as L, U and P such that $P \bullet A = L \bullet U$ with the following properties:

- L is a unit lower-triangular matrix
- U is an upper-triangular matrix
- P is a permutation matrix

The matrices L, U and P are called an LUP decomposition of the matrix A. Using an LUP decomposition for A, we can solve the equation $Ax = b$ by solving only triangular linear systems with the following steps:

- Multiply both sides of $Ax = b$ by P yielding the equivalent equation $PAx = Pb$
- Using LUP decomposition, we obtain $LUx = Pb$.

We can solve $LUx = Pb$ by solving two triangular linear systems when we define $y = Ux$ where x is the solution vector.

1. We solve the lower-triangular system $Ly = Pb$ by forward substitution, yielding y as the solution vector.
2. We solve the upper-triangular system $Ux = y$ by back substitution, yielding x as the solution vector.

The vector x is the solution vector to $Ax = b$, since the permutation matrix P is invertible:

$$Ax = P^{-1}LUx = P^{-1}Ly = P^{-1}Pb = b.$$

In the case that A is an $n \times n$ nonsingular matrix and P is absent we must find a factorization $A = LU$. We call the two matrices L and U an LU decomposition of A. The process of performing LU decomposition to solve the $Ax = b$ is called Gaussian elimination. Direct techniques such as Gaussian elimination reduce the system of linear equations to a triangular form and then use backsubstitution to solve the system.

Gaussian Elimination

Gaussian elimination is an algorithm used to solve a system of linear equations $Ax = b$, for the vector x. In general, the principle behind Gaussian elimination is to reduce the number of variables in a system of linear equations by performing elementary row operations on the augmented matrix Ab to reduce it to an echelon matrix (upper-triangular form matrix). This step is called the *forward-elimination* phase. The solution is then obtained by *backsubstitution* to diagonalize the matrix. At this point all the off-diagonal elements of the matrix have the value zero, and $x_i = b_i / A_{i,i}$. We start by subtracting multiples of the first equation from the other equations so that the first variable is removed from those equations. Then, we subtract multiples of the second equation from the third and subsequent equations so that now the first and second variables are removed from the equations. We continue this process until the upper-triangular is formed, which is the matrix U. The matrix L can be formed by row multipliers that cause variables to be eliminated.

Example: Consider the system of linear equations defined by

$$\begin{cases} x_1 + x_2 + x_3 = 4 \\ x_1 + 2x_2 + 2x_3 = 2 \\ -x_1 - 2x_2 - 2x_3 = 2 \end{cases} \Rightarrow \begin{bmatrix} 1 & 1 & 1 \\ 1 & 2 & 2 \\ -1 & -1 & 1 \end{bmatrix} \cdot \begin{bmatrix} x_1 \\ x_2 \\ x_3 \end{bmatrix} = \begin{bmatrix} 4 \\ 2 \\ 2 \end{bmatrix}$$

where

$$A = \begin{bmatrix} 1 & 1 & 1 \\ 1 & 2 & 2 \\ -1 & -1 & 1 \end{bmatrix}, b = \begin{bmatrix} 4 \\ 2 \\ 2 \end{bmatrix}, \text{ and we wish to solve for unknown } x = \begin{bmatrix} x_1 \\ x_2 \\ x_3 \end{bmatrix}.$$

$$\begin{bmatrix} 1 & 1 & 1 & 4 \\ 1 & 2 & 2 & 2 \\ -1 & -1 & 1 & 2 \end{bmatrix} \sim \begin{bmatrix} 1 & 1 & 1 & 4 \\ 0 & 1 & 1 & -2 \\ 0 & 0 & 1 & 3 \end{bmatrix} \Rightarrow \begin{cases} x_1 + x_2 + x_3 = 4 \\ x_2 + x_3 = -2 \\ x_3 = 3 \end{cases}$$

Backsubstitution

Backsubstitution solves $Ux = b$, where U is an upper-triangular matrix and x and b are vectors. Given the upper-triangular matrix U, we solve the n_{th} equation first and work backward to the first equation.

$$\begin{cases} x_1 & = 4 - x_2 - x_3 & \{\Rightarrow x_1 = 6 \\ x_2 & = -2 - x_3 & \{\Rightarrow x_2 = -5 \\ x_3 = 3\{\Rightarrow x_3 = 3 \end{cases}$$

The forward-elimination phase can be summarized as follows. First, we eliminate the first variable in all but the first equation by adding the appropriate multiple of the first equation to each of the others (elementary row operations), then we eliminate the second variable in all but the first two equations by adding the appropriate multiple of the second equation to each of the third through n_{th} equations, then we eliminate the third variable in all but the first three equations, etc. To eliminate the i_{th} variable in the j_{th} equation, we multiply the i_{th} equation by a_{ji} / a_{ii} and subtract it from the j_{th} equation. The row used to drive to zero all nonzero elements below the diagonal in column i is called the **pivot** row. In other words, the elements by which we divide during LU decomposition are called pivots, and they occupy the diagonal elements of the matrix U.

An important class of matrices for which LU decomposition always works correctly is the class of symmetric positive definite matrices. Such matrices require no pivoting, and the recursive method outlined above can be used without fear of dividing by 0. Forward substitution is similar to backsubstitution, and we solve the lower-triangular matrix L. A sequential algorithm to perform the Gaussian elimination method is shown below, followed by the implementation of the algorithm as a C program.

Procedure Gaussian-Elimination(A)
```
    begin    /* forward-elimination phase */
    for i = 1 to n do
        begin
        max = i
        for j = i + 1 to n do
            if (abs(a_{j,i}) >abs(a_{max,i})) then max = j
        for k = i to n + 1 do
        t = a_{i,k};   a_{i,k} = a_{max,k};   a_{max,k} = t
        for j = i + 1 to n do
            for k = n + 1 to i do
            a_{j,k} = a_{j,k} - a_{i,k} * a_{j,i} / a_{i,i}
        end
    end
    begin    /* back-substitution phase */
    for j = n to 1 do
        t = 0
        for k = j + 1 to n do
        t = t + a_{j,k} * x_k
        x_j = (a_{j,n+1} - t) / a_{j,j}
    end
End     Gaussian-Elimination
```

```
/* Sequential Gaussian Elimination algorithm included back substitution */
#define N       64
#define false   0
#define true    1
float   a[N][N + 1];
int     pivot[N], marked[N];
main (){
        int     Solution, i, j, seed;
        for     (i=0; i < N; i++)  {
                marked[i] = 0;      seed = I * i;
                a[i][N] = 0.0;
                for (j=0; j < N; j++)  {
                    a[i][j] = random(&seed);
                    a[i][N] = a[i][N] + j * a[i][j];
                }
        }        /* for */
        Solution = Gaussian_Elimination();
        if   (Solution ! = 0)   {
```

```
            Back_Substitution();
            for      (i=0; i < N; i++)
                printf("x[%d] = %10.5f\n", pivot[i], (a[i][N] / a[i][pivot[i]]) );
        }   /* then part of if */
        else
                printf("There is no solution");
        }   /*end main */
Gaussian_Elimination()    {
        int   i, j, k, picked;
        float tmp;
        for      (i = 0; i < N − 1; i++) {
            tmp = 0.0;
            for  (j=0; j < N; j++)  {
                if   (!marked[j] && (fabs(a[j][i]) > tmp) ) {
                    tmp = fabs(a[j][i]);
                    picked = j;
                }
            }
            marked[picked] = 1;   pivot[picked] = i;
            if       (fabs(a[picked][i] ) < 0.00000001)  {
                    return (false);
            }
            for  (j=0; j < N; j++)  {
                if   (!marked[j])  {
                    tmp = a[j][i] / a[picked][i];
        for  (k=i; k < N + 1; k++) a[j][k]=a[i][k]−a[picked][k]*tmp;
                }
            }
        }
    for  (i = 0; i < N; i++)
        if   (!marked[i])
            pivot[i] = N − 1;
    return(true);
    }   /* end Gaussian_Elimination */
Back_Substitution()   {
    float    coeff;
    int i, j;
    for  (i = N − 1; i ≥ 0; i−− ) {
        for  (j=0; pivot[j] != i; j++)
            coeff = a[j][N]/a[j][i];
            for  (j=0; j < N; j++)
                if   (pivot[j] < i)
                    a[j][N] = a[j][N] − coeff * a[j][i];
        }
    }   /* end Back_Substitution */
```

The running time of the backsubstitution phase is $O(n^2)$. Inspection of the forward-elimination phase identifies that, for each value of i, the k loop is iterated $(n - i + 2)$ times and the j loop $(n - i)$ times, thus the resulting inner loop is executed in $\displaystyle\sum_{i=1}^{n}(n - i + 2)(n - i)$. Therefore, the overall worst-case time complexity of the algorithm, including forward-elimination and back-substitution, is $O(n^3)$. In order to illustrate the parallel Gaussian elimination algorithm, we consider the following system of linear equations, which is the column-oriented version:

$$A = \begin{pmatrix} 1 & & & \\ -a_{21} & 1 & & \\ -a_{31} & -a_{32} & 1 & \\ -a_{41} & -a_{42} & -a_{43} & 1 \end{pmatrix} \quad x = \begin{pmatrix} x_1 \\ x_2 \\ x_3 \\ x_4 \end{pmatrix} \quad b = \begin{pmatrix} b_1 \\ b_2 \\ b_3 \\ b_4 \end{pmatrix}$$

where matrix A is reduced to a lower triangular form. The solution can be obtained as:

$$x_1 = b_1$$
$$x_2 = b_2 + a_{21} x_1$$
$$x_3 = b_3 + a_{31} x_1 + a_{32} x_2$$
$$x_4 = b_4 + a_{41} x_1 + a_{42} x_2 + a_{43} x_3$$

for which we can evaluate x_1, x_2, x_3, and x_4 in parallel. For a system with n linear equations, the algorithm requires n − 1 steps such that n − 1 processors are involved at the first step, and fewer processors thereafter.

Step 1: Evaluate in parallel all expressions of the form $b^{(1)}_i = b_i + a_{i1} x_1$ for $i = 2,\dots, n$, where $x_1 = b_1$ is known.

Step 2: Evaluate in parallel all expressions of the form $b^{(2)}_i = b^{(1)}_i + a_{i2} x_2$ for $i = 3,\dots, n$, where x_1 and x_2 are known.

...
...
...

Step k: Evaluate in parallel all expressions of the form $b^{(k)}_i = b^{(k-1)}_i + a_{ik} x_k$ for $i = k + 1,\dots, n$, where $(x_1, x_2, \dots , x_k)$ are known.

For a system with a relatively large number of processors, for example, of order n^3, we can express the solution as a product of elementary matrices that can easily be computed using the recursive techniques such as the recursive-doubling method [Modi 88].

On some parallel systems this approach does not seem promising, because the size of the system of equations under consideration is reduced at each stage, resulting in a considerable under utilization of processors. In general, there are three legitimate options as the fundamental unit of parallelism: the matrix element, the row and the column. If we associate a processor with every row, then the processors' interactions determine the identity of the pivot row. Once the pivot row is identified, then the algorithm must propagate the pivot row to the other rows, indicating that they may be reduced. In this approach, each processor is responsible for a single element of b, updating it along with its associated row. If we associate a processor with every column, then there is no need for processor interaction to determine the pivot row. The processor examines the entire column to find the element with the largest magnitude. Then it can compute the coefficient needed to reduce the rows and propagate the vector containing these coefficients. As we see, in this approach only a single processor is active when finding the pivot row, which indicates one of the disadvantages of the column-oriented approach.

For relatively small systems, the row-oriented version achieves higher performance on the Intel iPSC/2 and the Sequent Symmetry S81 parallel machines, whereas the column-oriented version achieves higher performance on the nCUBE 3200 parallel machine [Hatcher 91]. In general, the row-oriented version is the better alternative as the problem size increases.

Gauss-Jordan Elimination

The Gauss-Jordan elimination method is similar to Gaussian elimination, except that the coefficient matrix is diagonalized by further elementary row operations, specifically the elimination of nonzeroes above as well as below the diagonal. This method eliminates backsubstitution. In other words, Gauss-Jordan elimination reduces the system of linear equations directly into a diagonal form, thus eliminating the need for a backsubstitution phase, and this is its major advantage over Gaussian elimination. The weakness of this method is that it may sometimes prove numerically unstable, and some form of pivoting (such as column pivoting) should therefore be incorporated. In addition, the algorithm has the disadvantage of requiring 50% more floating point operations than Gaussian elimination. However, the algorithm has some interest in a parallel context, because it can be implemented with fewer processor interactions than Gaussian elimination followed by backsubstitution.

$$\textbf{Example:} \quad \begin{cases} x_1 + x_2 + x_3 = 4 \\ x_1 + 2x_2 + 2x_3 = 2 \\ -x_1 - x_2 + x_3 = 2 \end{cases}$$

$$
\begin{bmatrix} 1 & 1 & 1 & 4 \\ 1 & 2 & 2 & 2 \\ -1 & -1 & 1 & 2 \end{bmatrix} \sim \begin{bmatrix} 1 & 1 & 1 & 4 \\ 0 & 1 & 1 & -2 \\ 0 & 0 & 1 & 3 \end{bmatrix} \sim \begin{bmatrix} 1 & 0 & 0 & 6 \\ 0 & 1 & 0 & -5 \\ 0 & 0 & 1 & 3 \end{bmatrix} \Rightarrow \begin{bmatrix} x_1 = 6 \\ x_2 = -5 \\ x_3 = 3 \end{bmatrix}
$$

Figure 8.18 illustrates how Gaussian elimination and Gauss-Jordan elimination algorithms transform the matrix A for solving the system of linear equations Ax = b. The sequential Gauss-Jordan elimination algorithm is as follows:

Procedure Gauss-Jordan-Elimination(A)
    begin
    for k = 1 to n
            for j = k + 1 to n + 1
                $a_{kj} = a_{kj} / a_{kk}$
            for i = 1 to k − 1
                    for j = k + 1 to n + 1
                        $a_{ij} = a_{ij} − a_{ik} * a_{kj}$
            for i = k + 1 to n
                    for j = k + 1 to n + 1
                        $a_{ij} = a_{ij} − a_{ik} * a_{kj}$
    end
EndGauss-Jordan-Elimination

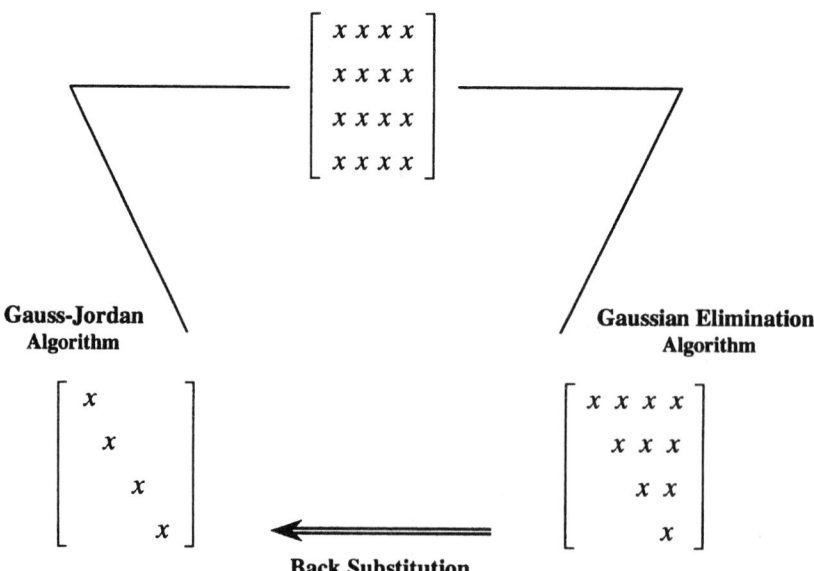

Figure 8.18. Solving the system of linear equations utilizing various algorithms.

In terms of parallel operations, Gaussian elimination takes $O(n)$ multiplication for the elimination phase and a further $O(n)$ multiplication for the back-substitution phase. The Gauss-Jordan method provides the solution in $O(n)$ time. Thus, the running cost of both methods utilizing n processors is $O(n^2)$. The following code represents the parallel version of the Gauss-Jordan elimination algorithm written in Dataparallel C adopted from [Hatcher 91], in which there are three variables associated with each processor as follows:

- The variable *rowptr*, which records the iteration in which the row serves as the pivot row.
- The variable *marked*, which is set to true once the row has been chosen as the pivot row.
- The array *coefficient*, which contains one row of A followed by a single element of b.

The program consists of two phases. In the first phase the processors perform a tournament to determine the pivot row. The flag is set to FALSE if the pivot element is too small; otherwise, it remains as TRUE. In the second phase, each processor reduces its row. In general, at the end of each iteration k, the only nonzero element in column k is the element in the pivot row. In the second phase each processor is active except the processor to which the pivot row is granted.

```
/* Parallel Gauss-Jordan Elimination algorithm written
       in Dataparallel C language */
#include     "math.h"
#define     N      64
#define     false   0
#define     true    1
#define     ID   (this − system)
domain row   {
int  rowptr;        char     marked; float     coefficient[N + 1];
                } system[N];
main ()
        {
        int  pivot_row, i, j, flag = true;
        float     pivot[N + 1], tmp;
        [domain system]. {
        int  seed;
        id = ID;
        marked = 0;
        seed = id * id;
        a[N] = 0.0;
        for  (i=0; i < N; i++)  {
```

```
                    a[i] = random(&seed);
                    a[N] = a[N] + i * a[i];
                    }   }
/* The following iterations reduce the matrix A to diagonal form */
for   (i=0; (i < N) && (flag != false); i++)    {
            [domain row]. {
                if   (!marked)    {
                    if (max_tournament(fabs(coefficient[i]),
                        id, &pivot_row) ) {
                    rowptr = i;
                    marked = 1;
                    }
                }
            pivot = system[pivot_row].coefficient;
                /* broadcast the pivot element */
            if   (fabs(pivot[i]) < 0.000001)      flag = false;
            if   ((flag != false) && (id != pivot_row) )   {
                tmp = coefficient[i] / pivot[i];
                for   (j = i; j ≤ N; j++)
                        coefficient[j] = coefficient[i] – pivot[j] * tmp;
            } }        }
/* The following part computes each element of x directly */
            if   (flag ! = false)          {
                for   (i = 0; i < N; i++) {
                pivot_row = system[i].rowptr;
                pivot = system[i].coefficient;
                printf("x[%d] = %10.5f\n", pivot_row, pivot[N]/pivot[pivot_row]);
                }   }
            else
            printf("There is no solution.");
}
```

8.5   Computing Determinants

If A is an $n \times n$ matrix, the **determinant** of A, denoted as $\det(A)$, can be defined as:

$$\det(A) = \begin{cases} a_{11} & \text{if } n = 1 \\ a_{11}\det(A_{11}) - a_{12}\det(A_{12}) + \ldots\ldots \\ + (-1)^{i+j}a_{ij}\det(A_{ij}) + \ldots\ldots\ldots \\ + (-1)^{n+1}a_{1n}\det(A_{1n}), & \text{if } n > 1 \end{cases}$$

where A_{ij} is the $(n - 1) \times (n - 1)$ matrix obtained from A by deleting row i and column j, when $n > 1$. The term $(-1)^{i+j} \det(A_{ij})$ is known as the cofactor of the element a_{ij}. In another notation, the determinant of matrix A can be defined as:

$$\det(A) = \sum_{\substack{i_1,\ldots,\,i_n \\ \text{all distinct}}} \wp(i_1,\ldots,i_n) A_{1,i_1} \ldots\ldots A_{n,i_n}$$

where $\wp(i_1,\ldots,i_n)$ is the parity of the permutation $\begin{pmatrix} 1 & \ldots\ldots & n \\ i_1 & \ldots\ldots & i_n \end{pmatrix}$.

Generally speaking, the determinant of an $n \times n$ matrix can be computed recursively from the determinants of n smaller $(n - 1) \times (n - 1)$ matrices obtained by deleting the first row and some column of the original matrix. Once the n sub-determinants are calculated, the determinants of the original matrix can be obtained very quickly. In other words, if A[i,j] denotes the $(n - 1) \times (n - 1)$ submatrix obtained from A by deleting the i_{th} row and the j_{th} column, then

$$\det(A) = \sum_{j=1}^{n} (-1)^{j+1} a_{1j} \det(A[1,j])$$

If $n = 1$ then the determinant is defined by $\det(A) = a_{11}$. The following properties are associated with the determinant of a square matrix A whose proofs are omitted here:

- If any row or any column of A is zero, then $\det(A) = 0$.
- The determinant of A is multiplied by λ if the entries of any one row or any one column of A are all multiplied by λ.
- The determinant of A is unchanged if the entries on one row or column are added to those in another row or column.
- The determinant of A equals the determinant of A^T.
- The determinant of A is multiplied by -1 if any two rows or columns are exchanged.

Determinants of matrices provide a clean and useful abstraction in linear algebra which can be used to solve a variety of problems, including:

- Testing whether matrix X is singular, meaning that the matrix does not have an inverse. A matrix X is singular if and only if $\det(X) = 0$. In other words, if $\det(A) \neq 0$, then A is said to be nonsingular, meaning that the inverse A^{-1} is guaranteed to exist. Conversely, if A^{-1} exists, then $\det(A) \neq 0$.
- Testing whether a set of d points lies on a plane in fewer than d dimensions. If so, the system of equations they define is singular, so $\det(X) = 0$.

- Testing whether a point lies to the left or right of a line or plane. This problem reduces to testing whether the sign of a determinant is positive or negative.
- Computing the area or volume of a triangle or tetrahedron. These quantities are a function of the magnitude of the determinant.

If A and B are n × n matrices, then some basic properties of determinants of matrices A and B are as follows:

- $\det(A \cdot B) = \det(A) \cdot \det(B)$
- The linear transformation represented by A is invertible if and only if $\det(A) \neq 0$.
- If A is a lower or upper-triangular matrix and D is a diagonal matrix, then $\det(D + A) = \det(D)$.

Several algorithms are available to evaluate determinants based on LU decomposition. They are discussed in Section 8.4. The determinant is simply the product of the diagonal elements of the LU decomposition of a matrix. Determinants also can be computed using matrix multiplication algorithms discussed in Section 8.3. The determinant can be calculated by the Gauss-Jordan elimination method, and even faster by other recursive algorithms of the divide-and-conquer family. For example, Brassard and Bratley [Brassard 96] used the Gauss-Jordan elimination method, which took a time proportional to n^3 for computing the determinant of an n × n matrix. They programmed an algorithm for an instance of a 10 × 10 matrix which consumed only one-hundredth of a second. It consumed about five and a half seconds for a 100 × 100 matrix. As a consequence, we can apply the parallel algorithms associated with these methods to construct the parallel algorithm for computing the determinant of a matrix. For example, parallel matrix multiplication, parallel Gauss-Jordan elimination and parallel divide-and-conquer methods can be used in developing the parallel algorithms to compute determinants.

8.6   Expression Evaluation

Consider arithmetic expressions consisting of operators such as +, −, *, and /, and operands denoted by numbers or letters. Such expressions are typically parenthesized to indicate precedence between operations. Expressions can be represented as expression trees, called parse trees. For example, consider the case in which an expression uses only binary operators. Such an expression corresponds to a binary tree, with operators in the internal vertices and operands in the external vertices, as shown in Figure 8.19, which depicts the parse tree for the expression

$$(((x + y) * z) - (w + ((a - (v + y)) / ((z + y) * x)))).$$

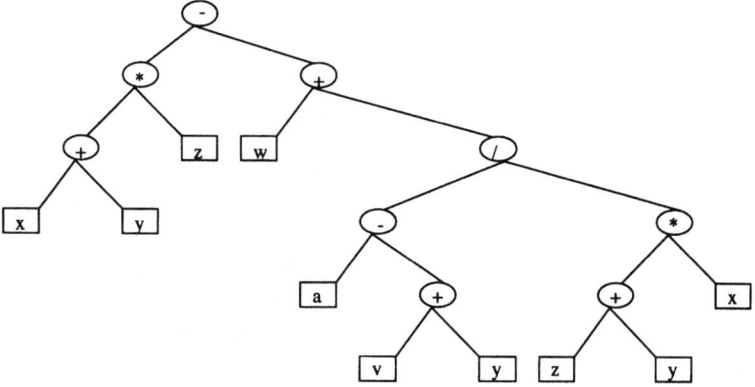

Figure 8.19. Tree representation of an arithmetic expression.

Given an expression tree, we can use a simple recursive procedure to compute the corresponding value of the expression, meaning that we recursively evaluate the two subtrees, then apply the operator to the computed values. Evaluation of an external vertex gives the current value of the associated variable. This is equivalent to a tree traversal, which is illustrated in the following procedure.

Procedure   Traversal(X:Linked-List)
      begin
          if $X \neq \phi$ then
             traverse (X.Left)
             traverse (X.Right)
          endif
      end
End   Traversal

The input to the algorithm is a string representing the arithmetic expression. To find the corresponding expression tree, we need to make fully bracketed expressions in which each subexpression is enclosed in the brackets. We can disregard all elements other than brackets to construct the expression tree of the fully bracketed expression. The expression is simple if each of the variables is used as an operand only once. E is a simple expression if it satisfies one of the following properties:

$E = x_i$, where x_i is a variable.
$E = \circ$ G, where G is a simple expression and $\circ \in \{+, -\}$.
$E = G \circ H$, where G and H are simple expressions involving sets of variables and $\circ \in \{+, -, *, /\}$.

For example, $(x_1 + x_2 + x_3) * x_4$ is a simple expression, but x^3 is not. Expression evaluation is of importance in its own right, but it is also indicative of the importance of trees in the process of translating computer programs from higher level languages to machine languages.

The evaluation of the arithmetic expressions in parallel and the concurrency in data flow architectures are closely related. In the arithmetic expressions, parallelism may be specified using a tree structure, and in data flow architectures concurrency may be expressed using a data-dependency graph. On a parallel computer, the evaluation of an arithmetic expression E is based on the selection of an equivalent expression E' for which several operations can be carried out simultaneously. Two expressions are equivalent if they take the same value for every assignment of values to the variables. For example, the following two expressions are equivalent with regard to the result value of the evaluations.

$$E = (x_1 x_2 + x_3)x_4 + x_5 \qquad\qquad E' = x_1 x_2 x_4 + x_3 x_4 + x_5$$

The order of evaluation of $E = (x_1 x_2 + x_3)x_4 + x_5$ on a serial computer may be indicated by

$$E = ((((x_1 \bullet x_2) + x_3) \bullet x_4) + x_5)$$

to address the precedence relation among the operators at the evaluation.

The equivalent expression $E' = x_1 x_2 x_4 + x_3 x_4 + x_5$, which is suitable for parallel computation, can be evaluated as

$$E' = (((x_1 \bullet x_2) \bullet x_4) + ((x_3 \bullet x_4) + x_5))$$

The rule of this evaluation is that we compute all the inner brackets at step 1, followed by all the next brackets at step 2, etc. In serial computation, the operations are executed sequentially. In parallel execution, the operations are carried out in the following steps:

Step 1: The products $x_1 x_2$ and $x_3 x_4$ are computed simultaneously.
Step 2: The product $x_1 x_2 \bullet x_4$ and the sum $x_3 x_4 + x_5$ are computed simultaneously.
Step 3: The sum is computed to produce E'.

The serial and parallel evaluations are illustrated in Figure 8.20. In order to compare the serial and parallel evaluations we can use three criteria: number of parallel or serial steps, number of processors used and total number of operations performed by the algorithm. The comparison of serial and parallel evaluations of the expression is depicted in Table 8.1. In this parallel execution, we are assuming that different operations can be carried out simultaneously. Thus, we have adopted an MIMD type of parallel computer. Using an SIMD computer, on which the additions and multiplications cannot be performed in parallel, four steps would be needed for the same evaluation. To be more precise, the type of parallel computers may influence the result of the expression evaluation. For example, the expression $E = (((x_1 \cdot x_2) + x_3) x_4 + x_5) \cdot x_6 + x_7$ has two equivalent expressions:

$E_1 = ((((x_1 \cdot x_2) (x_4 \cdot x_6)) + (x_3 (x_4 \cdot x_6))) + ((x_5 \cdot x_6) + x_7))$, and
$E_2 = ((((x_1 \cdot x_2) + x_3) \cdot (x_4 \cdot x_6)) + ((x_5 \cdot x_6) + x_7))$

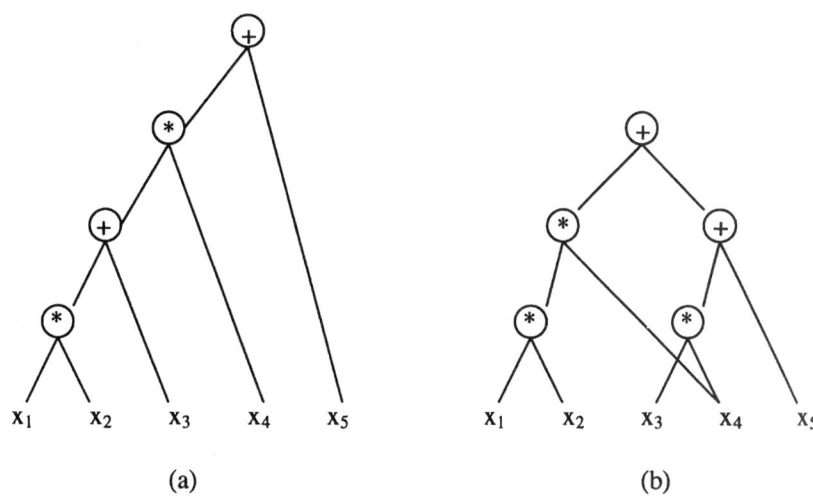

(a)   (b)

Figure 8.20. Expression evaluation trees. (a) Serial evaluation. (b) Parallel evaluation.

Table 8.1. Comparison of serial and parallel evaluations.

	Serial evaluation	Parallel evaluation
Number of steps	4	3
Number of processors	1	2
Total number of operations	4	5

Table 8.2 shows the required number of steps for the evaluation of the equivalent expressions on SIMD and MIMD computers.

Table 8.2. Comparison of SIMD and MIMD expression evaluations.

Expression	Number of Steps SIMD	Number of Steps MIMD
E_1	5	4
E_2	4	4

For further reading see Winograd [Winograd 75], Brent [Brent 74], Muller [Muller 76] and Kosaraju [Kosaraju 86]. A corollary follows from the examples that the obvious way to evaluate an expression tree in parallel is to assign one processor to each internal vertex and utilize an algorithm with the following outline:

repeat
    for each internal vertex x in parallel do
        if the value of the children of x are known then
            compute the value of x
            remove x's children from the tree
        endif
    endfor
until only root is left

where the number of iterations is equal to the height of the expression tree. The algorithm described takes time $O(\log n)$ using n processors, resulting in an overall running cost of $O(n \log n)$. If we reduce the number of processors required to $O(n/\log n)$ without increasing the time required, which is $O(\log n)$, the results are an improved algorithm that works in $O(n)$ running cost. To summarize the expression evaluation, we describe the results obtained by Brent, Winograd, Muller and Kosaraju for evaluating arithmetic expressions. The complexity of a simple expression of size n is summarized in Table 8.3.

Table 8.3. The complexity of expression evaluation obtained by [Kosaraju 86], [Muller 76], [Brent 74] and [Winograd 75], where T_{opt} is the lower bound complexity obtained for the expression evaluation.

complexity of simple expression with no divisions		
$T_{opt} \leq 2 \log_2(n) + O(1)$	with $O(n^{1.82})$ processors	[Kosaraju 86]
$T_{opt} \leq 2.08 \log_2(n) + O(1)$	with $O(n^{1.82})$ processors	[Muller 76]
$T_{opt} \leq \lfloor 4 \log_2(n-1) \rfloor$	with $(n-1)$ processors and $2(n-1)$ operations	[Brent 74]
$T_{opt} \leq O \log^2_2(n)$	with $\dfrac{3(n-1)}{2}$ operations	[Winograd 75]

complexity of simple expression with divisions		
$T_{opt} \leq 2.88 \log_2(n) + O(1)$	with $O(n^{1.44})$ processors	[Muller 76]
$T_{opt} \leq \lfloor 4 \log_2(n-1) \rfloor$	with $3(n-1)$ processors and $10(n-1)$ operations	[Brent 74]
$T_{opt} \leq O \log^2_2(n)$	with $\dfrac{5(n-1)}{2}$ operations	[Winograd 75]

8.7   Sorting

Sorting is the process of ordering a set of values into ascending (lowest to highest) or descending (highest to lowest) order. Sorting is used in compilers, editors, memory management and process management and is one of the most important operations performed in computers. The design of parallel sorting algorithms is highly dependent on the particular parallel architecture under consideration. There are several sequential sorting algorithms, such as ShellSort, MergeSort, QuickSort, TreeSort, HeapSort and BingoSort, which are comparision-based sorting algorithms.

In general, the algorithms for sorting are classified as:

- Internal Sorting
- External Sorting

All the previous sorting algorithms assume that the list of elements to be sorted is resident in memory, meaning they are internal sorting. In contrast to internal sorting, external sorting algorithms assume that since we can fit only a fixed number of elements into internal memory, the list of elements is originally assumed to reside in external memory, such as on a disk or magnetic tape. There are two approaches to sorting:

1. **Sorting by Merging.** In this method, the sequence to be sorted is divided into two subsequences of equal length. Each of the two subsequences is now sorted recursively. Finally, the two sorted subsequences are merged into one sorted sequence, thus providing the answer to the original problem.

2. **Sorting by Splitting.** In this method, the sequence to be sorted is divided into two subsequences of equal length such that each element of the first subsequence is smaller than or equal to each element of the second subsequence. This splitting operation is then applied to each of the two subsequences recursively. When the recursion terminates, the sequence is sorted.

There are several models of parallel computation for sorting algorithms. Some of the algorithms designed for parallel sorting are based on a network model of computation, in which a network of processors performs the sorting operations in parallel, comparing two elements and swapping them if necessary. We assume that the elements to be sorted are integer numbers and are resident in an array, and for simplicity we take the number of elements to be a power of 2. As is usual, we suppose that each element of the array to be sorted has a key which governs the sorting process. If the keys of the items to be sorted are in a vector Key[1...n], the operation of compare-and-exchange can be defined as follows:

Compare-and-Exchange(i,j)
   If Key[i] > Key[j]
      then Key[i] ⇐ Key[j]
         Key[j] ⇐ Key[i]

This indicates that two compare-and-exchange operations can be performed simultaneously if and only if they operate on disjoint entries of the vector Key. We describe odd-even and bitonic strategies discovered by Batcher [Batcher 68]. Both are based on parallel merge sort and have the same underlying computational structure of a binary tree. A binary tree sorting a list of elements of size n using n processors can be constructed as follows:

- The leaves of the tree are the elements that are to be sorted.
- The internal vertices of the tree are the compare-and-exchange operations of merging the two children of the vertex.

In other words, the leaves correspond to the Keys and the operation at non-leaf nodes is a merge of two sorted sequences. The result of each internal node is a sorted sequence of those Keys which are sorted at leaf descendants of the node. Thus, the final merge at the root of the tree provides the desired sorted sequence of all the inputs to the algorithm.

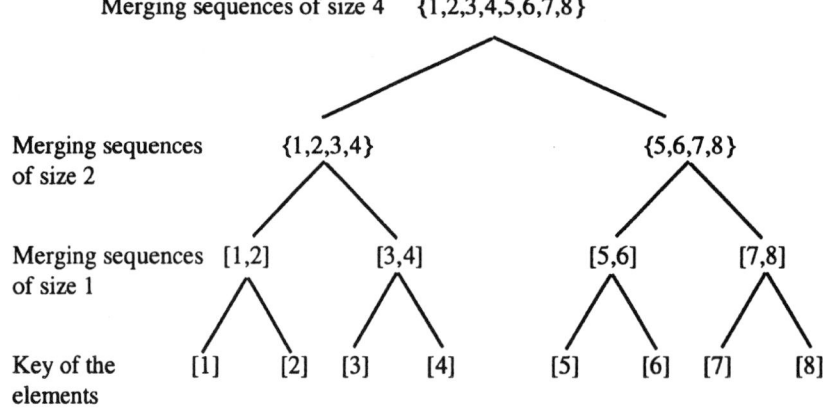

Figure 8.21. Merging operation of set of 8 elements. Root of tree provides sorted elements.

Figure 8.21 illustrates the merging operation when the number of elements to be sorted is 8. This structure provides that the merging on one level can be performed in parallel.

Odd-Even Network Sorting

The odd-even network sorting algorithm, also called the odd-even-merge-sorting algorithm, is based on the following properties. Given a set of elements $A = \{a_1, a_2, a_3, \ldots, a_n\}$, A_{odd} and A_{even} are defined as the set of elements of A with odd and even indices, respectively. For example, $A_{odd} = \{a_1, a_3, a_5, \ldots\}$ and $A_{even} = \{a_2, a_4, a_6, \ldots\}$ regarding a set of elements $A = \{a_1, a_2, a_3, \ldots, a_n\}$. Similarly, let a set of elements $B = \{b_1, b_2, b_3, \ldots, b_n\}$. We can then define the merge operation as:

$$Merge(A,B) = \{a_1, b_1, a_2, b_2, a_3, b_3, \ldots, a_n, b_n\}$$

For example, if $A = \{1,2,3,4\}$ and $B = \{5,6,7,8\}$ then

$$Merge(\{1,2,3,4\}, \{5,6,7,8\}) = \{1,5,2,6,3,7,4,8\}$$

Another operation we need is odd-even and is based on the parallel execution of compute-and-exchange(i, i + 1) for each even value of i, where $1 \le i \le n$. For example, Odd-Even$\{1,6,2,4,3,10\} = \{1,2,6,3,4,10\}$. The last operation is to join two sets of elements A and B and consists of the execution of two operations:

$$Join(A,B) = \{Merge(A,B), Odd\text{-}Even(A,B)\}$$

The odd-even network sorting algorithm can be illustrated by the following pseudocode.

Algorithm: Odd-Even(A,B,S)
```
    begin
    if A and B are of length 1
        then
Merge A and B using one Compare-and-Exchange operation
        else
        begin
        compute S_odd and S_even In Parallel do
        S_odd = Merge(A_odd,B_odd)
        S_even = Merge(A_even,B_even)
        S_odd-even = Join(S_odd,S_even)
        end
    endif
    end
```

Example: Suppose the set of elements $S = \{2,3,6,10,15,4,5,8\}$ and we start with $A = \{2,6,10,15\}$ and $B = \{3,4,5,8\}$, two sorted sets of elements. Then,

$$A_{odd} = \{2,10\} \qquad\qquad A_{even} = \{6,15\}$$
$$B_{odd} = \{3,5\} \qquad\qquad B_{even} = \{4,8\}$$

Now we see that

$$\text{Merge}(A_{odd}, B_{odd}) = \{2,3,5,10\}$$
$$\text{Merge}(A_{even}, B_{even}) = \{4,6,8,15\}$$

The join operation:

$$\text{Join}(A,B) = \{\text{Merge}(A,B), \text{Odd-Even}(A,B)\}$$

requires a merge operation, which results in $\text{Merge}(A,B) = \{2,4,3,6,5,8,10,15\}$, and an odd-even operation, which obtains the final sorted list of elements,

$$\text{Odd-Even}\{2,4,3,6,5,8,10,15\} = \{2,3,4,5,6,8,10,15\}$$

In this algorithm the recursive Merge operation has logarithmic depth. Using n processors the operations Merge and Join can be performed in one parallel step. Therefore, Merge of two sorted sequences of elements takes $O(\log n)$ time using n processors. Since the sequential time complexity of the best sorting algorithm for n elements is $O(n \log n)$, this formulation of odd–even sorting is cost-optimal, because its running cost is $O(n \log n)$ utilizing n processors.

Definition: A comparator is a circuit with two inputs and two outputs such that the inputs are on the left and the outputs on the right as shown in Figure 8.22. If the inputs are Input_1 and Input_2 and the outputs are Output_1 and Output_2, then the following properties are present:

- $\text{Output}_1 = \text{Min}(\text{Input}_1, \text{Input}_2)$, meaning the smaller input moves to the upper output
- $\text{Output}_2 = \text{Max}(\text{Input}_1, \text{Input}_2)$, meaning the larger input moves to the lower output

To be more precise, the inputs are exchanged when $\text{Input}_1 \leq \text{Input}_2$. Thus, a single comparator is able to sort two inputs, and the standard notation for a comparator when it is used in a network is the more compact diagram shown in Figure 8.23. The central idea is to assume that any number of comparators whose inputs and outputs are disjoint from each other can operate in parallel. A sorting network is a directed graph with the following properties:

- The interior vertices of the graph are comparators.
- The interior vertices provide the input for the graph.
- The exterior vertices of the graph are called the outputs.
- The data at the output vertices are the result of sorting the data that were at the input, or interior, vertices.

A corollary follows immediately from this definition that a merging network is defined as a sorting network with the property that if we subdivide the inputs into two subsets of equal sizes and insert sorted elements into each of these subsets, the output is the sorted result of merging the input sequences together. For example, Figure 8.24 illustrates a sorting network that sorts all possible sequences of three numbers utilizing three comparators. The rationale behind odd-even network sorting is that for any positive integer n, a merging network is a network built of comparators with two groups of n inputs and a single group of 2n outputs. Provided that two groups of inputs are already sorted and each input appears on one of the outputs, in which the outputs are also being sorted.

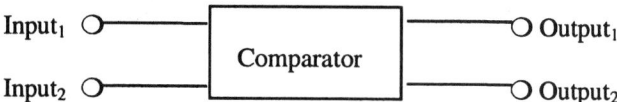

Figure 8.22. A comparator.

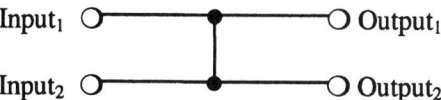

Figure 8.23. A comparator represented in a network sorting.

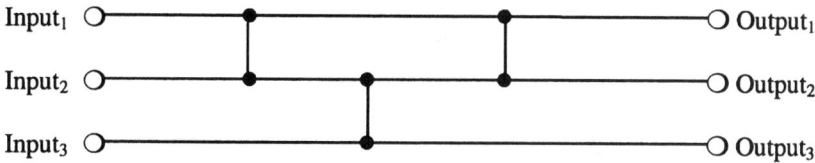

Figure 8.24. A sorting network on three inputs and utilizing three comparators.

Recalling the psuedocode of the algorithm, the following procedure utilizes *n* processors where half of them are used to execute the statement call OddEvenMerge(Odd[1:*n* / 2]) and the other half are used to execute the statement call OddEvenMerge(Even[1:*n* / 2]).

Procedure   OddEvenMerge(L[1:n])
    Model: PRAM computational model with n processors
    Input: L[1:n] of size n = 2^k where two sublists
              as [1:n/2] and L[n/2+1:n] are already sorted.
    Output: L[1:n] sorted list of elements.
    if   n = 2   then
        if   L[1] > L[2]   then   Interchange(L[1], L[2])
    endif

```
else     {separate list elements of odd and even indices}
     OddEvenSplit(L[1:n], Odd[1: n / 2], Even [1: n / 2])
     {recursively sort the elements of odd and even lists}
     OddEvenMerge(Odd[1: n / 2])
     OddEvenMerge(Even[1: n / 2])
     {interleave computation to identify a 2-subset of L[1:n]}
     for  1 ≤ i ≤ n / 2  do in parallel
             L[2i −1]  = odd[i]
             L[2i ]    = even[i]
     end in parallel
{perform Compare and Exchange to achieve a sorted list of elements}
     for  1 ≤ i ≤ (n / 2) −1  do in parallel
         if   L[2i] > L[2i + 1]  then
             Interchange(L[2i], L[2i + 1])
         endif
     end in parallel
endif
```
End OddEvenMerge

For instance, Figure 8.25 shows a merging network, illustrating how the inputs are transmitted to the sorted outputs.

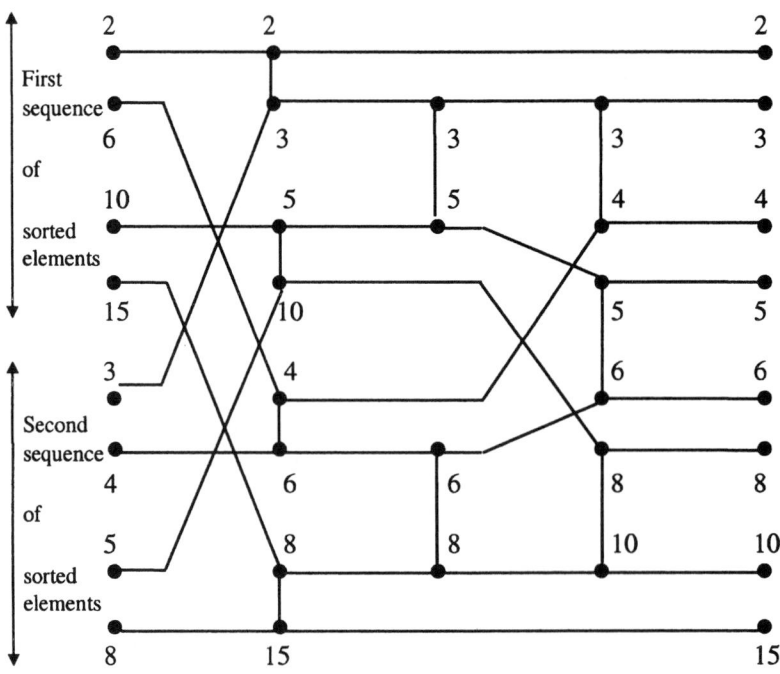

Figure 8.25. An odd-even merging network. Two sets of 4 sorted elements as input, and one set of 8 sorted elements as output.

Bitonic Network Sorting

Bitonic network sorting is based on performing compare-and-exchange operations on bitonic sequences. A sequence of numbers is called bitonic when it has the following properties:

- It starts increasing monotonically up to some point and then becomes monotonically decreasing, or
- It starts decreasing monotonically up to some point and then becomes monotonically increasing, or
- There exists a cyclic shift of indices so that either condition 1 or condition 2 holds.

The bitonic sorting network for sorting n elements contains (log n) stages. Each stage i consists of i columns of n/2 comparators, where each column performs compare-and-exchange operations on n wires.

For example, the sequence A = {2,6,10,15,8,5,4,3} is bitonic, and the sequence B = {3,2,1,4,6,8,7,5} is also bitonic since it is a cyclic shift of B' = {1,4,6,8,7,5,3,2}. Suppose S = {$a_1,a_2,...,a_n,b_1,b_2,...,b_n$}, where n = 2^k. The pseudocode of the bitonic sorting algorithm is as follows.

Algorithm: Bitonic-Network-Sorting(S)
　　Procedure Join(S)
　　　　　　Partition S into two monotonic sequences, S_1 and S_2
　　　　　　S1 consisting of the first n / 2 elements of S, and
　　　　　　S2 consisting of the second n / 2 elements of S.
　　　　　　S = Merge{S_1,S_2},
　　　　　　meaning that S is formed as S = {$a_1,b_1,a_2,b_2,...,a_n,b_n$}
　　　for all odd i, 1 ≤ i ≤ n, in parallel do
　　　　　Comparison-and-Exchange(i, i + 1)
　　　endfor
　　　End Join

　　　for j = 1 to k performing the loop logn times Join(S)
　　　{after the first execution the input to Join is the sequence output from}
　　　{the previous execution step}
　　　endfor
End Bitonic-Network-Sorting

Example: Suppose the set of elements S = {2,6,10,15,8,5,4,3} and S must be sorted in ascending order. S_1 = {2,6,10,15} and S_2 = {8,5,4,3} are two monotonic sequences of S in which the first is in increasing order and the second is in decreasing order. Given S = Merge{S_1,S_2} = {2,8,6,5,10,4,15,3} constructed in this way, the bitonic sorting algorithm is as follows. After the first bitonic halving operation we obtain

$$S = \{2,8,5,6,4,10,3,15\}$$

which is based on the compare-and-exchange operation of indices i and i + 1, where i is odd. In turn, the second bitonic halving operation yields

$$S = \{2,4,8,10,3,5,6,15\}$$

Consequently, the third and final bitonic halving operation provides

$$S = \{2,3,4,5,6,8,10,15\}$$

which is the sequence of sorted elements in ascending order. The operations Join, Merge, and Comparison-and-Exchange can be performed in one parallel step utilizing n processors. The time of the second loop dominates the running time of the algorithm, this indicates that the bitonic sorting takes O(log n) time using n processors. Therefore, the cost of the algorithm using n processors is O(n log n).

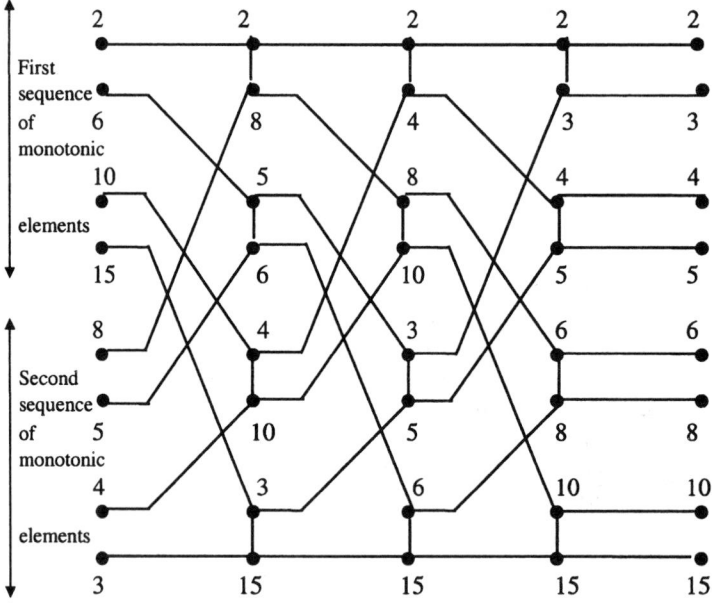

Figure 8.26. bitonic network sorting. Two monotonic set of elements as input, and one set of sorted elements as output.

Figure 8.26 illustrates bitonic sorting such that the first stage of comparators provides two bitonic sequences of four elements each. In the second stage, these two bitonic sequences are combined into one bitonic sequence, and in the third stage a single monotonic sequence is formed which is the sorted sequence of elements. The rationale behind this process is that a bitonic sequence of n elements can be split by comparison exchanges into two bitonic sequences half its length, such that the first sequence contains the n / 2 lower elements of the original sequence and the second sequence contains the n / 2 higher elements. Then it becomes possible to form a monotonic sequence of n elements by merging two such bitonic sequences.

Summary

Dramatic growth in the research and development of parallel computers has occurred during the last decade. Consequently, many standard algorithms have become inconvenient for the new technology, and new concepts and designs must be developed. In this chapter some of the important basic computational algorithms are discussed, including transitive closure, matrix multiplication, computing determinants, sorting, expression evaluation, system of linear equations and prefix computation. The parallel algorithms are presented in terms of one parallel model of computation called CREW PRAM (parallel random access machine), which consists of P processors sharing a common memory and allows several processors to read the same memory location simultaneously, but does not permit simultaneous writing to the same memory location.

We discussed prefix computation as a binary operation that might be applied to pairs of elements or a set of elements. We outlined the sequential and parallel prefix sums along with examples to illustrate the computation. We claimed that the problem of computing prefix sums in parallel could be solved on any binary tree in which the leaves correspond to the elements of the set. Utilizing the created tree, the algorithm consists of three steps: each internal vertex computes the sum of the entries in the leaves spanned by the vertex, each internal vertex passes the value computed to its right child, and the results are passed downward to the leaves. We illustrated parallel prefix computation on a hypercube with n processors in which x_i resided on the processor labeled p_i.

We can outline transitive closure as the process of determining the set of vertices that can be reached from a given vertex by traversing the edges of the graph in the indicated direction to determine whether or not there is a connected path between any two vertices. We can use the connectivity matrix to construct this set of vertices. We outlined several methods to compute the connectivity matrix, such as Floyd's algorithm, identity matrix, edge insertion, Warshall's algorithm, all-pairs shortest path, and Boolean matrix multiplication. We discussed the all-pairs shortest-paths method to construct the transitive closure based on the adjacency matrix of the graph utilizing two-dimensional mesh SIMD. In this model of computation, the k_{th} element of each row of the adjacency matrix was stored in the k_{th} processor of the corresponding row of processors. Indeed, the algorithm was based on the approach used for computing the connected components of the graph. We illustrated the parallel algorithm with an example.

Matrix multiplication provides many different opportunities for parallelizing on parallel architectures. We classified the matrices into two categories, dense and sparse, in which parallel matrix computation can be performed in two different forms, block partitioning and checkerboard partitioning. We outlined these two partitioning methods for matrix multiplication along with examples. We discussed matrix-vector multiplication based on block partitioning with two different approaches: one row per processor and one element per processor. We outlined the algorithm along with examples. Next, we discussed matrix-matrix multiplication. We outlined sequential and parallel algorithms, in which the parallel algorithm used two-dimensional mesh SIMD and three-dimensional mesh SIMD of processors. The two-dimensional mesh SIMD algorithm utilized n^2 processors, in which C_{ij} was the product of row i of matrix A and column j of matrix B. The three-dimensional mesh SIMD model of computation is ideally suited for matrix-matrix multiplication. We used a hypercube with n^3 processors and assumed the processors were arranged in an $n \times n \times n$ array such that for each 3-tuple (i,j,k) there was an associated processor p_x, where $x = in^2 + jn + k$. The model indicated that all processors were positioned on one or two of the coordinates (i,j,k) to form a hypercube of processors. We illustrated the problem with an example, in which the algorithm performed n^3 multiplication to compute n^2 elements of the product simultaneously and followed four steps:

1. The matrices were distributed over the processors such that A_{ij} and B_{ij} were stored in p_x, where $x = ni + j$.
2. A_{ij} and B_{ij} propagated to the rest of the processors.
3. The product $C_{ijk} = A_{ijk} * B_{ijk}$ was computed by processor p_{ijk}.
4. The sum $C_{0jk} = C_{ijk}$ was computed, where $0 \le i,j,k \le n - 1$.

In this chapter we surveyed several sequential algorithms used to solve systems of linear equations, and we outlined how to implement parallel versions of these algorithms. We examined the well-known Gaussian elimination method for solving arbitrary linear systems, including the backsubstitution phase. Then we discussed the Gauss-Jordan elimination method for solving linear systems, which discards the backsubstitution phase. We outlined the two phases of Gaussian elimination: forward elimination and backsubstitution. In the forward elimination phase, the augmented matrix Ab might be reduced to an echelon matrix. Then, the solution might be obtained by backsubstitution when the Ab is diagonalized. We outlined the sequential algorithm along with its implementation written in a C program. We discussed the parallel version that used n − 1 steps such that n − 1 processors were involved. We claimed that for small systems, the row-oriented version achieves higher performance on the Intel iPSC and the Sequent Symmetry S81, whereas the column-oriented version achieves higher performance on the nCUBE parallel systems. The Gauss-Jordan elimination eliminates for back substitution phase. We outlined the parallel algorithm along with its implementation written in Dataparallel C adopted from Hatcher.

We discussed the computing determinant of a matrix as a recursive procedure, in which the determinant of an $n \times n$ matrix can be computed recursively from the determinant of n smaller $(n - 1) \times (n - 1)$ matrices obtained by deleting the first row and some column of the original matrix. Expressions can be represented as expression trees called parse trees. Given an expression tree we can use a recursive procedure to compute the corresponding value of the expression. We outlined the sequential and parallel algorithms along with examples to illustrate expression evaluation. We compared serial and parallel evaluations with regard to the important criteria that are involved, such as number of steps, number of processors and total number of operations. We summarized the complexity of expressions with no divisions and divisions adopted from Kosaraju, Muller, Brent and Winogard with regard to the number of processors used. Sorting is an important utility in computational algorithms on both serial and parallel computers. We classified the sorting algorithms as internal and external, and discussed two sorting aspects, merging and splitting. We discussed two sorting algorithms, odd-even network sorting and bitonic network sorting. The odd-even sorting was based on the two set of elements A_{odd}, with odd elements, and A_{even}, with even elements. We performed two operations, merge and join, to construct the sorted set of elements. We outlined the parallel algorithm utilizing the comparator to represent the sorting network, in which the output of the network corresponded to the sorted elements.

Further, we looked at Batcher's bitonic merge algorithm, which was the basis for the sorting algorithms used in processor arrays organized as shuffle-exchange networks and hypercubes. Bitonic network sorting is based on performing compare-and-exchange operation on bitonic sequences. A sequence of numbers is called bitonic when it starts increasing monotonically up to some point and then becomes monotonically decreasing, or it starts decreasing monotonically up to some point and then becomes monotonically increasing. We outlined the algorithm along with an example for illustration. Books and papers that devote attention to computational algorithms include [Akl 93, Freeman 92, Roberts 76, Strassen 69]. Biswas [Biswas 87] has discussed the important issues of the Gauss-Jordan elimination method.

Exercises

1. Consider the standard nested loop for a matrix multiplication problem. Specify two orders in which the loops must be nested for efficient execution on an SIMD vector processor. On an MIMD shared-memory system.

2. Strassen suggested an algorithm for computing the product of two square matrices A and B with the following operations. If

$$A = \begin{pmatrix} A_{11} & A_{12} \\ A_{21} & A_{22} \end{pmatrix} \qquad B = \begin{pmatrix} B_{11} & B_{12} \\ B_{21} & B_{22} \end{pmatrix} \qquad C = \begin{pmatrix} C_{11} & C_{12} \\ C_{21} & C_{22} \end{pmatrix}$$

$Q1 = (A11 + A22)(B11 + B22)$

$Q2 = (A21 + A22)(B11)$

$Q3 = (A 11)(B12 - B22)$

$Q4 = (A22)(-B11 + B21)$

$Q5 = (A11 + A12)(B22)$

$Q6 = (-A11 + A21)(B11 + B12)$

$Q7 = (A12 - A22)(B21 + B22)$

Then

$C11 = Q1 + Q4 - Q5 + Q7$

$C21 = Q2 + Q4$

$C12 = Q3 + Q5$

$C22 = Q1 + Q3 - Q2 + Q6$

(a) Give the parallel execution time and the number of processors used.

(b) Compare the algorithm with one of the examples in Section 8.3.

3. Consider the problem of sorting very large arrays of numbers. Select a sorting algorithm and parallelize it as far as possible.

4. Program a 3×3 matrix multiplication on a one-dimensional linear array of processing elements using nine processing elements.

5. Write an algorithm for a processor array to evaluate the determinant of a matrix using the following formula:

$Det(A) = a_{11} a_{22} - a_{12} a_{21}$ for a 2×2 matrix.

$Det(A) = a_{11} a_{22} a_{33} + a_{12} a_{23} a_{31} + a_{13} a_{21} a_{32}$
$- a_{11} a_{23} a_{32} - a_{12} a_{21} a_{33} - a_{13} a_{22} a_{31}$ for a 3×3 matrix.

6. Forward substitution is an analog to the backsubstitution algorithm. It is used to solve lower triangular systems. Write a sequential forward substitution algorithm in pseudocode.

7. Describe a way to reduce the communication overhead of the row-broadcast step of the parallel Gaussian elimination algorithm by overlapping some of the communication and computation.

8. Quicksort is a recursive algorithm that repeatedly divides an unsorted sublist of elements into three smaller sublists with regard to a median value. One of the sublists contains values less than the median value, one of them contains values equal to the median, and the other sublist contains values greater than the median. The median value is located between the other two sublists. Quicksort is an example of an algorithm that uses the divide-and-

conquer approach. Devise a parallel quicksort algorithm for a UMA multi-processor system.

9. Use the odd-even sorting method to sort the following sequences.

    (a) 5, 8, 3, 2, 4, 6, 4, 1
    (b) 1, 3, 5, 7, 2, 4, 6, 8

10. Show how the following sequence of elements would be sorted by bitonic sorting approach: {7, 9, 10, 2, 3, 6, 16, 1, 14, 5, 15, 8, 4, 11, 13, 12}.

11. Design a parallel algorithm to obtain the inverse of an $N \times N$ matrix.

12. Develop a parallel algorithm to obtain the transpose of an $N \times N$ matrix on a two-dimensional mesh connected computer with N^2 processors.

13. Design an algorithm for sorting a sequence of numbers, sorted one per processor, on a De Bruijn interconnection network.

14. What is the difference between the Gaussian elimination and the Gauss-Jordan elimination methods.

15. Develop a tree of recursive parallel calls for Bitonic Sort for the initial input list T={2, 5, 7, 8, 6, 4, 3, 1}.

16. Develop a tree of recursive parallel calls to Sort and Merge a list of elements as T={1, 2, 3, 4, 5, 6, 7, 8}.

17. In a Sorting Network for sorting a list of size N elements, we assume that the list is input and output through N input and output wires, respectively. All other wires in the network connect Comparators together. Adopt a parallel sorting network for sorting a list of size 4.

18. Recalling the Odd-Even-Merge Sort algorithm presented in this chapter, show the high-level action of the algorithm for a sample list $L[1:N]$ of size 16 as

    {16, 22, 35, 40, 53, 66, 70, 85, 15, 18, 23, 55, 60, 69, 72, 78}.

Reference-Needed Exercises

19. Develop an efficient CREW PRAM sorting algorithm to sort an arbitrary list of N elements using P processors, where $P \geq N$ [Shiloach 81].

20. Prove that multiplication of two $N \times N$ matrices on the 2-D mesh SIMD model requires $O(N)$ data routing steps [Gentleman 78].

21. Gentleman's theorem assumes that every element of the A and B matrices is stored exactly once in the parallel computer and that no processing element

contains more than one element of either matrix. Are these assumptions realistic? Explain.

22. Prove that multiplication of two N×N matrices on a hypercube SIMD model with $N^3 = 2^{3Q}$ processors can be calculated in O(logN) time [Dekel 81].

23. Prove that the time complexity of sorting N elements on a one-dimensional mesh SIMD system with N processors using the odd-even sorting method is O(N [Habermann 72].

CHAPTER 9
Data Flow and Functional Programming

In the conventional (or imperative) programming languages the order of execution is determined by the program text and is referred to as the control flow of the program. In addition, it is possible to use the same variable name in different parts of a program and as a consequence of this the variable can be changed several times. In a sense, it is very difficult to detect any dependency that was involved between computations. This problem can be more complex if there is any transfer of flow control such as the *goto* statement in the computations.

In contrast, a data flow computation can be defined as one in which operations are executed in an order determined by the data interdependencies and the availability of resources. In general, the data flow model of computation attempts to introduce parallelism into the traditional control flow by looking at the process of computation from a different viewpoint. From the concept of dependency introduced in Chapter 3, we may conclude that the only dependency which could never be removed is data flow dependency, meaning that a data value must be produced before it can be used. In essence a data flow program is one in which the order of operations is determined by the availability of resources and the flow dependencies. In other words, in a data flow program, if the data are available for several instructions, these instructions may be executed in parallel. As such, the data dependencies must be deducible from the program to determine whether there are any data dependencies among the parallel executable instructions. This concept allows the employment of parallelism at the operator level. In fact, all data flow architectures have employed instruction level parallelism. For an overall introduction to data flow computation without any particular hardware approach the reader may refer to Sharp [Sharp 85, 87].

By contrast, a characteristic of the functional (or applicative) programming languages is that a program consists of an expression to be evaluated in the context of a number of function definitions. In a functional programming paradigm, the notion of a variable is similar to the mathematical sense. Application of a function to a variable can produce a new variable and a new value but it never changes the old value. The equivalence functional programming version of data flow programming can be achieved by inverting data flow to obtain functional or procedural parallelism. This is a powerful idea which we exploit in a functional programming language called SISAL. SISAL combines the best of functional programming with data flow programming to arrive at a solution to the parallel programming problem. Significant Fortran programs have been written in the functional language SISAL with good performance results.

In this chapter, we will discuss data flow and functional programming languages. In the data flow programming language section, the VAL data flow programming language is discussed to address the efficiency of data flow computation, and in the functional programming language section, SISAL is discussed to address the performance associated with the functional/data flow computation model.

9.1   Data Flow Programming

Data flow computation systems can be classified as *lazy evaluations* (also known as demand driven) or *greedy evaluations* (also known as data driven). In lazy evaluations the statement that produces the result of the program is identified and then the values required to calculate that statement are identified. This propagates back through the program until a statement that can be computed is reached and so the answer will be calculated. Greedy evaluation calculates all values as soon as possible. In this approach there is no need to calculate the flow through the program before calculating any values, but a disadvantage of greedy evaluation is that some values that are not required may be calculated. Most data flow languages are based on the single-assignment rule, stated as:

> A variable may be assigned only once in the area of the program in which it is active.

A program for a data flow computation consists of a symbolic representation of the computations as a network. The computation model is called the *data flow*. In this computation paradigm, computations move forward by nature of the availability of data values instead of the availability of instructions. A data flow computer is programmed by specifying what happens to data and ignores instruction order. To get a feeling for the difference we can consider the following example. Suppose there is a simple calculation to perform as given by the mathematical equation $X = B^2 - 4 * A * C$, where $*$ is multiplication and $=$ is assumed to be value assignment. Given inputs $A = 1$, $B = -2$, and $C = 1$, the control flow steps for computing X must be decomposed according to the operators involved, in the following operations:

Step	Calculation
1	$A = 1$
2	$B = -2$
3	$C = 1$
4	$T1 = A * C = 1$
5	$T2 = 4 * T1 = 4$
6	$T3 = B \wedge 2 = 4$
7	$X = T3 - T2 = 0$

where we have introduced the temporary variables T1, T2 and T3 to hold the intermediate results of the calculations. With regard to the control flow, the instructions are assumed to be executed in the order they are written, meaning that each instruction is performed one at a time in time step order. Consequently, 7 time steps were required, corresponding to the graph represented in Figure 9.1 (a).

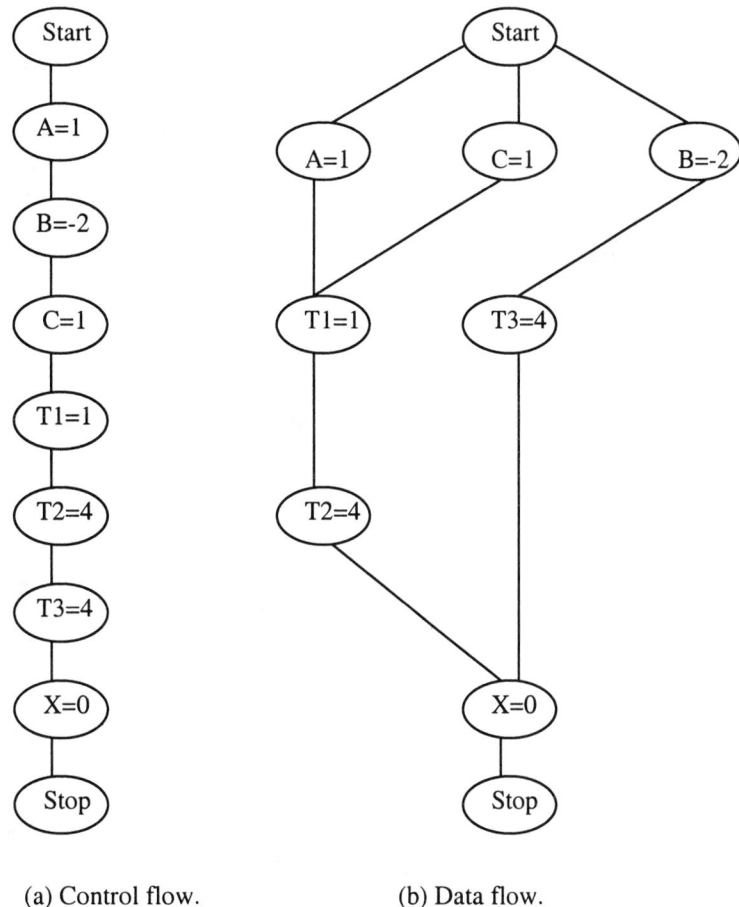

(a) Control flow.   (b) Data flow.

Figure 9.1. Computation of $X = B^2 - 4 * A * C$. (a) Control flow. (b) Data flow.

Now assume the same calculations are performed according to the availability of the data instead of the order of the instructions, which is the concept of data flow computation. The central control unit is replaced by distributed data-moving mechanism. In this scheme, the same calculation would be done in a different order:

Step	**Calculation**
1	A = 1; B = −2; C = 1
2	T1 = A * C = 1; T3 = B ^ 2 = 4
3	T2 = 4 * T1 = 4
4	X = T3 − T2 = 0

The graph representing this sequence of calculation is shown in Figure 9.1 (b). The arcs show data flow from one operation to the next.

The rationale behind this approach is that in a data flow programming model a copy of each result produced by a process is passed to each process wishing to consume that value. Processes are executed as soon as all the values required are available, or in the case of lazy evaluation, only when the value they produce is needed. There is no concept of sharing of data. Here, the nodes (circles) represent operators (processors) and arcs represent paths that carry either data or control values between them. Generally speaking, there is no concept of control flow and the flow of execution can be determined by the availability of the data. The important point of this example is that the two forms of calculation yield the same result. The only difference between these two forms is the underlying model used to represent computations. Control flow and data flow are alternate computational models that yield identical results. This is called the ***duality principle of computation***. If this principle can be applied to a complete program then the program can be executed in parallel utilizing a parallel architecture, meaning the availability of data determines the sequence of the execution.

This duality between the control flow and data flow is the basis on which it is possible to translate a control flow program into a data flow equivalent, and conversely. For example, Allen and Oldehoeft [Allen 80] developed algorithms for conversion of control flow programs to equivalent data flow programs. In addition, it is possible to program in the control flow languages and let the compiler convert the serial program into an equivalent parallel data flow program. While it is possible, it is not always desirable, because it may turn out that there are algorithms that might perform better than the generated parallel programs.

It is worth noting that control flow programming minimizes the use of hardware and this causes programmers to invent new algorithms. On the other hand, if we explicitly specify the parallelism, better and faster algorithms might be invented. Generally speaking, for maximum speed it is better to program in a language that explicitly expresses the parallelism than to rely on a compiler to detect and express the parallelism.

9.1.1   Data Flow Programming Language Principles

To represent a data flow program, a graph called a *data flow graph* is used which identifies the data dependencies between individual instructions. It represents the steps of a program and serves as an interface between architecture and programming language. The nodes in the data flow graph are called *actors*. They represent the operators and are connected by input and output arcs that carry tokens containing control values. In other words, the actor can be represented as an activity template as shown in Figure 9.2. It consists of fields for operation type, for storage of input tokens and for destination addresses.

A data flow notation requires five primitives, as illustrated in Figure 9.3, in which execution is expressed in terms of nodes firing when sufficient inputs are present. In the represented primitives, data items are viewed as tokens flowing along the edges connecting the nodes. A node fires the computation by taking the tokens on its input edges and placing the appropriate tokens on its output edges. The Gate node places a token on its output edge only if its control input is of the correct value. The Merge node (sometimes called union) fires when either of its input arcs contains a token.

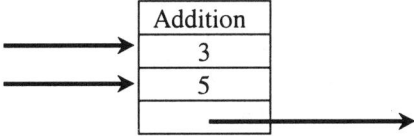

Figure 9.2. An activity template.

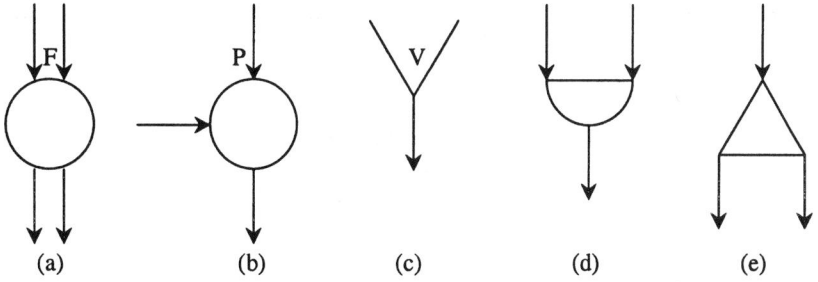

Figure 9.3. Primitives of data flow notations. (a) Primitive function. (b) Gate node (input is passed only if control matches predicate P). (c) Constant generator. (d) Nondeterministic Merge node (first input that arrives is passed on). (e) Copy node.

Some of the essential features associated with a data flow language are:

- The language follows the *single-assignment* rule, meaning that a variable is assigned a value by one statement only. The assignment can be viewed as the effect of providing a value and binding that value to the variable name appearing on the left side. In general, the same *variable name* cannot be used more than once on the left-hand side of any statement. A new name is given for any redefined variable and all subsequent references are changed to the new name. For example,

$$A := B + C;$$

$$A := A * D$$

should be converted into

$$E := B + C;$$

$$A := E * D$$

Thus, statement $A := A + 1$ is not allowed to be coded. Structured data types such as arrays and records are affected by the single-assignment rule and must be identified as single values. Of course, there is no unique way of performing this variable name change.

- It is required to restrict the scope in which a variable is used. This is called the *locality of effect*, which ensures that the instruction variables are not involved in data dependencies, which occur when data are produced by one node and used by some other nodes without influencing the computation performed by another node. Because of this issue, temporary names may be used in different sections associated with the variables.

- There should be no *global data space* of values or use of shared-memory locations.

- The language must be *applicative* oriented, meaning that values operate to produce more values. The values are used for other operations until the given operation is completed.

- The language is not suited to execute *loops* and usually only one type of iteration structure is allowed.

- The data flow language should be free of *side effects*. For example, if a procedure Q which is called by another procedure P changes some of the values of the variables of procedure P, this is called a side effect. A side effect can occur when a procedure or function changes the value of the variables in an enclosing subprogram.

- The data flow language should be free of *aliasing*, meaning that different formal parameters of a function refer to the same actual parameter whenever the function is activated. For example, if a procedure call ADD(A, A) indicates that the value of both parameters is A, then some of the statements could be simultaneously changing the same variable, which leads to inconsistencies.

Node Firing Methods

Node firing means that all input values (tokens) of the node are read, internal computation takes place and produced data become available on some or all of the subsequent nodes through some of the output arcs. The node then remains idle until data again become available on its input arcs. Tokens are placed on and removed from the arcs according to certain firing rules.

There are two node firing schemes employed in data flow computations, called *static* and *dynamic* data firing. In the static data firing system, a node fires only when each of its input arcs has a token and its output arcs are empty. Thus, a message indicating that a subsequent node has consumed its input token is required before the node fires. In the dynamic data firing system, a node fires when all its inputs have tokens, and the absence of tokens on its output arcs is not required. This can lead to the possibility of multiple tokens on an arc. There is a tagging system associated with this system to specify tokens with the appropriate data set. The tag carries information about when and how a token was generated and which data set it belongs to. The effect of node firing corresponds to removing the data from the input arcs, performing the defined computation, and placing the result on the output arcs to the receiving or destination nodes. A pictorial view of node firing is given in Figure 9.4.

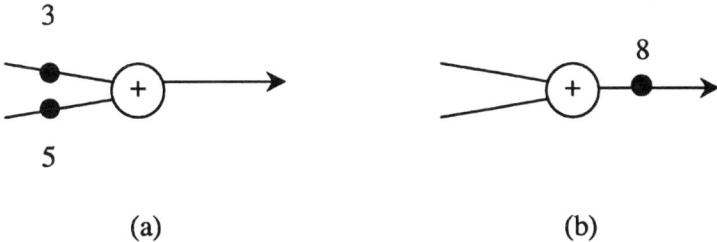

(a)   (b)

Figure 9.4. Node firing. (a) Before firing. (b) After firing.

Logically we may view each node of a data flow graph as a node data structure in memory. The data flow processor has a pool of processing elements (PE) that process instructions. Each instruction represents a specific instance of a firable node, consisting of the operation, its arguments and its destination addresses. The processor builds instructions in the node data structure. When a PE has finished executing an instruction, it generates a result packet which includes the result token and its destination address as well as any tags. The PE sends the result packet to the memory update system, which consists of an arbitrary number of memory update units which operate in parallel. The memory update system sends the result packet to the appropriate unit for processing. The memory update unit stores the result tokens in the destination locations and checks to see that the token corresponds to the argument in the node data structure. If so, the memory update unit notifies the fetch system and provides the address of the node data structure. The entire process continues until there is no firable instruction.

Data Flow Programming Languages

All data flow languages are functional or applicative languages in nature. A number of data flow languages have been proposed, including LUCID, proposed by Ashcroft [Ashcroft 77], Irvine (ID) developed at the University of California-Irvine by Arvind [Arvind 78], Value-Oriented Algorithmic Language (VAL) developed at MIT by Ackerman [Ackerman 79], HASAL [Sharp 85], and Lapse [Glauert 78]. In the following section, VAL is presented as an example of the data flow programming languages.

9.1.2   Value-Oriented Algorithmic Language (VAL)

VAL is a data flow language and was designed at MIT by Ackerman [Ackerman 79, McGraw 82, Dennis 79]. The objective was to provide a notation to illustrate an algorithm which can be executed in parallel on a parallel architecture. The language does not specify which parts of a program can be executed in parallel; rather, the parallel features are implicit. Execution of the statements is determined when the graph representation of a program is constructed. In addition, from the data flow graph of the program it is possible to determine which statements can be executed in parallel.

A programmer must write expressions and functions which take input values and produce a result without side effects. This indicates that when all the input values are available, an expression or function can be executed and cannot affect the execution of any other expression or function. In general, all expressions or functions which are ready to execute may be performed in parallel. VAL works on values which are assigned to variable names and they cannot be changed within the function or block in which they are defined. In this language, an array or record is not a collection of individual values and cannot be changed once it is assigned a value. In other words, arrays and records are considered to be equivalent to single scalar values.

Data Types

The supporting data types are integer, real, character and Boolean. The declaration is as follows when each variable is given an initial value.

```
A : REAL : = 0;
B : INTEGER : = 0;
C : CHARACTER : = 'x';
D : BOOLEAN : = TRUE;
```

The values that a BOOLEAN data type can have are TRUE and FALSE, known as the proper elements, and Undef[BOOLEAN] and Miss_elt[BOOLEAN], known as the error elements. These correspond to the situation in which the Boolean variable is undefined and the element value is missing. The Boolean operations include *and*, *or*, *not*, *equal* and *not equal*, with tests for *undef* and *miss_elt*. The defined data structures are arrays and records when the operations are chosen to support identification of concurrency for execution on a parallel processor.

Compound types can be constructed in three ways using the *array*, *record* and *oneof* definitions such that *oneof* corresponds to a union definition. The syntax consists of a type constructor giving the name of the compound type followed by the additional information within brackets. For example, an array type definition is in the form

type   XTYPE = array[INTEGER];

where the actual bounds of the array are associated with each individual array when it is used in the program execution. Since there is no bound information associated with the type, arrays of different sizes can be passed to a single procedure for execution. A two-dimensional array can be defined as follows:

type   XTYPE = array[array[INTEGER]];

where access to the elements is by using an integer index as the subscript. For example:

[1 : Expression1; 2 : Expression2];

creates an array with two elements such that the values associated with Expression1 and Expression2 become the values for the corresponding array elements and both elements can be specified and evaluated simultaneously. In general, it is possible to provide a long list of ordered pairs (name and value) which can be executed in parallel.

Consequently, if array *list* has four elements with the associated values {2,5,7,9} then the expression list[3:4] changes *list* to {2,5,4,9}, meaning that the value associated with element 3 is changed to 4. Similarly, list[6:3] provides element 5 the value miss_elt and element 6 the value 3. A record can be constructed in a fashion similar to an array. For example, a record type is defined as

type   XRECORD = record[FIELDS];

where FIELDS represent the identifiers and type associated with each component. For example,

record[A, B: Integer; C: Real; D: Character; E: Boolean];

represents a record of four fields A, B, C and D with associated data types, and

record[A:100; B:200; C; 12.5; D:'x'; E:FALSE];

establishes values of the five fields A, B, C, D and E for which the values can be computed and assigned simultaneously. Individual fields of a record may be accessed using the usual dot notation. VAL provides strong structured data type checking in which if two data types have identical structures they are equivalent to each other.

Expressions and Functions

In VAL the statements are constructed using expressions and functions to ensure there is no possibility of side effects occurring and any concurrency can be identified. For example:

```
function Class (Para : Boolean returns Integer);
                {Body of the Function}
endfun
```

defines a function named Class which returns an integer and has a single parameter Para of type Boolean. The scope of parameter is the entire function definition and the body of the function produces the returning result. In the statements of the body only the formal parameters (Para) and locally defined variables may be accessed, meaning that there is no access to global variables. This restriction ensures there is no possibility of side effects. In general, the environment defined by a function is available only during the execution of the function and not when the function returns a result. The *let-in* structure can be used to introduce one or more value identifiers, define their values and evaluate an expression. For example,

```
let   X : Integer; Y : Integer;
      X := A;
      Y := X + 20;
in
      X * Y
endlet
```

where A is accepted from the outside scope of this structure. In this way the environment of an expression can be expanded and possible concurrency in the data constructions or the evaluation of the expression can be introduced. Also, a value identifier may not be used until after it is defined and may be defined only once in a block. In contrast to conventional programming languages, a VAL function can return more than one value as a result of its execution. This can be achieved by writing a list of expressions separated by commas from each other. This is illustrated in the following function in which two expression values (X and Y) are returned from the function.

```
function Calc(A,B,C : Integer returns Integer Integer)
      let
          X : Integer := (A + B + C);
          Y : Integer := (A * B * C);
      in
          X , Y
   endlet
endfun
```

Parallel Expressions

Parallelism is represented in VAL by a parallel expression consisting of three parts:

- **A range specification**, which identifies which range of values in the named value will be used.
- **An environment expansion**, which identifies the operating environment of the expression such as the binding of the variable names.
- **A result accumulation**, which identifies how the results of the body of the expression will be combined and returned.

The range specification is identified by a forall structure which defines the scope of the parallelism. The parallel structure forall is expressed as:

```
forall_expression         : : =
    forall    name    in    [expression]
{, name in [expression] } [declaration-definition part]
    forall-body-part      {forall-body-part}
    endall
    forall-body-part   : : =
       construct expression | eval forall-op expression
    forall-op          : : =
             PLUS | TIMES | MIN | MAX | OR | AND
```

For example, in

```
forall   Calc   in [1,5]
```

Calc has the range 1 to 5 as the index value with the defined data type as integer. The body of the structure contains an environment expansion which is executed once for each element in the forall range. For example,

```
forall   Calc   in    [1,5]
```

indicates that 5 parallel environments can be in execution, and the results must be accumulated into one single block (an array) or one single element (a value). For example,

```
forall    Calc   in    [1,5]
          construct   Calc * Calc
endall
```

creates an array of 5 elements with the values 1, 4, 9, 16, and 25. And

```
forall    Calc   in    [1,5]
          eval Plus   Calc * Calc
endall
```

returns the value 55 associated with $1 + 4 + 9 + 16 + 25$. The if-then-else structure enables selection of expression results according to a test value with the following syntax:

```
Condition :: =   if      expression   then   expression
                 {else if  expression   then   expression}
                 else      expression
                 endif
```

where all values are passed to the construct and there are no value identifiers.

The for-iter structure is used as a loop structure which cannot be performed in parallel, because of data dependency between produced values in different iterations. That is, values produced in one iteration must be used in the next. For example, the following code computes the factorial of N, when the initialization part is enclosed between the reserved words **for** and **do** with the initial values.

```
for   I : Integer := 1;
      P : Integer := N;
do
      if P > 1    then
         iter
               I := I * P; P := P -1;
         enditer
      else
         I
      endif
endfor
```

The loop body, which appears between do and endfor, is repeatedly evaluated until a final result can be computed. It is worth noting that within such a construct (sequential in nature) it is valid to redefine the value of a variable, as in the statement $I := I * P$, where the old value of I has to be multiplied by P to produce the new value of I.

Matrix Multiplication

We consider the multiplication of two matrices to demonstrate the parallelism in the VAL data flow programming language. Two input arrays that correspond to a row and a column of two input matrices are declared as parameters to a function ARRAYMULT as follows:

```
function ARRAYMULT   (A : array [array[Integer]],
                      B : array [array[Integer]],
                      N : Integer
                      returns array[array[Integer]])
```

where N is the size of the array and the result is the product of two arrays A and B. The solution can be formed by finding the product of a row of A and a column of B and summing the values. This can be expressed by a **forall** structure using the **eval** construct by introducing a function INNERPROD.

Thus, a solution can be expressed as the following program:

```
function ARRAYMULT   (A : array [array[Integer]],
                      B : array [array[Integer]],
                      N : Integer
                      returns array[array[Integer]])
     forall  I  in [1, N]
             construct
             forall  J  in [1,N]
                     construct
                     INNERPROD(A[I], B[I], N)
             endall
     endall
endfun

function INNERPROD   (X : array [Integer], Y :
                          array [Integer],
                      N : Integer
                      Returns Integer)
     forall  I  in [1,N]
             eval
             plus X[I] * Y[I]
     endall
endfun
```

9.2 Functional Programming

While searching for a good parallel language, researchers and designers have observed the following:

- The data flow computation model is very similar to the functional programming language model of computation.
- In functional programming, the computation can be expressed in a serial fashion but interpreted in a parallel fashion.

This indicates that functional programming appears to unify the two theories of computation (conventional and data flow) into one. The most significant thing about the functional and data flow languages is the single-assignment feature, which means variables are assigned a value only once and maintain this value throughout the entire computation, meaning that there are no side effects. This property means that output and anti-dependencies are eliminated which simplifies analyzing the program before execution. Consequently, parallelism can be detected without global analysis of the program in functional programming languages.

A characteristic of the functional programming languages is that a program consists of an expression to be evaluated in the context of a number of function definitions. The value of any expression depends only on the values of its subexpressions and not on their order of evaluation. In functional programming, the semantics allow programmers to define data dependencies only among operations. As a result, functional programming languages are said to possess inherent parallelism because they do not insist on a predetermined ordering of instructions. It is left to the compiler and, in a parallel machine, to the run time system to determine the most appropriate order of instructions for the underlying architecture with regard to the scheduling of operations, the communication of data values and the synchronization of concurrent operations.

In addition, the clean and simple semantics of functional languages mean that the compiler is better able to detect parallelism automatically. For example, the functional programming languages research at University College London [Hansen 95, Best 96, Wilson 95] is based on the thesis that functional languages provided a much easier paradigm for the programming of parallel architectures. Some of the distinct features of parallel functional programming are:

- The parallelism may be dynamically rather than statically defined, since it is detected automatically by the compiler and scheduled by the run time system.
- Communication and synchronization between concurrent processes are handled transparently rather than being coded explicitly by the programmer.
- There are no extra language constructs and the same program will run without any changes on either a single processor or a multiprocessor computer system. Thus, it is not necessary to change the program when the number of processors in an underlying parallel machine changes.

Generally speaking, in functional programming we still need to deal with control flow, data dependencies and concurrency, but to a limited extent.

9.2.1 Functional Programming Language Principles

John Backus, the originator of Fortran, has been working on a purely Functional Programming language (FP) since the early 1970s. This section presents a review of Backus's idea of this language. In particular, we present the structure of a very simple language for functional programming called FP [Backus 78].

A functional programming language is based on the mathematical properties of functions with four independent components:

1. **A set of primitives** which are predefined by the language and correspond to the built-in operations of imperative languages.
2. **A set of functional forms** which are the procedures to combine functions to create new functions.
3. **The application operation** which is the built-in mechanism for applying a function to its arguments and producing a value.
4. **A set of data objects** which are the allowed members of the domain and range sets.

In addition, a functional language provides a method for binding a name to the new functions being defined. This provides a way that affects the language and avoids repetition of the function definition each time the function is to be invoked. In the functional computation paradigm, we think in terms of functions only. A function is as simple as mapping from a tuple to a value:

$$\text{Value} \leftarrow F(<x_1, x_2, \ldots, x_n>)$$

where $<x_1, x_2, \ldots, x_n>$ is a tuple, an ordered set of values. Indeed, $<x_1, x_2, \ldots, x_n>$ is an n-ary tuple or simply an n-tuple. Consequently, an n-ary function is a mapping from an n-tuple to a value. This is the basis of functional programming -- each function returns a value which is in turn used as an input to other functions and so on. Some of the essential primitives associated with a functional language are:

- **Selection operations:** FIRST is used to extract the first element of a sequence of elements, LAST is used to extract the last element, and TAIL is used to extract all the elements but the first element. For example,

$$x_1 \leftarrow \text{FIRST} : <x_1, x_2, \ldots, x_n>$$
$$x_n \leftarrow \text{LAST} : <x_1, x_2, \ldots, x_n>$$
$$<x_2, \ldots, x_n> \leftarrow \text{TAIL} : <x_1, x_2, \ldots, x_n>$$

- **Structuring operations:** The operations are used to combine, dissect or rearrange the elements. For example,

$\langle x_n, x_1, \ldots, x_{n-1} \rangle$ $\leftarrow$ ROTR : $\langle x_1, x_2, \ldots, x_n \rangle$ (ROTate Right)

$\langle x_2, \ldots, x_n, x_1 \rangle$ $\leftarrow$ ROTL : $\langle x_1, x_2, \ldots, x_n \rangle$ (ROTate Left)

$\quad$ n $\leftarrow$ LENGTH : $\langle x_1, x_2, \ldots, x_n \rangle$ (LENGTH)

$\langle x, x_1, x_2, \ldots, x_n \rangle$ $\leftarrow$ CONS : $\langle x, \langle x_1, x_2, \ldots, x_n \rangle \rangle$ (CONstruct Sequence)

- **Arithmetic operations:** These operations are applied to sequences of two elements and produce a new element as a result. We consider the ordinary arithmetic operations '+' for addition, '-' for subtraction, '*' for multiplication, 'div' for division and '|' for residue operation. For example the following returns the remainder of the division x by y.

$$ | : \langle x, y \rangle $$

- **Predicate operations:** These operations are used to produce results as truth values. We represent truth by T and false by F in which a predicate function yields either T or F.
- **Logical operations:** The operations that provide the combination of the truth values.
- **Identity operation:** The function ID yields the same element. For example,

$$ x \leftarrow ID : x $$

The most interesting feature of FP languages is the functional forms, because we are not used to functional forms in conventional programming languages. To introduce the power of functional forms in programming, we illustrate a few functional forms called Program-Forming-Operations (**PFO**) which Backus has suggested [Backus 78, 82].

Composition

This function is a mathematical function composition with the following syntax:

$$ (f \circ g) \; : X \equiv f : (\, g : X) $$

where the function form $\circ$ is defined to take two functions as the arguments and produce a result which is a function that is equivalent to the application of the first argument to the result of the application of the second argument. For example, if we define a composition function as

$$ make\_square \equiv Square \circ Square $$

then 16 is the produced result of *make_square*(2), where *Square* is the associated value of an expression that computes the square of a number.

Construction

The functional form [ ] has the following syntax:

$$[f_1, f_2, \ldots, f_n] : X \equiv <f_1 : X, f_2 : X, \ldots, f_n : X>$$

where it takes as arguments n functions and results in a function that is equivalent to applying each of the functions to the same argument and forming a sequence of the results. For example, assume we define individual functions for Maximum, Minimum, and Average of a sequence of numbers. If we define a construction as

[Maximum, Minimum, Average]

then <5, 1, 3> is the produced result of [Maximum, Minimum, Average]<1,2,3,4,5>, in which the construction is used to combine the results of applying the argument to individual functions.

Apply to All

The functional form Apply_to_All, denoted by α, has the following syntax:

$$\alpha f : <X_1, X_2, \ldots, X_n> = <f : X_1, f : X_2, \ldots, f : X_n>$$

which takes a function as argument and results in a function that is equivalent to applying the argument function to each element of the sequence and forming a sequence of the results.

Insert

The functional form Insert denoted by / has the following syntax:

$$/ f : <X_1, X_2, \ldots, X_n> = f : <X_1, / f : <X_2, \ldots, X_n>>$$

which takes a function as argument and results in a function which is equivalent to applying the argument function to successive elements of the sequence. For example, / + : < 1,2,3,4,5 > results 15, in which the function as the argument is + and is applied to the elements of the sequence with regard to the above syntax.

Functional Programming Languages

The evolution of functional programming languages is traced through the development of lambda calculus and combinatory calculus, Lisp, Iswin, FP, and ML to modern functional languages such as Miranda, Haskell, STRAND and SISAL [Szymanski 91, Wilkinson 99, Williams 90]. FP proved to be neither amenable to efficient execution nor rich enough in new language features of major research interest, and so FP has largely fallen by the wayside [Almasi 94]. Thus, FP was the inspiration for many new functional languages with new ideas for the design and implementation of such languages.

Gordon [Gordon 79] in the United Kingdom developed a programming language called ML that consisted of a deductive calculus called PPλ (Polymorphic Predicate calculus) together with an interactive programming language paradigm. It was called ML, for MetaLanguage, since it served as the common language for LCF, a proof-generating system for reasoning about recursive functions. David Turner, at the University of St. Andrews and later at the University of Kent, designed a series of three functional languages called SASL (St. Andrews Static Language), KRC (Kent Recursive Calculator), and Miranda [Turner 76, 81, 86] which introduced new syntactic issues in language design. Haskell is a general-purpose functional programming language developed by a committee which exhibits many new features in functional programming including higher order functions, lazy evaluation, static polymorphic typing, user defined data types, pattern matching and list comprehension. It has a rich set of primitive data types including lists, arrays, fixed precision integers, and floating point numbers. The design was influenced by languages as old as Iswin and as new as Miranda.

The name STRAND is based on the words STReam/AND, which were chosen to form a name for a functional programming language that supports streams (continuous data flows between tasks) and AND-parallelism (adjacent tasks are executed in parallel). STRAND88 [STRAND88 90, Lewis 92], developed by Strand Software Technologies, Inc., is available on numerous parallel and serial computers. STRAND combines the best of functional programming with data flow programming to achieve a solution to parallel programming problems. Applications written in STRAND run equally well on parallel and serial architectures, and applications are also portable across a wide variety of parallel computers. In STRAND a program is a collection of functions that consume processors dynamically, as many as needed. Hudak [Hudak 89] describes and compares different functional programming languages.

As a consequence of these projects, functional languages promote the construction of correct parallel programs by isolating the programmer from the complexities of parallel processing. They provide an easy-to-use and clean parallel programming model that facilitates algorithm development and simplifies compilation. Ease of programming, compatibility with parallel computers with regard to decomposition of computations, and expressive power are still claimed as strengths of this programming paradigm. In this section, we introduce SISAL (version 1.2), a functional programming language that executes programs on both serial and parallel computers. In SISAL a program is a collection of functions that consume a varying number of processors. SISAL exposes implicit parallelism through data independence and guarantees determinate results. SISAL programs are said to be referentially transparent and free of side effects and deadlock. The determination of data dependencies, scheduling of operations, communication of data values, and synchronization of concurrent operations are realized automatically by the compiler and run time system, and the programmer is not required to manage these operations. In general, a SISAL program defines a set of mathematical expressions in which names stand for specific values and computations progress without state. A SISAL program is translated into one or more machine-independent data flow graphs which contain all the information regarding the input and output dependencies among the operators that construct the program.

9.2.2 Stream and Iterations in Single Assignment Language (SISAL)

SISAL is a strongly typed general-purpose functional (applicative) programming language. It was defined in 1983 by McGraw [McGraw 83] (version 1.1) and revised in 1985 [McGraw 85] (version 1.2). SISAL was a descendant of the VAL data flow programming language and was a collaborative effort by Lawrence Livermore National Laboratory, Colorado State University, the University of Manchester, and Digital Equipment Corporation for use on both conventional and novel multiprocessor systems. It has a Pascal-like syntax and is designed to produce efficient code for large-scale scientific computations. SISAL is a functional programming language with no explicit parallel control constructs. A SISAL program is a collection of separated compiled files called compilation units in which each one includes a list of declared function names visible outside the unit, a list of corresponding function definitions, and possibly the definitions of additional functions. A function can take zero or more arguments and must return one or more values such that the data type of each argument and result is declared in a header. A function has access to its arguments and there are no side effects.

The latest version of SISAL is 2.0, which is similar to version 1.2 and includes some new features such as array comprehensions, which permit the definition of subregions of an array within a single expression. In this section SISAL 1.2 is presented as a prototype of this functional language. SISAL has several important semantic properties:

- All functions are mathematically defined, meaning that there are no side effects.
- Programs are referentially transparent, meaning that names are bound to values and not memory locations, which indicates there is no aliasing.
- The language is single assignment, meaning that a name is assigned a value only once.

As a consequence of these properties, the transformation from source code to data flow graph is trivial.

Some distinct objectives associated with the SISAL project are as follows:

- Define a general-purpose applicative language.
- Define a language-independent intermediate form for data flow graphs.

- Develop optimization techniques for high-performance parallel applicative computing.
- Develop a micro-tasking environment that supports data flow on conventional computer systems.
- Achieve execution performance comparable to Fortran.
- Validate the applicative style of programming for large-scale scientific applications.

The first three address the data flow computational objectives and the last three reflect the computing environment at Lawrence Livermore National Laboratory and other government facilities. In contrast to the data flow programming language projects that assume hardware support, the SISAL project was intended to define a language and an intermediate form independent of target architecture, then to develop the code generators and run time systems with regard to the specific target architecture. As a result of this approach, SISAL is running on uniprocessors, conventional shared-memory multiprocessors (MIMD architecture), the Cray X/MP, the Warp (Systolic Array architecture), the Connection Machine, the Mac II, and a variety of data flow architectures (RMIT/CSIRO, and Manchester).

Data Types

The supporting data types are integer, real, character, Boolean and double precision. It also supports the aggregate data types such as array, record, union and stream. All arrays are one dimensional, and multidimensional arrays are defined as arrays of arrays. For example, an n-dimensional array is an array of $(n-1)$-dimensional arrays. An array declaration specifies only the component type. The type, size and lower bound of an array are a function of execution. The components of a multidimensional array may have different length and lower bounds. For example, a one-dimensional array of integers is defined as:

type   OneDim = array[integer]

and a two-dimensional array of integers may be defined as an array of an array of integers:

type   twoDim = array[OneDim]

In general, any expression which has type array creates a new array. For example, in the following, the first expression creates an empty array of integers, the second builds an array of integers with lower bound 1, and the third builds a 2-dimensional array of integers.

X : = array OneDim [ ]
Y : = array OneDim [1: 1, 2, 3]
Z : = array TwoDim [1: array [1: 1, 2, 3], array [1: 4, 5, 6]]

A stream is a sequence of elements (values) of uniform data type and accessible in order, meaning that there is no random access to elements. A stream can have only one producer but more than one consumer. Each element of a stream is available as soon as it is produced, and the run time support system must provide concurrent execution of the elements associated with a stream with regard to producing and consuming. As a result, streams can express pipeline parallelism and are used for program input and output.

Parallel Expressions

SISAL is a functional programming language with no explicit parallel control constructs, but its data types and its constructs for expressing operations are designed to produce efficient code for large-scale scientific computations. SISAL supports both sequential and parallel loop expressions as follows:

- The **for initial** loop expression provides a mechanism to specify parallel iterations and allows references to values defined in other iterations. The expression consists of four components:
  1. **Initialization Part**, which defines all loop constructs, assigns an initial value to variables and is the first iteration of the loop.
  2. **Loop Body**, which appears before or after the body. If it appears before the body, the body might not execute, and if it appears after the body, the body executes at least once.
  3. **Termination Test**, which computes new values for the loop names, possibly based on their previous values. The rebinding of loop names to values is implicit and occurs between iterations. *Old* refers to previous values when it is the prefix of a loop name.
  4. **Result Clause**, which defines the results such that each result is the final value of a loop name or a reduction of the values assigned to a loop name during loop executions. The language supports seven reductions: *array of*, *stream of*, *catenate*, *sum*, *product*, *least* and *greatest*.
- The **for** loop expression provides a mechanism to specify independent iteration. It does not allow references to values defined in other iterations. The expression consists of three components:
  1. **A Range Generator**, which is a *dot* or *cross* product of a set of sequences or scatters. It specifies the order of reduction and defines the size and structure of aggregate objects.
  2. **A Loop Body**, which is a set of statements executed for each index, value or n-tuple.
  3. **A Return Clause**, which defines the results of the execution. Each result is a reduction of values defined in the loop body as stated in the **for initial** loop expression.

The **for initial** and **for** expressions are illustrated in the following examples.

```
for     initial                       for I in      1, N
        I : = 1;                           X := A[I] * B[I]
        X : = Y[1];                    returns value of sum X
        while I < N repeat            end for
               I : = old I + 1;
               X : = old X + Y[I];
        returns array of X
end for
```

A two-dimensional array can be defined as an aggregative object. For example, the following expression returns a two-dimensional array of n rows and m columns (a cross product of two sequences).

```
for I in  1,N cross J  in 1, M
     Returns array of (I * J)
end for
```

The SISAL Compiler

The SISAL compiler (Osc) is an extensive work of a prototype developed for the Hep multiprocessor [Oldehoeft 86]. The structure of Osc is shown in Figure 9.5, which is adapted from [McGraw 85] and illustrates the phases and subphases of the compilation process. The parser changes the source code to an intermediate form called IF1 which consists of data flow graphs with functional semantics. An IF1 program consists of one or more acyclic graphs made up of simple nodes (arithmetic operations such as addition, array and stream manipulation), compound nodes (one or more subgraphs to define structured expressions such as loop expressions), graph nodes, edges, and types. Similar to data flow computation, nodes denote operations, edges transmit data between nodes, and types describe the transmitted data. The linker, called IF1LD, is placed before the back end, because the entire program including any library routines can be optimized as a program. The first optimization phase, IF1OPT, is a machine-independent optimizer and performs conventional optimization such as function expansion, invariant code removal, common subexpression elimination, constant folding, loop fusion, and dead code removal. The second phase, IF2MEM, is an analyzer which preallocates array storage where compile time analysis or run time expressions can calculate their sizes. The next phase, IF2UP, restructures some graphs while preserving program correctness to help identify operations that can execute in place and improve chances for in-place operations at run time. The parallelizer, called IF2PART, defines the desired granularity of parallelism, meaning that the optimized IF2 is partitioned into parallel subtasks. In the last phase, CGEN translates the optimized IF2 graph into C code, which is then compiled using the local C compiler to produce an executable program.

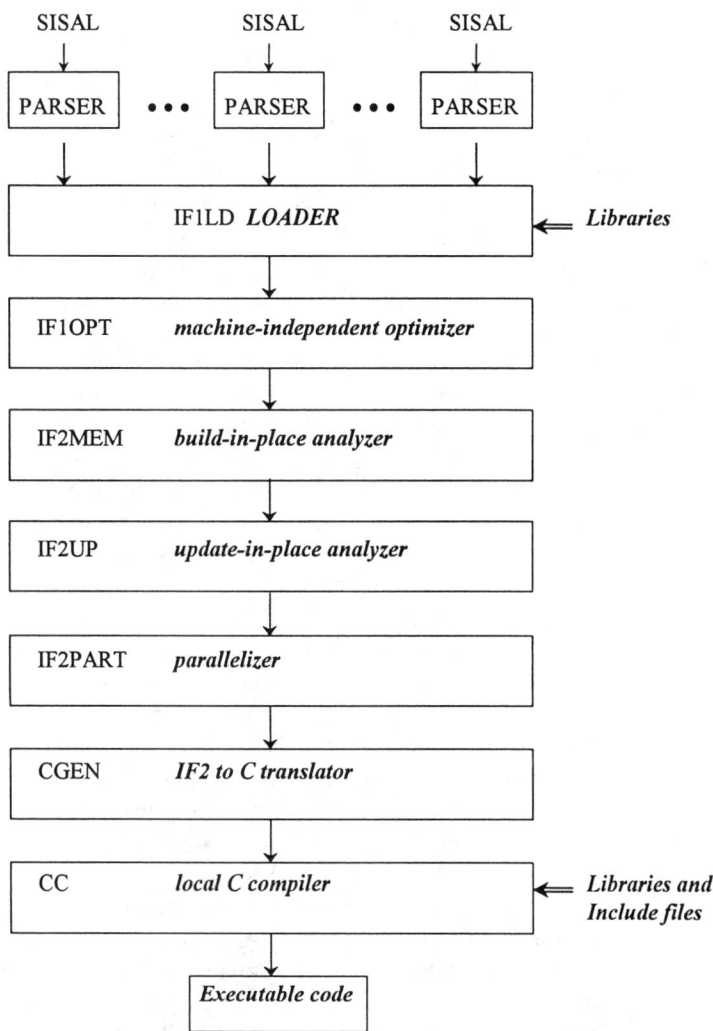

Figure 9.5. SISAL language processing [McGraw 85].

The C compiler is used as an intermediate form to increase system portability and allow experimentation with future optimization by manual editing. Library software linked during this phase of compilation provides support for parallel execution, storage management and interaction with the user. It is the responsibility of CGEN to recognize the code segments inserted during IF2 optimization and generate the appropriate packages as separate functions for parallel execution. In addition, synchronization primitives are added to coordinate parallel execution.

The Run Time System

The SISAL run time system is a microtasking kernel designed to support the parallel execution of loops associated with the SISAL programs. It provides dynamic storage allocation, implements operations on major data structures, and interfaces with operating systems for input and output and command line processing. If there are n participating processors, the system decomposes each loop into n slices. The run time system supports two queues of executable tasks called the *Ready List* and the *For Pool*.

At program initiation a command line specifies the number of operating system processes, called workers, to be created during the execution of the program. These workers are in the form of threads (lightweight processes) and their numbers vary over the program execution. A worker stays in one of three modes of operation, *for loop* work, *ready list* work or *idle* (because neither kind of work is available). After execution begins, the kernel creates and assigns a worker to each participating processor. The workers examine the *for pool* queue for a piece of a for loop expression (slice) to execute. A slice (one or more consecutive for bodies) is obtained and the thread stack already held by the worker is used to execute the code for the slice. If the slice terminates normally, the worker places the thread on the *Ready List* and returns to the *For Loop*; otherwise, the worker returns to the *For Loop* for another slice of the expression.

If during execution the slice must wait for completion of a storage request or the results of another loop selected for parallel execution, the worker will save its status on the appropriate list. When the event completes, a worker will restore the slice and continues its execution. The threads appear on the *ready list* queue as a result of being made executable by other events. At program initiation, a single thread for the main function is placed on the *Ready List*. All *Ready List* entries have been allocated to a thread stack, and upon obtaining a thread, execution may begin. If the thread terminates normally, the worker checks the parent context thread to see if it is waiting only for this thread to complete. If so, the worker places the parent thread on the *Ready List*, deallocates the associated stack and returns to the *Ready List* for more work; otherwise, it deallocates the stack and returns to the *Ready List*.

Feo [Feo 85] reported the evaluation of SISAL and Fortran codes. The comparison was the execution performance of equivalent SISAL 1.2 and Fortran versions of the Livermore Loops and four large scientific programs on a Sequent Balance 21000. Livermore Loops are a set of 24 scientific kernels from production codes run at Lawrence Livermore National Laboratory. They consist of computational structures, including independent parallel processes, recurrent processes, wavefronts and pipelines. For many years scientists have used the Loops to benchmark high-performance computers. The four scientific programs were Gauss-Jordan elimination, RICARD, SIMPLE and an instance of parallel simulated annealing. Four of the five SISAL programs ran as fast as the equivalent Fortran on a single-processor machine, and all five SISAL programs achieved good performance and speedup. It is worth noting that they did not rewrite or recompile the SISAL codes to run on multiple-processor architecture, they simply increased the number of participating workers at run time. Table 9.1 presents the execution times for the four scientific applications with regard to single and multiple processors.

Table 9.1. Execution times for four scientific programs (adopted from Feo 85).

Program	Fortran	SISAL (1)	SISAL	Processors	Speedup
Gauss-Jordan	54.0 s	54.5 s	8.8 s	10	6.2
RICARD	30.63 hr	31.0 hr	3.45 hr	10	9.0
SIMPLE	3081.3 s	3099.3 s	422.0 s	10	7.3
Simulated Annealing	476.6 s	956.2 s	267.8 s	5	3.6

In addition, a favorable performance comparison was reported between Fortran and SISAL [Cann 92]. In that comparison, a suite of eight benchmark programs coded in both Fortran and SISAL was compared on an 8-processor Cray Y-MP. The benchmark included the Livermore Loop (24 scientific kernels), the SIMPLE hydrodynamics program, and a weather prediction program. Compared with Fortran, the SISAL run time was 5% worse for the Livermore Loops, four times better for SIMPLE and almost six times better for the weather prediction program. As an example, the following pseudocode presents the complete SISAL source code for Loop 1, one of the 24 Livermore Loops.

```
type   double = double_real
type   OneD = array[double]

function Loop1( n : integer; Q, R, T : double; Y, Z :
         OneD returns OneD)
      for K in 1, n
      X : = Q + ( Y[K] * ( R * Z[K + 10] + T * z[K + 11]) )
      returns array of X
      end for
end function

function Main( rep, n : integer; Q, R, T : double; Y, Z :
         OneD returns OneD)
      for i in 1, rep
           X : = Loop1( n, Q, R, T, Y, Z );
      Returns value of X
      end for
end function
```

Summary

Control flow computing displays the common characteristic that the execution sequence of the program's statements is dictated by the order in which the statements are textually composed by the programmer. In other words, the instructions drive the program's execution. An alternative method of selecting statements for execution is to regard a statement as being ready for execution if the data that it requires are available. Hence the sequence in which the statements are textually composed is unlikely to be the order in which they are executed. In addition, if the data are available for more than one statement then these statements can be executed in parallel. This is referred to as data flow computing. In general, the data flow from one instruction to another and the order of execution of the instructions does not depend on the location of the instructions in memory. By contrast, a characteristic of functional computing is that the computation model consists of an expression to be evaluated in the context of a number of function definitions. In other words, a functional computing model is a set of functional forms for combining functions into new ones, and the application operation is a mechanism for applying a function to an argument and producing a value.

In this chapter, we have presented fundamental concepts of data flow and functional computing and illustrated the application of these concepts in the data flow and functional programming languages VAL and SISAL, respectively. We described both static and dynamic data-driven models that more or less assume data flow graphs as their computation model. The equivalent functional computing version of data flow computing can be achieved by inverting data flow to functional parallelism. This is a powerful mechanism which we exploited in a functional programming language.

We briefly discussed the data flow programming language principles and the essential features of a data flow language. VAL is a data flow language designed at MIT for data flow parallel programming. In VAL, statements are identified using expressions and functions to ensure that any concurrency can be identified. Parallelism is introduced by a parallel expression consisting of three parts: a range specification, an environment expansion, and a result accumulation. We introduced a matrix multiplication problem to address parallelism in VAL. We discussed the functional programming language components: a set of primitives, a set of functional forms, the application operation, and a set of data objects. Related to these components are the essential operations such as selection, structuring, arithmetic, predicate, logical and identity operations. A descendant of the VAL data flow programming language is a strongly typed functional programming language called SISAL. We discussed the SISAL functional programming language in terms of its semantic properties, data types, parallel expressions and compiler. SISAL combines the best of functional programming primitives with data flow programming primitives to achieve a solution to the parallel programming problem. The February 1982 issue of *Computer* is dedicated to data flow computing and is a good source to begin learning about the subject.

CHAPTER 10
Asynchronous Parallel Programming

Asynchronous parallelism is the most general form of parallelism, whereby processors operate freely on tasks, and global synchronization is not required. In place of the lockstep fashion of the various forms of synchronized parallelism, the asynchronous method relies on locks and explicit control flow.

In this chapter, we consider the programs that specify two or more sequences of actions to be performed concurrently within the same program. Each sequence of actions is performed by a process (task). In a program with several processes, each process performs actions in strict sequence, but several processes may be in progress at the same time. Multiprocess programs may be executed on a computer with a single processor or on a computer with multiple processors. A computer with one processor runs a multiprocess program by spending a little bit of execution time on one process, switching its attention to another process, and eventually picking up where it left off on the original process. This is called *interleaved concurrency*. On a computer with more than one processor, different processors may actually execute different processes at the same time. This is called *overlapped concurrency*. A programmer need not be concerned with the actual implementation of interleaved concurrency. In general, interleaved concurrency creates the illusion that all processes in programs are running simultaneously. Regardless of how concurrency is actually achieved, a programmer can imagine that there is a separate processor running each process. Such an imaginary processor is called a virtual processor. Multiprocess programs are designed for programs managing several concurrent activities in which one process manages each activity. Another reason for writing multiprocess programs is to allow programs to be finished more quickly. If concurrency is overlapped, a computation can be made to finish sooner by allowing parts that do not depend on each other to execute simultaneously on different processors.

Even if concurrency is interleaved, decomposing a computation into processes can allow work to proceed while one part of the computation is waiting for some external event such as the completion of an input or output operation. Depending on how concurrency is implemented, different virtual processors may appear to execute at different speeds. Ordinarily, no assumptions can be made about the relative progress of one process with respect to another. We say that such processes are *synchronous*. For processes to work cooperatively, they must be able to communicate. This means that the processes must be able to synchronize on occasion. We say that these processes are *asynchronous*. Concurrent programming is concerned with the following issues:

- A program depends on the relative speeds of different processes, for example when several processes examine and then update a single variable.
- Deadlock arises when no process can proceed because each process is waiting for some action that can be performed only by another waiting process.
- Debugging is difficult, because certain errors may depend on the timing of different processes. The timing of processes can vary from one execution of the program to another, meaning that such errors might not be reproduced.

The situations in which the processes interact can be divided into two categories:

- When processes wish to update a shared variable or a resource at the same time. This is described as *mutual exclusion*.
- When processes are cooperating on some operation and they must be correctly interleaved in time. This is described as *message-passing mechanism*.

The mutual exclusion mechanism is usually implemented by a lock which prevents all but one process access to the shared data at any instant in time. All other accesses must wait until the mutual exclusion lock is removed by the process that originally placed the lock on the data. The second major method is to send a message to all processes to inform them about the applicability of the access to the resource. This method can be employed by message-passing in distributed systems. Therefore in the concurrent programming environment we need to provide not only program and data structures similar to those required in a sequential programming environment but also methods to control the communication and synchronization of the concurrent processes.

In this chapter, three asynchronous parallel programming languages are considered. In particular, the language Modula-2 is considered as one language which uses shared variables for synchronization, whereas Ada and Occam are considered languages which perform message passing directly when communicating. Some typical problems in concurrent programming, known as bounded buffer problems or producer and consumer problems are programmed in the languages to illustrate the synchronization and communication techniques.

10.1   Parallel Programming with Ada

In 1957 the Department of Defense established the Higher Order Language Working Group to draw up the requirements for a language which would enable standardization of the programming language to be used in the embedded systems application area. The final choice was made in 1979 when the proposal developed by the team led by Jean Ichbiah at CII Honeywell Bull, France, was accepted. The language was renamed Ada in honor of Augusta Ada Byron. She had worked with Charles Babbage and is regarded as the world's first programmer. The first definitive version of the language was published in 1980. In general, it has been designed under sponsorship from the U.S. Department of Defense, and the objective was to come up with a language which would provide suitable facilities for real time programming of embedded systems. Embedded systems are systems in which the computer is only a part of the total system used for online monitoring and control, such as on a ship or missile. This new programming language paradigm is concerned when the main cause of errors in programs is the differences between machines, systems, languages and language implementations experienced when transporting and maintaining programs. In general, concurrent programming was done by calling the underlying operating system directly or by creating an operating system directly on the computer hardware. This made it practically impossible to transport programs from one system to another. By including a model of concurrent programming called tasking in the standard language, Ada makes this possible. Ada is designed for numerical computations, system programming, and applications with real time and concurrency requirements and was influenced by the Pascal programming language. It supports both a shared-memory and a message-passing model of computations.

Ada distinguishes itself from other languages in its concern with reliability. Consistency checks are performed when a program is being compiled so that errors can be caught as early as possible, even before a program is tested. In addition, checks are performed during program execution, so that unexpected conditions will be noticed soon after they arise, rather than after they indirectly cause other parts of the program to misbehave. These checks confine the effect of an error, so that an Ada program rarely addresses arbitrary storage or branches to an arbitrary address. There are mechanisms for recovering from a run time error when it is required to do so.

Clearly, this implies that some of the programming required will contain natural ways of expressing the handling of multiple concurrent activities. Ada offers standard and readable language concepts for the structuring of large programs, for the specification of the relationship between different modules of a program, for data abstraction and for programming distributed computing with tools for describing processes and the communication between them. It is important to emphasize that the design of Ada is more concerned with making programs easy to read than with minimizing the number of keystrokes needed to write a program. However, this is not a textbook of the Ada programming language, and simplifications may exist where a complete description would have caused digression from our main subject. Several good books on Ada are listed in the references [Schiper 89, Stammers 85, Cohen 96, Skansholm 97, Dongarra 89].

Language Model

The design of Ada introduced the following features:

- **System Programming,** for programs that are concerned with the underlying machine.
- **Real Time Systems,** for programs that must perform actions at particular times.
- **Distributed Systems,** for systems consisting of multiple main programs, possibly executing on different processors.
- **Information Systems,** for commercial applications.
- **Numerical Computations,** for programs that depend on the precise mathematical details of computations involving real numbers.
- **Safety and Security,** for programs whose reliability is so critical that extreme measures must be taken to ensure their correctness.

An Ada program consists basically of a procedure within which other procedures may be declared and called. Ada makes a careful distinction between the declaration part of a procedure, known as **elaboration**, in which variables and other constructs are declared, and the executable statements of the procedure. The overall structure of the Ada program is shown in the following:

```
MessageSystem:
   declare
        MessType = ........
        task Process1;
        task Process2;

        task Process3 is
                entry Get (mess: out MessType);
                entry Put (mess: in MessType);
        end Process3;

   --bodies for the tasks Process1, Process2 and Process3

begin
        --null body, since all the work is done by the tasks
end MessageSystem;
```

In this outline, we observe that there are three processes, and **Process3** is offering service facilities which will be used by the other two tasks. In this view, **Process3** is a passive process and the other two are active processes. In general, when *MessageSystem* is called, the elaboration of all its declarations takes place, including the initiation of the three processes, and the null body begins to execute. This body will not be terminated until each of its children is terminated.

The client/server paradigm is the rationale behind the Ada program construction. In the absence of a remote invocation, the client must make two calls, one to pass in data and the other to receive the reply after the input data have been processed. This can be outlined as follows.

```
Process  Server
   entry Request(SomeData)
   entry Reply(SomeOtherData)
   begin
         repeat
            select
               accept Request(SomeData)         do
                     SomeVariable = SomeData
               accept Reply(SomeOtherData)    do
                     SomeOtherData = SomeResult
            or
               terminate
            end select;
         forever
   end;
Process  Client
   begin
         Server.Request(Data)
         Server.Reply(Answer)
   end;
```

In general, a server process should not be affected by a client. Remote invocation allows the transaction to be represented as a single process interaction, meaning that the server does not need to know the identity of the client or indeed how many clients there are. This paradigm can be outlined as follows.

```
Process  Server          provides
   entry Request(SomeData, SomeOtherData)
Process  Client
   begin
         Server.Request(Data, Answer)
   end;
```

There are two distinctive goals of Ada, as follows:

1. To divide a large program into manageable smaller pieces (modules).
2. To write general software components that can be used in many programs.

Both of these goals are provided in Ada by *packages*. A *package* is a collection of related entities that can be used by other parts of the program. These entities may include variables, subprograms and type declarations. In this sense, an Ada *package* is very much like a general collection of software that can be incorporated in many different systems to fulfill particular needs. The description of a package in Ada consists of a *package declaration* describing the interface and a *package body* describing the implementation. A typical *package declaration* can be declared as follows:

```
package  identifier  is
      declaration;
      ...
      declaration
end   identifier;
```

where it consists of a sequence of declarations. A *package body* has the following form:

```
package  body  identifier  is
      declarative-part
begin
      {sequence of statements}
end   identifier;
```

where the sequence of statements is optional. Ada supports two kinds of subprograms. A subprogram may be either a *procedure* invoked by a procedure call statement to perform some action or a *function* invoked by evaluation of an expression to compute some value. The forms of a typical procedure and function are as follows:

```
procedure    identifier    (parameter-list) is
      declarative-part
begin
      {sequence of statements}
end   identifier;
function  identifier (parameter-list) return result-type is
      declarative-part
begin
      {sequence of statements}
end   identifier;
```

where the function is similar to the procedure except for the first line. Sixty-nine identifiers are reserved words in an Ada program and may not be given other meanings by the programmer. In general, the elements of a program can be combined to form *declarations* specifying the meaning of identifiers, *statements* specifying actions, and *pragmas* specifying information for the compiler (for example, task priority). Declarations, statements and pragmas always end with semicolons.

Architecture Model

Here, we are concerned with the applicability of the Ada tasking concept for the programming of distributed calculations. Thus, we have to choose a computational model consisting of more than one processor, with each one executing its own piece of code (a task) and with programmable communication between the processors. The language suggests that there is no relationship between the logical processes (the tasks) and the physical processors, but active tasks must be divided among the available processors. The availability of shared memory among all processors is not required if there is a solution for the system to establish communication between tasks which does not need shared memory. Thus, programs that contain global variables can execute with distributed memory allocated to those variables. Different processors might be given different tasks, and even if the tasks are identical (by task type), the processors should be capable of running asynchronously. If we use Ada for distributed computations, it will be most efficient when the system is parameterized with the following properties:

- The number P of available processors
- The size M of shared memory that can be accessed by tasks
- The size C of available communication channels
- The clock resolution facility for the presence of the vital processor

Asynchronous MIMD architecture fits the above requirements. The main characteristic of most other computational models is the determinism of execution caused by constraints on either the instructions performed by the different processors or the communication between processors. For example, SIMD in this category can be exploited while programming in Ada. In addition, some mechanism must be used for specifying the configuration of the distributed program, or the assignment of the program units making up the program to various parts of the underlying distributed system. The Distributed Systems feature of Ada provides a general model for describing distributed systems. The system is viewed as consisting of one or more *processor nodes* and zero or more *storage nodes*. The processor nodes may be a set of machines in the same room, a set of processors on the same board, or a set of operating system processes running on a single processor. A storage node is a set of storage locations that can be accessed by processor nodes, main memory, low-speed cache, high-speed cache or file storage systems, for example.

Process Definition

To conform with Ada terminology, the term "process" will be called **task** in this discussion. Tasks are the Ada concept for parallel executable program segments. The process level refers to the possibility of using process hierarchies. Such hierarchies may be constructed by nesting process declarations within process declarations. Some languages allow such nesting, but those with a flat process structure do not. For example, Ada allows nested dynamic processes (called tasks), whereas concurrent Pascal supports only static flat processes. When there are nested levels of processes, a relationship exists between processes, meaning that a process is the child process of the process in which it is declared. In this case, only when all children have terminated is it safe for the parent to be terminated. In Ada, tasks are hierarchically related but have remote invocation as their model of message passing. The task consists of two parts, its specification and its body. The task specification is the interface presented to other tasks and may contain entry specifications, which are a list of the services provided by the task. In general, an entry is exactly the same as a procedure declaration. This is made on purpose to allow substitution of a concurrent entry for a sequential procedure without changing a program. The task body contains the sequence of statements to be executed when any of its services are requested, which represents the dynamic behavior of the task.

For example, a task called A_Process can be declared as follows:

```
task   A_Process is
       --specification
end    A_Process;

task   body A_Process is
       --declarations
begin
       --body
end    A_Process;

begin --active here
       --parent
end;   --terminate here
```

where -- indicates comment in Ada programming language. The *specification* specifies the services the A_Process is offering to the other processes and the body details the implementation. When the **begin** of the parent is reached, the A_Process task becomes active and its body is executed. Then, the A_Process executes in parallel with the statements of its parent. A task has completed its execution when it has finished the execution of the sequence of statements that appears after its reserved word **begin**.

If several tasks are written in the same declarative part, they are executed in parallel with one another, including the parent task. For example, in the following case, all three tasks are executed in parallel whenever the **begin** of the parent task is reached.

```
task   A_Process is
       --specification
end    A_Process;

task   body  A_Process is
       --declarations
begin
       --body
end    A_Process;
task   B_Process is
       --specification
end    B_Process;

task   body  B_Process is
       --declarations
begin
       --body
end    B_Process;

begin --parent
       --all three tasks are active here
end;   --terminate here
```

In many applications, there is a need for several tasks to do the same thing simultaneously (such as to perform the same analysis on different sets of data). For this reason, Ada provides *task types*. Every task is associated with some task type, and all tasks associated with the same type have identical entries and identical statements to execute. An example is as follows:

```
task   type  Counter_Task_Type is
       --specification
end    Counter_Task_Type;
task   body  Counter_Task_Type is
begin
       --body
end    Counter_Task_Type;
```

A task type declaration must be accompanied by a *task body* which consists of the statements to be executed by the task. The declaration

Counter_1, Counter_2: Counter_Task_Type;

declares Counter_1 and Counter_2 to be two task objects each of which independently executes the task body above. Each one has its own copy of the variables declared in the task body. Task type declarations and task bodies can go in the declarative part of a subprogram body, a package body, a block statement, or a surrounding task body. Tasks may be declared or allocated. A task associated with a declared object begins execution when the object declaration is elaborated. A task associated with an allocated object begins execution upon creation of the object. A running task eventually terminates. Sequences of statements in an Ada program are *reentrant*. This means that several tasks may execute the same sequence of statements at the same time. For example, the statement

$$X := X + 1;$$

could be executed by several tasks, each having its own copy of the variable X. None of these tasks need be affected by the others.

Ada uses priority to control the interprocess synchronization in concurrent systems. Each task is given a *base priority*. A programmer can specify the initial base priority of a task and can change the base priority later. In addition to the base priority, a task has an *active priority*, which is the value actually considered when allocating processors to unblocked tasks and choosing the entry call to be serviced next. Normally the base priority and active priority of a task are the same. The initial base priority of a task can be specified by the Priority pragma in the following form:

pragma   Priority (expression);

where the expression is of type integer in a range defined by the implementation. This statement can be placed in a task type declaration or single task declaration to specify the initial base priority for all tasks of that task type. Whenever two tasks are competing for either the processor or an entry queue, the one with the higher priority will be chosen. A synchronization point is a point in computation at which a scheduling decision must be made with regard to the associated priority of the tasks; for example, at the conclusion of a rendezvous. If all tasks execute independently of each other, then the allocation of unique priorities will allow the behavior of each task to be predicted. An implementation must use a preemptive scheduler and employ time-slicing, which uses a timer to suspend the computation at a predefined time interval. In addition, the pragma may appear in the declarative part of the main subprogram to specify the priority of the task executing the main subprogram, and in this case, the expression is required to be treated as static.

Process Synchronization

The rules of scope will allow two or more tasks to access variables which are declared in the same or enclosing procedures, and as a result of this action, it is possible for conflicts to arise when multiple processes attempt to access the same data. Ada provides three mechanisms for tasks to synchronize and communicate: *shared variables, protected objects*, and *rendezvous*. A shared variable is a variable that is examined or modified by more than one task. Shared variables must be used with extreme caution because of to the possibility of one task modifying the variable while another task is examining it. This problem can be avoided through primitives defined in the Systems Programming feature. For example,

pragma   Atomic (*name*);

takes the name of a variable, or the name of a type, as a pragma argument. It stipulates two things about the named variable or about every variable of the named type:

- The variable is to be examined and updated atomically, meaning that it is impossible for one task to observe such a variable in a state in which it is partially updated by another task.
- No temporary copies of the variable are allowed, meaning that every examination of the variable must examine the variable itself, and every modification of the variable must immediately modify the variable itself.

A protected object holds data that can be shared by multiple tasks. A protected object can be manipulated through specific operations. In this case, while one task is executing an operation that modifies the object, any other task attempting to start an operation on that object is forced to wait until the operation started by the first task is complete. Objects of a *protected type* are called protected objects and can be manipulated only through high-level operations provided by the unit declaring the type. High-level operations of a protected type are called *protected operations*. For example, the following package declaration contains a *protected-type declaration*.

```
package     Protected_Queue   is
     protected type     Protected_Queue_Type is
          procedure   Enqueue (Item: in Integer);
          entry Dequeue (Item: out Integer);
          function Length return Natural;
     private
          Queue:    Queues.Queue_Type;
     end   Protected_Queue_Type
end   Protected_Queue
```

A protected-type declaration and its protected body together constitute a protected unit. Each Protected_Queue_Type object has a single component named Queue of type Queue_Type and three operations named Enqueue, Dequeue, and Length. A protected type can have three kinds of protected operations: *protected procedure*, such as Enqueue, *protected entries*, such as Dequeue, and *protected functions*, such as Length. If PQ is an object of a protected type and N is an object of type Integer, then the statement

$$PQ.Enqueue(N);$$

is a call on the protected procedure Enqueue of protected object PQ with parameter N. Similarly, the statement

$$PQ.Dequeue(N);$$

is a call on the protected entry Dequeue of protected object PQ with parameter N, and the expression on the right-hand side of the statement

$$N := PQ.Length;$$

is a call on the protected function Length of protected object PQ. The part of the protected-type declaration following the word **private** is called the *private part* of the protected-type declaration.

A rendezvous is an interaction during which two tasks synchronize and one provides a service to the other through an interface much like a procedure call. Ada allows a process to be synchronized with another process at particular points in their execution. The communication is synchronous, meaning that the first task to arrive must wait for the arrival of the second task. This synchronization point is called a rendezvous. Two tasks must meet in a rendezvous in order to communicate. However, the location of the rendezvous belongs to one of the tasks, which is called the **accepting** task. The other task, called the **calling** task, must know the identity of the accepting task and the name of the location of the rendezvous, which is called the **entry**. This indicates that when one task calls an entry of a second task and the second task accepts that call, a rendezvous takes place. The Ada rendezvous is a primitive with the following characteristics:

- Synchronous, unbuffered communication
- Asymmetric identification, meaning that the sender knows the identity of the receiver, but not the reverse
- Two-way data flow communication during a single rendezvous

It is clear that two processes wishing to make a rendezvous may not arrive at the point of synchronization at the same time, and in fact it is extremely unlikely that this will happen. A rendezvous between two Ada tasks is similar to a rendezvous between two people, meaning that whichever arrives at the appointed meeting place first waits for the other. Once the meeting is complete, each task continues about its own business independently. This indicates that when the two processes do meet, the entry code is executed jointly by the two processes, after which they part and go their separate ways. It is important to emphasize that both tasks are executing concurrently and independently, except at points where they synchronize. We illustrate this situation in Figure 10.1. The synchronization between tasks can be performed through *entries*. One task executes an *entry call*, which looks very much like a procedure call. Another task *accepts* the entry call. For instance, a task named Counter might have an entry declared as follows:

entry   Increment (Amount: **in** Integer; New_Total: **out** Integer);

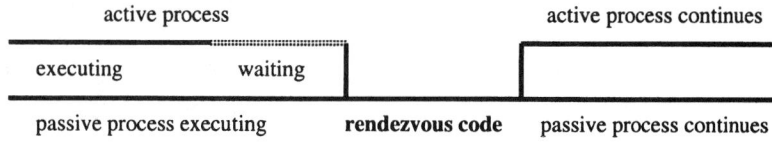

(a) The active process requests a rendezvous before the passive process is ready to receive the request and therefore has to wait.

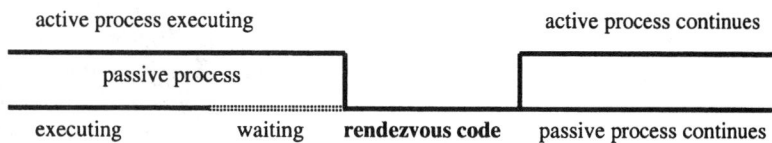

(b) The passive process has to wait pending the arrival of a request from the active process.

Figure 10.1. The synchronization between two processes.

This means that calls on the entry Increment can have the same form as calls on a procedure with two arguments of type Integer, the first of mode **in** and the second of mode **out**. Another task can communicate with task Counter by issuing an entry call like:

Counter.Increment(X, Y);

The task Counter accepts this entry by executing an *accept* statement such as the following:

```
accept   Increment(Amount: in Integer;
            New_Total: out Integer) do
      Total : = Total + Amount;
      New_Total := Total;
end   Increment;
```

where the *accept* statement is then executed with Amount representing the value of X and with Y receiving the value assigned to New_Total. This process is called a rendezvous for the duration of the execution of the *accept* statement. This *accept* statement may be empty when the only purpose is to have a synchronization.

Once the *accept* statement is complete, the task issuing the entry call Counter.Increment(X, Y) can go on with the next statement. As we see, a rendezvous is like a procedure call with the *accept statement* as a procedure body except that the *accept* statement is one of the steps executed in sequence by the task Counter. The completion of the entry call can occur only when the task Counter reaches the *accept* statement.

If a task executes a call on the entry Counter.Increment(X, Y) before Counter has reached the *accept* statement, the task executing the entry call is forced to wait. Similarly, if Counter reaches the *accept* statement before an entry call has been executed, it waits for some task to call the appropriate entry.

A Sample Program

In this program, we consider a solution to the bounded buffer problem, which occurs when several tasks called *Producers* wish to communicate a series of produced items to other tasks called *Consumers*. In the sequel it will be convenient to suppose that the buffer is of finite capacity, in to which the *Producers* deposit items and from which the *Consumers* remove items when ready. The synchronization must be performed in such a way that the *Producers* will not deposit items when the buffer is full and the *Consumers* will not try to remove items when the buffer is empty. In view of this disparity in the intensity of communication, the buffer itself must be regarded as a task called a passive task, which accepts requests from services from the active tasks, *Producers* and *Consumers*.

The outline of the program is illustrated in Figure 10.2, where the reserved words **in** and **out** indicate input and output parameters, respectively, and the statements between **do** and **end** perform the service associated with the entry procedure.

```
--BOUNDED BUFFER PROBLEM
    --specification of task allows items to be deposited and
        removed
    --from a buffer, meaning that it accepts calls to the
        procedures
    --Deposit and Remove from other tasks.
task   Bounded_Buffer   is
       entry Deposit(Item : in Message);
       entry Remove(Item : out Message);
```

```
end     Bounded_Buffer;
task    body    Bounded_Buffer    is
begin
        --statements
        accept Deposit(Item : in Message) do
        --statements
end;

        accept Remove(Item : out Message) do
        --statements
end;
end     Bounded_Buffer;


task    type    Producer    is
end     Producer;
task    body    Producer    is
        Item : =Message;
        begin
            loop
                --produce item
                Bounded_Buffer.Deposit(Item
                exit when Finished;
            end loop;
end     Producer;


task    type    Consumer    is
end     Consumer;
task    body    Consumer    is
        Item : =Message;
        begin
            loop
                --consume item
                Bounded_Buffer.Remove(Item
                exit when Finished;
            end loop;
end     Consumer;
```

Figure 10.2. A solution for the bounded buffer problem.

10.2   Parallel Programming with Occam

Occam was developed by the Inmos Company, whose main activity is the design and implementation of chips called transputers [Hoare 78, 85, Inmos 88, Jones 88]. The approach was based on the ideas originally developed by Tony

Hoare in the late 1970s. Occam is specifically designed to be used on transputers. A transputer is a single-chip computer with a processor, local memory and four specified input/output links (channels). A transputer is either a 16-bit or 32-bit processor providing 10 million instructions per second processing power with 2 Kbytes of memory. Each link is capable of transferring 10 megabits per second and the links enable transputers to communicate with each other. The links make it possible for any number of transputers to be joined together to form a network of computers with all the transputers capable of operating concurrently. Thus, an Occam program consists of several processes that can be mapped onto any number of these transputers, which can run in parallel and communicate by exchanging messages using the input/output links. In general, the number of transputers in the network can be increased or decreased and the program can be executed without changing its description. Figure 10.3 shows an architectural view of transputer systems, including two and four pipelined transputer systems.

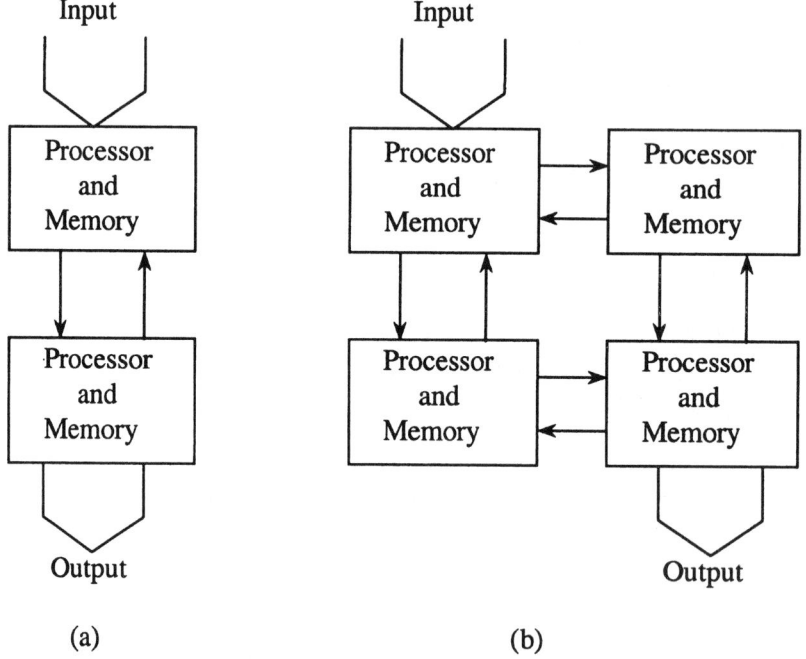

Figure 10.3. (a) Two pipelined transputer system. (b) Four pipelined transputer system.

The philosophy of Occam programming is that a large number of small concurrent processes communicate by fast channels (links) visible to both processes rather than synchronizing of access to main variables. Each Occam process can be resident on a separate transputer or a number of them can reside on a single transputer. The programmer can write the concurrent programs and remain ignorant of the number of transputers upon which the programs will eventually run. It is even possible to write an Occam program which can be run on a network of transputers which will determine the interconnection pattern automatically. There is a protocol associated with each link defining the signature of the data that can flow through the link. Communication is between each output statement and the corresponding input statement. In Occam, every link is used to connect exactly two processes, one of which performs output statements and the other input statements. This indicates that the behavior of the processes and their interconnection topology are defined before execution.

Generally speaking, Occam is a high-level programming language which is intended to be used for programming many interconnected or distributed computer systems, and the development centers around the concept of describing a system as a collection of concurrent processes. It lacks many high level programming language features such as recursion, data types and pointers. However, it includes different concepts of concurrency and communication as those are available in other languages such as Ada. The concurrent programming model is based on the synchronous communication (rendezvous) used in the Ada programming language. This indicates that two processes must meet in a rendezvous in order to communicate. The first process to arrive must wait for the arrival of the second process. It is important to emphasize that both processes are executing concurrently and they are synchronized only at the rendezvous. There is no terminate alternative and the termination must be programmed explicitly.

In Occam an action that can be performed in parallel is called a process, and every statement (even a low-level assignment statement) has to be declared as a process. It is up to the programmer to specify explicitly whether processes will be combined in sequence or in parallel for execution. This indicates that Occam encourages concurrent programming by setting its syntax very similar to that of sequential programming. In general, Occam primitives are a subset of Ada primitives, and the examples of Occam programming can easily be translated into Ada.

Principles of Processes

There are three primitive processes, as follows:

- **Assignment** process, which changes the value of a variable.
- **Input** process, which receives a value from a channel.
- **Output** process, which sends a value through a channel.

An input process is represented by the statement

Channel ?   variable

meaning that a value is received from the channel (or from a process) and placed in the variable.

Example: user   ?   x

means that a value is received from a process called **user**.
   An output process is declared by the statement

                Channel !   expression

meaning that a value is output along the channel.

Example: user   !   x

means that a value is sent to a process called **user**. An assignment process is indicated by

$$x := x + 1$$

which increments the value of x by 1.

   Example: Assume processes A and B square their inputs and pass them on to process C which adds them together.

user	?	x	process A receives a value from the user
C	!	x * x	process A passes the square to process C
user	?	y	process B receives a value from the user
C	!	y * y	process B passes the square to process C
A ?	x ‖	B ? y	process C accepts two inputs which may arrive in any order from processes A and B
user	!	x + y	user receives the sum of the inputs from process C

As we can see, processes A and B perform a sequence of sequential operations, and C accepts the inputs from A and B in any order to perform a sequence of operations.

Principles of Constructors

In addition to these three primitive processes, processes can be combined to make three constructors for forming more complex processes, as follows:

- **SEQ**: Sequential constructor causes its component processes (statements) to be executed one after another sequentially and terminates when the last component is finished.
- **PAR**: Parallel constructor causes its component processes to be executed concurrently and terminates when all components are finished.

- **ALT**: Alternative constructor chooses one of its component processes from among several processes for execution and terminates when the selected process is finished.

In addition, there is a conditional process which selects the first component process whose Boolean expression is true for execution and then terminates, and a repetitive process which executes the component process for as long as the Boolean expression is true. These three processes could have been combined into one Occam program, as follows, in which we can declare the channels as well as the constructors.

```
CHAN      intoa,    intob,    outtoc1, outtoc2, result:
PAR
      VAR x:
      SEQ
          intoa    ?  x
          outtoc1  !  x * x
      VAR x:
      SEQ
          intob    ?  x
          outtoc2  !  x * x

      VAR x, y, SUM:
      SEQ
          PAR
                outtoc1  ?  x
                outtoc2  ?  y
          SUM := x + y
      user   !  SUM.
```

Occam allows processes to be named and parameters to be used to describe them. This can allow the above program to be rewritten as follows:

```
PROC  square(CHAN in, out)  =
      VAR x:
      SEQ
          in ?  x
          out    !  x *x
PROC  sum(CHAN in1, in2, out)  =
      VAR x, y, SUM:
      SEQ
          PAR
                in1    ?  x
                in2    ?  y
```

```
            SUM := x + y
         out   !   SUM
CHAN   intoa, intob, outtoc1, outtoc2, result:
PAR
         square(intoa, outtoc1)
         square(intob, outtoc2)
         sum(outtoc1, outtoc2, result).
```

In the program, a local variable must be used to hold a value which is the input of the process. This can be accomplished by

VAR   variable_name:

where the variable cannot be accessed outside the scope of the process, it will be associated with the process that follows, and it has been declared without data type. The sum of the input values of process C can be calculated using an assignment process utilizing the variable SUM to store the result.

To enable the program to deal with a series of input values, a loop should be introduced. This can be achieved by the use of a repetitive process to form an infinite loop. For example, assume there are two adder processes with similar characteristics acting in parallel such that each one accepts an input value and performs an addition process. They could be declared as follows:

```
CHAN      In1,  In2:
CHAN      Out1, Out2:
VAR       Sum1, Sum2:
SEQ
    Sum1  : = 0
    Sum2  : = 0
    PAR
            - - FIRST ADDER PROCESS
            While TRUE
                    VAR   Item1:
                    SEQ
                            In1   ?   Item1
                            Sum1  :=  Sum1 + Item1
                            Out1  !   Item1
            - - SECOND ADDER PROCESS
            While TRUE
                    VAR   Item2:
                    SEQ
                            In2   ?   Item2
                            Sum2  :=  Sum2 + Item2
                            Out2  !   Item2
```

The constructor **PAR** indicates that any following processes can be executed in parallel, in this case two adder processes. Both processes proceed independently and receive values from different channels. They sum these values and output the values to other channels. Thus, PAR and SEQ can be followed by any number of component processes, each starting on a new line as a separate process. When a process has a number of channels associated with it and wants to select one of the component processes, the alternative constructor has been provided. In general, when a process encounters such a constructor it means that one of several alternative actions or processes may be chosen at that stage of the execution. There is a guard associated with each process of the alternative constructor to introduce a different choice criterion for each process. The guard can consists of a Boolean expression followed by an input. The Boolean expression must be true for the process to be selected. Thus, if the condition is true and input is provided, the component process can be selected; otherwise, the next component will be checked. For example,

$$(x > 0) \quad \& \qquad input1 \quad ? \qquad number1$$

indicates that the value of x is positive and a value is input from channel input1. An alternative constructor waits until at least one of the processes is ready to execute. One of the ready component processes is then selected at random and executed. After execution of the process the constructor terminates. The following example illustrates the use of the ALT constructor with two component processes, each requiring an input before execution.

```
ALT
    - - FIRST ADDER PROCESS
(value > 0) &  input1    ? number1
            Sum := Sum + number1
    - - SECOND ADDER PROCESS
                input2    ? number2
            Sum := Sum + number2
```

The first process has a Boolean expression which must be true before it is chosen. If the conditions of both processes are satisfied, then one of the processes is chosen at random and executed. If only one process is ready, that alternative component is chosen. If neither processes is ready then the alternative process waits. The replicator constructor is provided to enable the constructors SEQ, PAR and ALT to execute some number of times. It takes the following forms:

```
SEQ   i = [0 FOR N]
PAR   i = [0 FOR N]
ALT   i = [0 FOR N]
```

where the initial value of i is zero, it is increased by 1, and it is iterated N times.

For example, the construct

$$\text{PAR} \quad i = [0 \text{ FOR } 10]$$

creates 10 replicated parallel processes, each with value of i in the range 0 to 9.

Communicating Processes

In the above example, the processes do not communicate with one another since each one operates on its own variables, which are not shared with or required by the other parallel process. If the processes wish to communicate then the same channel must be used by both processes to form a communication link between them. One of the processes may output to the channel while the other one inputs from the same channel. In general, a process may communicate with any number of channels. Here, we present a simple Occam program that runs on several processors and performs inpterprocess communication utilizing the main memory of the system. The main memory consists of 1 Mbyte of multiported RAM used to hold the source and destination data for the interprocess communication. The program causes each process running on a processor to transmit messages to its nearest neighbors in the hypercube. The processes then conclude by printing a message indicating their position in the hypercube and the processes from which they have received a message.

It is worth noting that the nearest neighbors to a processor are those whose processor numbers differ by one bit when that processor number is represented in binary notation. For example, processor number 7 (binary 111) has nearest neighbors 3 (binary 011), 5 (binary 101), and 6 (binary 110). The number of the link that connects two adjacent processors is equivalent to the bit position of the differing bit plus one. It can therefore be seen that processor number 7 communicates with processor number 3 over link number 3 (bit position 2 plus 1), and processor number 5 communicates with processor number 4 over link number 1 (bit position 0 plus 1).

```
1    DEF    dimension = 3
2    VAR neighbor[dimension]
3    DEF recvaddr = #80000:
4    PUTBYTE(processor, #40000)
5    SEQ
6        Set.links(4, 1, 2, 3)
7        SEQ i = [1 FOR dimension]
8            PAR
9                byte.slice.output(i, #40000, 1)
10               byte.slice.input(i, recvaddr + (i - 1), 1)
11           release.links
12           hkeep(status)
13           hwrite.string("Processor Number ",0,processor,status)
```

```
14      hwrite.int(processor, 0, processor, status)
15      hwrite.string(" Received Messages from Processor
            Numbers #",  0, processor, status)
16      SEQ i = [0 FOR dimension]
17         SEQ
18            GETBYTE(neighbor[i], recvaddr + i)
19            hwrite.int(neighbor[i], 0, processor, status)
20            hwrite.string(" ", 0, processor, status)
21      hwriteln(0, processor, status)
22      hrelease(status)
```

The interpretation of the program is as follows:

- Line 1 declares a constant that represents the number of dimensions in the cube, meaning that the program uses eight (2^3) processors.
- Line 2 declares an array that holds the processor number of all processors sending messages to this processor.
- Line 3 declares a constant that represents the address in main memory where processor values received from neighboring processors are stored.
- Line 4 stores this processor number at byte address 40000 (hexadecimal) in main memory.
- Line 5 is an Occam control structure indicating the sequential execution of the following statements. The control structure encloses all statements from lines 6 through 22. This is the Occam method of representing control structure hierarchy.
- Line 6 wires the link multiplexors for a particular pattern of communication between processors; for example, links 1 to 4 will be activated.
- Line 7 is an Occam-style DO loop structure to be executed sequentially. This encloses lines 8 to 10.
- Line 8 is an Occam control structure performing the statements in parallel and enclosing lines 9 and 10.
- Line 9 indicates that one byte of data is output to link i from an address in main memory.
- Line 10 indicates that one byte of data is input on link i to a different address in main memory.
- Line 11 unwires the links from this communication.
- Lines 13 to 22 display the termination message of this interprocess communication to address which processor number (processor address in the hypercube) receives messages from neighboring processors in an 8-processor system as represented in the following.

Processor Number 0 Received Messages from Processor Numbers 1 2 4
Processor Number 1 Received Messages from Processor Numbers 0 3 5
Processor Number 2 Received Messages from Processor Numbers 0 3 6
Processor Number 3 Received Messages from Processor Numbers 1 2 7

Processor Number 4 Received Messages from Processor Numbers 0 5 6
Processor Number 5 Received Messages from Processor Numbers 1 4 7
Processor Number 6 Received Messages from Processor Numbers 2 4 7
Processor Number 7 Received Messages from Processor Numbers 3 5 6

Matrix Multiplication Program

We present the matrix multiplication using a square array of transputers. The program calculates C = AB, where C, A and B are all square matrices. Each transputer performs a simple calculation such as multiplying two input values and adding them to a third value. The calculated values are then passed to neighboring transputers using the associated output links. Assume the following matrices in a 4-transputer system:

$$A = \begin{bmatrix} 2 & 3 \\ 4 & 5 \end{bmatrix} \qquad B = \begin{bmatrix} 3 & 4 \\ 5 & 6 \end{bmatrix}$$

where the algorithm inputs the values of matrix A from the west and matrix B from the north to transputers as illustrated in Figure 10.4. Figure 10.4 (a) provides the input data to transputers. The top left transputer calculates the product of its input values, stores the result in its local memory and transfers the output to its south and east neighboring transputers as shown in Figure 10.4 (b). Now three transputers can operate in parallel by producing the product of their input values from neighboring transputers as illustrated in Figures 10.4 (c) and (d). The calculation continues until all input values are used by the transputers to produce the final product as shown in Figure 10.4 (e).

The Occam program is presented as follows such that all the transputers are declared in an array of size 2 ∗ 2. The input values are input from the NORTH and WEST channels, multiplied and added to the local value C, after which the values are output on SOUTH and EAST channels. The channels are required for passing the results between transputers, and the procedure MULT is used to express the individual transputers in the array of transputers.

```
DEF SIZE = 2
PROC   MULT(CHAN  NORTH, SOUTH, EAST, WEST) =
       VAR A, B, C
       SEQ
          C : = 0
          SEQ   I = [0 for SIZE]
                SEQ
                   PAR
                         NORTH ? A
                         WEST  ? B
                   C := C + (A * B)
                   PAR
```

```
                    SOUTH ! A
                    EAST  ! B:
CHAN COLUMN[SIZE * (SIZE + 1)]:
CHAN ROW[SIZE * (SIZE + 1)]:
PAR
        PAR   I = [0 FOR SIZE]
            PAR J = [0 FOR SIZE]
                MULT  (COLUMN[((SIZE +1) * I) + J],
                    COLUMN[(((SIZE +1) * I) + (J+1))],
                    ROW[(SIZE*I)+J],
                        ROW[(SIZE*(I+1))+J])
```

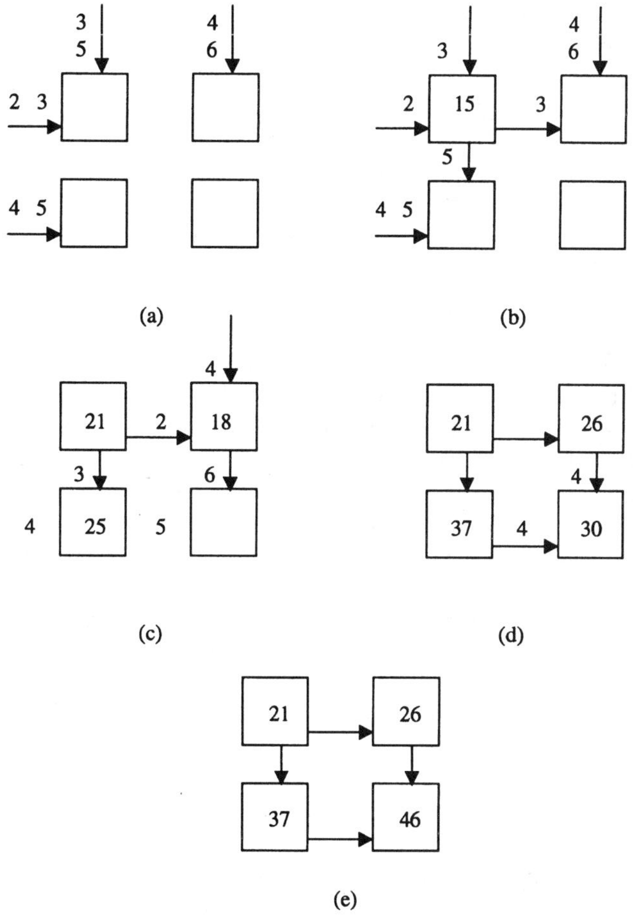

(a)   (b)

(c)   (d)

(e)

Figure 10.4. Occam matrix multiplication program with 4-transputer system.

10.3   Parallel Programming with Modula-2

Modula was a special-purpose language designed by Wirth [Wirth 77] for programming large systems and also real time control systems. Modula was based on the Pascal programming language but included important structuring features of multiprocessing facilities such as processes, interface modules and signals. An interface module is the same as the monitor structure, and a signal is similar to a condition variable. The language Modula-2 [Wirth 85] is referred to as a direct successor of Modula, which is itself a descendent of Pascal. Modula-2 combined some of the better features of both Pascal and Modula, and it was designed primarily for implementation on a conventional single processor, meaning that it required less facilities for controlling the interaction of processes.

The fact is, it was via Modula that the facilities for handling concurrency were introduced. The language has no mechanism for mutual exclusion or synchronization. During the design, the direct implementation of processes and monitors was removed and the tools for handling process creation and switching between processes were simplified and were based on co-routines with transfer procedures. In general, on a single-processor system the type of parallelism which is provided is more described as quasi-parallelism since the single processor is switched between different processes in such a way that only one process is active at any time.

Thus the parallelism within Modula-2 is the illusion of the execution of concurrent processes, because of a design decision that the implementation would run on a single-processor architecture. In Modula-2 the program is used to describe several processes that interact with each other, but only one process is active at any time. A sufficient tool to handle this type of execution is the co-routine. Thus a process in Modula-2 is represented as a co-routine, and the words are used interchangeably. A co-routine is executed independently (not concurrently) from other co-routines, and control is passed between co-routines via specific statement in their codes. A program is terminated if any of the co-routines reaches the end of its procedure body, and when a program terminates all its co-routines are automatically terminated. The main points to note about the Modula-2 language support for the representation of concurrent programs are:

- The Modula-2 facilities are low level compared with those provided in the monitor-based languages. This means that these facilities are easy to implement and the language is easy to transport.
- Modula-2 allows the synchronization operations to be defined by the programmer, meaning that programmers can define their own concurrency primitives.

- Modula-2 allows transfer of control from one process to another to be defined explicitly. Such an operation can be achieved by adding an explicit switching facility to support concurrency.

Principles of Constructs

The main constructs of Modula-2 are *procedures* and *modules*. The role of a procedure is similar to that in most other programming languages. A feature which provides related definitions to be grouped together and which can restrict access to certain variables is called a *module*. The module is one of the most important features introduced by Modula-2. It has the following structure:

```
module   module-name;
   import       lists;
   export       lists;
   data declarations;
   procedures;
begin
   statement-1
   statement-2
   ...
   statement-m
end       module-name;
```

A program can be partitioned into several modules, each one containing its own constructs, variables, procedures, types, and import and export lists such that the declarations are enclosed between the reserved words **module** and **end**. The variables of the module that are available outside the module are listed in the *export list* and all other variables are invisible outside the module. Conversely, the only external variables which can be used inside the module appear in an *import list*. This indicates that the only variables which can be used outside the module by another module are those listed in the export list. Modules are perhaps the most important feature of Modula-2. Modules can be either local or separately compiled. In both cases the visibility of variables is controlled by the use of import. Local modules essentially differ from procedures in their control over the scope and visibility of variables. In general, some of the advantages of the modules can be stated as:

- Modules can be used to define processes.
- Modules can be used to start the execution of processes.
- Modules can be used to perform process synchronization by explicit operations.

- Modules can be compiled individually; thus, when one module is altered, only that module needs to be recompiled.
- New programs can be constructed from existing programs.
- Modules help to separate program development.
- Modules extend the language and allow details of the implementation to be hidden.

Process Creation and Switching

Modula-2 does not provide processes as syntactic units. In Modula-2 a co-routine has the same syntax as a procedure and can be used to change an existing procedure into a process. In Modula-2 each co-routine is represented by a process variable which is a pointer to the actual process, and all references to the process are made through its process variable. To use co-routines it is necessary to import procedures from a library called SYSTEM using two primitives named NEWPROCESS procedure (for process creation) and TRANSFER procedure (for process switching). The procedure NEWPROCESS is a primitive that turns a procedure into a process with four parameters:

PROCEDURE NEWPROCESS(P:PROC; A:ADDRESS; S:CARDINAL; VAR N:PROCESS);

where
1. P is the name of a procedure with no parameter. It is to be turned into a co-routine and constitutes the code of the process. A Modula-2 program terminates when any one of its co-routines reaches the final end in the procedure that constitutes its code. PROC is a standard type defined to indicate a procedure with no parameters.
2. A is the address of a region of memory that can be used by this co-routine which provides the process workspace. The workspace of a process is usually defined as an array variable. The address can be determined by using the standard function ADR, and values of type ADDRESS are pointers to locations in memory.
3. S is the size of the associated workspace obtained by using the function SIZE. The size is to be chosen to reflect the number of local variables. Thus, the user has to decide the size of the process workspace before the call to NEWPROCESS.
4. N is the process variable which is assigned to the newly created process, and by this variable the process can be identified in the system. NEWPROCESS assigns a value to the variable N, which is a reference to the created process. N is of type PROCESS which is exported from the library module SYSTEM.

A graphical representation of a process creation using procedure NEWPROCESS, in which the variable N holds the base address of the process, is illustrated in Figure 10.5 in which the variable N holds the base address of the process.

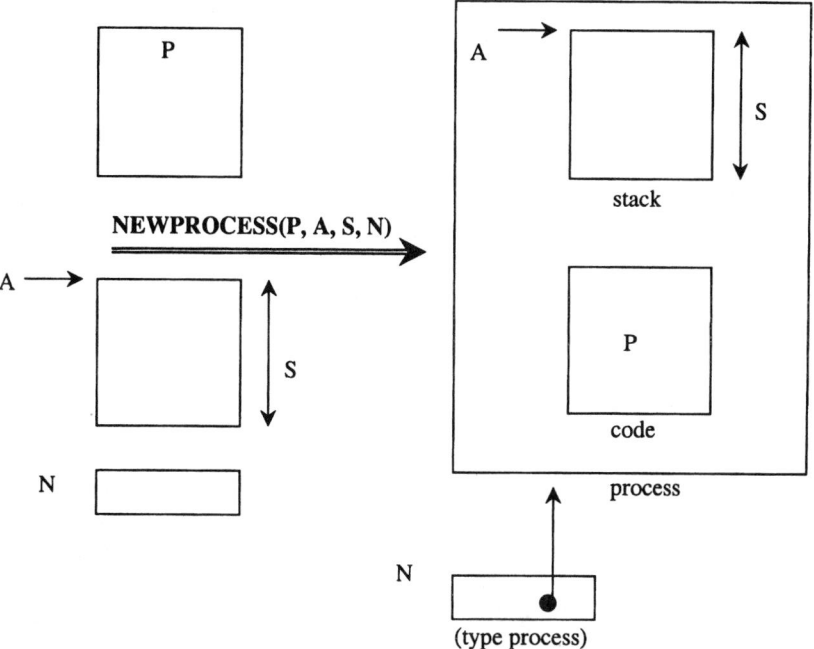

Figure 10.5. Illustration of process creation.

The procedure type mechanism in Modula-2 is used to pass this procedure as an argument to NEWPROCESS. Initially, the program counter contains the address of the first instruction of the procedure P which constitutes the process code. For example, given the following declarations:

```
const Length = 100;
type  Space = array [0..Length-1] of WORD;
var   ADD: Space; Player: PROCESS;
Procedure   GAME;
   ...
   ...
   ...
```

then, the statement

NEWPROCESS(GAME, ADR(ADD), SIZE(ADD), PLAYER);

can create a new process named PLAYER which will execute the procedure called GAME provided by the address space ADD. To be more precise, a process can be created by a call to the procedure NEWPROCESS, and the number of processes is not determined statically. A process created cannot be executed until the execution is granted and will not be released from the processor until this release is explicitly requested. A process can be activated or resumed by calling another system procedure named TRANSFER, which is also exported from library module SYSTEM. The procedure TRANSFER identifies within each process the points at which its execution can be suspended (released from the processor) as well as which process can be granted for the next step of execution. This indicates that a process continues its execution until it decides to give up the processor and then it specifies which process is to be executed next.

The statement at which control is to be passed is identified by a system procedure known as the TRANSFER procedure, with two parameters:

PROCEDURE TRANSFER(VAR N1, N2:PROCESS);

where
1. N1 is the name by which the state of the running co-routine is saved.
2. N2 indicates which co-routine can take control, where the state of that co-routine can be created from the information in this parameter.

In general, the TRANSFER procedure suspends the running process associated with N1 with its state variables saved and activates the process associated with N2. After the completion of TRANSFER, the process associated with N1 is identified as a suspended process, meaning that its resumption is possible by a subsequent call to the TRANSFER procedure. When the process associated with N1 resumes, it continues execution at the point with exactly the same state as when it was suspended. In this way the activities of the created processes are explicitly scheduled. A graphical representation is illustrated in Figure 10.6.

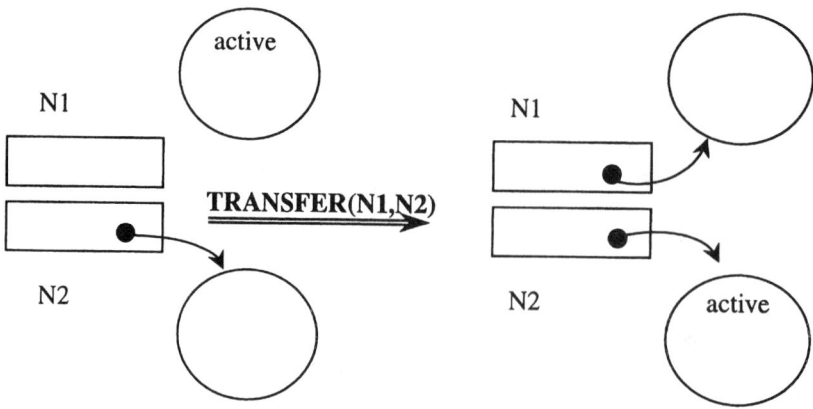

Figure 10.6. Illustration of process switching.

These two procedures are provided in module SYSTEM and are called through the definition part as illustrated in the following code:

```
definition  module   SYSTEM;
type   ADDRESS; WORD; PROCESS;
procedure TRANSFER(var N1; N2:PROCESS);
procedure NEWPROCESS(P:PROC;A:ADDRESS;S:CARDINAL;
    var   N: PROCESS);
end   SYSTEM;
```

The module SYSTEM is a standard module which contains the data types and procedures which refer to low-level operations that are required by a particular architecture or implementation. In general, the declaration of a procedure type specifies the number and type of all parameters and the type of the value returned, if any. For example, the declaration

```
Type  utility  = Procedure (Integer) : Integer
```

declares **utility** as a procedure type. Values of that type must be procedures that have a single parameter of type integer and return a value of type integer. If we declare a variable **specific** as

```
Var    specific : utility
```

then the assignment statement

specific : = *temp*

assigns *temp* to **specific** in which *temp* is a procedure declared in the program with a specification matching that type.

Consequently, the following statement

x : = **specific**(y)

actually invokes *temp*. Similarly, a value of type **utility** can be passed as an argument to a procedure that has a parameter of type **utility**. Generally speaking, a process is implemented by means of a co-routine which is a set of local variables and statements specifying its activities. A co-routine is created by a call to a system procedure NEWPROCESS. It is activated by another system procedure TRANSFER. TRANSFER is used to identify within a co-routine explicit scheduling points, that is the points at which one co-routine resumes another co-routine. A resumed co-routine continues execution in the same state as it was before it relinquished control. In this way control can be transferred among various processes in the system.

A Sample Program

In the following, there is a program consisting of four processes in which three of them are created by calls to NEWPROCESS and the fourth performs the main part. The TRANSFER in each procedure indicates the switching between processes.

```
Module      Sample;
FROM        SYSTEM    IMPORT
            PROCESS, TRANSFER, NEWPROCESS;
Var         P1, P2, P3, P4: PROCESS;
Procedure   Sample1;
begin
   loop
   ...
   TRANSFER(P1, P2);
   ...
   end
End         Sample1;

Procedure   Sample2;
begin
   loop
   ...
   TRANSFER(P2, P3);
   ...
   end
End         Sample2;

Procedure   Sample3;
begin
   loop
   ...
   TRANSFER(P3, P1);
   ...
   end
End         Sample3;

begin
   NEWPROCESS(Sample1,..., ..., P1);
   NEWPROCESS(Sample2,..., ..., P2);
   NEWPROCESS(Sample3,..., ..., P3);
   TRANSFER(P4, P1);
End         Sample;
```

Process Synchronization

Shared variables can be used for synchronization purposes among processes and the processes must access such variables under conditions of mutual exclusion.

A Modula-2 solution encapsulates these shared variables in a module which performs the function of a monitor structure and guarantees mutual exclusion of processes. Modula-2 has a concept known as *signal* and a *condition variable* to identify a queue associated with waiting processes inside a monitor. The *signal* is used to synchronize processes, and each signal is associated with a particular *condition variable*. If the *condition variable* is not true, a process should be delayed. Conversely, if the *condition variable* is found to be true, one of the delayed processes can be resumed. Two operations which are performed on a *signal* are identified by WAIT and SEND and are associated with delaying and resuming a waited process.

Consequently, Modula-2 provides synchronization between processes by means of explicit transfer primitives. A monitor structure and its associated operations can be used to provide for the designation of concurrent processes and for controlling their interaction. The mutual exclusion associated with monitors can be implemented by associating each monitor with a unique *semaphore*. A monitor can be constructed on top of a kernel that supports the abstraction of a semaphore. A kernel is usually provided in the form of a separately compiled module made up of two parts:

1. A definition part that defines the exported objects (here, of type semaphore) and the procedures P, V, Initsemaphore, CreateProcess and StartSystem.

2. An implementation part which constitutes the body of the module (here, the definition of the type Semaphore, the procedures bodies and the data structures handled by the kernel).

The data structures handled by the kernel are a record of type *ProcessDescriptor* and *SemaphoreDescriptors*. A process descriptor contains a flag (to indicate the process is ready or waiting for a signal), the process reference (a field of type PROCESS which designates the process), a link that provides the process to be inserted into a list and two list pointers:

• The Ready list, in which the active process is always the process at the head of this list.

• The Waiting list, which is associated with the semaphore variable.

The flag is an integer used in the implementation of a wait with delay. If this field contains a value different from zero, it means that the process is waiting for a delay to expire and is therefore not ready. When the flag is decremented by one, the process becomes ready. The kernel uses co-routines to support the abstraction of concurrent processes. If we view the kernel together with the hardware on which it executes as a single system and calls to the kernel as abstract

operations, then each co-routine appears to be a process, meaning that we refer
to these co-routines as processes. The kernel supports the abstraction of process
synchronization, and the processes synchronize through calls to procedures
WAIT and SEND and otherwise appear to run asynchronously. Consequently,
to synchronize concurrent processes by using a monitor with condition variables, a module named KERNEL is provided with five parameters: StartProcess,
SEND, WAIT, Queue and Init. The definition module which contains the list of
exported operations and illustrates an implementation of a kernel in Modula-2 is
presented as follows:

```
definition module      KERNEL;

export Qualified SIGNAL, StartProcess,
       SEND, WAIT, Queue, Init;
type  SIGNAL;

procedure   StartProcess(P:PROC; N:CARDINAL);
   (* start a concurrent process with *)
   (* associated program P and workspace N *)
procedure   SEND(var S:SIGNAL);
   (* a process waiting to receive *)
   (* signal S can be resumed *)
procedure   WAIT(var S:SIGNAL);
   (* the running process waits until it *)
   (* receives a signal S from some other process *)
procedure   Queue(S:SIGNAL) : BOOLEAN;
   (* one process is waiting for signal S *)
   (* meaning that queue is not empty *)
procedure   Init(var S:SIGNAL);
   (* initializes the associated queue *)
   (* for signal S to empty *)

end      KERNEL;
```

Process switching occurs only on calls to WAIT and SEND procedures. When a
process attempts to enter a monitor, any process within the monitor must have
its control point at a call to SEND or WAIT. Therefore, mutual exclusion is
automatically ensured. We have assumed a single-processor system, meaning
that mutually exclusive access to kernel variables cannot be violated as a result
of concurrent calls to the kernel by two processes executing on different processors. The rationale behind this idea is that if Modula-2 programs are specified
for execution on a system with a single processor and the processors can be
switched between processes only at specific points, then it is not necessary to
provide mutual exclusion. A new process is created by a call to StartProcess(P,
N) in which a procedure P and a workspace size N are passed as arguments. A

user of the kernel can create a new signal by declaring a variable of type SIGNAL and calling Init(S) to initialize it, meaning that it initializes the signal S and every signal must be initialized before it is used. The procedure Queue(S) is a Boolean function that tests whether the list associated with the signal passed as an argument is empty, meaning that at least one process is waiting to receive the signal S. The procedure WAIT(S) links the descriptor of the executing process to the end of the list associated with the signal passed as an argument, meaning that it suspends the execution of the process which executes it until a signal S is received. Then WAIT searches the list for the next ready process, and if there is none indicates a deadlock situation. The procedure SEND(S) deletes the process descriptor at the head of the list associated with the signal passed as an argument and passes control to the associated process, which causes one of the processes waiting for signal S to resume execution. This indicates that the processes waiting for a signal are treated in a first-in-first-out fashion by the system.

Consequently, this module can provide more detailed control over parallel processing than the use of the TRANSFER procedure in Modula-2. We consider the bounded buffer problem to illustrate the use of the synchronization features of Modula-2 in which several processes (the producers) wish to communicate with other processes (the consumers). This is to be implemented using a buffer of finite capacity such that the producers deposit items into the buffer and the consumers remove items from the buffer. The processes must be synchronized in such a way that the producers will not deposit items when the buffer is full and the consumers will not consume items when the buffer is empty. A solution to this problem is given in Figure 10.7.

The solution is formulated in terms of a module BoundedBuffer which performs the monitor mechanism for synchronization between producer and consumer. In this solution Count is the number of items in the buffer and Pointer specifies the position of the next item in the buffer. The module BoundedBuffer imports the required features and procedures (SIGNAL, SEND, WAIT, INIT-Signal) from the earlier module Kernel and exports those procedures which permits another process to use, in this case, the Deposit and Remove procedures. To synchronize the consumers and producers accessing the buffer, two signals are required: *notempty*, which will delay a consumer if there is nothing in the buffer to be removed, and *notfull*, which will delay a producer if there is no more space left in the buffer for an item to be deposited.

```
definition module       BoundedBuffer;
    export Qualified Deposit;
    export Qualified Remove;
    procedure   Deposit (var Item:MESSAGE);
    procedure   Remove (var Item:MESSAGE);
end         BoundedBuffer;
```

```
implementation module    BoundedBuffer[1];
   from   Kernel        import
   SIGNAL, SEND, WAIT, INITSignal;
   export    Deposit, Remove;
   const N = 20;
   var    Buffer: array[0..(N-1)] of MESSAGE;
          notfull, notempty: SIGNAL;
          Pointer: [0..N-1];
          Count  : [0..N-1];

   procedure    Deposit(Item:MESSAGE);
   begin
          if Count = N then WAIT(notfull) end;
          Buffer[(Pointer + Count) mod N] : = Item;
          Count = Count + 1;
          SEND(notempty);
   end    Deposit;

   procedure    Remove(var Item:MESSAGE);
   begin
          if Count = 0 then WAIT(notempty) end;
          Item = Buffer[Pointer];
          Count = Count - 1;
          Pointer = (Pointer + 1) mod N;
          SEND(notfull);
   end    Remove;
begin
Count = 0;
Pointer = 0;
INITSignal(notempty);
INITSignal(notfull);
end    BoundedBuffer;
```

Figure 10.7. Modula-2 solution for the producer and consumer problem.

Summary

In the parallel processors, processes represent independent actions which can be executed in parallel. This indicates that we need to provide facilities to controling the interaction of such processes. In parallel systems represented by array and vector processors, the computation is performed in a lock-step or over-

lapped fashion. This processing is called synchronous parallelism. As a consequence, the machines in this category do not have the synchronization problems
associated with multiprocessors and multicomputers.

Asynchronous parallelism is the most general form of parallelism, whereby
processors operate freely on tasks, without regard for global synchronization. In
place of the lock-step fashion of the various forms of synchronized parallelism,
the asynchronous method relies on locks and explicit control flow. The mutual
exclusion mechanism is usually implemented by a lock which prevents all but
one process to access the data at any instant in time. All other accesses must
wait until the mutual exclusion lock is removed by the process that originally
placed the lock on the shared data. The second major method is to send a message to all processes to inform them about the applicability of the data access.
This method can be employed by message passing in distributed systems. In this
chapter we presented three asynchronous parallel programming languages, Ada,
Occam, and Modula-2. The message-passing approach has been used in high-
level programming languages such as Ada and Occam. They use the two basic
operations, send and receive, to exchange messages among parallel processes.

Ada was a general-purpose language strongly supported by the U.S. Department of Defense and designed for numerical computations, system programming and applications with real time and concurrency requirements.
Among its features are packages and generics, designed to aid the construction
of large modular programs. In Ada the transfer of data is direct and synchronized. Ada was probably the best example available of a state-of-the-art concurrent programming language, but it was not intended for fine-grained parallelism.
An Ada program consists of a procedure, in which Ada makes a careful distinction between the declaration part, known as elaboration, and the other parts,
known as executable statements. We discussed the architecture model and process definition to address synchronization and communication between processes. In Ada the processes rendezvous to exchange information and then continue their activity in parallel and independently. A classic example known as
the bounded buffer problem addressed the structure of an Ada program.

The Occam programming language was developed by the Inmos Company
to be used on transputers, which is a single-chip computer with a processor, local memory and four specified input and output channels. The Occam programmer assumes the parallel computation environment as a group of MIMD
processes interacting through synchronous message passing. Although the Occam programming language was developed for a particular architecture,
(transputers), it is an architecture-independent programming language, since it
can be ported to other machines, interconnected or distributed computer systems. We discussed the principles of processes, and constructors to address the
communication mechanism used in Occam. A classical example known as the
matrix multiplication problem addressed the structure of an Occam program.

Modula-2, which was a direct successor of Modula, was designed for programming large and real time systems. Modula-2 combined the block and type
structure of Pascal with the module constructs of Modula for defining abstract

data types primarily for a conventional single-processor system. This indicates that fewer facilities for controlling the interaction of processes were required. Modula-2 was a general-purpose language at a relatively low level of design, meaning that it provided visibility of the underlying hardware to be useful for concurrency. A process in Modula-2 is implemented utilizing a co-routine, which is a set of local variables and statements describing the process activities. We discussed the principles of constructs, process creation and switching, including an example to illustrate process switching. Modula-2 provides synchronization between processes by explicit transfer primitives such as semaphores and monitors. Modula-2 supports a concept known as signal and a condition variable to identify a queue associated with waiting processes inside a monitor. To synchronize concurrent processes by using a monitor with condition variables, a module named kernel was provided with five parameters: StartProcess, Send, Wait, Queue, and Init, in which processes switching occurred only on calls to Wait and Send primitives. In addition to interface modules that support monitors, Modula-2 uses device modules to implement abstract I/O, allowing more flexibility in interfacing with the kernel. A classic example, known as the bounded buffer problem, addressed the structure of the Modula-2 program. A good reference about this programming language is [Riley 87].

CHAPTER 11
Data Parallel Programming

SIMD computers operate as data parallel computers by having the same instruction executed by different processing elements but on different data and all in a synchronous fashion. In an SIMD machine the synchronization is built into the hardware, meaning that the processing elements operate in lock-step fashion. A simple example is to add the same constant to each element of the array as illustrated by the following C code:

```
for   (I = 0; I ≤ N; I++)      {
      A[I] = A[I] + K;
      B[I] = B[I] + A[I];  }
```

where the statement A[I] = A[I] +K can be executed simultaneously by processing elements on an SIMD machine using a different index I, $0 \leq I \leq N$. This is illustrated in Figure 11.1. The synchronization between the processing elements is performed after the execution of the instruction. The next step of the computation proceeds with the execution of the statement B[I] = B[I] + A[I] utilizing processing elements in the same fashion as above.

In general, this parallel computation refers to the degree of parallelism at the instruction level. Such languages are called data parallel programming languages, and programs written in these languages are called data parallel programs. Data parallel programs are naturally suited to SIMD computers, meaning that a global control unit broadcasts the instructions to the processing elements, which contain the data, and the processing elements execute the instructions synchronously.

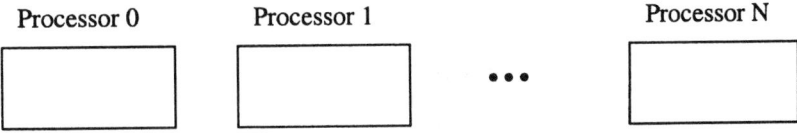

Figure 11.1. Data parallel computation on SIMD machine.

Since data parallel languages hide many architectural characteristics from the programmer, data parallel code is easier to write and to debug, because the parallelism is explicitly handled by hardware synchronization and flow control. In SIMD computation, the control unit to carry out the lock-step execution of SIMD programs enforces the synchronization. However, the ease of programming comes at the expense of increased compiler complexity. Compilers for data parallel languages must map virtual processors onto physical processors, generate code to communicate data, and enforce synchronous instruction execution.

Data parallel computation can be implemented on either SIMD or MIMD computers, depending on the grain size and operation mode adopted. MIMD machines are more general than SIMD machines because they have multiple control units. This capability can be used to advantage when combined with the data parallel programming paradigm and large-grained applications. However, the strict synchronous execution of a data parallel program on an MIMD computer results in inefficient code since it requires global synchronization after each instruction. One solution to this problem is to relax the synchronous execution of instructions. Synchronization takes place when processors need to exchange data. Thus, data parallelism can be exploited on an MIMD computer even without using an explicit data parallel programming language. This can be explained as follows.

Assume there is a *parallel construct* associated with the parallel programming language to specify data parallel operations in which n instances of the statements in the body can be executed simultaneously. One value of the loop variable I is valid in each instance of the body, meaning that the first instance has I = 0, the next I = 1, and so on. A pictorial view of this alternative data parallel computation is illustrated in Figure 11.2. On such a data parallel computation model, instances of the body can be executed on different processing elements (processors) but the whole construct will not be completed until all instances of the body have been executed.

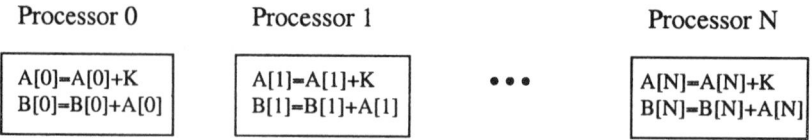

Figure 11.2. Alternative data parallel computation.

When we write in data parallel style on a MIMD machine, the result is an SPMD (Single Program Multiple Data) program in which each processor executes the same program asynchronously. In general, SPMD programs are easier to write and debug than arbitrary MIMD programs. From another point of view,

SPMD programs are a special class of SIMD programs which emphasize medium-grain parallelism and synchronization at the subprogram level rather than at the instruction level. In this sense, this data parallel programming model applies to both synchronous SIMD and loosely coupled MIMD computers. As a consequence, a programming structure we may use is SPMD programming, which means that a single source program is written and each processor will execute its personal copy of this program, although independently and not in a synchronous fashion. The source program can be constructed so that parts of the program are executed by certain computers and not others, depending on the identity of the computers.

Data parallelism often leads to a high degree of parallelism involving thousands of concurrent data operations, and it is applied to fine-grain parallelism. This is rather different from control parallelism, which offers a much lower degree of parallelism at the instruction level. Data parallel languages are modified directly from standard serial programming languages. For example, Fortran 90 is specially designed for data parallelism, and Thinking Machine Corporation designed C* for programming the Connection Machines. A number of commercial parallel computers typically programmed in the data parallel programming mode are available. The names of the companies and their machines are:

- Thinking Machine Corporation, the Connection Machine (CM)
- MasPar Computer, the MP series
- Active Memory Technology, Distributed Array Processor (DAP)
- Wavetracer Corporation, Data Transport Computer (DTC)

Thinking Machine Corporation introduced the Connection Machine Model CM-1 in 1986. An improved version of CM-1 was CM-2, introduced in 1987, with several modifications to increase memory capacity, performance and overall reliability. The company introduced CM-5 in 1991. A general view of Connection Machine architecture is presented in Chapter 1. C* is a data parallel programming language suitable for programming the Connection Machines. C* is an extension of the C programming language specified by the American National Standard Institute (ANSI), meaning that programs written in C compile and run correctly under C*. A Digital Equipment Corporation vice-president formed MasPar in 1988, and the company retains an association with DEC. The company produces a single range of SIMD machines, the MP-1 series, which consists of five models. The range supports a UNIX operating system, ANSI-compatible C and MasPar Fortran (MPF), which is an in-house version of Fortran 90, and an advanced graphical programming environment. The machine consists of processing elements (RISC-like) grouped into clusters of 16 on the chips and connected in a 2-D lattice. A front-end computer (typically a VAX) drives the machine. A general view of this architecture is presented in Chapter 1. Programs written in C and Fortran are executed on the front-end computer and contain procedures written in MPL (MasPar Programming Language).

When the procedures are called, they are executed inside the Data Parallel Unit (DPU). In general, the Array Control Unit (ACU) broadcasts each instruction to all processing elements in the PE Array. Each processing element in the array then executes the instruction simultaneously.

One data parallel programming language is Parallaxis-III, a structured programming language for data parallel programming on SIMD machines which was developed by Thomas Bräunl in 1989. The language is based on sequential Modula-2 but is extended by machine-independent parallel constructs. In Parallaxis an abstraction is achieved by declaring a processing element configuration in functional form and specifying the number, arrangement, and connections between processing elements. With this approach an application program can be constructed independent of the actual computer hardware. Other languages, such as MultiC, pC++ [Bodin 91], and DataParallel C [Hatcher 91] have extended C to data parallel capability as well. The language C* is an extension of the C programming language which supports data parallel programming. Similarly, *Lisp is an extension of the common Lisp programming language for data programming. Other data parallel languages are NESL [Blelloch 90], DINO [Rosing 90] and CM Fortran [Thinking Machine Corporation 93].

11.1   Data Parallel Programming with C*

In 1987, the Thinking Machine Corporation announced the availability of C*, which is an extension of the C programming language designed to support data parallel programming for Connection Machines. It provides a new data type based on classes in C++, a synchronous execution model and some extensions to C syntax. It supports all standard C operations and a few new operations for data parallel programming. In 1990, Thinking Machine announced C*, version 6.0, with different syntax and semantics from the prior versions of C*, for programming CM-2 parallel computers. C* is also available for the CM-5.

The system software of the Connection Machine is based on the operating system, and programmers feel like they are programming an SIMD computer consisting of a front-end uniprocessor attached to a back-end parallel processor. The front-end processor stores the sequential variables and executes the control structure of the parallel programs, issuing commands to the processing elements whenever necessary. Programs have ordinary sequential control flow and do not need any new synchronization mechanism. Indeed, programmers can use familiar programming languages and programming constructs. The front-end can read or write data from or to the local memories of the processing elements. The back-end processors store the parallel variables and execute the parallel portions of the program, each of which has its own local memory. In general, there is only one single flow of control, meaning that at any time either the front-end processor is executing a sequential operation or the back-end processing elements are executing a parallel operation. The processing elements are adaptable, meaning that the programmer can select the size and shape of the processing elements for whatever purpose. For this reason, the processing elements are referred to as *virtual processors*. In addition, the configuration of the back-end processing elements is adaptable between different points in the same program. The programmer's view of C* programming on the Connection Machine is shown in Figure 11.3. Pointers are used for interprocessor communication. A synchronous computation model is assumed by C* in which all instructions are issued from the front end. This allows different processors to have different memory layouts, because they may hold different kinds of data. A structure type called *domain* allows the specification of the memory layout.

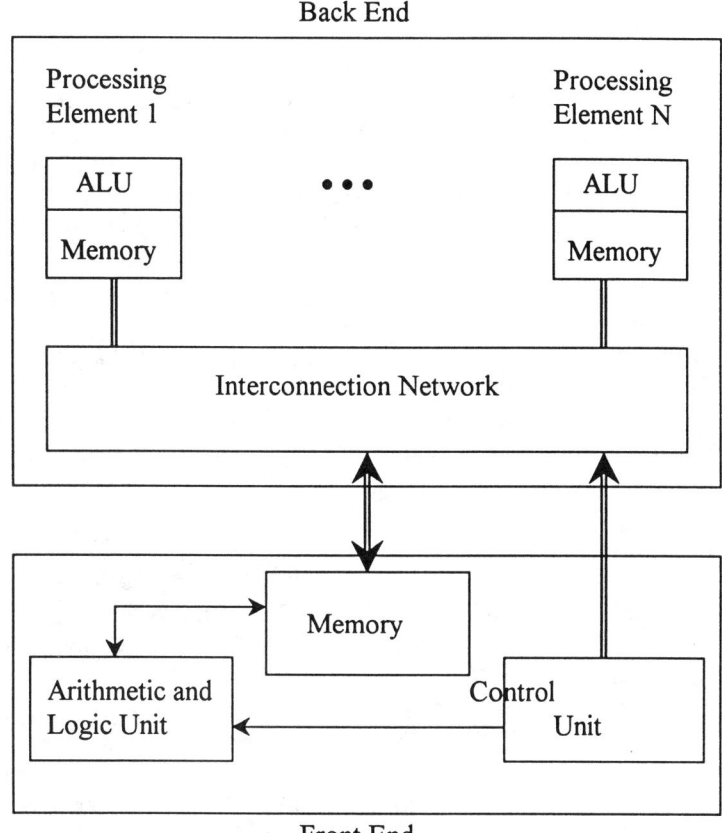

Figure 11.3. Structure of data parallel C* programming model.

Accordingly, the C* code is divided into serial and parallel portions. The code that belongs to a *domain* is parallel and is executed by many data processors, whereas the serial code is executed by the front-end processor. The data are divided into scalar and parallel portions, described by the keywords *mono* and *poly*, respectively. *Mono* data are stored in the memory of the front end whereas *poly* data are stored in the memory of the data processors. In general, at compile time the data are distinguished and scalar operators are extended to operate on parallel data. In addition, there is a new statement in C*, which is the selection statement. It can be used to activate the multiple processors. The C* compiler parses the C* source code, performs data flow analysis and then translates the parallel code into a series of function calls that might be invoked for execution.

11.1.1 Parallel Variables

C language constructs such as data types, operators, structures, pointers and functions are all supported in C*. C* has two types of variables, scalar and parallel. A scalar variable is identical to an ordinary C variable and is allocated in the front-end processor. A parallel variable is allocated on all processing elements and has as many elements as the number of processors. C* introduces the notion of a *shape*, which specifies the way a parallel variable is defined. A *shape* is a template for parallel data and defines how many elements of a parallel variable exist and how they are organized. Each element occupies one position within the shape and contains a single value, meaning that each element can be thought of as a single scalar variable.

In general, by declaring a variable to be of *shape* data type, programmers indicate that they want the ability to perform parallel operations on that variable. For example, the variable declaration

```
shape [10][10] class;
```

specifies a template for a parallel variable with two dimensions and 100 positions. Similarly, the following declares a *shape* of rank four with 5 positions along each axis:

```
shape [5][5][5][5] fourclass;
```

where the declaration specifies a template for parallel variable fourclass containing a total of $5 \times 5 \times 5 \times 5 = 625$ positions. A shape is defined by specifying how many dimensions it has, which is referred to as its rank, and the number of elements or positions (number of processors) in each of its dimensions. A dimension can be referred to as an axis. We can access individual elements of the parallel variable. After a *shape* is specified, parallel variables of that *shape* type can be declared. Parallel variables have a data type, a storage class and a shape. The following statement declares the parallel variable class1 of type integer and shape class.

```
shape [10][10] class;
int : class class1;
```

This declaration creates a parallel variable class1 with 100 positions, each of which is allocated to a different processor. We can access individual elements of the parallel variable class1 by using left indexing. For example, [0]class1 indicates the value of the class1 that resides on the first processor. Similarly,

```
int : fourclass grade[100];
```

declares the 625-position parallel variable grade in which each element is an array of 100 integers. Generally speaking, a shape can reflect the logical organization of the application's data. For example, we can declare a cube *shape* to represent the data of a three-dimensional problem. C* supports the C aggregate data types such as parallel structures and parallel arrays, such that we can declare an entire structure as a parallel variable. For example, consider the following declarations:

```
shape [10][10] class;
struct    list
        {
        int    id;
        float gpa;
        char  grade;
        };
```

where a parallel structure list1 of type *struct list* and *shape* class can be declared as follows:

```
struct    list: class list1;
```

Members of a parallel structure can be accessed by dot notation; for example, list1.id identifies the structure member id in the parallel structure list1.

11.1.2 Parallel Operations

If the operands of an operation are scalar, the C* code behaves exactly as standard C code and the operation is performed on the front-end computer. The situation is different when one or more operands are declared as parallel variables. For example, consider the simple assignment statement:

```
x = y + z;
```

where all three variables are declared as parallel variables. This assignment adds the value of y at the defined shape position to the value of z at the corresponding shape position and stores the result as the value of x in that shape position. Note that the variables x, y and z must be declared with the same shape. Parallel operations occurs in the context of a *with* statement. The *with* statement activates the positions of a *shape*, setting up a context in which variables of that data type can be used in parallel. For example, given the following declarations:

```
shape [10][10]    class;
integer: class x, y, z;
with  (class)     {
      x = y + z;
      }
```

the *with* statement performs an element-wise addition on each component of y and z and stores the resulting values in the corresponding components of x. In other words, it performs a separate addition of the values of y and z in each position of the shape and assigns the result to the element of x in that position.

In general, before we can perform operations in parallel, they must be of the same *shape* (*current shape*), and the *with* statement selects a *current shape* and allows operations on parallel data simultaneously. We can use many *with* statements in a program, making different shapes active at different times. C* has a set of built-in operators, shown in Table 11.1, which are called reductions and which reduce parallel values to scalar values. The result of these operations is a reduction. For example, the following C* program computes the sum of all 100 values of x and stores it in the scalar variable total. In general, the reduction operator += sums the values of all active elements of the parallel variable x and assigns this sum as the value of the scalar variable total.

```
main(){
      integer total;
      with (class)    {
          total = (+= x);
                        }
  }
```

Table 11.1. C* language reduction operators.

Operator	Meaning
+=	Sum of parallel variable elements values
-=	Negative of sum of parallel variable elements values
&=	Bitwise AND of values
^=	Bitwise XOR of values
|=	Bitwise OR of values
>?=	Maximum of values
<?=	Minimum of values

C* also supports a new statement called *where* to provide the ability to perform operations on a subset of the elements of a parallel variable. The positions to be operated on are called *active positions*, and selecting the active positions of a shape is known as *setting the context*. For example, the following segment results in the evaluation of y + z as the value of x only at those positions in the shape where the value of x is greater than zero.

```
with   (class)   {
       where    (x > 0)   {
                          x = y + z;
                          }
                }
```

The *where* statement can include the *else* statement, which reverses the set of active positions, meaning that the active positions when the *where* statement was executed are made inactive, and similarly, the inactive positions are changed to active. For example,

```
with   (class)   {
       where    (x > 0)   {
                          x = y + z;
       else
                          x = y - z;
                          }
                }
```

specifies that the value of y + z and y - z are evaluated as the result of those positions of x in the shape, where the value of x is greater than zero or less than zero, respectively. In addition, C* supports parallel variables and shapes as arguments in standard C functions. This indicates that parallel variables and shapes can be used as arguments to and returned from functions. For example, in the following code a function is called with a parallel variable x of *type* integer and *shape* class.

```
int    add_values (int: class x)   {
       printf("The sum of the elements is %d: ", += x);
       }
```

In addition, it is allowed to use different versions of a function, meaning that functions can be overloaded. The *overload* statement is used to specify the name of the function to be overloaded. For example, the following statements can involve three different meanings of the function, indicating that the function calculate is overloaded:

```
int    calculate(int x);
int    calculate(int x, int y);
int    calculate(int: class x);
```

11.1.3 Parallel Communication

There are two methods of interprocess communication supported in C*, as follows:

- **Grid communication,** in which parallel variables of the same shape can communicate with each other by their coordinates.
- **General communication,** in which the value of any element can be transferred to any other element, whether or not the parallel variables are the same shape.

The function *pcoord* provides a grid communication between parallel variables in C*. The function, when passed a dimension number, returns each element of a parallel variable to its position within the dimension of the shape, meaning that it provides a self-index for a parallel variable along a specified axis of its shape. In grid communication, data can be transferred only a fixed distance along each dimension. For example,

```
[pcoord(0) + 1] source2 = source1;
```

sends *source1* values to the elements of *source2* which are located one coordinate higher along axis 0. Figure 11.4 illustrates the function *pcoord* in which the shape has dimension [3][3] with regard to the execution of the statement:

```
source2 = [pcoord(0)+1][pcoord(1)+1]source1
```

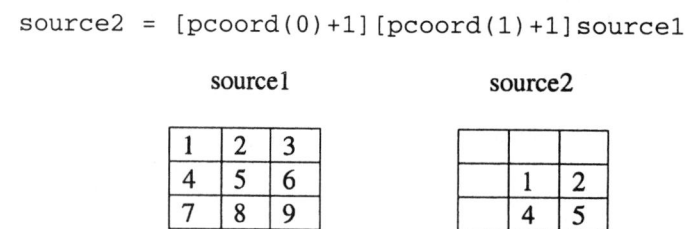

Figure 11.4. Grid communication of a shape with [3][3] dimension.

As a consequence, C* uses the concept of left indexing to provide communication between different shapes as well as within a shape. In addition, *get* and *send* operations are provided in C*. For example, the general form of a *send* operation and a *get* operation is as follows:

```
[index] source2 = source1;
source2 = [index]source1;
```

where index, source2, and source1 are parallel variables of rank one, as illustrated in Figure 11.5.

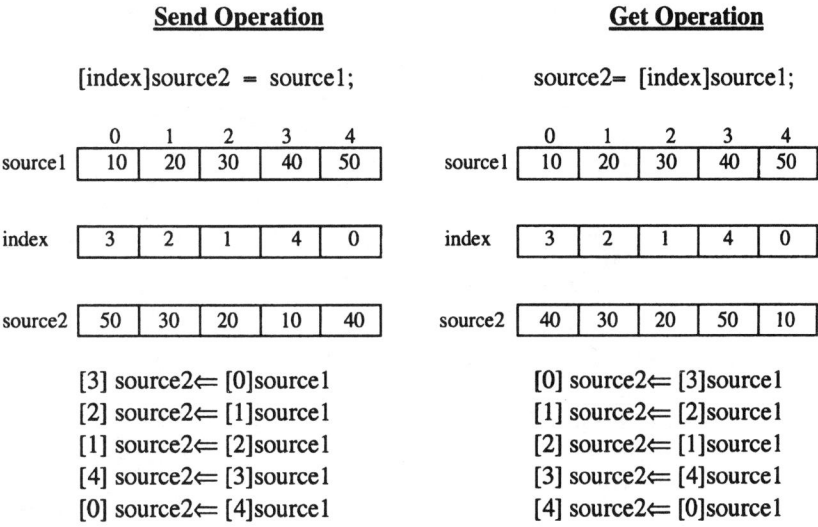

Figure 11.5. Illustration of the *send* and *get* communication operations.

Example: Matrix Multiplication in C*

The program multiplies two $N \times N$ matrices **A** and **B** to result in a product matrix **C**. The program uses $N \times N$ virtual processors as shown by $N = 256$ in line 5. A single shape called **Mesh**, which is a two-dimensional grid of size 256×256, is defined in line 6, which resembles the topology used for matrix multiplication. In general, each shape position computes an element of the product matrix. Line 13 is the start of the **with** statement which puts us in a parallel context. In lines 15 to 17 we perform a circular shift of the elements of matrix **A** such that at the end of this loop each processor has the required row elements of matrix **A**. Similarly, lines 19 to 21 perform a circular shift of the elements of matrix **B** so that at the end of this loop each processor has the required column elements of matrix **B**. In both loops for the circular shifts, the left index of the variable **Buffer** is computed modulo N to achieve wraparound communication. Finally, in line 23 each processor computes one element of the product matrix **C**.

It is worth noting that the program does not specify how many processors are used. In general, virtual processors do not result in the best formulation, and it is recommended to use explicit mapping, meaning that virtual processors are mapped onto physical processors. Virtual processors may be mapped onto physical processors in many different ways, and the best mapping leads to a better formulation. For example, a two-dimensional shape of virtual processors may be mapped onto four processors using block-checkerboard mapping.

```
/* Matrix Multiplication program using 256x256 */
/* virtual processors */
/* The line numbers are for reference purposes */
/* and are not part of the program */

1   #include <stdio.h>
2   #include <stdlib.h>
3   #include <ctype.h>
4   #include <cscomm.h>
5   #define  N   256

6   shape [N][N]Mesh;
7   int:Mesh A[N];
8   int:Mesh B[N];
9   int:Mesh C;
10  int:Mesh Buffer;

11  main ()
         {
12        int   i;
13        with  (Mesh)
              {
14            Buffer = A[pcoord(1)];
15            for   (i = 1; i < N; i++)  {
16                Buffer = [pcoord(0)]
                      [(pcoord(1)+1) %% N]Buffer;
17                A[(pcoord(1)+i) % N] = Buffer;
                  }

18        Buffer = B[pcoord(0)];
19        for   (i = 1; i < N; i++)  {
20                Buffer = [(pcoord(0)+1) %% N]
                      [pcorrd(1)]Buffer;
21                B[(pcoord(0)+i) % N] = Buffer;
                  }

22        for   (i = 0; i < N; i++)
23                C += A[i]*B[i];
              }
         }
```

Example: PI Computation Program

The program is written in C* version 6.0 for a Connection Machine with 8192 processing elements. In line 1 we define **Intervals** to address the number of rectangles. A single shape called **Span**, which is a one-dimensional shape of size 8192 * 16, is defined in line 2 which corresponds to the set of subintervals. Two scalar variables and one variable of type shape are declared in lines 4, 5, and 7, respectively. Line 6 is used for the parallel context with the **with** statement. Line 8 computes the midpoint of each rectangle on the **x** axis. In line 9 we compute the height of the function curve at each of the midpoints. The heights are added and stored as the value of the scalar variable **Sum**. In line 10 we multiply the total height computed as the value of the scalar variable **Sum** by the scalar variable **Width**, which is the width of the rectangles. Finally, the total area as the result is printed in line 11.

```
1   #define Intervals (8192*16)
2   shape [Intervals] Span;

3   main ()
         {
4   double Sum;
5   double Width = 1.0 / Intervals;

6       with (Span)
             {
7             double:Span X;
8             X = (pcoord(0) + 0.5) * Width;
9             Sum = (+= (4.0 / (1.0 + X * X) ) );
             }

10      Sum *= Width;
11      printf ("Estimation of PI is %15.12f", Sum);
         }
```

11.2   Data Parallel Programming with Fortran 90

In the early 1990s Fortran 90 was adopted as an ANSI standard programming language. Fortran 90 is a data parallel programming language which is an augmented version of Fortran 77 with new features such as pointers, user-defined data types, modules, recursive subroutines, dynamic storage allocation, array operations, new intrinsic functions and abstract data types. In addition, it supports extended computational capabilities involving arrays; for example, dot product and matrix computations.

A Fortran 90 programmer has a model of parallel computation similar to a Parallel Random Access Machine (PRAM), as shown in Figure 11.6, which consists of the following components:

- A CPU
- A Scalar Arithmetic Logic Unit
- A Vector Arithmetic Logic Unit
- Shared Memory

where the CPU executes sequential instructions by accessing variables stored in the shared memory. The vector unit stores and fetches data to and from the shared memory, which is controlled by the CPU, to execute the parallel operations.

As a consequence, the compiler partitions the arrays, distributes them onto multiple processor memories and generates concurrent code for computations using these arrays. In general, Fortran 90 supports implicit parallelism by allowing basic Fortran 77 operations and functions to operate on array-valued operands. The basic idea of data parallelism in Fortran 90 is based on array names, meaning that expressions with one array name address all its elements and can be processed concurrently. The array assignment statement and array intrinsic functions are the features that are relevant to data parallel programming. Fortran 90 supports intrinsic functions to manipulate and construct arrays and to perform gather and scatter operations.

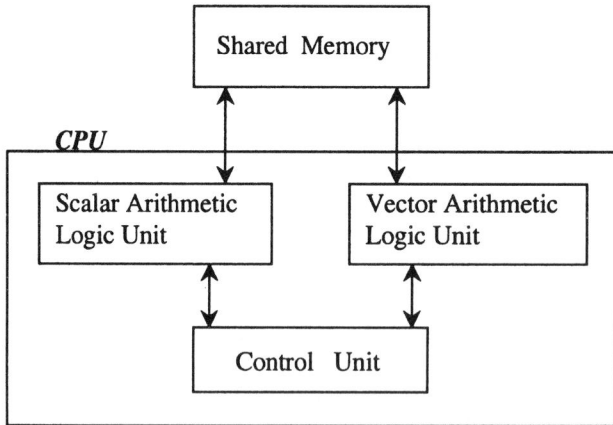

Figure 11.6. Pictorial view of the Fortran 90 parallel computation model.

11.2.1 Variable Declarations

To declare a variable it is required to provide the following, as shown in Figure 11.7:

- *Type* is any of the valid Fortran data types, such as REAL, INTEGER, CHARACTER, LOGICAL, etc.
- *Kind* is an optional suffix that is used with some types to further define *type*. For example, in the following (LEN = 10) is a *kind* that is used to define a CHARACTER type variable that can hold up to 10 characters. LEN means *length* in characters.

  ```
  CHARACTER    (LEN = 10)   ::  . . .
  ```

- [*,attribute*] is a list of Fortran attributes that define special characteristics of the variables in *Variable-List*. Attributes are separated from *type* and from each other by commas.
- :: separates the type description from the variables that will conform to that description.
- *Variable-List* is a list of variable names, separated by commas, which will have the properties defined on the left side of the : : .

This indicates that the programmer may specify explicitly the *kind* as well as the *type* of the variables, as in the following example.

```
INTEGER (kind = long) PRODUCT
INTEGER (kind = short) TOTAL
```

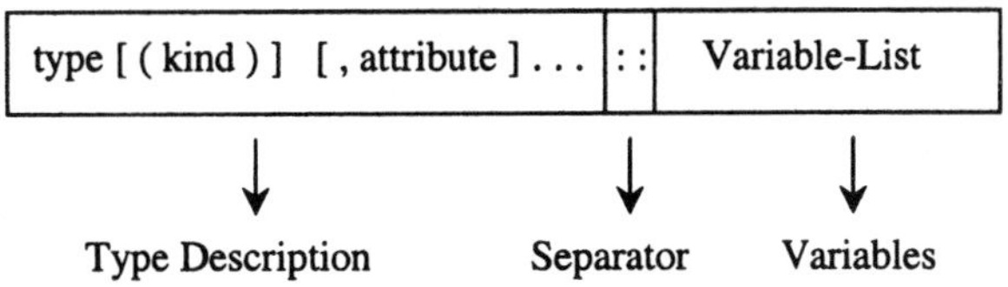

Figure 11.7. Variable declaration.

11.2.2 Array Assignment Statements

Array variables are declared exactly the same way as simple variables, with one exception: the DIMENSION attribute must be used to specify array variables.

The following statement declares an integer array variable Square-Array with ten elements.

```
INTEGER, DIMENSION (1 : 10) :: Square-Array
```

The attribute, DIMENSION (1 : 10) makes Square-Array an array variable, where "(1 : 10)" defines the bounds of Square-Array by specifying how many data elements an array has. All of an array's declared bounds together implicitly define its dimensionality or shape. Array variable Square-Array is called a one-dimensional array, because it has only one set of bounds. Fortran 90 allows a variety of scalar operations to be applied to entire arrays, meaning that the scalar operation is applied to each element of the array. For example, the following scalar operation assigns the sum of X + Y to Z.

```
INTEGER X, Y, Z
Z = X + Y
```

We can apply the same operation to arrays A and B and scalar C. For example, if A and B are 10-element one-dimensional arrays, both

```
INTEGER A(10), B(10), C
DO I = 1, 10, 1
   A(I) = B(I) + C
END DO
```

and

```
A = B + C
```

assigns each element A(I) of A the sum B(I) + C, where I = 1,2,...,10. Other examples are:

```
A = SQRT(A), computes square root of each element,
   A(I) = SQRT(A(I)), I = 1,2,...,10.
A = A * 2,   doubles each element of A,
   A(I) = A(I) * 2, I = 1,2,...,10.
```

Multidimensional arrays can be treated the same as one-dimensional arrays; there are just more sets of bounds. One can think of a two-dimensional array as a grid of boxes in which two subscripts are required to access a single array position. For example, given an array A(1:100, 1:100), the following statement gives the upper-left quadrant:

```
A(1:50, 1:50)
```

We can describe sections of arrays as well. For example, the following two statements

```
Square-Array(1 : 5)
Square-Array(1 : 10 : 2)
```

refer to the first 5 elements of Square-Array and the elements with odd indices, respectively. An array section is represented by specifying a range for one or more subscripts. A range is represented by a triplet that has the following form:

```
Lower-bound : Upper-bound : Stride
```

Figure 11.8 illustrates examples of array sections of array A(1:3, 1:6), an array with three rows and six columns. Different array components do not need to have corresponding subscripts. For example, the following statement can compute the sum A(I) = B(I) + C(I + 1), for I = 1,2,...,7, as illustrated in Figure 11.9.

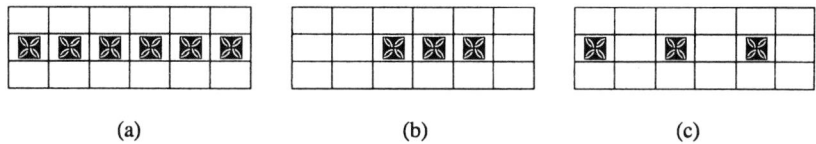

(a)   (b)   (c)

Figure 11.8. Array sections. (a) A(2, :), all elements of row 2. (b) A(2, 3:5), elements 3,4 and 5 of row 2. (c) A(2,1:6:2), elements 1,3, and 5 of row 2.

$$A(1:5) = B(1:5) + C(2:6)$$

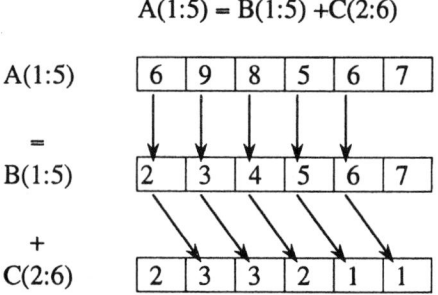

Figure 11.9. Using different array subscripts.

The *where* construct is used to allow an operation on a subset of the array elements. It restricts the array elements on which an operation is performed. For example, the following statement replaces each element of the array that is greater than 10 with its square root plus 100.

```
where (Square-Array > 10)Square-Array =
sqrt(Square-Array)+100
```

In general, the *where* construct divides array elements into two groups, one group corresponding to the elements for which the expression is true and the second group corresponding to the elements for which the expression is false, as shown in the following form:

```
where (logical-expression)
       True-part elements
elsewhere
       False-part elements
end where
```

11.2.3 Array Intrinsic Functions

Intrinsic means "built in" or "part of," and intrinsic functions are those that come in a library for use with a compiler. The intrinsic functions may be used without declaring or describing them in any way, and they are completely known to the compiler. The machine language code for intrinsic functions is added to programs in the linking process, which produces the executable version of the program. All intrinsic functions that apply to scalar values can also be applied to arrays, meaning that the function is applied to each individual array element. A representative selection of intrinsic functions is listed in Table 11.2.

Table 11.2. Selected intrinsic functions.

Intrinsic Functions	Returned value
MAXVAL(A)	Maximum value of A
MINVAL(A)	Minimum value of A
SUM(A)	Sum of A elements
PRODUCT(A)	Product of A elements
MAXLOC(ARRAY)	Indices of maximum value in A
MINLOC(ARRAY)	Indices of minimum value in A
MATMUL(A,B)	Matrix multiplication, A*B
DOT_PRODUCT(A,B)	Vector dot product, A.B
TRANSPOSE(A)	Transpose of A
CSHIFT(A,SHIFT,DIM)	Rotation of elements of A

In general, some of the intrinsic functions return a scalar value (MAXVAL, MINVAL, SUM, PRODUCT), and some of the functions (CSHIFT) return a new array of the same size and shape. For example, if A is a 10-element one-dimensional array, the following two array assignments create the arrays Left and Right with A shifted to the left one element and A shifted to the right one element, respectively, as illustrated in Figure 11.10.

```
Integer   A(10), Left(10), Right(10)
Left    = CSHIFT(A, +1)
Right   = CSHIFT(A, −1)
```

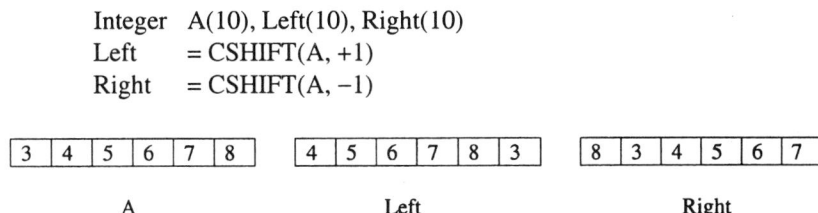

| A | Left | Right |

Figure 11.10. Illustration of CSHIFT function.

Example: PI Computation Program

The program is written in Fortran 90 to compute PI (π) using numerical integration. In line 1 we define *Intervals* to address the number of rectangles. Line 2 declares parameter *Long* to define real variables with 15 digits of precision and exponents ranging from 10^{-50} through 10^{+50}. The variables are declared in lines 4 and 5 as *PI*, *Width*, *X*, and *Y*. Line 6 computes the width of each interval. The array *Id* is initialized in line 7 (declared in line 3) and represents the interval number associated with the array elements. Line 8 computes the midpoint of each interval in parallel and line 9 calculates the height of the function curve associated with each of these points in parallel. In line 10 we multiply the total height computed as the returned value of the *Sum* function by the scalar variable *Width* to result in the total area *PI*, which is printed in line 11.

```
1      Integer        parameter : : Intervals = 131072
2      Integer        parameter : : Long = Selected(15, 50)
3      Integer, Dimension (Intervals) : : Id
4      Real (Kind = Long)  PI, Width
5      Real (Kind = Long), Dimension(Intervals) : : X, Y
6      Width = (1.0 - Long) / Intervals
7      Id = ( / (I, I = 1, Intervals) / )
8      X = (Id - 0.5) * Width
9      Y = 4.0 / (1.0 + X * X)
10     PI = Sum(Y) * Width
11     Print 2, PI
12 2   Format("Estimated PI is", F15.12)
13     Stop
14     End
```

Summary

Think of SIMD systems as a single control unit directing the activities of a number of processing elements, each performing the same instruction by fetching and manipulating its own local data. The data parallel programming approach is characterized by a relatively large number of synchronous processes executing a single instruction stream. One must suitably define the fundamental unit of parallelism in order to execute a data parallel algorithm efficiently on parallel hardware.

The imperative language approach is the one that has received the most attention. In particular, the Fortran-based languages reflect the initial use of parallel computing. In this sense, several different approaches have been developed. Some are languages with explicit parallel features and parallelizing compilers that take a sequential program and detect any inherent parallelism. These language approaches have been developed for machines based on the shared-memory and distributed-memory models. The distributed-memory model has received considerable attention because it appears to be scalable to higher orders of parallelism, whereas the other model is not. Another approach is the explicit method of programming using message passing. However, the effort required to implement the message-passing model can become large due to the inherent complexities of the technique. The SPMD model of programming overcomes such drawbacks by requiring the specification of the data distribution scheme. An SPMD program is a special class of SIMD program which emphasizes a medium-grain level of parallelism. In other words, it applies to both synchronous SIMD and asynchronous MIMD parallel computation models.

In this chapter, we discussed two data parallel programming languages, C* and Fortran 90, which were described as extensions of C and Fortran for specifying concurrency, locality, communication and mapping. The data parallel programming language C* was designed by Thinking Machine Corporation for its Connection Machine processor array. The language C* is a major language for data parallel programming and has been implemented on a number of SIMD and MIMD parallel computers. We outlined the structure of the data parallel C* programming model, which consisted of two parts: front end and back end. The front end consisted of a single processor machine and the back end was a collection of processing elements connected to an interconnection network. The language supports two types of variables, scalar and parallel, in which the scalar variable is allocated to the front-end processor and the parallel variable can be allocated on all processing elements. C* supports a shape keyword that lets the programmer provide the shape and size of parallel data. We discussed the constructs of the language, including parallel variables, parallel operations and parallel communication. We categorized parallel communication into two methods: grid communication and general communication. There is one new statement type called the selection statement which is used to activate multiple processors. We outlined two examples, matrix multiplication and PI computation, to address the program structure, process creation, mapping, synchronization and communication mechanisms.

Fortran 90 is a data parallel programming language which was an augmented version of Fortran 77, with new features such as pointers, user-defined data types, modules, recursion, dynamic memory allocation, array operations, new intrinsic functions, abstract data types and input-output facilities. We discussed the structure of a Fortran 90 program, including features such as variable declarations, array assignment statements and array intrinsic functions. We listed some of the array intrinsic functions that are used in the language. We illustrated a PI computation program to address the computation of the array elements in parallel fashion.

Generally speaking, in keeping with the design methodology of algorithms, C* and Fortran 90 allow mapping decisions to be changed independently of other aspects of a design. Several surveys provide comparative studies of various parallel programming languages and paradigms. In particular, they discuss concurrency based on synchronous and asynchronous system. A representative set of references include [Burns 93, Bernstein 87, 93, Bustard 88, Snow 92, Meyer 91, Fortune 78].

Exercises

1. Define the following terms:
   Data flow languages   Logic languages
   Imperative languages   Functional languages
   Applicative languages   Declarative languages
   Procedural languages   Sequential languages

2. The current Thinking Machines C* compiler demands that the size of each dimension of a shape be a power of 2. Suppose you want to compute the integral using exactly 100,000 rectangles. Modify the program PI presented in this chapter to effect this change.

3. Let us say a language is more high level if the programmer does not have to manage the number of processes explicitly; i.e., if the programmer can think in terms of the parallelism of the problem, rather than the parallelism of the underlying architecture. Using this criterion, rank the following high-level parallel programming languages from most high level to least high level and justify your ranking: C*, Ada, Occam and C-Linda.

4. Construct a Modula-2 program which will output the messages Hello and Mello alternately.

5. Write a DataParallel C program for the implementation of Gaussian elimination as explained in Chapter 8.

6. Write a DataParallel C program for implementation of Gauss-Jordan algorithm explained in Chapter 8.

7. Write a C-Linda program to create 100 parallel processes to perform some function on the first 100 integers.

8. Write a matrix multiplication program using microthreads.

9. Write a parallel version of the shortest-path problem using the thread.

10. Write a program to create a user-specified number of chares using the CHARM parallel programming language.

11. Write a program to illustrate the pack and unpack primitives used in the CHARM parallel programming language.

12. Write a program to illustrate a read-only variable in the CHARM parallel programming language.

13. Write a PCN program to call a Fortran procedure named power(a,b,c) to compute $c = a^b$.

14. Write a PCN program to implement a divide-and-conquer algorithm for summing the elements of an array. The task of summing an array is recursively decomposed into the tasks of summing the left and right subarrays.

15. Write a PCN program to illustrate a match operator to extract the elements of the tuple t.

16. Explain the PVM computation model for the SPMD parallel programming paradigm.

17. Write a PVM program to implement a parallel sorting algorithm that works as follows. One process (the manually started process in PVM) has the list to be sorted. It then spawns a second process and sends it half of the list. At this point, there are two processes, each of which spawns a process and sends them one-half of their already halved lists. This continues until a tree of appropriate depth is constructed. Each process then independently sorts its portion of the list, and a merge phase follows in which sorted sublists are transmitted upwards along the tree edges, with intermediate merges being done at each node.

18. If X is a 50-element one-dimensional array, what is the interpretation of the following codes?

```
DO I = 1, 50, 1
   X(I) = 5 * X(I)
END DO
```
and
```
X = X * 5
```

19. Write an Occam program representing a simple buffer which repeatedly inputs a value and then outputs it.

20. Devise an Occam program which represents the producer and consumer problem.

21. Devise a C-Linda program which represents the producer and consumer problem.

22. Write an EPT program which reads a text file and a string. The program reads the text for all the occurrences of the string in parallel form.

23. It is required to provide the facility of a Stack including procedures Pop and Push in Modula-2 language. Write a Modula-2 module to implement stack data structure.

CHAPTER 12
Artificial Intelligence and Parallel Processing

Artificial Intelligence (AI) has been defined as an area of computer science that is concerned with computer systems that exhibit human intelligence, meaning they allow computers to emulate human behavior. The activities that are involved in AI are classified as: natural language processing, automatic programming and theorem proving, robotics, machine vision and pattern recognition, modeling and representing knowledge, learning new information, intelligent data retrieval, expert systems, problem solving and planning, and game playing [Winston 92]. In general, there are two components associated with artificial intelligence: *knowledge* and *reasoning*. There are different methods to represent knowledge and various approaches of reasoning this knowledge. The computer programs that perform this process are said to exhibit artificial intelligence.

There are several aspects of artificial intelligence which suggest that the application of some form of parallel computation and distributed systems might be appropriate. Parallel processing techniques not only can improve the processing speed, but also can make possible the tackling of large applications that are often difficult if not impossible to handle on a single-processor machine. There are two main areas in which parallel processing can contribute to the study of intelligence systems:

- Production Systems
- Reasoning Systems

In this chapter, the goal is to identify specific processing requirements for these two important AI paradigms. In production systems, the sources of parallelism are identified and parallel execution models and parallel programming languages are presented. In reasoning systems, also called knowledge processing, which are composed of a set of separate modules and a set of communication paths between them, semantic networks represent a viable approach to the adoption of parallel processing. Both general-purpose parallel computers and special-purpose parallel computers may be used for reasoning systems.

12.1 Production Systems

The production system was proposed as a model of human information processing, and it continues to play an important role in AI. Some production system models stress the sequential nature of production systems; for example, the manner in which short-term memory is modified over time by the rules. Other models stress the parallel aspect, in which all productions match and fire simultaneously, no matter how many there are. Both types of models have been used to explain timing data from experiments on human problem solving. A production system program consists of an unordered collection of If-Then statements and is characterized by three components as follows:

- **System State**, also called the *database of knowledge* or *declarative knowledge*, is one of the core concepts of AI-based systems. It is also called *working memory* and stores various facts and rules about the particular application.
- **Production Rules**, which allow the system to change from one state to another, are also called *production memory* or *procedural knowledge*. Each rule has a precondition, and when it is satisfied by any rules in the database, the rule itself can be applied.
- **Control System**, which manages the execution of production rules, allowing the system to evolve according to some desired criteria, is also called the *inference engine* or *control knowledge*. In general, the control system chooses which applicable rule in the working memory should be applied.

In general, databases fall into two classes, databases of objects and databases of rules. It is worth noting that the effectiveness of an AI system depends heavily on the size of its database, so that there is continual pressure to increase the amount of data involved. To solve real and complex production systems often requires tens of thousands of facts and rules which is very difficult to implement on sequential computers. The applicability of production systems has been limited by their slow execution speed. A production rule has the following form:

$$\text{If} \qquad B_1 \& B_2 \& \dots \& B_n \qquad \text{Then} \qquad A_1 \& A_2 \& \dots \& A_m$$

where B_1, B_2, ..., B_n are conditions that constitute the left-hand side of the production rule, and A_1, A_2, ..., A_m are the operations that constitute the right-hand side of a production rule. If the conditions are satisfied, then the rule is applicable, meaning that the database knowledge can be modified according to the operations. By convention, the If part of a production rule is called its LHS (left-hand side), and its Then part is called its RHS (right-hand side). The inference engine (interpreter) is responsible for matching production conditions to the database and deciding which rule should be activated in order to produce the solution. The interpreter executes a production system by performing the following operations:

- Match
- Resolve or conflict resolution
- Execute or act

The basic components of a production system are shown in Figure 12.1.

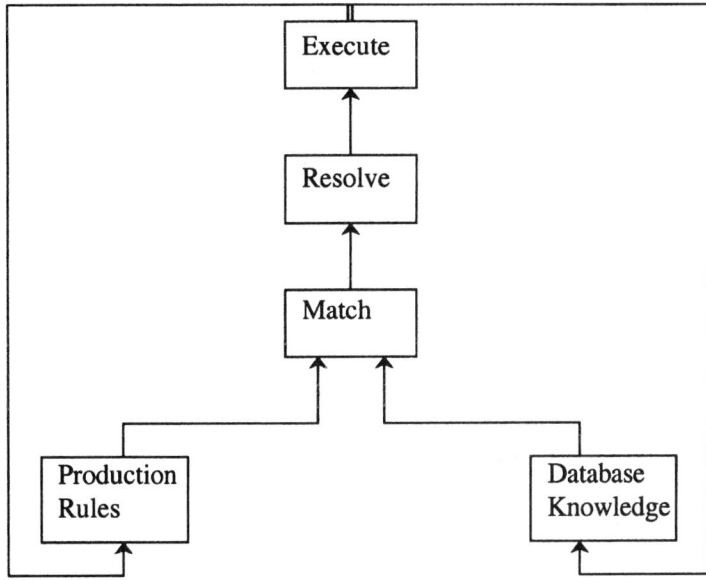

Figure 12.1. Computation model of a production system.

In the *match* phase, the inference engine selects appropriate rules for the problem domain. Then, the problem is to find the set of rules that match the database of knowledge. This can be performed by comparing the rule conditions against the components of the database. As a result of this comparison, rules whose conditions match the database of knowledge are applicable for activation. In the *resolve* phase, called resolution or unification, the inference engine selects the appropriate rule among all candidates that will make sense to execute, meaning that it selects one production rule with a satisfied LHS. As a result of this unification, one rule is selected from all eligible rules. In the last phase, called *execute*, the execution can be performed. This consists of adding, modifying or removing components from the database knowledge, meaning that the RHS of the selected production is executed. In general, a production system can be modeled as a positively weighted digraph, called a *State Space Graph*, where each vertex in the graph is the state of the system, and a directed edge from vertex v to vertex w is a path from v to w indicating the production rule that transfers state v into state w. Given some initial state r (root vertex in the directed graph), we are interested in whether or not we can find a path from r to a *goal* state. A control system for the problem is then simply a search strategy for reaching a *goal* state starting from the initial state r. Typically, the problem is stated as, find any, some or all solutions, in addition to the paths to the solutions, for particular goal.

As a consequence, we can say that a production system is a computer system that has provisions for storing facts and rules and for applying these rules to perform reasoning on the input fact the system is presented with. When the set of rules corresponds to a domain of expert knowledge, the result is called an expert system. In other words, expert systems are AI systems with the ability to perform at the level of a human expert within a specific task domain. For some expert systems, such as MYCIN, which is used to diagnose and recommend therapy for disease, a trained knowledge engineer extracts information from medical experts and then incorporates it into a computer program which would provide the combined wisdom of the experts. MYCIN was written in the Lisp programming language, which is generally acknowledged to be harder to learn compared with the other AI programming languages, e.g., Prolog. These production systems perform useful reasoning based on a set of built-in rules obtained from a human expert. For example, present systems contain up to 10,000 rules and facts and present an equal degree of potential parallelism. Since the production systems can have many rules, the operation suggests several opportunities for parallel processing and provides employment for many processing elements. One way is to assign each rule to its own processing element, which can then search the working memory for facts in parallel with all the other processing elements simultaneously, rather than using sequential methods, meaning that special parallel processing techniques are required for this new computational paradigm.

12.2 Reasoning Systems

Reasoning is the process by which new information is extracted from a knowledge base. A characteristic of the knowledge base of reasoning systems is that only a small portion of the knowledge is stated explicitly, and more knowledge could be made explicit via an inference mechanism. Some of the reasoning techniques for knowledge-based systems include recognition, inheritance, classification, generalization and unification. In general, the reasoning system consists of a set of separate modules, also called agents since each module is acting as a problem-solving entity, and a set of communication paths between them. The supporting architectures range from tightly coupled systems in which there is a completely centralized control mechanism to a shared-memory system in which both control and knowledge are fully distributed. In fact, most reasoning systems lie somewhere in the middle. Some of the distinctive features associated with the reasoning systems are as follows:

- **Modularity**, meaning that the system maintains a collection of modules rather than one huge one.
- **Reliability**, meaning that problem solving can continue even if one of the agents fails.
- **Heterogeneous unification**, meaning that problem-solving techniques and knowledge representation may vary for different parts of a reasoning problem.

One of the important issues involved in the design of reasoning systems is how the actions of the individual agents can be coordinated so that they work effectively. In general, there are two approaches in the design of reasoning systems:

1. **Multi-Agent Planning**, in which one agent is in charge, called the master agent, and decomposes the goal into subgoals which are assigned to the various other agents, called slaves. The slaves perform the tasks and report their results. They may communicate with other agents if necessary to accomplish their results.
2. **Single-Agent Planning**, in which no one agent is in change, although there is a single shared goal among all the agents. They must cooperate both in forming the final result and in executing the associated tasks.

We need a way to represent models of agents, including what they know, what they can do, and what their goals are. Also, it is possible for each agent to build a model of both itself and the other agents with which it must interact. In addition, the architecture of the reasoning system must provide a mechanism for ensuring that the activities of the various agents in the system are coordinated so that the overall problem-solving system achieves its goal, as well as a communication structure that enables information to be passed back and forth among agents.

12.3   Parallelism Analysis

Parallelism in production systems involves decomposing problems and matching expressions containing variables. In general, the application can inolve which type of parallelism is most appropriate and profitable. For example, if a problem is deterministic (has only a few matching rules and facts for any particular subgoal), then the problem may exhibit large-grained parallelism. Parallelism in production systems provides the opportunity for parallel processing, in that the method for solving the problem divides it into tasks that can be executed on different processing elements, and the solution can be constructed from the partial solutions that the processing elements have provided. Generally speaking, there are four sources of parallelism in production systems, as follows:

Task Parallelism

In task parallelism, several cycles are executed simultaneously. The amount of task parallelism available depends upon the nature of the application. For example, in a medical diagnosis AI system, each production rule firing might be dependent on the previous rules, thus providing a chain of reasoning. However, if the system were diagnosing five patients simultaneously, then production rules involving different patients would not interact with one another and could be executed in parallel fashion. In general, task parallelism is a very effective approach.

Match Parallelism

Match parallelism corresponds to parallel versions of the unification phase of the algorithm, meaning that overlap occurs between phases of the production system cycle. In match parallelism, multiple processors are used to speed up the handling of individual match-resolve-act cycles. The paradigm is suited for decomposable problems and the matching of expressions containing variables. Since AI systems spend nearly all of their computation time in the matching phase, it was expected that match parallelism would lead to speedup. There is less optimism today for match parallelism, which corresponds to parallel versions of the unification algorithm used by Prolog [Almasi 94].

OR Parallelism

In OR-parallelism, multiple paths to the same goal are taken in parallel. It comes from trying to solve many parts of one problem at once, or pursuing solutions to a number of subgoals at the same time. It is also called parallelism within a rule. It is called OR-parallelism because success may come from executing the first subgoal or the second, and so on. If all solutions to a query are required, then every subgoal must be examined, and OR-parallelism is highly beneficial. On the contrary, if the goal can be satisfied by producing just one subgoal solution, then OR-parallelism may perform considerable unnecessary computations and is not highly beneficial. As a consequence, OR-parallelism is best suited for applications in which all solutions are required.

Generally speaking, in OR-parallelism the problems are different, indicating that no cooperation and communication or minimal cooperation and communication between the different activities are required. This can involve managing a large and distributed data space. Problems in which one query can produce multiple answers are well matched to OR-parallelism; i.e., database systems. An important aspect of OR-parallelism is that backtracking is eliminated in the execution model. More information on OR-parallelism is found in the paper by Ciepielewski [Ciepielewski 91], who reviewed the scheduling problems in OR-parallel Prolog.

AND Parallelism

In AND-parallelism, the portions of a conjunctive goal are pursued in parallel, meaning that the paradigm tries to solve two or more subgoals in parallel. It involves trying to achieve one goal in several ways at once and works on different problems each as a potential solution to the original goal. It is also called parallelism between rules. In general, to solve the original problem (goal), a series of sets of subgoals are produced in which all subgoals in a subgoal set are working on the same problem. For each set, all subgoals must be solved in order to provide the solution; thus the name AND-parallelism. If there is no solution to a subgoal in a subgoal set, backtracking occurs to a previous subgoal set. Because the subgoals are working on the same query, they share a set of data and variables, indicating the need for cooperation and communication between processes. An advantage of AND-parallelism is that it may produce a single solution more quickly, since different parts of the problem are solved independently, in contrast to OR-parallelism.

AND-parallelism can be classified into two categories, *Restricted AND-parallelism* and *Stream AND-parallelism*, with regard to the concurrent evaluation of shared variables. In restricted AND-parallelism, a compile time analysis and/or a run time system is used to prevent the possibility of conflicts, in which two subgoals share one or more variables. This indicates the paradigm assumes that the arguments being evaluated concurrently are independent of each other. Stream AND-parallelism is the concurrent evaluation of processes that share variables, in which the value of the shared variable is propagated between the processes. When looking for one solution, AND-parallelism provides more speed than OR-parallelism, since the resources are considered on a single potential solution. Combinations of AND-parallelism and OR-parallelism are also possible.

12.4   Parallelizing AI Algorithms

Many AI systems can be solved efficiently by parallel methods, but it is not always a simple matter to convert a sequential algorithm into an efficient parallel one. For example, the analysis of rule dependencies is one of the most important issues involved in constructing parallel algorithms of AI systems. In production systems, for a pair of rules, three dependencies are defined, as follows:

1. **Inhabit dependency**, in which firing of one production rule deletes or adds new rules to the database of knowledge of AI systems.
2. **Output dependency**, in which new rules (added by the firing of one production rule) are deleted by the firing of another production rule.
3. **Enable dependency**, in which new rules (added by the firing of one production rule) satisfy one of the existing production rules, indicating that one of the existing production rules is enabled to be fired.

Divide-and-Conquer is a method for solving a problem by dividing it into subproblems, solving them possibly in parallel, and combining the results [Skiena 97]. If the subproblems are small enough, they are solved directly; otherwise, they are solved by applying the divide-and-conquer method recursively. Parallel divide-and-conquer algorithms can be applied easily in AI systems and become more interesting when they involve cooperation and direct communication among the processes solving the subproblems.

Systolic programming is another approach used in AI systems. Systolic programming [Shapiro 84], which is also called parallelism with locality and pipelining, is based on overlap and balances computation with communication. The approach applies to general-purpose parallel computers. In this scheme, two aspects of the execution of the program need explicit attention. One is the mapping of processes to processors, which should provide the locality of the algorithm by using the locality of the architecture. Another aspect is the communication pattern employed by the processes. In this approach the mapping is done using a special notation which is called a *Logo-Like Turtle* program. Each process is associated with a position and a heading. A goal in the body of a clause may have a Turtle program associated with it. The activation of the Turtle program determines the position and heading of the new process. Using this notation, complex process structures can be mapped with regard to desired architecture. In general, the performance of many systolic algorithms depends on routing communication in a specific pattern. This approach has been used in AI systems utilizing the Concurrent Prolog logic programming language.

The **Rete matching algorithm** is an example of parallel pattern matching that has been developed at Carnegie-Mellon University and is used by the OPS5 Production System Language [Forgy 82]. The Rete algorithm is an efficient method for comparing a large collection of patterns to a large collection of objects. The Rete algorithm was first described in 1974 by Forgy [Forgy 74].

The pattern matcher can be viewed as a *black box* with one input and one output as follows:

{Changes to working memory}

⇓

Black Box

⇓

{Changes to production rules}

in which the black box receives information about the changes that are made to working memory and determines the changes that must be made in the production rules to keep it consistent. The Rete algorithm uses a data flow architecture (tree-structured sorting network) to perform the match operations, which are the principal component of the black box. The basic idea of this matching algorithm is to construct a data graph from the conditions of all productions and then to perform the match operation by invoking elements of database knowledge in the form of *tokens*. The root of the graph is called a *common node* which is followed by the constant nodes corresponding to different classes and is the input to the black box. Each of the nodes has two inputs so that it can join two paths in the network into one. The first of the two-input nodes joins the linear sequences for the first two patterns, and the second two-input node joins the output of the first with the sequence for the third pattern, and so on. The two-input nodes test every inter-element feature that applies to the elements they process. Finally, after two-input nodes, the interpreter builds a special terminal node to represent the production. This node is attached to the last of the two-input nodes. A token is an ordered pair consisting of a tag and a list of data elements. The token tag is either +, meaning addition to the database of knowledge, or -, meaning deletion from the database of knowledge. When an element is modified, two tokens are sent to the black box, one indicating that the old form of the element has been deleted from working memory and the other indicating that the new form of the element has been added. The result of the match between the elements of working memory and the network is stored as states of the nodes in a data flow graph.

Although the Rete algorithm was developed for use in production systems interpreters, it can be used for other purposes, including image processing and pattern recognition. In general, the algorithm is efficient even when it processes large sets of patterns and objects. In this algorithm, the patterns are compiled into a data graph program to perform the match process.

12.5   Parallelizing AI Architectures

Once the parallelism analysis is completed and an execution model is selected, there remains the issue of mapping the problem into a multiprocessor architecture or designing a special architecture for the parallelism application. For example, the Columbia DADO Production-System Machine [Stolfo 86] is a parallel architecture designed for rule-driven production system applications. It is a tree-structured MIMD parallel architecture. A commercial version of this prototype with up to 8191 processing elements built on the 32-bit Motorola 68020 was announced by the Fifth Generation Computer Group in 1987 [Moto-Oka 82, Bishop 86] with two different characteristics, as follows:

- One version for rule-based, sorting and matching problems
- One version for signal interpretation problems

SOAR, developed by Larid [Larid 87], is another production system architecture with two distinctive characteristics as follows:

1. It is intended as an architecture for building integrated AI systems.
2. It is intended as a model of human intelligence.

The system provides both sequential and parallel aspects of production systems by operating in cycles. For example, in the *elaboration phase* of the processing cycle, the production rules are fired in parallel, and in the *decision phase*, operators and states are chosen in parallel, thus setting the stage for another elaboration phase.

One attempt to implement production systems using parallel processing was the mapping of the ***Rete Match Algorithm*** into a multiprocessor. This was done because most of the execution time of production systems is spent in the match phase. The hardware architecture developed by Moldovan [Moldovan 89] and extended by Kuo [Kuo 91] consisted of a message-passing multiprocessor attached to a host computer as shown in Figure 12.2. The set of production rules is partitioned into disjoint subsets of rules by an interpreter in the host computer, with each subset allocated to one processor. The database is also partitioned as a result of the intersection of the original database with the union of the preconditions of each rule subset. The remaining part of the database knowledge is stored in the host computer. The interconnection network is the means through which the interprocess communication is performed. As a consequence, rules in the database are treated as the corresponding rule preconditions distributed over the processing elements. Each processing element consists of three components as follows:

1. **Program Memory**, which consists of rules assigned to the processing element.

2. **Data Memory**, which consists of a database subset of rules.
3. **Control Memory**, which consists of the addresses of the rules associated with the processing element and the variables that can be used during the unification process.

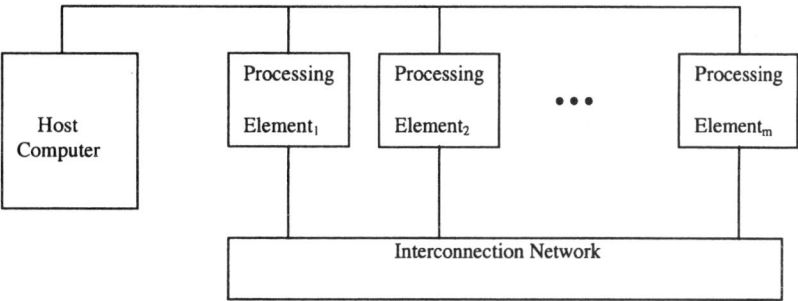

Figure 12.2. Message-passing architecture for production systems [adopted from Moldovan 92].

Message-passing systems also provide an alternative approach for agents in a reasoning system to communicate with each other. In such a framework, the agents are able to direct their messages to those agents that are most likely to be able to do what needs to be done. An example of a message-passing system is MACE [Gasser 87], which provides a general architecture for reasoning systems. A MACE system consists of five kinds of components as follows:

1. Problem-solving agents, which are specialized to a problem domain.
2. System agents, which provide such facilities as command interpretation, error handling and tracing.
3. Facilities, which are built-in functions that agents can use for such things as pattern matching and simulations.
4. A database of knowledge, which maintains descriptions of the agents.
5. Kernels, one for each processor, which handle such functions as message routing and input/output transfers.

This architecture supports many of the kinds of reasoning systems. Semantic networks are used for reasoning systems, in which knowledge is represented associatively and structurally. Processing elements, called node units, represent concepts and entities in the knowledge base representation and the links represent relations between nodes, which allow the exchange of information between processors. The Semantic Network Array Processor (SNAP) computer system developed at the University of Southern California is shown in Figure 12.3.

A semantic network connects the processors such that each processor preserves many semantic network nodes and their relations. The interconnection network is responsible for message exchange and knowledge base transfers. The system consists of an array of processors, one or more controllers, an interconnection network and input/output devices.

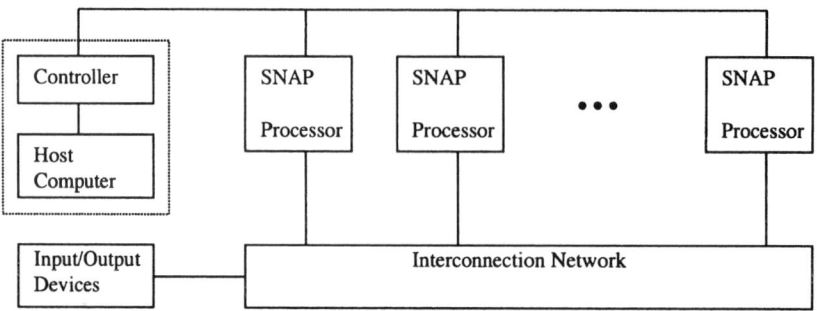

Figure 12.3. SNAP architecture.

Each processor, called a SNAP processor, consists of four components as follows:

- An Instruction Unit (IU), which controls the operation of the processor.
- A Relation Memory (RM), which provides the main memory and stores semantic network nodes and relations.
- A Marker Control Unit (MCU), which provides the storage and processing functions for markers associated with semantic network nodes within the processor.
- A Communication Unit (CU), which acts as the interface between the processor and the interconnection network.

Two forms of knowledge are stored in each processor, and it is easy to convert from one to another.

1. Permanent knowledge is provided by the user and is stored in the relation memory (RM).
2. Temporary knowledge is stored in the marker control unit (MCU).

For each semantic network node stored in the relation memory, there is a memory space in the marker control unit to store markers corresponding to that node. The SNAP instruction set consists of powerful instructions specific to knowledge processing. The instructions are divided into seven categories: node maintenance, marker node maintenance, search, logical, propagate, marker supplemental and data retrieval. The instructions are used to program knowledge processing applications on the SNAP system. For more detail about the SNAP architecture refer to [Moldovan 93].

In general, the application program can perform operations to manipulate the various markers in the knowledge base, meaning that it generates markers at one or more nodes which are propagated and activate other nodes.

12.6 Parallelizing AI Programming Languages

In procedural languages, computations are driven by the instructions. A class of languages for which the order of the execution of subproblems is not specified is called declarative languages. A more precise statement is that declarative programming languages are based on an abstract formalism in which there is no implicit state that can be modified by constructs in the language.

Operationally, declarative programs can be viewed as an abstract computational model, like the Turing Machine, the Lambda Calculus, and the Random Access Machine. A computation in this model is a goal-driven deduction from the statements of the program. The computation is nondeterministic, meaning that for each state of the computation, there may be several possible transitions, like the search models. Two examples of declarative programming languages are *functional languages*, whose model of computation is the *functions*, and *logic languages*, whose model of computation is based on *relations*. This programming paradigm has an obvious relationship to the idea of parallel processing, since the possibility is left open to implement processes in a parallel fashion as resources will permit. In this section, we discuss the benefits of parallelism in AI programs. An example of a production system language is **OPS5**, developed at Carnegie-Mellon University by Brownston [Brownston 85] and used in several expert systems. In OPS5, working memories consist of several hundred objects, and each object has between ten and one hundred associated attribute-value pairs. An object together with its attribute-value pairs is called a *working memory element* (WME). For example, the following element

WME: (Phys-Object ↑Name Apartment ↑Weight Small ↑At 10-Street ↑On South)

declares an object of class Phys-Object which is named Apartment. It has 4 properties:

- Its name (↑ Name)
- Its weight (↑ Weight)
- Its location (↑ At)
- Its support (↑ On)

where the symbol ↑ is used to distinguish properties from values. This element specifies a physical object as an apartment on the south at location 10 Street where weight is small. For example, the following working element

WME: (Expression ↑Name Expression10 ↑Arg1 5 ↑Arg2 A ↑Op *)

declares an object of class Expression which is named Expression10 and has 5 as its first argument, A as its second argument, and * as its operator.

Generally speaking, the LHS of a production consists of a sequence of patterns, meaning a sequence of partial descriptions of working memory elements. When a pattern P describes an element E, P is said to match E. A pattern matches a working memory element if every attribute value in the pattern occurs in the corresponding position in the working memory element. Thus, the pattern

(Expression   ↑Arg2 10 ↑Op *)

would match the element

(Expression   ↑Name Expr20 ↑Arg1 X ↑Arg2 10 ↑Op *)

Most interpreters in AI applications are developed based on two representatives of the logic programming and functional programming languages, called Prolog and Lisp. The number of parallel logic programming languages has grown, and a good overview and comparison can be found in the survey paper by Shapiro [Shapiro 89]. A program written in these languages is a set of clauses, and the user starts the computation by specifying a goal. Its evaluation is carried out by a network of very small, fine-grained logic processes to be proved in parallel. Communication channels among the processes are shared streams in which data items flow. Generally speaking, the great potential parallelism in logic programs steams from two forms:

- AND parallelism, in which several goals or subgoals are solved at once
- OR parallelism, in which a goal is solved in many ways at once

The two types of parallelism are implemented in different parallel logic programming languages. For example, parallel Prolog models include Concurrent Prolog [Shapiro 89], Parlog [Clark 86], FGHC (Flat Guarded Horn Clauses) [Tick 91] and Guarded Horn Clauses [Ueda 85], all of which are examples of stream AND-parallelism. A detailed description of the language OR-parallel Prolog can be found in the book by Tick [Tick 91]. Ali and Karlsson [Ali 90] described an OR-parallel language named Muse. Ciepielewski [Ciepielewski 91] offers detailed information about OR-parallelism and reviews the scheduling problems in OR-parallel Prolog.

Brogi and Ciancarini [Brogi 91] detailed a concurrent logic programming language named Shared Prolog. A Shared Prolog program is composed of a set of parallel agents that are Prolog programs extended by a guard mechanism which rules synchronization and communication. The programmer controls the granularity of parallelism, communication and synchronization of agents via a centralized data structure called the *blackboard*. The blackboard model of problem solving consists of partitioning the knowledge about a particular problem into several subsets. The idea behind this separation is to keep domain knowledge separated from control knowledge and to organize communication via a central data structure, named the blackboard. A blackboard architecture consists of three components: a number of knowledge sources, a blackboard, and a control module. In general, in Shared Prolog, processes communicate via the blackboard, meaning that it is designed as an operating environment in which theories (agents) are dynamically connected to and disconnected from a running system. Shared Prolog communication mechanisms can be compared with those of Concurrent Prolog.

In the following, we briefly discuss the Prolog logic programming, language as well as two representatives of the parallel declarative languages, called Concurrent Prolog and Multilisp, which are used as logic and functional programming languages in AI applications.

Prolog Logic Programming Language

Logic programming languages are declarative languages whose basis is logical relationships and which are used to develop production systems. The practical importance of this branch of mathematics is that it represents a formalized method of reasoning utilizing inferences and deductions. The most popular logic programming language is Prolog, originally developed by Alain Colmerauer, Philippe Roussel, and their colleagues of the d'Intelligence Artificielle (University of Marseille) to be a theorem-proving language [Clocksin 87]. Prolog entered in the fourth generation programming languages as a good language for database management, and into the fifth generation as a logic programming language in the field of artificial intelligence. Its developers called it Prolog as an abbreviation for *programming en logique*. Prolog is a very high level programming language which is based on automatic theorem proving. Its built-in control scheme is based on a specific method for searching state space, and it appears to be a suitable language for production systems. Prolog is not a parallel programming language, but logic programming appears to offer parallelism in the execution of the programs. A Prolog program consists of several independent components, as follows:

Horn clause: A Prolog program is described as a series of logical assertions, each of which is called a *Horn clause*. A clause in the form

$$A \Leftarrow B_1, B_2, ..., B_n$$

where only a single term appears on the left-hand side is called a Horn clause. A is the *head* (goal) of the clause, and $B_1, B_2, ..., B_n$ forms the *body* (subgoals) of the clause. The clause above can be interpreted as either of the following:

- A logical statement that if all the Bs are satisfied (true), then A is satisfied (true)
- A procedure for producing a state that satisfies condition A, similar to:

```
Procedure A
     Begin
          Call B₁
          Call B₂
          ...
          Call Bₙ
     End
```

Such a clause is interpreted as follows: "To execute procedure A, call B_1 and call B_2 and ... and call B_n." The fact that Prolog programs are composed only of Horn clauses and not of arbitrary logical expressions has two important consequences. The first is that because of the uniform representation, a simple and efficient interpreter can be developed. The second is that the logic of the Horn clause system is decidable.

Query: This is the given input to a program, which is treated as a goal to be proved. The query is a question from the system and the answer is true or false.

Predicates: The As and Bs in the clause are predicates in the logic sense, and they represent relations; for instance, that something is a property of something else.

Resolution: This is a theorem-proving method which starts by trying to prove the negation of the *Query* (goal) and searches for a contradiction.

Unification: This is the search process of finding the general substitution of variables that makes two literally identical.

Backward reasoning is applied to try to prove the goal given the assertions in the program. The program is read top to bottom, left to right, and searching is performed in a depth-first fashion with backtracking. The unification of a goal with the head of a clause is the basic computation step of the interpreter, as well as that of Prolog and other logic programming languages. In general, the unification of two terms involves finding a substitution of values for variables in the terms which makes the two terms identical. This process is a simple and powerful form of pattern matching and is the basis and the only data manipulation primitive in the logic programming languages.

Generally speaking, the state of a computation consists of a goal G and a substitution (assignment of values) θ and is denoted by a pair (G; θ). A computation begins with an initial state, consisting of the initial goal to be proven and the empty substitution ∈, and progresses nondeterministically from state to state according to the following transition rules, called Reduce and Fail. A computation can be viewed as an attempt to prove the initial goal of the program. At each state, the goal represents a statement whose proof will establish the initial goal, and the substitution represents the values computed so far for variables used in the computation, including the initial goal variables. A computation ends in a state whose goal is either *true* or *fail*. In the *true* case, the computation is successful, it corresponds to a successful proof of the initial goal, and the substitution in the terminal state is called the *answer substitution* of the computation. In the *fail* case, the proof fails. A successful computation has the property that its initial goal, generated by the answer substitution, is a logical consequence of the program. Figure 12.4 shows an example of a simple knowledge base represented in standard logic notation and in Prolog. A key difference between the logic and the Prolog representations is that the Prolog interpreter has a fixed control strategy, and so the assertions in the Prolog program define a particular search path to an answer to any question. In contrast, the logical assertions define only the set of answers they justify, and they say nothing about how to choose among those answers if there is more than one. Because Prolog performs an exhaustive depth-first search when trying to unify its variables, program execution can be very inefficient in both speed of execution and use of memory. Thus, it is up to the programmer to write procedures that minimize both search time and memory usage or to adopt another approach to make the program execution efficient; i.e., parallel processing.

(Prolog)	(Logic)
apartment(X) :- pet(X), small(X).	$\forall x: pet(x) \wedge small(x) \Rightarrow apartment(x)$
pet(X) :- cat(X).	$\forall x: cat(x) \vee dog(x) \Rightarrow pet(x)$
pet(X) :- dog(X).	$\forall x: poodle(x) \Rightarrow dog(x) \wedge small(x)$
dog(X) :- poodle(X).	poodle(fluffy)
small(X) :- poodle(X).	
poodle(fluffy).	

Figure 12.4. Logic and Prolog representations of axioms.

Prolog is an AI language that had a prominent role in the launching of the Fifth Generation Computer Project and seems well matched to production systems. Several projects, most notably the Japanese, attempted to show that the logic programming language Prolog would be efficient in describing AI applications for parallel execution. To do this, their computer needed to be intelligent, meaning it had to be able to learn, associate, make inferences, make decisions, and behave in ways we consider to encompass human reasoning. They designed a computer system using Prolog as its core language. The project included the development of the Prolog-like parallel logical programming language KL-1 [Lipkis 83]. It included some operating system functions as well as modularity and concurrent processing. As an experiment, 64 computers running KL-1 were connected in parallel under the operating system PIMOS (Parallel Inference Machine Operating System) [Chikayama 88]. Time efficiencies were measured at 5-8 mega LIPS (Logical Inference Per Second). The target for this project was the development of knowledge and information processing capabilities. Research and development are continuing, with a new goal of connecting 1000 parallel computers to achieve 200 mega LIPS speed. The Japanese have also developed a Prolog-based language called Extended Self-Contained Prolog (ESP) [Fuchi 87] for programming many Fifth Generation projects on PCs and workstations which run in a UNIX environment.

Prolog is sufficiently organized for parallel processing. If there is a rule:

$$t_G : - t_1, t_2, \ldots, t_n$$

with goal t_G, and we have n processors available, we can resolve all n subgoals simultaneously. This sort of parallel execution is AND-parallelism, because in a clause such as A : – B, C we will attempt to prove B and C concurrently in order to prove A. AND-parallelism requires that subgoals be independent of each other. Backward reasoning is then applied to construct the general solution with regard to subsolutions. In general AND-parallelism involves concurrent processing across different time levels. OR-parallelism, which eliminates backtracking, is substantially easier. If all the processing at a given time occurs in parallel, we would have an example of OR-parallelism. OR-parallelism works concurrently on clauses such as:

$$A : - B.$$

$$A : - C.$$

meaning that we can prove A is true by proving either B or C. Thus, we work concurrently on both B and C, stopping when either B or C is resolved. In this example, only the successful resolution is visible to the user. When Prolog announces that A is true, we may not know or care whether B or C is also true. This is called nondeterminism, which is a feature associated with closed systems, in which only the successful resolution is important as the answer.

Shapiro [Shapiro 89] characterized Prolog as a sequential simulation of a parallel computational model and described a parallel language called Concurrent Prolog, which he designed. He added two syntactic constructs to logic programming, namely read-only annotation of variables and the commit operator, both of which are used to control the parallel computation.

12.6.1 Concurrent Prolog Logic Programming Language

Parallel Prolog models have been addressed by three well-known concurrent logic programming languages: Concurrent Prolog [Shapiro 89], Guarded Horn Clauses [Ueda 85], and Parlog [Clark 86]. Indeed, the difference between the various logic programming languages, such as Prolog, Guarded-Horn Clauses, and Concurrent Prolog, lies in the way they deduce consequences from the facts and rules. However, the deduction mechanism used by all these logic programming languages is based on the abstract interpreter for logic programs, as shown in Figure 12.5.

```
Input:    A Logic program P and a Goal G
Output:   GℜR, which is an instance of G proved from P,
          or failure.

Algorithm:Initialize the resolvent to be G, the input goal.
          While the resolvent is not empty do
              (* choose a goal A in the resolvent and *)
              (* a copy of a clause. *)
              A* ⇐ B₁,B₂,...,Bₖ,  k ≥ 0, in P,
              (* such that A and A* are unifiable with a *)
              (* substitution ℜ, and exit if such a goal *)
              (* and clause do not exist. *)
              Remove A and add B₁,B₂,...,Bₙ to the resolvent.
              Apply ℜ to the resolvent and to G.

          If the resolvent is empty then output G, otherwise
          output failure.
```

Figure 12.5. Interpretation of a logic program.

Concurrent logic programming involves high-level programming languages for parallel and distributed systems which offer a wide range of execution to AI systems. Being logic programming languages, they preserve many advantages of the logic programming model, including the logical reading of programs and computations and the convenience of representing data structures with logical terms and manipulating them using unification. Operationally, the model of computation consists of a dynamic set of concurrent processes which communicate by instantiating shared logical variables, synchronize by waiting for variables to be initialized, and make nondeterministic choices with regard to the availability of values of variables.

Concurrent Prolog is a logic programming language designed in 1982 for concurrent programming and parallel execution on AI systems. Concurrent Prolog is a single-assignment logic programming language, meaning that a logical variable can be assigned to a nonvariable term only once during a computation. The language embodies data flow synchronization and guarded commands as its basis for control mechanisms. In a concurrent processing environment, processes are abstract entities. Each process can be viewed as the generalization of the execution thread of sequential programs. Different issues are involved, such as interprocess communication, change of state, creation of new processes and termination. Concurrent Prolog provides the essential components of concurrent computation, such as concurrent actions, indeterminate actions, communication, processes creation and termination. A compiler of Concurrent Prolog was developed with a speed of more than 10,000 reductions per second, which is more than a quarter of the speed of the underlying Prolog system. In general, the computational model of Concurrent Prolog embodies these notations.

Principles of Concurrent Prolog

A Concurrent Prolog program consists of the following independent components:

- **Goal:** A goal $P(T_1,T_2,\ldots,T_n)$ can be viewed as a process in which the argument constitutes the data state of the process.
- **Network of Processes:** A network of processes (called a conjunctive goal) is defined by its processes and by the way they are interconnected. The variables shared between the goals in the conjunction determine an interconnection scheme. The actions a process can take depend on its state. The basic action of a process is the *process reduction* operation. Process reduction refers to the unification of the process with the head of a clause and its replacement by the processes specified in the body of the clause. In general, this action depends on whether its arguments can be unified with the arguments of the head of a given clause. AND-parallelism can be achieved by reducing several processes in parallel. In this sense, communication can be achieved by the assignment of values to shared variables, which is caused by the unification that occurs during process reduction. OR-parallelism can be achieved by reducing a process. Given a process to be reduced means that all clauses applicable may be tried in parallel.
- **Communication Channel:** A communication channel (shared-memory single-assignment variable or shared logical variable) provides a way in which two or more processes may communicate with each other to exchange information. A logical variable can be shared between two or more processes (subgoals) and can serve a group of processes. A logical variable can be assigned only once during a computation. In general, a logical variable can be viewed as a communication channel capable of transmitting one message or as a shared variable capable of receiving one value. As a consequence, it is convenient to view shared logical variables as analogous to communication channels and as analogous to shared memory variables. The single-assignment restriction has been adopted as a suitable primitive for parallel programming included logic programming.
- **Rules and Facts:** Rules and facts (clauses of a logical program) are the instructions for process behavior. In general a process is involved in two actions, *control* and *data*. Control actions include termination, iteration, branching and creation of new processes. The control actions are specified by clauses of logic programming. The data actions in-

clude communication and various operations on data structures, such as testing and construction.

Clause Primitives

The clauses can specify the activities that are involved with processes, such as termination, iteration, branching, state change and creation of new processes. In general this is called *process reading of logic programs*.

- **Termination:** In general, a unit clause, or a definite clause with an empty body, such as

$$P(T_1, T_2, \ldots, T_n)$$

  specifies that a process can reduce itself to an empty set of processes and thus can be terminated. This indicates that the clause is unifiable, meaning that it can be unified with another clause to produce the empty clause (NULL).

- **Change of data and program state:** A clause with one literal in the body specifies that a process can change its state. For example, a clause such as:

$$P(T_1, T_2, \ldots, T_n) \Leftarrow Q(S_1, S_2, \ldots, S_m)$$

  indicates that if a process is in the state unifiable with $P(T_1, T_2, \ldots, T_n)$, then its state can be changed to $Q(S_1, S_2, \ldots, S_m)$. In this sense, the program state is changed to Q / m (branch) and the data state to $(S_1, S_2, \ldots, S_m)$. In general, this kind of clause is an iterative clause.

- **Create new processes:** A clause can indicate that a process can replace itself with several new processes. For example, a general clause of the form

$$P(T_1, T_2, \ldots, T_n) \Leftarrow S_1, S_2, \ldots, S_m$$

  specifies that if a process is in the state unifiable with $P(T_1, T_2, \ldots, T_n)$, then it can be replaced with m new processes as determined by $S_1, S_2, \ldots, S_m$. As a consequence of this, the resolvent (the current set of goals of the interpreter) is viewed as a network of concurrent processes, where each goal is a process.

Process Synchronization and Communication

In Concurrent Prolog, once a process has reduced itself using some clause, the process is committed to it and the actions must be completed. The resulting computational behavior is called *committed-choice-nondeterminism*, or sometimes *indeterminacy*. To ensure that processes make correct choices of actions, Concurrent Prolog is provided with primitives to delay process reduction until enough information is available for a correct choice to be made. There are two synchronization and control primitives associated with Concurrent Prolog:

- **Read-Only** is indicated by a "?" and can be applied to logical variables. For example, X? indicates that logical variable X is a read-only variable. As a consequence, a read-only variable can receive a value only through the instantiation of its corresponding write-enabled variable. This can be performed by a unification action. A unification that attempts to instantiate a read-only variable suspends until that variable becomes instantiated. For example, the unification of X? with a can be suspended until $f(X,Y?)$ with $f(a,Z)$ succeeds by the unifier $\{X = a, Z = Y?\}$. In other words, if we assume two distinct sets of variables, write-enabled and read-only variables, the read-only operator ? is then a one-to-one mapping from write-enabled to read-only variables. The mapping is written in postfix notation. For every write-enabled variable X, the variable X? is the read-only variable corresponding to it.
- **Commit Operator** "|" is used to separate the right-hand side of a rule into a *guard* and a *body*, meaning that it creates a guarded clause. For example, the guarded clause:

$$A \Leftarrow G_1, G_2, ..., G_m \mid B_1, B_2, ..., B_n$$

where m,n $\geq$ 0 indicates that A is true if the G's and the B's are true. Thus, the guard is a new primitive to ensure that processes make correct choices of actions by postponing process activation. In general, Concurrent Prolog allows G's (the goals in the guard) to be called to the program, meaning that guards can be nested recursively.

Stream Communication is the basis of process communication in Concurrent Prolog. In this scheme, the communicating processes, typically one sender and one receiver process, share a variable; i.e., X. In this sense, the sender process that wants to send a sequence of messages (M1, M2, M3,...) issues [M1 | X1] in order to send M1, then initiates X1 to [M2 | X2] to send M2, then assigns X2 to [M3 | X3] and so on. The receiver process examines the read-only variable X? and attempts to unify the variable with [M1 | X1]. If the unification is successful, then the message M1 can be processed, and the iteration is continued with X1 waiting for the next message. The approach can be applied for one sender and multiple receivers, provided that all receivers have read-only access to the original shared variable. A receiver that creates a new process can append the generated process in the group of receivers by proving it a read-only reference to the current stream variable.

Quicksort Example

The recursive structure of Concurrent Prolog with the availability of logical variables makes it a perfect approach for specifying a recursive process network. An example is quicksort, in which the program creates two tree networks as follows:

1. One tree is called the *Partition Processes tree*, which decomposes the input list into smaller lists.
2. The second tree is called the *Append Processes tree*, which concatenates these lists.

In general, the process network is based on the divide-and-conquer algorithm and is useful for searching purposes. Figure 12.6 shows the Concurrent Prolog program for quicksort. In this program, the variables Smaller and Larger serve as communication channels between partitions and the two quicksort processes.

```
1  Quicksort([X | XS], YS) ←
      Partition(XS?, X, Smaller, Larger),
2      Quicksort(Smaller?, SS),
3      Quicksort(Larger?, LS),
4      Append(SS?, [X | LS?], YS).
5  Quicksort([ ], [ ]).
6  Partition([Y | IN], X, [Y | Smaller], Larger) ←
      X≥Y | Partition(LN?, X, Smaller, Larger).
7  Partition([Y | IN], X, Smaller, [Y | Larger]) ←
      X<Y | Partition(LN?, X, Smaller, Larger).
8  Partition([ ], X, [ ], [ ]).
9  Append([X | XS], YS, [X | ZS]) ←
      Append(XS?, YS, ZS).
10 Append([ ], XS, XS).
```

Figure 12.6. A Concurrent Prolog QuickSort program.

The program consists of three kind of clauses, the quicksort clause, the partition clause, and the append clause. The line numbers are not part of the program and are used for reference purposes only. The program can be illustrated as follows.

In line 1, we sort list [X | XS] to result in YS. Partitioning XS with respect to X gives Smaller and Larger elements. Lines 2 and 3 indicate that sorting Larger and Smaller lists results in LS and SS, respectively. Line 4 means that appending [X | SS] to LS gives YS, and line 5 indicates that sorting the empty list produces the empty list. In line 6, we partition list [X | IN] with respect to X to result in [Y | Smaller] and Larger if $X \geq Y$. In line 7 list [Y | IN] is partitioned with respect to Y to result in Smaller and Larger elements. Line 8 indicates that partitioning an empty line produces two empty lists. In line 9, two lists are appended to result in a new list. Line 10 is used to append an empty list. It is worth noting that the recursive clause of quicksort says that a quicksort process whose first argument is a list can replace itself with a network of four processes: one partition process, two quicksort processes and one append process. It then specifies their interconnection and initialization as the first element in the list, causing the second argument of append to be X, which is the partitioning element.

Matrix-Matrix Multiplication Example

Figure 12.7 illustrates a Concurrent Prolog program for multiplying two matrices. The program is based on the systolic algorithm that pipelines two matrices on the rows and columns of a processor array. It is assumed that the two input matrices are represented by a stream of streams of their columns and rows respectively. The program produces a stream of streams of the rows of the output matrix. The program uses a grid of P processes for computing the inner products of each row and column.

```
MM([ ], __ , [ ]).
MM([X | XS], YS, [Z | ZS]) ←
    VM(X, YS?, Z)@right,
    MM(XS?, YS, ZS)@forward.
VM(__, [ ], [ ]).
VM(XS,[Y | YS], [Z | ZS])  ←
    P(XS?, Y?, Z), VM(XS, YS?, ZS)@forward.
P([X | XS], [Y | YS], Z)  ←
    Z := (X * X) + Z1, P(XS?, YS?, Z!).
P([ ], [ ], 0).
```

Figure 12.7 Matrix-matrix multiplication.

12.6.2 Multilisp Functional Programming Language

A characteristic particularly associated with artificial intelligence programs but also found elsewhere is the search problem. Lisp is an existing sequential programming language used in AI programs, particularly for search problems. Parallel Lisp models have been addressed by three well-known concurrent functional programming languages: MultiLisp [Halstead 86, 88], Qlisp [Gabriel 88] and the Paralation Model [Sabot 88]. In this section, we briefly discuss Multilisp as one of the representatives of the parallel functional programming languages used in AI programs.

Multilisp, which is known as a *parallel symbolic computing language*, is a modification of the Lisp language and was developed at MIT for experiments in parallel symbolic programming. In general, the symbolic computation emphasizes rearrangement of data, because symbolic programs are more likely to be written in a language such as Lisp or Smalltalk. The structure of symbolic computations generally seems to favor recursions on composite data structure such as trees, lists and sets as the major source of concurrency. Programming languages such as Qlisp and Multilisp include constructs to take advantage of these sources of concurrency. Multilisp is a version of the Lisp-like programming language Scheme, in which the language is extended to allow the programmers to specify concurrent execution of programs. Multilisp also works in the sequential execution environment, meaning that it allows Lisp programs written without the intention of parallelism to be executed. Multilisp provides two properties that distinguish the language from the other functional programming languages:

- Lexical scooping, which promotes modularity
- Procedural scooping, which indicates that the procedures may be passed as arguments

As a consequence, procedures may be passed freely as arguments, returned as values of other procedures, stored in other data structures and treated in the same way as any other kind of value.

Concurrency can be introduced into a Multilisp program by a **future** construct, in which (**future** X) creates a process to concurrently evaluate X. This allows concurrency between the computation of a value and the use of that value. When the evaluation of X results in a value, that value replaces the **future**. In this scheme, any process that needs to have the **future's** value will be suspended until the value is available. In Multilisp, **future** is the only primitive for process creation. There is a one-to-one mapping between processes and the **future** whose values they have created to compute. Thus, every process terminates by resolving its associated **future** to some value. A process T examines or touches a **future** when it performs an operation that causes T to be suspended if the **future** is not yet resolved. The **future** construct is related to the idea of lazy evaluation, meaning that an expression is not evaluated until its value is demanded by some other part of a program. This indicates that any expression in a program is not evaluated immediately; instead, a suspension is created and returned, and evaluation is delayed until the suspension is removed. Multilisp provides a **delay** primitive that implements lazy evaluation. Generally speaking, **future** provides a style of computation much like that used in designing graph-reduction architectures and data flow architectures.

Example: The Multilisp program uses binary trees represented by nodes, in which each node corresponds to a set of elements. The program manipulates elements of these sets which are represented by integers, ordered pairs, character strings or whatever. Each interior node of the tree is a triple, as shown in Figure 12.8. It has three components – a left and right child and a discriminant part -- and corresponds to the larger element as shown in Figure 12.9.

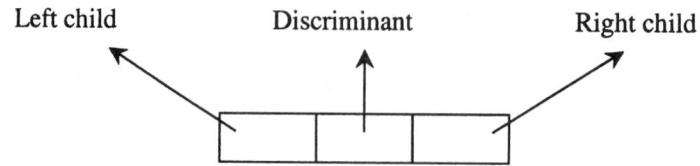

Figure 12.8. An interior node in the search tree.

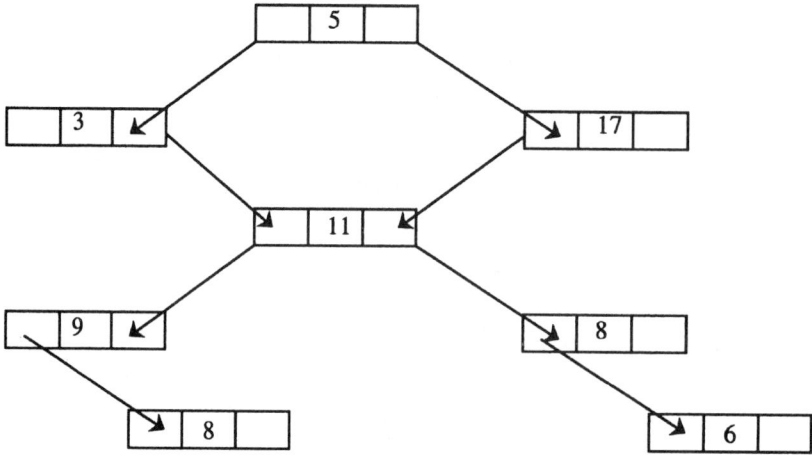

Figure 12.9. A search tree generated by the nodes.

We can use a Lisp function **leaf?** to identify the two types of nodes associated with the tree. For example, (left? X) returns true if X is a leaf node and false if X is an interior node. A Lisp function (make_node L D R) generates a new interior node whose left child is L, whose right child is R, and whose discriminant is D. The function (left-child N), (right-child N) and (discriminant N) returns the left child, right child, and discriminant of N, respectively. The following procedure inserts an element **elt** into a structure **tree**. The procedure copies the tree nodes to be modified and returns a new tree, meaning that there are no side effects on the existing nodes and tree. The procedure is a straight-forward version of the Lisp procedure for insertion except for its use of the **future** primitive.

```
(defun insert (elt tree)
(if (empty-tree? tree)
    elt
    (if (leaf? tree)
```

```
(if    (elt < tree elt)
       (make-node tree tree elt)
       (make-node elt elt tree)
(if (elt <(discriminant tree) elt)
       (make-node (left-child tree)
           (discriminant tree)
           (future (insert elt (right-child tree))))
       (make-node (future (insert elt (left-child tree)))
           (discriminant tree)
           (right-child tree))))))))    )
```

In the case of an empty tree, **insert** returns **elt** (a single leaf node) as the resulting tree. In the case of a nonempty tree, if tree is a leaf, **insert** returns an interior node with **elt** and **tree** as children. If tree is an interior node, **insert** determines whether **elt** belongs in the left or right subtree of tree and returns a new interior node with the same discriminant and left and right children. If ·**future** were not used, then an **insert** performed to an interior node would not return until its recursive call to **insert** had returned, meaning that no result would be generated until the new tree had been completely constructed. With the use of **future**, however, **insert** can construct a new node and return it without waiting for the completion of recursive calls to **insert**. This indicates that the use of **future** allows **insert** to return even before the insertion has been completed.

As we see, **future** give us a way to represent partially computed values, meaning that they can be released for use while they are still being processed. This indicates that the **future** primitive associated with the Multilisp language is an effective tool for exposing parallelism, but **future** does not provide the information needed to properly schedule the processes. Generally speaking, synchronization is not available using conventional fork-join primitives. Instead, synchronization can be achieved through the use of the **PCALL** primitive, or the scheduling of the processes could be dictated by assigning priorities to the processes.

A complete Multilisp language has been implemented on an experimental shared-memory multiprocessor system called Concert at MIT under the supervision of Halstead [Halstead 86]. The Concert multiprocessor system consists of 32 MC68000 processors and a total of 20 megabytes of memory. In a more recent paper, Kranz [Kranz 89] describes a compiler-based Multilisp implementation for a shared-memory Encore Multimax multiprocessor for up to 12 processors.

12.7 Neural Networks or Parallel Distributed Processing

A very different approach to build the intelligent programs is Neural Networks or Artificial Neural Networks (ANN) [Hagan 96, Russell 95]. The neural networks are suitable for solving problems that do not have a specific algorithm to achieve the output from the inputs. A simple schematic of a biological neuron consists of a cell body that has a number of branches called dendrites and a single branch called the axon. The axons are used for transmitting the information between neurons. Dendrites receive signals from other neurons. The point of contact between an axon of one cell and a dendrite of another cell is called a synapse. At the synapse the transmission of information from one cell to another cell occurs. When these combined impulses exceed a certain threshold, the neuron fires and an impulse passes down the axon. Figure 12.10 is a simplified schematic diagram of two biological neurons connected to each other.

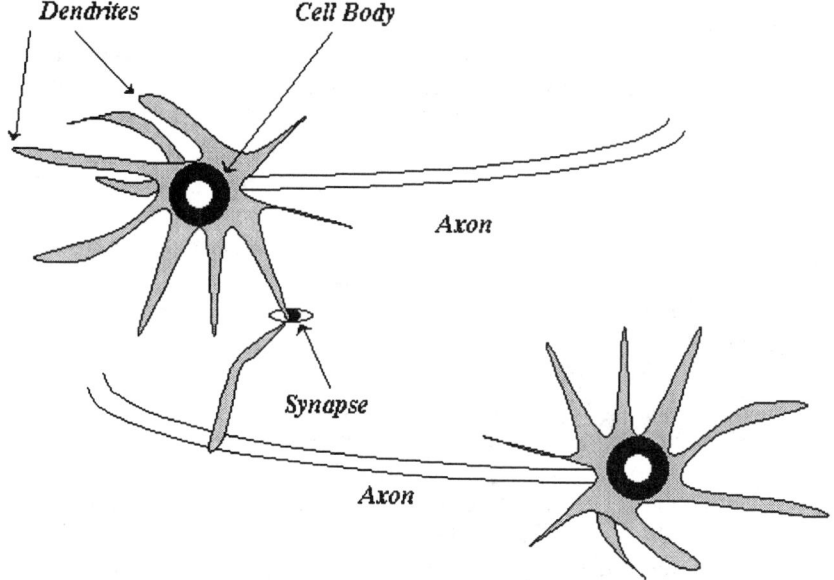

Figure 12.10. Schematic view of two neurons.

It is the arrangement of neurons and the strengths of the individual synapses, determined by a complex chemical process, that has established the function of the neural networks. Artificial neural networks do not approach the complexity of the biological neurons. There are, however, two key similarities between biological and artificial neural networks. First, the building blocks of both networks are simple computational devices that are highly interconnected. Second, the connections between neurons determine the function of the network. It is worth noting that even though biological neurons are very slow when are compared with the electrical circuits, the brain is able to perform many tasks much faster than any conventional computer. This is because of the massively parallel structure of biological neural networks, meaning that all of the neurons are operating at the same time.

Since biological brains are examples of massively parallel structures, densely interconnected, and self-organized computational networks, they are representatives as ideal prototype which special purpose hardware can be modeled. Artificial neural networks share this parallel structure, meaning that their parallel structure makes them ideally suited for implementation using parallel processors. Generally speaking, artificial neural architectures provide a natural model for parallelism, because each neuron is an independent unit, meaning that can be treated as a processing element. Hillis [Hillis 85] has commented on the fact that humans get faster to process a task as they acquire more knowledge about it, while conventional computers tend to slow down. This is because of sequentially searching a knowledge base, whilst massively parallel architectures like the human brain would not suffer from this consequence. Hopfield [Hopfield 82] introduced a neural network as a theory of memory. A Hopfield network has the following features:

- Distributed Memory
- Distributed Asynchronous Control
- Fault Tolerance

The neurons in this network are initialized with the input vector, then the network iterates until the output converges. In general the network operates as follows. A random unit is chosen, if any of its neighbors are active, the unit computes the sum of the weights on the connections to those active neighbors. If the sum is positive, the unit becomes active, otherwise it becomes inactive. Another random unit is chosen and the process repeats until the network reaches a stable state. This process is called parallel relaxation. Hopfield's major contribution was to show that given any set of weights and any initial state, his parallel relaxation algorithm would eventually put the network into a stable state which is correspond to one of its solutions. In general, parallel relaxation is nothing more than a search, albeit of different style. The perceptron network models a neuron by taking a weighted sum of its inputs and sending the output 1 if the sum is greater than some adjustable threshold value [Rich 91]. In general, a typical ANN can be characterized by having the following components:

- A large number of very simple neuron-like processing elements.
- A large number of weighted connections between the elements. The weights on the connections encode the knowledge of a network.
- Highly parallel and distributed control.
- An emphasis on learning internal representations automatically.

Although ANN can be implemented on conventional computers, they are intended to be implemented on parallel architectures. The neuron-like processing elements are arranged in layers, in which the neurons in one layer receive their inputs from those in another layer and send their outputs to the neurons in a third layer. The connection between the neurons have weights associated with them, in which if two neurons are not connected the corresponding weight is 0; otherwise, it represents the influence of one neuron over the other connected to it. All neurons sum the values received from their dendrites to update their state. The value of the weights are determined by the learning algorithms.

In recent years, several ANN prototypes have been developed [Cohen 83, Hopfield 85, Hopfield 86, Zitti 89, Hecht-Nielsen 91, Takefuji 92, and Karayiannis 93]. However, most of them are simulated by software, in which the implementation is flexible, but it is slow. Thus, the most promising approach of ANN implementation is through the hardware, specially the parallel architecture. Figure 12.11 illustrates a layered model of an ANN consisting of a number of neuron-like processing elements.

Input   (Neuron-Like Processing Elements)   Output

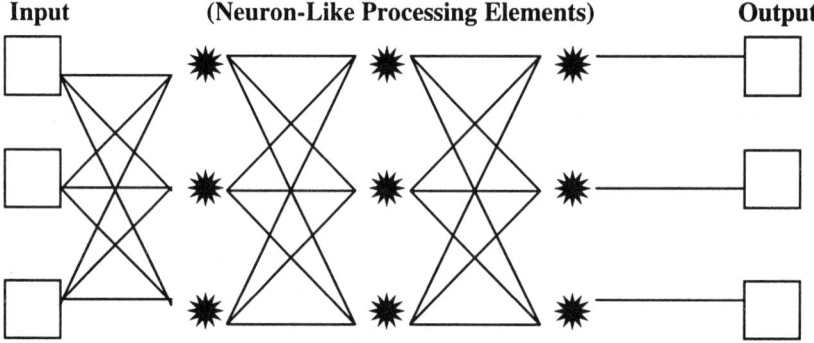

Figure 12.11. Schematic view of an ANN.

In this model each neuron has multiple inputs and its output is connected to different number of processing elements. As a consequence, data presented as input will produce an output pattern. A programmable analog neural network processor consisting of 256 neural circuits and a total of 2048 programmable resistors physically located on 16 boards developed by Fisher [Fisher 91]. The system was used as a massively parallel analog control processors. It was used to demonstrate the applications of neural network learning to the problem of real time adaptive mirror control. The C programming language was used to write an extensive library of routines that can be used as part of programs within the system. The processors are separated from the other components to allow the system to be expanded in a modular fashion. Other ANN systems include simulations executed on MIMD architectures by Zitti [Zitti 89].

Summary

Rule-based and reasoning systems are among the most important paradigms for knowledge representation and processing. They include applications such as natural language processing, machine translation, planning, image processing and many other areas associated with artificial intelligence. In this chapter we identified specific processing requirements for rule-based and reasoning systems. We discussed the production systems as models of human information processing with three components: System State, Production Rules and Control System. We outlined the structure of a production rule as the basis for Match, Resolve, and Execute operations. We briefly explained the distinctive features associated with the reasoning systems, such as modularity, reliability, and heterogeneous Unification. We outlined two approaches in the design of reasoning systems: single-agent planning and multi-agent planing, which are similar to the master/slave paradigms. In the parallelism analysis, we outlined four sources of parallelism in production systems: task parallelism, match parallelism, OR-parallelism and AND-parallelism. There are different methods involved in parallelizing AI algorithms, such as divide-and-conquer, systolic programming, and pattern matching. For example, the rete matching algorithm developed at Carnegie-Mellon University is employed by the OPS5 production system language to parallelize AI applications.

A tree-structured MIMD machine called DADO is designed for rule-based systems. It consists of up to 8191 processing elements and was announced by the Fifth Generation Computer Group in 1987 with two different characteristics: one version for rule-based applications, and the other version for signal interpretation applications. Another example of a message-passing MIMD machine for reasoning systems is MACE, which consists of five different components: problem-solving agents, system agents, facilities, a database of knowledge, and kernels. We described the Semantic Network Array Processor (SNAP) computer developed at the University of Southern California for message exchange and knowledge base transfers. We discussed the parallelizing AI programming languages with a brief discussion of the Prolog logic programming language. We outlined the potential parallelism in logic programs folded in two forms, known as OR-parallelism and AND-parallelism. We outlined the basic components of a logic programming system: query, predicates, resolution, and unification. Parallel Prolog models have been addressed by three well-known concurrent logic programming languages: Concurrent Prolog, Guarded Horn Clauses and Parlog. We outlined the Concurrent Prolog developed by Shapiro as a logic programming language for concurrent programming and parallel execution of AI applications. We discussed the computational model, which consists of a network of processes, communication channels, rules and facts, clause primitives, and process synchronization and communication. The traditional quicksort and matrix multiplication examples presented to address the concurrent Prolog program structure.

Lisp is a functional programming language used in AI systems, particularly for search problems. Parallel Lisp models were addressed by three well-known functional programming languages: Multilisp, Qlisp and the Paralation Model. We outlined Multilisp, developed by Halstead and known as a parallel symbolic computing language. Concurrency is introduced into Multilisp programming by a future construct which creates a process. The synchronization mechanism involved in the language is achieved through the use of the PCALL primitive. A complete Multilisp language implemented on an experimental shared-memory multiprocessor system called Concert at MIT consists of 32 processors and a total of 20 megabytes of memory.

We outlined briefly the artificial neural networks that are suitable for solving problems that do not have a well-defined algorithm to map the input to the output. Instead, a collection of representative samples is used to train the network, which adapts itself to produce the desired output when presented with the example input. Artificial neural networks are similar to biological neurons in terms of their behaviors of learning, recognizing, and applying relationships between objects. A typical network might be formed by a large number of simple neuron-like processing elements with a parallel and distributed control. A standard reference for the Prolog logic programming language is Clocksin and Mellish [Clocksin 87], and a good reference is [Crookes 88]. Parallelism in logic programs is discussed by [Gregory 87, Shapiro 86, 89]. A representative set of books and papers discussing neural networks includes [Hecht-Nielson 91, Hopfield 82, 85, 86, Karayiannis 93]. Parallelism in neural networks is discussed in a book by Takefuji [Takefuji 92].

Exercises

1. Define the following terms:
    OR-parallelism   Artificial intelligence
    AND-parallelism   Rule-based systems
    Production systems   Reasoning systems
    Logic   Expert systems

2. What are the main differences between a typical database and a typical knowledge base?

3. Consider a production system with four rules, which is to be mapped into a three-processor message-passing system with an interconnection as shown below. The parallelism matrix and the communication matrix derived from the rule interconnection are given by P and C, respectively.

$$P = \begin{pmatrix} 1\,0\,1\,0 \\ 0\,1\,1\,0 \\ 1\,1\,1\,0 \\ 0\,0\,0\,1 \end{pmatrix} \qquad C = \begin{pmatrix} 1\,0\,1\,0 \\ 0\,1\,1\,0 \\ 1\,1\,1\,0 \\ 0\,1\,0\,1 \end{pmatrix}$$

The problem is to compute the allocation cost, consisting of the communication cost and the parallelism cost, given by the following two allocation matrices:

$$X_1 = \begin{pmatrix} 0\,1\,0 \\ 1\,0\,0 \\ 0\,1\,0 \\ 1\,0\,0 \end{pmatrix} \qquad X_2 = \begin{pmatrix} 1\,0\,0 \\ 0\,1\,0 \\ 1\,0\,0 \\ 0\,0\,1 \end{pmatrix}$$

Rules	Processor		Rules	Processor
1	2		1	1
2	1		2	2
3	2		3	1
4	1		4	3

Decide which allocation scheme is better when the allocation cost is

$$E = \sum_{Col} \sum_{Row} E_c + \frac{1}{2} \sum_{Col} \sum_{Row} E_p \qquad E_c = (X^T C X).D \quad E_p = XX^T.L$$

where D is the distance matrix characterizing the interconnection network and L is the parallelism loss of allocation, in which $P_{ij} = 1$ implies $L_{ij} = 0$.

4. Prove that whether a set of compatible rules in a production cycle is executed either sequentially or in parallel, the same changes to the working memory are produced.

5. Outline the most important operations in knowledge processing and identify computer architecture features that might provide efficient implementations of these operations.

6. Show how a speech understanding system could be built using a MACE-style architecture.

7. Explain the structure of a working memory in the OPS5 production system language.

8. What is the difference between OR-parallelism and AND-parallelism?

9. Describe the operations of a production system.

10. What value do we give a future created by an expression such as (future (/ 3 0)), which has been asked to perform a division by zero?

11. Write a logic program for defining list intersection.

12. Consider the four-rule production system below:

R1:	If	P(A,B) & N(B,C) $\Rightarrow$ M(A,B)
R2:	If	R(C,D) & N(B,C) $\Rightarrow$ Q(C,D)
R3:	If	R(C,D) & N(D,A) $\Rightarrow$ P(D,E)
R4:	If	M(B,D) & Q(A,C) $\Rightarrow$ N(B,C)

(a) Design the interconnection network among four rules that minimizes the communication cost (one rule per processor).

(b) Derive the parallelism matrix and the communication matrix.

13. Dijkstra's shortest-path algorithm is too inefficient for most search-oriented applications, since the shortest-path tree can grow to be quite large, even exponentially large. Explain the reason for its inefficiency and propose a new search paradigm that leads to an efficient algorithm.

Reference-Needed Exercises

14. Contrast expert systems and neural networks in terms of knowledge representation, knowledge acquisition and explanation. Give one domain in which the expert system approach would be more promising and one domain in which the neural network approach would be more promising.

15. Write a logic program to number the leaves of a tree in ascending order from left to right.

Bibliography

[Accetta 86] M. Accetta, R. Baron, D. Golub, R. Rashid, A. Tevanian, and M. Young. "Mach: A New Kernel Foundation for UNIX Development," Proceedings Summer 1986 USENIX Conference, pp. 93-112, 1986.

[Ackerman 79] W. B. Ackerman and J. B. Dennis. "VAL: A Value Oriented Algorithmic Language," Technical Report MIT/LC/STR-218, Laboratory of Computer Science, MIT, 1979.

[Aho 86] A. V. Aho, R. Sethi, and J. D. Ullman. "Compilers: Principles, Techniques and Tools," Addison-Wesley Publishing Company, 1986.

[Ahuja 86] S. Ahuja. "Linda and friends," IEEE Computer, Vol. 18, No. 8, pp. 26-34, 1986.

[Ali 90] M. Ali and R. Karlsson. "Full Prolog and Scheduling OR-Parallelism in Muse," International Journal of Parallel Programming, Vol. 19, No. 6, pp. 445-475, 1990.

[Akl 82] S. G. Akl, D. T. Barnard, and R. J. Doran. "Design, Analysis and Implementation of a Parallel Tree Search Algorithm," IEEE Transactions on Machine Analysis and Artificial Intelligence, Vol. 4, pp. 192-203, 1982.

[Akl 97] S. G. Akl. "Parallel Computation: Models and Methods," Prentice-Hall Publishing Company, Upper Saddle River, New Jersey, 1997.

[Allen 80] S. J. Allen and A. Oldehoeft. "A flow analysis procedure for the translation of high-level languages to a dataflow language," IEEE Trans. Computers, Vol. C-29, No. 9, pp. 826-831, 1980.

[Almasi 94] G. Almasi and A. Gottlieb. "Highly Parallel Computing," Benjamin/Cummings Publishing Company, 1994.

[Alton 77] D. A. Alton and D. M. Eckstein. "Parallel graph-processing using depth-first search," Conference on Theoretical Computer Science, University of Waterloo, pp. 21-29, 1977.

[Amdahl 67] G. M. Amdahl. "Validity of the Single-Processor Approach to Achieving Large-Scale Computer Capabilities," AFIPS Conference Proceedings, Vol. 30, pp. 483-485, 1967.

[Anaratone 86] M. Anaratone, E. Rnould, T. Gross and H. T. Kung. "Wrap architecture and implementation," Proceedings of the 13th Annual International Symposium on Computer Architecture, pp. 346-356, 1986.

[Arvind 78] V. Arvind, K. P. Gostelow, and W. Plouffe. "The ID Report. An Asynchronous Programming Language and Computing Machine," Technical Report 114a, Department of Information and Computing Science, University of California, 1978.

[Arvind 81] V. Arvind and V. Kathail. "A multiple processor data flow machine that supports generalized procedures," Computer Architecture News, Vol. 9, pp. 291-302, 1981.

[Ashcroft 77] A. Ashcroft and W. Wadge. "LUCID, a nonprocedural language with iteration," Communication ACM, Vol. 20, pp. 519-526, 1977.

[Atallah 84] M. Atallah and U. Vishkin. "Finding Euler tour in parallel," Journal of Computer and System Sciences, Vol. 29, pp. 330-337, 1984.

[Backus 78] J. W. Backus. "Can Programming Be Liberated from the von Neumann Style? A Functional Style and Its Algebra of Programs," Communication of ACM, Vol. 21, No. 8, pp. 613-641, 1978.

[Backus 82] J. W. Backus. "Functional Level Computing," IEEE SPECTRUM, Vol. 19, pp. 22-27, August 1982.

[Baron 92] R. J. Baron. "Computer Architecture," Addison-Wesley Publishing Company, 1992.

[Batcher 68] K. E. Batcher. "Sorting Networks and Their Applications," Proceedings of the AFIPS Spring Joint Computer Conference, April 30-May2, Vol. 32, pp. 307-314, 1968.

[Bell 92] G. Bell. "Ultracomputer: A Teraflop Before Its Time," Communications of ACM, Vol. 35, No. 8, pp. 27-47, 1992.

[Ben-Ari 90] M. Ben-Ari. "Principles of Concurrent and Distributed Programming," C.A.R. Hoare Series Editor, Prentice-Hall Publishing Company, 1990.

[Banerjee 93] U. Banerjee. R. Eigenmann, A. Nocilau, and D. A. Padua. "Automatic program parallelization," Proceedings of IEEE Vol. 81. No. 2, pp. 211-243, 1993.

[Bentley 80] J. L. Bentley. "A parallel algorithm for constructing minimum spanning trees," Journal of Algorithms, pp. 21-23, 1980.

[Berman 84] F. Berman and L. Snyder. "On mapping parallel algorithms into parallel architectures," 1984 International Conference on Parallel Processing, pp. 307-309, 1984.

[Bishop 86] P. Bishop. "Fifth Generation Computers: Concepts, Implementations and Uses," Ellis Horwood Series on Computers and Their Applications, Chichester, UK, 1986.

[Blank 90] T. Blank. "The MasPar MP-1 Architecture," COMPCON Proceedings, pp. 20-24, 1990.

[Blelloch 90] G. Blelloch. "Vector Models for Data Parallel Computing," MIT Press, 1990.

[Bodin 91] F. Bodin, P. Beckman, D. B. Gannon, S. Narayana and S. Yang. "Distributed pC++: Basic ideas for an object parallel language," Proc. Supercomputing, pp. 273-282, 1991.

[Bokhari 81] S. H. Bokhari. "On the Mapping Problem," IEEE Transactions on Computers, Vol. C-30, pp. 207-214, 1981.

[Borgi 91] F. Brogi and A. Ciancarini. "A Logic Programming Language," Proceedings of the ACM Conference on Functional Languages and Computer Architecture, pp. 171-178, 1991.

[Boruvka 26] O. Boruvka. "O jistém problém minimálním," Práca Moravské Prírodovédecké Spolecností, Vol. 3, pp. 37-58, 1926.

[Brassard 96] G. Brassard and P. Bratley. "Fundamentals of Algorithmics," Prentice-Hall Publishing Company, 1996.

[Brent 74] R. P. Brent. "The parallel evaluation of general arithmetic expressions," Journal of the Association of Computer Machinery, Vol. 21, No. 2, 1974.

[Brownston 85] L. R. Brownston, R. Farrell, E. Kant, and N. Martin. "Programming Expert Systems in OPS5: An Introduction to Rule-Based Programming," Addison-Wesley Publishing Company, 1985.

[Burkhardt 92] H. Burkhardt. "Technical Summary of KSR-1," Kendell Square Research Corporation, 170 Tracer Lane, Waltham, MA 02154, 1992.

[Cann 92] D. Cann. "Retire Fortran? A debate rekindled," Communication of the ACM, Vol. 35, No. 8, pp. 81-89, 1992.

[Chandy 91] M. Chandy and S. Taylor. "An Introduction to Parallel Programming," Jones and Bartlett Publishing Company, 1991.

[Chandy 88] M. Chandy and J. Misra. "Parallel Program Design: A Foundation," Addison-Wesley Publishing Company, 1988.

[Chaudhuri 92] P. Chaudhuri. "Parallel Algorithms: Design and Analysis," Advances in Computer Science Series, Prentice-Hall Publishing Company, 1992.

[Chiang 83] Y. P. Chiang and K. S. Fu. "Matching parallel algorithms and architecture," 1983 International Conference on Parallel Processing, pp. 374-380, 1983.

[Christofides 76] N. Christofides. "Worst-case analysis of a new heuristic for the traveling salesman problem," Research Report No. 388, Management Sciences, Carnegie-Mellon University, Pittsburgh, PA, 1976.

[Ciepielewski 91] A. Ciepielewski. "Scheduling in OR-parallel Prolog systems: Survey and open problems," International Journal of Parallel Programming, Vol. 20, No. 6, pp. 421-451, 1991.

[Chikayama 88] T. Chikayama, H. Sato, and T. Miyazaki. "Overview of the Parallel Inference Machine Operating System (PIMOS)," Proceedings of the International Conference on Fifth Generation Computer Systems, Tokyo, pp. 230-251, 1988.

[Christy 90] P. Christy. "Software to Support Massively Parallel Computing on the MasPar MP-1," COMPCON Proceedings, pp. 29-33, 1990.

[Clark 86] K. L. Clark and S. Gregory. "Parlog: Parallel programming in logic," ACM Transactions on Programming Languages and Systems, Vol. 8, No. 1, 1986.

[Clocksin 87] W. F. Clocksin and C. S. Mellish. "Programming in Prolog," Springer-Verlag Publishing Company, 3rd Ed., 1987.

[Cohen 83] M. A. Cohen and S. G. Grossberg. "Absolute stability of global pattern formation and parallel memory storage by competitive neural networks," IEEE Trans. Systems Man Cybernetics 13-5, pp. 815-826, 1983.

[Cohen 96] N. H. Cohen. "Ada as a Second Language," McGraw-Hill Publishing Company, 2nd Ed., 1996.

[Dasgupta 90] S. Dasgupta. "A hierarchical taxonomic system for computer architectures," Computer, Vol. 23, No. 3, pp. 64-74, 1990.

[Dekel 81] E. Dekel, D. Nassimi and S. Sahni. "Parallel matrix and graph algorithms," SIAM Journal on Computing, Vol. 10, No. 4, pp. 657-675, 1981.

[Dennis 80] J. Dennis. "Data flow supercomputers," IEEE Computers, Vol. 13, pp. 48-56, 1980.

[Dennis 79] J. B. Dennis. "The Varieties of Data Flow Computers," Proceedings of the International Conferences in Distributed Computing Systems, pp. 430-439, 1979.

[Dijkstra 59] E. W. Dijkstra. "A note on two problems in connection with graphs," Numerische Mathematik, Vol. 1, pp. 269-271, 1959.

[Doeppner 87] T. W. Doeppner. "A Threads Tutorial," Computer Science Technical Report CS-87-06, Brown University, 1987.

[Douglas 78] J. Douglas. "Automatic Partitioning of Programs in Multiprocessor Systems," COMPCON Proceedings, pp. 175-178, 1980.

[Feo 85] J. T. Feo, D. C. Cann, and R. R. Oldehoeft. "A Report on the Sisal Language Project," Lawrence Livermore National laboratory, Technical Paper UCID-211159, Lawrence Livermore National Laboratory, Livermore, CA, 1985.

[Ferguson 88] C. Ferguson and R. Korf. "Distributed Tree Search and its Application to Alpha-Beta Pruning," Proceedings of the 1988 National Conference on Artificial Intelligence, 1988.

[Finkel 82] R. A. Finkel and J. P. Fishburn. "Parallelism in alpha-beta search," Artificial Intelligence, Vol. 19, No. 1, pp. 89-106, 1982.

[Fisher 91] W. A. Fisher, R. J. Fujimoto, and R. C. Smithson. "A Programmable Analog Neural Network Processor," IEEE Trans. on Neural Networks, Vol. 2, No. 2, pp. 210-216, 1991.

[Fisher 83] J. A. Fisher. "Very long instruction word architectures and the Eli-512," Proceedings of the 10th Annual International Symposium on Computer Architecture, pp. 140-150, 1983.

[Fitzgerald 86] K. Fitzgerald and R. Rashid. "The integration of virtual memory management and interprocess communication in Accent," ACM Trans. Computer Systems, Vol. 4, No. 2, pp. 147-177, 1986.

[Floyd 62] R. W. Floyd. "Algorithm 97: Shortest Path," Communications of the ACM, Vol. 5, No. 6, pp. 345, June 1962.

[Flynn 66] M. J. Flynn. "Very high-speed computing systems," Proceedings of the IEEE, Vol. 54, No. 12, pp. 1901-1909, December, 1966.

[Forgy 82] C. L. Forgy. "Rete: A fast algorithm for the many pattern-many object pattern match problem," Artificial Intelligence, Vol. 19, pp. 17-37, 1982.

[Forgy 74] C. L. Forgy. "A Network Match Routine for Production Systems," Department of Computer Science, Carnegie-Mellon University, 1974.

[Fortes 85] J. A. B. Fortes and D. I. Moldovan. "Parallelism detection and transformation techniques useful for VLSI algorithms," Journal of Parallel and Distributed Computing, Vol. 2, pp. 277-301, August 1985.

[Foster 95] I. Foster. "Designing and Building Parallel Programs," Addison-Wesley Publishing Company, 1995.

[Foster 94] I. Foster. "Designing and Building Parallel Programs," Addison-Wesley Publishing Company, 1994.

[Foster 92] I. Foster, R. Olson and S. Tuecke. "Productive parallel programming: The PCN approach," Scientific Programming, Vol. 1, pp. 51-66, 1992.

[Foster 91] I. Foster. "Program Transformation Notation: A Tutorial, "Technical Report ANL-91/38, Argonne National Laboratory, 1991.

[Foster 89] I. Foster and S. Taylor. "Strand: New Concepts in Parallel Programming," Prentice-Hall Publishing Company, 1989.

[Fox 91] G. Fox, S. Hiranandani, K. Kennedy, C. Koelbel, and U. Kemer. "FORTRAN D Language Specification," Rice University Technical paper TR90-141, 1991.

[Fox 87] G. Fox, S. Otto and A. J. Hey. "Matrix algorithms on a hypercube I: Matrix multiplication," Parallel Computing, Vol. 4, pp. 17-31, 1987.

[Fuchi 87] K. Fuchi and K. Furukawa. "The Role of Logic Programming in the Fifth Generation Computer Project," New Generation Computing, Vol. 3, No. 5, pp. 3-23, 1987.

[Gabow 82] H. Gabow and O. Kariv. "Algorithms for edge colouring bipartite graphs and multigraphs," SIAM Journal of Computing, Vol. 11, No. 1, pp. 117-129, 1982.

[Gabriel 88] R. Gabriel and J. McCarthy. "Qlisp," In Parallel Computation and Computers for Artificial Intelligence, ed. J. Kowalik., Boston:Kluwer, 1988.

[Gasser 87] L. Gasser, C. Braganza, and N. Herman. "Implementing Distributed Artificial Intelligence Systems using MACE," Proceedings of the Third IEEE Conference on Artificial Intelligence Applications," pp. 315-320, 1987.

[Geist 94] A. Geist, A. Geguelia, J. Dongarra, W. Jiang and V. Sunderam. "PVM: Parallel Virtual Machine, A User's Guide and Tutorial for Networked Parallel Computing," MIT Press, 1994.

[Gelernter 85] D. Gelernter. "Generative communication in Linda," ACM Transactions Programming Languages and Systems, Vol. 7, No. 1, pp. 80-112, 1985.

[Gentleman 78] W. Gentleman. "Some complexity results for matrix computations on parallel computers," Journal of the ACM, Vol. 25, No. 1, pp. 112-115, 1978.

[Gibbons 87] A. M. Gibbons and W. Rytter. "Fast parallel algorithms for edge-colouring of some tree structured graphs," FCT, 1987.

[Gibbons 88] A. Gibbons, and W. Rytter. "Efficient Parallel Algorithms," Cambridge University Press, 1988.

[Glauert 78] J. Glauert. "A Single Assignment Language for Data Flow Computing," Master's thesis, University of Manchester, 1978.

[Gordon 79] M. J. Gordon, R. Milner and C. Wadsworth. "Edinburgh LCF," Springer-Verlag LNCS 78, Berlin, 1979.

[Goscinski 91] A. Goscinski. "Distributed Operating Systems: The Logical Design," Addison-Wesley Publishing Company, 1991.

[Graham 85] R. L. Graham and P. Hell. "On the history of the minimum spanning tree problem," Annals of the History of Computing, Vol. 7, pp. 43-57, 1985.

[Gurd 85] J. R. Gurd, C. C. Kirkham and I. Watson. "The Manchester prototype dataflow computer," Communication of the ACM, Vol. 28, No. 1, pp. 34-52, 1985.

[Gustafson 88] J. Gustafson. "Reevaluating Amdahl's Law," Communications of the ACM, Vol. 31, No. 5, pp. 532-535, 1988.

[Habermann 72] A. Habermann. "Parallel Neighbor Sort," Technical Report, Carnegie-Mellon University, Pittsburgh, PA, 1972.

[Hagan 96] M. T. Hagan, H. B. Demuth, and M. Beale. "Neural Network Design," PWS Publishing Company, 1996.

[Hagersten 90] E. Hagersten, S. Haridi, and D.H. Warren. "The Cache-Coherent Protocol of the Data Diffusion Machine," in Cache and Interconnect Architectures in Multiprocessors, edited by M. Dubois, 1990.

[Hagersten 92] E. Hagersten, A. Landin, and S. Haridi. "DDM: A Cache-Only Memory Architecture," Computer, Vol. 25, No. 9, pp. 44-54, September 1992.

[Halstead 88] R. Halstead. "Parallel computing using Multilisp," in Parallel Computation and Computers for Artificial Intelligence, ed. J. Kowalik, Boston:Kluwer, 1988.

[Halstead 86] R. Halstead. "Parallel Symbolic Computing," IEEE Computer, Vol. 19, No. 8, pp. 35-43, August 1986.

[Halstead 86] R. Halstead, T. Anderson, R. Osborne and T. Sterling. "Concert: Design of a multiprocessor development system," Proceeding of the 13th Annual International Symposium on Computer Architecture, pp. 40-48, 1986.

[Hamacher 96] V. C. Hamacher, Z. G. Vranesic, and S. G. Zaky. "Computer Organization," The McGraw-Hill Publishing Company, 1996.

[Hanlon 66] A. G. Hanlon. "Content addressable and associative memory systems - A survey," IEEE Transactions on Electronic Computers, Vol. EC-15, No. 4, pp. 509-521, 1966.

[Hatcher 91] P. Hatcher and M. Quinn. "Data Parallel Programming on MIMD Computers," MIT Press, 1991.

[Hayes 78] J. P. Hayes. "Computer Architecture and Organization," McGraw-Hill Publishing Company, 1978.

[Hecht-Nielson 91] R. Hecht-Nielson. "Neurocomputing," Addison-Wesley Publishing Company, 1991.

[Hillis 85] D. W. Hillis. "The Connection Machine," MIT Press, 1985.

[Hiraki 91] K. Hiraki, S. Sekiguchi and T. Shimada. "Status of SIGMA-1: A data flow supercomputer," in Advanced Topics in Data Flow Computing, eds. J. L. Gaudiot and L. Bic, Prentice-Hall Publishing Company, 1991.

[Hiranandani 92] S. Hiranandani, K. Kennedy, and C. W. Tseng. "Compiling Fortran-D for MIMD Distributed Memory Machines," Communications of the ACM, Vol. 35, No. 8, pp. 66-80, 1992.

[Hiranandani 93] S. Hiranandani, K. Kennedy, and C. W. Tseng. "Preliminary Experiences with the Fortran-D Compiler," Proceedings, Supercomputing 1993, pp. 338-350, November 1993.

[Hoare 85] C. A. R. Hoare. "Communicating Sequential Processes," Prentice-Hall Publishing Company, 1985.

[Hoare 78] C. A. R. Hoare. "Communicating sequential processes," Communication of ACM, Vol. 21, No. 8, pp. 666-677, 1978.

[Hockney 87] R. W. Hockney. "Classification and evaluation of parallel computer systems," Springer-Verlag Lecture Notes in Computer Science, No. 295, pp. 13-25, 1987.

[Hockney 88] R. W. Hockney and C. R. Jesshope. "Parallel Computers 2," Adam Hilger, Bristol and Philadelphia, 1988.

[Hopfield 82] J. J. Hopfield. "Neural networks and physical systems with emergent collective computational abilities," Proceedings of the National Academy of sciences USA, Vol. 79, No. 8, pp. 2554-2558, 1982.

[Hopfield 85] J. J. Hopfield and D. W. Tank. "Neural computation of decisions in optimization problems," Biological Cybernetics, Vol. 52, No. 3, pp. 141-152, July 1985.

[Hopfield 86] J. J. Hopfield and D. W. Tank. "Computing with Neural Circuits," Science, Vol. 233, pp. 625-633, August 1986.

[Hudak 89] P. Hudak. "Functional programming languages," ACM Computing Surveys, Vol. 21, No. 3, pp. 359-411, 1989.

[Hwang 93] K. Hwang. "Advanced Computer Architecture: Parallelism, Scalability, and Programmability," McGraw-Hill Publishing Company, 1993.

[Hyatt 89] R. Haytt, B. Suter and H. Nelson. "A parallel alpha-beta tree searching algorithm," Parallel Computing, Vol. 10, pp. 299-308, 1989.

[Inmos 88] Inmos Corporation. "Occam 2 Reference Manual," Prentice-Hall International, Hemel Hempstead, 1988.

[Intrepid Group 94]. Intrepid Group. "CHARM: User's Guide and Reference Manual," Department of Electrical and Computer Engineering, University of Iowa, November 1994.

[Jaja 92] J. Jaja. "An Introduction to Parallel Algorithms," Addison-Wesley Publishing Company, 1992.

[Jarnik 30] V. Jarnik. "Ojistém problému minimálnim," Práce Moravské Prírodovéd Spolecnosti, Vol. 6, pp. 57-63, 1930.

[Jones 88] G. Jones and M. Goldsmith. "Programming in Occam 2," Prentice-Hall Publishing Company, 1988.

[Kale 94] L. V. Kale, B. Ramkumar, A. B. Sinha, and A. Gursoy. "The Charm Parallel Programming Language and System: Part I   Description of Language Features," Parallel Programming Laboratory, Department of Computer Science, University of Illinois at Urbana-Champaign, 1994.

[Karayiannis 93] N. B. Karayiannis and A. K. Venetsanopoulos. "Artificial Neural Networks," Academic Press, Inc., 1993.

[Keller 79] R. M. Keller. "A loosely coupled applicative multiprocessing system," AFIPS Conference, Vol. 48, pp. 613-622, 1979.

[Kosaraju 86] S. R. Kosaraju. "Parallel evaluation of division-free arithmetic expressions," STOC, pp. 231-239, 1986.

[Kranz 89] D. Kranz, R. Halstead and E. Mohr. "Mul-T: A high-performance parallel Lisp," ACM SIGPLAN Notices, Vol. 24, No. 7, pp. 81-90, 1989.

[Kruskal 56] J. B. Kruskal. "On the shortest spanning subtree of a graph and the traveling salesman problem," Proceedings of the American Mathematical Society, Vol. 7, pp. 48-50, February 1956.

[Kuck 84] J. Kuck, R. H. Kuhn, B. Leasure, and M. Wolfe. "The Structure of an Advanced Retargatable vectorizer," in Kai Hwang editor, Tutorial on Supercomputers, IEEE Press, pp. 163-178, 1984.

[Kumar 94] V. Kumar, A. Grama, A. Gupta, and G. Karypis. "Introduction to Parallel Computing: Design and Analysis of Algorithms," The Benjamin/Cummings Publishing Company, 1994.

[Kumar 87] V. Kumar and V. N. Rao. "Parallel depth-first search, part II: Analysis," International Journal of Parallel Programming, Vol. 16, No. 6, pp. 501-519, 1987.

[Kung 78] H. T. Kung and C. E. Leiserson. "Systolic Arrays for VLSI," I. S. Duff and G. N. Stewart (eds.), Sparse Matrix Proceedings, SIAM, 1978.

[Kuo 91] S. Kuo and D. I. Moldovan. "Implementation of Multiple Rule Firing Production Systems on Hypercube," Journal of Parallel and Distributed Computing, Vol. 13, No. 4, pp. 383-394, 1991.

[Lai 84] T. H. Lai and S. Sahni. "Anomalies in Parallel Branch and Bound Algorithms," Communications of the ACM, pp. 594-602, 1984.

[Lampson 80] B. W. Lampson and D. D. Redell. "Experience with Processes and Monitors in Mesa," Communications of the ACM, Vol. 23, No. 2, pp. 105-117, 1980.

[Larid 87] J. E. Larid, A. Newell and P. Rosenbloom. "Soar: An architecture for general intelligence," Artificial Intelligence, Vol. 33, No. 1, 1987.

[Lawrence 82] S. Lawrence. "Introduction to the Configurable, Highly Parallel Computer," Computer, Vol. 15, pp. 47-56, January 1982.

[Lawrie 75] D. Lawrie. "Access and Alignment of data in array processors," IEEE Trans. Computers, C-24(12), pp.1145-1155, 1975.

[Leighton 92] F. T. Leighton. "Introduction to Parallel Algorithms and Architectures: Arrays, Trees, Hypercubes," Morgan Kaufmann Publishers, San Mateo, California, 1992.

[Leighton 83] F. T. Leighton. "Parallel computation using meshes of trees," in Proceedings 1983 International Workshop on Graph Theoretic Concepts in Computer Science, 1983.

[Levesque 89] J. M. Levesque, and J. L. Williamson. "A guidebook to Fortran on supercomputers," Academic Press, Inc., 1989.

[Lewis 92] T. Lewis and H. El-Rewini. "Introduction to Parallel Computing," Prentice-Hall Publishing Company, 1992.

[Li 85] H. Li, C-C. Wang and M. Lavin. "Structured process: A new language attribute for better interaction of parallel architecture and algorithm," 1985 International Conference on Parallel Processing, pp. 247-254, 1985.

[Lipkis 83] T. A. Lipkis and J. G. Schmolze. "Classification in the KL-ONE Knowledge Representation System," Proceedings of Eighth International Joint Conference on Artificial Intelligence, Vol. 1, pp. 330-332, 1983.

[Loral Instrumentation 86] "LDF 100 Getting Started Manual," Document No. 49055665(A), 1986.

[Loveman 93] D. Loveman. "High Performance Fortran," IEEE Parallel and Distributed Technology, Vol. 1, No. 1, pp. 25-42, 1993.

[Luger 93] G. F. Luger, and W. A. Stubblefield. "Artificial Intelligence: Structures and Strategies for Complex Problem Solving," The Benjamin/Cummings Publishing Company, 1993.

[Mago 79] G. Mago. "A network of microprocessors to execute reduction languages," International Journal of Computer and Information Sciences, Vol. 8, No. 6, pp. 349-471, 1979.

[Mankovich 87] T. Mankovich, V. Popescu and H. Sullivan. "CHoPP principles of operation," Proceedings of the 2nd International Supercomputer Conference, pp. 2-10, 1987.

[MasPar Computer Corporation 91] "The MP-1 Family of Massively Parallel Computers," MasPar Computer Corporation, 1991.

[McGraw 83] J. R. McGraw et al. "SISAL: Streams and Iterations in a Single Assignment Language," Reference Manual, Version 1.1, Lawrence Livermore National Laboratory, Livermore, CA, 1983.

[McGraw 85] J. R. McGraw et al. "SISAL: Streams and Iterations in a Single Assignment Language," Reference Manual, Version 1.2, Lawrence Livermore National Laboratory, Livermore, CA, 1985.

[McGraw 82] J. R. McGraw. "The VAL Language: Description and Analysis," ACM Transactions on Programming Languages and Systems, Vol. 4, No. 1, pp. 44-82, January 1982.

[Mehlhorn 95] K. Mehlhorn and S. Naher. "LEDA, a platform for combinatorial and geomatric computing," Communications of the ACM, Vol. 38, pp. 96-102, 1995.

[Miller 84] R. Miller and Q. F. Stout. "Computational Geometry on a mesh-connected computer," Preceedings of the 1984 International Conference on Parallel Processing, pp. 66-73, 1984.

[Moldovan 93] D. Moldovan. "Parallel Processing: From Applications to Systems" Morgan Kaufmann Publisher, 1993.

[Moldovan 92a] D. I. Moldovan, W. Lee, and C. Lin. "SNAP: A Marker Propagation for Knowledge Processing," IEEE Transactions on Parallel and Distributed Systems, Vol. 3, No. 4, pp. 397-410, 1992.

[Moldovan 92b] D. I. Moldovan, W. Lee, C. Lin, and M Chung. "SNAP: Parallel Processing Applied to AI," Computers, Vol. 25, No. 5, pp. 39-50, 1992.

[Moldovan 89] D. I. Moldovan. "RUBIC: A Multiprocessor for Rule-Based Systems," IEEE Transactions on Systems, Man and Cybernetics, Vol. 19, No. 4, pp. 699-706, 1989.

[Moler 86] C. Moler and D. S. Scott. "Communication Utilities for the iPSC," IPSC Technical Report, No. 2, Intel Scientific Computers, August 1986.

[Monien 90] B. Monien, R. Feldmann, P. Mysliwietz, and O. Vornberger. "Parallel Game Tree Search by Dynamic Tree Decomposition," in Parallel Algorithms for Machine Intelligence and Vision, edited by V. Kumar, Springer-Verlag Publishing Company, 1990.

[Moto-oka 82] T. Moto-oka. "Fifth Generation Computer Systems," North-Holland Publishing Company, 1982.

[Muller 76] D. E. Muller and F. P. Preparata. "Restructuring of arithmetic expressions for parallel evaluation," Journal ACM, Vol. 23, pp. 534-543, 1976.

[Nassimi 80] D. Nassimi and S. Sahni. "Finding connected components and connected ones on a mesh-connected parallel computer," SIAM Journal on Computing, Vol. 9, No. 4, pp. 744-757, 1980.

[Nath 83] D. Nath, S. N. Maheshwari and C. P. Bhatt. "Efficient VLSI networks for parallel processing based on orthogonal trees," IEEE Transactions on Computers, Vol. C-32, pp. 21-23, 1983.

[Nickolls 90] J. R. Nickolls. "The Design of the MasPar MP-1: A Cost Effective Massively Parallel Computer," COMPCON Proceedings, pp. 25-28, 1990.

[Oldehoeft 86] R. R. Oldehoeft, D. Cann and S. Allen. "Sisal: Initial MIMD performance results," Proceedings of the 1986 Conference on Algorithms and Hardware for Parallel Processing, pp. 120-127, 1986.

[Powley 90] C Powley, C. Ferguson, and R. Korf. "Parallel Heuristic Search: Two Approaches," in Parallel Algorithms for Machine Intelligence and Vision, edited by V. Kumar, Springer-Verlag Publishing Company, 1990.

[Prim 57] R. C. Prim. "Shortest connection networks and some generalizations," Bell Systems Technical Journal, Vol. 36, pp. 1389-1401, 1957.

[Quinn 94] M. Quinn. "Parallel Computing: Theory and Practice," McGraw-Hill Publishing Company, 1994.

[Quinn 84] M. J. Quinn and N. Deo. "Parallel Graph Algorithms," Computing Surveys, Vol. 16, No. 3, pp. 319-348, September 1984.

[Rashid 86] R. Rashid. "Experiences with the Accent Network Operating System," Networking in Open Systems, Lecture Notes in Computer Science, Vol. 248, pp. 259-269, 1986.

[Rashid 81] R. Rashid and G. Robertson. "Accent: A communication oriented network operating system kernel," ACM Operating Systems Review, Vol. 15, No. 5, pp. 64-75, 1981.

[Reghbati 78] E. Reghbati and D. G. Corneil. "Parallel Computations in Graph Theory," SIAM Journal on Computing, Vol. 7, No. 2, pp. 230-237, 1978.

[Rich 91] E. Rich and K. Knight. "Artificial Intelligence," McGraw-Hill Publishing Company, 1991.

[Rosing 90] M. Rosing, R. B. Schnabel and R. P. Weaver. "The DINO Parallel Programming Language," Technical Report CU-CS-501-90, Computer Science Department, University of Colorado, Boulder, CO, 1990.

[Russell 95] S. Russell and P. Norvig. "Artificial Intelligence: A Modern Approach," Prentice-Hall Publishing Company, 1995.

[Sabot 88] G. Sabot. "The Paralation Model: Architecture-Independent Parallel Programming," MIT Press, 1988.

[Sahni 85] S. Sahni. "Concepts in Discrete Mathematics," Camelot Publishing Company, 2nd Ed., 1985.

[Sakai 91] S. Sakai, Y. Kodama and Y. Yamaguchi. "Prototype implementation of a highly dataflow machine," Proceedings of the International Parallel Processing Symposium, 1991.

[Savage 84] C. Savage. "A systolic design for connectivity problems," IEEE Transactions on Computers, Vol. C-33, pp. 99-104, 1984.

[Sejnowski 80] M. C. Sejnowski, E. T. Upchurch, R. N. Kapur, D. P. Charlu, and G. J. Lipovski. "An Overview of the Texas Reconfigurable Array Computer,".AFIPS Computer Conference, pp. 631-641, June, 1980.

[Shapiro 89] E. Y. Shapiro. "The family of concurrent logic programming languages," ACM Computing Surveys, Vol. 21, No. 3, 1989.

[Shapiro 86] E. Shapiro. "Concurrent Prolog: A Progress Report," Computer, Vol. 19, No. 8, pp. 44-58, 1986.

[Shapiro 84] E. Y. Shapiro. "Systolic Programming: A Paradigm of Parallel Processing," Proceedings of the FGCS, 1984.

[Sharp 85] J. A. Sharp. "Data Flow Computing," Ellis Horwood Series on Computers and Their Applications, Wiley, 1985.

[Sharp 87] J. A. Sharp. "An Introduction to Distributed and Parallel Processing," Blackwell Scientific Publications, 1987.

[Shaw 84] D. Shaw. "SIMD and MSIMD variants of the NON-VON supercomputer," COMPCON Proceedings, pp. 360-363, 1984.

[Shiloach 81] Y. Shiloach and U. Vishkin. "Finding the maximum, merging, and sorting in a parallel computation model," Journal of Algorithms, Vol. 2, pp. 88-102, 1981.

[Shiva 96] S. Shiva. "Pipelined and Parallel Computer Architectures," Harper Collins College Publishers, 1996.

[Siegel 87] H. T. Siegel, T. Schwederski, J. T. Kuehn and N. J. Davis. "An Overview of the PASM Parallel Processing System," in Tutorial Computer Architecture, Edited by D. D. Gajski et al., IEEE, pp. 387-407, 1987.

[Skansholm 97] J. Skansholm. "Ada 95: From the Beginning," Addison-Wesley Publishing Company, 3rd Ed., 1997.

[Skiena 97] S. Skiena. "The Algorithm Design Manual," Springer-Verlag Publishing Company, 1997.

[Skillicorn 88] D. B. Skillicorn, "A taxonomy for computer architectures," Computer, Vol. 21, No. 11, pp. 46-57, 1988.

[Sollin 77] M. Sollin. "An algorithm attributed to Sollin," in Introduction to the Design and Analysis of Algorithms, edited by S. Goodman and S. Hedetmiemi, McGraw-Hill Publishing Company, 1977.

[Stolfo 86] S. J. Stolfo and D. P. Miranker. "The DADO Production System Machine," Journal of Parallel and Distributed Computing, Vol. 3, pp. 269-295, 1986.

[STRAND88 90] STRAND88. User Manual, Buckingham Release 1990, Artificial Intelligence Limited, Greycaine Rd., Watford, Hertfordshire WD2 4JP England, 1990.

[Sullivan 77] H. Sullivan. "A large scale homogeneous, fully distributed parallel machine," Proceedings of the 4th Annual Symposium on Computer Architecture, pp. 105-124, 1977.

[Syre 77] J. Syre, D. Comte and N. Hifdi. "Pipelining, parallelism, and anachronism in the ALU system," Proceedings of the 1977 International Conference on Parallel Processing," pp. 87-92, 1977.

[Takefuji 92] T. Takefuji. "Neural Network Parallel Computing," Academic Press, Inc., 1992.

[Tanenbaum 85] A. S. Tanenbaum, and R. Renesse. "Distributed Operating Systems," Computing Surveys, Vol. 17, No. 4, pp. 419-470, 1985.

[Tanenbaum 92] A. S. Tanenbaum. Modern Operating Systems, Prentice-Hall Publishing Company, 1992.

[Tanenbaum 90] A. S. Tanenbaum. R. Renesse, H. Staveren, G. Sharp, and S. Mullender, "Experiences with the Amoeba Distributed Operating System," Communications of ACM, Vol. 33, No. 12, pp. 46-63, 1990.

[Thinking Machines Corporation 93]. "The CM Fortran Reference Manual, Version 2.1," Thinking Machine Corporation, 1993.

[Thinking Machines Corporation 91], "Connection Machine Model CM-5," Technical Summary, 1991.

[Thinking Machines Corporation 90], "Connection Machine Model CM-2," Technical Summary, 1990.

[Thinking Machines Corporation 90], "The CM-2 Technical Summary," Thinking Machine Corporation, 1990.

[Tick 91] E. Tick. "Parallel Logic Programming," MIT Press, 1991.

[Treleaven 82] P. C. Treleaven, D. R. Brownbridge, and R. P. Hopkins. "Data-driven and demand-driven computer architecture," ACM Computing Surveys, Vol. 14, No. 1, pp. 93-143, 1982.

[Tucker 88] L. W. Tucker, and G. G. Robertson. "Architecture and Application of the Connection Machine," Computer, Vol. 21, pp. 26-38, August, 1988.

[Turner 86] D. A. Turner. "An Overview of Miranda," ACM SIGPLAN Notices, Vol. 21, No. 12, pp. 158-166, 1986.

[Turner 85] D. A. Turner. "Miranda: A non-strict functional language with polymorphic types," in Functional Programming Languages and Computer Architecture, Springer-Verlag LNCS 201, pp. 1-16, 1985.

[Turner 81] D. A. Turner. "The semantic elegance of applicative languages," Proceedings of the 1981 Conference on Functional Programming Languages and Computer Architecture, ACM, pp. 85-92, 1981.

[Turner 76] D. A. Turner. "SASL Language Manual," Report, University St. Andrews, 1976.

[Ueda 85] K. Ueda. "Guarded Horn Clauses," in Proceedings of Logic Programming '85, ed. E. Wada. Springer-Verlag Publishing Company, 1985.

[Veen 86] A. Veen. "Dataflow machine architecture," ACM Computing Surveys, Vol. 18, No. 4, pp. 365-396, 1986.

[Winograd 75] S. Winograd. "On the parallel evaluation of certain arithmetic expressions," Journal of the Association of Computer Machinery, Vol. 22, No. 4, 1975.

[Winston 92] P. H. Winston. "Artificial Intelligence," Addison-Wesley Publishing Company, 1992.

[Wirth 85] N. Wirth. "Programming in Modula-2," Springer-Verlag Publishing Company, 1985.

[Wirth 77] N. Wirth. "Modula: A language for modular programming," Software Practice and Experience, Vol. 7, pp. 3-35, 1977.

[Wulf 72] W. A. Wulf and C. G. Bell. "C.mmp: A multiminiprocessor," Proceedings of AFIPS Conference, pp. 765-777, 1972.

[Yoo 83] Y. Yoo. "Parallel Pocessing for Some Network Optimization Problems," Ph.D. dissertation, Computer Science Dept., Washington State University, Pullman, 1983.

[Zitti 89] E. Zitti, D. Caviglia, G. Bisio, and G. Parodi. "Neural Networks on a Transporter Array," Department of Biophysical and Electronic Engineering of Genoa, Italy, 1989.

[Zomaya 96] Y. H. Zomaya. "Parallel & Distributed Computing Handbook," McGraw-Hill Publishing Company, 1996.

Glossary

ACU	Array Control Unit, 11,480
AI	Artificial Intelligence, 229,232,425,501-517,524
ALU	Arithmetic and Logic Unit, 14,19,35
AM	Associative Memory, 12,60
ANN	Artificial Neural Network, 527,529-530
ANSI	American National Standard Institute, 10,479,489
BB	Branch and Bound, 336-340
BFS	Breadth First Search, 329-332
C.mmp	Computer with multi-mini-processor, 29-30,81,90
CAM	Content Addressable Memory, 60,103
CM	Connection Machine, 479-480
CM-1	Connection Machine-1, 8,12,81,479
CM-2	Connection Machine-2, 3,12-13,50,72,169,224,479-480
CM-5	Connection Machine-5, 12,23,27,51,81,169,224,479-480
Cm	Computer module, 29
COMA	Cache-Only Memory Architecture, 64
CR	Concurrent Read, 62-63
CRCW	Concurrent Read Concurrent Write, 101-105,315,356
CREW	Concurrent Read Exclusive Write, 101,265,271,308,353
CU	Control Unit, 14
CU	Communication Unit, 512
CW	Concurrent Write, 62-63,323
DAP	Distributed Array Processor, 3,50,70,80,219,479
DCC	Dual Channel Disk Controler, 29
DDDP	Distributed Data Driven Processor, 44,50
DDG	Data Dependence Graph, 113
DDM	Data Difussion Machine, 44,65
DDM1	Data Driven Machine-1, 41,49
DDP	Distributed Data Processor, 49,52
DDP	Data Driven Processor, 40-43
DDPA	Data Driven Processor Array, 49
DFG	Data Flow Graph, 35-43,119,133,415,417,429,509
DFS	Depth First Search, 324-331,352
DGL	Loral Data Graph Language, 49
DPU	Data Parallel Unit, 11,480

Author Index

Subject Index